DR. JANG'S SAT* 800

MATH WORKBOOK

FOR THE NEW SAT

Simon Jang and Tiffany T. Jang

Published in the United States by CreateSpace Publishing, North Charleston, SC.

Jang, Simon.
Dr. Jang's SAT 800 Math Workbook: For The New SAT/ Simon Jang and Tiffany T. Jang
517p. 28 cm.
1. SAT (Educational test)—Study guides. 2. Mathematics—Examinations—Study guides. 3. Mathematics / Study & Teaching. 4. Study Aids / SAT. 5. Redesigned SAT – 2016
378.1664 - dc23

ISBN-10: 1517637430
ISBN-13: 978-1517637439

www.DrJang800.com

Cover photo and design by Jennifer Jang

Table of Contents

How This Book Can Help You

For more than 10 years, we have taught math to students in both the high school and the private setting. One thing we noticed throughout our years of teaching is that there is a lack of good learning material for students of any level studying for the math section of the SAT exam. To remedy this, we have produced this book. It contains all the material you need to know to get a great score. Through our years of teaching, we have reached the conclusion that anyone can get an excellent math score on the SAT in a short period of time provided that he or she focuses on the content required for the test and the skills to tackle the questions quickly and easily.

Required Content Knowledge
In this book, we divide the required content knowledge into four chapters based on the guideline provided by the College Board for the 2016 redesigned SAT Math:

- Chapter One: Heart of Algebra
- Chapter Two: Problem Solving and Data Analysis
- Chapter Three: Passport to Advanced Math
- Chapter Four: Additional Topics in Math

Within each chapter, we explore all necessary sub-concepts in depth and provide numerous practice questions mimicking those on the actual SAT.

The problems and techniques in this book will help train and prepare students for the redesigned math section of the new SAT. The breakdown of topics in this book reflects the topics emphasized on the new SAT. Working on the problem solving skills sections will help students build a strong sense of intuition for solving problems and making educated guesses.

Problem Solving Skills
Within each concept section, the problems are grouped into three difficulty levels:

- Easy
- Medium
- Hard

The critical thinking advices, answers, and detailed explanations are located to the right of the problems. Students can refer to the answers easily but can also cover the page if they want to attempt the problem on their own.

1500+ Practice Problems and 10 Mock Tests
In addition to a thorough overview of materials, this book provides over 1500 practice problems for you to reinforce your understanding of the material and pinpoint the weak areas you need to improve on.

There are some parts of questions needed to be answered without a calculator, of which the symbol of a no-calculator sign, , has been added at the end of questions. For other questions, without a no-calculator sign, acceptable calculators are allowed.

The ten SAT Math mock tests located at the back of book closely mimic the actual exam and provide more even practice. By taking these mock exams with a timer under test-like conditions, students will be even more prepared to master the real test.

About the Authors

Dr. Simon Jang and Mrs. Tiffany Jang have been teaching in public high schools and in their own private tutoring studio for more than 10 years. They have developed a unique and proven SAT Math learning system that suits the students' needs and helps them efficiently prepare for the Math section of the SAT. Over the years, their innovative methods and effective teaching materials have benefitted not only their students' scores, but also their students' endeavors in college and beyond.

Dr. Jang received a Ph.D in Chemical Engineering from New York Polytechnic University. He worked as a software developer before he became a high school teacher. He has been teaching math, physics, and chemistry in New Jersey public high schools for many years. He has dedicated his spare time to developing innovative and effective methods of teaching high school math, chemistry, and physics in his established tutoring studio.

Tiffany Jang earned a Master's degree in Library and Information Sciences from the University of Wisconsin-Madison and a Master's degree in Computer Science from the New Jersey Institute of Technology. After several years of teaching high school math, now she is working as a school librarian in the New Jersey public school system.

They have spent years developing innovative teaching methods and effective learning materials. Their methods can both introduce a new student to the subject and remedy a student's weaknesses to help them efficiently prepare for the SAT Math exam.

Acknowledgements

We would like to acknowledge the help and support from our daughters, Jennifer and Justine, both of whom are currently studying Mathematics at the Massachusetts Institute of Technology, as well as the countless students over the years who have provided feedback on our system. Special thanks to our parents back in Taiwan for their help and support as well. Without the help of everyone around us, this enormous project would never even have been conceptualized.

About the Redesigned SAT Math Test

Know what content knowledge is included
According to the College Board, a nonprofit organization that administers the Scholastic Assessment Test (SAT*), mathematics in the new SAT, launched in March 2016, covers content knowledge up to Algebra II. The new SAT Math increases emphasis on critical thinking, problem solving, and data analysis skills.

Four areas of math will be focused on the new SAT Math:

- Heart of Algebra (33%)
- Problem Solving and Data Analysis (29%)
- Passport to Advanced Math (28%)
- Additional Topics in Math (10%)

Know how the test is organized
The SAT Math exam lasts a total of 80 minutes with two portions of test, Math Test – Calculator and Math Test – No Calculator. Within each portion, SAT Math questions range from easy to hard, with the easier problems at the beginning and the more difficult ones at the end. There are 58 questions, 78% of which are four-option multiple choice questions and 22% are grid-in response questions. Here is the breakdown of the redesigned SAT Math content specifications:

New SAT Math Testing Time (80 minutes)	38 questions with calculators 20 questions without calculators	55 minutes 25 minutes
Types of Questions (58 questions)	45 multiple choice with 4 options 13 grid-in questions	78% 22%
Content Areas	Heart of Algebra ▪ Analyzing and fluently solving equations and systems of equations ▪ Creating expressions, equations, and inequlities ▪ To represent relationships between quantities and to solve problems ▪ Rearranging and interpreting formulas	19 questions 33%

Content Areas	Problem Solving and Data Analysis ▪ Creating and analyzing relationships using ratios, proportions, percentages, and units ▪ Describing relationships shown graphically ▪ Summarizing qualitative and quantitative data	17 questions 29%
	Passport to Advanced Math ▪ Rewriting expressions using their structure ▪ Creating, analyzing, and fluently solving quadratic and higher-order equations ▪ Manipulating polynomials purposefully to solve problems	16 questions 28%
	Additional Topics in Math ▪ Making area and volume calculations in context ▪ Investigating lines, angles, triangles, and circles using theorems ▪ Working with trigonometric functions	6 questions 10%

Know how the SAT is scored

On the new SAT, test-takers will **not be penalized** for incorrect answer in multiple choice questions. The redesigned SAT will be administered both in print and by computer. The top score will return to 1600, which includes the 800 points from the math section and 800 points from the evidence-based reading and writing.

What to do before the test

- Get a good night's sleep.
- Have your photo ID, admission ticket, No. 2 pencils, erasers, watch, and a scientific or graphing calculator ready the night before.
- Have a nutritious but not too filling breakfast.
- Be there 15 minutes before the test is expected to start.

What to be aware of during the test

- Read the questions completely and carefully.
- Solve the easy questions with caution; careless mistakes tend to occur when solving easy questions too confidently.
- Don't struggle on one question for too long. Mark the question and work on it at the end.
- Check the scantron frequently to make sure the bubbles are filled in correctly and on the right question number.

About SAT Math Problem Solving Strategies

There are two types of math questions on the SAT

- 45 multiple-choice questions
- 13 grid-in questions

Strategies and some shortcuts to solving SAT questions

When taking a math test, you have to think mathematically. To think mathematically, you must become familiar with some keywords and their definitions or mathematical equivalents:

- Even Integer: $2n$
- Odd Integer: $2n + 1$
- Order of Operation: Follow the PEMDAS Rules
- Union, Intersection, and Venn diagram
- GCF (Greatest Common Factor) and LCM (Least Common Multiple)
- Prime Numbers
- Common Denominator
- Multiplying and Dividing Exponents
- Percent and Percent Change
- Ratio and Proportion: Direct Proportion and Inverse Proportion
- Average, Sum, Median, and Mode
- Rate
- Probability of an Event
- Parallel Lines and Their Transversals
- Triangles and Special Triangles
- Interior and Exterior Angles of a Triangle
- Polygons
- Area of Geometric Figures

Read questions carefully and underline or circle the most important key points, such as "average," "sum," "maximum," etc. so that you can catch the scope of the question quickly. One of the most important aspects that you must get used to in SAT Math test is the reading comprehension feature. You will need excellent reading comprehension skills to translate word problems into math problems.

Pay attention to hints in the questions that you can use to decide whether or not to use shortcuts to solve the problem. Do not use shortcuts without understanding the question first. Certain types of example questions can be easily solved by shortcuts. Some examples are shown below.

Shortcuts

1. Plugging in Easy Numbers: If a question is along the lines of "which of the following must be true or must NOT be true," and the answer choices contain variables, you can try to assign an easy number to the variable to find the answer.

Example 1: If X, Y and Z represent consecutive positive odd integers, which of the following is NOT true?

a) X + Y + Z is an odd integer
b) X + Y is an even integer
c) $\frac{Z-X}{2}$ is an even integer
d) $\frac{X+Y}{2}$ is an odd integer

This question looks complicated, but if we plug in, X = 1, Y = 3, and Z = 5, you will find out that only answer (d) is not true. Of course, make sure that the numbers you plug in satisfy the requirements. 1, 3, and 5 are obviously consecutive positive odd integers.

Example 2: If $|x| < 1$, which of the following is the greatest?

a) 2
b) $1 - x$
c) $1 + x$
d) $2x$

Instead of solving this inequality, you can easily find the right answer (a) by plugging in a value of x that satisfies the inequality. If we plug in $x = \frac{1}{2}$, we see that the answer (a) is the greatest.

Example 3: The figure below shows a square and a right triangle. What is the area of shaded region?

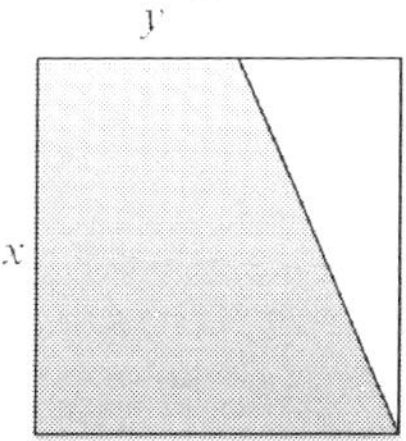

a) $\frac{x(x+y)}{2}$
b) $\frac{(x^2+y^2)}{2}$
c) xy
d) $2xy$

To find the answer fast, we can plug in $x = 5$ and $y = 3$. If we do this, the shaded region has area $5^2 - \frac{1}{2}(2)(5) = 20$. Only (a) gives an equivalent answer.

2. In geometry, when you are given a set of parallel lines and possibly a transversal, many times the degree of two angles end up being congruent or supplementary. Many times you can tell which one is which just by looking at the graph (but this is not always the case and sometimes graphs are not drawn to scale).

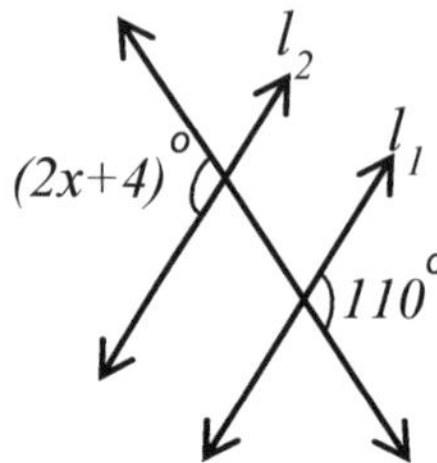

Example 4: In the figure above, if $l_1 \parallel l_2$, what is the value of x?

a) 45
b) 53
c) 57
d) 60

Since we have two parallel lines and a transversal, there are only two different types of angles here: angles with degree equal to 110° and angles supplementary to 110°. By just looking at that graph, we can tell, $2x + 4 = 110$, so $x = 53$. Answer is (b).

3. Sometimes if you can't solve the problem mathematically, you can still use logic to eliminate the answer choices. The more answer choices you can eliminate, the higher the probability of you answering a question right.

Example 5: John can complete a job in 20 minutes. Bob can complete the same job in 40 minutes. If they work together, approximately how many minutes will it take them to complete the job?

a) 60 minutes
b) 40 minutes
c) 30 minutes
d) 15 minutes

If they work together, the job should be completed faster than 2 Bobs and slower than 2 Johns. The only reasonable answer should be between 10 to 20 minutes. Answer is (d).

Example 6: Sam drove to work at an average speed of 50 miles per hour from her house and then returned along the same route at an average speed of 40 miles per hour. If the entire trip took her 2.25 hours, what is the entire distance, in miles, for the round trip?

a) 90
b) 100
c) 120
d) 125

In this problem, since distance = time × speed, the entire distance is between 40×2.25 and 50×2.25 miles. The reasonable answer is 100 miles, answer (b).

4. Take advantage of your calculator during the calculator portion of the test. Learn to use a calculator efficiently by practicing. As you approach a problem, focus on how to solve that problem and then decide whether the calculator will be helpful. Using a calculator may help to prevent you from careless mistakes and save you some time performing calculations. However, a calculator will not solve a problem for you. You must understand the problem first. Keep in mind that every SAT Math question can be solved without a calculator and some questions can be solved faster mentally than with a calculator.

Example 7: What is the average (arithmetic mean) of 192, 194, and 196? We can get the answer, 194, without using a calculator since the median of three consecutive odd integers is also the average.

5. When applicable, use the plug-and-chug technique to solve a question backwards. This method works best when you see simple numbers as answer choices. Plug the numbers from the answer choices into the question until you find the right one. Plug-and-chug is sometimes faster than setting up an equation.

Example 8: Together, Ken, Justin, and Tiff have read a total of 65 books. Justin read 3 times as many books as Ken and Tiff read 3 times as many books as Justin. How many books did Ken read?

a) 12
b) 9
c) 7
d) 5

Plugging and chugging this question is faster than setting up an equation. You can start with plugging in the number from choice (c) and notice that the number 7 is too big, so you pick a smaller number, (d), to plug in. Thus you arrive at the right answer, (d).

6. Working backwards can sometimes help you organize your thoughts in order to solve a word problem. First, identify what the question is asking. Then, ask yourself what data you might need. Finally, look for the data you need from the question, and use it to solve the problem.

Example 9: On an Algebra exam, class A has 10 students taking the test and an average score of 90. Class B has 20 students taking the test and an average score of 85. What is the average score of all the students in both class A and B?

- By reading the last sentence, we know the question is asking for the average of all the students.
- In order to answer this question, we will use the formula to find averages:

$$Average = \frac{Total\ Score}{Number\ of\ Students}$$

- The total number of students is 10 + 20 and the total score is $10 \times 90 + 20 \times 85$.
- Finally, set up an equation to solve this problem.

$$\frac{10 \times 90 + 20 \times 85}{10 + 20} = 86.666$$

7. Most of the word problems can be translated from English into mathematical expressions by following a few guidelines:

a) Keywords in the problem can help translating the words into algebraic expressions. For instance, the words "greater than," "more," and "increase" indicate addition and "less than," "fewer," and "decrease" indicate subtraction. "2 times" refers to multiplying a number or a variable by 2, and "is" indicates equality in an equation. If the question mentions finding "a number" without specifying the value of the number, assign a variable for that number and then solve for the value of the variable.

b) When dealing with percent problems, the following keywords usually translate to the following actions:

- Percent in decimal form → divide by 100
- Decimal in percent form → multiply by 100
- 'is' → =
- 'of' → ×
- 'what' or 'a number' (the value you are solving for) → $\boldsymbol{x}$

Examples:

a) What is 15% of 60?

b) 20% of what number is 16?

c) What percent of 20 is 5?

Solutions:

a) $x = \frac{15}{100} \times 60 = 9$

b) $\frac{20}{100} \times x = 16$
$x = 80$

c) $\frac{x}{100} \times 20 = 5$
$x = \frac{5 \times 100}{20}$
$x = 25\%$

c) If a geometry question is given in words, make a sketch and label points according to the question. It becomes easier to find the answer once you have drawn your own sketch.

8. It's okay to trust their geometric figures unless when it is stated that the figure is not drawn to scale. You may estimate the answer based on the figure itself if you cannot solve the problem or you run out of time. If it is stated that the figure is not drawn to scale, you may redraw the figure based on the data presented.

Know some tricks about grid-in questions

- Grid in only one digit per column.
- There is no penalty for wrong answers, so answer all the grid-in questions.
- There are no negative answers.
- Mixed numbers need to be changed to improper fractions. (Grid in $\frac{3}{2}$ instead of $1\frac{1}{2}$. $1\frac{1}{2}$ is not acceptable and will be read as $\frac{11}{2}$.)
- Either fraction or decimal form is acceptable.
- Decimals can be rounded or truncated but answers rounded to fewer digits than space available will be marked wrong.
  - The answer $\frac{16}{21}$ should be entered as .761 or .762 (note: $\frac{16}{21} = 0.7619$), but not 0.76.
  - Don't add a 0 in the far left column except when the answer is 0.
- Don't waste time rounding your decimal answer.
- Don't waste time to reduce fractions.

About the Diagnostic Test in This Book

This diagnostic test contains 58 questions on topics that are most frequently found on the SAT Math test. The purpose of the diagnostic test is to allow you to measure your level of proficiency and identify your weakest areas.

It is important that you take this diagnostic test to find out your weakest areas and then study those areas accordingly. All the questions in the diagnostic test are on a medium to hard level on the actual SAT. So if you quite comfortable with some of these questions, you should be able to do well on SAT Math test in those areas. If you have no idea how to solve a question, you should leave a mark on the question and spend more time studying that area in the future.

After taking the diagnostic test and checking the solutions, group each question based on your confidence level when you were solving it:

1. Low: Questions that you skipped or had absolutely no idea how to solve.
2. Medium: Questions that you may be able to solve but are not completely familiar with and/or made careless mistakes on.
3. High: Questions that you are very confident and you know how to solve.

For the topic areas you have confidence low, you need to read through the concept overviews on each section, try to understand them, and do questions from easy to hard on the problems solving skills sections. Remember, only after recognizing your problem areas, you can tackle them by lots of practices.

For those areas that you have medium confidence in, you may quickly glance at the concept overviews to see if there are some concepts or tricks that you don't know and then jump straight to the medium and hard level practice problems.

If you still have time after dealing with low and medium confidence questions, you can focus on the hard-level questions of the topics you have high confidence in. By doing so, you will improve your skills across the board and become a master of the SAT Math test. Practice makes perfect!

SAT Math Diagnostic Test

Evaluating Algebraic Expressions

1. If $z = \frac{12x^4}{y}$, what happens to the value of z when both x and y are doubled?
   a) z is multiplied by 32.
   b) z is multiplied by 16.
   c) z is multiplied by 8.
   d) z is doubled.

Evaluating Variables in Terms of Another

2. A right circular cylinder with radius 3 and height 7 has a volume v, In terms of v, what is the volume of the right circular cylinder with radius 3 and height 14?
   a) $v + 7$
   b) $7v$
   c) $5v$
   d) $2v$

Solving Equations

3. A litter of milk can fill up 3 large cups or 5 small cups. If there are 12 large cups and 10 small cups, about how many litters of milk will be needed to fill up all the cups?
   a) 6
   b) 4
   c) 3
   d) 2

Solving Linear Equations

4. If a linear function passes through the points (1, s), (3, t) and (5, 10), what is the value of $2t - s$?
   a) 2
   b) 4
   c) 8
   d) 10

Solving Quadratic Equations

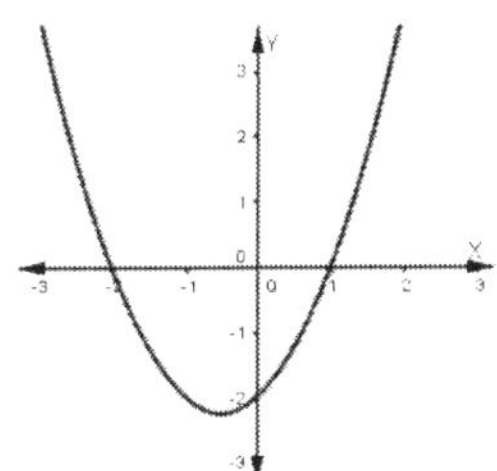

5. Which of the following equations best describes the curve in the figure above?
   a) $y = x^2 - 2$
   b) $y = x^2 + x - 2$
   c) $y = x^2 + x + 2$
   d) $y = x^2 + x$

Solving Systems of Equations

6. There is $180 of cash in John's pocket. John only has 10 and 20 dollar bills. If John has a total of 13 bills, how many 20 dollar bills are in his pocket?

Solving Inequalities

7. If $x < 5 < \frac{1}{x-1}$, then x could be which of the following?
   a) 5
   b) 1
   c) $\frac{7}{6}$
   d) $\frac{10}{3}$

Word Problems

8. Six erasers cost as much as 3 pencils. If Matt bought one eraser and one pencil for $1.50, how much does one pencil cost in dollars?
   a) 0.25
   b) 0.50
   c) 0.75
   d) 1.00

Rate Word Problems

9. Sam drove from home at an average speed of 50 miles per hour to her working place and then returned along the same route at an average speed of 40 miles per hour. If the entire trip took her 2.25 hours, what is the entire distance, in miles, for the round trip?
   a) 90
   b) 100
   c) 120
   d) 125

Percent Word Problems

10. A store sells a certain brand of TVs for $550 each. This price is 25 percent more than the cost at which the store buys one of these TVs. The store employees can purchase any of these TVs at 20 percent off the store's cost. How much would it cost an employee to purchase a TV of this brand?
   a) $352
   b) $330
   c) $413
   d) $440

Ratio and Proportion Word Problems

11. A recipe of a cake for 8 people requires 1.2 pounds of flour. Assuming the amount of flour needed is directly proportional to the number of people eating the cake, how many pounds of flour are required to make a big cake for 240 people?
   a) 20
   b) 26
   c) 30
   d) 36

Unions and Intersections of Sets

12. For an end of the year party, Mrs. Scott ordered 40 slices of pizza for her class. Among those slices of pizza, 16 were topped with mushroom and 14 were topped with chicken. If 15 slices contained neither mushroom nor chicken, how many slices of pizza must be topped with both mushroom and chicken?
   a) 3
   b) 5
   c) 7
   d) 9

Ratios, Proportions, and Rates

13. If y is inversely proportional to x and y is equal to 12 when x is equal to 8, what is the value of y when $x = 24$?
   a) $\frac{1}{6}$
   b) 4
   c) 1
   d) $\frac{1}{4}$

14. If y is directly proportional to x and y is equal to 40 when x is equal to 6, what is the value of y when $x = 9$?
   a) 40
   b) 45
   c) 50
   d) 60

15. Freddy's family owns two different types of cars, a sedan and an SUV. The sedan has gas mileage of 25 miles per gallon, and the SUV has gas mileage of 20 miles per gallon. If both cars use the same amount of gasoline and the sedan travels 100 miles, how many miles does the SUV travel?

Percents

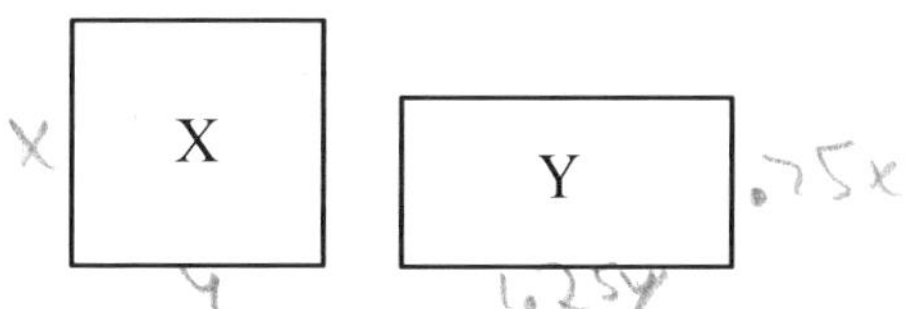

16. Two rectangles X and Y are shown below. If the width of rectangle Y in the figure below is 25 percent less than the width of rectangle X and the length of rectangle Y is 25 percent greater than the length of rectangle X. What is the area of rectangle Y compared to the area of rectangle X?
    a) The area of rectangle Y is 25 percent less than the area of rectangle X.
    b) The area of rectangle Y is 6 percent less than the area of rectangle X.
    c) Both rectangles have the same area.
    d) The area of rectangle Y is 6 percent greater than the area of rectangle X.

Averages

17. Which of the following could be the sum of 8 numbers if the average of these 8 numbers is greater than 9 and less than 10?
    a) 85
    b) 83
    c) 82
    d) 79

Data Analysis

Auto Sales

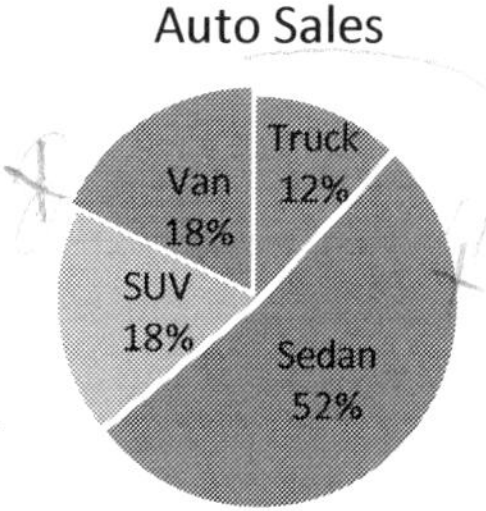

18. The pie graph above represents the automobiles that were sold by a dealer in 2010, according to their records. If the dealer sold 40 more Sedans than all others combined, how many automobiles did it sell altogether?

Counting Rules

19. A school will send a team of one math teacher and two science teachers to work on a project. If the school has 5 math teachers and 6 science teachers, how many of such teams are possible?

Probability

20. A bag contains red, blue, and green marbles. The probability of pulling out a red marble randomly is $\frac{1}{4}$ and the probability of pulling out a blue marble randomly is $\frac{1}{5}$. Which of the following could be the total number of marbles in the bag?
    a) 10
    b) 12
    c) 18
    d) 20

Sequence Patterns

486, 162, ...

21. In the sequence above, each term after the 1st term is $\frac{1}{3}$ of the term preceding it. What is the 5th term of this sequence?

Symbol Functions

22. For all numbers j and k, Let \$ be defined by $j\$k = j - k + 3$. What is the value of (3\$6) \$2?
    a) 0
    b) 1
    c) 2
    d) 3

Logic

23. Helen threw a fair six sided dice 5 times. Each throw showed a different number according to the following rules:

The first roll was greater than 5.
The second roll was less than 3.
The third roll was 4.
The fourth roll was the same as the first roll.
The fifth roll was an even number.

Which of the following must be true?

a) Helen could have rolled a 6 more than three times.
b) Helen could have rolled a 5 only one time.
c) Helen rolled more even numbers than odd numbers.
d) Helen rolled 3 at least once.

Factors and Multiples

24. What is the greatest three-digit integer that has the factors 10 and 9?

a) 100
b) 900
c) 955
d) 990

25. Which of the following must be a factor of x if x is a multiple of both 9 and 12?

a) 8
b) 24
c) 27
d) 36

Fraction Operations

26. If $x = -\frac{1}{2}$, what is the value of $\frac{1}{x} - \frac{1}{x+1}$?

a) −4
b) −2
c) 4
d) 2

Algebraic Factoring

27. If $x^2 - y^2 = 15$, and $x - y = 3$, what is the value of $x + y$?

a) 1
b) 3
c) 5
d) 10

Functions

28. The quadratic function f is given by $f(x) = ax^2 + bx + c$, where a and c are positive real numbers. Which of the following is the possible graph of $f(x)$? 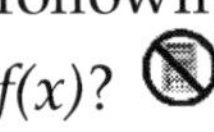

a)

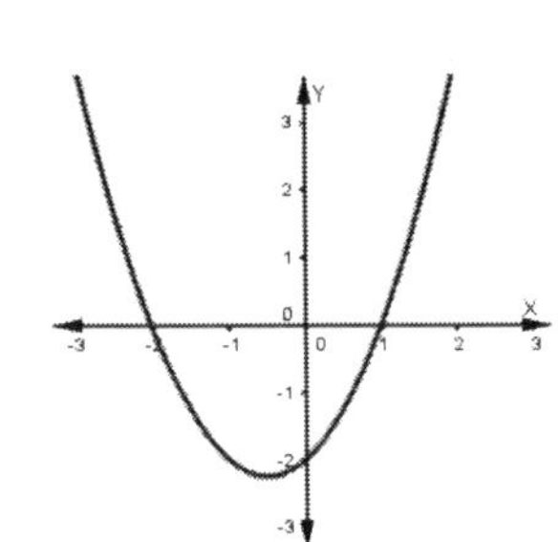

b)

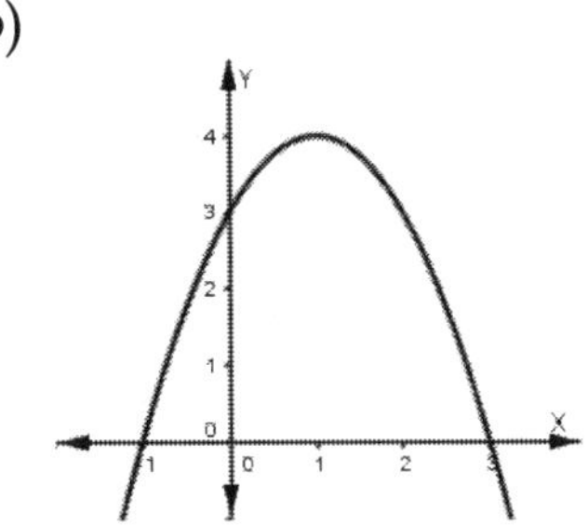

c)

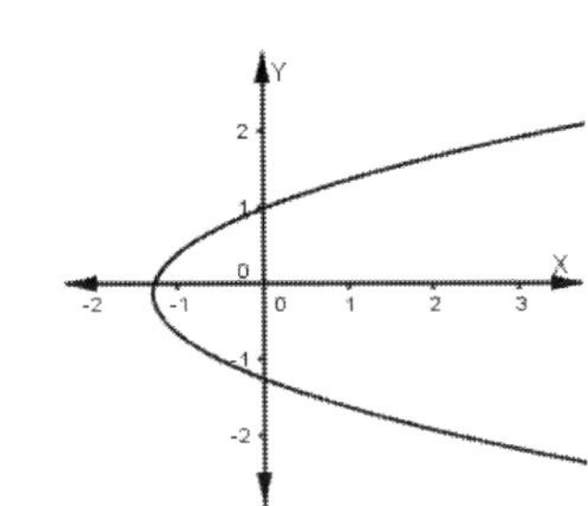

d)

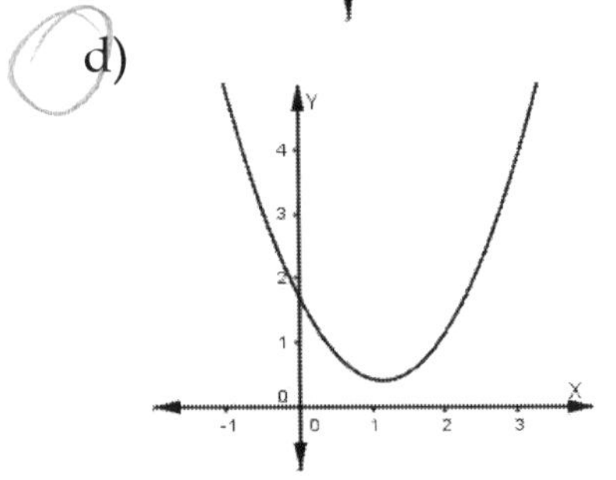

Complex Numbers

29. Which of the following is the expression $\frac{3-2i}{4+3i}$ equivalent to?

    a) $\frac{12-4i}{7}$
    b) $\frac{6+17i}{25}$
    c) $\frac{6-10i}{7}$
    d) $\frac{6-17i}{25}$

30. If $3 - 2i$ is a root of $2x^2 + ax + b = 0$, then b = ?

    a) 7.5
    b) -7.5
    c) 26
    d) It cannot be determined.

Quadratic Functions and Equations

31. Which of the following could be a graph of the equation $y = ax^2 + bx + c$, where $b^2 - 4ac = 0$?

    a)

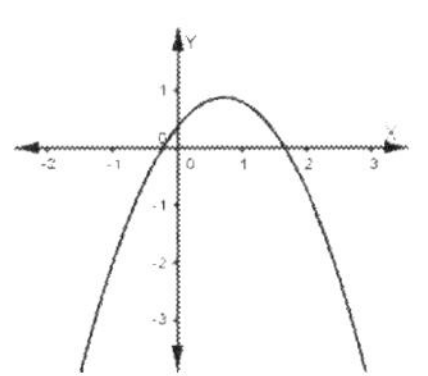

    b)

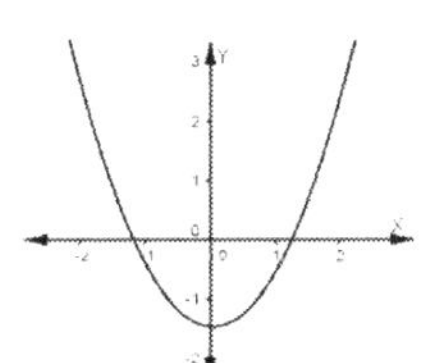

    c)

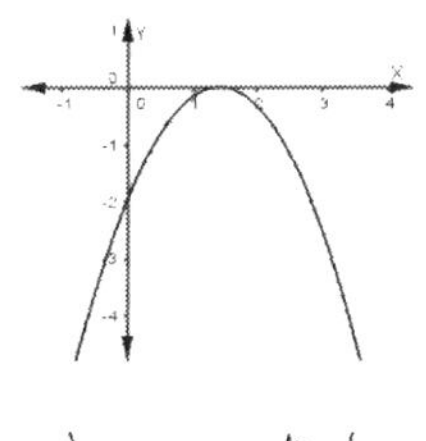

    d)

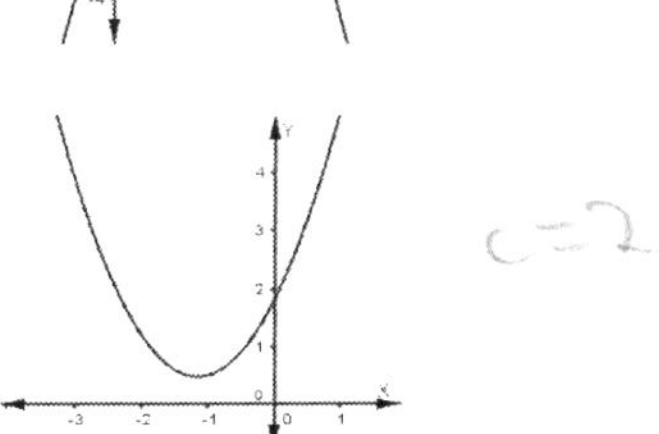

32. A baseball is hit and flies into a field at a trajectory defined by the equation $d = -1.2t^2 + 100$, where t is the number of seconds after the impact and d is the horizontal distance from the home plate to the outfield fence. How many seconds have passed if the ball is 50 meters away from the outfield fence ?

    a) 3.78
    b) 4.33
    c) 5.12
    d) 6.45

Polynomials

33. What is the remainder when $2x^4 - 3x^3 + 4x^2 - 5x + 6$ is divided by $x - 3$?

    a) 108
    b) 96
    c) 87
    d) 75

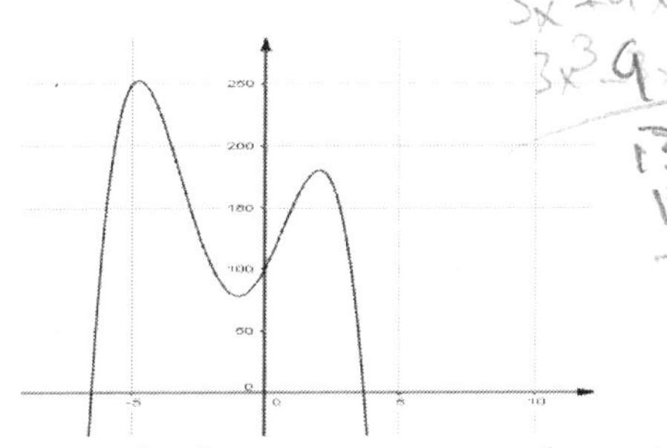

34. The graph above represents the function $y = -x^4 - 5x^3 + 14x^2 + 40x + c$. Which of the following could be the value of c?

    a) -100
    b) -7
    c) 4
    d) 100

Exponent Operations

35. If $8 = a^y$, then $8a^2$ =?

    a) a^{y^2}
    b) a^{y+2}
    c) $8a^y$
    d) a^{8y}

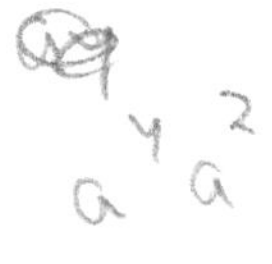

Roots and Radical Operations

36. If $x^{\frac{3}{2}} = \frac{1}{27}$, then what does x equal?

a) -9
b) −3
c) $\frac{1}{9}$
d) $-\frac{1}{9}$

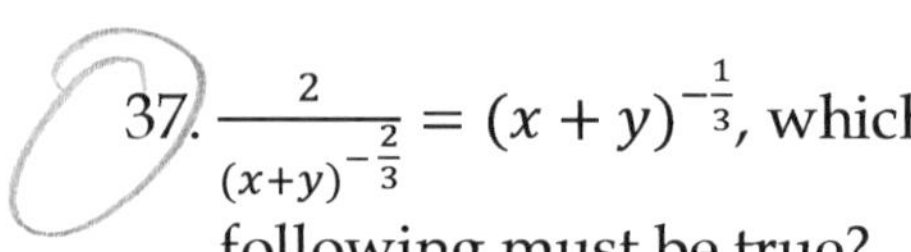

37. $\frac{2}{(x+y)^{-\frac{2}{3}}} = (x+y)^{-\frac{1}{3}}$, which of the following must be true?

a) $x = 0$
b) $\sqrt{x+y} = 2$
c) $\sqrt{x+y} = \frac{1}{2}$
d) $x + y = \frac{1}{2}$

Lines and Angles

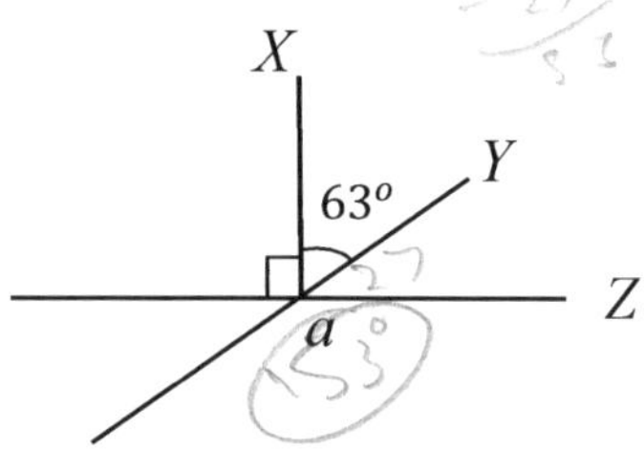

38. What is the value of a in the figure above?

Parallel Lines and Their Transversal

39. In the figure below, $\overline{AB} \parallel \overline{CD}$ and $\overline{CD} \perp \overline{BC}$. What is the value of $x + y$?

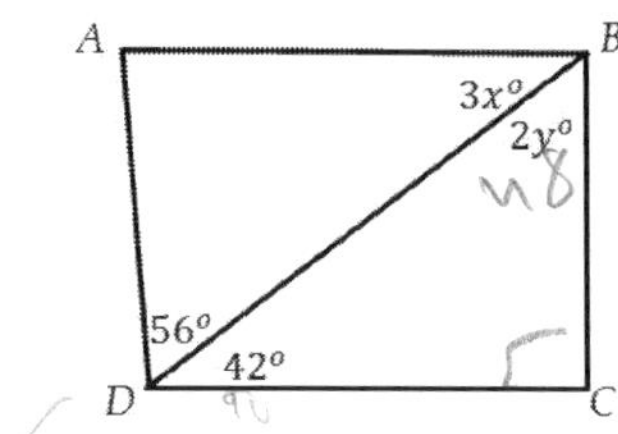

a) 21
b) 34
c) 36
d) 38

Triangle Interior and Exterior Angles

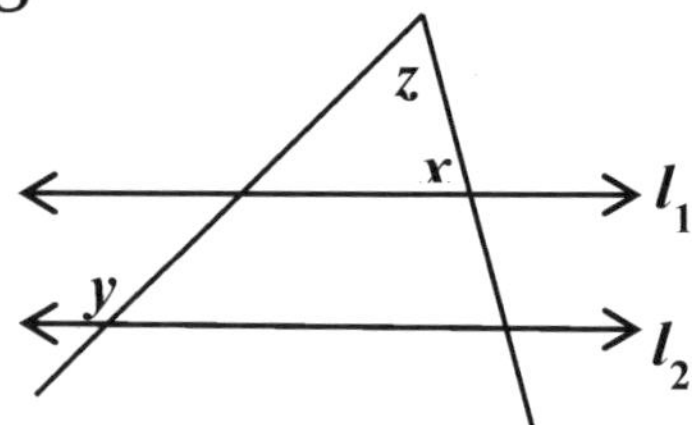

40. In the figure above, if $l_1 \parallel l_2$, what does z equal in terms of x and y?

a) $x - y$
b) $y - x$
c) $180° - y + x$
d) $180° - x - y$

Special Triangles

41. In the figure below, AB = 2. What is the length of AD?

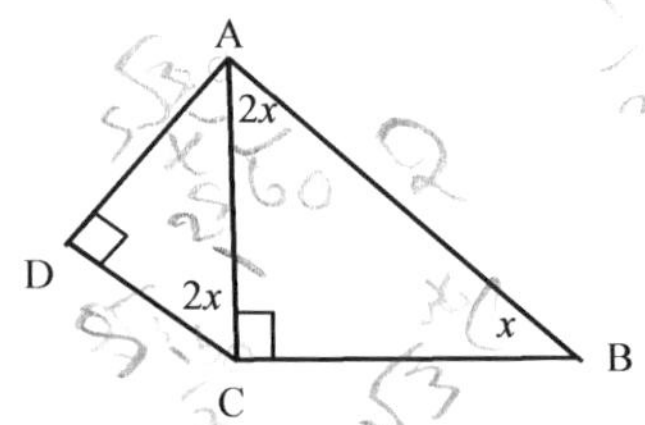

a) $\sqrt{3}$
b) 1
c) $\frac{1}{2}$
d) $\frac{\sqrt{3}}{2}$

Similar Triangles

42. In the figure below, point D is the mid-point of $\overline{AB}$ and point E is the mid-point of $\overline{AC}$. If AB = 10, AC = 12, and DE = 7, what is the perimeter of quadrilateral DBCE?

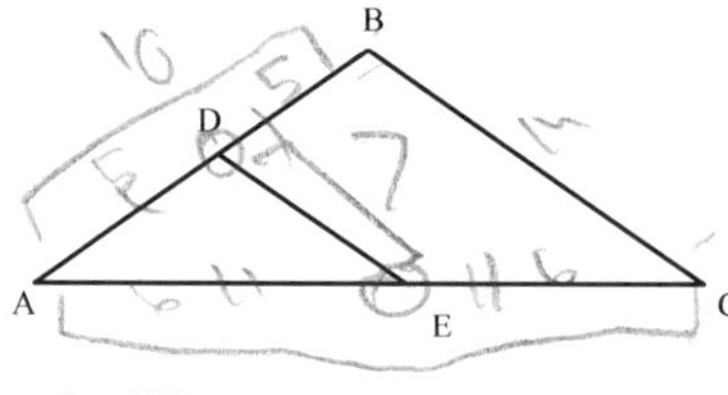

a) 29
b) 30
c) 31
d) 32

Areas of Triangles

43. In the figure below, the area of the shaded region is 26 square units. What is the height of the smaller triangle?

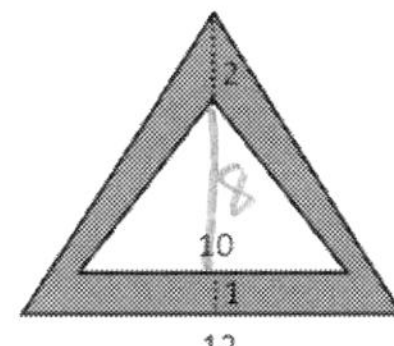

Triangle Inequality Theorem

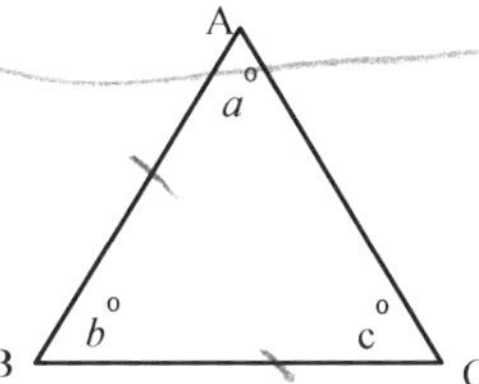

Note: Figure not drawn to scale.

44. The triangle above is isosceles and $a < b$. Which of the following must be FALSE?
    a) AB = BC
    b) BC = AC
    c) AC = AB
    d) a = c

Polygons

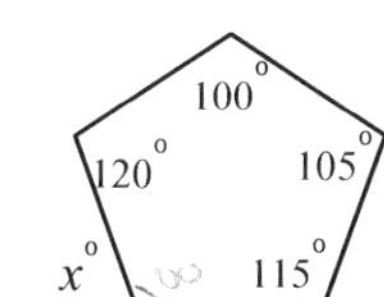

Note: Figure not drawn to scale.

45. The figure shown above is composed of five straight line segments, what is the value of x?

Parallelograms

46. In quadrilateral ABCD, $m\angle A = m\angle B = 128°$, and $m\angle D$ is $10°$ less than 5 times of $m\angle C$. Find $m\angle D$.

Areas of Polygons

47. If the parallelogram above has side lengths all equal to 12, what is the area of this parallelogram?
    a) 72
    b) $72\sqrt{2}$
    c) $72\sqrt{3}$
    d) 144

Segments of a Circle

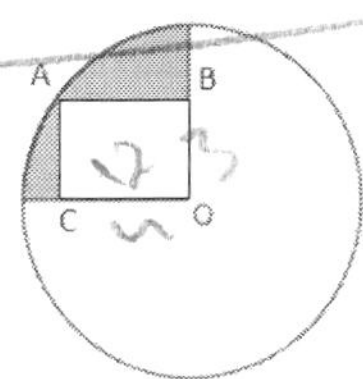

48. In the figure above, rectangle ABOC is drawn in circle O. If OB = 3 and OC = 4, what is the area of the shaded region?
    a) $6\pi - 3$
    b) $\frac{25\pi}{4} - 12$
    c) $25\pi - 12$
    d) $\frac{25\pi}{4} - 3$

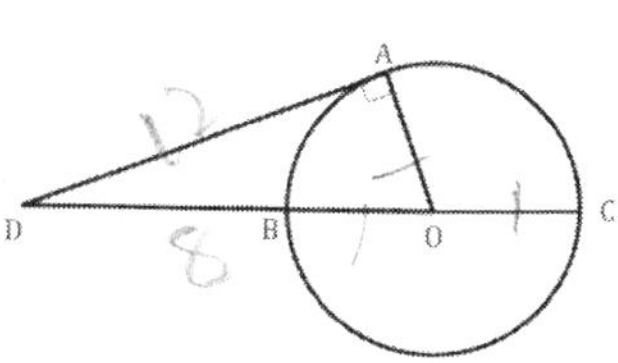

49. Point O is the center of the circle in the figure above. If DA = 12 and DB = 8, what is the area of the circle?

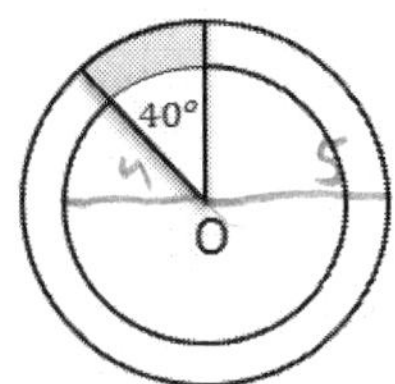

50. In the figure above, O is the center of the two circles. If the bigger circle has a radius of 5 and the smaller circle has a radius of 4, what is the area of shaded region?
    a) 3π
    b) 2π
    c) π
    d) $\frac{2}{3}\pi$

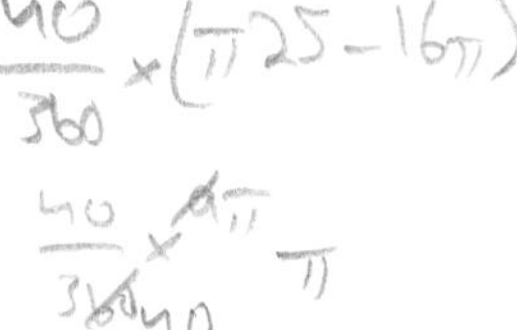

Cubes

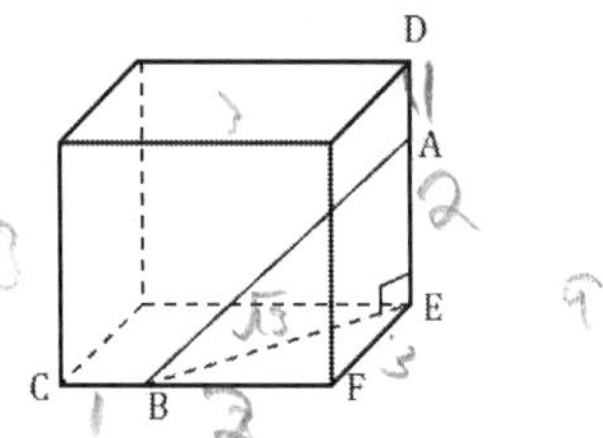

51. The cube shown above has edges of length 3. If $\overline{CB} = \overline{AD} = 1$, what is the length of $\overline{AB}$?

Volumes and Surface Areas

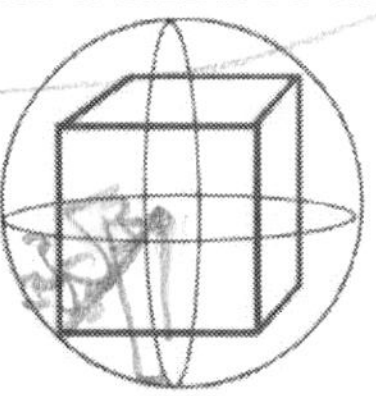

52. A cube is inscribed in a sphere as shown in the figure above. Each vertex of the cube touches the sphere. If the diameter of this sphere is $3\sqrt{3}$, what is the volume of the cube?
    a) 8
    b) 27
    c) 36
    d) 48

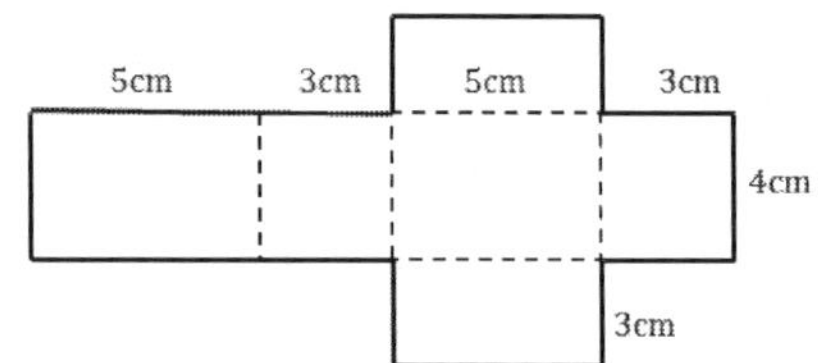

53. If the figure above is folded along the dashed lines, a rectangular box will be formed. What is the volume of the box in cubic centimeters?
    a) 15
    b) 20
    c) 40
    d) 60

Coordinate Geometry

54. Which of the following is the equation of a parabola whose vertex is at (–3, –4)?
    a) $y = (x + 3)^2 - 4$
    b) $y = (x - 3)^2 + 4$
    c) $y = (x - 4)^2 - 3$
    d) $y = x^2 - 4$

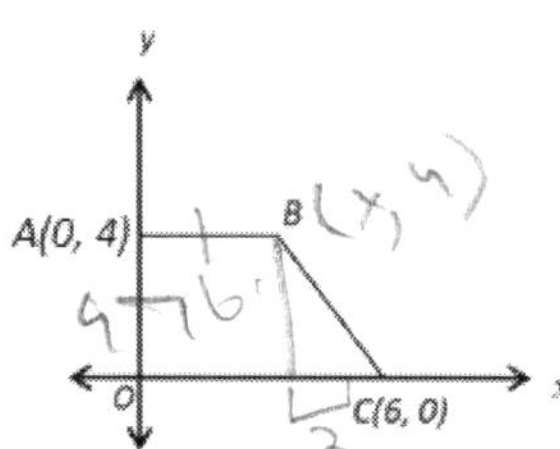

55. In the xy-coordinate plane, AB is parallel to the x-axis. If AO = AB, what is the area of quadrilateral ABCO?
    a) 12
    b) 16
    c) 18
    d) 20

56. If the center of the circle defined by $x^2 + y^2 - 4x + 2y = 20$ is (h, k) and the radius is r, then $h + k + r = ?$

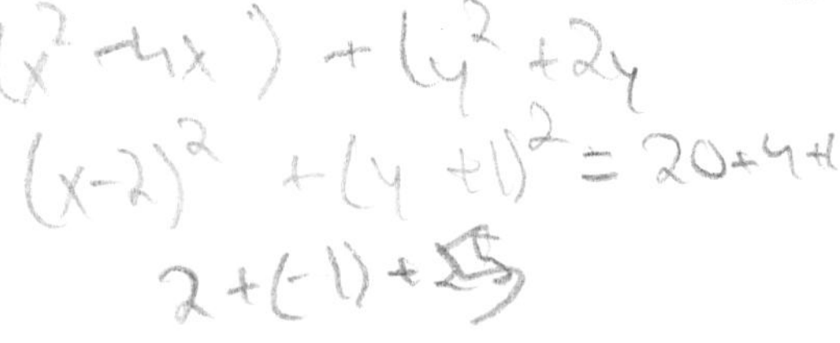

Trigonometric Functions and Their Inverses

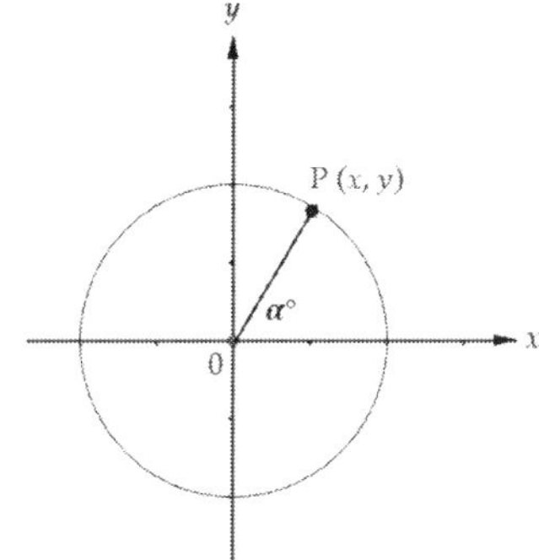

Note: Figure not drawn to scale.

57. On the unit circle above, if the values of sine and cosine of the angle $\alpha°$ are equal, what is the sum $x + y$?
    a) $2\sqrt{2}$
    b) $\sqrt{2}$
    c) $\frac{\sqrt{2}}{2}$
    d) $\frac{\sqrt{2}}{3}$

58. The graph of $y = 3\cos(2x) + 3$ intersects the y–axis at what value of y?
    a) 3
    b) 6
    c) 9
    d) 0

Diagnostic Test Answer Keys:

1. C	2. D	3. A	4. D	5. B	6. 5	7. C	8. D	9. B	10. A
11. D	12. B	13. B	14. D	15. 80	16. B	17. D	18. 1000	19. 75	20. D
21. 6	22. B	23. C	24. D	25. D	26. A	27. C	28. D	29. D	30. C
31. C	32. D	33. A	34. D	35. B	36. C	37. D	38. 153	39. D	40. B
41. D	42. D	43. 8	44. B	45. 80	46. 85	47. C	48. B	49. 78.5	50. C
51. 4.12	52. B	53. D	54. A	55. D	56. 6	57. B	58. B		

Diagnostic Test Answer Explanations:

1. *Answer: (c)*
   $\frac{12(2x)^4}{(2y)} = 2^3\left(\frac{12x^4}{y}\right)$

2. *Answer: (d)*
   $v = \pi(3)^2 \times 7$
   $v_2 = \pi(3)^2 \times 14$
   $\frac{v}{v_2} = \frac{\pi(3)^2 \times 7}{\pi(3)^2 \times 14} = \frac{1}{2}$
   $v_2 = 2v$

3. *Answer: (a)*
   12 large cups need 4 litters and 10 small cups need 2 litters.
   The amount of milk needed:
   4 + 2 = 6 litters

4. *Answer: (d)*
   The line segment connecting the first two points must have the same slope as the line segment connecting the last two points.
   $\frac{10-s}{5-1} = \frac{10-t}{5-3}$
   $\frac{10-s}{4} = \frac{10-t}{2}$
   $40 - 4t = 20 - 2s$
   $4t - 2s = 20$
   $2t - s = 10$

5. *Answer: (b)*
   From the graph, there are two roots, −2 and 1.
   $y = (x+2)(x-1) = x^2 + x - 2$

6. *Answer: 5*
   Let x be the number of \$20 bills and y be the number of \$10 bills.
   $x + y = 13,\ y = 13 - x$
   $20x + 10y = 180$
   $20x + 10(13 - x) = 180$
   $130 + 10x = 180$
   $10x = 50$
   $x = 5$

7. *Answer: (c)*
   $5 < \frac{1}{x-1},\ \frac{1}{5} > x - 1$
   $1 < x < \frac{6}{5}$

8. *Answer: (d)*
   Let the price of one eraser be x and the price of one pencil be y. The price of 6 erasers = the price of 3 pencils.
   $6x = 3y,\ x = \frac{1}{2}y$
   The Price of One Eraser = $\frac{1}{2}$ *the Price of One Pencil.*
   $x + y = 1.50$
   $\frac{1}{2}y + y = 1.50$
   Solve for y to get the price of one pencil \$1.00.

9. *Answer: (b)*
   Let one trip have x miles.
   $Time = 2.25 = t_1 + t_2 = \frac{x}{50} + \frac{x}{40}$
   $2.25 = x\left(\frac{1}{50} + \frac{1}{40}\right)$
   $x = 50$
   Total Distance = 2 × 50 = 100

10. *Answer: (a)*
    Store's Cost × (1 + 25%) = 550
    Store's Cost = $\frac{550}{1.25} = 440$
    20 percent off the store's cost:
    $440 \times (1 - 0.2) = 352$

11. *Answer: (d)*
    $\frac{8\ People}{1.2\ Pounds} = \frac{240\ People}{x\ Pounds}$
    $8x = 1.2 \times 240$
    x = 36 pounds of flour

12. *Answer: (b)*
Use Venn diagram: Mushroom ∪ Chicken = Total – (No Mushroom ∩ No Chicken)
= Mushroom + Chicken – (Mushroom ∩ Chicken)
Mushroom ∪ Chicken = 40 − 15 = 16 + 14 − (Mushroom ∩ Chicken)
25 = 30 − (Mushroom ∩ Chicken)
Mushroom ∩ Chicken = 5

13. *Answer: (b)*
$8 \times 12 = y \times 24$
$y = 4$

14. *Answer: (d)*
$\frac{40}{6} = \frac{y}{9}$
$y = 60$

15. *Answer: 80*
Small car uses $\frac{100}{25} = 4$ *gallons*
SUV Miles = 4 × 20 = 80 miles

16. *Answer: (b)*
Let X's width be w and length be l. Then Y's width is 0.75w and length is 1.25l.
Area of Y = 0.75w × 1.25l = 0.9375wl = 93.75% of area of X.
100% − 93.75% = 6.25% (less)

17. *Answer: (d)*
Sum = Number of Elements × Average
$9 \times 8 < Sum < 10 \times 8$
$72 < Sum < 80$

18. *Answer: 1000*
Solve this problem using proportions.
There were 4% (52% − 48%) more Sedans sold than all other cars combined.
4% : 40 = 100% : x
x = 1,000 cars

19. *Answer: 75*
This is combination. The number of ways to select m objects from n objects (n ≥ m), where order does not matter:
$C_m^n = \frac{n!}{m!(n-m)!}$
Math: $C_1^5 = 5$
Science: $C_2^6 = 15$
Total number of arrangements:
$5 \times 15 = 75$

20. *Answer: (d)*
The total number of marbles should be a common multiple of 4 and 5.
The LCM of 4 and 5 is 20, so the total number of marbles has to be a multiple of 20.

21. *Answer: 6*
The Fifth Term $= 486 \times (\frac{1}{3})^4 = 6$

22. *Answer: (b)*
Find the 3$6 first.
3$6 = 3 – 6 + 3 = 0
0$2 = 0 −2 + 3 = 1

23. *Answer: (c)*
List of results: 6, less than 3, 4, 6, even.
Only (c) could meet all the conditions.

24. *Answer: (d)*
Find the greatest number that ends in 0 and where the sum of the digits is divisible by 9.

25. *Answer: (d)*
The LCM of 12 and 9 is 36.

26. *Answer: (a)*
$$\frac{1}{-\frac{1}{2}} - \frac{1}{-\frac{1}{2}+1} = -2 - 2 = -4$$

27. *Answer: (c)*
$x^2 - y^2 = (x - y)(x + y)$
$3(x + y) = 15, x + y = 5$

28. *Answer: (d)*
A positive value of a will make the quadratic function's graph open upward and a positive value of c will show that the function has a positive y-intercept.

29. *Answer: (d)*
Rationalize the denominator.
$$\frac{3-2i}{4+3i} \times \frac{4-3i}{4-3i} = \frac{(3-2i)(4-3i)}{16+9} = \frac{6-17i}{25}$$

30. *Answer: (c)*
If (3 – 2i) is a root of the quadratic equation, then its conjugate (3 + 2i) is also the root of the equation.
The product of the roots is $\frac{b}{2}$*; the sum of the roots is* $-\frac{b}{a}$.
$(3 - 2i)(3 + 2i) = 13 = \frac{b}{2}$
$9 - (-4) = 13 = \frac{b}{2} \rightarrow b = 26$

31. *Answer: (c)*
The discriminant, $b^2 - 4ac$, *of a quadratic equation reveals the type of its roots.*
When $b^2 - 4ac = 0$, *the quadratic equation two equal, real roots.*
- *When* $b^2 - 4ac > 0$, *the quadratic equation has two unequal, real roots.*
- *When* $b^2 - 4ac < 0$, *the quadratic equation has no real roots.*

32. *Answer: (d)*
$50 = -1.2t^2 + 100$
$t = 6.45$

33. *Answer: (a)*
Remainder Theorem states if a polynomial $P(x)$ *is divided by* $x - r$, *its remainder is* $P(r)$.
$P(3) = 2 \times 3^4 - 3 \times 3^3 + 4 \times 3^2 - 5(3) + 6 = 108$

34. *Answer: (d)*
c is the y-intercept which is equal to 100.

35. *Answer: (b)*
$8a^2 = a^y \times a^2 = a^{y+2}$

36. *Answer: (c)*
$x^{\frac{3}{2}} = \frac{1}{27}$
$x = (\frac{1}{27})^{\frac{2}{3}}$
$\frac{1}{27} = 3^{-3}$
$x = (3^{-3})^{\frac{2}{3}} = 3^{-2} = \frac{1}{9}$

37. *Answer: (d)*
$\frac{2}{(x+y)^{-\frac{2}{3}}} = (x+y)^{-\frac{1}{3}}$,
$2 = (x+y)^{-\frac{2}{3}}(x+y)^{-\frac{1}{3}} = (x+y)^{-1}$
$x + y = \frac{1}{2}$

38. *Answer: 153*
$a + (90 - 63)° = 180°$
$a = 153°$

39. *Answer: (d)*
$3x = 42$
$x = 14$
$2y + 42 = 90$
$y = 24$
$x + y = 14 + 24 = 38$

40. *Answer: (b)*
$y = x + z$ *(exterior angle theorem and corresponding angles)*
$z = y - x$

41. *Answer: (d)*
$2x + x = 90°$
$x = 30°$
These are two special 30–60–90 right triangles.
$AB = 2$
$AC = \frac{1}{2} \times 2 = 1$
$AD = \frac{\sqrt{3}}{2} \times AC = \frac{\sqrt{3}}{2}$

42. *Answer: (d)*
Point D is the mid-point of $\overline{AB}$ *and point E is the mid-point of* $\overline{AC}$, *so* $\frac{AD}{AB} = \frac{AE}{AC} = \frac{1}{2}$
Therefore, $\Delta ADE \sim \Delta ABC$ *by SAS Similarity theorem*
$AB = 10$
$DB = 5$
$\frac{1}{2} = \frac{DE}{BC}$
$DE = 7$
$BC = 14$
$EC = \frac{1}{2}AC = 6$
Perimeter of DBCE $= 5 + 7 + 14 + 6 = 32$

43. *Answer: 8*
If h is the height of smaller triangle, then the height of the big triangle is h + 3.
Area of Big Δ *– Area of Small* $\Delta = 26$
$\frac{1}{2}(h + 3) \times 12 - \frac{1}{2}h \times 10 = 26$
$6h + 18 - 5h = 26$
$h = 8$

44. *Answer: (b)*
If $a < b$, *then* $BC < AC$.

45. *Answer: 80*
The sum of all interior angles of a pentagon is $(5 - 3) \times 180 = 540°$.
$540 = 120 + 100 + 105 + 115 + (180 - x)$
$x = 80$

46. *Answer: 85*
$A + B + C + D = 360°$
$128° + 128° + 5x - 10° + x = 360°$
$x = 19°$
$5x - 10° = 85°$

47. *Answer: (c)*

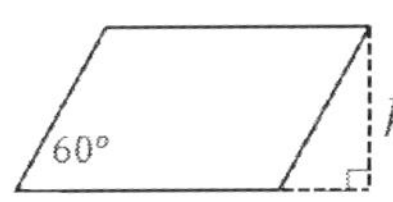

Area = Base × Height = $12 \times 12 \times \frac{\sqrt{3}}{2} = 72\sqrt{3}$

48. *Answer: (b)*
OA is the radius of the circle and the shaded area is the area of the quarter circle minus the area of the rectangle.
Radius = $\sqrt{OB^2 + OC^2} = \sqrt{3^2 + 4^2} = 5$
Shaded Area = Area of $\frac{1}{4}$ *Circle – Area of Rectangle =*
$\frac{1}{4}(\pi \times 5^2) - 4 \times 3 = \frac{1}{4} \times 25\pi - 12 = \frac{25\pi}{4} - 12$

49. *Answer: 78.5*
$DA^2 + OA^2 = OD^2$
$12^2 + r^2 = (8 + r)^2 = 64 + 16r + r^2$
$r = 5$
Area = $\pi \times 5^2 = 78.54$

50. *Answer: (c)*
Area = $\frac{40}{360}(\pi \times 5^2 - \pi \times 4^2) = \pi$

51. *Answer: 4.12*
$BF = 2$
$EF = 3$
$EA = 2$
$AB = \sqrt{EA^2 + EB^2} = \sqrt{EA^2 + BF^2 + EF^2}$
$AB = \sqrt{2^2 + 2^2 + 3^2} = \sqrt{17} = 4.123$

52. *Answer: (b)*
Let x be the length of one side of the cube.
Diameter of Sphere = Diagonal of Cube
Diagonal of Cube = $\sqrt{x^2 + x^2 + x^2} = x\sqrt{3}$
$\sqrt{x^2 + x^2 + x^2} = 3\sqrt{3}$
$x\sqrt{3} = 3\sqrt{3}$
$x = 3$
Volume of Cube = $3^3 = 27$

53. *Answer: (d)*
After folding, the height of the box will be 3 cm, the length will be 5 cm, and the width will be 4cm.
Volume = 3 cm × 4 cm × 5 cm = 60 cm^3

54. *Answer: (a)*
The equation of a parabola with vertex (h, k) is $y = (x - h)^2 + k$.
$(h, k) = (-3, -4)$
$y = (x + 3)^2 - 4$

55. *Answer: (d)*
This is a trapezoid of whose area is equal to $\frac{1}{2}(AB + OC) \times OA$.
Area = $\frac{1}{2}(4 + 6) \times 4 = 20$

56. *Answer: 6*
Rewrite the equation in standard form.
$x^2 + y^2 - 4x + 2y = 20$
$(x^2 - 4x + 2^2) + (y^2 + 2y + 1^2) = 20 + 2^2 + 1^2 = 25$
$(x - 2)^2 + (y + 1)^2 = 5^2$
The center of circle is $(2, -1)$ *and the radius is 5.*
$h + k + r = 2 - 1 + 5 = 6$

57. *Answer: (b)*
In the first Quadrant, only when $\alpha = 45$, $cos(\alpha°) = sin(\alpha°) = \frac{\sqrt{2}}{2}$
For a unit circle:
$x = y = \frac{\sqrt{2}}{2}$
$x + y = \sqrt{2}$

58. *Answer: (b)*
The graph of $y = 3\cos(2x) + 3$ *intersects the y-axis at* $x = 0$.
$y = 3\cos(2 \times 0) + 3 = 3\cos(0) + 3$
$= 3 \times 1 + 3 = 6$

Chapter 1 Heart of Algebra

I. Algebraic Expressions

A. Evaluating Algebraic Expressions

Concept Overviews

Variables

A variable is a letter or symbol that represents a value that is usually unknown or subject to change. An **algebraic expression** is made up of one or more **terms**. For instance, the expression $x^2 + 4x + 4$ is made up of three terms: x^2, $4x$, and 4, with x being the variable. The **coefficient** of a term is the constant in front of the variable and is multiplied by the variable. The **base** of a term is another name for the variable.

To raise a number to the nth power is the same as multiplying n copies of that number. The **power** of a term is the number to which the variable or the base has been raised. For instance, 3^2 has a power of 2. To evaluate it, $3^2 = 3 \times 3 = 9$. The **exponent** is the same as the power.

Like Terms

Terms that share a base and the same power are called like terms. For instance, the terms x, $3x$, and $8x$ are like terms because these terms all have the same base, x, and the same exponent (the exponent is one because it is not explicitly stated). The terms $3x$ and $3x^2$ are **unlike terms**, because the variables have different exponents.

Addition and Subtraction of Algebraic Expressions Consist of Combining Like Terms

To add like terms, combine them by adding their coefficients, for example, $3x + 4x = 7x$. To subtract like terms, subtract their coefficients, for example, $9a^2 - 6a^2 = 3a^2$.

Multiply and Divide Terms with Same Base

To **multiply** terms with same base , multiply the coefficients of the terms and add the exponents: $(3b^4)(2b^3) = 6b^7$. To divide terms with same base, divide the coefficients of the terms and subtract the exponents: $\frac{15x^5}{5x^2} = 3x^3$.

- The **reciprocal** of a number x is equivalent to $\frac{1}{x}$ where x is not 0.
- To divide by a fraction term is the same as multiplying by its reciprocal. For instance: $\frac{x^5}{\frac{1}{x^2}} = x^5 \times x^2 = x^7$

Distributive Law

Use the **distributive law** when multiplying algebraic expressions with more than one term. The distributive law states that in order to get rid of the parentheses, each element within the parentheses should be multiplied by the term outside.

Examples:

$$A(B + C) = AB + AC$$
$$A(B - C) = AB - AC$$

- Rules for removing the parentheses: if there is no coefficient in front of the parentheses and simply a +, remove the parentheses. This is equivalent to distributing +1. If the sign before the parentheses is –, change the sign of every term inside and take away the parentheses. This can be thought of as distributing -1.
  For instance, $x^2 - (-2x^2 + 3x - 1) = x^2 + 2x^2 - 3x + 1 = 3x^2 - 3x + 1$

- Use **FOIL** to multiply a binomial by another binomial

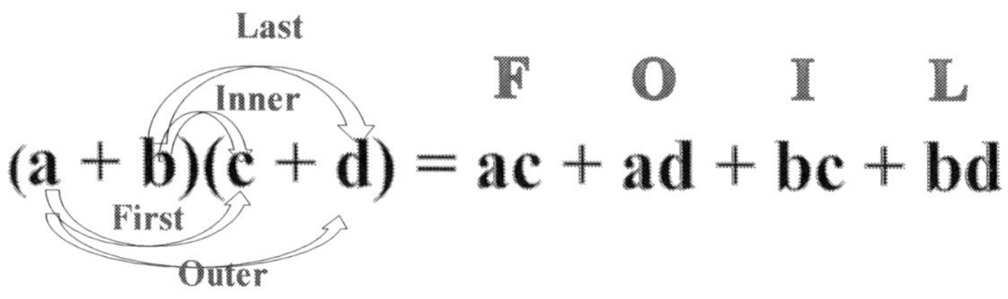

Last

Inner

F O I L

$$(a + b)(c + d) = ac + ad + bc + bd$$

First

Outer

Example: $(x + 3)(x - 1) = x^2 - x + 3x - 3$
$= x^2 + 2x - 3$

- To multiply two polynomials consisting of three or more terms, multiply each term in the first polynomial by each term in the second polynomial.

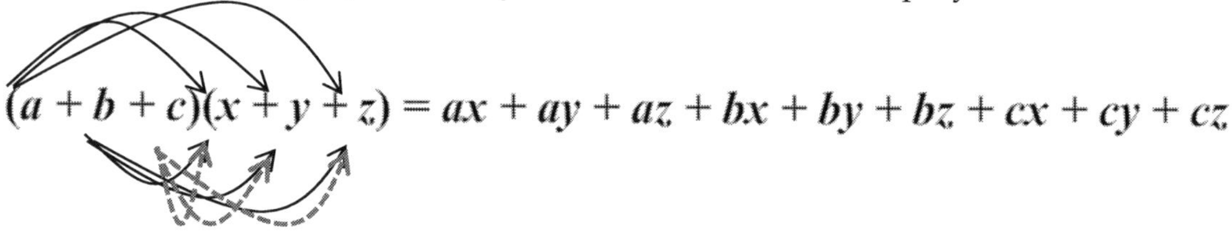

$$(a + b + c)(x + y + z) = ax + ay + az + bx + by + bz + cx + cy + cz$$

Example: $(x^2 + x + 1)(2x^2 - x - 1)$
$= 2x^4 - x^3 - x^2$
$+2x^3 - x^2 - x$
$+ 2x^2 - x - 1$
$= 2x^4 + x^3 - 2x - 1$

Evaluate an Expression

To evaluate an expression by substitution is to replace a variable by its value and then perform the calculations.

Example: Evaluate $x^2 + 3x + 5$ when $x = -1$

Solution: Substitute x with -1, so $(-1)^2 + 3(-1) + 5 = 1 - 3 + 5 = 3$.

Problem Solving Skills

Easy

1. If $x = 3$, what is $2y(6 - 5x)$ in terms of y?
   a) $12y - 30$
   b) $12y$
   c) $12y - 10$
   d) $-18y$

Answer: (d)

Replace x with 3 in the equation.
$x = 3$, $2y(6 - 5 \times 3) = 2y \times (-9)$
$= -18y$

2. If $f(x) = \frac{x^2+35}{x^2-10}$, what is the value of $f(5)$?
   a) 0
   b) 3
   c) 4
   d) 7

Answer: (c)

Plug the number 5 into the function.
$f(5) = \frac{5^2 + 35}{5^2 - 10}$
$\frac{60}{15} = 4$

3. If $a = \left|\frac{1}{x+2}\right|$ and $b = \frac{1}{y}$, what is the value of $a + b$ when $x = -3$ and $y = -3$?
   a) $\frac{1}{6}$
   b) $\frac{1}{4}$
   c) $\frac{2}{3}$
   d) $\frac{1}{2}$

Answer: (c)

$a + b = \left|\frac{1}{-3+2}\right| + \frac{1}{-3}$

$1 - \frac{1}{3} = \frac{2}{3}$

4. If $x = 5$ and $y = -4$, then $x^2 + xy + y^2 =$?
   a) 4
   b) -12
   c) 0
   d) 21

Answer: (d)

Plug in $x = 5$ and $y = -5$.

$(5)^2 + (5)(-4) + (-4)^2 = 21$

5. If $x + y = 8$, $y = z - 3$, and $z = 1$, then what is the value of x?
   a) 10
   b) 3
   c) -8
   d) -6

Answer: (a)

If $z = 1$, then $y = 1 - 3 = -2$.

$x + (-2) = 8$
$x = 10$

6. If $a - 2b = 12$, $b - c = 5$, and $c = -1$, what is the value of a?
   a) 6
   b) 12
   c) 16
   d) 20

Answer: (d)

If $c = -1$, then $b - (-1) = 5$.
$b + 1 = 5$
$b = 4$
$a - 2(4) = 12$
$a = 20$

7. If $x = \frac{5}{3}yz$, what is the value of y when $z = 6$ and $x = 40$?
   a) 2
   b) 4
   c) 10
   d) 12

Answer: (b)

If $x = 40$ and $z = 6$, then $40 = \frac{5}{3}(y)(6)$.

$y = \frac{120}{5 \times 6} = 4$

8. If $4 + \sqrt{k} = 7$, then k =?
   a) 3
   b) 6
   c) 9
   d) $\sqrt{3}$

Answer: (c)

If $4 + \sqrt{k} = 7$, then $\sqrt{k} = 3$.

Square both sides: $k = 9$

9. If $x = 4y$ and $y = 2$, what is the value of $5x$?
   a) 4
   b) 10
   c) 20
   d) 40

Answer: (d)

Plug $y = 2$ into the first equation.

$x = 4(2) = 8$
$5x = 5(8) = 40$

10. If one soft drink costs $0.40 and one burger cost $2, which of the following represents the cost, in dollars, of S soft drinks and B burgers?
    a) S × B
    b) .8S × B
    c) 2.4(B + S)
    d) 2B + 0.4S

Answer: (d)

Total = 2 × B + 0.4 × S

11. What is the least value of integer x such that the value of $2x - 1$ is greater than 9?
    a) 7
    b) 6
    c) 5
    d) 4

Answer: (b)

$2x - 1 > 9$

$2x > 10$
$x > 5$
The least value of integer is 6.

12. If $\frac{x+y}{z} = 9$, $\frac{x}{y} = 8$, and $\sqrt{x} = 4$, what is the value of z?
    a) 1
    b) 2
    c) 3
    d) 4

Answer: (b)

If $\sqrt{x} = 4$, then $x = 4^2 = 16$.
$\frac{x}{y} = \frac{16}{y} = 8 \rightarrow y = 2$
$\frac{16+2}{z} = 9 \rightarrow z = 2$

13. If $x - y = 7$, $y = 2z + 1$, and $z = 3$, what is the value of x?
    a) −14
    b) −12
    c) 10
    d) 14

Answer: (d)

$y = 2z + 1 = 2 \times 3 + 1 = 7$
$x - y = 7$
$x - 7 = 7$
$x = 14$

14. If $x + 2y = 5$, what is the value of $x + 2y - 5$?

Answer: 0

$(x + 2y) - 5 \rightarrow 5 - 5 = 0$

15. If $\frac{x}{y} = 4$, $x = 8z$, and $z = 7$, what is the value of y?

a) 12
b) 13
c) 14
d) 16

Answer: (c)

Plug the value of z into x = 8z.
$x = 8 \times 7 = 56$
$\frac{x}{y} = 4 \rightarrow \frac{56}{y} = 4 \rightarrow 4y = 56 \rightarrow$
$y = 14$

16. If $a = \frac{3}{5}xy$, what is the value of y when $x = 2$ and $a = 24$?

a) 10
b) 20
c) 35
d) 40

Answer: (b)

Plug x = 2 and a = 24 into the equation.
$a = \frac{3}{5}xy \rightarrow 24 = \frac{3}{5} \times 2 \times y$
$y = \frac{24 \times 5}{2 \times 3} = 20$

17. If $f(x) = \frac{2-x^2}{x}$ for all nonzero x, then $f(1)$=?

a) 1
b) 2
c) 3
d) 4

Answer: (a)

Plug x = 1 into the function.
$f(1) = \frac{2-(1)^2}{1} = \frac{1}{1} = 1$

18. If $3(x - 5) = 15$, what does $\frac{x-5}{x+5}$ equal?

Answer: $\frac{1}{3}$

$3(x - 5) = 15$
$x - 5 = 5 \rightarrow x = 10$
$\frac{x-5}{x+5} = \frac{5}{10+5} = \frac{5}{15} = \frac{1}{3}$

19. If $ab + 3b = a - 2c$, what is the value of b when $a = -2$ and c = −1?

Answer: 0

Plug a = −2 and c = −1 into equation.
$(-2)b + 3b = -2 - 2 \times (-1)$
$-2b + 3b = 0 \rightarrow b = 0$

20. If $(x^2 - 3x + 4)(2x + 1) = ax^3 + bx^2 + cx + d$ for all values of x, what is the value of c?

a) −5
b) 4
c) 5
d) 2

Answer: (c)

Two polynomials are the same when the coefficients of corresponding terms are equal.
FOIL: $(x^2 - 3x + 4)(2x + 1) =$
$2x^3 - 5x^2 + 5x + 4$
$= ax^3 + bx^2 + cx + d$
$a = 2$, $b = -5$, $c = 5$, and $d = 4$

21. If $x = y(y - 2)$, then $x + 3$ =?

a) $y^2 - y$
b) $y^2 - 3y$
c) $y^2 - 2y + 2$
d) $y^2 - 2y + 3$

Answer: (d)

FOIL: $x = y(y - 2) = y^2 - 2y$
$x + 3 = y^2 - 2y + 3$

Medium

22. Which of the following is not equal to $6x^2$?
    a) $2x^2 + 4x^2$
    b) $2x + 4x$
    c) $(2x)(3x)$
    d) $(6x)(x)$

Answer: (b)

$2x + 4x = 6x \neq 6x^2$

23. If $z = \frac{12x^4}{y}$, what happens to the value of z when both x and y are doubled?
    a) z is multiplied by 32.
    b) z is multiplied by 16.
    c) z is multiplied by 8.
    d) z is doubled.

Answer: (c)

$\frac{12(2x)^4}{(2y)} = 2^3 \times \frac{12x^4}{y}$

24. If $\frac{x}{2} = 0$, what is the value of $1 + x + 2x^2 + 3x^3 =$?
    a) 2
    b) 1
    c) 0
    d) 3

Answer: (b)

$\frac{1}{2}x = 0$
$x = 0$
$1 + 0 + 2(0)^2 + 3(0)^3 = 1$

25. If n is a positive integer and $\frac{n}{2^n} = \frac{1}{4}$ then $n =$?
    a) 1
    b) 3
    c) 4
    d) 5

Answer: (c)

Apply either cross multiplication or trial and error to find the answer.
$4n = 2^n$
$n = 4$

26. If $x = 3$, $y = 5$, what is the value of $2 \times (\frac{x}{y})^2 \times y^2$?
    a) 5
    b) 10
    c) 15
    d) 18

Answer: (d)

$2 \times (\frac{3}{5})^2 \times 5^2 = 18$

27. If I and J are integers and $2I + 3J = 17$, which of the following CANNOT be a value of J?
    a) −1
    b) 1
    c) 2
    d) 3

Answer: (c)

$2I = 17 - 3J$
2I is an even number, so 17 – 3J must be even.
J must be an odd number.

28. $f(x) = \frac{x^3 - 5}{x^2 - 2x + 8}$, then what is $f(3)$?

a) 0
b) 2
c) 4
d) 6

Answer: (b)

$f(3) = \frac{3^3 - 5}{3^2 - 2(3) + 8} = \frac{22}{11} = 2$

29. $x = -4$ and $y = 2$, what is the value of $|\sqrt[3]{xy} - 5y|$?

a) 12
b) 18
c) -12
d) 24

Answer: (a)

Plug in the values of x and y.
$|\sqrt[3]{-4 \times 2} - 10|$
$= |\sqrt[3]{-27} - 9|$
$= |-2 - 10|$
$= |-12| = 12$

30. If $\frac{6x}{\sqrt{x+1}} = 3\sqrt{2}$, what is one possible value of x?

a) - 7
b) - 1
c) 0
d) 1

Answer: (d)

Take square on both sides of the equation: $(\frac{6x}{\sqrt{x+1}})^2 = (3\sqrt{2})^2$
$\frac{36x^2}{x+1} = 18$
$36x^2 = 18x + 18$
$2x^2 = x + 1 \rightarrow x = 1 \text{ or } -\frac{1}{2}$

31. If $x > y > 0$, which of the following is less than $\frac{x}{y}$?

a) $\frac{3}{2}$
b) $\frac{y}{x}$
c) $\frac{2y}{x}$
d) $\frac{3y}{2x}$

Answer: (b)

If $x > y > 0$, *then* $(\frac{x}{y} > 1)$ *and* $(\frac{y}{x} < 1)$.

32. The table below gives values of the quadratic function $f(x)$ at selected values of x. Which of the following defines $f(x)$?

x	0	1	2	3
f(x)	5	7	13	23

a) $f(x) = x^2 + 5$
b) $f(x) = x^2 + 1$
c) $f(x) = 2x^2 - 5$
d) $f(x) = 2x^2 + 5$

Answer: (d)

Plug in x = 0 and x= 1 to try out until the answer found.

(d) $2(0)^2 + 5 = 5$
$2(1)^2 + 5 = 7$

33. If $(x + y)^2 = 49$ and $(x - y)^2 = 29$, what is the value of xy?

a) 2
b) 5
c) 6
d) 10

$(a+b)^2$
$a^2 + 2ab + b^2$

Answer: (b)

$(x + y)^2 - (x - y)^2 = (x^2 + y^2 + 2xy) - (x^2 + y^2 - 2xy) = 4xy$
$49 - 29 = 4xy$
$xy = 5$

Hard

Questions 34 – 35 refer to the following information:

The Doppler effect is the change in frequency of a wave while its source is moving. The Doppler effect formulas shown below are used to calculate the frequency of sound as a result of relative motion between the source and the observer.

If the source is moving toward an observer at rest, the change of observed frequency can be calculated by:

$$f_{observed} = f_{original}\left(\frac{v_{sound}}{v_{sound} - v_{source}}\right)$$

If the observer is moving toward the sound and the source moving closer to the observer, the change of frequency can be calculated by:

$$f_{observed} = f_{original}\left(\frac{v_{sound} + v_{observer}}{v_{sound} - v_{source}}\right)$$

$f_{observed}$ = observed frequency
$f_{original}$ = frequency of the original wave
v_{sound} = speed of the sound
$v_{observer}$ = speed of the observer
v_{source} = speed of the source

34. Standing on the side walk, you observe an ambulance moving toward you. As the ambulance passes by with its siren blaring, you hear the pitch of the siren change. If the ambulance is approaching at the speed of 90 miles/hour and the siren's pitch sounds at a frequency of 340 Hertz, what is the observed frequency, in Hertz? Assume the speed of sound in air is 760 miles/hour.
    a) 302
    b) 324
    c) 386
    d) 419

Answer: (c)

The source is moving toward an observer at rest.

$f_{observed} = f_{original}\left(\frac{v_{sound}}{v_{sound} - v_{source}}\right)$

$v_{observer} = 0\ miles/hour$
$v_{source} = 90\ miles/hour$
$v_{sound} = 760\ miles/hour$
$f_{observed} = 340 \times \left(\frac{760}{760 - 90}\right)$
$= 386\ Hertz$

35. If you are driving a car at the speed of 30 miles/hour while an ambulance is approaching to you at the speed of 60 miles/hour, what is the observed frequency of the siren, in Hertz? Assume that the ambulance sounds at a frequency of 340 Hertz and the speed of sound in air is 760 miles/hour.
    a) 362
    b) 384
    c) 409
    d) 439

Answer: (b)

The observer is moving toward the sound.

$f_{observed} = f_{original}\left(\frac{v_{sound} + v_{observer}}{v_{sound} - v_{source}}\right)$

$v_{observer} = 30\ miles/hour$
$v_{source} = 60\ miles/hour$
$v_{sound} = 760\ miles/hour$
$f_{observed} = 340 \times \left(\frac{760 + 30}{760 - 60}\right)$
$= 383.7\ Hertz$

36. If $x = -5$ and $y = 3$, what is the value of $x^2(2y + x)$?
   a) -275
   b) -75
   c) -25
   d) 25

Answer: (d)

$(-5)^2 \times (2 \times 3 + (-5)) = 25$

37. If a and b are consecutive odd integers, where $a > b$, which of the following is equal to $a^2 - b^2$?
   a) 4
   b) $2a - 2b$
   c) $2b + 4$
   d) $4b + 4$

Answer: (d)

If a and b are consecutive odd integers and $a > b$, then $a = b + 2$.

$a^2 - b^2 = (a + b)(a - b)$
$= (b + 2 + b)(b + 2 - b)$
$= 2(2b + 2)$
$= 4b + 4$

38. If $\frac{a^3}{b^2}$ is an integer, but $\frac{2a+9}{b}$ is not an integer, which of the following could be the values of a and b?
   a) $a = 2,\ b = 1$
   b) $a = 3,\ b = 2$
   c) $a = 5,\ b = 5$
   d) $a = 6,\ b = 4$

Answer: (c)

Try out the values of a and b from answer choices.

a) $\frac{2^3}{1^2}, \frac{13}{1}$
b) $\frac{3^3}{2^2}, \frac{15}{2}$
c) $\frac{5^3}{5^2}, \frac{19}{5}$
d) $\frac{6^3}{4^2}, \frac{21}{4}$

39. Which of the following expressions must be negative if $x < 0$?
   a) $x^4 - 2$
   b) $x^3 - 3$
   c) $x^4 - 3x^2 - 1$
   d) $x^6 + 3x^2 + 1$

Answer: (b)

If $x < 0$, then the result of an odd power of x is negative and the result of an even power of x is positive.

B. Evaluate One Variable in Terms of Another

Concept Overviews

One Variable in Terms of Another
An equation that contains two variables can be written so that the value of one variable is given in terms of the other. For instance, $y = 3x + 3$ is an equation with two variables, x and y, in which the value of variable y is written in terms of the other variable x. The value of y is $3x + 3$.

Steps to Evaluate One Variable in Terms of Another

1) Combine like terms.
2) Isolate the terms that contain the variable you wish to solve for.
3) Move all other terms to the other side of the equation.
4) Divide all terms by the desired variable's coefficient to calculate the variable in terms of the other.

Example: If $4a + 8b = 16$, what is the value of a in terms of b?
Solution: $4a = 16 - 8b$, Isolate $4a$ on one side of the equation, move $8b$ to the other side of the equation and change the sign of $8b$ to negative.
$a = 4 - 2b$, after dividing all terms by 4, the value of a in terms of b is $4 - 2b$.

Problem Solving Skills

Easy

1. If $xy^3 = z$, $z = ky^2$, and $ky \neq 0$, which of the following is equal to k? (no calculator)
   a) xy
   b) $\frac{x}{y}$
   c) $x - 1$
   d) $x + y$

Answer: (a)
$xy^3 = z = k\,y^2$

$k = \frac{xy^3}{y^2} = xy$

2. If $2x + y = x + 5$, what is y in terms of x? (no calculator)
   a) $5 - x$
   b) $x + 5$
   c) $1 - 5x$
   d) $1 - 2x$

Answer: (a)

Isolate the terms that contain the variable you wish to solve for and then move all other terms to the other side of the equation.
$2x + y = x + 5$
$y = x + 5 - 2x$
$y = -x + 5$

3. If $5x = 4y$ and $2y = 5z$, what is the value of x in terms of z?
   a) z
   b) $2z$
   c) $3z$
   d) $4z$

Answer: (b)

Substitute 2y with 5z in the first equation.
$5x = 2(2y) = 2(5z) = 10z$
$x = 2z$

4. If x and y are positive and $3x^2y^{-1} = 27x$, what is y^{-1} in term of x?
   a) $\frac{x}{9}$
   b) $\frac{9}{x}$
   c) $\frac{x^2}{9}$
   d) $\frac{x}{3}$

Answer: (b)

Divide by $3x^2$ on both sides of the equation $3x^2y^{-1} = 27x$.
$y^{-1} = \frac{27x}{3x^2} = \frac{9}{x}$

Medium

5. If $x^{-1}y = 5$, what does y equal in term of x?
   a) $-5x$
   b) x
   c) $-x$
   d) $5x$

Answer: (d)

$x^{-1} = \frac{1}{x}$
$x^{-1}y = 5$
$\frac{y}{x} = 5 \rightarrow y = 5x$

6. A right circular cylinder with radius 3 and height 7 has a volume v, In terms of v, what is the volume of the right circular cylinder with radius 3 and height 14?
   a) $v + 7$
   b) $7v$
   c) $5v$
   d) $2v$

Answer: (d)

$v = \pi (3)^2 \times 7$
$v_2 = \pi (3)^2 \times 14$
$\frac{v}{v_2} = \frac{\pi(3)^2 \times 7}{\pi(3)^2 \times 14} = \frac{1}{2}$
$v_2 = 2v$

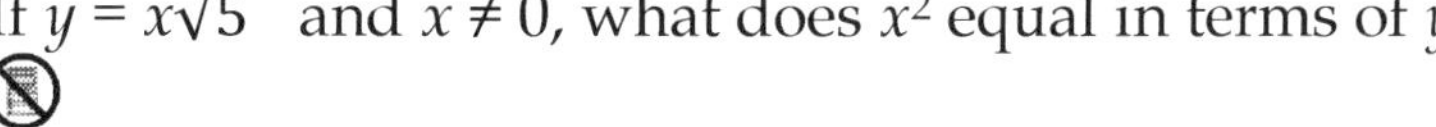

7. If $y = x\sqrt{5}$ and $x \neq 0$, what does x^2 equal in terms of y?
   a) $\frac{y^2}{5}$
   b) $5y^2$
   c) $\frac{25}{y^2}$
   d) $\frac{y^2}{25}$

Answer: (a)

Divide by $\sqrt{5}$ on both sides of the equation $y = x\sqrt{5}$.

$x = \frac{y}{\sqrt{5}}$ *(Then square both sides.)*
$x^2 = \frac{y^2}{5}$

8. The price of green tea leaves is D dollars for 5 ounces and each ounce makes x bottles of green tea drink. In terms of D and x, which of the following expressions shows the cost of making 1 bottle of green tea drink?
   a) $5Dx$
   b) $\frac{5D}{x}$
   c) $\frac{5x}{D}$
   d) $\frac{D}{5x}$

Answer: (d)

$D = 5\ ounces \times \frac{x\ Bottles}{Ounce} \times Price\ of\ One\ Bottle$

$Price\ of\ One\ Bottle = \frac{D}{5x}$

Hard

9. If $x = 2z + 4$ and $y = 1 + 4z^2$, what is y in terms of x? 
   a) $x^2 + 8x + 17$
   b) $x^2 - 8x + 17$
   c) $4x^2 - 8x + 17$
   d) $4x^2 - 8x + 68$

Answer: (b)

Replace z in terms of y.
$z = \frac{x-4}{2}$
$y = 1 + 4(\frac{x-4}{2})^2$
$y = 1 + (x - 4)^2$
$y = 1 + x^2 - 8x + 16$
$y = x^2 - 8x + 17$

10. If $x = 2(3z^2 + z + 4)$ and $y = -z + 3$, what is x in terms of y?

   a) $6y^2 - 38y - 68$
   b) $6y^2 + 38y - 132$
   c) $6y^2 - 38y + 68$
   d) $6y^2 + 38y + 68$

Answer: (c)

Write z in terms of y.
$z = 3 - y$
$x = 2[3(3 - y)^2 + (3 - y) + 4)$
$x = 2[\ 3(y^2 - 6y + 9) + 7 - y]$
$x = 2(3y^2 - 18y + 27 + 7 - y\ )$
$x = 2(3y^2 - 19y + 34)$
$= 6y^2 - 38y + 68$

11. If $x = y^2$ for any positive integer x, and if $z = x^3 + x^4$, what is z in terms of y?
   a) $y^2 + y^3$
   b) y^3
   c) $y^6 + y^3$
   d) $y^6 + y^8$

Answer: (d)

Replace x with y^2.

$z = (y^2\ )^3 + (y^2\ )^4 = y^6 + y^8$

12. If $x = 2y^2 + 3y + 4$ and $z = -y + 1$, what is x in terms of z?

   a) $2z^2 - 7z - 9$
   b) $2z^2 - 7z + 7$
   c) $2z^2 + 7z + 9$
   d) $2z^2 - 7z + 9$

Answer: (d)

Plug in y = 1 – z to the first equation and then apply FOIL method and the distributive law.
$x = 2(1 - z)^2 + 3(1 - z) + 4$
$x = 2z^2 - 7z + 9$

II. Solving Equations

A. Solving Equations

Concept Overviews

Definition of Equation
An **equation** is a statement that two expressions are equal. The both sides of the equation are equal. The key of solving for a variable in the equation is to isolate the variable on one side and everything else on the other side of the equal sign.

Opposite Operations
To isolate variables, use operations that are opposite to the existing operations in the equation in order to move variables or numbers between both sides of an equation and keep the two sides equal.

Using opposite operations is very important for solving an equation. Some pairs of opposite operations include + verses − , × verses ÷, and square verses square root.

Problem Solving Skills

Easy

1. If $3x + 2 = 5$, what is the value of $3x - 6$?
   a) -1
   b) -2
   c) -3
   d) 1

Answer: (c)

Subtract 8 on both sides.

$3x + 2 - 8 = 5 - 8 = -3$
$3x - 6 = -3$

2. If $a^2 - 1 = b^3$, and $2a = 6$, which of the following could be the value of b?
   a) -1
   b) 0
   c) 1
   d) 2

Answer: (d)

$2a = 6$
$a = 3$
$3^2 - 1 = b^3$
$8 = b^3 = 2^3$
$b = 2$

3. If $x \times y = x$ for all values of x, what is the value of y?
   a) $-x$
   b) -1
   c) 0
   d) 1

Answer: (d)

Divide by x on both sides.

$y = 1$

4. If $-3x + 8 = -2x - 7$, what is the value of x?
   a) 15
   b) 3
   c) -3
   d) -15

Answer: (a)

Isolate x on one side of equation and use opposite operations.
$-3x + 8 = -2x - 7$
$-3x + 8 - 8 + 2x$
$= -2x - 7 - 8 + 2x$
$-x = -15 \rightarrow x = 15$

5. If $3x - 2 = 7$, then $2x + 5 =$?
   a) 10
   b) 11
   c) 12
   d) 14

Answer: (b)

Use opposite operations.
$3x - 2 = 7$
$3x - 2 + 2 = 7 + 2$
$3x = 9 \rightarrow x = 3$
$2(3) + 5 = 11$

6. If $\frac{3x}{5} = \frac{3}{2}$, then x=?
   a) $\frac{2}{5}$
   b) $\frac{5}{2}$
   c) $\frac{1}{5}$
   d) 3

Answer: (b)

Use cross multiplication to solve fraction equations.
$\frac{3x}{5} = \frac{3}{2}$
$2 \times 3x = 3 \times 5$
$6x = 15$ *(divide both sides by 6)*
$x = \frac{15}{6} = \frac{5}{2}$

7. If $m^2 + 8 = 39$, then $m^2 - 7 =$?
   a) 31
   b) 29
   c) 26
   d) 24

Answer: (d)

$m^2 + 8 = 39$
$m^2 = 31$
$m^2 - 7 = 31 - 7 = 24$

8. If $3(x + 5) = 18$, then what is the value of x?
   a) 1
   b) 3
   c) 6
   d) 9

Answer: (a)

Divide both sides by 3.
$3(x + 5) = 18$
$x + 5 = 6$
$x = 1$

9. If $\frac{x + 2y}{x} = 0$, what is the value of x?
   a) $-2y$
   b) 0
   c) $2y$
   d) y^2

Answer: (a)

If a fraction is equal to zero, its numerator must be equal to zero.
$x + 2y = 0$
$x = -2y$

10. If $0.3x + 2 = 5.6$, what is the value of x?
   a) 3.6
   b) 1.2
   c) 36
   d) 12

Answer: (d)

$0.3x = 5.6 - 2 = 3.6$
$x = \frac{3.6}{0.3} = 12$

11. If $9x + 3 = 21$, then $5x + 10 =$?
   a) 20
   b) 30
   c) 32
   d) 34

Answer: (a)

$9x + 3 = 21$
$9x = 18$
$x = 2$
$5(2) + 10 = 20$

12. If $8 \times 27 \times 64 = x^3$, what is the value of x?
   a) 6
   b) 12
   c) 18
   d) 24

Answer: (d)

$8 \times 27 \times 64 = 2^3 \times 3^3 \times 4^3 = x^3$
$x = 2 \times 3 \times 4 = 24$

13. If $\frac{x^2}{2\times 3} = 6 \times 5$, what is the value of x^2?
   a) 60
   b) 90
   c) 120
   d) 180

Answer: (d)

$x^2 = 6 \times 5 \times 2 \times 3 = 180$

14. If x, y, and z are positive numbers and $xyz = x^2$, which of the following must equal x?
   a) yz
   b) xy
   c) xz
   d) 1

Answer: (a)

Divide both sides by x.

$xyz = x^2$
$yz = x$

15. If $3x - x = x - 5$, then $x =$?
   a) 10
   b) 5
   c) −1
   d) −5

Answer: (d)

$3x - x = 2x$
$2x = x - 5$
$x = -5$

16. If $(0.0010) \times y = 10$, then $y =$?
   a) 0.01
   b) 0.001
   c) 100
   d) 10000

Answer: (d)

Divide both sides by 0.001.
$(0.0010) \times y = 10$
$y = \frac{10}{0.001} = 10000$

17. If $\frac{3}{x} + x = 5 + \frac{3}{5}$, then x can be equal to which of the following?
   a) 1
   b) 2
   c) 3
   d) 5

Answer: (d)

Compare both sides of the equation and find the corresponding terms.
$x = 5$

18. If $x^3 + 6 = x^3 + y$, then y =?
    a) −6
    b) −3
    c) 6
    d) 3

Answer: (c)

Definition of equation. Both sides of the equation are equal.

$x^3 + 6 = x^3 + y$
$y = 6$

19. If $\frac{\sqrt{x}+y}{\sqrt{x}+5} = 1$, then y = ? (no calculator)
    a) 1
    b) 3
    c) 5
    d) 8

Answer: (c)

$\sqrt{x} + y = \sqrt{x} + 5$
$\sqrt{x} + y = \sqrt{x} + 5$
$y = 5$

20. If $3(x + 6) = 21$, what is the value of x? (no calculator)
    a) 1
    b) 3
    c) 5
    d) 7

Answer: (a)

Divide both sides by 3.
$3(x + 6) = 21$
$x + 6 = 7$
$x = 1$

21. If $\frac{x}{y} = 6$ and $\frac{x}{z} = 3$, then what does z equal when $y = 2$?
    a) 2
    b) 4
    c) 6
    d) 8

Answer: (b)

If $y = 2$, then $x = 12$.
$\frac{12}{z} = 3$
$12 = 3z$
$z = 4$

22. If $2\sqrt{3x^2} + 7 = 19$, what is the value of x?
    a) 2
    b) 3
    c) $2\sqrt{3}$
    d) $3\sqrt{2}$

Answer: (c)

$2\sqrt{3x^2} = 12$

$\sqrt{3x^2} = 6$
$3x^2 = 36$
$x^2 = 12$
$x = \sqrt{12} = \pm 2\sqrt{3}$

23. If $\frac{y}{y-3} = \frac{4}{3}$, then what does y equal to?
    a) 4
    b) 8
    c) −8
    d) 12

Answer: (d)

$\frac{y}{y-3} = \frac{4}{3} \rightarrow$ *cross multiply*
$3y = 4(y - 3) = 4y - 12$
$y = 12$

24. If $-a^4 + b^2 = -a^4 + 4$, then b could equal to?
    a) −4
    b) −2
    c) 1
    d) 3

Answer: (b)

Because this is an equation, both sides are equal.
$-a^4 + b^2 = -a^4 + 4$
$b^2 = 4 \rightarrow b = \pm 2$

25. If $\frac{2x+4}{x+1} = \frac{4}{3}$, then what is the value of x?
   a) -12
   b) -4
   c) -2
   d) 2

Answer: (b)

Apply Cross Multiplication.
$\frac{2x+4}{x+1} = \frac{4}{3}$
$3(2x + 4) = 4(x + 1)$
$6x + 12 = 4x + 4$
$2x = -8$
$x = -4$

26. If $3(x + y)(x - y) = 30$ and $x - y = 5$, what is the value of $x + y$?
   a) 1
   b) 2
   c) 3
   d) -1

Answer: (b)

$3 \times 5 \times (x + y) = 30$
$x + y = 2$

27. If $3(x - 3) = 9$, what is the value of x?
   a) -6
   b) -10
   c) 6
   d) 10

Answer: (c)

Divide both sides by 3.
$3(x - 3) = 9$
$x - 3 = 3$
$x = 6$

28. If $\frac{x}{3} = \frac{3x}{z}$ and $z \neq 0$, what is the value of z?
   a) 9
   b) 6
   c) 4
   d) 3

Answer: (a)

Apply cross multiplication.
$\frac{x}{3} = \frac{3x}{z}$
$\frac{1}{3} = \frac{3}{z}$
$z = 3 \times 3 = 9$

29. If $3x^2 = 2y = 12$, what is the value of x^2y?

Answer: 24

Divide each term by 3.
$x^2 = \frac{12}{3} = 4$
$y = \frac{12}{2} = 6$
$x^2 y = 4 \times 6 = 24$

30. If $\frac{x}{x-2} = \frac{43}{41}$ then x?
   a) 39
   b) 43
   c) -41
   d) -39

Answer: (b)

Apply cross multiplication or simply observe that both numerators exceed their denominator by 2, therefore $x = 43$.
$41x = 43(x - 2) = 43x - 86$
$2x = 86$
$x = 43$

31. If 3,500 = 100(3x + 5), then x =
   a) $\frac{1}{10}$
   b) 1
   c) 10
   d) 100

Answer: (c)

Divide both sides by 100.
$3{,}500 = 100(3x + 5)$
$35 = 3x + 5$
$3x = 30$
$x = 10$

32. If 7,373 = 73(x + 1), then x =?
   a) 10
   b) 11
   c) 100
   d) 101

Answer: (c)

Divide both sides by 73.
$7{,}373 = 73(x + 1)$
$\frac{7373}{73} = x + 1$
$101 = x + 1$
$x = 101 - 1 = 100$

33. If 2x – 36 = 16, then x – 18 =?
   a) 1
   b) 3
   c) 5
   d) 8

Answer: (d)

Divide both sides by 2.
$2x - 36 = 16$
$x - 18 = 8$

34. If 3x + 2 = 13, then 6x − 2?
   a) 20
   b) 24
   c) 26
   d) 28

Answer: (a)

$3x = 11$
$6x = 22$
$6x - 2 = 2(3x) - 2$
$= 2 \times 11 - 2 = 20$

Medium

35. If $xy = 4$, $z - y = 3$, and $2z = 10$, what is the value of $x + y + z$?

Answer: 9

Solve for z first. Then solve for y, and finally solve for x.
$2z = 10 \rightarrow z = 5$
$5 - y = 3 \rightarrow y = 2$
$x(2) = 4 \rightarrow x = 2$
$x + y + z = 9$

36. A litter of milk can fill up 3 large cups or 5 small cups. If there are 12 large cups and 10 small cups, about how many litters of milk will be needed to fill up all the cups?
   a) 3
   b) 4
   c) 5
   d) 6

Answer: (d)

12 large cups need 4 litters and 10 small cups need 2 litters.

The amount of milk needed:
4 + 2 = 6 litters

37. If $x^3 + 2y = 0$, which of the following must be true?
   a) $x^3 = -2y$
   b) $xy = y$
   c) $x = \frac{2y}{x}$
   d) $x^3 = y^2$

Answer: (a)

$x^3 + 2y - 2y = -2y$

$x^3 = -2y$

38. If $2a + 3b = 2b$, which of the following must equal $6a + 3b$?
   a) 0
   b) 1
   c) b
   d) $3b$

Answer: (a)

$2a + 3b = 2b, \quad 2a + b = 0$

$6a + 3b = 3(2a + b) = 0$

39. If $\frac{x+y}{x-y} = 4$ and $y \neq 0$, what is the value of $\frac{x}{y}$?

Answer: $\frac{5}{3}$

Cross multiply and then divide both sides by y.

$\frac{x+y}{x-y} = 4 \rightarrow x + y = 4(x - y)$

$\frac{x}{y} + 1 = 4(\frac{x}{y} - 1)$

$\frac{x}{y} + 1 = 4\frac{x}{y} - 4$

$\frac{x}{y} = \frac{5}{3}$

40. If $\frac{6}{\sqrt{x+4}} = 2$, what is the value of x?
   a) -5
   b) -3
   c) 5
   d) 3

Answer: (c)

$\frac{6}{\sqrt{x+4}} = 2$

$\sqrt{x+4} = \frac{6}{2}$

$\sqrt{x+4} = 3$

$x + 4 = 9 \rightarrow x = 5$

41. If $\frac{5}{q} = \frac{4}{3}$, what is the value of q in fraction?

Answer: $\frac{15}{4}$

Apply cross multiplication.

$3 \times 5 = 4 \times q$

$q = \frac{15}{4}$

42. If $|3r - 5| = 10$ and $|r + 2| = 7$, then what is the value of r?
   a) 5
   b) 3
   c) -3
   d) -5

Answer: (a)

There are two possible solutions for each equation after taking out the absolute value sign, one where the inside is positive and one where the inside is negative.

$|3r - 5| = 10$

$3r - 5 = 10$ or $3r - 5 = -10$

$r = 5$ or $-\frac{5}{3}$

Only $r = 5$ satisfies both equations.

43. If k is a constant and $2x + 7 = 4kx + 7$ for all values of x, what is the value of k?
   a) 2
   b) $\frac{1}{2}$
   c) 0
   d) $\frac{2}{3}$

Answer: (b)

Because the equation is true for all values of x, the two expressions have the same coefficients for corresponding terms.
$4k = 2$
$k = \frac{1}{2}$

44. $\frac{2x - y}{y} = \frac{1}{3}$, what is the value of $\frac{x}{y}$?

Answer: $\frac{2}{3}$

$\frac{2x - y}{y} = 2(\frac{x}{y}) - 1$
$2(\frac{x}{y}) - 1 = \frac{1}{3}$
$2(\frac{x}{y}) = \frac{4}{3}$
$\frac{x}{y} = \frac{2}{3}$

$$|x - 1| = 2$$
$$|y + 2| = 3$$

45. In the equations above, given that $x < 0$ and $y > 0$, what is the value of $x - y$?
   a) 1
   b) 2
   c) 0
   d) -2

Answer: (d)
There are two possible solutions for each equation after taking out the absolute value sign, one where the inside is positive and one where the inside is negative.
$x - 1 = 2$ or $x - 1 = -2$
$x = 3$ (violate $x < 0$) or $x = -1$
$y + 2 = 3$ or $y + 2 = -3$
$y = 1$ or $y = -5$ (violate $y > 0$)
$x - y = -1 - 1 = -2$

Hard

$$\sqrt{x + 2} = x - 1$$

46. For all values of x greater than 1, the equation above is equivalent to which of the following?
   a) $x = x^2$
   b) $x = x^2 - 1$
   c) $x = x^2 - 2x - 1$
   d) $x = x^2 - 2x + 1$

Answer: (c)

Square both sides of the equation.
$(\sqrt{x + 2})^2 = (x - 1)^2$
$x + 2 = x^2 - 2x + 1$
$x = x^2 - 2x - 1$

47. $\frac{1}{3}(6x^3 - 3x^2 + 3x + 9) = ax^3 + bx^2 + cx + d$, for all values of x, where a, b, c, and d are all constants, what is the value of $a + b + c + d$?

Answer: 5

Because the equation is true for all values of x, the two expressions have the same coefficients for corresponding terms.
$\frac{1}{3}(6x^3 - 3x^2 + 3x + 9) = 2x^3 - x^2 + x + 3 = ax^3 + bx^2 + cx + d$
$a = 2$, $b = -1$, $c = 1$, and $d = 3$
$a + b + c + d = 5$

48. If $x > 1$ and $\frac{12}{\sqrt{x-1}} = 4$, what is the value of x?

Answer: 10

Apply cross multiplication.

$$\frac{12}{\sqrt{x-1}} = \frac{4}{1}$$

$\sqrt{x-1} \times 4 = 12$

$\sqrt{x-1} = 3$

$x - 1 = 9$

$x = 10$

49. A parallel circuit has two or more paths for current to flow through and has more than one resistor as shown below. In a house, there are many electrical appliances that connect in parallel so they would not affect each other when their switches are turned on or off.

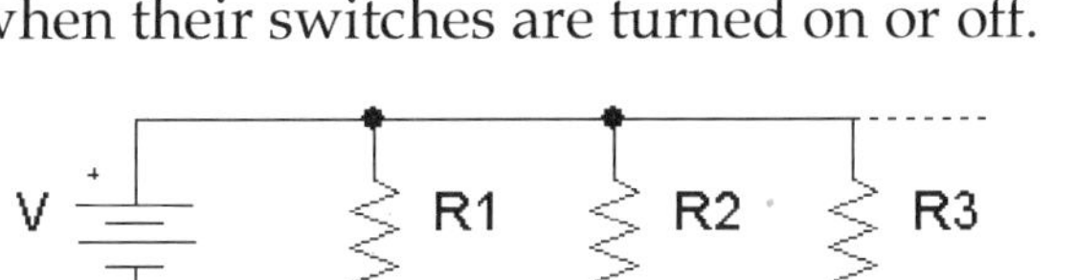

The total resistance, R_{Total}, in a parallel circuit can be calculated by the following formula:

$$\frac{1}{R_{Total}} = \frac{1}{R_1} + \frac{1}{R_2} + \frac{1}{R_3}$$

If three resistors are connected together in parallel and the resistors have values of 20 ohm, 30 ohm, and 60 ohm respectively, what is the total resistance of the circuit?

a) 15 ohm
b) 10 ohm
c) 8 ohm
d) 5 ohm

Answer: (b)

$$\frac{1}{R_{total}} = \frac{1}{20} + \frac{1}{30} + \frac{1}{60} = \frac{1}{10}$$

$R_{total} = 10\ ohm$

B. Solving a Linear Equation

Concept Overviews

Slope of Two Points $= \frac{Rise}{Run} = \frac{y_2 - y_1}{x_2 - x_1}$

Slope-intercept Form: $y = mx + b$ where m is the slope and b is the y-intercept. A linear equation written as slope-intercept form has the properties illustrated by the following graph:

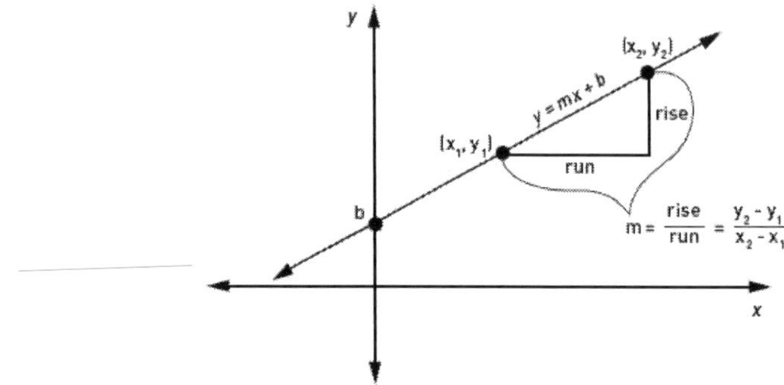

Point-slope Form: From the graph below, the equation of a line passing through the point $(x_1, y_1)$with the slope of m can be expressed as: $y - y_1 = m(x - x_1)$

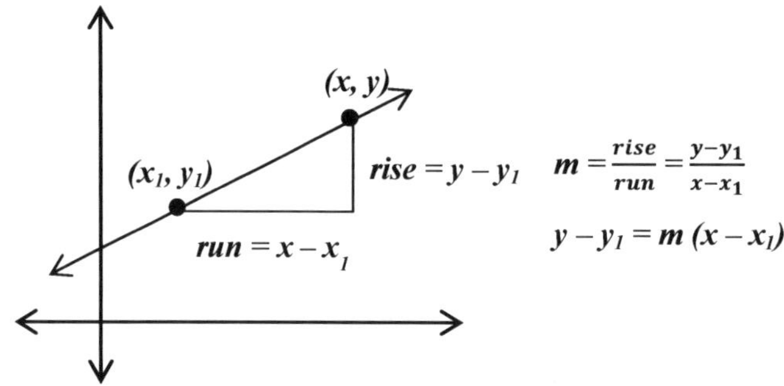

The slope of a linear equation $ax + by + c = 0$ will be $-\frac{a}{b}$.

Two lines are perpendicular if their slopes are opposite reciprocals, i.e., the product of their slopes is –1.

Two different lines are parallel if their slopes are equal but they are not the same line.

Problem Solving Skills

Easy

x	−1	1	2	3
y	5	1	−1	−3

1. Which of the following equations satisfies the relationship between x and y in the table above?
   a) $y = x + 6$
   b) $y = 2x - 3$
   c) $y = 2x + 3$
   d) $y = -2x + 3$

Answer: (d)

Slope $= \frac{Rise}{Run} = \frac{5-1}{-1-1} = -2$

$y - 5 = -2(x + 1)$ *(Point-Slope Form)*

$y = -2x + 3$

2. What is the y-intercept of the linear equation $7y - x = -14$?
   a) -4
   b) -2
   c) 0
   d) 2

Answer: (b)

The y-intercept occurs when $x = 0$.
$7y - 0 = -14$
$y = -2$

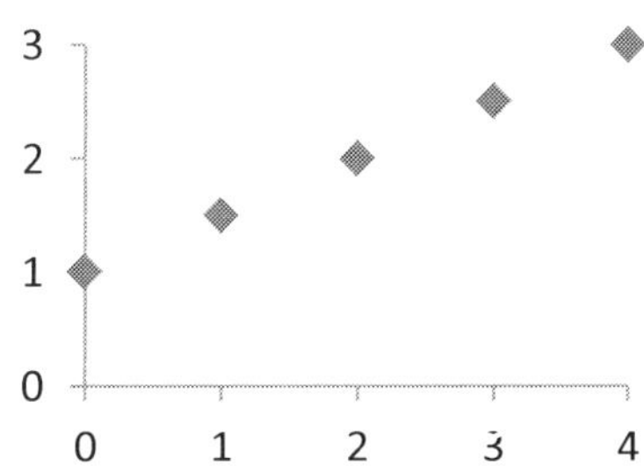

3. Which of the lines described by the following equations best fits those points above?
   a) $y = 0.5x - 1$
   b) $y = 0.5x + 1$
   c) $y = -0.5x - 1$
   d) $y = -0.5x + 1$

Answer: (b)

Slope $= \frac{Rise}{Run} = \frac{2-1}{2-0} = 0.5$
y-intercept $= 1$
$y = 0.5x + 1$

x	0	1	2	3
$f(x)$	−1	1	3	5

4. The table above gives values of the linear function f for several values of x. Which of the following defines $f(x)$?
   a) $f(x) = x - 1$
   b) $f(x) = x + 1$
   c) $f(x) = 2x - 1$
   d) $f(x) = 2x + 1$

Answer: (c)

Slope $= \frac{Rise}{Run} = \frac{1-(-1)}{1-0} = 2$ *and*
y-intercept $= -1$
$y = 2x - 1$

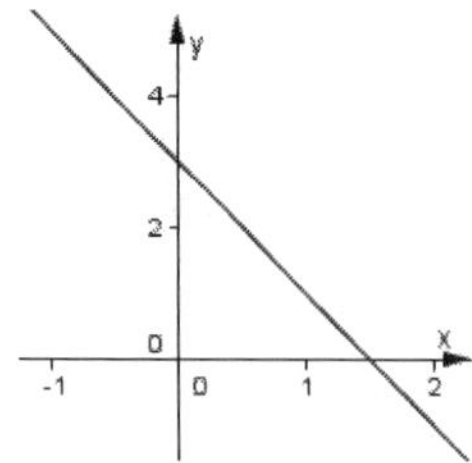

5. What is the equation of line shown in the figure above?
   a) $y = 2x + 3$
   b) $y = -x + 3$
   c) $y = -2x - 3$
   d) $y = -2x + 3$

Answer: (d)

$Slope = \frac{Rise}{Run} = \frac{0-3}{1.5-0} = -2$
y-intercept = 3
$y = -2x + 3$

x	-1	3	j
$f(x)$	1	j	k

6. In the table above, if $f(x) = 3x + 4$, what is the value of k?
   a) 19
   b) 25
   c) 37
   d) 43

Answer: (d)

Plug x = 3 into the function.
$y = 3 \times 3 + 4 = 13 = j$
When $x = j = 13$,
$y = 3 \times 13 + 4 = 43 = k$

7. Line l has an undefined slope and contains the point (1, −3). Which of the following points is also on line l?
   a) (0, 3)
   b) (−1, −3)
   c) (0, −3)
   d) (1, −2)

Answer: (d)

A"undefined slope" means a perpendicular line with a constant x-coordinate which is 1.
Only (d) has x-coordinate of 1.

8. What is the slope of a line that passes through the points (1, −1) and (−1, 5)?
   a) −3
   b) −2
   c) 0
   d) 2

Answer: (a)

$Slope = \frac{Rise}{Run} = \frac{5-(-1)}{-1-1} = -3$

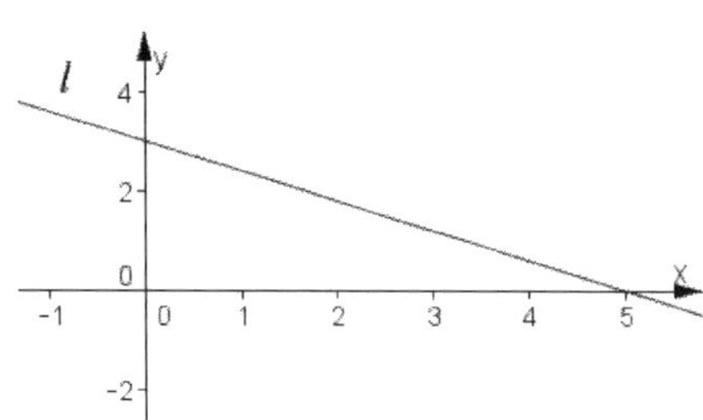

9. In the figure above, what is the slope of line l?
   a) $\frac{1}{4}$
   b) $\frac{1}{2}$
   c) $\frac{2}{5}$
   d) $-\frac{3}{5}$

Answer: (d)

$Slope = \frac{Rise}{Run} = \frac{3-0}{5-0} = -\frac{3}{5}$

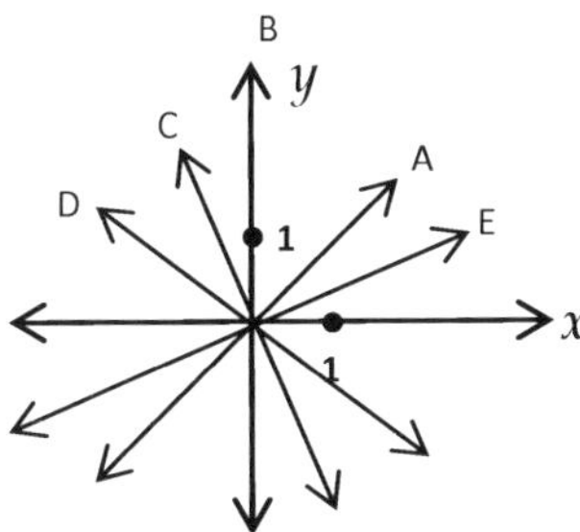

10. In the xy-coordinate system above, which of the following lines has a slope closest to 1?
    a) A
    b) B
    c) C
    d) D

Answer: (a)

Line A has the slope closest to 1.

11. Which of the following is the graph of a linear function with a negative slope and a negative y-intercept?
    a)

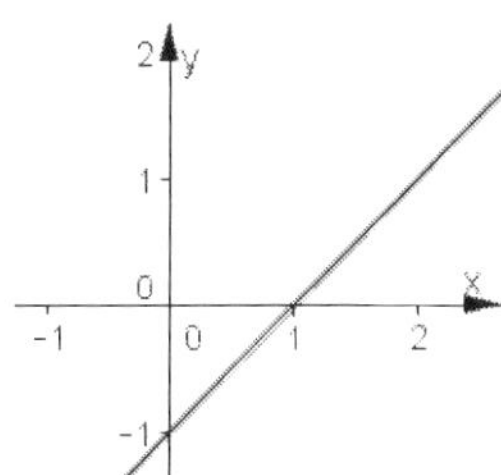

    b)

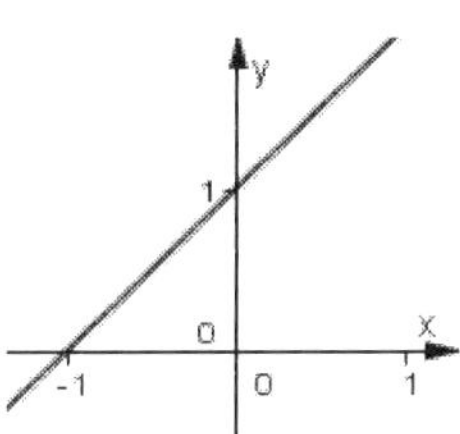

    c)

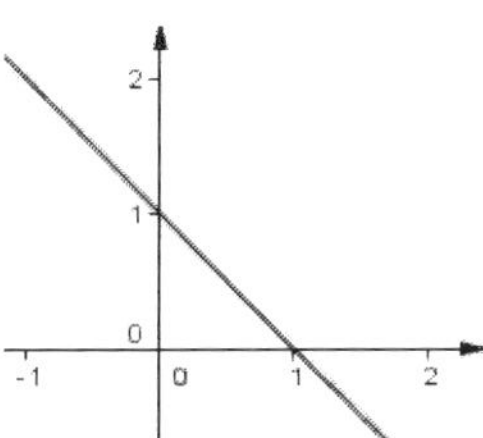

    d)

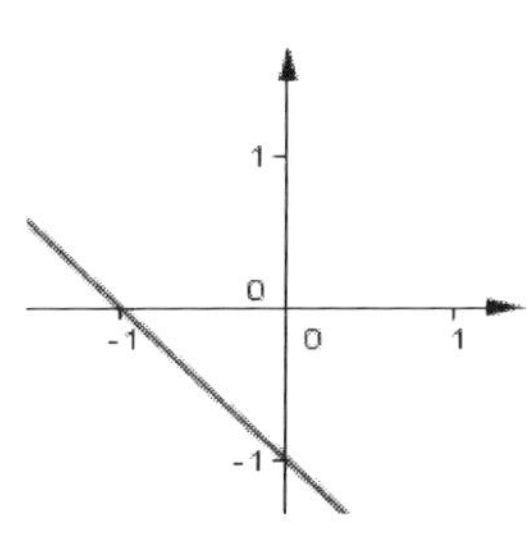

Answer: (d)

A line with a negative slope descends from left to right (d) has a negative slope and a negative y-intercept.

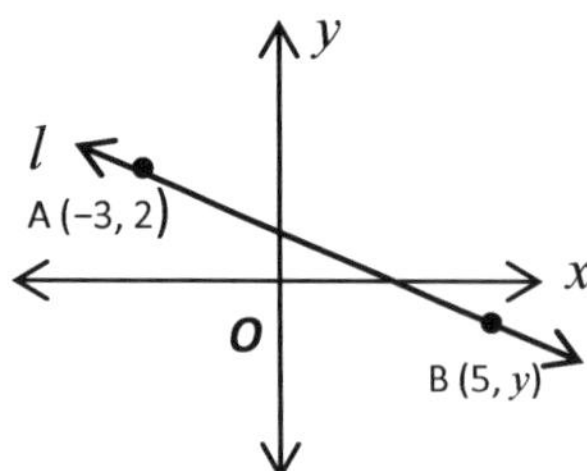

12. In the figure above, the slope of line l is $-\frac{1}{2}$. What is the value of y?
    a) $\frac{1}{2}$
    b) 1
    c) $-\frac{1}{2}$
    d) -2

Answer: (d)

$slope = \frac{y-2}{5-(-3)} = -\frac{1}{2}$

$y - 2 = -4$
$y = -2$

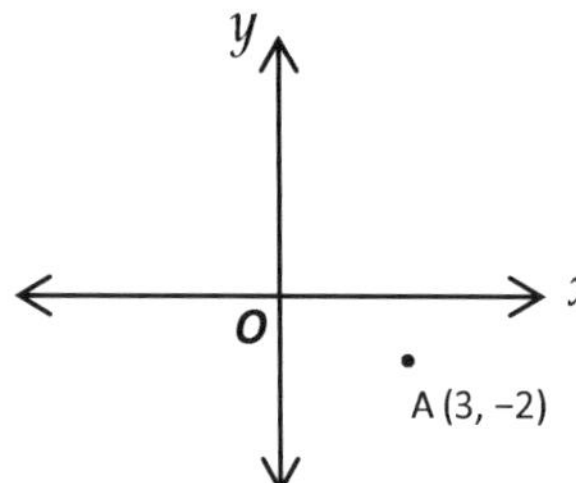

13. In the figure above, a line is to be drawn through point A so that it has a slope of 1. Through which of the following points must the line pass?
    a) (−5, 1)
    b) (−4, 1)
    c) (1, 4)
    d) (1, −4)

Answer: (d)

$slope = 1 = \frac{y-(-2)}{x-3}$

$x - 3 = y + 2$
$y = x - 5$
Out of 5 answer choices, only (1, −4) satisfies the equation $y = x - 5$.

14. If $3x + 1 = a$, then $6x + 5$?
    a) $a + 3$
    b) $a - 3$
    c) $2a$
    d) $2a + 3$

Answer: (d)

$3x = a - 1$
$6x = 2 \times (3x) = 2 \times (a - 1)$
$= 2a - 2$
$6x + 5 = 2a - 2 + 5 = 2a + 3$

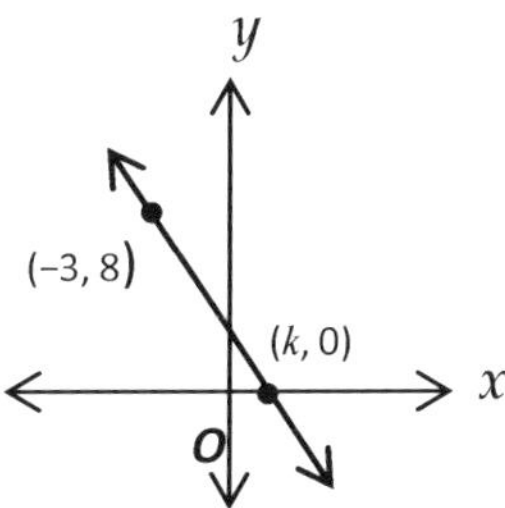

15. In the figure above, the slope of the line through points (-3, 8) and (k, 0) is −2. What is the value of k?
    a) 4
    b) 3
    c) 2
    d) 1

Answer: (d)

$Slope = \frac{Rise}{Run} = \frac{0-8}{k-(-3)} = -2$
$k + 3 = 4$
$k = 1$

Medium

16. If a linear function passes through the points (1, s), (3, t) and (5, 10), what is the value of $2t - s$?
    a) 2
    b) 8
    c) 10
    d) 12

Answer: (c)

The line segment connecting the first two points must have the same slope as the line segment connecting the last two points.
$\frac{10-s}{5-1} = \frac{10-t}{5-3}$ *and* $\frac{10-s}{4} = \frac{10-t}{2}$
$40 - 4t = 20 - 2s \rightarrow 2t - s = 10$

17. Which two lines are perpendicular to each other?
    a) $y = x - 1; x = 1$
    b) $y = x + 1; x = 1$
    c) $y = -1; x = 1$
    d) $x = -1; x = 1$

Answer: (c)

The value of the y coordinate is constant for a horizontal line.

18. What is the y-intercept of the line that passes through the points (1, 1) and (5, 13)?
    a) −2
    b) −1
    c) 1
    d) 2

Answer: (a)

$Slope = \frac{13-1}{5-1} = 3$

$y - 1 = 3(x - 1)$ *(point-slope form)*
$y = 3x - 2$
y-intercept $= -2$

19. Which of the following could be the coordinates of point R in a coordinate plane, if points P(1, 1), Q(-l, 5), and R(x, y) lie on the same line?
    a) (0, 2)
    b) (2, −1)
    c) (0, −2)
    d) (2, 2)

Answer: (b)

$Slope = \frac{Rise}{Run} = \frac{5-1}{-1-1} = -2$
Point-slope-form: $y - 1 = -2(x - 1)$
The point (2, −1) satisfies the above equation.

20. In the xy-plane, the line with equation $y = 3x - 9$ crosses the x-axis at the point with coordinates (a, b). What is the value of a?
    a) 3
    b) -2
    c) −1
    d) 2

Answer: (a)

The line intersects the x-axis when $y = 0$.

$0 = 3x - 9$
$x = 3$
$a = 3$

21. In the xy-plane, the line $x - 2y = k$ passes through point $(4, -1)$. What is the value of k?
    a) 6
    b) 4
    c) 2
    d) −2

Answer: (a)

Plug in the values for x and y into the equation.

$4 - 2(-1) = k = 6$

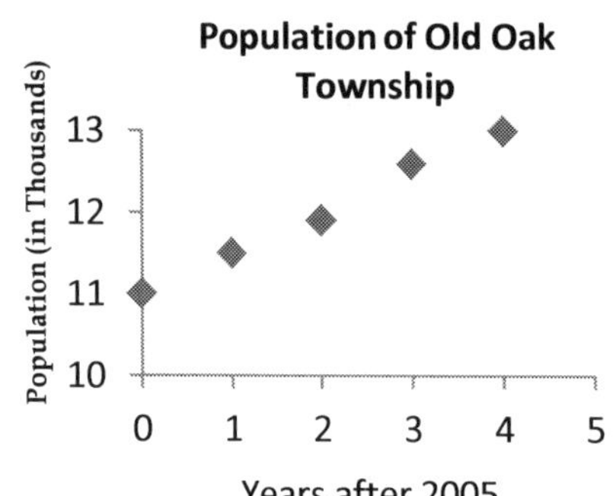

22. The graph above shows the population of Old Oak Township since 2005. If y represents the population, in thousands, and x represents the number of years after 2005, which of the following equations best describes the data shown?
    a) $y = x + 11$
    b) $y = 2x + 11$
    c) $y = 2x - 11$
    d) $y = \frac{1}{2}x + 11$

Answer: (d)

Find the slope and y-intercept from the graph.

Slope $= \frac{1}{2}$
y-intercept $= 11$
$y = \frac{1}{2}x + 11$

23. Point Q lies on the line with equation $y + 4 = 2(x - 1)$. If the x-coordinate of Q is 3, what is the y-coordinate of Q?
    a) 2
    b) 1
    c) 0
    d) −1

Answer: (c)

$y + 4 = 2(3 - 1)$

$y = 0$

24. The figure above shows the graph of the line $y = mx + b$, where m and b are constants. Which of the following best represents the graph of the line $y= 2mx + b$?

a)

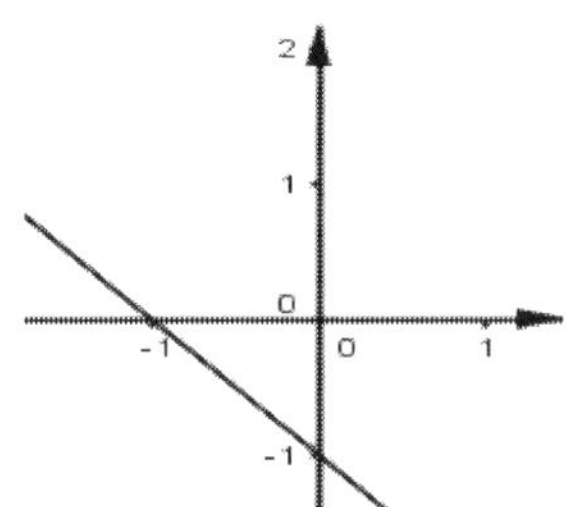

b)

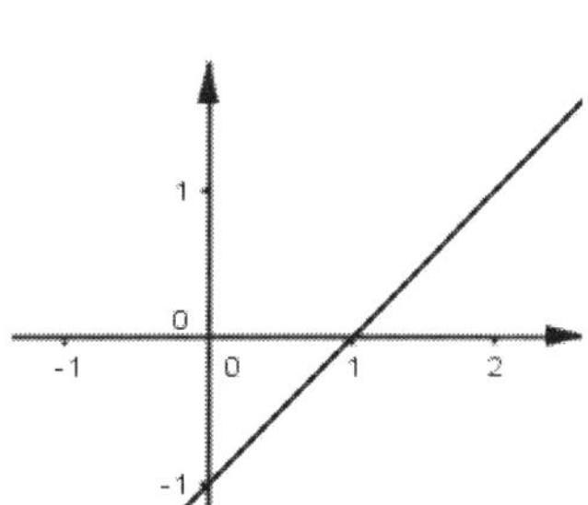

c)

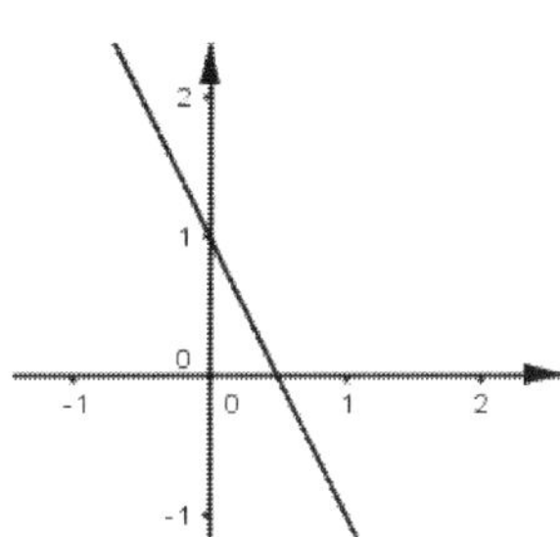

d)

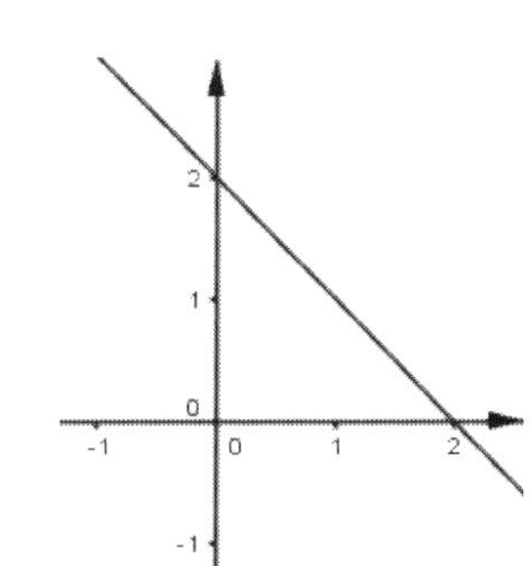

Answer: (c)

From the graph, slope equals −1 and y-intercept is 1.

$m = -1,\ b = 1$

$y = 2mx + b = -2x + 1$

(with negative slope and positive y-intercept)

25. What is the product of the slopes of all four sides of a rectangle if all four sides' slopes are not equal to zero?
    a) -2
    b) −1
    c) 0
    d) 1

Answer: (d)

The product of the slopes of two perpendicular lines is −1.
The product of the slopes of all four sides of rectangle is
$-1 \times (-1) = 1$.

26. Which of the following is an equation of the line that is perpendicular to the y-axis and passes through the point (1, –1)?
    a) $y = 1$
    b) $y = -1$
    c) $y = x$
    d) $y = -x$

Answer: (b)

The line perpendicular to the y-axis is a horizontal line. The value of the y coordinate is constant for a horizontal line.

$y = -1$

27. The equation of line l is $x - 2y = 3$. Which of the following is an equation of the line that is perpendicular to line l?
    a) $y = x + 2$
    b) $y = -x + 2$
    c) $y = 2x - 1$
    d) $y = -2x + 1$

Answer: (d)

$x - 2y = 3$
$y = \frac{1}{2}x - 1.5$

Line l has a slope of $\frac{1}{2}$.
A line that is perpendicular to line l would have a slope of -2.

28. In the figure above, line l passes through the origin. What is the value of $\frac{b}{a}$?
    a) 1
    b) 1.5
    c) 2
    d) 2.5

Answer: (d)

$\frac{b-0}{a-0} = \frac{5-0}{2-0}$

$\frac{b}{a} = \frac{5}{2} = 2.5$

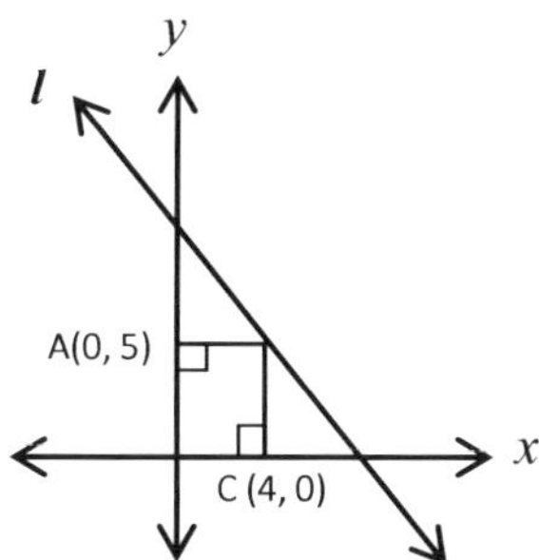

29. In the figure above, if line l has a slope of –2, what is the x-intercept of l?
    a) 6
    b) 6.5
    c) 7
    d) 13

Answer: (b)

Line l intersects the x-axis at (x, 0) and has a slope of −2.

$\frac{0-5}{x-4} = -2$

$-2x + 8 = -5$

$x = \frac{13}{2} = 6.5$

Hard

30. In the xy-coordinate plane, lines m and n are perpendicular. If line m contains the points (0, 0) and (3, 1), and line n contains the points (2, 3) and (1, a), what is the value of a?
    a) −6
    b) −3
    c) 6
    d) 3

Answer: (c)

If two lines are perpendicular, then the product of their slopes is −1.

$\frac{1-0}{3-0} \times \frac{3-a}{2-1} = -1$

$3 - a = -3$

$a = 6$

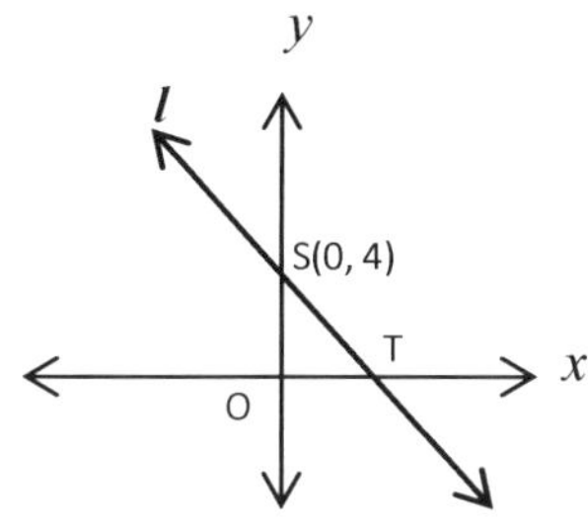

31. If the slope of line l is −1 as shown above, what is the area of ΔSOT?
    a) 2
    b) 4
    c) 6
    d) 8

Answer: (d)

Slope $= \frac{Rise}{Run} = \frac{0-4}{T} = -1$

$T = 4$

Area $= \frac{1}{2} \times 4 \times 4 = 8$

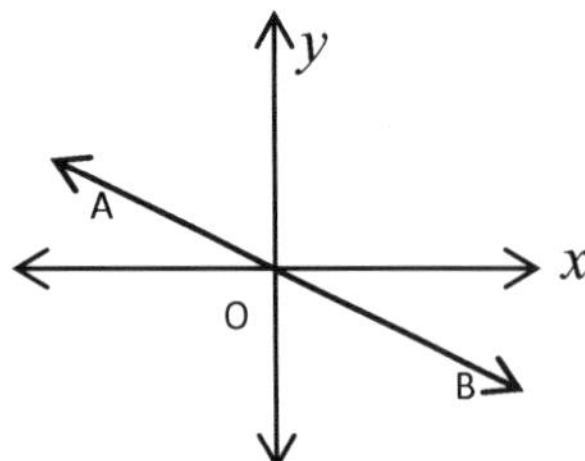

32. The coordinates of point A in the figure above are (a, b), where $|a| > |2b|$. Which of the following could be the slope of AB?
    a) -1
    b) $-\frac{1}{2}$
    c) $-\frac{1}{3}$
    d) $\frac{2}{3}$

Answer: (c)

A line with a negative slope descends from left to right; therefore, the slope of the line in the graph is negative.

$|x| > |2y|$

$\frac{1}{2} > |\frac{y}{x}|$

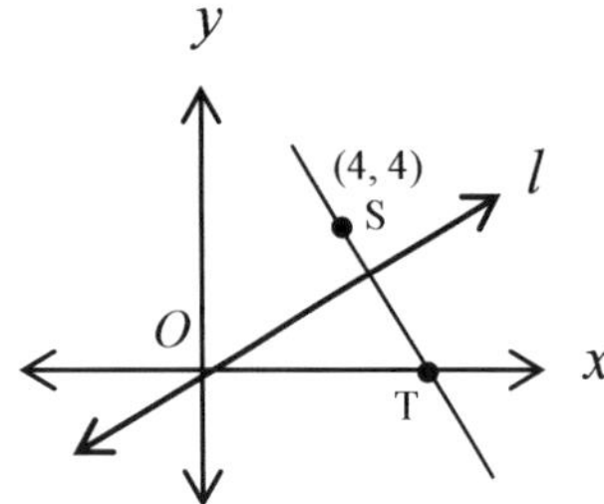

33. Line l intersects ST between S and T and also passes through the origin. Which of the following could be line l's slope?
    a) -2
    b) -1
    c) $\frac{1}{2}$
    d) $\frac{3}{2}$

Answer: (c)

OT has a slope of 0 and OS has a slope of 1 so the slope of line l should be between 0 and 1.

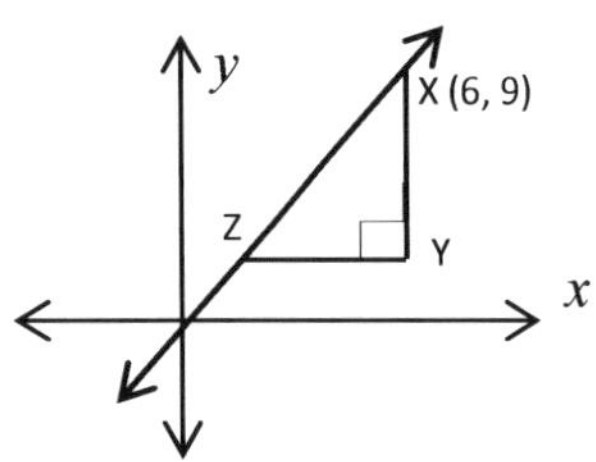

34. In the figure above, if two legs of ΔXYZ are parallel to the x and y axes respectively, what is the ratio of the longer leg to the shorter leg of ΔXYZ?
    a) 1
    b) $\frac{4}{3}$
    c) $\frac{3}{2}$
    d) 2

Answer: (c)

This line passes through the origin and the point (6, 9), so the slope of the line is 1.5. Therefore the ratio of the length of the vertical piece divided by the ratio of the length of the horizontal piece is 1.5.

$\frac{9}{6} = \frac{3}{2} = 1.5$

35. In the xy-plane, line l passes through the origin and is perpendicular to the line $2x - y = b$, where b is a constant. If the two lines intersect at the point $(2a, a + 1)$, what is the value of b?

a) -1
b) $-\frac{5}{2}$
c) 0
d) $\frac{1}{2}$

Answer: (b)

The slope of line $2x - y = b$ is 2. Line l is perpendicular, so it should have a slope of $-\frac{1}{2}$. We also know that it passes through the origin.

$y = -\frac{1}{2}x$

$a + 1 = -\frac{1}{2}(2a)$

$2a = -1, \quad a = -\frac{1}{2}$

point $(-1, \frac{1}{2})$ passing through

$2x - y = b$

Solve for b.

$-2 - \frac{1}{2} = -\frac{5}{2}$

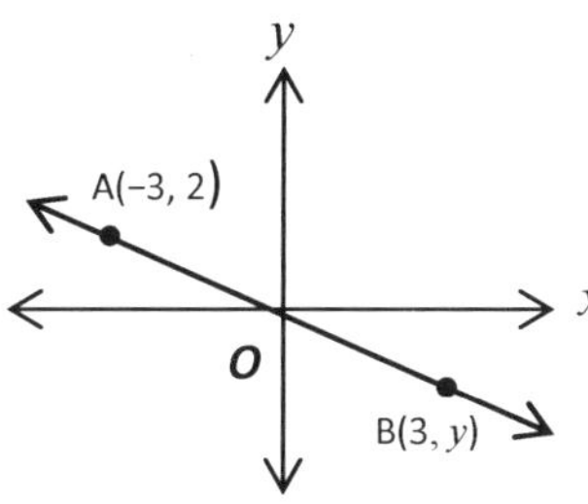

36. In the figure above, line AB passes through the origin. If the x-coordinate of point B is 3, what is the y-coordinate of B?

a) -5
b) -4
c) -3
d) -2

Answer: (d)

Slope of OA = Slope of OB

$\frac{0-2}{0-(-3)} = \frac{y-0}{3-0}$ → *Cross multiply*

$3y = -6$

$y = -2$

C. Solving a System of Equations

Concept Overviews

There must be at least one equation given in order to solve for one variable. In the same vein, at least two equations must be given to solve two variables, at least three equations for three variables, and so on. **In order to solve a system of equations, there must be at least the same number of equations given as the variables being solved for.** In the real world, tools such as matrices or computer algorithms are necessary to solve complicated system of equations. On the SAT, however, it is sufficient to use the following two methods:

- **Substitution**

Example: Solve the following system of equations by substitution:

$x - y = 1$ (1)
$2x + 3y = 7$ (2)

Solution: $x = y + 1$, from the first equation

$2(y+1) + 3y = 7$, because they are equivalent, substitute x with $y + 1$ into the second equation

$2y + 2 + 3y = 7$
$5y = 5$
$y = 1$
$x = y + 1$
$= 1 + 1$
$= 2$
$x = 2$ and $y = 1$

- **Elimination**

Example: Solve the following system of equations by elimination:

$3x - y = 3$ ---(1)
$x + 2y = 15$ ---(2)

Solution: In order to eliminate y, multiply equation (1) by 2.

$2(3x - y) = 3 \times 2$ ---(3), add equations (2) and (3).
$2(3x - y) + (x + 2y) = 3 \times 2 + 15$
$6x - 2y + x + 2y = 21$, cancel out $-2y$ and $2y$.
$7x = 21$
$x = 3$, plug in the value for x into equation (1).
$3 \times 3 - y = 3$
$y = 6$
$x = 3$ and $y = 6$

Problem Solving Skills

Easy

1. $y = x + 1$ and $x + 2y = 8$, what is the value of x?
   a) 1
   b) 2
   c) 3
   d) −2

Answer: (b)

Use the substitution method.
$y = x + 1$
$x + 2(x + 1) = 8$
$3x + 2 = 8$
$x = 2$

2. There are 25 high school seniors who are taking the total of 112 AP classes this year. Some of them take 4 APs and the others take 5. How many seniors are taking 5 APs?
   a) 11
   b) 12
   c) 13
   d) 14

Answer: (b)

Let x be the number of students taking 5 APs and y be the number of students taking 4 APs.
$x + y = 25$
$y = 25 - x$
$5x + 4y = 112$ *(substitution rule)*
$5x + 4(25 - x) = 112$
$x + 100 - 112$
$x = 12$

3. At the school cafeteria, there are 30 tables and each table can seat either 2 or 4 students. If there are a total 80 students in one of the lunch sections, how many tables must seat exactly 4 students in this lunch section?
   a) 9
   b) 10
   c) 11
   d) 12
   e) 13

Answer: (b)

Let x be the number of tables that seat 4 students and y be the number of tables that seat 2 students.
$x + y = 30$
$y = 30 - x$
$4x + 2y = 80$ *(substitution rule)*
$4x + 2(30 - x) = 80$
$2x + 60 = 80 \rightarrow x = 10$

4. What is the value of x if $x + 2y = 6$ and $x + y = 5$?
   a) 2
   b) 3
   c) 4
   d) 5

Answer: (c)

Substitute y with $5 - x$.

$x + 2(5 - x) = 6$
$x = 4$

5. If $3a - b = 3$ and $a + 2b = 15$, then $a + b$?
   a) −2
   b) −4
   c) 9
   d) 5

Answer: (c)

It is easier to use the method of elimination for this question.
$3a - b = 3$ (1)
$6a - 2b = 6$ (1a)
$a + 2b = 15$ (2)
Add (1a) and (2) to eliminate b.
$(1) + (2) \rightarrow 7a = 21 \rightarrow a = 3$
$3 \times 3 - b = 3 \rightarrow b = 6$
$a + b = 9$

Medium

6. If $\frac{x}{w} = 28$ and $5yw = 3$, then xy =?

Answer: $\frac{84}{5}$

$\frac{x}{w} \times 5yw = 5xy = 28 \times 3 = 84$
$xy = \frac{84}{5}$

$$3x - 4y = 8$$
$$5x + 3y = 23$$

7. Based on the above system of 2-equations, which of the following values will $(x + y)$ equal?
   a) 10
   b) 8
   c) 7
   d) 5

Answer: (d)

Use the method of elimination.
$(3x - 4y = 8) \times 5$
$15x - 20y = 40$ (1)
$(5x + 3y = 23) \times (-3)$
$15x - 9y = -69$ (2)
Add the equations (1) and (2) to eliminate x.
$-29y = -29 \rightarrow y = 1$
$3x - 4 \times 1 = 8 \rightarrow x = 4$
$x + y = 5$

8. If $2x - 3y = 11$and $x = y + 4$, what is the value of x?

Answer: 1

Substitute y with x – 4.
$2x - 3(x - 4) = 11$
$-x + 12 = 11 \rightarrow x = 1$

9. If $5 \leq x \leq 7$ and $-3 \leq y \leq 1$, which of the following gives the set of all possible values of xy?
   a) $-15 \leq xy \leq 7$
   b) $0 \leq xy \leq 7$
   c) $-21 \leq xy \leq 5$
   d) $-21 \leq xy \leq 7$

Answer: (d)

Try out different combinations of x and y.
$-21 \leq xy \leq 7$

10. If $3x - z = 2y$ and $3x + 5y - z = 28$, what is the value of y?
   a) 3
   b) 4
   c) 5
   d) 6

Answer: (b)

Try to eliminate z
$3x - z = 2y$ (1)
$3x + 5y - z = 28$ (2)
$(1) - (2) \rightarrow -5y = 2y - 28$
$28 = 7y \rightarrow y = 4$

11. There is $180 of cash in John's pocket. John only has 10 and 20 dollar bills. If John has a total of 13 bills, how many 20 dollar bills are in his pocket?

Answer: 5

Let x be the number of $20 bills and y be the number of $10 bills.
$x + y = 13 \rightarrow y = 13 - x$
$20x + 10y = 180$
$20x + 10(13 - x) = 180$
$130 + 10x = 180$
$10x = 50 \rightarrow x = 5$

D. Solving an Inequality

Concept Overviews

Definition of an Inequality: When comparing two real numbers, one number is greater than, less than, or equal to the other number.

- $a > b$ means a is greater than b.
- $a < b$ means a is less than b.
- $a \geq b$ means a is greater than or equal to b.
- $a \leq b$ means a is less than or equal to b.

To solve inequalities, follow rules that are similar to those applicable to equations. Isolate the variable that needs to be solved for on one side, move all other numbers or constants to the other side, and combine the like terms.

All the rules and techniques used in solving an equation apply to solving an inequality EXCEPT for multiplication and division by a **negative. When you multiply or divide both sides by a negative number, reverse the direction of the inequality**.

Example: $4 > 3$, but if you multiply –1 on both sides, the inequality becomes $-4 < -3$.

The inequality is not preserved when both sides are multiplied by zero.

Absolute Value Inequality
The absolute value of a number is the distance from that number to the zero-mark on the number line. The absolute value of any number is always nonnegative.

- If $|x - a| \leq b$, all values of x are between $a - b$ and $a + b$, inclusive, on the number line:
  $a - b \leq x \leq a + b$

  Example: $|x - 1| \leq 3$
  $-3 \leq x - 1 \leq 3$
  $1 - 3 \leq x \leq 1 + 3$
  $-2 \leq x \leq 4$

- If $|x - a| \geq b$, all values of x are either less than or equal to $a - b$ or larger than or equal to $a + b$ on the number line: $x \geq a + b$ *or* $x \leq a - b$.

  Example: $|x - 1| \geq 3$
  $3 \leq x - 1$ *or* $x - 1 \leq -3$
  $1 + 3 \leq x$ *or* $x \leq 1 - 3$
  $x \geq 4$ *or* $x \leq -2$

Problem Solving Skills

Easy

1. There are 15 boxes of apples in the storage room. Each box has at least 21 apples, and at most 28 apples. Which of the following could be the total number of apples in the storage room?
   a) 200
   b) 250
   c) 300
   d) 350

Answer: (d)

Set up the inequality for the number of apples and then multiply the inequality by 15.

$(21 < x < 28) \times 15$
$315 < 15x < 420$

2. Alex has less money than Bob and Bob has less money than Chris. If a, b, and c represent the amounts of money that Alex, Bob, and Chris have, respectively, which of the following is true?
   a) $a < b < c$
   b) $c < b < a$
   c) $b < a < c$
   d) $a < c < b$

Answer: (a)

"Alex has less money than Bob" $\rightarrow a < b$
"Bob has less money than Chris" $\rightarrow b < c$

$a < b < c$

3. If $x > y$, $w < z$, and $x < w$, which of the following must be true?
   I. $y < z$
   II. $w < y$
   III. $x < z$
   a) None
   b) II and III
   c) I and II
   d) I and III

Answer: (d)

Draw a number line and locate w, x, y and z on the line.

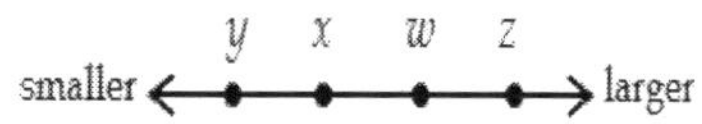

Only (I) and (III) are correct.

4. If $0 < xy$ and $y < 0$, which of the following statements must be true?
   I. $x < 0$
   II. $x < y$
   III. $x > 0$
   a) I only
   b) III only
   c) I and II
   d) II and III

Answer: (a)

$xy > 0 \rightarrow$ *both x and y must have the same sign. (Both are positive or both are negative.)*

$y < 0$ *and* $x < 0$

5. If $0 > x > y$, which of the following is less than $\frac{x}{y}$?
   a) 1
   b) 2
   c) xy
   d) $\frac{x}{2y}$

Answer: (d)

If $0 > x > y$, then $\frac{y}{x} > 1 > \frac{x}{y} > 0$.

6. If $x - 1 > 2$ and $x + 2 < 7$, which of the following could be a value for x?
   a) 1
   b) 2
   c) 3
   d) 4

Answer: (d)

Solve the inequalities.

$x - 1 > 2 \rightarrow x > 3$
$x + 2 < 7 \rightarrow x < 5$
Combine them together.
$3 < x < 5$

7. If $5x < 3y$ and $6y < 7z$, which of the following is true?
   a) $5x < 7z$
   b) $5x > 7z$
   c) $10x < 7z$
   d) $10x = 7z$

Answer: (c)
Multiply both sides of the first equation by 2.
$(5x < 3y) \times 2 \rightarrow 10x < 6y$ (1)
$6y < 7z$ (2)
(1) + (2): $10x < 6y < 7z$

8. Given that $4x + 3 < 12$, which of the following cannot be the value of x?
   a) 3
   b) 2
   c) 1
   d) 0

Answer: (a)

$4x + 3 < 12$, $4x < 12 - 3$
$4x < 9 \rightarrow x < 2.25$

9. If $|3 - 2y| < 11$, which of the following is a possible value of y?
   a) −6
   b) −4
   c) 5
   d) 10

Answer: (c)

There are two possible solutions for the inequality after taking out the absolute value sign.
$3 - 2y < 11$ or $3 - 2y > -11$
$3 - 2y < 11 \rightarrow 3 - 11 < 2y \rightarrow -4 < y$
$3 - 2y > -11 \rightarrow 3 + 11 > 2y \rightarrow 7 > y$
Combine both results of the inequalities: $-4 < y < 7$

10. If $a + 3b < a$, which of the following must be true?
   a) $a > 0$
   b) $a = 0$
   c) $a < 0$
   d) $b < 0$

Answer: (d)

Subtract a from both sides.
$a + 3b < a$
$a + 3b - a < a - a$
$3b < 0$
$b < 0$

11. If 3 less than x is a negative number and if 1 less than x is a positive number, which of the following could be the value of x?
    a) 3
    b) 2
    c) 1
    d) 0

Answer: (b)

"3 less than x is a negative" →
$x - 3 < 0$
$x < 3$
"1 less than x is a positive" →
$x - 1 > 0$
$x > 1$
Combine them together: $1 < x < 3$

12. If $x + y = 13$ and $x < 7$, then which of the following must be true?
    a) $y > 0$
    b) $y < 13$
    c) $y = 6$
    d) $y > 6$

Answer: (d)

Substitute x with (13 – y).
$x < 7$
$13 - y < 7$
$13 - 7 < y$
$6 < y$

13. Which of the following conditions would make $2x - y < 0$?
    a) $2x = y$
    b) $x > 0$
    c) $y > 0$
    d) $2x < y$

Answer: (d)

If $2x - y < 0$, *then* $2x < y$.

Medium

14. If $x < 5 < \frac{1}{x-1}$, then x could be which of the following?
    a) 5
    b) 1
    c) $\frac{1}{5}$
    d) $\frac{7}{6}$

Answer: (d)

$5 < \frac{1}{x-1}$
$\frac{1}{5} > x - 1$

$1 < x < \frac{6}{5}$

15. If $|y| < 1$ and $y \neq 0$, which of the following statements is always true?
    I. $y < 3y$
    II. $y^2 < y^3$
    III. $y^2 < \frac{1}{y^2}$
    a) I only
    b) II only
    c) III only
    d) I and III

Answer: (c)

$|y| < 1 \rightarrow -1 < y < 1$
If $-1 < y < 1$, *then* $0 < y^2 < 1$.

$\frac{1}{y^2} > 1$
$0 < y^2 < 1 < \frac{1}{y^2}$
Only (III) is always true.

16. If $|x| < 1$, which of the following is the greatest?
   a) 2
   b) $1 - x$
   c) $1 + x$
   d) $2x$

Answer: (a)

$|x| < 1 \rightarrow -1 < x < 1 \rightarrow$
$-1 < -x < 1$, *therefore,*
b). $0 < 1 - x < 2$
c). $0 < 1 + x < 2$
d). $-2 < 2x < 2$

So among those answer choices the number 2 is the greatest value. Shortcuts: Plug $x = 0.5$ into each answer choice and compare the results. This method works better when you try different values to verify your answer.

17. What is the smallest positive integer value of x for which $2x - 7 > 0$?

Answer: 4
If $2x - 7 > 0$, *then* $2x > 7$.
$x > 3.5$
So the smallest positive integer is 4.

18. If x is an integer and $2x + 1$ is the median of three different integers $2x + 1$, $x - 1$, and $3x - 1$, which of the following could be a possible value of x?
   a) -1
   b) 0
   c) 1
   d) 3

Answer: (d)
If $x - 1 < 2x + 1 < 3x - 1$, *then*
$x - 1 < 2x + 1 \rightarrow -2 < x$ *and*
$2x + 1 < 3x - 1 \rightarrow 2 < x$.
Therefore, $2 < x$
If $3x - 1 < 2x + 1 < x - 1$, *then*
$3x - 1 < 2x + 1 \rightarrow x < 2$ *and*
$2x + 1 < x - 1 \rightarrow x < -2$
Therefore, $x < -2$
In conclusion, $2 < x$ *or* $x < -2$
Only answer (d) is correct.

19. When the positive integer P is increased by 30 percent, the result is between 9 and 10. What is the value of P?

Answer: 7

When P increases 30%, the new value of P becomes 1.3P.
$9 < 1.3P < 10$
$\frac{9}{1.3} < P < \frac{10}{1.3}$
$6.9 < P < 7.69$
$P = 7$

20. The scores of a math class midterm are between 75 and 93. Which of the following inequalities can be used to determine the range of a student's midterm score, represented by h in this class?
   a) $|h - 75| < 18$
   b) $|h - 93| < 18$
   c) $|h - 84| < 18$
   d) $|h - 84| < 9$

Answer: (d)

Find the mid-value of 75 and 93.

$\frac{75 + 93}{2} = 84$
$84 - 75 = 9$
$93 - 84 = 9$
$|h - 84| < 9$

21. If $|5 - 2x| < 3$, which of the fol1owing is a possible value of x?
    a) 3
    b) 4
    c) 5
    d) 6

Answer: (a)

If $|5 - 2x| < 3$, then $-3 < 5-2x < 3$.
$-3 - 5 < -2x < 3 - 5$
$-8 < -2x < -2$
$8 > 2x > 2 \rightarrow 4 > x > 1$

22. If the side length of a square is an integer and the area of this square is less than 25 but greater than 15, what is the perimeter of the square?

Answer: 16

Let the side length = d, the area of the square = d^2.
$15 < d^2 < 25$
$\sqrt{15} < d < 5 \rightarrow$ *d can only be 4.*
$4 \times 4 = 16$

Hard

Questions 23 – 24 refer to the following information:
Jenny has a summer job at an ice cream shop. She needs to order a few boxes of small cups and a few boxes of large cups. The storage room can hold up to 30 boxes. Each box of small cups costs $20 and each box of large cups costs $30. A maximum of $720 is budgeted for cups.

23. If x represents the number of boxes of small cups and y represents the number of boxes of large cups that Jenny can order, which of the following systems of equations represents the number of each she could order?

a) $\begin{cases} x \geq 0 \\ y \geq 0 \\ x + y \leq 30 \\ 20x + 30y \leq 720 \end{cases}$

b) $\begin{cases} x \geq 0 \\ y \geq 0 \\ x + y < 30 \\ 20x + 30y < 720 \end{cases}$

c) $\begin{cases} x \geq 0 \\ y \geq 0 \\ x + y > 30 \\ 20x + 30y > 720 \end{cases}$

d) $\begin{cases} x \geq 0 \\ y \geq 0 \\ x + y \geq 30 \\ 20x + 30y \leq 720 \end{cases}$

Answer: (a)

The number of boxes must be greater or equal than zero. The storage room can hold up to 30 boxes and the maximum of $720 can be spent, therefore the answer is a).

$\begin{cases} x \geq 0 \\ y \geq 0 \\ x + y \leq 30 \\ 20x + 30y \leq 720 \end{cases}$

24. Which of the following graphs represents the number of boxes of each type of cup she could order?

a)

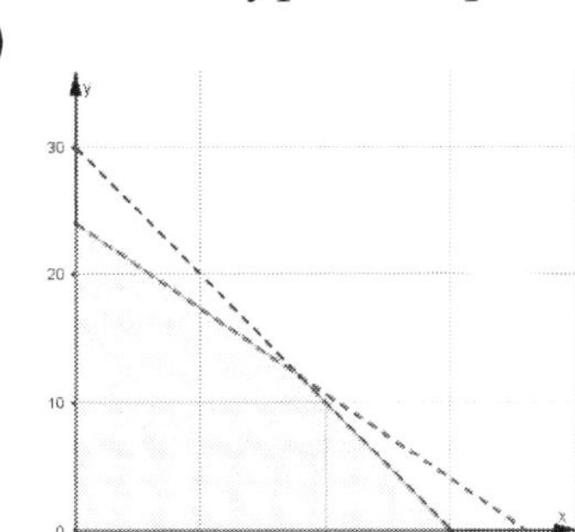

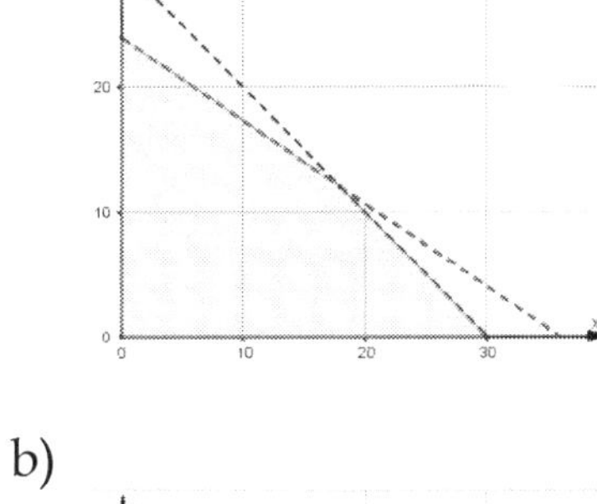

b)

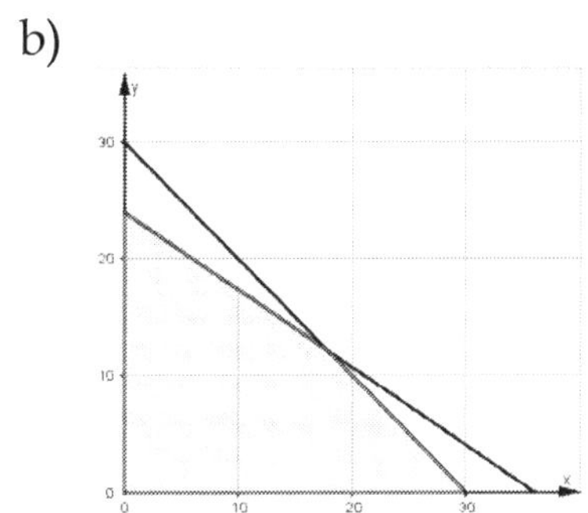

c)

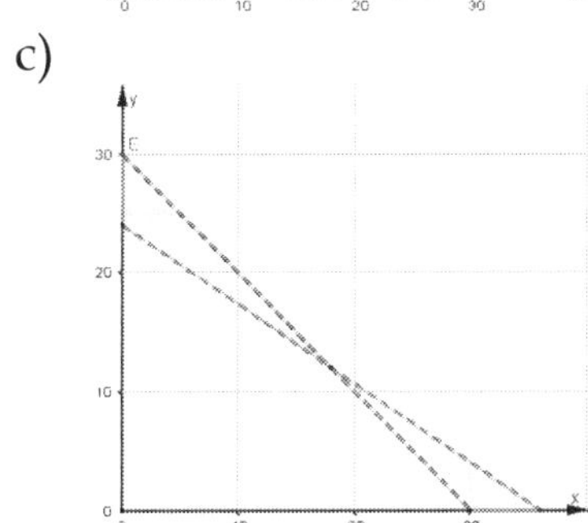

d)

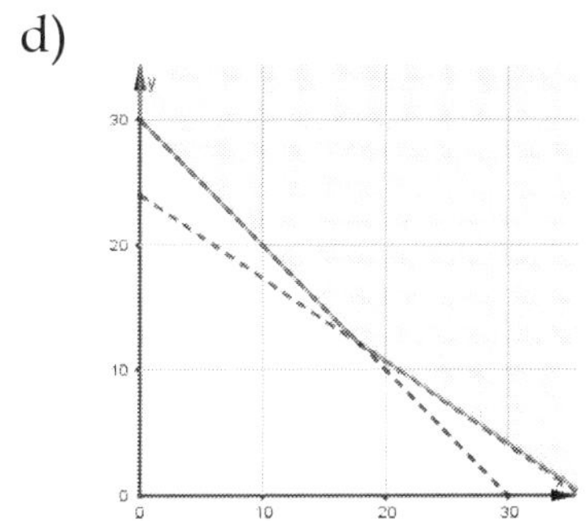

Answer: (b)

Only answer b) depicts the correct system of equations of the previous question.

$$\begin{cases} x \geq 0 \\ y \geq 0 \\ x + y \leq 30 \\ 60x + 100y \leq 1000 \end{cases}$$

25. If $x + 2 < y + 1 < 0 < z$, which of the following must be true?

I. $-y > -x$
II. $x z < y z$
III. $x + y < z - 1$

a) I only
b) II only
c) III only
d) II and III only

Answer: (d)

$x + 2 < 0 \rightarrow x < 0$
$y + 1 < 0 \rightarrow y < 0$
$x + 2 < y + 1 \rightarrow x < y$
$z > 0$ and $x + y + 1 < 0$
(The sum of two negatives x and $(y + 1)$ is negative.)
Therefore $-x > -y$, $xz < yz$, and $x + y < z - 1$.
Only (II) and (III) are true.

26. If $x > 0$, $y > 2$, and $2x + y = 5$, and x is an integer, what is the value for x?
   a) 1
   b) 2
   c) 3
   d) 4

Answer: (a)

$2x + y = 5$, $y = 5 - 2x$
Given that $y > 2$,
$5 - 2x > 2$ (substitution rule)
$5 - 2 > 2x$
$3 > 2x$
$1.5 > x$

27. If w is a positive number and $w > w^2$, which of the following statements is true?
   I. $w^2 > w^3$
   II. $w > \frac{w}{3}$
   III. $w > w^3$
   a) I, II
   b) II, III
   c) I, II, and III
   d) I only

Answer: (c)

w is a positive number and
$w < w^2$.
$w^2 - w > 0$
$w(1 - w) > 0$
$w > 0$ and $1 - w > 0$
$-w > -1$, $w < 1$
So $0 < w < 1$.
If $0 < w < 1$, then any number multiplied by w produces a number smaller than the original number. Therefore $w^2 > w^3$, $w^3 > w^4$, and so on.
I, II, III are all correct.

$$f(x) = |x - 6|$$

28. For the function defined above, what is the value of c such that $f(2c) < c$?
   a) −3
   b) −1
   c) 1
   d) 3

Answer: (d)

Substitute 2c for x and solve for c.
$|2c - 6| < c$
$-c < 2c - 6 < c$
$-c < 2c - 6 \rightarrow 2 < c$
$2c - 6 < c \rightarrow c < 6$
Therefore $2 < c < 6$

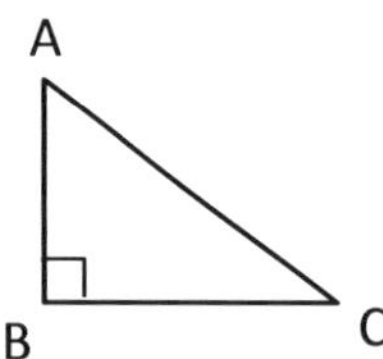

29. In the figure above, ΔABC is a right triangle and $\overline{AB}$ has the length of 5. If the area of ΔABC must be more than 25 but less than 35 and all three sides' lengths are positive integer, what is one possible value of AC?
   a) 10
   b) 11
   c) 12
   d) 13

Answer: (d)
Area of $\Delta ABC = \frac{1}{2} AB \times BC$
$= 2.5 \times BC$
$25 < 2.5 \times BC < 35$
$10 < BC < 14$
Apply the Pythagorean theorem.
$AC^2 = AB^2 + BC^2 = 5^2 + BC^2$
$AC = \sqrt{25 + BC^2}$
See if BC equals 11, 12, or 13.
$AC = \sqrt{25 + 12^2} = 13$

III. Word Problems

Concept Overviews

Translating from English to Algebraic Expressions
Keywords in the problem can help translating the words into algebraic expressions. For instance, the word "increase" indicates addition and "less" indicates subtraction. "2 times" refers to multiplying a number or variable by two, and "is" indicates equality in an equation.

If the question mentions finding "a number" without specifying the value of the number, assign a variable for that number and then solve for the value of the variable.

The following table lists the most common phrases and their translations.

Operations	Keywords	Sample Phrases	Algebraic Expressions
Addition	plus sum added to more than increased by	three plus a number the sum of a number and 3 three added to a number three more than a number a number increased by 3	$x + 3$
Subtraction	difference minus subtracted from less than decreased by reduced by deducted from	the difference of a number and three a number minus 3 three subtracted from a number three less than a number a number decreased by three a number reduced by three three deducted from a number	$x - 3$
Multiplication	of multiply times twice product of multiplied by	30% of 50 is 15. multiplying 3 by a number four times a number twice a number the product of a number and three a number multiplied by five	$0.3 \times 50 = 15$ $3x$ $4x$ $2x$ $3x$ $5x$
Division	divided by quotient of	a number divided by 3 the quotient of a number and 3	$\frac{x}{3}$
Equal	equal is is equal to	Three multiplied by a number equals 4. Half of 20 is 10. The sum of 5 and 4 is equal to 9.	$3x = 4$ $\frac{1}{2} \times 20 = 10$ $5 + 4 = 9$

Examples: Translate each of the following into an algebraic expression.

1. Three more than four times a number: $4x + 3$
2. Five times the sum of a number and two: $5(x + 2)$
3. Eleven subtracted from the product of two and a number: $2x - 11$
4. The quotient of two less than a number and twice the number: $\frac{(x-2)}{2x}$
5. The sum of a number and its reciprocal is equal to three: $x + \frac{1}{x} = 3$
6. Six times the difference of a number and two is equal to twice the number: $6(x - 2) = 2x$
7. The product of a number and five is increased by the number: $5x + x$
8. Eight less than five times a number divided by twice the number: $\frac{(5x-8)}{2x}$
9. The product of two numbers, if one number is three less than twice the other number: $x(2x - 3)$
10. If nine times a number is reduced by five, the result is three less than the number: $9x - 5 = x - 3$
11. The sum of three consecutive odd integers is 51: $x + (x + 2) + (x + 4) = 51$
12. The sum of three consecutive even integers is 36: $x + (x + 2) + (x + 4) = 36$
13. The product of the sum and difference of two numbers is equal to 15: $(x + y)(x - y) = 15$

Problem Solving Skills

Easy

1. A chef has 100 slices of bread, 80 slices of ham, and 65 slices of tomato. If he needs to make sandwiches each with 2 slices of bread, 2 slices of ham, and 1 slice of tomato, find the maximum number of sandwiches he can make?
   a) 100
   b) 80
   c) 65
   d) 40

Answer: (d)

The maximum number of sandwiches occurs when the chef uses up all the 80 slices of ham with 2 slices for each sandwich.

2. To make picture frames, Jen needs to cut 4 pieces of molding, each 9 inches long, to make one picture frame. She bought a 10-foot long molding to start her project. How many feet of molding will be left after she makes as many picture frames as possible?
   a) 4
   b) 3
   c) 2
   d) 1

Answer: (d)

$4 \times 9 = 36$
36 inches = 3 feet, so each frame needs 3 feet of molding.
10 divided by 3 has a remainder of 1.

1 foot will be left after making 3 frames.

3. When twice a number is reduced by 25, the result is 225. What is the number?

Answer: 125

$2a - 25 = 225 \rightarrow a = 125$

4. During a lunch in the school cafeteria, if Kristin paid \$3.50 for her lunch from her pocket and borrowed \$1.50 from a friend, how much did she spend for this lunch?

Answer: 5

If she spent x money, then $3.5 - x = -1.5$.
$3.5 - x = -1.5 \rightarrow x = 5$

5. A smartphone costs \$30 less than four times the cost of a basic cell phone. If the smartphone and the basic phone together cost \$570, how much more does the smartphone cost than the basic phone?
   a) \$216
   b) \$330
   c) \$415
   d) \$450

Answer: (b)

Let the price of a basic phone be x, then the price of a smartphone is $4x - 30$*. Solve the equation* $x + (4x - 30) = 570$*, and get* $x = 120$*. Therefore, a basic phone costs \$120 while a smartphone costs* $4 \times 120 - 30 = \$450$.
$450 - 120 = 330$

6. The width of Mitchell's room is 2 feet less than its length. If the width of his room is 12 feet, what is the area of his room in square feet?
   a) 120
   b) 140
   c) 148
   d) 168

Answer: (d)

The width of the room is 12 and the length is 12 + 2.

$12 \times 14 = 168$

7. A car rental company charges \$60 per day for the first 5 days, and \$45 a day for each day after that. How much will Tom be charged if he rents a car for two weeks?
   a) \$465
   b) \$685
   c) \$705
   d) \$735

Answer: (c)

Two Weeks = 14 Days.

$60 \times 5 + 45 \times 9 = 705$

8. To find out how much time Wilson needs to spend on transportation each day to and from school, he notices that it takes 25 to 32 minutes to go to school and 30 to 45 minutes to return home. What is the range of time that Wilson needs to spend for his round trip to and from school?
   a) 25 minutes to 45 minutes
   b) 30 minutes to 45 minutes
   c) 32 minutes to 45 minutes
   d) 55 minutes to 1 hour and 17 minutes

Answer: (d)

The minimum total time is 25 + 30 = 55 minutes; the maximum total time is 32 + 45 = 77 minutes.

77 minutes = 1 hour and 17 minutes

9. If x is 7 more than y, and y is 5 less than z. What is x when $z = 5$?
   a) -9
   b) -5
   c) 7
   d) 9

Answer: (c)

If $x = y + 7$, then $y = z - 5$.

If $z = 5$, then $y = 0$.
$x = 0 + 7 = 7$

10. It takes between 6 and 8 minutes for Joe to run one mile up to the hill during a marathon. The amount of time it takes for him to run a mile down the hill is 2 to 3 minutes shorter than the time it takes him to run up the hill. What is the range of possible times it would take Joe to run one mile down the hill?
    a) 4 and 5 minutes
    b) 3 and 6 minutes
    c) 5 and 7 minutes
    d) 6 and 8 minutes

Answer: (b)

Running down the hill saves 2 to 3 minutes. Therefore the minimum amount of time would be $6 - 3 = 3$ minutes and the maximum amount of time would be $8 - 2 = 6$ minutes.

11. A, B, and C are three points on a line in that order. If $\overline{AB} = 25$ and $\overline{BC}$ is 10 less than $\overline{AB}$, what is the length of $\overline{AC}$?
    a) 40
    b) 38
    c) 35
    d) 32

Answer: (a)

$BC = 25 - 10 = 15$

$AC = AB + BC = 25 + 15 = 40$
Given that the points A, B, C are in order.

12. A parking lot charges $5.00 maintenance fee per day to use its parking space. In addition, there is a charge of $3.25 per hour. Which of the following represents the total charge, in dollars, to park a car in the parking lot for m hours in one day?
    a) $5m + 3.25$
    b) $(5 + 3.25)m$
    c) $5 + 3.25 + m$
    d) $5 + 3.25m$

Answer: (d)

Parking m hours costs $3.25 × m plus $5 maintenance fee per day, so the total charge would be $5 + 3.25m$.

13. Mr. Jones has taught math for 8 years less than twice as long as Miss Carter. If Miss Carter has taught Math for m years, which of the following indicates the number of years that Mr. Jones has taught?
    a) $2m + 8$
    b) $m + 8$
    c) $2m - 8$
    d) $2m$

Answer: (c)

8 years less than 2 times m years $\rightarrow 2m - 8$

14. Triangles A, B, and C are different in size. Triangle A's area is twice the area of triangle B, and triangle C's area is four times the area of triangle A. What is the area of triangle C, in square inches, if the area of triangle B is 10 square inches?
    a) 20
    b) 40
    c) 60
    d) 80

Answer: (d)

$A = 2B$,
$C = 4A$

If $B = 10$, then
$A = 20$, and $C = 4 \times 20 = 80$.

15. Mr. Smith's air conditioner is broken and it will cost \$360 to repair it. A new energy-efficient air conditioner, costing \$1200, will save Mr. Smith \$20 per month on his electric bill. If Mr. Smith decides to buy the new air conditioner, after how many months will he break even?
    a) 30
    b) 32
    c) 40
    d) 42

Answer: (d)

First find the difference between the cost of the new AC and the cost of repairing the old one. Then divide the difference by the amount saved per month:

$1200 - 360 = 840$
$840 \div 20 = 42$

16. John plans to work m days to earn n dollars to buy his own car. But due to his sickness, he took x days off. What is the additional amount of average salary that he must earn for the $m - x$ remaining work days in order to buy the car?
    a) $\frac{n}{(m-x)m}$
    b) $\frac{nx}{(m-x)m}$
    c) $\frac{m-x}{n}$
    d) $\frac{n(x-m)}{mx}$

Answer: (b)

If John earns n dollars in m days, he earns an average of $\frac{n}{m}$ dollars a day. If he earns n dollars in $(m - x)$ days, then he earns an average of $\frac{n}{(m-x)}$ dollars a day.

Find the difference between $\frac{n}{(m-x)}$ and $\frac{n}{m}$:
$$\frac{n}{(m-x)} - \frac{n}{m} = \frac{nx}{(m-x)m}$$

17. The local route from Maya's house to her college is 4 miles longer than the expressway. When she drives by the local route and returns by the expressway, the round trip is 30 miles. How many miles does Maya have to drive if she goes to school through the expressway?
    a) 13
    b) 15
    c) 17
    d) 19

Answer: (a)

Let the express way be x miles between Maya's house and her college. The local route would be $x + 4$ miles, which means that the round trip would be $x + (x + 4) = 30$.
$x = 13$

18. If a rectangle of perimeter 18 has a width that is 3 less than its length, what is its area?
    a) 12
    b) 18
    c) 27
    d) 36

Answer: (b)

Let the length = x, then the width = x – 3.

The perimeter: $2x + 2(x - 3) = 18$
$x = 6$
Area = Length × Width
$= 6 \times 3 = 18$

19. If $x^2 - 5x - 6 = 0$, what are the possible values of x?
    a) –1, 6
    b) 1, –6
    c) –1, –6
    d) 2, –3

Answer: (a)

Use trinomial factoring.
$x^2 - 5x - 6 = (x - 6)(x + 1) = 0$
$x = 6$ *or* -1

Subtract 5 from y
Divide this difference by 5
Multiply this quotient by 5

20. After completing the operations described above, which of the following is showing the result?
    a) $\frac{y-5}{5}$
    b) $\frac{y}{5}$
    c) $\frac{y+5}{5}$
    d) $y - 5$

Answer: (d)

Since division and multiplication are the inverse functions to each other, the last two operations will cancel each other. Hence, it will only need to perform the first operation: subtract 5 from y.

21. The sum of x and the square of y is equal to the square root of the difference between x and y. Which of the following mathematic expressions represents the statement above?
    a) $x + y^2 = (\sqrt{x} - y)^2$
    b) $x + \sqrt{y} = \sqrt{x - y}$
    c) $(x + y)^2 = \sqrt{x} - \sqrt{y}$
    d) $x + y^2 = \sqrt{x - y}$

Answer: (d)

Sum of x and the square of y → $x + y^2$
Square root of the difference between x and y → $\sqrt{x - y}$

$x + y^2 = \sqrt{x - y}$

22. Which of the following is an equation you would use to find x if it is given that 10 more than the product of x and 5 is 30?
    a) $5(x - 10) = 30$
    b) $5x - 10 = 30$
    c) $5(x + 10) = 30$
    d) $5x + 10 = 30$

Answer: (d)

10 more than the product of x and 5 → $10 + 5x$

$5x + 10 = 30$

23. Joan has $23 and wants to buy a dozen of red pens at $0.50 each and two dozens of blue pens at $0.75 each. Without counting sales tax, how much more money does she need?
   a) $1.00
   b) $1.75
   c) $1.50
   d) $2.00

Answer: (a)

The cost of buying 12 red pens:
$12 \times 0.5 = 6$
The cost of buying 24 blue pens:
$24 \times 0.75 = 18$
Joan would need 6 + 18 = $24, so she has $1.00 short.

24. $\frac{1}{5}$ of 100 is equal to what percent of 400?
   a) 5 %
   b) 10 %
   c) 15 %
   d) 20 %

Answer: (a)
$\frac{1}{5}$ *of* $100 \rightarrow \frac{1}{5} \times 100$
$20 = \frac{x}{100} \times 400$
$20 = 4x \rightarrow x = 5$
Therefore, $\frac{1}{5} \times 100 = 20$, *which is equal to* $400 \times 5\% = 20$

25. If $y > 0$, what is 25 percent of $40y$?
   a) $10y$
   b) $12y$
   c) $14y$
   d) $20y$

Answer: (a)

25 percent of 40y $\rightarrow$
$25\% \times 40y = 10y$

26. A number a is multiplied by $\frac{1}{3}$. The product is then multiplied by 27, which results in 81. What is the value of a?
   a) 3
   b) 6
   c) 9
   d) 18

Answer: (c)

$a \times \frac{1}{3} \times 27 = 81$

$a = 9$

27. Ken, Justin, and Tiff have read a total of 65 books from the library. Justin read 3 times as many books as Ken and Tiff read 3 times as many as Justin. How many books did Ken read?
   a) 12
   b) 9
   c) 7
   d) 5

Answer: (d)

Let k be the number of books Ken read, j be the number of books Justin read, and t be the number of books Tiff read.
$j = 3k$
$t = 3j = 3(3k) = 9k$
Given that $k + j + t = 65$
Substitute for j and t:
$k + 3k + 9k = 65 \rightarrow k = 5$

28. If 0.01 percent of y is 1, what is 1 percent of y?
   a) 1
   b) 100
   c) 0.1
   d) 0.01

Answer: (b)
Given that $0.01\% \times y = 1$
$y = 10000$
1% *of* $y \rightarrow 1\% \times 10000 = 100$

29. If 10 percent of 40 percent of a positive number is equal to 20 percent of y percent of the same positive number, find the value of y.
   a) 10
   b) 15
   c) 20
   d) 35

Answer: (c)

$10 \times 40 = 20y \quad y = 20$

$\frac{10}{100} \times \frac{40}{100} \times A = \frac{20}{100} \times \frac{y}{100} \times A$

$\frac{10 \times 40}{100 \times 100} = \frac{20y}{100 \times 100}$

Therefore $10 \times 40 = 20y$

$y = 20$.

30. Which of the following is the expression that represents the statement that the value of the cube of y multiplied by the value of the square root of z, all subtracted from five–sevenths of the square of x equals x?
   a) $\frac{5x^2}{7} - y^3\sqrt{z} = x$
   b) $\frac{5x^2}{7} - y^2\sqrt{z} = x$
   c) $\frac{5x^2}{7} - \sqrt{y^3z} = x$
   d) $\frac{5}{7}x^2 - y^3z^2 = x$

Answer: (a)

Translate the expression to an algebraic equation.

31. When $3x$ is added to 28 and the sum is divided by 6 subtracted from x, the result equals 5. What is the value of x?
   a) 12
   b) 18
   c) 24
   d) 29

Answer: (d)

$\frac{3x + 28}{x - 6} = 5$

$3x + 28 = 5(x - 6)$

$3x + 28 = 5x - 30$

$58 = 2x$

$x = 29$

32. If you multiply $(x - 2)$ by 5, and then divide this product by x, the result is 4. What is the value of x?
   a) 2
   b) 10
   c) 12
   d) –10

Answer: (b)

$\frac{5(x - 2)}{x} = 4$

$x = 10$

33. Christine has y dollars to buy new videos from a video store. The member's price of any video is x dollars each. Christine needs to pay a membership fee of 25 dollars to become a member. Which of the following represents the maximum number of videos that she can buy from this video store?
   a) $\frac{y - 25}{x}$
   b) $\frac{y}{x} - 25$
   c) $xy - 25$
   d) $\frac{y}{x - 25}$

Answer: (a)

She has $y - 25$ *dollars to buy videos.*

$\frac{y - 25}{x}$

34. Which of the following represents the statement "When the square of the sum of x and y is added to the sum of the squares of x and $2y$, the result is 5 less than z"?
   a) $x^2 + y^2 + (x + 2y)^2 = z - 5$
   b) $(x + y)^2 + x^2 + 2y^2 = z - 5$
   c) $(x + y)^2 + (x + 2y)^2 = z - 5$
   d) $(x + y)^2 + x^2 + (2y)^2 = z - 5$

Answer: (d)

The square of the sum of x and y $\rightarrow (x + y)^2$
The sum of the squares of x and 2y $\rightarrow x^2 + (2y)^2$

$(x + y)^2 + x^2 + (2y)^2 = z - 5$

35. After 20 customers entered a deli store and 4 customers left, there were 3 times as many customers as there were at the beginning. How many customers were in that deli store at the very beginning?
   a) 6
   b) 7
   c) 8
   d) 12

Answer: (c)

Let x be the number of customers originally, then $x + 20 - 4 = 3x$.

$x = 8$

The difference of 5a and the square root of 2b is equal to the sum of the squares of 3a and 4b.

36. Which of the following is an expression for the statement above?
   a) $5a - \sqrt{2b} = (3a + 4b)^2$
   b) $5a - \sqrt{2b} = (3a)^2 + (4b)^2$
   c) $5a - \sqrt{2b} = (3a)^2 + 4b$
   d) $5a - \sqrt{2b} = 3a^2 + 4b$

Answer: (b)

$5a - \sqrt{2b} = (3a)^2 + (4b)^2$

37. A total of x students went on a field trip transported by the number of y school buses. Each bus could seat a maximum of z students. If one bus had half of the seats empty and the remaining buses were filled, which of the following describes the relationship between x, y, and z?
   a) $zy - \frac{1}{2}z = x$
   b) $\frac{x}{y} - \frac{1}{2}z = x$
   c) $x - \frac{1}{2}z = zy$
   d) $y - \frac{1}{2}z = x$

Answer: (a)

There are (y − 1) buses, each of which is filled with z students.

$z(y - 1) + \frac{z}{2} = x$
$zy - z + \frac{z}{2} = x$
$zy - \frac{z}{2} = x$

38. If 4 less than twice a number is equal to 20. What is 5 more than 3 times the number?
   a) 8
   b) 12
   c) 41
   d) 29

Answer: (c)

Let the number be x.
$2x - 4 = 20$
$x = 12$
$3x + 5 = 36 + 5 = 41$

39. There was the same number of blue marbles and green marbles in a bag. After 5 blue marbles were taken out, there were twice as many green marbles as blue marbles in the bag. How many marbles were originally in the bag?
    a) 10
    b) 15
    c) 18
    d) 20

Answer: (d)

Let x be the original number of blue or green marbles, after 5 blue marbles were taken, then (x – 5) blue marbles left.
$(x - 5) = \frac{1}{2}x \rightarrow x = 10$
There were originally 10 blue marbles and 10 green marbles in the bag, which makes a total of 20 marbles in the bag.

40. If 25 % of m is 20, what is 15% of m?
    a) 12
    b) 15
    c) 20
    d) 24

Answer: (a)

$25\% \times m = 20$
$m = 80$
$15\% \text{ of } 80 \rightarrow 15\% \times 80$
$15\% \times 80 = 12$

41. If $\frac{3}{5}$ of a number is 21, what is $\frac{1}{7}$ of that number?

Answer: 5

Let the number be x.
$\frac{3}{5}x = 21 \rightarrow x = 35$
$\frac{1}{7} \times 35 = 5$

42. The sum of $5x$ and 3 is equal to the difference of $2x$ and 3. Which of the following represents the above statement?
    a) $5x + 3 = 2x - 3$
    b) $5(x + 3) = 2(x - 3)$
    c) $5x - 3 = 2x + 3$
    d) $5x - 3 = 2x - 3$

Answer: (a)

Convert words into algebraic expressions.
$5x + 3 = 2x - 3$

43. The difference of two consecutive numbers is equal to k. What is a possible value of k?
    a) 2
    b) $\frac{1}{2}$
    c) 1
    d) –2

Answer: (c)

Let the two consecutive numbers be x and (x + 1).
$(x + 1) - x = k$
$k = 1$

44. Jenny reads 10 pages of her reading every weekday and 15 pages more each day during the weekend. Which of the following represents the total pages of reading she finishes in n weeks, where n is an integer?
    a) $30n$
    b) $50n$
    c) $70n$
    d) $100n$

Answer: (d)

Jenny reads 10 pages each day from Monday to Friday and (10 +15) pages each day on Saturday and Sunday.
The pages she finishes in one week: $10 \times 5 + 25 \times 2 = 100$
100n pages for n weeks

Medium

45. After 8 new customers entered the grocery store and 2 customers left the store, there were three times as many customers in the store as there were before. How many customers were originally in the grocery store?
    a) 1
    b) 2
    c) 3
    d) 4

Answer: (c)

Let x be the number of customers before the changes. After adding 8 new customers and subtracting 2 customers who left, the number of customers equals three times as many as x.
$x + 8 - 2 = 3x$
$x = 3$

46. In a certain skiing resort, daily entrance costs \$60. However, a triple ticket for three days can be bought for \$150. How much money can be saved by buying a triple ticket rather than buying three daily tickets?
    a) \$20
    b) \$30
    c) \$40
    d) \$55

Answer: (b)

It costs 3 × 60 = \$180 to buy three daily entrance tickets; a triple ticket good for 3 days costs \$150. You would save 180 − 150 = 30 dollars.

47. Six erasers cost as much as 3 pencils. If Matt bought one eraser and one pencil for \$1.50, how much does one pencil cost in dollars?
    a) 0.25
    b) 0.50
    c) 0.75
    d) 1.00

Answer: (d)

Let the price of one eraser be x and the price of one pencil be y.
The Price of 6 Erasers = the Price of 3 Pencils.
$6x = 3y \rightarrow x = \frac{1}{2}y$
The Price of One Eraser = $\frac{1}{2}$ the Price of One Pencil.
$x + y = 1.50$
$\frac{1}{2}y + y = 1.50 \rightarrow y = 1.0$
The price of one pencil is \$1.00.

48. When the average (arithmetic mean) of a list of grades is multiplied by the number of students, the result is n. What does n represent?
    a) the number of the grades
    b) the average of the grades
    c) the sum of the grades
    d) the range of the list of the grades

Answer: (c)

This is the definition of "sum."

49. Helen had to pay off her student loan \$24,000 on a twelve-year payment plan. The amount she paid each year for the first six years is three times as much as the amount she paid each of her remaining years. How much did she pay the first year?
   a) \$3000
   b) \$2000
   c) \$1500
   d) \$1000

Answer: (a)

Let the first year payment be \$x and each of her last 6 years be \$y.
$x = 3y$ *and* $6x + 6y = 24000$
$18y + 6y = 24000$
$y = 1000$
$x = 3000$
The first year payment is \$3000.

50. A school fundraising event aims to raise \$1000 by purchasing muffins for m dollars each and then selling them at $\frac{7m}{5}$ dollars each. How many muffins do they need to sell to reach their goal?
   a) $\frac{5000}{m}$
   b) $\frac{2500}{m}$
   c) $400m$
   d) $2500m$

Answer: (b)

Let l be the number of muffins they need to sell in order to make a profit of \$1000, so that
$l \times \left(\frac{7m}{5} - m\right) = 1000.$
$\frac{2m}{5} \times l = 1000$
$l = 1000 \times \frac{5}{2m} = \frac{2500}{m}$

51. By doing her chores, Jessica's parents pay Jessica m dollars on Monday, \$1 more than twice as much on Tuesday as on Monday, and \$2 more than triple as much on Wednesday as on Monday. How many dollars does she earn during these three days?
   a) $6m + 3$
   b) $3m + 3$
   c) $6m + 1$
   d) $3m + 1$

Answer: (a)

Jessica earns m dollars on Monday, and then she earns 2m + 1 on Tuesday and 3m + 2 on Wednesday.
The total amount of dollars she earns for these three days:
$m + (2m + 1) + (3m + 2) = 6m + 3$

52. To rent a single movie from a DVD lending machine, Mrs. Kinney was charged \$1 for the first day. For every day afterwards, she must pay a rental fee of \$1 plus a late fee of \$.50. If she paid a total of \$7, how many days did she keep the DVD?
   a) 2
   b) 3
   c) 4
   d) 5

Answer: (d)

Let n be the number of days that Mrs. Kinney kept the DVD.

$1 + 1 \times (n - 1) + 0.5 \times (n - 1) = 7$

$n = 5$

53. If John gives Sally $5, Sally will have twice the amount of money that John will have. Originally, there was a total of $30 between the two of them. How much money did John initially have?

a) 25
b) 21
c) 18
d) 15

Answer: (d)

Let J be the amount of money John initially had and S be the amount of money Sally initially had. Together, they originally had $30.
$J + S = 30 \rightarrow J = 30 - S$
After John gives Sally $5, John will have J − 5 dollars and Sally will have S + 5 dollars.
$S + 5 = 2(J - 5)$
Solve this system of equations.
$J = \$15$

54. By 7 AM, $\frac{1}{4}$ of all students were in school. Half an hour later, 80 more students arrived, raising the attendance to $\frac{3}{4}$ of the total students. How many students are in this school?

a) 300
b) 320
c) 240
d) 160

Answer: (d)

Let m be the total number of students in the school. $(\frac{1}{4} \times m)$ *students arrive by 7 AM and 80 students arrive half an hour later. The total number of students that have arrived would be*
$\frac{1}{4} \times m + 80 = \frac{3}{4} \times m.$
$m = 160$ *students*

55. A cube has 3 faces painted yellow and the remaining faces painted blue. The total area of the blue faces is 27 square inches. What is the volume of this cube, in cubic inches?

a) 9
b) 27
c) 36
d) 64

Answer: (b)

Let x be the length of the side. The area of one face is x^2*. The total area of the three blue faces is then* $3x^2$*, which is equal to 27.*
$3x^2 = 27, \quad x = 3$
If we know the length of the side, we can solve for the volume of cube.
$x \times x \times x = 3 \times 3 \times 3 = 27$

56. The rate for a long distance call is $1.00 for the first minute and $.75 for each additional minute. Which of the following represents the cost, in dollars, of a phone call made for n minutes?

a) $1.75n$
b) $1.00 + n$
c) $1.00 + 0.75(n - 1)$
d) $1.00 + 1.75(n - 1)$

Answer: (c)

Each additional minute costs $.75.

For the n-minute phone call, the total cost would be the first minute ($1.00) plus additional (n − 1) minues ($0.75(n − 1)), so the total cost of n minute call is
$1.00 + 0.75(n - 1)$ *dollars.*

57. If 7 more than twice a certain number is equal to the product of 3 and the number, what is the number?

Answer: 7

Let x be the number.
$2x + 7 = 3x$
$x = 7$

58. A company sells boxes of marbles in red and green. Helen purchased a box of marbles in which there were half as many green marbles in the box as red ones and 20 marbles were green. How many marbles were in Helen's box?
   a) 67
   b) 60
   c) 34
   d) 20

Answer: (b)

Let g be the number of green marbles and r be the number of red marbles.
Translate "half as many green marbles as red ones" into an algebraic statement: $g = \frac{1}{2}r$
Plug $g = 20$ *into the equation to get* $r = 40$.
$20 + 40 = 60$

59. Bob needs two 60" pieces of duct tape to protect each window in his house during hurricane season. There are 12 windows in the house. Bob had an m-foot roll of duct tape when he started. If no tape was wasted, which of the following represents the number of feet of duct tape left after he finished taping all of his windows?
   a) $m - 240$
   b) $m - 120$
   c) $m - 60$
   d) $m - 20$

Answer: (b)

Every window needs 2 pieces of tape and each piece of tape is 60 inches long, so $60 \times 2 = 120$ *inches needed for each window.*
Twelve windows, in total, would need 12×120 *inches of tape.*
12 × 120 inches = 120 feet

(m − 120) feet left after the use.

60. Mrs. Alan's class of 23 students will have a 3-day educational camp. Each student is expected to use one pack of index card each day. If index cards are bought as a box of six packs, how many boxes will Mrs. Alan have to buy?
   a) 10
   b) 11
   c) 12
   d) 13

Answer: (d)

The total number of boxes of index cards needed is 23 × 3 = 69.
Since index cards are bought in 6-pack boxes,
$69 \div 6 = 11.5$
12 boxes will be needed for the entire camp.

61. The rectangle ABCD below is divided into 16 smaller identical rectangles. The ratio of the length to the width of each small rectangle is 3 to 1. If the area of the rectangle ABCD is 48 square units, what is the length of DE?

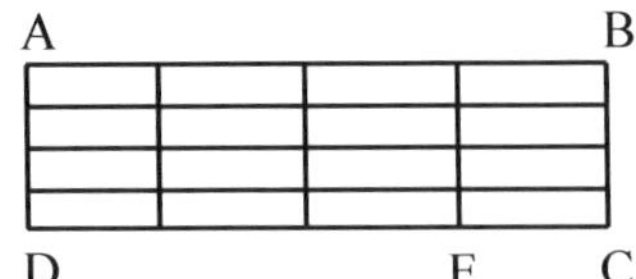

   a) 1
   b) 3
   c) 8
   d) 9

Answer: (d)

The ratio of the length to the width of each small rectangle is 3 : 1, so the ratio of the length to the width of the rectangle ABCD is also 3 :1.
Let x be the width and thus 3x be the length of the rectangle ABCD, then $3x \times x = 48$.
$x = 4$
Hence the length AD = 4 and the length AB = 3 × 4 = 12
The length of each smaller rectangle is $\frac{12}{4} = 3$*, so the length of DE would be 3 × 3 = 9.*

62. If $x > 0$, what is 50% of $30x$?
   a) $1.5x$
   b) $15x$
   c) $150x$
   d) $1500x$

Answer: (b)

$50\ \%\ of\ 30x \rightarrow 50\ \% \times 30x$
$50\ \% \times 30x = \frac{1500x}{100} = 15x$

63. How old was William 5 years ago if a years ago he was b years old (given that $a > 5$ and $b > 5$)?
   a) $a + b$
   b) $a + b + 5$
   c) $b - a - 5$
   d) $a + b - 5$

Answer: (d)

Let x be the current age.
$x - a = b; x = a + b$
Current Age $= a + b$
William's Age 5 Years Ago $=$ $a + b - 5$

64. 3 times a number is the same as the number itself. What is the number?

Answer: 0

Let the number be a.
$3a = a$
$3a - a = 0 \rightarrow a = 0$

65. Which of the following is equivalent to $\frac{1}{3}$ of 51% of 330?
   a) 51% of 110
   b) 17% of 110
   c) 51% of 330
   d) 49% of 110

Answer: (a)

$\frac{1}{3}$ *of 51 percent of 330* $\rightarrow$
$\frac{1}{3} \times 51\% \times 330$
$= 51\%$ *of 110*
$= 17\% \times 330$

66. If x is $\frac{3}{4}$ of y, y is $\frac{2}{3}$ of z, and $z > 0$, and then what is x in terms of z?
   a) $\frac{3}{4}z$
   b) $\frac{1}{2}z$
   c) $\frac{1}{4}z$
   d) $2z$

Answer: (b)

$x = \frac{3}{4}y = \frac{3}{4}\left(\frac{2}{3}z\right)$
$x = \frac{1}{2}z$

67. If the product of 0.6 and a number is equal to 1, what is the number?

Answer: $\frac{5}{3}$ *or 1.66*

$0.6a = 1$
$a = \frac{1}{0.6} = \frac{10}{6} = \frac{5}{3} = 1.666$

68. Find the product of 10 and the sum of m and 10. Then, find one-tenth of the difference between that product and 10. In terms of m, what is the final result?
   a) $m - 1$
   b) $m - 10$
   c) $m + 9$
   d) $m + 10$

Answer: (c)

$\frac{10(m + 10) - 10}{10}$
$= \frac{10(m + 10 - 1)}{10}$
$= m + 9$

69. If 14% of x is equal to 7% of y, which of the following is equivalent to y?
    a) 200% of x
    b) 20% of x
    c) 2% of x
    d) 98% of x

Answer: (a)

$\frac{14}{100}x = \frac{7}{100}y$

$y = \frac{14}{100} \times \frac{100}{7}x$

$y = 2x = 200\%x$

70. Among the 12 colleges Helen applied to, 3 are her top schools. How many admissions would Helen have to receive to guarantee that she can get into at least one of her top schools?
    a) 8
    b) 9
    c) 10
    d) 11

Answer: (c)

12 − 3 = 9
She applied to 9 schools that are not her top choices. If all 9 of these schools accept Helen, then the 10th school which accepts her must be one of her top schools.
9 + 1 = 10

Hard

71. As a part of a store's shoe sale, the first pair of shoes costs x dollars, and each additional pair on sale costs m dollars less than the first pair. Which of the following represents the total cost if a customer buys n pairs of shoes?
    a) $nx + m(n-1)$
    b) $nx - m(n-1)$
    c) $x + (n-1)(x-m)$
    d) $x + n(x-m)$

Answer: (c)

The first pair costs x dollars. Each additional pair costs $(x - m)$ dollars. Therefore the cost of n pairs of shoes would be the price of the first pair plus the cost of the additional $(n - 1)$ pairs.
$x + (n-1)(x-m)$

72. A construction site orders certain inches length of pipe cut between $18^1/_{12}$ and $17^{11}/_{12}$ inches long. If they use a pipe that is x inches long, which of the following represents all possible values of x?
    a) $|x - 17| < \frac{1}{12}$
    b) $|x - 17| > \frac{1}{12}$
    c) $|x - 18| < \frac{1}{12}$
    d) $|x - 18| > \frac{1}{12}$

Answer: (c)

$17\frac{11}{12} < x < 18\frac{1}{12}$

$\frac{1}{2}(17\frac{11}{12} + 18\frac{1}{12}) = 18$

$17\frac{11}{12} - 18 < x - 18 < 18\frac{1}{12} - 18$

$-\frac{1}{12} < x < \frac{1}{12}$

$|x - 18| < \frac{1}{12}$

73. Mrs. Matt provides some markers to her Arts class. If each student takes 3 markers, there will be 2 markers left. If 6 students take 4 markers each and the rest of students take 1 marker each, there will be no markers left. How many students are in Mrs. Matt's Arts class?

Answer: 8

Let x be the number of students in Mrs. Matt's Arts class.
$3x + 2 = 6 \times 4 + (x - 6) \times 1$
$x = 8$

74. In the gym, a sports ball rack is stacked with 15 basketballs and 15 volleyballs. After Bob took 6 basketballs and 5 volleyballs, Steve took 8 more balls from the rack. What is the maximum number of volleyballs that Steve took in order for there to be more volleyballs than basketballs remaining on the rack?
   a) 8
   b) 6
   c) 4
   d) 3

Answer: (c)

After Bob took 6 basketballs and 5 volleyballs, there were 9 basketballs and 10 volleyballs left. For the 8 balls that Steve took: Let number of volleyballs be V and the number of basketballs be B.

$8 = V + B$ (1)

$10 - V > 9 - B$

$1 > V - B$ (2)

Add the equations (1) and (2):

$9 > 2V$

The most number of V is 4.

75. The cost of a long-distance call using phone company A is $1.00 for the first three minutes and $.25 for each additional minute. The same call using the phone company B is charged flat rate at $0.30 per minute for any amount of time. For a call that lasts *t* minutes, the cost using company A is the same as the cost using the company B, what is the value of *t*?
   a) 5
   b) 10
   c) 15
   d) 20

Answer: (a)

$1 + (t - 3) \times 0.25 = 0.30t$

$t = 5$

76. The daily cost of phone services in a business building is $.18 per hour from 8 AM through 5 PM, and $.08 per hour at any other hours of the day. Which of the following expressions represents the cost, in dollars, of the phone service starting from 8 AM and lasting for 20 hours a day over 30 days?
   a) 30 × 9(.18) + 30(20 – 9)(.8)
   b) 30(.18) + 30(20 – 9)(.8)
   c) 30 × 9(.18) + 30(20 – 9)
   d) 30 × 9(.18) + 30(.8)

Answer: (a)

In order to find the daily price, add the cost from the rush hours, which is 9 (hours) × (.18), and the cost from the additional hours, which is (20 − 9)(hours) × (.8).

Multiply the daily cost by 30 to find the total cost for 30 days.

77. If K is a positive integer, find the least value of K for which 27K is a perfect cube?
   a) 1
   b) 3
   c) 8
   d) 9

Answer: (a)

$27K = 3^3K$

Look for the least cube number which is 1.

78. The price of a pizza at the pizza store includes:
 i. The basic charge
 ii. An additional charge for each topping
 If the price of a 2-topping pizza is \$22 and the price of a 5-topping pizza is \$34, what is the price of a 7-topping pizza?

Answer: 42

Let the initial charge be x dollars and the charge for one topping be y dollars.
$x + 2y = 22$ (1)
$x + 5y = 34$ (2)
Subtract (1) from (2).
$3y = 34 - 22 = 12 \rightarrow y = 4$
$x = 14$
The price for 7-topping :
$x + 7y = 14 + 28 = 42$

79. The fee of a car rental includes:
 i. a basic rental fee
 ii. an additional charge for every 20 miles
 If the fee to rent a car and drive 60 miles is \$210 and the fee to rent a car and drive 160 miles is \$260, how much does it cost to rent a car and drive 250 miles?

Answer: 305

If the basic fee is \$x and every 20 miles is charged \$y, then
$x + 3y = 210$ (1)
$x + 8y = 260$ (2)
Subtract (1) from (2).
$5y = 260 - 210 = 50$
$y = 10 \rightarrow x = 180$
The rental to travel 250 miles:
$x + \frac{450}{20}y = 180 + \frac{250}{20} \times 10 = \$305$

80. If the sum of three consecutive even integers is 108 and m represents the largest of the three integers, which of the following represents the statement above?
 a) $3m + 6 = 108$
 b) $m + 2 = 54$
 c) $m - 2 = 54$
 d) $m - 2 = 36$

Answer: (d)

$(m - 4) + (m - 2) + m = 108$

$3m - 6 = 108$
$m - 2 = 36$

81. The square of the sum of x and 1 is equal to y. If y is the square of the difference of x and 2, what is the value of x?
 a) 2
 b) $\frac{1}{2}$
 c) $-\frac{1}{2}$
 d) $-\frac{1}{4}$

Answer: (b)

$(x + 1)^2 = y$ *and* $y = (x - 2)^2$
$(x + 1)^2 = (x - 2)^2$
$x^2 + 2x + 1 = x^2 - 4x + 4$
$6x = 3$
$x = \frac{1}{2}$

82. If $2x - y$ is equal to 80% of $5y$, what is the value of $\frac{y}{x}$?
 a) $\frac{5}{2}$
 b) $\frac{2}{5}$
 c) $\frac{5}{3}$
 d) $\frac{3}{5}$

Answer: (b)

$2x - y = .8 \times 5y$
$2x - y = 4y$
$2x = 5y$
$\frac{y}{x} = \frac{2}{5}$

83. If x and y are non-zero integers, what is x percent of y percent of 2500?

a) xy
b) $4xy$
c) $10xy$
d) $\frac{1}{4}xy$

Answer: (d)

x percent of y percent of 2500 →
$\frac{x}{100} \times \frac{y}{100} \times 2500 = \frac{xy}{4}$

84. If $\frac{2}{5}$ of k is 20, what is $\frac{3}{5}$ of k

a) 50
b) 40
c) 30
d) 20

Answer: (c)

$\frac{2}{5} \times k = 20$
$k = 20 \times \frac{5}{2} = 50$
$\frac{3}{5} \times 50 = 30$

85. The value of $5n - 7$ is how much greater than the value of $5n - 8$?

a) 15
b) 1
c) $10n + 1$
d) $5n - 1$

Answer: (b)

Find the difference between the two expressions.
$(5n - 7) - (5n - 8) = 1$

86. How much less than $r + 4$ is $r - 7$?

Answer: 11

Find the difference between the two expressions.
$(r + 4) - (r - 7) = 11$

87. For b > a, the product of 3 and (b − a) is equal to the average of a and b. If b is 49, what is a?

a) 21
b) 28
c) 32
d) 35

Answer: (d)

Let the smaller number be a, then
$\frac{49 + a}{2} = 3 \times (49 - a)$.
$49 + a = 6(49 - a)$
$49 + a = 294 - 6a$
$7a = 245$
$a = 35$

88. How much money was originally in Sue's checking account if she withdrew m dollars, deposited n dollars, and now has l dollars in her checking account?

a) $l + m - n$
b) $l - m - n$
c) $m + n - l$
d) $m + n + l$

Answer: (a)

If there were x dollars in the account originally, then the total dollars now is:
$l = x - m + n$
$x = l + m - n$

Chapter 2 Problem Solving and Data Analysis

I. Unions and Intersections of Sets

Concept Overviews

Union and Intersection

- The **Union** of two sets, denoted by **A∪B,** is the set of elements which are in **either** set. It is similar to the "OR" logic among the sets.

  Example: Let set *A = {1, 2, 3}* and set *B = {3, 4, 5}*, the union of sets A and B is the set of elements that are included in ***A* or *B***, i.e. A∪B = *{1, 2, 3, 4, 5}*.

- The **Intersection** of two sets, denoted by **A∩B,** is the set of elements which are in **both** sets. It is similar to the "AND" logic among the sets.

  Example: The intersection of set *A* and set *B*, as the example above, is the set of elements that are included in *A* and *B*, i.e. A∩B = {3}.

Venn Diagram

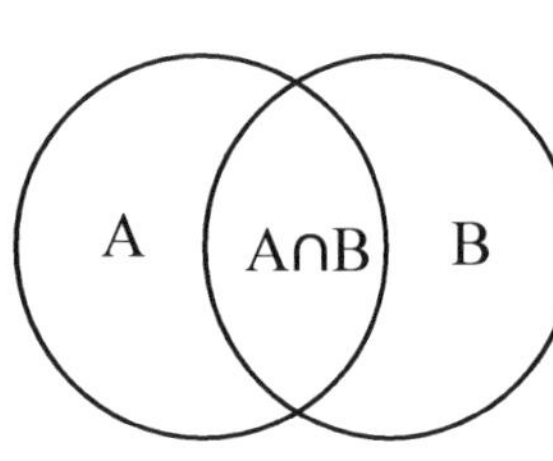

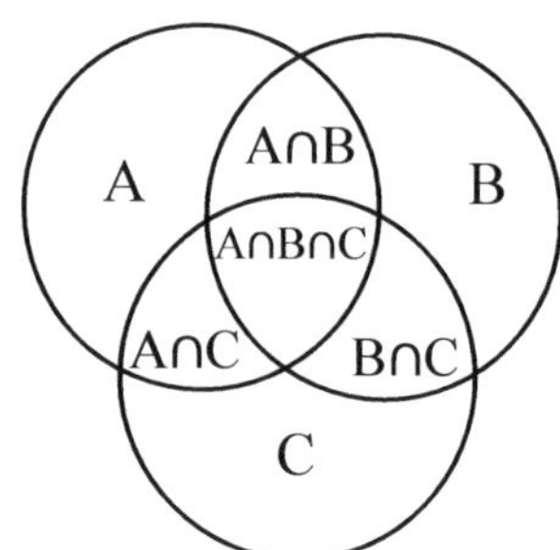

$$\{A\cup B\}=\{A\}+\{B\}-\{A\cap B\}$$

$$\{A\cup B\cup C\}=\{A\}+\{B\}+\{C\}-\{A\cap B\}-\{B\cap C\}-\{C\cap A\}+\{A\cap B\cap C\}$$

Example: In a class of 50 students, 18 students take chemistry, 26 students take biology, and 2 students take both chemistry and biology.

a) How many students in the class are enrolled in either chemistry or biology?

Solution: {Enrolled in either chemistry or biology} = {Enrolled in chemistry} + {Enrolled in biology} – {Enrolled in both chemistry and biology}
= 18 + 26 − 2 = 42

b) How many students in the class are **not** enrolled in either chemistry or biology?

Solution: {**Not** *enrolled in either chemistry or biology*} = total students − *{Enrolled in either chemistry or biology}*
= 50 − 42 = 8

Problem Solving Skills

Easy

Set X = {21, 22, 23}
Set Y = {22, 23, 24, 25, 26}

1. Sets X and Y are shown above. How many numbers are in the intersection of set X and set Y?
   a) Two
   b) Three
   c) Four
   d) Seven

Answer: (a)

only 22 and 23 are both in set X and set Y.

2. If A is the set of positive integers, B is the set of odd integers, and C is the set of integers multiple of 3, which of the following will be in all three sets?
   a) 24
   b) 18
   c) 15
   d) –21

Answer: (c)

The only odd positive integer that is also a multiple of 3 is 15.

3. Set A contains all odd positive numbers less than 10 and set B contains all prime numbers less than 20. What is the difference between the number of elements in the union of the two sets and the number of elements in their intersection?

Answer: 7

Union of two sets:
{1, 2, 3, 5, 7, 9, 11, 13, 17, 19}
Intersect of two sets: { 3, 5, 7 }

10 – 3 = 7

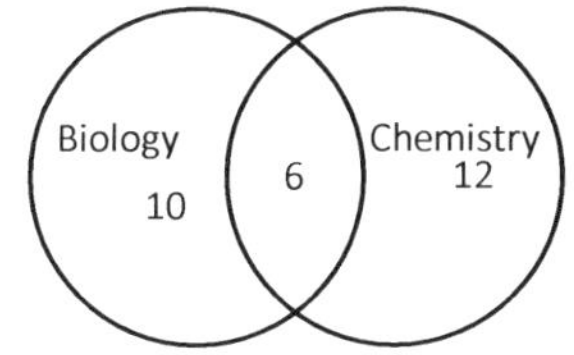

4. The Venn diagram above shows the distribution of 28 students in a class who took biology, chemistry, or both. If there are total 30 students in this class, what percent of the students did not take either chemistry or biology?
   a) 5%
   b) 6.7%
   c) 9%
   d) 10%

Answer: (b)

$30 - (10 + 12 + 6) = 2$
$\frac{2}{30} = 0.067 = 6.7\%$

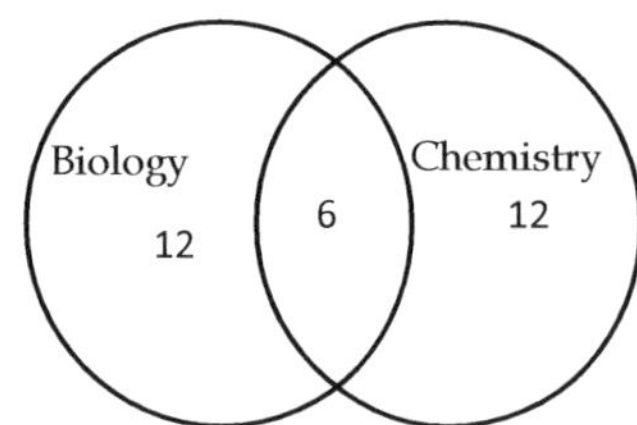

5. The Venn diagram above shows the distribution of 30 students in a class who took biology, chemistry, or both. If there are total 30 students in this class, what percent of the students studied chemistry?
   a) 30%
   b) 40%
   c) 50%
   d) 60%

Answer: (d)

Among the total 30 students, there were (6 + 12) students studied chemistry.

$\frac{18}{30} = 0.6 = 60\%$

Medium

6. What is the intersection of X and Y if X is the set of positive multiples of 3 and Y is the set of positive multiples of 4?
   a) the set of all positive integers
   b) the set of all positive real numbers
   c) the set of positive multiples of 12
   d) the set of positive multiples of 4

Answer: (c)

The common multiples of 3 and 4 will be the multiples of 12.

7. For an end of the year party, Mrs. Scott ordered 40 slices of pizza for her class. Among those slices of pizza, 16 were topped with mushroom and 14 were topped with chicken. If 15 slices contained neither mushroom nor chicken, how many slices of pizza must be topped with both mushroom and chicken?
   a) 3
   b) 5
   c) 7
   d) 9

Answer: (b)

Use Venn diagram:
Mushroom ∪ Chicken = Total – (No Mushroom ∩ No Chicken) = Mushroom + Chicken – (Mushroom ∩ Chicken)

Mushroom ∪ Chicken = 40 − 15 = 16 + 14 − (Mushroom ∩ Chicken)
25 = 30 − (Mushroom ∩ Chicken)
Mushroom ∩ Chicken = 5

Hard

8. If set A = {1, 3, 7, 10, 15} and set B consists of all the odd positive integers less than or equal to 13, how many elements are in the union of the two sets?
   a) 0
   b) 3
   c) 8
   d) 9

Answer: (d)

$A \cup B = A + B - (A \cap B)$
$A = \{1, 3, 7, 10, 15\}$
$B = \{1, 3, 5, 7, 9, 11, 13\}$
$A \cap B = \{1, 3, 7\}$
Number of Elements in $(A \cup B) = 5 + 7 - 3 = 9$

9. Set X has x elements and set Y has y elements. If they have exactly w elements in common, how many elements are in set X or set Y but not in both set X and Y?
   a) $x + y$
   b) $x + y - w$
   c) $x + y - 2w$
   d) $x + y + 2w$

Answer: (c)

There are $(x - w)$ members belong to X only and $(y - w)$ members belong to Y only.

$(x - w) + (y - w) = x + y - 2w$

Questions 10 – 11 refer to the following information:

Planetary Data of Solar System

Planet	*Distance from the Sun (billion meters)*	*Orbital Period (Earth years)*
Mercury	*57.9*	*0.241*
Earth	*149.6*	*1.0*
Mars	*227.9*	*1.88*
Saturn	*Z*	*29.5*
Uranus	*2870*	*84.0*
Planet X	*20,000*	*Y*

The chart above shows our Solar System's planetary data applied to the Kepler's Third Law, which states that the square of the period of any planet is proportional to the cube of its distance from the Sun. For any planets in the Solar System, the square of the orbital period divided by the cube of its distance from the Sun should be a constant.

10. If Saturn has the period of 29.5 Earth years, find its distance from the Sun, in billion meters? (Round your answer to the nearest whole number.)

Answer: 1428

Kepler's Third Law:

$$\frac{(Orbital\ Period)^2}{(Distance\ from\ the\ Sun)^3} = K$$

$$\frac{29.5^2}{(Distance\ from\ the\ Sun)^3} = \frac{1^2}{149.6^3}$$

$Distance = 1428\ billion\ meters$

11. If Planet X is 20,000 billion meters away from the Sun, what is its orbital period, in Earth years? (Round your answer to the nearest whole number.)

Answer: 1546

$$\frac{(Orbital\ Period)^2}{20000^3} = \frac{1^2}{149.6^3}$$

$Orbital\ Period =$
$1546\ Earth\ years$

II. RATIOS, PROPORTIONS, AND RATES

CONCEPT OVERVIEWS

Setting up a Ratio

- A **ratio** is a comparison between two numbers or two measures with the same unit.
- Ratios can be expressed as a fraction. For example, 1 : 2 can be written as $\frac{1}{2}$.
- Ratios can be reduced like a fraction. For example, 6 : 9 can be reduced to 2 : 3.

Setting up a Proportion

- A **proportion** is an equation relating two fractions or ratios.
- The phrase "*a* to *b* is equal to *c* to *d*" can be converted into an equation using ratios ($a : b = c : d$) or fractions ($\frac{a}{b} = \frac{c}{d}$), both of which can be solved by cross-multiplication.

Example 1: The proportion of x in $\frac{2}{3}$ is equal to $\frac{1}{3}$. What is x?

Answer: $\frac{x}{\frac{2}{3}} = \frac{1}{3}$ (apply cross-multiplication)

$3x = \frac{2}{3}$

$x = \frac{2}{9}$

Example 2: What proportion of $\frac{2}{3}$ is $\frac{1}{3}$?

Answer: $x \times \frac{2}{3} = \frac{1}{3}$

$x = \frac{3}{2} \times \frac{1}{3} = \frac{1}{2}$

Two variables are **directly proportional** if an increase in one is directly correlated with an increase in another. For example, in the following

$$\frac{x_1}{y_1} = \textbf{coefficient of proportionality}$$

- x_1 and y_1 are directly proportional, and their ratio is called the coefficient of proportionality. If we do not change the coefficient of proportionality, then if we increase or decrease x_1, we increase or decrease y_1 respectively by the same factor.

Two variables are **inversely proportional** if an increase in one is directly correlated with a decrease in another. For example, in the following

$$x_2 \times y_2 = \textbf{coefficient of proportionality (inverse)}$$

- x_2 and y_2 are inversely proportional. This can also be written as

$$x_2 = \frac{k}{y_2}$$

where k is the coefficient of inverse proportionality.

Solve a Proportion

To solve a problem involving ratios, you can often write as a proportion and solve it by **cross_multiplication**. For example, what proportion to10 is equal to the proportion of 3 out of 5? This problem can be written as $x : 10 = 3 : 5$. Changing the ratios to a fraction gives you $\frac{x}{10} = \frac{3}{5}$. Applying cross-multiplication gives you $5x = 30$. Solving for x gives you $x = 6$.

To solve conversions between units or scales, you can use ratios. Write the conversion's ratios so that you can cross out the unwanted unit.

Example: How many feet is 18 inches?

Answer:

$$\frac{1\ foot}{12\ inches} = \frac{x\ feet}{18\ inches}$$

$$\frac{18\ \cancel{inches}}{12\ \cancel{inches}} = \frac{x\ \cancel{feet}}{1\ \cancel{foot}}$$

$x = 1.5$ (18 inches × 1 foot/12 inches = 1.5 feet)

Rate and Work

A **rate** is a ratio that compares two different kinds of numbers, such as miles per hour or dollars per pound.

Rate Formula: $Rate = \frac{Distance}{Time}$

Example 1: Bob walks up and down a hill to get to school. He walks at 3 miles per hour up a hill and 4 miles per hour down a hill. The hill is 1 mile upwards and 1 mile downwards. What is his average rate?

Hint: If you get a question about the average rate traveled over several trips at different rates, you need to find the total distance and divide by the total time. Most people will think that they can average the two rates, 3.5 in this case – this does not work because you spend less time walking downhill and so you spend more than 50% of the time walking the slower rate.

Solution: The total distance traveled is obviously 2 miles (1 mile up and 1 mile down). The total time spent traveling is

$$1\ mile \times \frac{1\ hour}{3\ miles} + 1\ mile \times \frac{1\ hour}{4\ miles} = \frac{7}{12}\ hours$$

If we traveled 2 miles in $\frac{7}{12}$ hours, then we have traveled an average rate of

$$\frac{2\ miles}{\frac{7}{12}\ hours} = \frac{24}{7}\ miles\ per\ hour = 3.43\ miles\ per\ hour$$

(Applying rate formula: $Rate = \frac{Distance}{Time}$)

So the average rate is **less** than the arithmetic average between the two rates (3.43 < 3.5). This is because we spend more time traveling the slower rate.

Example 2: A plane travels from New York to San Francisco at 500 miles per hour. However, there is a headwind (a wind blowing against the direction of motion) of 100 miles per hour. When the plane flies back from San Francisco to New York, the same wind is now a tailwind (a wind blowing in the direction of motion) of 100 miles per hour. Each trip is 3000 miles. What speed does the plane actually travel at for both trips? What is the combined rate of travel for the entire trip?

Hint: If there are currents or winds involved, add the speed of the current or wind when it is moving along the direction of motion and subtract the speed of the current or wind when it is moving against the direction of motion.

Answer: The speed of the plane flying from New York to San Francisco is

$$500\ mph - 100\ mph = 400\ mph$$

The speed of the plane flying from San Francisco to New York is

$$500\ mph + 100\ mph = 600\ mph$$

Using the technique we used in the previous example to calculate the average rate. First, we find the total distance traveled, which is 3000 × 2 = 6000 miles. Then, we find the time traveled:

$$3000\ miles \times \frac{1\ hour}{400\ miles} + 3000\ miles \times \frac{1\ hour}{600\ miles} = 12.5\ hours$$

So the average rate is

$\frac{6000\ miles}{12.5\ hours} = 480\ mph$ (Applying rate formula: $Rate = \frac{Distance}{Time}$)

Total Time Worked $= \frac{1}{Rate\ of\ Work}$. If there is more than one person working, then the total rate is equal to the sum of each person's rate.

Example 1: It took Joe 5 hours to paint a house. What is his rate of painting?

Answer: Rate of painting $= \frac{x\ house}{1\ hour} = \frac{1\ house}{5\ hours}$, applying cross multiplication to find x.

$x = \frac{1}{5}$ houses per hour

Example 2: Once again, Joe takes 5 hours to paint a house. How much of a house can he paint in 1 hour?

Hint: Set up a fractional equation and then cross multiply.

Answer: $\frac{5\ hours}{1\ house} = \frac{1\ hour}{x\ houses}$, applying cross multiplication to find x.

$x = \frac{1}{5}$ houses per hour.

Example 3: Joe's friend Bob joins him in painting a house. Bob takes 3 hours to paint a house. What is their total rate of painting?

Hint: If there is more than one person painting, then the total rate is equal to the sum of each person's rate.

Answer: We calculate the total rate by adding two persons' rates:

Joe: $\frac{1}{5}$ houses per hour

Bob: $\frac{1}{3}$ houses per hour

Total rate: $\frac{1}{5} + \frac{1}{3} = \frac{8}{15}$ houses per hour

If some objects must be counted as whole numbers, then their total should be the multiple of the sum of the ratios. For example, if the ratio is 1:2:3 for different colors of marbles in the bag, then the total number of marbles in the bag must be a multiple of (1 + 2 + 3).

Example: The ratio of boys to girls in Ms. Johnson's class is 5 to 6. Which of the following CANNOT be the number of students in her class?

a) 11
b) 22
c) 33
d) 45

Answer: Since the ratio of boys to girls is 5 : 6, the total number of students must be a multiple of 11, (5 + 6). Only choice *(d)* is not the multiple of 11. Answer is *(d).*

Problem Solving Skills

Easy

1. If an object travels at 15 feet per minute, how many feet does it travel in 1.5 seconds?
   a) 22.5
   b) 1
   c) 0.1
   d) $\frac{3}{8}$

Answer: (d)

1.5 seconds $= \frac{1.5}{60}$ *minutes = 0.025 minutes*
Distance = 0.025 minutes×15 feet/minute = .375 feet $= \frac{3}{8}$ *feet*

2. How many pounds of flour are needed to make 15 rolls of bread if 20 pounds of flour are needed to make 100 rolls of bread?
   a) 3
   b) 4
   c) 5
   d) 3.5

Answer: (a)

20 pounds : 100 rolls = x : 15 rolls

$\frac{20\ pounds}{100\ rolls} = \frac{x\ pounds}{15\ rolls}$

Cross multiply: $100x = 20 \times 15$
$x = 3$ *pounds*

3. The ratio of 1.5 to 1 is equal to which of the following ratios?
   a) 1 to 2
   b) 2 to 1
   c) 3 to 1
   d) 3 to 2

Answer: (d)

You can multiply the numerator and denominator by the same factor to get an equivalent ratio.
$1.5 \times 2 : 1 \times 2 = 3 : 2$
Or just simply convert the ratios to decimals and compare, such as $3 \div 2 = 1.5$.

4. A certain graph chart shows ♥ = 500 viewers in a particular TV show. Approximately how many viewers are represented by the symbols ♥♥♥♥?
   a) 1000
   b) 2000
   c) 3500
   d) 4500

Answer: (b)

4♥ = 4 × 500 = 2000 viewers

5. Worker A can install a toy in 12 minutes. Worker B takes 10 minutes to install the same toy. In 5 hours, how many more toys can be installed by worker B than by worker A?
   a) 10
   b) 8
   c) 7
   d) 5

Answer: (d)

Worker A can finish $5 \times \frac{60}{12} = 25$ *toys in 5 hours. Worker B can finish* $5 \times \frac{60}{10} = 30$ *toys in 5 hours.*

$30 - 25 = 5$ *toys*

6. How many gallons are needed to travel 550 miles for a certain car that needs 17.5 gallons to travel 350 miles?
   a) 17.5
   b) 20
   c) 27
   d) 27.5

Answer: (d)

Write out the problem as an equation and cross-multiply.
17.5 gallons : 350 miles = x gallons : 550 miles

$\frac{17.5\ gallons}{350\ miles} = \frac{x\ gallons}{550\ miles}$

Cross multiply: $350x = 17.5 \times 550$

$x = \frac{17.5 \times 550}{350} = 27.5\ gallons$

7. How many more minutes would it take to burn a full 640 gallon tank of gasoline for a certain rocket engine that can burn a full 480 gallon tank in 15 minutes?
   a) 5
   b) 10
   c) 15
   d) 20

Answer: (a)

480 : 15 = m : 640

$\frac{480\ gallons}{15\ minutes} = \frac{640\ gallons}{m\ minutes}$

m = 20 minutes
20 − 15 = 5 more minutes

8. If 60 pounds of force can stretch a spring 5 inches, how many inches will the spring be stretched by a force of 84 pounds? Assume the force needed to stretch a spring varies directly with its stretch distance.
   a) 10
   b) 9
   c) 7
   d) 6

Answer: (c)

$\frac{60\ pounds}{5\ inches} = \frac{84\ pounds}{X\ inches}$

x = 7 inches

9. If John has \$90.00 and he spends \$30 on video games and \$25 on food, what fraction of the original \$90.00 does John have left?

Answer: $\frac{7}{18}$

$\frac{90 - 30 - 25\ Dollars}{90\ Dollars}$

$\frac{35}{90} = \frac{7}{18}$

10. John takes 8 minutes to bike 3 miles. At this rate, how many minutes will it take him to bike 4.5 miles?
    a) 10
    b) 12
    c) 14
    d) 16

Answer: (b)

8 minutes : 3 miles = x minutes : 4.5 miles

x = 12

11. If $\frac{x}{y} = \frac{4}{5}$, what is the value of $\frac{10x}{4y}$ =?
    a) 1
    b) 2
    c) 3
    d) 4

Answer: (b)

$\frac{10x}{4y} = \frac{10}{4} \times \frac{x}{y}$

$\frac{10 \times 4}{4 \times 5} = 2$

12. The number of lollipops Sam gets on her birthday varies directly with her age. If Sam got 15 lollipops when she was 6 years old, how many lollipops will she get when Sam is 18 years old?
    a) 45
    b) 50
    c) 55
    d) 60

Answer: (a)

Since Sam's lollipops and age are directly proportional, solve for the coefficient of proportionality and use that constant to find the missing number of lollipops.

$\frac{Lollipops}{Age} = k$

$\frac{15\ Lollipops}{6\ Years} = \frac{x\ Lollipops}{18\ Years}$

$x = 45$

13. How many toy parts can a machine make in 10 minutes if this machine can make 36 toy parts in 1 hour?
    a) Two
    b) Three
    c) Five
    d) Six

Answer: (d)

36 parts : 60 minutes = x parts : 10 minutes

$60x = 36 \times 10 = 360$

$x = 6$

14. If a small dog can run 12 miles in 1.5 hours and a mountain cat can travel twice as far in half the time, what was mountain cat's speed, in miles per hour?
    a) 18
    b) 24
    c) 28
    d) 32

Answer: (d)

The mountain cat's speed is 4 times of dog's speed.

Dog's Speed $= \frac{12\ Miles}{1.5\ Hours} = 8$ *miles/hour*

8 miles/hour $\times$ *4 = 32 miles/hour*

15. A jaguar can run at speeds up to 70 miles per hour. About how many miles can a jaguar run in 5 seconds?
    a) 0.1
    b) 0.2
    c) 0.3
    d) 0.4

Answer: (a)

1 hour = 3600 seconds

70 miles : 3600 seconds = x miles : 5 seconds

$3600x = 70 \times 5$

$x = \frac{350}{3600} \sim 0.1$ *miles*

16. For a certain type of heater, the increase in gas bills is directly proportional to the temperature setting (in Fahrenheit). If the gas bills increased by $20 when the temperature setting is increased by 4 degrees Fahrenheit, by how much will expenses increase when the temperature setting is increased by 10 degrees Fahrenheit?
    a) $35
    b) $40
    c) $50
    d) $60

Answer: (c)

$\$20 : 4^{\circ} F = \$x : 10^{\circ} F$

$4x = 200$

$x = \$50$

17. If $\frac{20}{x} = \frac{y}{14}$, what is the value of xy?
   a) 300
   b) 280
   c) 210
   d) 240

Answer: (b)

Cross multiply.
$20 \times 14 = xy = 280$

18. Kim spent 2.5 hours installing 700 square feet of solar panels. At this rate, how many hours will she require to install 4200 square feet of solar panels?

Answer: 15

$\frac{2.5Hhours}{700\ sq\ ft} = \frac{x\ Hours}{4200\ sq\ ft}$
$x = \frac{2.5 \times 4200}{700} = 15\ hours$

19. A worker can complete the assembly of 10 toys in 20 minutes. At the same rate, how many minutes does he need to assemble 20 toys?

Answer: 40

$\frac{Toys}{Minutes} = \frac{10}{20} = \frac{20}{x}$
$10x = 20 \times 20$
$x = 40$

20. Rachel has either blue or black pens in her pencil case. If the ratio of the number of blue pens to the number of black pens is $\frac{1}{4}$, Rachel could have the following number of pens in her pencil case EXCEPT?
   a) 8
   b) 15
   c) 20
   d) 30

Answer: (a)

The total number of pens is a whole number and a multiple of (1 + 4).

8 is not a multiple of 5.

21. If $x \neq 0$ and x is inversely proportional to y, which of the following is directly proportional to $\frac{1}{x^3}$?
   a) $\frac{1}{y^3}$
   b) $-\frac{1}{y^3}$
   c) y^3
   d) y^2

Answer: (c)

If "x is inversely proportional to y", then $xy = k$.
Raise power of 3 on both sides:
$(xy)^3 = k^3$
$x^3y^3 = k^3 \rightarrow y^3 = k^3\ (\frac{1}{x^3})$
So $\frac{1}{x^3}$ *directly proportional to* y^3

22. Sam drove from home at an average speed of 50 miles per hour to her working place and then returned along the same route at an average speed of 40 miles per hour. If the entire trip took her 2.25 hours, what is the entire distance, in miles, for the round trip?
   a) 90
   b) 100
   c) 120
   d) 125

Answer: (b)

Let one trip have x miles.

$Time = 2.25 = t_1 + t_2 = \frac{x}{50} + \frac{x}{40}$
$2.25 = x(\frac{1}{50} + \frac{1}{40})$
$x = 50$
$Total\ Distance = 2 \times 50 = 100$

23. The fruits provided in the student lounge contain pears, apples, and oranges. The ratio of the numbers of pears to apples is 3 : 4 and the ratio of the numbers of pears to oranges is 2 : 5. Find the ratio of the numbers of apples to oranges?
   a) 3 : 10
   b) 8 : 15
   c) 10 : 3
   d) 15 : 8

Answer: (b)

Use the same ratio number to compare.
pear : apple = 3 : 4 = 6 : 8
pear : orange = 2 : 5 = 6 : 15
apple : orange = 8 : 15

24. In a 100 mile biking competition, John biked at an average of 8 miles per hour for the first h hours. In terms of h, where $h < 12.5$, how many miles remained until the end after h hours?
   a) $8h$
   b) $100 - 8h$
   c) $108h$
   d) $100 - h$

Answer: (b)

Total – Past $= 100 - 8 \times h$

25. A machine can assemble toys at the rate of one toy per second. If the machine works 10 hours a day, how many days does it take the machine to assemble 720,000 toys?
   a) 20
   b) 1,00
   c) 2,000
   d) 10,000

Answer: (a)

Time = Total ÷ Rate

$\text{Time} = \frac{720000}{10 \times 60 \times 60 \times 1} = 20 \text{ days}$

26. A bike traveled 84 miles in 4 hours. At this rate, how many miles would the bike travel in 5 hours?
   a) 67
   b) 90
   c) 100
   d) 105

Answer: (d)

This is a ratio problem.

$\frac{84}{4} = \frac{x}{5}$ *(cross multiply)*
$x = 105$

Medium

27. If y is inversely proportional to x and y is equal to 12 when x is equal to 8, what is the value of y when $x = 24$?
   a) $\frac{1}{6}$
   b) $\frac{1}{4}$
   c) 4
   d) 2

Answer: (c)

$8 \times 12 = y \times 24$

$y = 4$

28. If y is directly proportional to x and y is equal to 40 when x is equal to 6, what is the value of y when $x = 9$?
    a) 60
    b) 55
    c) 50
    d) 45

Answer: (a)

$\frac{40}{6} = \frac{y}{9}$

$y = 60$

29. On a map, $\frac{1}{3}$ of an inch represents 18 miles. If a river is 45 miles long, what is its length, in inches, on the map?
    a) $\frac{5}{6}$
    b) $\frac{1}{2}$
    c) $\frac{1}{3}$
    d) 1

Answer: (a)

$\frac{1}{3}$ *inches : 18 miles*
$=$ *x inches : 45 miles*

$\frac{\frac{1}{3}\ inches}{18\ miles} = \frac{x\ inches}{45\ miles}$

$x = \frac{15}{18} = \frac{5}{6}$ *inches*

30. Machine A makes 200 toys per hour. Machine B makes 300 toys per hour. If both machines begin running at the same time, how many minutes will it take the two machines to make a total of 1000 toys?
    a) 150
    b) 130
    c) 120
    d) 100

Answer: (c)

Total Time $= \frac{Total\ Toys}{Total\ Rate}$

Total Rate = 200 toys/hour + 300 Toys/Hour = 500 toys/hour

Total Time $= \frac{1000\ toys}{500\ toys/hour}$
= 2 hours = 120 minutes

31. The ratio of 2.5 to 30 is the same as the ratio of x to 6. What is the value of x?
    a) $\frac{1}{2}$
    b) $\frac{1}{4}$
    c) 1
    d) 2

Answer: (a)

$2.5 : 30 = x : 6$

$x = \frac{1}{2}$

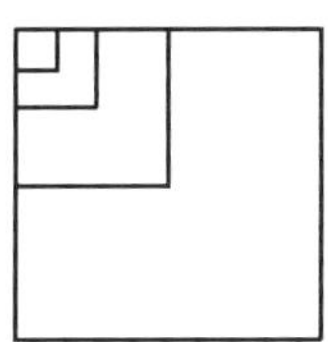

32. In the figure above, each square is one-fourth of the area of the square immediately larger than it. The area of the smallest square is what fraction of the area of the biggest square?

Answer: $\frac{1}{64}$

The Area of the Smallest Square $=$
$\frac{1}{4} \times \frac{1}{4} \times \frac{1}{4} \times$ *(the Area of the Biggest Square)*
$\frac{1}{4^3} = \frac{1}{64}$

33. Vehicle A ran 15 miles an hour for 4 hours. The total distance A traveled was twice the distance of Vehicle B after Vehicle B traveled 5 miles an hour for X hours. What is X?
    a) 6
    b) 5.5
    c) 5
    d) 4.5

Answer: (a)

Total Distance A Traveled = Rate × Time = 15 miles/hour × 4 hours = 60 miles
Total distance B traveled :
5 miles/hour × X hours
$= \frac{1}{2} \times 60$ *miles*
= 30 miles
$X = \frac{30\ miles}{5\ miles/hour} = 6$ *hours*

34. At a pet's store, if the ratio of cats to dogs is 12 to 5, which of the following could be the total number of cats and dogs?
    a) 70
    b) 75
    c) 80
    d) 85

Answer: (d)

The total number of dogs and cats must be a multiple of (12 + 5) since it must be an integer.

Only 85 is a multiple of 17.

35. In Sam's birthday party, if the ratio of the boys to girls is 3 to 4, which of the following could be the total number of boys and girls in the party?
    a) 12
    b) 14
    c) 18
    d) 20

Answer: (b)

The total number of boys and girls must be a multiple of (3 + 4) since it must be an integer.

Only 14 is a multiple of 7.

36. The number of cats is inversely proportional to the number of mice in the city park. One year ago, there were 20 cats and 70 mice in the park. How many cats are in the park if there are 140 mice in the park today?
    a) 10
    b) 20
    c) 30
    d) 40

Answer: (a)

The product of the number of cats and the number of mice must be constant at all time
Cats × Mice = constant, inversely proportional
x *= number of cats*
$20 \times 70 = x \times 140$
$x = 10$

37. A recipe of a cake for 8 people requires 1.2 pounds of flour. Assuming the amount of flour needed is directly proportional to the number of people eating the cake, how many pounds of flour are required to make a big cake for 240 people?
    a) 20
    b) 25
    c) 30
    d) 36

Answer: (d)

$$\frac{8\ People}{1.2\ Pounds} = \frac{240\ People}{x\ Pounds}$$

$8x = 1.2 \times 240$
$x = 36$ *pounds of flour*

38. The ratio of I to 3J is the same as the ratio of I + 1 to 3J + 4. Which of the following must be true if I and J are positive numbers?

    i. I = J
    ii. $I = \frac{3}{4}$
    iii. $I = \frac{3}{4}J$

    a) None
    b) i only
    c) ii only
    d) iii only

Answer: (d)

$\frac{I}{3J} = \frac{I+1}{3J+4}$

$3IJ + 4I = 3IJ + 3J$
$4I = 3J$
$I = \frac{3}{4}J$

39. The ratio of action movies to dramas in Albert's DVD collection is 4 to 3. If the total number of DVDs in the collection is greater than 20 but less than 30, what could be a possible number of DVDs in Albert's collection?

Answer: 21, 28

The total number should be a multiple of (4 + 3).

The numbers between 20 and 30 and a multiple of 7 are 21, and 28.

40. To make fruit punch, grapefruit juice, orange juice, and lemonade are mixed in with a ratio of 5:3:2 by volume, respectively. In order to make 5 liters of this drink, how much orange juice, in liters, is needed?

    a) 1
    b) 1.5
    c) 2
    d) 2.5

Answer: (b)

Every 10 liters, (2 + 3 + 5), of drink, 3 liters of orange juice will be needed. So 5 liters of this drink, we need $\frac{3}{10} \times 5$ *of orange juice.*
Orange Juice $= 0.3 \times 5 = 1.5$ *liters*

41. If each cubical block has edges of length 6 inches, what is the number of such blocks needed to fill a rectangular box with inside dimensions of 30 inches by 36 inches by 42 inches?

Answer: 210

Calculate how many for each side and multiply them together.

$\frac{30}{6} \times \frac{36}{6} \times \frac{42}{6} = 5 \times 6 \times 7 = 210$

42. Gina drove at an average of 30 miles per hour from her house to a bookstore. Along the same route, she returned at an average of 60 miles per hour. If the entire trip took her 1 hour, how many miles did Gina drive in total?

Answer: 40
Let one trip have x miles.
Total Time $= t_{go} + t_{back}$
$1 = \frac{x}{30} + \frac{x}{60} = x(\frac{1}{30} + \frac{1}{60})$
$x = 20$
Total: $2 \times 20 = 40$ *miles*

43. If a certain kind of bird can fly at 5 feet per second, how many feet can it fly in half an hour?

Answer: 9000
Distance = Time × Speed
Half an Hour = 30 × 60 seconds
Total Feet =
5 × 30 × 60 = 9,000 ft.

44. Freddy's family owns two different types of cars, a sedan and an SUV. The sedan has gas mileage of 25 miles per gallon, and the SUV has gas mileage of 20 miles per gallon. If both cars use the same amount of gasoline and the sedan travels 100 miles, how many miles does the SUV travel?

Answer: 80

Small car uses $\frac{100}{25} = 4$ *gallons*
SUV miles $= 4 \times 20 = 80$ *miles*

Hard

Questions 45 – 46 refer to the following information:

The fluid dynamics continuity model states that the rate at which mass enters a system is equal to the rate at which mass leaves the system. The rate of mass at any cross section in a pipe is the product of the cross sectional area and the speed of the fluid.

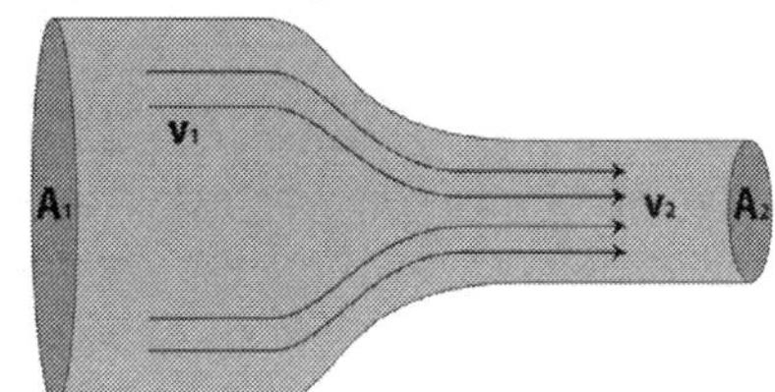

45. If water runs through a pipe with cross sectional area 0.4 m² at a speed of 6 m/s, calculate the speed of the water in the pipe when the pipe tapers off to a cross sectional area of 0.3 m².
    a) 8.0 m/s
    b) 7.5 m/s
    c) 7.0 m/s
    d) 5.5 m/s

Answer: (a)

$A_1V_1 = A_2V_2$
$0.4 \times 6 = 0.3 \times V_2$
$V_2 = 8\ m/s$

46. If water enters a certain type of garden hose with a diameter of 1.5 cm at a speed of 5 m/s, calculate the speed of water when it travels to the nozzle, which has diameter 0.7 cm.
    a) 30.66 m/s
    b) 22.96 m/s
    c) 17.23 m/s
    d) 14.21 m/s

Answer: (b)

$A_1V_1 = A_2V_2$
$\pi\left(\frac{1.5}{2}\right)^2 \times 5 = \pi\left(\frac{0.7}{2}\right)^2 \times V_2$

$V_2 = 22.96\ m/s$

47. Sean needs to finish reading his book in four days. He read $\frac{1}{3}$ of the book on the first day, $\frac{1}{4}$ of the book on the second day, $\frac{1}{5}$ of the book on the third day. If he has 13 pages to finish on the fourth day, how many pages are there in the book?

Answer: 60

Find out the last portion of pages and set up ratio equation
The last portion of pages: $1 - \frac{1}{3} - \frac{1}{4} - \frac{1}{5} = \frac{13}{60} = \frac{13}{total} = \frac{13}{x}$
$x = 60$

48. In a mixture of flour and sugar, the ratio of flour to sugar is 5 to 3 when measured by cups. How many cups of sugar will be used for 4 cups of this mixture?

Answer: 1.5

$\frac{Sugar}{Total} = \frac{3}{5+3} = \frac{x}{4}$

$8x = 12$

$x = 1.5$ *cups*

49. Let the function f be defined by $f(t) = 5(t^3 - 4)$. When $f(t) = -155$, what is the value of $2 - t$?
    a) 4
    b) 5
    c) 6
    d) 7

Answer: (b)

$5(t^3 - 4) = -155$

$t^3 - 4 = \frac{-155}{5} = -31$

$t^3 = -27$

$t = -3$

$2 - t = 2 - (-3) = 5$

50. To get a job done, a machine needs to produce x boxes of toys, in which each box contains y toys. If this machine produces an average of z toys per minute, how many hours will it take to finish the job?
    a) $\frac{xy}{z}$
    b) $\frac{xy}{60z}$
    c) $\frac{xyz}{60}$
    d) $\frac{60z}{xy}$

Answer: (b)

$Hours = \frac{Total\ Works}{Work\ per\ Hour}$

Total Toys $= xy$

Number of Toys Per Hour $= z \times 60$

$Hour = \frac{xy}{60z}$

51. Bob drove to the school at an average rate of 30 miles per hour. He returned home along the same route at an average rate of 40 miles per hour. If his entire trip took 42 minutes, how many miles did he drive on his way back from school?

Answer: 12

Let one trip have x miles.

$Time = \frac{Miles}{Rate}$

Total Time (hours) $= t_{go} + t_{back}$

$\frac{42}{60} = \frac{x}{30} + \frac{x}{40} = x(\frac{1}{30} + \frac{1}{40})$

$x = 12$ *miles*

Questions 52 – 53 refer to the following information:

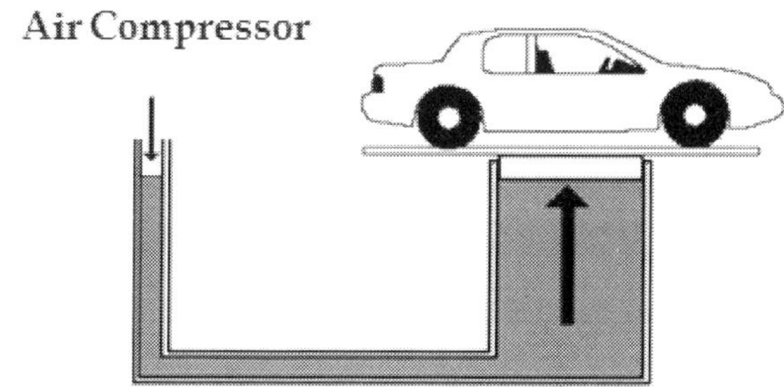

The hydraulics system in the figure above uses liquids to create pressure and lift heavy objects. The pressure from one end of the hydraulics system (the air compressor)

will always be equal to the pressure on the other end (the car). Pressure is defined as force divided by the cross sectional area:

$$Pressure = \frac{Force}{Area}$$

52. The cross sectional area of the cylinder underneath the car is 700 cm^2 and the cross sectional area of the cylinder at the end with the air compressor is 8 cm^2. If a car is lifted by a force of 2,800 kg, what force should be exerted by the air compressor?
    a) 32 kg
    b) 28 kg
    c) 24 kg
    d) 20 kg

Answer: (a)

$$\frac{Force_1}{Area_1} = \frac{Force_2}{Area_2}$$
$$\frac{2800}{700} = \frac{x}{8}$$
$$x = 32\ kg$$

53. In order to lift a car by a force of 2,800kg, a 5 kg force is applied at the air compressor end. Find the ratio of the radii of the cylinder at the car end to the air compressor end.
    a) 27.3
    b) 25.5
    c) 23.7
    d) 15.3

Answer: (c)

$$\frac{Force_1}{Area_1} = \frac{Force_2}{Area_2}$$
$$\frac{2800}{\pi r_1^2} = \frac{5}{\pi r_2^2}$$
$$\frac{r_1}{r_2} = \sqrt{\left(\frac{2800}{5}\right)} = 23.7$$

III. Percentages

Concept Overviews

A percentage is a ratio of a part to a whole expressed as a fraction of 100. To calculate the percentage that a part represents in the whole, use the percent formula:

$$\text{Percentage} = \frac{Part}{Whole} \times 100\%$$

- Identify the part and the whole and then set up an equation using the percent formula.
- If you are performing **operations on percentages**, convert them into fractions first.

Example: A baseball pitcher won 28 out of 35 games he pitched. How many percent of his games did he win?
Answer: the percentage of winning $= \frac{28}{35} \times 100\% = 80\%$

Changing Decimals to Percentages
Multiply a decimal by 100 to get the equivalent percentage.

$$\text{Percentage} = \text{Decimal} \times 100\%$$

Example: 0.25 is equal to 0.25×100%, which is equal to 25%?

Changing Fractions to Percentages
Change a fraction into a decimal by dividing the denominator into numerator. Then convert the decimal into a percentage.

Example: Write $\frac{2}{5}$ as a percent.
Solution: $\frac{2}{5} = 0.4$
$0.4 \times 100\% = 40\%$
Therefore, $\frac{2}{5}$ is equal to 40%.

Changing Percentages to Decimals
Divide the percentage by 100 and get rid of the percent sign (%).

The easy way to divide a number by 100 is to move the decimal point two places to the left.

Example: Convert 35% to a decimal.

Solution: 35 (without the % sign) divided by 100 is equal to 0.35. The easy way to divide 35 by 100 is to move the decimal point two places to the left. 35.0 is equivalent to 0.35.

Changing Percentages to Fractions

Write the percent as a fraction out of 100 and reduce the fraction.

$$\text{Fraction} = \frac{\textit{The Percent (without the \% sign)}}{100}$$

Example: Change 40% into a fraction.

Answer: Fraction $= \frac{40}{100} = \frac{2 \times 20}{5 \times 20} = \frac{2}{5}$

Percent Change (Percent Increase and Percent Decrease)

The percent change is defined as the percent of the initial value that was gained or lost.

$$\text{Percent Change} = \frac{\textit{Final Value} - \textit{Initial Value}}{\textit{Initial Value}} \times 100\%$$

- Percent Change > 0 → Percent Increase
- Percent Change < 0 → Percent Decrease

Example: The population of a small town was 1200 in last year and became 1260 this year. What was its population percent change from last year to this year?

Answer: Percent Change $= \frac{\textit{This Year's Population} - \textit{Last Year's Population}}{\textit{Last Year's Population}} \times 100\%$

$= \frac{1260 - 1200}{1200} \times 100\% = 5\%$

Keywords: When dealing with percent problems, the following keywords usually translate to the following actions:

- Percent in decimal form → divide by 100
- Decimal in percent form → multiply by 100
- 'is' → =
- 'of' → × *(multiplication)*
- 'what' or 'a number' → ***x*** (the value you are solving for)

Example 1: 5 is what percent of 20?

Answer: $5 = \boldsymbol{x} \times 20$

$x = \frac{5}{20} = 0.25$

$0.25 \times \mathbf{100\%} = 25\%$

Changing 0.25 into a percent is equal to 25%.

Therefore, *5 is 25% of 20.*

Example 2: What is 15% of 60?
Answer: $x = \frac{12}{100} \times 60 = 9$

Example 3: 20% of what number is 16?
Answer: $\frac{20}{100} \times x = 16, \quad x = 80$

Example 4: What percent of 20 is 5?
Answer: $\frac{x}{100} \times 20 = 5$
$x = \frac{5 \times 100}{20} = 25\%$

Example 5: If 40 percent of 20 percent of a number is 20, what is the number?
Answer: Changing 40% into decimal form gives you 0.4. Changing 20% into decimal form gives you 0.2.
$0.4 \times 0.2 \times x = 20$
$x = \frac{20}{0.4 \times 0.2} = 250$

Discount: You might be asked a question that gives you two of the following: discount rate of an item, the original price of the item, and/or the total amount of money saved from purchasing the item at a discount, and asked to find the third term. To do this, you should use the discount formula:

Total Discount = Original Price × Discount Rate

Or if you are solving for or given the sale price of the item, you can either subtract the discount from the original price to get the sale price:

Original Price – Original Price × Discount Rate = Sale Price

or multiply the original price by (1 – Discount Rate):

Sale Price = Original Price × (1 – Discount Rate)

Example 1: In a department store, a $50 T-shirt is marked "20% off." What is the sale price of the T-shirt?
Answer: Converting 20% to a decimal gives you 0.2.
Total Discount = $\$50 \times 0.2 = \$10$
Sale Price of the T−shirt = $\$50 - \$10 = \$40$

Example 2: An object that regularly sells for $125 is marked down to $100. What is the discount percentage?
Answer: *Total Discount* = $\$125 - \$100 = \$25$
$\$25 = \$125 \times \textit{Discount Rate}$
$\textit{Discount Rate} = \frac{25}{125} = 0.2$
Changing 0.2 to percent gives you 20%.
The discount rate is equal to 20%.

Simple Interest

When you put money in a bank, you usually earn something called interest. This is money the bank pays you for leaving money (principal) with them. Simple interest can be calculated with the simple interest formula:

Total Interest Earned = Interest Rate × Principal × Time

When you are using the interest formula, be careful of units and make sure your time units match with your interest rate units!

Example: A bank is offering its customers 3% simple interest rate annually on savings accounts. If a customer deposits \$2,500 in the account, without cashing out, how much money will be in his saving account after 4 years?

Answer: Changing 3% to decimal gives you 0.03.

Total Interest Earned = *0.03×\$2,500× 4 =\$300*

Money in Account = *\$2,500 + \$300 = \$2,800*

After 4 years, his saving account will have *\$2,800.*

Compound Interest

Compound interest is the interest added to the principal of a deposit so that the interest earned also earns interest continuously. A formula for calculating annual compound interest is as follows:

$$A = P\left(1 + \frac{r}{100}\right)^t$$

A is the amount of money, in dollars, generated after t years by a principal amount P in a bank account that pays an annual interest rate of r%, compounded annually.

Example: How much would you need to deposit in your bank account today with an annual interest rate of 3% compounded annually in order to get \$10,000 in your back account after 10 years? (Round your answer to the nearest dollar and ignore the dollar sign when gridding your response.)

Answer: $10000 = P\left(1 + \frac{3}{100}\right)^{10}$

$10000 = P \times (1.3439)$

$P = \$7{,}441$

Problem Solving Skills

Easy

1. If 70 percent of x is 28, then what is 30 percent of x?
   a) 16
   b) 12
   c) 14
   d) 12

Answer: (b)

$\frac{70}{100} \times x = 28$

$x = 40$

$40 \times 0.3 = 12$ *(Note: 30% = 0.3)*

2. 50 percent of 210 is the same as 35 percent of what number?
   a) 340
   b) 300
   c) 350
   d) 275

Answer: (b)

This sentence can be translated into: $\frac{50}{100} \times 210 = \frac{35}{100} \times A$

$A = \frac{50}{35} \times 210 = 300$

3. If 60 percent of 30 percent of a number is 36.54, what is the number?

Answer: 203

This can be translated into $0.6 \times 0.3 \times A = 36.54$.

$A = \frac{36.54}{0.6 \times 0.3} = 203$

4. Based on Mrs. Johnson's grading policies, if a student answers 90 to 100 percent of the questions correctly in a math test, she will receive a letter grade of A. If there are 60 questions on the final exam, what is the minimum number of questions the student would need to answer correctly to receive a grade of A?
   a) 34
   b) 38
   c) 42
   d) 54

Answer: (d)

$90\% = \frac{Correct\ Answers}{Total\ Questions}$

$\frac{x}{60} = \frac{90}{100}$ *(cross multiply)*

$x = \frac{90 \times 60}{100} = 54$

5. If John earns $3,000 a month and he saves $600 out of his salary, what percent of John's earnings is his monthly savings?
   a) 15%
   b) 20%
   c) 25%
   d) 30%

Answer: (b)

$Percent = \frac{Part}{Whole} \times 100$

$\frac{600}{3000} \times 100 = 20$

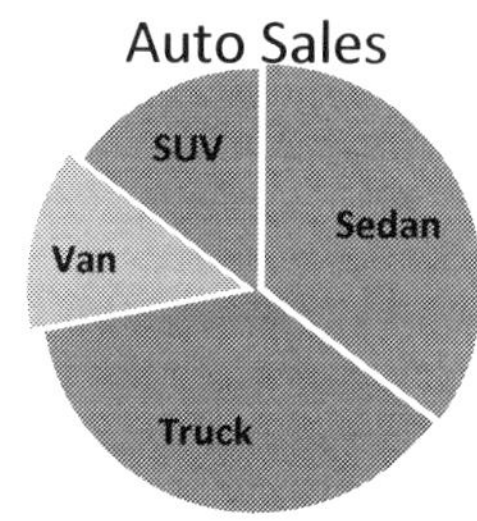

6. According to the circle graph above, how many types of automobiles represent less than 30 percent of the total sales?
   a) 0
   b) 1
   c) 2
   d) 3

Answer: (c)

30% is slightly more than $\frac{1}{4}$ *(25%) of the whole graph.*
From the graph above, two types of automobiles make up less than $\frac{1}{4}$ *of the whole graph.*

7. If 25 percent of x is 250, what is x percent of 50?
   a) 50
   b) 500
   c) 520
   d) 550

Answer: (b)

Translate "25 percent of x is 250" into an algebraic equation:
$\frac{25}{100} \times x = 250; x = 1000$
"x percent of 50" $\rightarrow 50 \times \frac{1000}{100} = 500$

8. The percent increase from 6 to 15 is equal to the percent increase from 12 to what number?
   a) 20
   b) 22
   c) 24
   d) 30

Answer: (d)

$\frac{15-6}{6} = \frac{x-12}{12}$ *(cross multiply)*
$9 \times 12 = 6(x - 12)$
$18 = x - 12$
$x = (18 + 12) = 30$

Medium

9. In a certain year at Lion High School, exactly 68 out of the 400 students are taking AP Chemistry. What percent of students are NOT taking AP Chemistry that year?
   a) 15
   b) 17
   c) 50
   d) 83

Answer: (d)

Percentage of people taking AP Chemistry: $\frac{68}{400} \times 100 = 17\%$

Percentage NOT taking AP Chemistry: $100\% - 17\% = 83\%$

10. If x is the least possible integer for which 35 percent of x is greater than 7.7, what is the value of x?
    a) 22
    b) 23
    c) 24
    d) 25

Answer: (b)

$\frac{35}{100} \times x > 7.7$
$x > \frac{770}{35}$
$x > 22$
$x = 23$

11. A family spent $350 on utilities in January. Due to the weather, they spent 20% more in February. How much did they spend on utilities in February?

Answer: 420

"20% more of 350" $\rightarrow 350 \times (1 + 0.2) = 420$
$x = 420$

12. In a recent town election, 75 percent of the 16,000 people voted. Of the voting people, 60 percent voted for current mayor and 120 votes were invalid. How many people voted for other candidates?

Answer: 4680

Total Vote – Vote for Current Mayor – Invalid Vote = Vote for Other Candidates
Total Vote: $16000 \times 0.75 = 12000$
Vote for Current Mayor: $12000 \times 0.6 = 7200$
Vote for Others: $12000 - 7200 - 120 = 4680$

13. Two rectangles X and Y are shown above. If the width of rectangle Y in the figure above is 25 percent less than the width of rectangle X and the length of rectangle Y is 25 percent greater than the length of rectangle X. What is the area of rectangle Y compared to the area of rectangle X?
    a) The area of rectangle Y is 25 percent less than the area of rectangle X.
    b) The area of rectangle Y is 6 percent less than the area of rectangle X.
    c) Both rectangles have the same area.
    d) The area of rectangle Y is 6 percent greater than the area of rectangle X.

Answer: (b)

Let X's width be w and length be l. Then Y's width is 0.75w and length is 1.25l.

Area of Y = 0.75w × 1.25l = 0.9375wl = 93.75% of area of X. 100% − 93.75% = 6.25% (less)

Questions 14 – 15 refer to the following information:
Percent error is useful for determining the precision of a calculation. Percent error close to zero means the calculation is very close to the target value. The formula to measure percent error is:

$$Percent\ Error = \frac{Measured\ Data - Actual\ Data}{Actual\ Data} \times 100\%$$

14. The density of water at 4°C is known to be 1.00 g/mL. If Anny experimentally found the density of water be 0.9975 g/mL, what would be her percent error?
    a) 1.25%
    b) −1.25%
    c) 0.25%
    d) −0.25%

Answer: (d)

$Percent\ Error = \frac{0.9975-1}{1} \times 100\%$
$= -0.25\%$

15. Frank got his lab report back with "8.0% error" written in red on it. If he had examined the boiling point of an unknown liquid to be 92 °C, what could be the actual boiling point for his unknown liquid?
    a) 90.5 °C
    b) 85.2 °C
    c) 80.3 °C
    d) 75.1 °C

Answer: (b)

$8\% = \frac{92 - x}{x} \times 100\%$
$9200 = 108x$
$x = 85.2\ °C$

16. There are 860 students in the class of 2013, and 45% are boys. How many girls are in the class of 2013?

Answer: 473

Number of Girls =
860 − Number of Boys
Boys: 860 × 0.45 = 387
Girls: 860 − 387 = 473

17. The percent increase from 10 to 14 is equal to the percent increase from 15 to what number?

Answer: 21

$\frac{14-10}{10} = \frac{x-15}{15}$
$4 \times 15 = 10 \times (x - 15)$
$60 = 10x - 150 \rightarrow x = 21$

18. The price of a pair of shoes was first increased by 10 percent and then decreased by 25 percent. The final price was what percent of the original price?
    a) 80%
    b) 82.5%
    c) 85%
    d) 87.5%

Answer: (b)

Let the original price be 100, then the final price is 100 × (1 + 0.1) × (1 − 0.25) = 82.5.

19. A movie company invited a total of 500 people to complete their review survey after watching a new release movie. Of the 380 people who finished that survey so far, 55 percent are female and 45 percent are male. Assuming all 500 people will eventually complete the survey, how many of the rest of the respondents must be male in order for half of the total respondents to be male?

Answer: 79

We need 250 males but only 380 × 0.45 surveyed so far.

250 − 380 × 0.45 = 79

20. If the length of a rectangle is increased by 20% and the width of the same rectangle is decreased by 20%, how does the area of the rectangle change?
    a) It is increased by 10%.
    b) It is increased by 4%.
    c) It is unchanged.
    d) It is decreased by 4%.

Answer: (d)

"increased by 20%" means to multiply by (1 + 0.2); "decreased by 20%" means to multiply by (1 − 0.2).
new area = (1 + 0.2)(1 − 0.2) = 0.96
4% less than its original

21. A car salesman's monthly pay consists of $1000 plus 2% of his sales. If he got paid $3,000 in a certain month, what was the dollar amount, in thousands, of his sales for that month?

Answer: 100

Let his car sales be $x, then
$3000 = 1000 + 0.02 \times x$
$3000 - 1000 = 0.02x$
$x = \$100,000$

Questions 22 – 23 refer to the following information:
According to research, 90 percent of 20 to 36 month-old children in the United States need to have received measles vaccination in order to achieve herd immunity. In 2013, California did not meet the vaccination goal and

Colorado, Ohio, and West Virginia had 86 percent of 20 to 36 month-olds received the vaccination.

22. If 89 percent of 20 to 36 month-olds received the measles vaccination in California in 2013 and the total number of 20-36 month-olds in California in 2013 is 1.41 million, which of the following could be the number of 20-36 month-olds who have received the measles vaccination in California in 2013?
    a) 1.24 million
    b) 1.25 million
    c) 1.26 million
    d) 1.27 million

Answer: (b)

The measles vaccination percentage in California is 89%. The number of 20 to 36 month-olds who had received measles vaccination in California need to be 1.41 million × 0.89 = 1.2549 million.

23. If the total number of 20 to 36 month-olds in Ohio in 2013 is 0.235 million, how many of 20 to 36 month-olds in Colorado have received the measles vaccination in 2013?
    a) 224,600
    b) 205,100
    c) 202,100
    d) 145,300

Answer: (c)

0.235 million × 0.86 = 0.2021 million = 202,100

Questions 24 – 25 refer to the following information:

The unemployment rate is officially defined as the percentage of unemployed individuals divided by all individuals currently willing to work. To count as unemployed, a person must be 16 or older and have not held a job during the week of the survey. According to the Bureau of Labor Statistics, below is a comparison of the seasonally adjusted unemployment rates for certain states for the months of August and September 2015.

State	Rate (August 2015)	Rate (September 2015)
Nebraska	2.8	2.9
Hawaii	3.5	3.4
Texas	4.1	4.2
Wisconsin	4.5	4.3
Connecticut	5.3	5.2
New Jersey	5.7	5.6
Oregon	6.1	6.2
Alaska	6.6	6.4

24. Among those states shown in the table above, how many states have their unemployment rate drop from August 2015 to September 2015?
    a) 5
    b) 4
    c) 3
    d) 2

Answer: (a)

5 states, Hawaii, Wisconsin, Connecticut, New Jersey, and Alaska, have unemployment rate drop among those states shown above.

25. If about 251,400 residents of New Jersey were unemployed in September 2015, approximately how many New Jersey residents were willing to work in September 2015?
    a) 44,900
    b) 1,407,800
    c) 3,251,600
    d) 4,489,200

Answer: (d)

Let the number of residents who were willing to work be x.

$$\frac{251{,}400}{x} = 5.6\%$$
$$5.6x = 25{,}140{,}000$$
$$x = 4{,}489{,}286 \approx 4{,}489{,}200$$

Hard

26. A store sells a certain brand of TVs for $550 each. This price is 25 percent more than the cost at which the store buys one of these TVs. The store employees can purchase any of these TVs at 20 percent off the store's cost. How much would it cost an employee to purchase a TV of this brand?
    a) $352
    b) $330
    c) $413
    d) $586

Answer: (a)

Store's Cost × (1 + 25%) = 550

Store's Cost $= \frac{550}{1.25} = 440$

20 percent off the store's cost:

$440 \times (1 - 0.2) = 352$

27. If increasing 50 by x percent is equal to the result of decreasing 70 by x percent, what is the value of x?

Answer: 16.6 or 16.7

$$50 \times (1 + x) = 70 \times (1 - x)$$
$$50 + 50x = 70 - 70x$$
$$x = 0.1667 = 16.67$$

28. There are 12 more men than women enrolled in a cooking class. If there are M men enrolled, then, in terms of M, what percent of those enrolled are men? 🚫
    a) $\frac{100M}{M+12}\%$
    b) $\frac{100M}{M-12}\%$
    c) $\frac{100M}{2M+12}\%$
    d) $\frac{100M}{2M-12}\%$

Answer: (d)

There are (M – 12) women in the class.

Percent of Men in Class $= (\frac{M}{total}) \times 100\%$

$$= \frac{100M}{M + M - 12}\% = \frac{100M}{2M - 12}\%$$

IV. AVERAGES

CONCEPT OVERVIEWS

Average

The average of a set of values is equal to the sum of all values in that set divided by the number of values.

$$Average = \frac{Sum\ of\ Terms}{Number\ of\ Terms} \quad \text{(the average formula)}$$

The key to solving arithmetic average problems is using the average formula.

Example: John has the following scores on his math tests this semester: 80, 85, 89, and 90. What is his average score on his math tests that semester?

Answer: $John's\ Average = \frac{80 + 85 + 89 + 90}{4} = 86$

The average score of all of John's math tests is 86.

Sum of All Values in the Set

If you are given an average and asked to find the sum of all values in the set, multiply the average by the number of terms in the set.

$$\text{Sum of Terms} = \text{Average} \times \text{Number of Terms}$$

Number of Terms in the Set

On the other hand, if you are given an average and a sum and asked to find the number of terms in the set, divide the sum by the average to get the number of terms.

$$\text{Number of Terms} = \frac{Sum\ of\ Terms}{Average}$$

Example: The average score of a math quiz in a class is 81 and the sum of the scores is 1215. How many students are in this class?

Answer: Number of Students $= \frac{1215}{81} = 15$

Finding the Missing Number

If you know the average of a set, the number of items in that set, and the sum of all but one of the values, then you can find the value in that set missing from the sum by subtracting the sum from the average times the number of items.

Example: There were 4 tests in Joe's Algebra class. So far he received the following scores on his tests: 83, 93, and 87. What score does he need on the last test in order to get an average score of 90 and above?

Hint: The current sum (with one score missing) is 83 + 93 + 87 = 263. He wants an average of 90 or above.

Answer: $90 \times 4 - 263 = 360 - 263 = 87$.

Joe needs to get at least an 87 to get an average of 90 or above.

Mean, Median, and Mode

- **Mean:** The usual arithmetic average of a set.

  Example: The mean of the set {2, 6, 4, 5, 3} is $\frac{2+6+4+5+3}{5} = 4$.

- **Median:** The middle element (or average of two middle elements) when a set is sorted from least to greatest. If the set has an odd number of elements, the median is the middle element. If the set has an even number of elements, the median is the average of the two middle elements.

  Example 1: What is the median of the set {3, 11, 6, 5, 4, 7, 12, 3, 10}?
  Hint: Sort the numbers in order first: {3, 3, 4, 5, 6, 7, 10, 11, 12}
  Answer: There are 9 numbers in the set, so the median is the middle element in the sorted set. The median is 6.

  Example 2: What is the median of the set {3, 11, 6, 5, 4, 7, 12, 3, 10, 12}?
  Hint: Sort the numbers in order: {3, 3, 4, 5, 6, 7, 10, 11, 12, 12}
  Answer: There are 10 numbers in the set, so the median number is the average of the two middle numbers, 6 and 7. The median is 6.5.

- **Mode:** The value(s) that appear most often in the set.

  Example: What is the mode of the set {7, 13, 18, 24, 9, 3, 18}?
  Hint: Sort the numbers in order: {3, 7, 9, 13, 18, 18, 24}
  Answer: The number which occurs most often is 18. Therefore, the mode is 18.

Problem Solving Skills

Easy

1. The average (arithmetic mean) of 5, 14, and x is 15. What is the value of x?
   a) 25
   b) 26
   c) 27
   d) 28

Answer: (b)

The average of these three numbers is 15, so the sum will be $3 \times 15 = 45$.
$5 + 14 + x = 45$
$x = 45 - 19 = 26$

2. Mary has the following scores on 7 quizzes in Algebra class: 84, 79, 83, 87, 81, 94, and 87. What was the median score of all of her Algebra quizzes?
   a) 81
   b) 84
   c) 85
   d) 86

Answer: (b)

Sort the scores in order.

79, 81, 83, 84, 87, 87, 94
The median is 84.

3. If the average (arithmetic mean) of 7 numbers is greater than 25 and less than 30, which of the following could be the sum of the 7 numbers?
   a) 150
   b) 170
   c) 190
   d) 210

Answer: (c)

$7 \times 25 < Sum < 7 \times 30$

$175 < Sum < 210$

4. Which of the following sets of numbers has an average (arithmetic mean) that is equal to its median?
   a) {-2, −1, 1}
   b) {-2, −1, 1, 2, 3}
   c) {1, 2, 3, 6}
   d) {1, 2, 3, 4, 5}

Answer: (d)

Sort all the numbers in the set from least to greatest. If there are odd amount of numbers in a set, then median is the middle number. If there are even amount of numbers in the set, median is the average of the two middle numbers.

a) *Average* $= -\frac{2}{3}$ *Median* $= -1$
b) *Average* = 0.6 *Median* = 1
c) *Average* = 3 *Median* = 2.5
d) *Average* = 3 *Median* = 3

5. X is a set of numbers whose average (arithmetic mean) is 5. Y is a set that is created by doubling and adding 3 to each number in X. What is the average of the numbers in the set Y?
   a) 10
   b) 11
   c) 12
   d) 13

Answer: (d)

If we double and add 3 to each element in X, we will double and add 3 to the mean of X as well.

$5 \times 2 + 3 = 13$

6. Let A represents the average of all winter monthly heating bills for John's family. What is the result of multiplying A by the number of months in winter?
   a) The average of all heating expenses for John's family in the year.
   b) The highest monthly heating bill for John's family that winter.
   c) The sum of the gas bills for the whole year for John's family.
   d) The sum of the heating expense in winter for John's family.

Answer: (d)

Multiplying the average by the number of elements (months) in the set gives you the sum of all the elements.

7. If the average of $3a$, $4a$, and $5a$ is equal to 8, what is a equal to?

Answer: 2

The average of 3a, 4a and 5a is equal to 4a.

$4a = 8 \rightarrow a = 2$

8. The median of a set of 13 consecutive integers is 35. What is the greatest of these 13 integers?
   a) 37
   b) 38
   c) 40
   d) 41

Answer: (d)

The median is the 7th number of 13 consecutive integers. That means there are 6 integers less than the median and 6 integers greater than the median. The greatest integer is the 6th consecutive integer after 35.
$35 + 6 = 41$

9. If the average (arithmetic mean) of 2, X, and Y is 3, what is the value of X + Y?
   a) 4
   b) 5
   c) 7
   d) 8

Answer: (c)

$X + Y + 2 = 3 \times 3 = 9$
$X + Y = 7$

10. The average score of John's 5 math tests is 75. If the teacher decides not to count his lowest score, which is 55, what will be John's new average score?
    a) 78
    b) 79
    c) 80
    d) 81

Answer: (c)

John's original average is 75 for 5 tests.
$5 \times 75 = 375$ *(sum of 5 tests)*
$375 - 55 = 320$ *(sum of 4 tests)*
$\frac{320}{4} = 80$ *(average of 4 tests)*

11. If the average (arithmetic mean) of x and $2x$ is 12, what is the value of x?

Answer: 8

$x + 2x = 2 \times 12$
$3x = 24$
$x = 8$

12. The average (arithmetic mean) of the weights of 15 boxes of oranges is x pounds. In terms of x, what is the total weight of the boxes, in pounds?
    a) $15 + x$
    b) $15 - x$
    c) $15 \div x$
    d) $15x$

Answer: (d)

Sum of All Elements = Number of Elements × Average
Total Weight $= 15 \times x$

13. If the sum of 4 numbers is between 61 and 63, then the average (arithmetic mean) of the 4 numbers could be which of the following?
    a) 15
    b) 15.2
    c) 15.5
    d) 16

Answer: (c)

$\frac{61}{4} < \text{Average} < \frac{63}{4}$

$15.25 < \text{Average} < 15.75$

14. Joe goes on a business trip that includes 3 different types of transportation: bike, bus, and airplane, in that order. If all three transportations take roughly the same amount of time, which of the following could be the graph of the distance traveled by the three transportations?

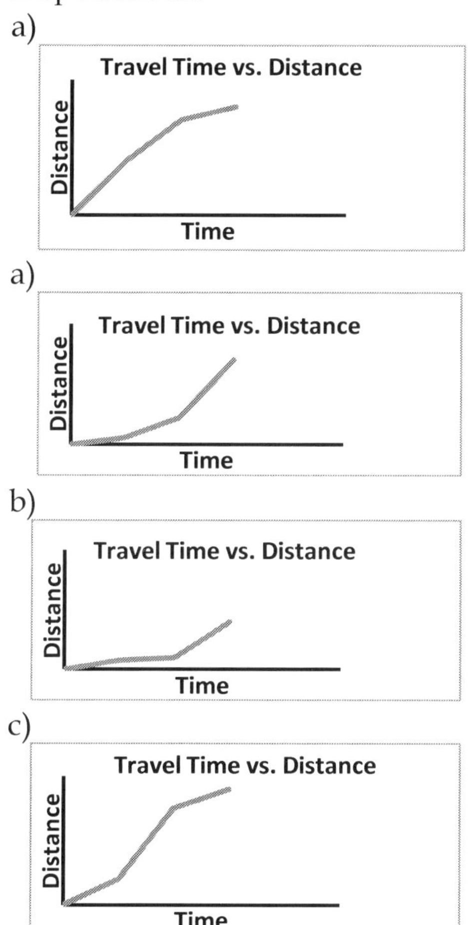

Answer: (b)

The higher the speed of the vehicle, the steeper (greater) the slope of the graph. Since bikes are slower than buses which are slower than planes, the graph must have three segments of increasing slope.

Medium

15. If the sum of 7 numbers is between 41 and 43, then the average (arithmetic mean) of the 7 numbers could be which of the following?
    a) 5
    b) $5\frac{1}{2}$
    c) 6
    d) $6\frac{1}{2}$

Answer: (c)

$Average = \frac{Sum}{7}$

$\frac{41}{7} < Average < \frac{43}{7}$

$5.85 < Average < 6.14$

16. On a certain test, the highest possible score is 100 and the lowest is 0. If the average score of 5 students is 82, what is the lowest possible score of the fifth student?
    a) 0
    b) 5
    c) 7
    d) 10

Answer: (d)

The lowest possible score is equal to the lowest score a student can get if each of other four students got the highest possible score (otherwise we can always increase another student's score and decrease the lowest score). Thus, each of other four students must get 100. Total Score = $5 \times 82 = 410$*; Lowest Score* $= 410 - 400 = 10$

17. If a solution of iodine and alcohol contains 3 ounces of iodine and 13.5 ounces of alcohol, how many ounces of alcohol need to evaporate so that the ratio of iodine to alcohol is 2 to 5?
    a) 6
    b) 7
    c) 8
    d) 9

Answer: (a)

Only alcohol can evaporate. Let x be the amount of alcohol evaporated in ounces.

$\frac{3}{13.5 - x} = \frac{2}{5}$ *(cross multiply)*

$15 = 27 - 2x$

$x = 6$

Math Midterm	
Scores	*Number of Students*
100	*1*
95	*3*
90	*5*
85	*8*
80	*3*

18. The scores of the math midterm for every student in Sam's class are shown in the table above. Sam, who was the only student absent, will take the test next week. If Sam receives a score of 95 on the test, what will be the median score for the test?
    a) 75
    b) 82.5
    c) 85
    d) 87.5

Answer: (c)

For an odd set, the median is the score in the middle when scores listed in order.

If we include Sam, the median will be the 11th highest score which is 85.

19. On an Algebra final exam, class A has an average score of 90 with 10 students. Class B has an average score of 85 with 20 students. When the scores of class A and B are combined, what is the average score of class A and B?
    a) 82
    b) 82.5
    c) 83
    d) 86.7

Answer: (d)

*This is **not** the average of the averages since the classes have different number of students! The final average is the sum of all students' scores divided by the total number of students. We know that the sum of all the students' scores in one class is just the average multiplied by the number of students.*

Average $= \frac{10 \times 90 + 20 \times 85}{10 + 20} = 86.67$

20. If the average (arithmetic mean) of x, y, and z is k, which of the following is the average of w, x, y and z?
   a) $\frac{k+w}{2}$
   b) $\frac{2k+w}{3}$
   c) $\frac{3k+w}{3}$
   d) $\frac{3k+w}{4}$

Answer: (d)

$k = \frac{x+y+z}{3}$

$x + y + z = 3k$

Average: $\frac{x+y+z+w}{4} = \frac{3k+w}{4}$

21. If 8 out of 24 students in a math class get a perfect score, then the class average (arithmetic mean) on this test will be 91 points out of 100. What was the average score for the remaining students?
   a) 86
   b) 86.5
   c) 87.5
   d) 88

Answer: (b)

To find the average score for the remaining students, we need to find the total score of all the remaining students and divide that by the number of remaining students.
There are 24 – 8 = 16 remaining students who did not get a perfect score. The sum of all scores is 24× 91 (which includes the test scores for the 8 that got a perfect score).
$24 \times 91 - 8 \times 100 = 1384$
Average: $\frac{1384}{24-8} = 86.5$

3, 5, 7, 9

22. In the list above, if we add a positive integer P to the list, which of the following could be the median of the new list of five numbers?
   I. 5
   II. 6
   III. 7
   a) I only
   b) I, II only
   c) I, III only
   d) I, II, III

Answer: (d)

P can be any positive integer, so there are a few cases.

P < 5: The median would be 5.
P = 6: The median would be P.
P > 7: The median would be 7.

23. On a biology test with total of 100 points, a class of 21 students had an average of 93. If 5 of the students had a perfect score, what was the average score for the remaining students?
   a) 89
   b) 90
   c) 91
   d) 91.5

Answer: (c)

Once again, the average gives a way to calculate the total score of all the students. Deduct from that sum the sum of the test scores that were perfect and divide by the remaining number of students.
Average: $\frac{Sum}{21} = 93$
Sum of all scores: $21 \times 93 = 1953$
Deduct 5 perfect scores:
$1953 - 500 = 1453$
New Average $= \frac{1453}{21-5} = 90.8 \sim 91$

24. Which of the following could be the sum of 8 numbers if the average of these 8 numbers is greater than 9 and less than 10?
    a) 85
    b) 83
    c) 82
    d) 79

Answer: (d)

Sum = Number of Elements × Average
$9 \times 8 < Sum < 10 \times 8$
$72 < Sum < 80$

Hard

25. We start out with a set of 7 numbers. We subtract 3 from 3 of these numbers. If the average (arithmetic mean) of these seven numbers was 11 originally, what is the new average?
    a) 7.5
    b) 8
    c) 8.5
    d) 9.7

Answer: (d)

Average: $\frac{Sum\ of\ Terms}{Number\ of\ Terms}$

$\frac{7 \times 11 - 3 \times 3}{7} = 9.7$

26. If the average (arithmetic mean) of 12, 16 and x is equal to x, what is the value of x?
    a) 9
    b) 10
    c) 14
    d) 16

Answer: (c)

Average: $\frac{12 + 16 + x}{3} = x$

$28 + x = 3x$
$28 = 2x$
$x = 14$

27. The average (arithmetic mean) of 24 exam scores is 88. After removing the highest and lowest scores from the set, the average of the remaining 22 exam scores is 89. What is the sum of the scores of the 2 exams that were removed?
    a) 150
    b) 152
    c) 154
    d) 156

Answer: (c)

We have two pieces of information: the average of the original set of scores (from which we can get the sum of the scores by multiplying by the number of scores) and the average of the scores after taking out two exams (from which we can also find the sum of the remaining scores).
Subtract, and we will get the sum of the scores that were removed.
$24 \times 88 - 22 \times 89 = 154$

28. If the average (arithmetic mean) of a and b is m, which of the following is the average of a, b, and c?
    a) $\frac{2m+c}{3}$
    b) $\frac{m+c}{2}$
    c) $\frac{2m+c}{2}$
    d) $\frac{m+2c}{2}$

Answer: (a)

The Average of a, b, and c is equal to the sum of a, b, and c divided by 3.
$a + b = 2m$
$a + b + c = 2m + c$
Average: $\frac{2m + c}{3}$

29. Class A has X students and class B has Y students. The average of the test scores of class A is 80, and the average of the test scores of class B is 90. When the scores of class A and B are combined, the average score is 88. What is the ratio of X to Y?
    a) $\frac{1}{2}$
    b) $\frac{1}{3}$
    c) $\frac{1}{4}$
    d) $\frac{2}{3}$

Answer: (c)

We want to find $\frac{X}{Y}$.

Average: $\frac{Sum\ of\ Terms}{Number\ of\ Terms}$

$\frac{80X + 90Y}{X+Y} = 88$ *(cross multiply)*

$80X + 90Y = 88 \times (X + Y)$

$80X + 90Y = 88X + 88Y$

$2Y = 8X$

$\frac{X}{Y} = \frac{2}{8} = \frac{1}{4}$

30. N students have an average of K scores on a math test. Another 3 students were absent and received zeroes on the test. What is the average score of this math test in terms of N and K, taking into accounts all of the students?
    a) $\frac{NK}{3}$
    b) $\frac{NK}{K+3}$
    c) $\frac{NK}{N+3}$
    d) $\frac{N-3}{K}$

Answer: (c)

Average $= \frac{Total\ Score}{Number\ of\ Students}$

Average $= \frac{K \times N}{N+3}$

31. Which of the following CANNOT affect the value of the median in a set of nonzero unique numbers with more than two elements?
    a) Increase each number by 5
    b) Double each number
    c) Increase the smallest number only
    d) Decrease the smallest number only

Answer: (d)

The median of an odd-numbered set is the number in the middle when all numbers in the set have been sorted in numerical order. In an even-numbered set, it is the average of the two middle elements.
We can change the median by:
i. Changing the value of the median
ii. Changing order of numbers so that we have a new median
Choices (a) and (b) change all values so the median will be changed. Choice (c) could result in a new median if the number changed becomes the new median. Choice (d) reduces the element that is already the smallest, and we know that there are more than 2 elements, so the median does not get changed.

V. DATA ANALYSIS

CONCEPT OVERVIEWS

Reading and Interpreting Graphs, Charts, and Tables

SAT data analysis questions use graphs, charts, and tables to organize information.

Bar graphs use horizontal or vertical bars to represent data.

Example: The bar graph below shows the number of students taking honors and AP classes. For math classes, there are 20 students taking math honors and 15 students taking AP math.

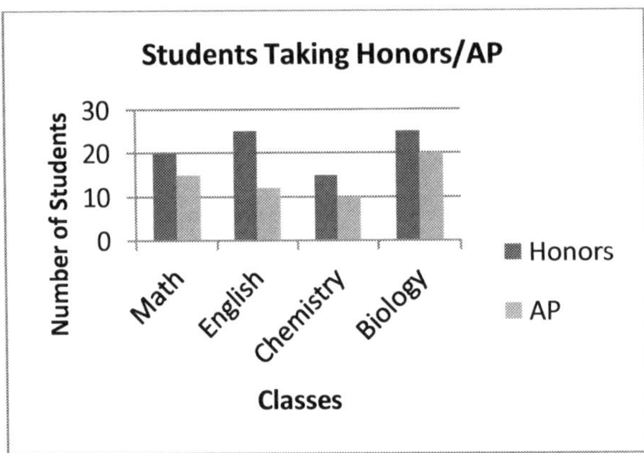

Pictographs use pictures to represent data. There is usually a scale provided that gives you an idea of what each picture represents.

Example: The pictograph below shows the car sales data from 1971 to 2010. The scale clearly states that each car represents 2 million cars. In the pictograph, we can see that the years 2001-2010 are drawn with four cars, which represents a total of 8 million cars sold. In the years 1981-1990, the pictograph shows $2\frac{1}{2}$ cars sold, which represents 5 million cars.

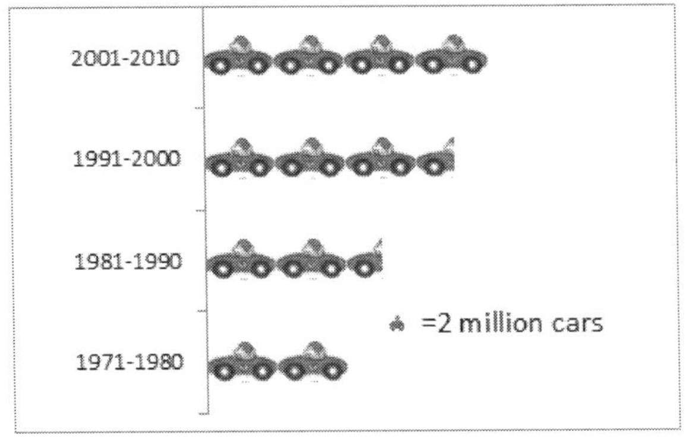

Car Sales from 1971 to 2010

Pie graphs use a circle (or pie) to display data. Pie graphs can be used to determine the proportion of an item out of a whole as well as ratios of different items to each other.

Example: The pie graph below shows Ellen's family's monthly expenses and the proportion of each expense out of all of their expenditures.

As we can see from the graph, food takes up about $\frac{1}{4}$ of all expenditures, and utilities take up about $\frac{1}{5}$ of all expenditures. The ratio of food expenditures to taxes is about 1:1.

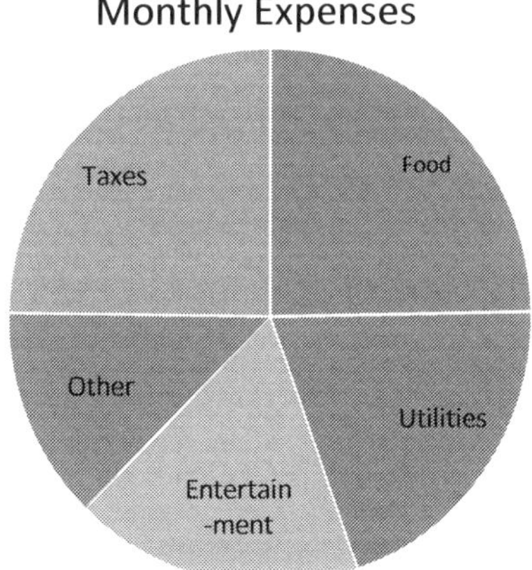

Sometimes you are asked to the value of a sector given the total value. You can figure out the proportion of the sector in the pie and solve for the missing value:

$$\text{Proportion of Sector in Pie} = \frac{Value\ of\ the\ Sector}{Total\ Value}$$

Example: If the Ellen's family's total expenses are \$6000 per month, approximately how much do they pay in taxes per month?

Solution: Taxes take up around $\frac{1}{4}$ of the total pie.

$$\frac{1}{4} = \frac{Taxes}{6000}$$

$$Taxes = \$1500$$

Tables represent data in rows and columns. Tables are simple to understand. The top entry of a column usually explains the contents of that column. Elements are corresponded to all the other elements in the same row.

Example: The table below shows the number of students taking AP classes in school. The entry that contains a '1' under 'Number of APs' corresponds to the entry that contains a '6' under 'Number of Students.' In other words, there are 6 students taking 1 AP class.

Students Taking AP Classes	
Number of Aps	*Number of Students*
1	6
2	4
3	5
4	4

Line graphs record a change in data. Usually this change is graphed over time. Time is usually graphed on the x-axis.

Example: The line graph below records car sales (in millions) over four years.

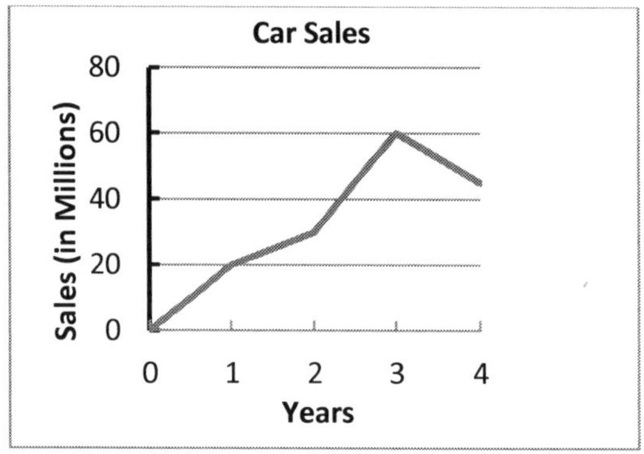

Scatterplots are similar to line graphs, but show the individual data points instead of connecting them with a line. Like line graphs, scatterplots show trends in the data.

Example: The scatterplot below shows the wolf population in a safari every 5 years.

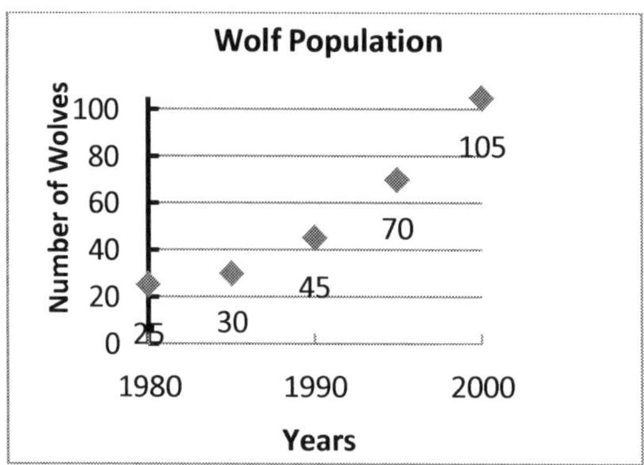

Tips to solve data analysis questions with graphs:

- Always look through the question first to check what the question is asking.
- Read the titles and axes to see what the graph is trying to show.
- Collect information from the graph as needed.
- Perform operations on the data you collected.

Problem Solving Skills

Easy

1. From the graph below, John sold how many more cars in year 3 than the sum of cars sold in years 1 and 2?

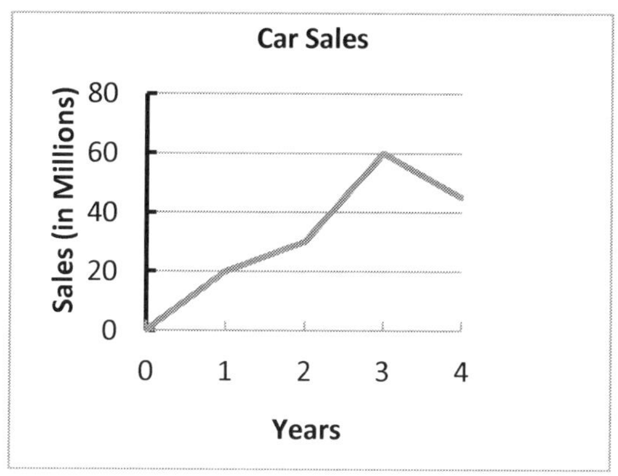

a) 10
b) 15
c) 20
d) 25

Answer: (a)

Year 1 + Year 2 = 20 + 30 = 50 cars
Year 3 = 60 cars

60 − 50 = 10 cars

2. The pictogram below shows the number of car sales in Company G over the years from 1971 to 2010. How many cars (in millions) were sold from 1971 to 2000?

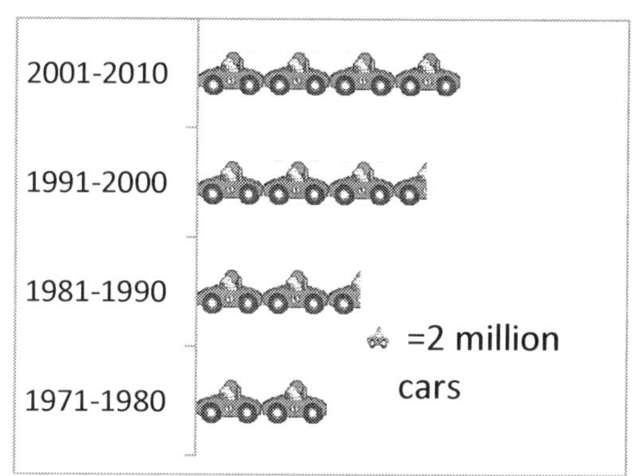

a) 8
b) 10
c) 12
d) 16

Answer: (d)

From 1971 to 2000 there are (2 + 2.5 + 3.5) × 2 million = 16 million

3. According to the graph below, how many students are taking honors classes altogether?

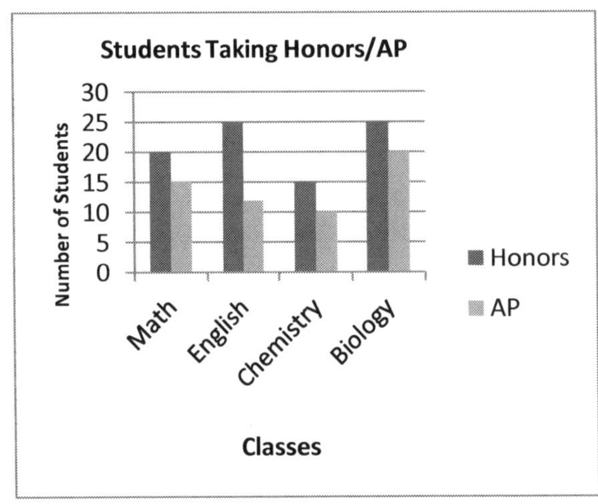

a) 75
b) 80
c) 85
d) 90

Answer: (c)

Total = (20 + 25 + 15 + 25) = 85

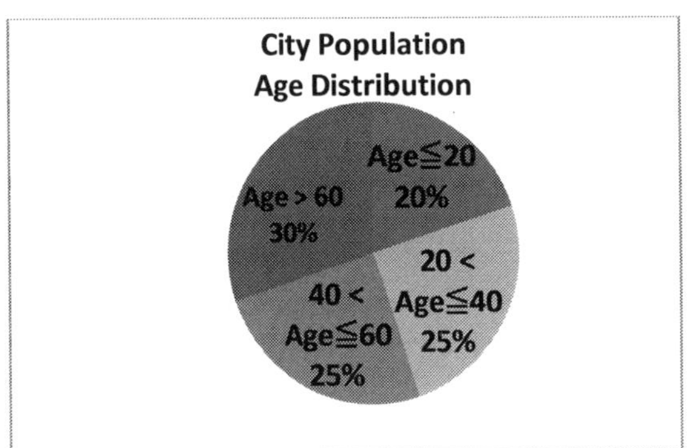

4. Town A has a population of 25,000 and the chart above shows their age distribution. How many people are 40 years or younger?
   a) 5000
   b) 8000
   c) 10,000
   d) 11,250

Answer: (d)

The number of population 40 years or younger:
(25% + 20%) × 25,000
= 45% × 25,000 = 0.45 × 25,000
= 11,250

5. What is the percent increase of sales from the third to the fourth year in the chart below?

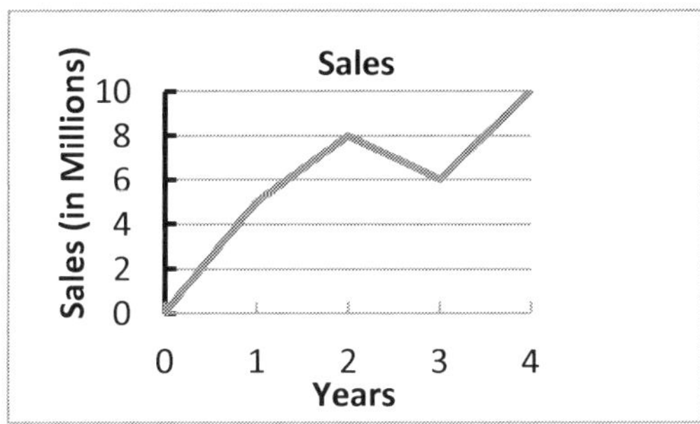

a) 40%
b) 55%
c) 65%
d) 67%

Answer: (d)

Percent increase =

$$\frac{4^{th}\text{ Year Sales} - 3^{rd}\text{ Year Sales}}{3^{rd}\text{ Year Sales}} \times 100\%$$

From the graph, sales in the 3rd year is 6 million and sales in the 4th year is 10 million.

Percent Increase $= \frac{10-6}{6} \times 100\% = 67\%$

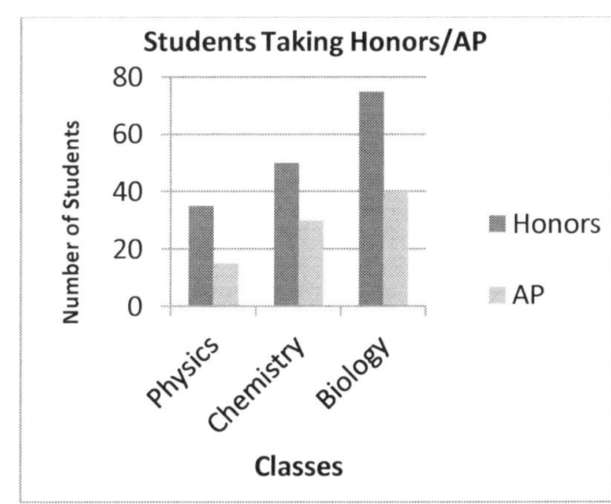

6. The bar graph above shows the distribution of students in each science class in Livingston High School last year. Which of the following pie graphs most accurately displays the breakdown AP classes taken at Livingston High School (provided each student only takes 1 AP)?
   a)

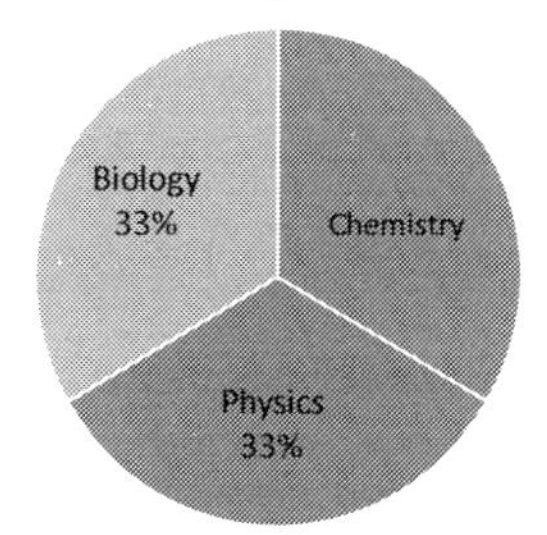

Answer: (b)

There are 15 students in AP Physics, 25 students in AP Chemistry and 40 students in AP Biology class. There are a total of 15 + 25 + 40 = 80 students in AP classes.

AP Physics $= \frac{15}{80} \times 100\% = 19\%$

AP Chemistry $= \frac{25}{80} \times 100\% = 31\%$

AP Biology $= \frac{40}{80} \times 100\% = 50\%$

b)

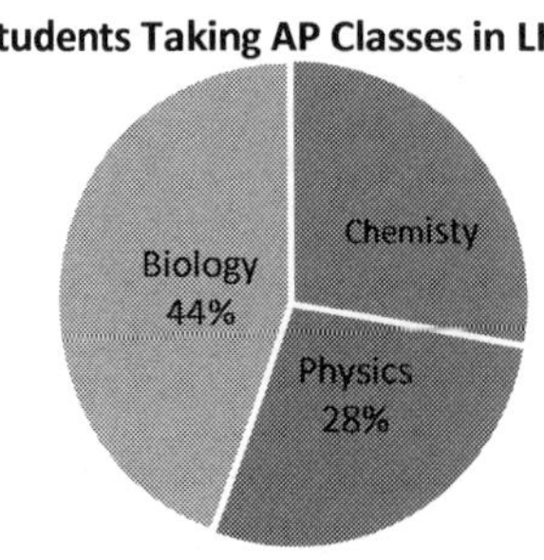

c)

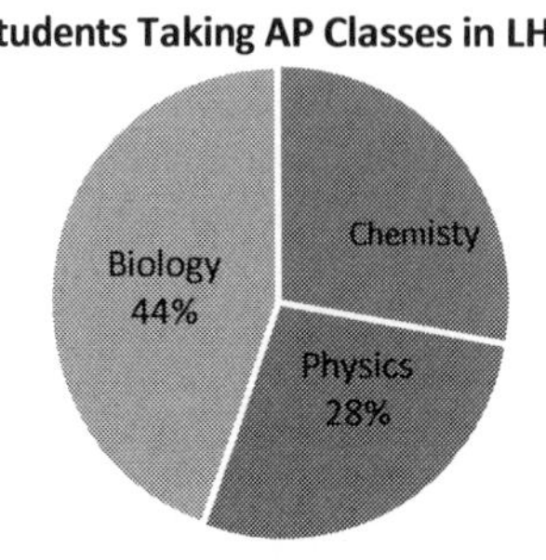

d)

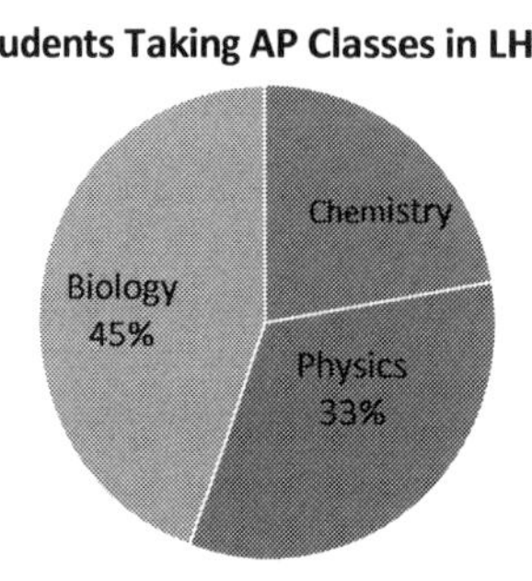

7. According to the graph below, how many employees have salary less than or equal to $40,000?

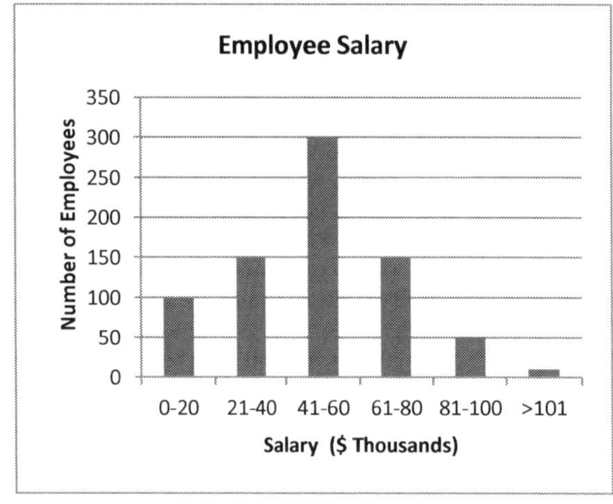

a) 100
b) 150
c) 250
d) 300

Answer: (c)

According to the bar graph, there are 100 + 150 =250 employees with a salary of $40,000 or less.

8. The chart below shows the results of a swimming race. If all the students started at the same time, who finished second?

Swimming Race Results	
Student	*Time (in seconds)*
Grant	*57.55*
Robert	*56.94*
Larry	*55.81*
Adam	*56.02*
Chris	*57.41*

a) Grant
b) Robert
c) Larry
d) Adam

Answer: (d)

Adam has the 2nd shortest time listed.

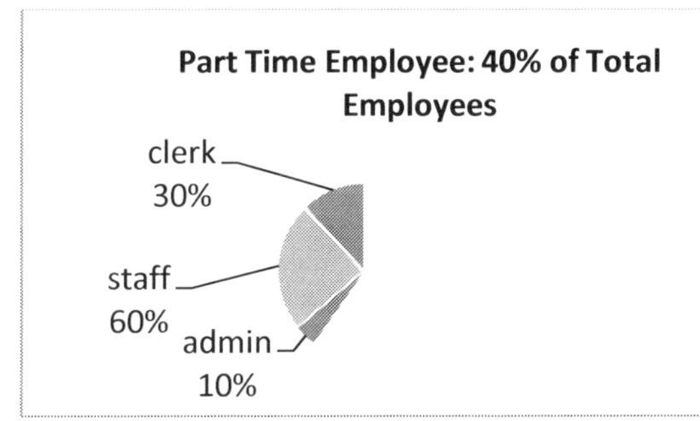

9. According to the graphs above, the total number of full-time employees is how many more than the total number of part time employees at Oak Town High School?

a) 20
b) 40
c) 50
d) 60

Answer: (b)

Number of Full Time Employees = 15 + 45 + 60 = 120 employees.
Full time employees comprise of 60% of the total.
0.6 × Number of Employees = 120 employees
Number of Employees = 200 employees
Part Time Employees = 200 × 0.4 = 80 employees
Full Time Employees – Part Time Employees = 120 − 80 = 40

10. According to the graphs below, how many part-time staff members are at Oak Town High School?

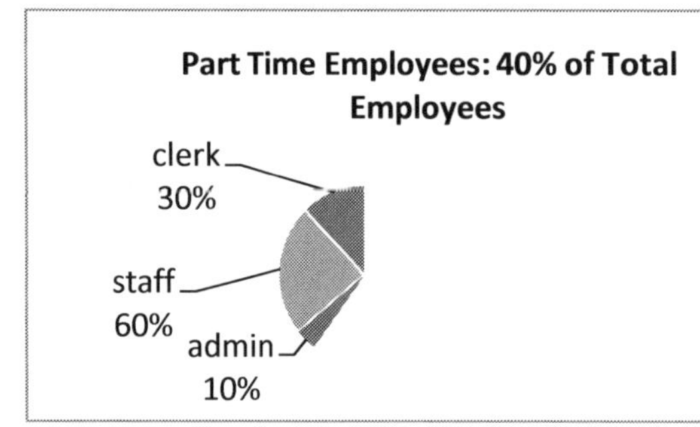

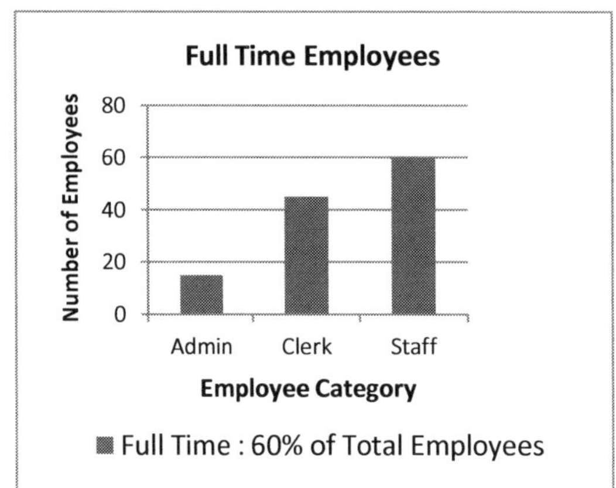

a) 48
b) 50
c) 52
d) 54

Answer: (a)

The total number of employees is 200.
The part time staff comprise of 60% of all part time employees.

Number of Part Time Staff Members =
$(200 \times 0.4) \times 0.6 = 48$ staff members

11. Of the following, which is the closest approximation of the cost per ticket when one purchases a book of 6?

Bus Ticket Price	
Number of Bus Tickets	*Price*
1	*7.5*
Book of 6	*40*
Book of 12	*75*

a) $6.67
b) $6.70
c) $6.80
d) $6.90

Answer: (a)

$\frac{\$40}{6\ Tickets} = \$6.67$ *per ticket*

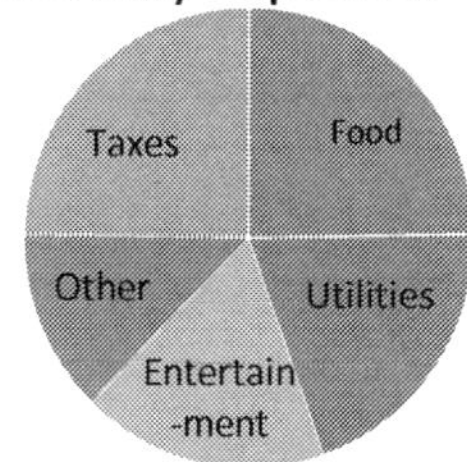

12. The pie graph above shows Ellen's family's monthly expenses and the proportion of each expense out of all of their expenditures. If the family's total expenses are \$3000 per month, approximately how much do they pay on taxes per month?
    a) \$500
    b) \$600
    c) \$700
    d) \$750

Answer: (d)

Taxes take up around $\frac{1}{4}$ of the total pie, which translates to 25% of total expenses.

Taxes = \$3000 × 0.25 = \$750

Votes in Favor of Building a New Sewer System in Orange County		
Town	*Yes*	*Total Population*
A	*30%*	*25,000*
B	*60%*	*40,000*
C	*45%*	*15,000*
D	*40%*	*20,000*

13. The table above shows voting results of 5 towns for support of building a new sewer system in Orange County. What is the percent of total residents that voted "Yes" for building a new sewer system?
    a) 45%
    b) 46%
    c) 50%
    d) 52%

Answer: (b)

Total Votes of "Yes"= 25,000 × 0.3 + 40,000 × 0.6 + 15,000 × 0.45 + 20,000 × 0.4 = 46,250 votes
Total Population = 25,000 + 40,000 + 15,000 + 20,000 = 100,000 people
Percent that Voted "Yes" = $\frac{46250}{100000} \times 100\% = 46.25\%$

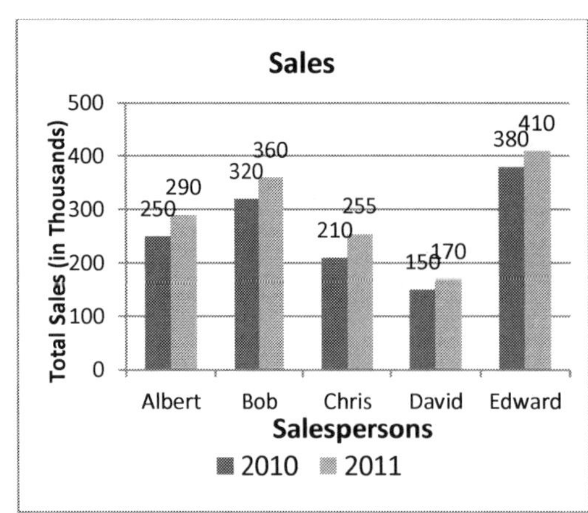

14. Which salesperson had the greatest increase in the number of units sold from 2010 to 2011 according to the graph above?
    a) Albert
    b) Bob
    c) David
    d) Chris

Answer: (d)

Chris had an increase of 255 − 210 = 45 units, the greatest increase shown.

15. What would be the least amount of money needed to purchase exactly 21 tickets according the table below?

Bus Ticket Price	
Number of Bus Tickets	*Price*
1	*7.5*
Book of 6	*40*
Book of 12	*75*

    a) $155
    b) $142.5
    c) $137.5
    d) $135

Answer: (c)

The lowest price for 21 tickets is to purchase 1 book of 12, 1 book of 6 and 3 single tickets.

$75 + $40 + $7.5 × 3 = $137.5

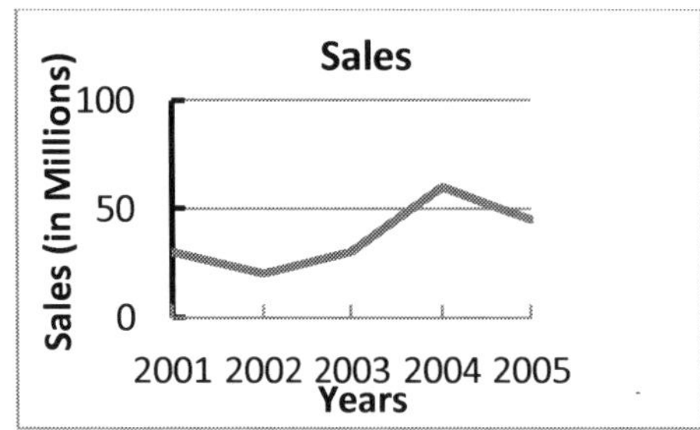

16. Which of the following is closest to the decrease in sales in millions between 2004 and 2005 according to the graph above?
    a) 10
    b) 12
    c) 15
    d) 20

Answer: (c)

2004 Sales = 60 million units
2005 Sales = 45 million units

60 − 45 = 15 million units

Questions 17 – 18 refer to the chart below:

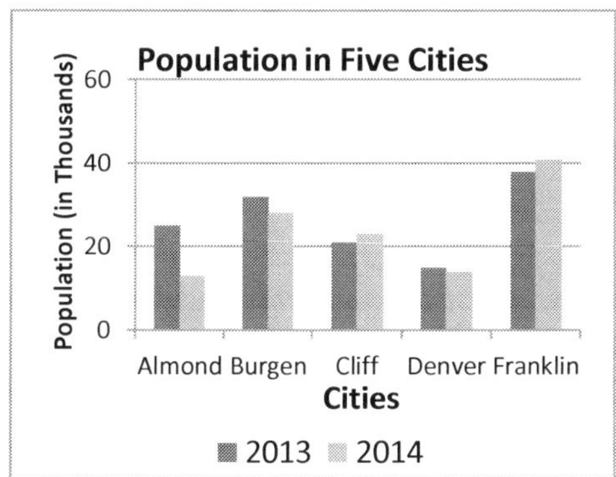

17. Which of the following cities had a population in 2014 that was approximately 50% less than its population in 2013?
    a) Almond
    b) Burgen
    c) Cliff
    d) Denver

Answer: (a)

Almond's population in 2014 is around double its population in 2013.

18. The total population in all five cities increased by approximately what percent from 2013 to 2014?
    a) 10%
    b) 9%
    c) –10%
    d) –9%

Answer: (d)

Total Population in 2013 = 25 + 32 + 21 + 15 + 37 = 130 thousand.
Total Population in 2014 = 13 + 28 + 22 + 14 + 41 = 118 thousand. $\frac{118-130}{130} \times 100\%$ *= –9.2% ~ –9%*

19. The following graph shows a certain brand of smartphone sales in four different continents. How many of the continents shown below had fewer sales in 2011 than 2010?

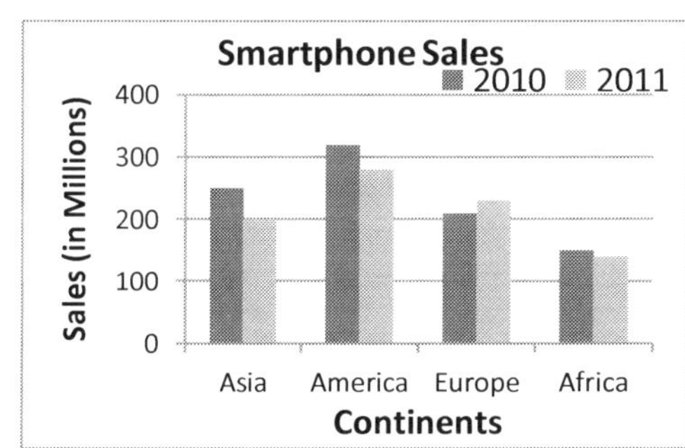

    a) 0
    b) 1
    c) 2
    d) 3

Answer: (d)

Asia, America, and Africa have had fewer sales in 2011 than in 2010.

Medium

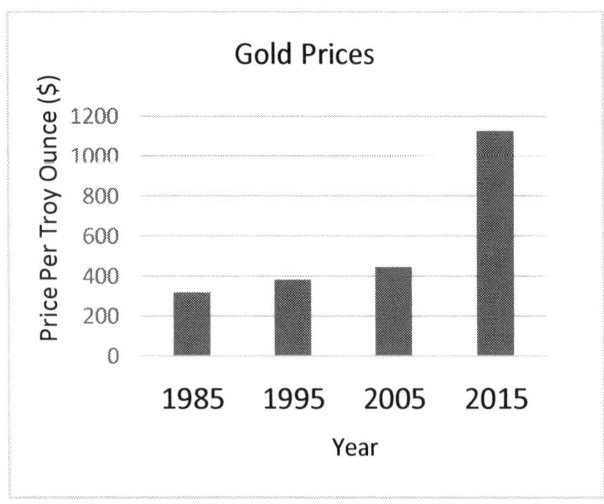

Annual Average Gold Price from 1985 to 2015
(U.S. dollars per troy ounce)

20. The figure above shows the change of the annual average gold price between 1985 and 2015, in U.S. dollars per troy ounce. A troy ounce is a traditional unit of gold weight. In 1985, a troy ounce of gold had an annual average price of around $317. Based on the information shown, which of the following conclusions is valid?
    a) A troy ounce of gold cost more in 1995 than in 2005.
    b) The price more than doubled between 2005 and 2015.
    c) The percent increase from 1985 to 2015 is more than 300%.
    d) The overall average gold price between 1985 and 2015 is around US $550.

Answer: (d)

Percent Change: $\frac{1100-310}{310} \times 100\% \approx 255\%$

Overall Average: $\frac{310+390+420+1100}{4} = \$550$

21. According to the table below, auto parts with different grades can be used for different number of years before they must be replaced. How many years can parts with grade A last?

Grades of Auto Parts	
Grade	*Max Years of Operation*
D	*3 years*
C	*20% more than D*
B	*15 % more than C*
A	*10 % more than B*

Answer: 4.55

If A is " x% more" than B, this means $B = A \times (1 + \frac{x}{100})$

$A = (1 + 0.1) \times B$
$= (1.1) \times (1 + 0.15) \times C$
$= 1.1 \times 1.15 \times (1 + 0.2) \times D$
$= 1.1 \times 1.15 \times 1.2 \times 3 = 4.55$ *years*

Questions 22 – 23 refer to the following information:

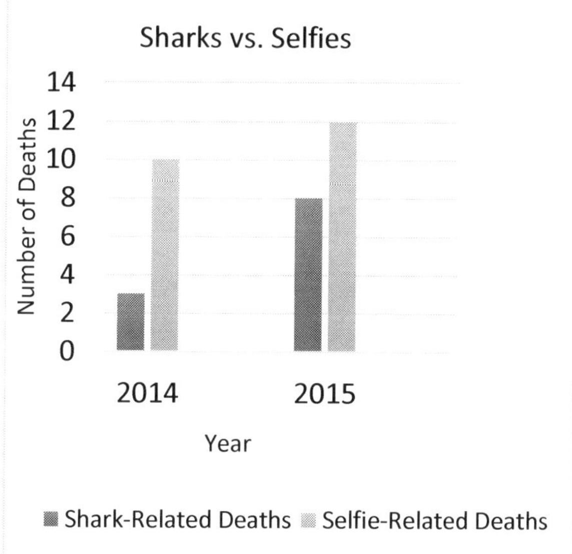

News outlet *Reuters* reports that taking a selfie is actually a dangerous endeavor, and that many people have been injured or died while taking a selfie. The figure above shows that more people around the world have died by taking selfies than by shark attacks in the years of 2014 and 2015. There have been twelve recorded selfie deaths in 2015 compared to eight people dying from shark attacks. The most common selfie-related deaths have been due to falling or being hit by a moving vehicle.

22. What is the percent change of total deaths from 2014 to 2015?
    a) 50%
    b) 70%
    c) 100%
    d) 233%

Answer: (c)

Total selfie-related deaths: 10 + 12 = 22
Total shark-related deaths: 3 + 8 = 11
Percent Increase $= \frac{22-11}{11} \times 100\% = 100\%$

23. What is the difference between the percent changes of shark-related deaths and selfie-related deaths from 2014 to 2015?
    a) 20%
    b) 147%
    c) 167%
    d) 187%

Answer: (b)

Percent change of selfie-related deaths: $\frac{12-10}{10} \times 100\% = 20\%$
Percent change of shark-related deaths: $\frac{8-3}{3} \times 100\% = 167\%$
Difference: $167\% - 20\% = 147\%$

24. The scatter plot below shows the wolf population in a safari every 5 years. If w is the number of wolves present in the park and t is the number of years since the study began in 1980, which of the following equations best represents the wolf population in the safari?

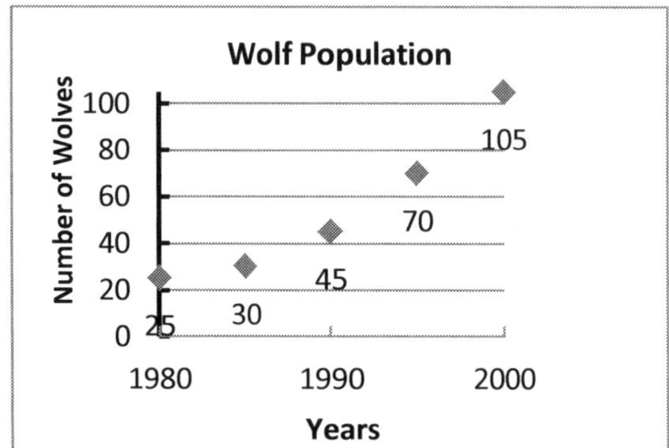

a) $w = 25 + t$
b) $w = 25 + 5t^2$
c) $w = 25 + 0.2t^2$
d) $w = (25)(0.2)^{(t/5)}$

Answer: (c)

Plot numbers into your calculator and test:
Year 1980, $t = 0$, $w = 25$
Year 1985, $t = 5$, $w = 30$
Only (a) and (c) satisfy, but (a) is a linear equation which contradicts the shape of the graph.

25. In Old Bridge High School each class period is 1 hour and 20 minutes long, each break in between periods is 5 minutes long and lunch (between 2nd and 3rd period) is 45 minutes long. If 4th period is to end at 2:30, what time should the school day begin?

a) 8:00
b) 8:15
c) 8:30
d) 8:45

Answer: (b)

The total time spent in school is 4 periods + lunch + 2 breaks (between periods 1 and 2, and periods 3 and 4).
Total Time = 4 ×(1 hour 20 minutes) + 45 minutes + 2 × 5 minutes= 6 hours 15 minutes
6 hours 15 minutes before 2:30PM is 8:15 AM.

26. The table below, describing number of students who passed or failed the Algebra I final exam, is partially filled in. Based on the information in the table, how many females have failed?

Algebra I Final Exam Results			
	Pass	*Fail*	*Total*
Male	*125*		
Female			*145*
Total	*230*		*305*

a) 35
b) 40
c) 45
d) 50

Answer: (b)

The Number of Students Passing = the Number of Males Passing + the Number of Females Passing

230 = 125 + the Number of Females Passing

The Number of Females Passing = 105
Total Number of Females = Number of Females Passing + Number of Females Failing
The Number of Females Failing = 145 − 105 = 40

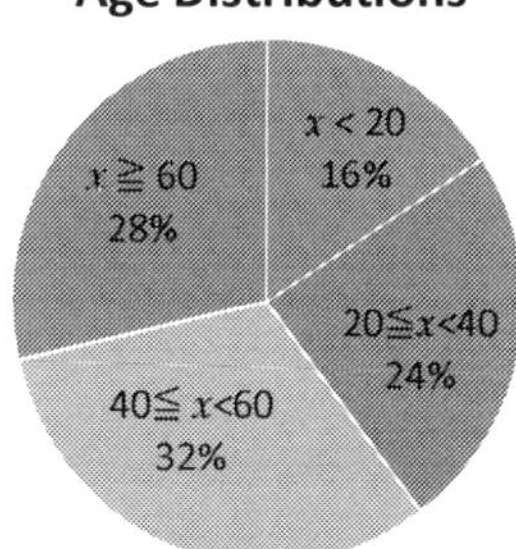

27. If there are 4180 residents ranging in age from 40 to 59 in Green Village County according to the graph above, approximately how many residents are under the age of 20?
    a) 2000
    b) 2100
    c) 2200
    d) 2300

Answer: (b)

This is a proportion problem.

Percent of residents 40 to 59 years old: 32%.
Percent of residents under 20: 16%
32% : 4180 = 16% : x
x = 2090

28. The percent decrease from the 1995 population to the 2000 population was the same as the percent decrease from the 2005 population to the 2010 population. According to the graph below, what was the 2010 population in Springfield?

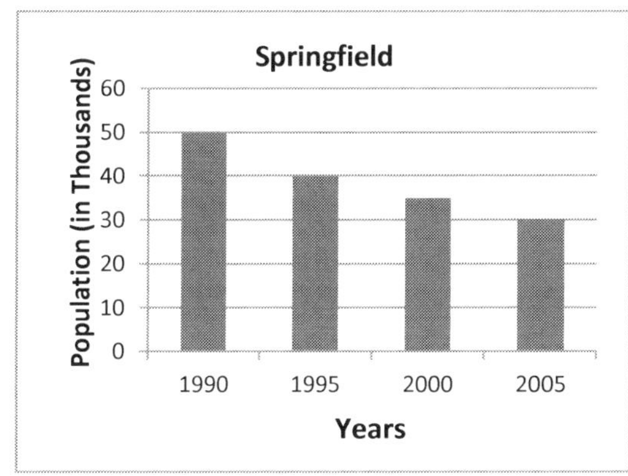

    a) 25,000
    b) 26,000
    c) 26,250
    d) 26,500

Answer: (c)

The percent decrease from the 1995 to the 2000 was $\frac{40-35}{40} \times 100\% = 12.5\%$

Let the 2010 population be x.
$12.5\% = \frac{30-x}{30} \times 100\%$
$\frac{12.5}{100} = \frac{30-x}{30}$ *(cross multipls)*

375 = 3000 − 100 x
x = 26.25
Since the graph is in thousands, the population was 26,250.

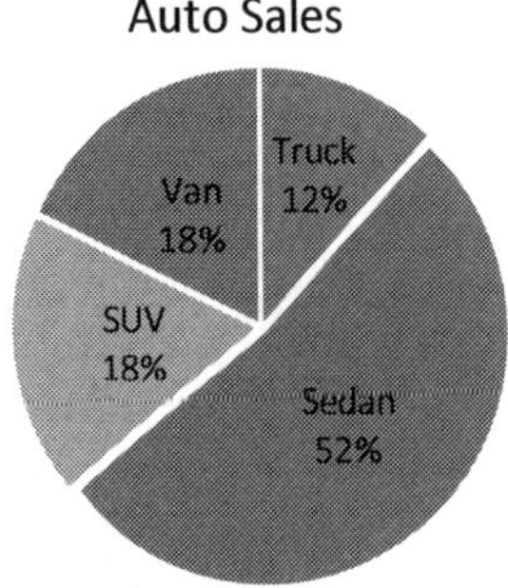

29. The pie graph above represents the automobiles that were sold by a dealer in 2010, according to their records. If the dealer sold 40 more Sedans than all others combined, how many automobiles did it sell altogether?
   a) 1,000
   b) 1,150
   c) 1,500
   d) 2,000

Answer: (a)

Solve this problem using proportions.
There were 4% (52% − 48%) more Sedans sold than all other cars combined.

4% : 40 = 100% : x
x = 1,000 cars

Hard

30. In a charity donation event, based on the chart below, how much money did women on the Red Team raise in this event?

Charity Donation Event			
	Blue Team	*Red Team*	*Total*
Men	*$4,500*		*$11,300*
Women			*$3,500*
Total		*$10,500*	

   a) $3,000
   b) $3,500
   c) $3,700
   d) $4,300

Answer: (c)

$11,300 (Total Raised by Men) = $4500 + $ Raised by Red Team Men
$ Raised by Red Team Men = $6800
Total Number of Men = $ Raised by Red Team Men + $ Raised by Red Team Women
$10500 = $6800 + $ Raised by Red Team Women
$ Raised by Red Team Women = $3700

31. In a charity donation event, based on the chart below, how much money did women on the Red Team raise in this event?

Charity Donation Event			
	Blue Team	*Red Team*	*Total*
Men	*$4,500*		*$11,300*
Women			*$3,500*
Total		*$10,500*	

   a) $3,000
   b) $3,500
   c) $3,700
   d) $4,300

Answer: (c)

$11,300 (Total Raised by Men) = $4500 + $ Raised by Red Team Men
$ Raised by Red Team Men = $6800
Total Number of Men = $ Raised by Red Team Men + $ Raised by Red Team Women
$10500 = $6800 + $ Raised by Red Team Women
$ Raised by Red Team Women = $3700

Number of Hours of TV Watched

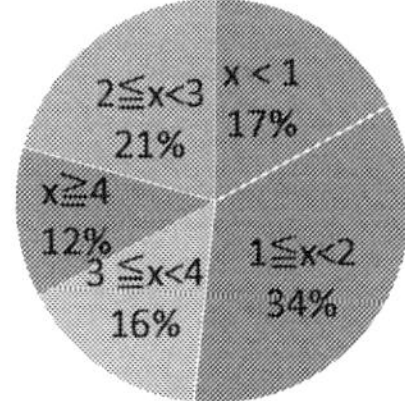

32. The graph above shows breakdown of the average number of hours of TV watched per day. 1000 people were surveyed, and all but 120 people surveyed responded to the question. If x is the number of hours spent, about how many respondents watch TV for more than 3 hours a day?
    a) 200
    b) 220
    c) 250
    d) 280

Answer: (c)

Watching TV for more than 3 hours a day includes those who answered with 3 ≦x ≦4 and 4 ≦ x, which make up around 28% (12% + 16%) of those who answered.
Total Respondents = 1000 − 120 = 880 people
880 × 28% = 246 ~ 250 people

33. The table below shows test scores for seven students. If the median score is 70, then the score for David could be any of the following EXCEPT?

Test Scores	
Student	*Scores*
Alan	*80*
Bill	*63*
Cindy	*57*
David	*X*
Eric	*98*
Frank	*74*
Gina	*70*

    a) 59
    b) 65
    c) 69
    d) 72

Answer: (d)

Since 70 is the median, x should less than or equal to 70.

All of the answers are possible except (d).

34. The number of books that have been checked out of the town public library in a particular week was recorded in the table below. If the median number of books checked out for the whole week was 93, which of the following could have been the number of books checked out on Saturday and Sunday, respectively, of the same week?

Town Library Checkout Records	
Day of the Week	*Number of Books Checked Out*
Monday	*87*
Tuesday	*91*
Wednesday	*92*
Thursday	*93*
Friday	*96*

a) 88 and 92
b) 89 and91
c) 90 and 97
d) 94 and 97

Answer: (d)

If the median number of books checked out for the whole week was 93, the number of books checked out on both Saturday and Sunday should be more than 93.

35. The table below shows the number of students in Mr. Jang's class that are taking 1, 2, 3, or 4 AP classes. After a new student joined the class (not shown in the table), the average (arithmetic mean) number of AP classes per student became equal to the median. How many AP classes is the new student taking?

Students Taking AP Classes	
Number of APs	*Number of Students*
1	6
2	4
3	5
4	4

a) 2
b) 3
c) 4
d) 5

Answer: (d)

There are 20 students after a new student joined the class. If the student is taking 2 or less APs, the median is 2. If the student is taking more than 2 APs, the median is 2.5.
If median is 2 and the new average is 2, then the new student needs to take $20 \times 2 - (6 \times 1 + 4 \times 2 + 5 \times 3 + 4 \times 4) = -5$ *AP classes (which is not possible).*

If the median is 2.5 and the new average is 2.5, then the new student needs to take $20 \times 2.5 - (6 \times 1 + 4 \times 2 + 5 \times 3 + 4 \times 4) = 5$ *AP classes.*

VI. COUNTING AND PROBABILITY

A. COUNTING RULES

CONCEPT OVERVIEWS

Multiplication Principle of Counting
If an event A happens in p possible ways and an event B happens independently in q possible ways, and then the total number of possible ways that event A **AND** B happen is $p \times q$ ways.

Example: Suppose that there are 5 different main course items and 6 different side dishes. How many different orders can a customer buy one main course and one side dish?
Hint: Because the customer is ordering a main course AND a side dish, use the Multiplication Principle.
Answer: $5 \times 6 = 30$

Addition Principle of Counting
If an event A happens in p possible ways and an event B happens in q different ways, and then the total number of possible ways that either event A **OR** event B happens is $p + q$ ways.

Example: Suppose that there are 4 seafood main dishes and 6 chicken main dishes. How many different ways can a customer choose a main dish?
Hint: Because the customer can choose a seafood dish OR a chicken dish, use the Addition Principle.
Answer: $4 + 6 = 10$

Venn Diagram: $n\{A \text{ or } B\} = n\{A\} + n\{B\} - n\{A \text{ and } B\}$

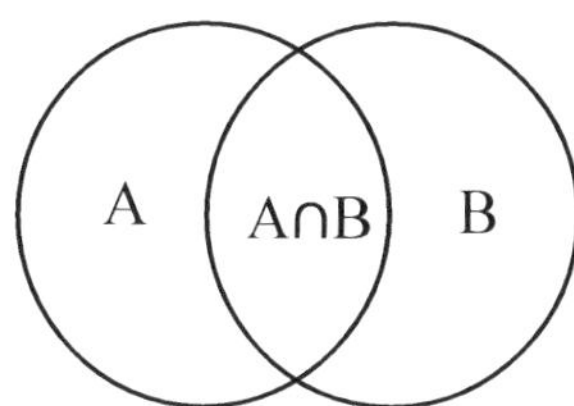

n!: The **factorial** of a whole number n is the product of all the positive integers less than or equal to n.

$$n! = n \times (n-1) \times (n-2) \times \ldots \times 2 \times 1.$$

Example: $5! = 5 \times 4 \times 3 \times 2 \times 1 = 120$

- ***0!*** is defined to be equal to 1.

$$0! = 1$$

Permutations: A permutation is a selection of objects from a set where the order of selection matters. For example, a selection of *apple, pear, apple* is different from a selection of *pear, apple, apple*.

The number of ways to select ***M*** objects from ***N*** objects, ***(N ≥ M)***, where the order of the objects chosen is important is

$$\boldsymbol{P_M^N = \frac{N!}{(N-M)!}}$$

Example: Mary, Sam, Eric, and Lucy are running for student council positions, president, secretary and treasurer. In how many ways can these positions be filled?

Answer: This is to select 3 positions from 4 candidates and order is important. For instance, Mary being elected as president is different from being elected as secretary. Therefore this is a permutation question. The answer is P_3^4 which is equal to $\frac{4!}{1!} = 4 \times 3 \times 2 \times 1 = 24$.

Combinations: In combinations, the order of selection does not matter. For example, a selection of *apple, pear, apple* is the same as a selection of *pear, apple, apple*.

The number of ways to select *m* objects from *n* objects ($n \geq m$), where order does not matter, is:

$$\boldsymbol{C_m^n = \frac{n!}{m! \times (n-m)!}}$$

Example: Joe has four marbles with different colors in his pocket and he randomly pulls out three at one time. How many different color arrangements of marbles are possible?

Answer: Pulling out three out of 4 marbles from Joe's pocket means that order is not important and therefore makes this a combination. The answer is C_3^4 which is equal to $\frac{4!}{3! \times 1!} = 4$.

The number of ways to arrange *n* distinct objects in order is ***n!.***

Example: In how many ways can five different books be placed on the book shelf?

Answer: The number of ways to arrange five books in order is *5!.*
$5! = 5 \times 4 \times 3 \times 2 \times 1 = 120$

Problem Solving Skills

Easy

1. A restaurant offers a choice of one side dish when a main course is ordered. Customers can choose from a list of 5 different main courses and 6 different side dishes. How many different combinations are there of one main course and one side dish?
   a) 11
   b) 16
   c) 20
   d) 30

Answer: (d)

Because the customer is ordering a main course AND a side dish, use the Multiplication Principle.

Total number of choices: $5 \times 6 = 30$

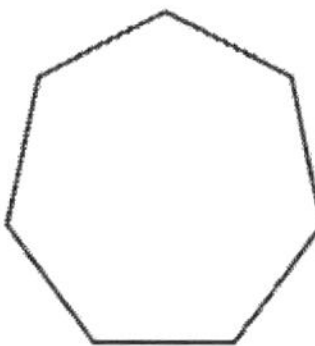

2. What is the total number of distinct line segments that must be drawn in the interior of the heptagon, as shown above, to connect all pairs of the vertices?
   a) 7
   b) 8
   c) 14
   d) 28

Answer: (c)

Each of the 7 vertices has to be connected to each of its 4 non-adjacent vertices, but this double counts the number of line segments needed because each line segment connects two vertices.
$(7 \times 4) \div 2 = 14$

3. For a salad dish, each customer can choose from 5 types of vegetables and 4 types of dressings. How many distinct salad dishes containing one type of vegetable and one dressing are there?
   a) 20
   b) 16
   c) 14
   d) 8

Answer: (a)

One vegetable AND one dressing, so use the Multiplication Principle.
$5 \times 4 = 20$

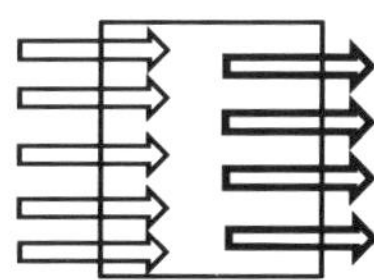

4. The figure above shows an indoor parking lot with the rectangular arrows indicating the different entrances and exits. What is the total number of distinct ways that a driver can enter and exit the parking lot?
   a) 9
   b) 5
   c) 4
   d) 20

Answer: (d)

Because cars entering the parking lot will also exit, so use the Multiplication Principle.

Total number of ways: $5 \times 4 = 20$

5. There are 5 sizes and 6 colors of T-shirts available for LHS students. How many different combinations of T-shirt color and size can students choose?
   a) 11
   b) 16
   c) 17
   d) 30

Answer: (d)

To find the total number of combinations of color AND size, use the Multiplication Principle.

$5 \times 6 = 30$

6. A box contains red, blue and green pens. If one pen is chosen at random, the probability that a red pen will be chosen is two times the probability for a blue pen and three times the probability for a green pen. If there are 12 red pens in the box, how many pens are in the box?
   a) 20
   b) 22
   c) 24
   d) 28

Answer: (b)

Red : Blue : Green $= 1 : \frac{1}{2} : \frac{1}{3}$
$= 12 : 6 : 4$

Total number of pens:
$12 + 6 + 4 = 22$

7. How many different positive four-digit integers can be formed if the digits 1, 2, 3, and 4 are each used exactly once?
   a) 10
   b) 12
   c) 14
   d) 24

Answer: (d)

$4 \times 3 \times 2 \times 1 = 24$

8. As a part of a vacation package, a travel agent offers 3 choices for the destination, 7 choices for the hotel chain and 2 choices for car rental companies. How many distinct vacation packages are there with a destination, hotel, and car rental company?
   a) 52
   b) 42
   c) 21
   d) 12

Answer: (b)

We want to find all distinct packages, so we want to solve for the total number of combinations. The total number of combinations of one hotel AND one car rental can be found by using the Multiplication Principle.
$3 \times 7 \times 2 = 42$

Medium

9. How many different positive 2-digit integers are there such that the tens digit is less than 5 and the units digit is even?
   a) 20
   b) 16
   c) 14
   d) 12

Answer: (a)

There are 4 choices for the tens digit and 5 choices for the units digit.

$4 \times 5 = 20$

10. There are 5 red, 5 green, 5 blue, and 5 yellow letters, each of which is inside one of twenty identical, unmarked envelopes. What is the least number of envelopes that must be selected in order to have at least 3 letters of same color?
    a) 4
    b) 8
    c) 9
    d) 12

Answer: (c)

If 2 letters for each color have been picked, then the next pick has to make at least one color triple.

$2 \times 4 + 1 = 9$

11. A school choir consists of one row of singers, half of which are boys and the other half girls. Which of the following must be true?
    a) The first person and the last person have different genders.
    b) There are two girls next to each other.
    c) If there are two adjacent boys, there are also two adjacent girls.
    d) If the last two are girls, there are at least two adjacent boys.

Answer: (d)

There are no rules about how to arrange boys and girls, so (a) and (b) are incorrect.
If there is one girl at each end, then two boys must be adjacent. Therefore, (c) is wrong.
If the last two seated are girls, then two boys must be adjacent. (d) is correct.

12. In the thirty days of June, for every day it rained, it did not rain for four days. The number of days it rained in June was how many days less than the number of days it did not rain?

Answer: 18
Rain Days : Dry Days = 1 : 4

$$\frac{\text{The Number of Rain Days}}{\text{30 Days}} = \frac{1}{1+4}$$

Apply cross multiplication.
The Number of Rain Days = 6
$30 - 6 = 24$
The Number of Dry Days = 24
$24 - 6 = 18$

13. The above design is to be painted using a different color for the face, the eyes (both of which have to be the same color), the nose, and the mouth. If 6 different colors are available, how many different designs are possible?
    a) 120
    b) 240
    c) 360
    d) 720

Answer: (c)

6 colors can be used to paint face, then 5 of the remaining colors can be used for the eyes, and 4 choices remain for the nose. There are 3 color left for the mouth. It doesn't matter in what order you paint the face, the number of color choices will always be 6, 5, 4, and 3 for the first, second, third, and fourth part.

$6\times 5 \times 4 \times 3 = 360$

14. There are four different games: Monopole, Good, Words with Ends, and Turner. Each of four friends wants to play a different game. How many different arrangements of who wants to play what are possible?

Answer: 24

The number of ways to arrange n distinct objects in order is n!.
4! = 4 × 3 × 2 × 1 = 24

15. There are four points A, B, C, and D on line *l*, and another four points W, X, Y, and Z on a different line parallel to line *l*. How many distinct lines can be drawn that include exactly two of these 8 points?

Answer: 16

Each of the four points on line l can be connected to each of the four points on the parallel line.
4 × 4 = 16

16. A school will send a team of one math teacher and two science teachers to work on a project. If the school has 5 math teachers and 6 science teachers, how many of such teams are possible?

Answer: 75

This is combination. The number of ways to select m objects from n objects (n ≥ m), where order does not matter:

$$C_m^n = \frac{n!}{m!\,(n-m)!}$$

Math: $C_1^5 = 5$
Science: $C_2^6 = 15$
Total number of arrangement:
5 × 15 = 75

Hard

17. If there are 7 points in a plane, no three of which are collinear, how many distinct lines can be formed by connecting two of these points?
    a) 18
    b) 20
    c) 21
    d) 22

Answer: (c)

This is combination. The number of ways to select m objects from n objects (n ≥ m), where order does not matter:

$$C_m^n = \frac{n!}{m!\,(n-m)!}$$

To choose any two points among the 7 points: $C_2^7 = 21$

18. How many combinations of three dishes can be prepared if you have the recipes for 10 dishes?

Answer: 120

This is combination. The number of ways to select m objects from n objects (n ≥ m), where order does not matter:

$$(C_m^n = \frac{n!}{m!(n-m)!})$$

To choose 3 from 10: $C_3^{10} = 120$

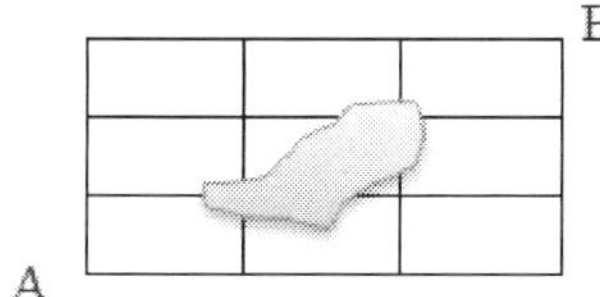

19. Bob wants to get from point A to point B by travelling along the gridlines in the figure above. He either moves up or to the right at every intersection. How many different paths can be drawn from A to B that does not include points inside the lake?
    a) Two
    b) Four
    c) Six
    d) Eight

Answer: (b)

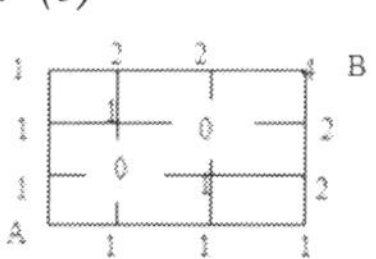

Mark a number on each vertex to indicate the number of ways to get to that vertex from A. The 1s on the leftmost column and bottommost row indicate that there is only 1 possible path from A. The path cannot reach the two points inside the lake, so we put 0s at those points. For each unlabeled vertex, add the number of the vertex to the left of it with the number of the vertex below it. This will be the number of ways to reach that vertex from A. Therefore there are 4 paths from A to B

20. 10 players participate in a tennis tournament. A game involves two players and each player plays three games with each of the other nine players. How many games will be played in total at this tournament?
    a) 90
    b) 120
    c) 132
    d) 135

Answer: (d)

This is combination. The number of ways to select m objects from n objects ($n \geq m$), where order does not matter:

$$C_m^n = \frac{n!}{m!\,(n - m)!}$$

Choose any 2 players from 10 players to play a match.
$C_2^{10} = 45$
Each match has 3 games.
45 × 3 = 135 games

21. If x and y are positive integers and $2x + 5y = 37$, what is the sum of all possible values of x?
    a) 22
    b) 26
    c) 29
    d) 34

Answer: (d)

List out all the possible pairs of (x, y) and here y can only be an odd number. Therefore,
(x , y) =
(16, 1), (11, 3), (6, 5), (1, 7).
Sum of x Values = 16 + 11 + 6 +1 = 34

B. Probability Formula

Concept Overviews

Probability of an Event

Probability problems are very similar to counting problems. The **probability** of an event occurring is equal to the ratio of successful events to the total possible events.

$$\textbf{Probability of an Event} = \frac{\textit{Number of Successful Events}}{\textit{Total Number of Possible Events}}$$

Example: What is the probability of rolling a number less than 4 when you roll one dice?

Solution: Probability of Rolling a Number < 4 $= \frac{Rolling\ 1,2,or\ 3}{6} = \frac{3}{6} = \frac{1}{2}$

Sometimes probability problems take place over a multi-dimensional sample space. In these problems, use familiar geometric concepts to find the **geometric probability** of an event.

$$\textbf{Geometric Probability} = \frac{\textit{Size of Target Space}}{\textit{Size of Sample Space}}$$

where size could refer to the length, area, or volume of the space.

Example: The diagram below shows 2 concentric circles, with radii 1 and 3 respectively. What is the probability that a randomly selected point in the diagram will fall in the shaded region?

Solution: The shaded region is the target, therefore the probability of falling in the shaded region is:

$$\frac{Size\ of\ the\ Target}{Total\ Size} = \frac{Size\ of\ Small\ Circle}{Size\ of\ Big\ Circle} = \frac{\pi(1)^2}{\pi(3)^2} = \frac{1}{9}$$

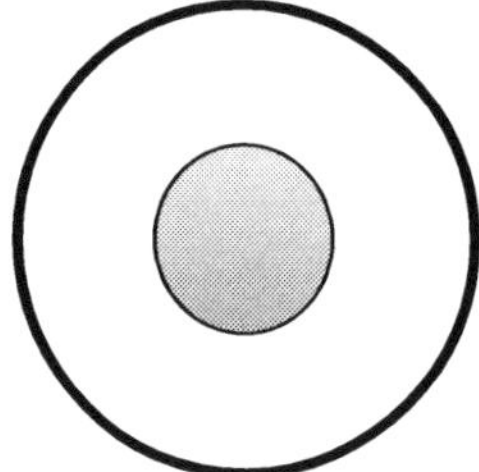

Problem Solving Skills

Easy

1. There are 10 red boxes, 15 blue boxes, and 20 white boxes. If a blue marble is randomly placed into one of these boxes, what is the probability that it will be placed in a box that is the same color as it?

Answer: $\frac{1}{3}$

Probability = $\frac{\textit{Number of Successful Events}}{\textit{Total Number of Possible Events}}$

$\frac{15}{15+10+20} = \frac{1}{3}$

2. 36 marbles, all of which are red, blue, or green, are placed in a bag. If a marble is picked from the bag at random, the probability of getting a red marble is $\frac{1}{4}$ and the probability of getting a blue marble is $\frac{1}{3}$. How many green marbles are in the bag?

Answer: 15

The probability of getting green marbles: $1 - \frac{1}{4} - \frac{1}{3} = \frac{5}{12}$

$\frac{5}{12} = \frac{x}{36}$, $x = 15$

3. In a high school pep rally, a student is to be chosen at random. The probability of choosing a freshman is $\frac{1}{8}$. Which of the following cannot be the total number of students in the pep rally?
   a) 20
   b) 24
   c) 32
   d) 80

Answer: (a)

The total number of students must be a multiple of 8. Note that the number of students must be a whole number.

Only (a) is not a multiple of 8.

4. At an intersection, a complete cycle of the traffic light takes 60 seconds. Within each cycle, the green light lasts for 30 seconds and the yellow light 10 seconds. If a driver arrives at the intersection at a random time, what is the probability that the light is red?

Answer: $\frac{1}{3}$

The red light takes 20 seconds.

$60 - 30 - 10 = 20$

Probability of Red Light = $\frac{20}{60} = \frac{1}{3}$

5. For every 20 cars sold by a dealer, 8 of them were red. What is the probability that a car sold that is selected at random would be red?

Answer: $\frac{2}{5}$ *or .4*

$\frac{8}{20} = \frac{2}{5}$

6. The center of a circle is the origin of a rectangular coordinate plane. If (−4, 0), (0, 4), and (4, 0) are three points on the circumference of the circle, what is the probability that a randomly picked point inside the circle would fall inside the triangle formed by those three points?
   a) $\frac{1}{2}$
   b) $\frac{1}{3}$
   c) $\frac{1}{\pi}$
   d) $\frac{2}{\pi}$

Answer: (c)

Radius of the Circle = 4

Area of the Circle = $\pi (4)^2 = 16\pi$

Area of the Triangle = $\frac{1}{2} \times 4 \times 8 = 16$

Probability = $\frac{16}{16\pi} = \frac{1}{\pi}$

7. The figure below shows a top view of a container with a square-shaped opening and which is divided into 5 smaller compartments. The side of the overall square is double the length of the side of the center square and the areas of compartments A, B, C, and D are all equal. If a baseball is thrown into the box at random, what is the probability that the baseball is found in compartment A?

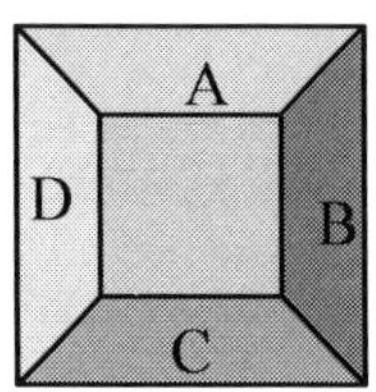

Answer: $\frac{3}{16}$

Find the ratio of the total area to the area of A.

If the total area is 1, the small square area in the middle will be $\frac{1}{4}$.

Area of A $= \frac{1-\frac{1}{4}}{4} = \frac{3}{16}$

Probability $= \frac{3}{16}$

Medium

8. Bella has 5 blue pens, 6 black pens, and 5 red pens in her pencil case. She takes out a pen at random and puts it aside because the pen is not blue. She then takes out a second pen randomly from her pencil case. What is the probability that the second pen will be a blue pen?

Answer: $\frac{1}{3}$

After first taking, there are 5 blue pens and a total of 15 pens left in her pencil case.
Probability to get a blue pen:
$\frac{5}{15} = \frac{1}{3}$

9. A bag contains red, blue, and green marbles. The probability of pulling out a red marble randomly is $\frac{1}{4}$ and the probability of pulling out a blue marble randomly is $\frac{1}{5}$. Which of the following could be the total number of marbles in the bag?
   a) 10
   b) 12
   c) 18
   d) 20

Answer: (d)

The total number of marbles should be a common multiple of 4 and 5.
The LCM of 4 and 5 is 20, so the total number of marbles has to be a multiple of 20.

10. If a number is picked randomly from a set of numbers consisting of j positive numbers and k negative numbers, the probability of getting a positive number is $\frac{3}{8}$. What is the value of $\frac{j}{k}$?

Answer: $\frac{3}{5}$

The probability of picking a positive number is $\frac{3}{8}$ *so the probability of picking a negative number is* $\frac{5}{8}$.

$\frac{j}{k} = \frac{\frac{3}{8}}{\frac{5}{8}} = \frac{3}{5}$

11. A bag contains 15 tennis balls, 6 of which are yellow, 4 pink, and the rest blue. If one ball is randomly chosen from the bag, what is the probability that the ball is blue?

Answer: $\frac{1}{3}$

The number of blue balls : $15 - 6 - 4 = 5$

Probability $= \frac{5}{15} = \frac{1}{3}$

12. Kat has some coins in her purse. Of the coins, 6 are pennies. If she randomly picks one of the coins from her purse, the probability of picking a penny is $\frac{1}{3}$. How many coins are in her purse?

Answer: 18

$\frac{6}{Total\ Coins} = \frac{1}{3}$

Total Coins = 18

Hard

13. The figure above represents seven chairs that will be assigned randomly to seven students, one student per chair. If Sam and Chris are two of the seven students, what is the probability that each will be assigned a chair indicated by an *X*?

Answer: $\frac{1}{21}$ *or .047, or .048*

The arrangement that we want is an arrangement where five students choose from 5 chairs and two students (Sam and Chris) choose from the 2 chairs marked with an X. Then we will divide the number of special arrangements by the number of possible arrangements, where Sam and Chris are not constrained to the two chairs with Xs.

Probability $= \frac{Special\ Arrangements}{Total\ Arrangements}$

Total Arrangements = 7! = 5040

Special Arrangements = 5! × 2! = 240

$P = \frac{240}{5040} = \frac{1}{21} = 0.0476$

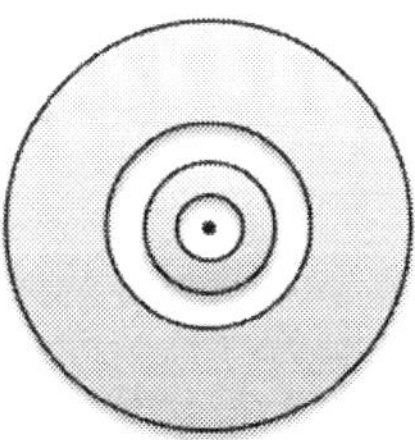

14. The diagram above shows 4 concentric circles, with diameters 2, 4, 6, and 10 respectively. What is the probability that a randomly selected point in the diagram will fall in the shaded region?

Answer: .76

Total Area – White Area = Shaded Area

$\pi (5)^2 - \pi (3)^2 + \pi (2)^2 - \pi (1)^2 = 19\pi$

Probability $= \frac{Shaded\ Area}{Total\ Area} = \frac{19\pi}{25\pi} = \frac{19}{25} = 0.76$

15. Linda's purse contains 4 quarters, 5 dimes, 2 nickels, and 4 pennies. If she takes out one coin at random, what is the probability that the coin is worth less than 10 cents?

Answer: $\frac{2}{5}$ *or* .4

If the coin is worth less than 10 cents, then the coin must be either a penny or a nickel.
Probability $= \frac{2+4}{4+5+2+4} = \frac{2}{5}$

16. On a certain farm, every fifth tomato picked is rotten, and every fourth tomato picked is green. If a famer randomly picks a tomato from the farm, what is the probability that the tomato will be both green and rotten?

a) $\frac{1}{8}$
b) $\frac{1}{10}$
c) $\frac{1}{15}$
d) $\frac{1}{20}$

Answer: (d)

For every multiple of the LCM of 4 and 5, there will be a tomato that is both green and rotten.
LCM of 4 and 5 is 20.
Probability $= \frac{1}{20}$

17. A bag contains red, green, and blue marbles. The probability of randomly pulling out a red marble from the bag is $\frac{1}{4}$ and the probability of randomly pulling out a blue marble is $\frac{3}{7}$. Which of the following could be the total number of marbles in the bag?

a) 11
b) 22
c) 28
d) 35

Answer: (c)

Total number of marbles must be a common multiple of 7 and 4.

LCM of 7 and 4 is 28.
So 28 is one possible number of marbles in the bag.

VII. LOGIC AND PATTERN

A. SEQUENCE PATTERN

CONCEPT OVERVIEWS

Sequence and Pattern

A **sequence** is a group of objects, almost always numbers, which are in a certain order. The order can be defined by some rules, such as the following:

- **Arithmetic Sequence**: An arithmetic sequence is constructed by adding the same number to each term to get the next term. This number is called the **common difference.** If the common difference is 1, one possible sequence would be 1, 2, 3, 4… If the common difference is 3, one possible sequence would be 1, 4, 7, 10, 13….

  To find the nth term in an arithmetic sequence:

  $$a_n = a_1 + (n - 1) \times d$$

  Where a_n is the nth term, a_1 is the first term, and d is the common difference in the sequence.

  To find the sum of first n^{th} term in an arithmetic sequence:

  $$S_n = \frac{n}{2} \times (a_1 + a_n)$$

  Where a_n is the nth term and a_1 is the first term in the sequence.

- **Geometric Sequence**: A geometric sequence is constructed by multiplying the same number each time to get the next term. This number is called the **common ratio**. If the common ratio is 2, one possible sequence would be 2, 4, 8, 16, 32… If the common ratio is 10, one possible sequence would be 5, 50, 500, 5000….

  To find the nth term in a geometric sequence:

  $$a_n = a_1 \times r^{(n-1)}$$

  Where a_n is the nth term, a_1 is the first term, and r is the common ratio in the sequence.

  To find the sum of first n^{th} term in a geometric sequence:

  $$S_n = \frac{a_1(r^n - 1)}{r - 1}$$

  Where a_1 is the first term, and r is the common ratio in the sequence. $r \neq 1$.

To find a missing number in a sequence, figure out the rules or the pattern for the sequence and then apply the rules to find the missing number. Carefully examine at least 3 of its consecutive numbers to figure out a pattern and use additional data to verify this pattern.

In a sequence, if a pattern repeats itself every m consecutive terms, the nth term of the sequence is the same as the pth term, where p is the remainder of n divided by m. The remainder indicates the position within each cycle of the pattern and thus the value of the term.

Example: A sequence like 2, 3, 5, 7, 2, 3, 5, 7, 2, 3, 5...... repeats every 4 terms. In order to find the 2013rd term, you can find the remainder of 2013 ÷ 4 which is 1. Therefore the number of the 2013rd term is same as the 1st term in this sequence which is 2. If the remainder is 0 that term would be equal to the last term of the cycle. Therefore the 2012nd term of the above sequence is 7, which is the last term of the cycle of 2, 3, 5, 7.

Problem Solving Skills

Easy

1. In the sequence 1, 3, 9, x, 81, ... what is the value of x?
   a) 12
   b) 18
   c) 27
   d) 36

Answer: (c)

Examine the first few terms to figure out the pattern. This is a geometric sequence constructed by multiplying the common ratio 3 each time to get the next term.
$9 \times 3 = 27$
$x = 27$

2. A total of 729 students participate in a school pep rally event. If every 30 minutes, $\frac{2}{3}$ of the students leave, after 2 hours, how many students will be still staying at the pep rally?

Answer: 9

Every 30 minutes, $\frac{1}{3}$ of the students still stay.
$729 \times \frac{1}{3}$; $729 \times (\frac{1}{3})^2$; $729 \times (\frac{1}{3})^3$
After two hours, the number of students staying:
$729 \times (\frac{1}{3})^4 = 9$

2, 7, 14, 15, 26, 29, 32, 37, 41

3. Based on the sequence of numbers above, a second sequence is generated by increasing each odd-valued term by 5 and decreasing each even-valued term by 3. What is the difference between the total sum of the elements in the original sequence and the total sum of the second sequence?
   a) 4
   b) 6
   c) 10
   d) 13

Answer: (d)

There are 5 odd-valued terms and 4 even-valued terms in this sequence.
$5 \times 5 - 4 \times 3 = 13$

7, 23, 71, 215, ...

4. The leading term in the sequence above is 7, and each successive term is formed by multiplying the preceding term by x and then adding y. What is the value of y?
   a) 1
   b) 2
   c) 3
   d) 4

Answer: (b)

Use trial and error. Plug in each of the values from the answer choices.
$7 \times 3 + 2 = 23$
$23 \times 3 + 2 = 71$
$71 \times 3 + 2 = 215$
$y = 2$

1, 5, 17, *t*, 161, ...

5. In the sequence above, what is the value of t?
   a) 34
   b) 51
   c) 53
   d) 68

Answer: (c)

Examine the first few terms to figure out the pattern.
This is a sequence constructed by multiplying the previous term by 3 and then adding 2 to the product each time to get the next term.
$1 \times 3 + 2 = 5$; $5 \times 3 + 2 = 17$;
$17 \times 3 + 2 = 53$; $t = 53$

6. In a sequence of numbers, the leading term is 3. Each successive term is formed by adding 2 to its preceding term and then multiplying the result by 2. What is the fifth term in the sequence?
   a) 108
   b) 110
   c) 114
   d) 216

Answer: (a)

$((((((((3 + 2) \times 2) + 2) \times 2) + 2) \times 2) + 2) \times 2) = 108$

7. A sequence with first value of 5 is constructed by adding 7 to the term immediately preceding it. Which term in this sequence is equal to $5 + 54 \times 7$?
   a) The 56th term
   b) The 55th term
   c) The 54th term
   d) The 53rd term

Answer: (b)

The Value of Nth Term $= 5 + (N - 1) \times 7$
$5 + (N - 1) \times 7 = 5 + 54 \times 7$
$N - 1 = 54$
$N = 55$

Medium

7, −7, −1, ...

8. The sequence above starts with 7. Each even-numbered term is found by multiplying the previous term by −1, and each odd-numbered term is found by adding 6 to the previous term. What is the 101st term of the sequence?
   a) −7
   b) 7
   c) 1
   d) −1

Answer: (b)

Sometimes list out more items to find out the pattern.
7, −7, −1, 1, 7, −7, ...
The numbers repeat every 4 terms.
$101 \div 4 = 25$ *and remainder is 1, so the value of 101th term is the same as the value of 1st term, which is 7.*

−3, −2, −1, 0, 3, 2, 1, 0, −3, −2, −1, 0

9. The first twelve terms of a sequence are shown above. What is the sum of the first 95 terms?

Answer: 0

Observe that every 8 terms sum to 0.
95 ÷ 8 has a remainder 7, so the total sum of the sequence is equal to the sum of the first 7 terms.
$-3 + (-2) + (-1) + 0 + 3 + 2 + 1 = 0$

a, b, c

10. In the sequence above, if each term after the first is d more than the preceding term, what is the sum of a, b, and c in terms of a and d?
   a) $a + d$
   b) $a + 2d$
   c) $2a + d$
   d) $3(a + d)$

Answer: (d)

The first three terms can be rewritten as a, a+d, a+2d.
The Sum of the Sequence $= a + a + d + a + 2d = 3a + 3d = 3(a + d)$

0.202002000200002. . .

11. The decimal number above consists of only 2s and 0s. The first 2 is followed by one 0, the second 2 is followed by two 0s, and the third 2 is followed by three 0s. If such a pattern goes on, how many 0s are between the 105th 2 and the 108th 2?

Answer: 318

Following the pattern, find the number of 0s between the 105th 2 and the 108th 2.
105 + 106 + 107 = 318 zeroes

12. The nth term of a sequence has a value of $3n - 1$. The 29th term is how much greater than the 24th term?
   a) 5
   b) 7
   c) 10
   d) 15

Answer: (d)

The difference of two consecutive terms is 3. There are 5 consecutive terms between the 24th and the 29th terms.
$3 \times 5 = 15$
The other way to solve this question is to calculate the terms outright.
29th Term: $3(29) - 1 = 86$
24th Term: $3(24) - 1 = 71$
$86 - 71 = 15$

k, 2k, 4k...

13. In the sequence above, k is the leading term and each successive term is 2 times the preceding term. If the sum of the first 6 terms is 315, what is the value of k?

Answer: 5
$k + 2k + 4k + 8k + 16k + 32k = 63k = 315$
$k = 5$

1, −2, 4, …

14. The first term of the sequence above is 1, and every term after the first term is −2 times the preceding term. How many of the first 100 terms of this sequence are less than 100?
   a) 53
   b) 54
   c) 57
   d) 58
   e) 60

Answer: (a)

Among the first 100 terms, there are 50 negative numbers and 4 positive numbers less than 100: 1, 4, 16, and 64.
Total numbers less than 100 = 50 + 4 = 54

15. The first term of a sequence of numbers is −1. If each term after is the product of −3 and the preceding term, what is the 5th term of the sequence?
   a) 27
   b) −27
   c) −81
   d) 81

Answer: (c)

−1, 3, −9, 27, −81

16. Each term in a sequence of numbers is greater than the term before it and the difference between any two consecutive terms is constant. If the 15th and 20th terms in the sequence are −10 and 15, respectively, what is the 30th term?

Answer: 65

Because the difference between any two consecutive terms is constant, the difference between every consecutive 5 terms is constant as well.
The difference of every 5 terms is 25.
15th term: −10
20th term: 15
25th term: 40
30th term: 65

16, 10, 13 …

17. In the sequence above, the first term is 16 and the second term is 10. Starting with the third term, each term is found by averaging the two terms before it. What is the value of the first non-integer term found in the sequence?

Answer: $\frac{23}{2}$

List out several more terms until you hit a non-integer.
16, 10, 13, $\frac{23}{2}$

486, 162, …

18. In the sequence above, each term after the 1st term is $\frac{1}{3}$ of the term preceding it. What is the 5th term of this sequence?

Answer: 6

The Fifth Term $= 486 \times (\frac{1}{3})^4 = 6$

Hard

19. If the fraction $\frac{1}{7}$ equals the repeating decimal 0.1428571428571.., what is the 203rd digit after the decimal point of the repeating decimal?
    a) 1
    b) 4
    c) 5
    d) 8

Answer: (c)

Every 6 digits are repeated. The remainder of 203 divided by 6 is 5 so the 203rd digit is same as the 5th digit after the decimal point, both of which are 5.

2, 2, 4, 4, 4, 4, 6, 6, 6, 6, 6, 6, ...

20. The sequence above is made up of a list of positive even numbers. Each even number n appears in the sequence n times. On which term in the sequence does the number 10 first appear?

Answer: 21

The number 2 appears twice, the number 4 appears four times, and so on. The number of terms up to integer 8 appears 2 + 4 + 6 + 8 = 20 times.
The number 10 first appears in the sequence right after the last 8.
20 + 1 = 21

21. In a sequence of numbers, each term after the first term is 2 greater than $\frac{1}{3}$ of the preceding term. If a_o is the first term and $a_o \neq 0$, which of the following represents the ratio of the first term to the second term?
    a) $\frac{3a_0}{a_0+8}$
    b) $\frac{3a_0}{a_0+6}$
    c) $\frac{2a_0}{a_0+6}$
    d) $\frac{a_0+2}{3a_0}$

Answer: (b)

1st Term $= a_o$,
2nd Term $= 2 + \frac{1}{3} \times a_o$
Ratio $= \frac{a_0}{2+\frac{1}{3}a_0} = \frac{3a_0}{a_0+6}$

22. In a sequence of numbers, each term after the first term is 4 greater than $\frac{1}{4}$ of the preceding term. If a_o is the first term and $a_o \neq 0$, which of the following represents the ratio of the third term to the second term?
    a) $\frac{a_0+16}{4}$
    b) $\frac{a_0+6}{4a_0}$
    c) $\frac{a_0+4}{4a_0}$
    d) $\frac{a_0+80}{4a_0+64}$

Answer: (d)

1st Term $= a_0$
2nd Term $= 4 + \frac{1}{4} \times a_0$
3rd Term $= 4 + \frac{1}{4}\left(4 + \frac{1}{4}a_0\right)$
$= 5 + \frac{1}{16}a_0$
Ratio $= \frac{5+\frac{1}{16}a_0}{4+\frac{1}{4}a_0} = \frac{a_0+80}{4a_0+64}$

B. Symbol Functions

Concept Overviews

Sometimes the SAT test will use strange symbols that define an invented operation.

To solve these kinds of questions, follow the formula defined in the problem and substitute any given values into the expressions given.

Problem Solving Skills

Easy

1. If $x♣y$ is defined by the expression $x(x + y) + y(x - y)$, what is the value of 3♣2 =?
   a) 52
   b) 48
   c) 20
   d) 17

Answer: (d)

Substitute x with 3 and y with 2 into the given formula.

3♣2 = 3(3 + 2) + 2(3 – 2) = 17

2. If ♥x♥ is defined by ♥x♥ = $3x - x \div 3$, then ♥9♥ =?
   a) 30
   b) 27
   c) 24
   d) 21

Answer: (c)

Substitute x with 9.

♥9♥ = 3 × 9 – 9 ÷ 3 = 27 – 3 = 24

$$\begin{array}{r} E\,G \\ +\,E\,F \\ \hline G\,F\,3 \end{array}$$

3. The above shows the sum of two 2-digit numbers. If none of the digits E, F, and G are zero, what is value of the digit E?
   a) 2
   b) 4
   c) 6
   d) 8

Answer: (c)

In this addition, G must be 1, because the largest sum of two 2-digit numbers is 199.

F = 2
2E = 12
E = 6

4. For all positive integer a and b, let a ♦ b to be defined *as* $\frac{a+b}{a-b}$. What is the value of 7♦3 ?

Answer: 2.5

Replace a with 7 and b with 3.

7 ♦ 3 = $\frac{7+3}{7-3}$ = 2.5

5. A 'triple-factor" is an integer greater than 1 with exactly three positive integer factors: itself, its square root, and 1. Which of the following is a triple-factor?
   a) 81
   b) 64
   c) 49
   d) 36

Answer: (c)

The square root of the number must be a prime number.

Only $\sqrt{49}$ is a prime number.

Medium

6. For all numbers j and k, Let \$ be defined by $j\$k = j - k + 3$. What is the value of (3\$6) \$2?
   a) 0
   b) 1
   c) 2
   d) 3

Answer: (b)

Find the 3\$6 first.

3\$6 = 3 – 6 + 3 = 0
0\$2 = 0 − 2 + 3 = 1

7. For all numbers m and n,
   m ☺ $n = 3m + 2n$
   m ☻ $n = 2m + 3n$
   What is the value of ($\frac{1}{6}$ ☺ $\frac{1}{4}$) ☻ 6?

Answer: 20

($\frac{1}{6}$ ☺ $\frac{1}{4}$) = $\frac{1}{6} \times 3 + \frac{1}{4} \times 2 = 1$
1 ☻ 6 = 2 × 1 + 3 × 6 = 20

8. If M is a positive integer, let *M* be defined as a set of all factors of M. Each of the elements in the three sets *6*, *12*, and *15* can also be found in which of the following sets?
   a) *6*
   b) *60*
   c) *72*
   d) *90*

Answer: (b)

Looking for all the factors of 6, 12 and 15, all of which are also the factors of 60.

9. Let <I, J> be defined as any integer greater than I but less than J, such as <–2, 4> = { –1, 0, 1, 2, 3}. Which of the following has the same elements as the intersection of <–1, 6> and <2, 8>?
   a) <–1, 3>
   b) <–3, 2>
   c) <1, 8>
   d) <2, 6>

Answer: (d)

Intersection of <–1, 6> and <2, 8>
= {0, 1, 2, 3, 4, 5} ∩ {3, 4, 5, 6, 7}
= {3, 4, 5}
The intersection has three elements.
(d) has 3 same elements {3, 4, 5}.

10. A student folded many paper planes of different colors in the following order: red, orange, yellow, green, blue, indigo and purple. If he finished 46 paper planes, and started with red, what color was the last paper plane?
    a) yellow
    b) green
    c) blue
    d) red

Answer: (b)

The student used 7 colors in total. Divide the number of planes he made by 7 and use the remainder to find the color of the last plane.

$46 \div 7 = 6$ with remainder 4
The color for the 4th plane is green.

Hard

11. For all positive integers x, let $\sharp x\sharp$ be defined to be $(x-1)^2$. Which of the following is equal to $\sharp 8\sharp - \sharp 7\sharp$?
    a) $\sharp 2\sharp + \sharp 1\sharp$
    b) $\sharp 3\sharp + \sharp 2\sharp$
    c) $\sharp 4\sharp + \sharp 2\sharp$
    d) $\sharp 4\sharp + \sharp 3\sharp$

Answer: (d)

Find $(8-1)^2 - (7-1)^2$.
$(8-1)^2 - (7-1)^2 = 13$
Find the answer that is also equal to 13.
(d): $(4-1)^2 + (3-1)^2 = 13$

12. For all positive integers j and k, let $j \triangle k$ be defined as the sum of the quotient and remainder when j is divided by k. What is the result after the operation of $26 \triangle 3$?

Answer: 10

26 divided by 3 has a quotient 8 and a reminder 2.
$8 + 2 = 10$

13. Let $\langle x \rangle$ is defined as $\langle x \rangle = x^2 + x$ for all values of x. If $\langle k \rangle = \langle k+2 \rangle$, what is the value of k^2?

Answer: $\frac{9}{4}$

Set $\langle k \rangle = k^2 + k$ equal to
$\langle x+2 \rangle = (x+2)^2 + x + 2$.
$k^2 + k = (k+2)^2 + (k+2)$
$k^2 + k = k^2 + 4k + 4 + k + 2$
$-6 = 4k$
$k = -\frac{3}{2} \rightarrow k^2 = \frac{9}{4}$

14. For all positive integer a, let ♥a be defined as the product of all even factors of a^2. For example, ♥6= 36 × 18 × 12 × 6 × 4 × 2. What is the value of ♥4?

Answer: 1024

♥4 = 16 × 8 × 4 × 2 = 1024

15. For all numbers m and n, let $m!!n$ be defined by $m!!n = m^2 - n^2$. If p and q are different positive integers, which of the following can be negative?
    I. p!!q
    II. (p + q) !!p
    III. p!! (p + q)
    a) II only
    b) III only
    c) I and III
    d) I, II, III

Answer: (c)

$p!!q = p^2 - q^2$
When $p < q$, $p!!q < 0$
$(p+q)\,!!p = (p+q)^2 - p^2 > 0$
$p!!\,(p+q) = p^2 - (p+q)^2 < 0$
Only (I) and (III) can be negative.

16. For all numbers p and q, let $p@q$ be defined by $p@q = (p + 2)^2 \times (q - 1)^2$, what is the value of 7@5?
    a) 1381
    b) 1296
    c) 743
    d) 527

Answer: (b)

Replace p with 7 and q with 5.

$7@5 = (7 + 2)^2 \times (5 - 1)^2 = 1296$

17. For positive integers a, b, and c, let $(a\ \Omega\ b\ \Omega\ c)$ to be defined by $(a\ \Omega\ b\ \Omega\ c) = a^b - 2ac + c$. What is the value of $(2\ \Omega\ 3\ \Omega\ 4) = ?$
    a) 2
    b) 4
    c) −4
    d) −2

Answer: (c)

$(2\ \Omega\ 3\ \Omega\ 4) = 2^3 - 2 \times 2 \times 4 + 4 = -4$

18. If a ≥ b, a♣b = $\sqrt{a - b}$, what is the value of 39♣3?

Answer: 6

39♣3 = $\sqrt{39 - 3} = 6$

19. If (⧖j) is the greatest odd integer smaller than j, and (⸙j) is the smallest even integer larger than j, what is the value of [⧖ (4.45) – (⸙0.99)]?

Answer: 1

⸙0.99 = 2, ⧖(4.45) = 3
[⧖(4.45) – (⸙0.99)] = 3 – 2 = 1

20. Let $*m$ be defined as $*m = m^2 + 4$ for all values of m. If $*x = 2x^2$, which of the following could be the value of x?
    a) −2
    b) 1
    c) $\sqrt{2}$
    d) $-\sqrt{2}$

Answer: (a)

$*x = x^2 + 4,\ x^2 + 4 = 2x^2$
$x^2 = 4$
$x = \pm 2$

C. Logic

Concept Overviews

The statement "If *A*, then *B*" does not imply the statement "if *B*, then *A*".

Example 1: If it is snowing, then it is cold outside. However, we cannot conclude that if it is cold outside, then it is snowing.

Example 2: If a geometry shape is a square, then it is a rectangle. However we cannot say if a geometry shape is a rectangle, then it is a square.

"**If A is true, then B is true**" implies that "**If B is false, and then A is false**".

Example 1: If it is snowing, then it is cold outside. We can conclude that if it is not cold outside, it must not be snowing.

Example 2: If he misses the bus then he will be late. If we know that he was not late, then we can conclude that he did not miss the bus.

Example 3: If a number is divisible by 4, then it is divisible by 2. This implies that if a number is not divisible by 2, then it is not divisible by 4.

If we know the following two statements **"If A is true, then B is true"** and **"If B is true, then C is true"**, we can conclude the following: **"If A is true, then C is true."**

Example: If John receives a grade C and above in math final exam, then he will pass math class. If he passes math class, then he can graduate from high school. This implies that if John receives a grade C and above in math final exam, then he will graduate.

One strategy to test whether a statement is true is to try special cases that may disprove the statement.

Example: Mitchell just had a cup of drink from a store that sells only soda and tea. Which of the following statements must be true?

a) The cup of drink is tea.
b) The cup of drink is not a coke.
c) The cup of drink is not green tea.
d) The cup of drink is not decaf coffee.

Solution: a) Mitchell may have had a cup of soda. False
b) Coke is a type of soda, and is thus a possible drink. False
c) Green tea is a type of tea, and is thus a possible drink. False
d) The store did not sell coffee, so this is TRUE.
Answer is (d).

A good problem-solving strategy is to list out all of the logical statements and check whether each choice fits the statements.

1	2	3	4

Example 1: The graph above shows four labeled colored boxes which are placed in a row. Each box is painted a different color. There is a red box next to a blue box. The green box is next to a red box and a yellow box. Which of the labeled boxes could be painted red?

a) 1 only
b) 2 only
c) 3 only
d) 2 or 3

Solution:

According to the descriptions in the problem the red box is next to the blue box and the green box and the green box is next to the yellow box. In order from left to right, only the two configurations YGRB and BRGY can satisfy those conditions.
Answer is *(d)*.

Example 2: Eric sometimes reads historical fiction novels in the library. Betsy never reads mystery novels in the library.
If the two statements above are true, which of the following statements must also be true?

I. Eric never reads mystery novels.
II. Betsy sometimes reads historical fiction novels.
III. Eric and Betsy never read mystery novels in the library together.

a) I only
b) II only
c) III only
d) I and III

Solution:

Check each statement whether it is true.

(I) Eric never reads mystery novels. This is not always true because we only know Eric sometimes reads historical fiction novels.
(II) Betsy sometimes reads historical fiction novels. We are not sure about that either.
(III) Eric and Betsy never read mystery novels in the library together. This is true because we know Betsy never reads mystery novels Therefore, they never read mystery novels in the library together.
Answer is *(c)*.

Example 3: Some integers in set X are odd.
If the statement above is true, which of the following must also be true?

b) If an integer is odd, it is in set X.
c) If an integer is even, it is in set X.
d) All integers in set X are odd.
e) Not all integers in set X are even.

Solution:

a) This is not necessarily true. We know that some integers that are odd are in set X, but not all odd integers.
b) This is not necessarily true. We do not have any information about even integers.
c) This is not necessarily true.
d) This is true. We know some integers in set X are odd, which means that not all integers in set X are even.

Answer is *(d)*.

Problem Solving Skills

Easy

1. At the Essex High School, some students on the math team are also on the bowling team and none of the students on the bowling team are on the tennis team. Which of the following statements must also be true?

   a) None of the students on the math team are also on the tennis team.
   b) More students on the math team than are on the bowling team.
   c) More students are on the bowling team than on the math team.
   d) Some of the students on the math team are not on the tennis team.

Answer: (d)

The students on both math and bowling teams will not be on tennis team.

2. Mr. Lee just had dinner at a restaurant that offered only soup and barbecue. Which of the following must be true?

   a) Mr. Lee just had a tofu soup.
   b) Mr. Lee just had a barbecue.
   c) Mr. Lee did not order a big salad.
   d) Mr. Lee did not have barbecue ribs.

Answer: (c)

Since the restaurant offered only either soups or barbecues, Mr. Lee would not have ordered a big salad.

3. In a game, an integer is randomly picked. If the integer picked is smaller than 0, the square of that integer is shown. If the integer picked is greater than 0, the integer itself is shown. If the integer shown is 16, which of the following could have been the integer picked? 🅝

    I. 16

    II. -4

    III. 4

    a) I
    b) II
    c) III
    d) I, II

Answer: (d)

If 16 was picked, then 16 would have been shown. If −4 was picked, then $(-4)(-4) = 16$ would also have been shown. If 4 was picked, then 4 would have been shown.

So only 4 could not have been picked.

4. At Old Town High School, some members of the math club are on the tennis team and no members of the tennis team are freshmen. Which of the following must also be true? 🅝
    a) No members of the math club are freshmen.
    b) Some members of the math club are freshmen.
    c) Some members of the math club are not freshmen.
    d) More tenth graders are on the tennis team than are on the math club.

Answer: (c)

Some students on math club also on tennis team in which there are no freshmen.

Medium

5. When an integer is multiplied by itself, which of the following cannot be the last digit of its product?
    a) 8
    b) 6
    c) 5
    d) 4

Answer: (a)

Try 1^2, 2^2, 3^2, 4^2, 5^2, 6^2, 7^2, 8^2, 9^2, and 0^2. None of these examples would have produced 8 in the units digit.

6. Helen threw a fair six sided dice 5 times. Each throw showed a different number according to the rules:

    The first roll was greater than 5.
    The second roll was less than 3.
    The third roll was 4.
    The fourth roll was the same as the first roll.
    The fifth roll was an even number.

    Which of the following must be true?
    a) Helen could have rolled a 6 more than three times.
    b) Helen could have rolled a 5 only one time.
    c) Helen rolled more even numbers than odd numbers.
    d) Helen rolled 3 at least once.

Answer: (c)

List of results: 6, less than 3, 4, 6, even.

Only (c) could meet all the conditions.

All integers in set X are negative.

7. If the statement above is true, which of the following must also be true?
   a) If an integer is negative, it is in set X.
   b) If an integer is positive, it is in set X.
   c) All integers in set X are positive.
   d) Not all integers in set X are positive.

Answer: (d)

If X only contains negative integers, then there are no positive integers in set X.

Hard

8. The scale in a small seafood store can only weigh objects greater than 2 pounds. A customer wanted to know the individual weight for lobsters A, B, and C. He weighed them in pairs and got the following results,
   The lobsters A and B weighed 3 lbs.
   The lobsters B and C weighed 4 lbs.
   The lobsters A and C weighed 5 lbs.

   What is the weight of the lobster B?
   a) 1 pounds
   b) 2 pounds
   c) 3 pounds
   d) 4 pounds

Answer: (a)

$(A + B) + (B + C) + (C + A) = 2(A + B + C) = 3 + 4 + 5 = 12$

$A + B + C = 6$
$6 - (A + C) = B = 6 - 5 = 1$

Marble 1 is red.
Marble 2 has the same color as marble 3.
Marble 3 is blue.
Marble 4 has the same color as marble 6.
Marble 5 is not orange.
Marble 6 is orange.
Marble 7 is not the same color as marble 1.

9. If a bag contains 20 marbles that are red, orange, or blue, and the 7 marbles chosen follow the rules above, which of the following must be true?
   a) Only one red marble is drawn.
   b) At most two red marbles are drawn.
   c) Two red marbles are drawn.
   d) At least three blue marbles are drawn.

Answer: (b)

Marble 1 is red, and marble 5 could be either red or blue. Therefore at most two red marbles are drawn.

10. In a certain card game, there are three types of card worth 2 points, 5 points, or 9 points. How many different combinations of these cards are possible in order to get a total of 19 points?
    a) One
    b) Two
    c) Three
    d) Four

Answer: (d)

There are 4 different combinations as below:

22222225, 222229, 22555, and 559

Chapter 3 Passport to Advanced Math

I. Factors and Multiples

Concept Overviews

Prime Number: An integer number greater than 1 that has only two positive divisors: 1 and itself.

- Prime numbers up to 50: 2, 3, 5, 7, 11, 13, 17, 19, 23, 29, 31, 37, 41, 43, 47

Prime Factorization: The prime factorization of an integer x is to find all the prime numbers that multiply together equal to x.

Example: 36 is equal to $2 \times 2 \times 3 \times 3$.

GCF (Greatest Common Factor) of Two Integers: the largest integer that divides exactly into both integers.

Example: GCF of 24 and 30 is 6.

LCM (Least Common Multiple) of Two Integers: the smallest integer that is divisible by both integers. For example, LCM of 24 and 30 is 120.

We can use ladder method to figure out GCF and LCM of two integers.

2	24	30
3	12	15
	4	5

GCF of 24 and 30 is $2 \times 3 = 6$ (numbers on the side)
LCM of 24 and 30 is $2 \times 3 \times 4 \times 5 = 120$ (all the numbers on the side and bottom)

Euclid's Algorithm: The GCF of two numbers does not change when you replace either number with the difference between the two numbers (the larger number minus the smaller number).

Example: The GCF of 168 and 189 is equal to the GCF of 168 and 21, $(189 - 168)$, which is 21.

Total Number of Factors

To find the total number of unique factors of any integer, write that integer as the product of powers of the prime numbers in its **prime factorization**. For example, if an integer can be written as $x^a y^b z^c$ where x, y, z are prime numbers and a, b, c are positive integers, then the total number of unique factors it has is $(a + 1) \times (b + 1) \times (c + 1)$.

Example: How many unique factors does the number 24 have?
Solution: Since 24 is equal to 2 × 3 × 4, it has a total of (1 + 1) × (1 + 1) × (1 + 1) = 8 factors. If you list them out, they are 1, 2, 3, 4, 6, 8, 12, and 24.

Example: How many unique factors does the number 1800 have?
Solution: The number 1800 has a total 36 factors because 1800 is equal to $2^3 \times 3^2 \times 5^2$ and $(3 + 1) \times (2 + 1) \times (2 + 1) = 36$.

Problem Solving Skills

Easy

1. In a toy factory production line, every 10th toy has their electronic parts checked and every 5th toy will have their safety features checked. In the first 150 toys, what is the probability that a toy will have both its electronic parts and safety features checked?

Answer: $\frac{1}{10}$

The LCM of 10 and 5 is 10.
The every 10th toy will have both of their electronic parts and safety features checked.
There are 15 such toys (150 divided by 10).
$\frac{15}{150} = \frac{1}{10}$

2. A supermarket has brand A juice smoothie on sale every 7 days and has brand B juice smoothie on sale every 4 days. Within a year (365 days), how many times does this supermarket have both brands of juice smoothie on sale on the same day?
   a) 9
   b) 12
   c) 13
   d) 24

Answer: (c)

The LCM of 7 and 4 is 28.

Every 28 days, A and B will be on sale on the same day.
$\frac{365}{28} = 13.035$

Medium

3. Which of the following must be a factor of x if x is a multiple of both 9 and 12?
   a) 8
   b) 24
   c) 27
   d) 36

Answer: (d)

The LCM of 12 and 9 is 36.

4. If x, y, and z are all integers greater than 1 and $xy = 14$ and $yz = 21$, which of the following must be true?
   a) $z > x > y$
   b) $y > z > x$
   c) $y > x > z$
   d) $x > z > y$

Answer: (b)

The only common factor of 14 and 21 other than 1 is 7, so $y = 7$.
$y = 7$
$x = \frac{14}{7} = 2$
$z = \frac{21}{7} = 3$

5. If x, y and z are three different prime numbers greater than 2 and $m = x \times y \times z$, how many positive factors, including 1 and m itself, does m have?
   a) 9
   b) 8
   c) 6
   d) 4

Answer: (b)

$m = x \times y \times z = x^1 \times y^1 \times z^1$

The total number of factors including 1 and m is $(1 + 1) \times (1 + 1) \times (1 + 1) = 8$.

6. If the area of a rectangle is 77 and its length and width are integers, which of the following could be the perimeter of the rectangle?
   a) 36
   b) 37
   c) 38
   d) 39

Answer: (a)

The length and width of the rectangle must be factors of 77. There are only two ways to factor 77, into 7×11 and 1×77.
$77 = 7 \times 11$
Perimeter $= 2\ (7 + 11) = 36$ *(a)*
$77 = 1 \times 77$
Perimeter $= 2(1 + 77) = 156$ *(not included)*

Hard

7. How many positive factors does the number 24 have?
   a) 4
   b) 5
   c) 7
   d) 8

Answer: (d)

$24 = 2^3 \times 3^1$
Number of positive factors:
$(3 + 1) \times (1 + 1) = 8$

8. If x is the greatest prime factor of 34 and y is the greatest prime factor of 49, what is the value of $x - y$?
   a) 8
   b) 9
   c) 10
   d) 15

Answer: (c)

The greatest prime factor of 34 is 17 and the greatest prime factor of 49 is 7.
$x + y = 17 - 7 = 10$

II. Operations on Fractions

Concept Overviews

A Fraction is a number of the form $\frac{a}{b}$ where a and b are integers and b is not a zero. A fraction can be expressed as a terminating or repeating decimal.

- When you multiply the top and bottom of a fraction by the same amount, it doesn't change its value, such as $\frac{2}{5} = \frac{2 \times 3}{5 \times 3} = \frac{6}{15}$.

- To add two fractions with different denominators, you must first convert both fractions to a **common denominator**, a common multiple of the two denominators. Then convert both fractions to equivalent fractions with the common denominator. Finally, add the numerators and keep the common denominator.

  Example: Add the two fractions $\frac{2}{3}$ and $\frac{-2}{5}$.
  Solution: Find the common denominator of 3 and 5. Use the common Denominator 15:
  $\frac{2}{3} + (\frac{-2}{5}) = (\frac{2}{3})(\frac{5}{5}) + (\frac{-2}{5})(\frac{3}{3}) = \frac{10-6}{15} = \frac{4}{15}$

- To multiply two fractions, the resulting numerator is the product of the two numerators and the resulting denominator is the product of the two denominators.

  Example: $\frac{2}{5}(\frac{-3}{7}) = \frac{2 \times (-3)}{5 \times 7} = \frac{-6}{35} - \frac{6}{35}$

- To divide one fraction by another, first **invert** the second fraction (find it's **reciprocal**), then multiply the first fraction by the inverted fraction.

  Example: $\frac{3}{5} \div \frac{6}{7} = \frac{3}{5} \times \frac{7}{6} = \frac{3 \times 7}{5 \times 6} = \frac{21}{30} = \frac{7}{10}$

- To simplify a fraction: Find the greatest common factor of the numerator and denominator and divide both numerator and denominator by the GCF.

  Example: $\frac{15}{20} = \frac{3 \times 5}{4 \times 5} = \frac{3}{4}$

- **Cross multiplying** is a way to solve an equation that involves a variable as part of two equal fractions.

  Example: If $\frac{9}{x} = \frac{3}{5}$, what is the value of $\boldsymbol{x}$?

  Solution: Applying cross multiplying: $x \times 3 = 9 \times 5$ $\quad x = \frac{45}{3} = 15$

Problem Solving Skills

Easy

1. If a movie is 120 minutes long, what fraction of the movie has been completed 20 minutes after it begins?
   a) $\frac{1}{5}$
   b) $\frac{1}{6}$
   c) $\frac{1}{4}$
   d) $\frac{1}{3}$

Answer: (b)

$\frac{20}{120} = \frac{1}{6}$

2. In a poll, 25 people supported the current city mayor, 14 people were against him, and 6 people had no opinion. What fraction of those polled supported the city mayor?

Answer: $\frac{5}{9}$

$\frac{Part}{Whole} = \frac{25}{25+14+6} = \frac{25}{45} = \frac{5}{9}$

3. Every Monday through Friday after school, John spends 1.5 hours playing tennis with his school team and 1.5 hours practicing violin for the school orchestra. What fraction of the total number of hours in these five days did he spend on his after school activities?
   a) $\frac{1}{5}$
   b) $\frac{1}{6}$
   c) $\frac{1}{8}$
   d) $\frac{1}{9}$

Answer: (c)

$\frac{Part}{Whole} = \frac{1.5+1.5}{24} = \frac{3}{24} = \frac{1}{8}$

4. Which of the following numbers is between 1 and 2?
   a) $\frac{8}{9}$
   b) $\frac{7}{3}$
   c) $\frac{10}{4}$
   d) $\frac{11}{9}$

Answer: (d)

$1 < \frac{11}{9} < 2$

Medium

5. An integer is divided by 3 more than itself. If the fraction is equal to $\frac{5}{6}$, what is the value of this integer?
   a) 12
   b) 15
   c) 18
   d) 20

Answer: (b)

$\frac{x}{x+3} = \frac{5}{6}$

$6x = 5(x+3)$ *(Cross multiply)*

$x = 15$

6. An hour-long workshop included 10 minutes of self-studies. What fraction of the hour-long workshop were self-studies?

Answer: $\frac{1}{6}$

$\frac{10}{60} = \frac{1}{6}$

7. If $x = -\frac{1}{2}$, what is the value of $\frac{1}{x} - \frac{1}{x+1}$?
   a) 2
   b) -2
   c) 4
   d) -4

Answer: (d)

$\frac{1}{-\frac{1}{2}} - \frac{1}{-\frac{1}{2}+1} = -2 - 2 = -4$

Hard

8. Monday morning, Johnson starts out with a certain amount of money that he plans to spend throughout the week. Every morning after that, he spends exactly $\frac{1}{2}$ the amount he has left. 6 days later, on Sunday morning, he finds that he has $5 left. How many dollars did Johnson originally have Monday morning?

Answer: 320

*Let's say Johnson has $x on Monday. On Sunday, he will have:*$(\frac{1}{2} \times \frac{1}{2} \times \frac{1}{2} \times \frac{1}{2} \times \frac{1}{2} \times \frac{1}{2})x$ *dollars left.*

$\frac{x}{2^6} = 5$

$x = 5 \times 2^6 = 320$ *dollars*

9. One-fourth of a bottle originally contains grape juice. It is then filled to the top with a fruit juice mix with equal amounts of orange, grape, and apple juices. What fraction of the final mixture is grape juice?

Answer: $\frac{1}{2}$

$\frac{1}{4}$ *of the bottle is originally grape juice. Then* $\frac{3}{4}$ *of the bottle is filled with a mixture that is* $\frac{1}{3}$ *grape juice. The fraction that is grape juice is equal to:*

$\frac{\text{Amount of Grape Juice}}{\text{Amount of All Juice}} = \frac{\frac{1}{4} + \frac{3}{4}(\frac{1}{3})}{1} = \frac{1}{2}$

III. Algebraic Factoring

Concept Overviews

Factoring out Common Factors

A **common factor** is a nonnegative number (other than one) or expression that divides into each term of a list. For instance, the common factors of $2x^5$, $4x^4$, $6x^2$, $2x$ are 2, x, and $2x$.

Factoring by Grouping

When you have a polynomial that consists of four terms without common factors, one strategy is to factor "in pairs". To factor "in pairs", split the expression into two pairs of terms, and then factor the pairs separately.

Example: Factor $x^3 - 7x^2 - 2x + 14$.

Solution: Group in pairs:

$x^3 - 7x^2 - 2x + 14 = (x^3 - 7x^2) - (2x - 14)$

Factor out common factors from each pair:

$x^3 - 7x^2 - 2x + 14 = x^2(x - 7) - 2(x - 7) = (x - 7)(x^2 - 2)$

Factoring by the Difference of Two Squares

An expression which has one square subtracted by another square can be factored into the sum of the two variables multiplied by the difference of the two variables.

$$x^2 - y^2 = (x + y)(x - y)$$

Example: Factor $x^2 - 1$.

Solution: $x^2 - 1$ can be written as $x^2 - 1^2$. So $x^2 - 1 = (x + 1)(x - 1)$.

Similarly, $x^4 - 16 = [(x^2)^2 - 4^2)] = (x^2 + 4)(x^2 - 4)$.

Furthermore, $x^2 - 4$ can be rewritten as $x^2 - 2^2 = (x + 2)(x - 2)$.

Therefore, $x^4 - 16 = (x^2 + 4)(x + 2)(x - 2)$.

Factoring Trinomial

- **How to factor $x^2 + bx + c$ where b and c are integers:**
  First, by FOIL we know that $(x + m)(x + n) = x^2 + (m + n)x + mn$. Therefore, by backwards logic, in order to factorize $x^2 + bx + c$, numbers m and n must be found such that $m + n = b$ and $mn = c$.

- **How to factor $ax^2 + bx + c$ where a, b and c are integers and $a \neq 1$:**
  a) Set $ax^2 + bx + c$ equal to $a(x + \frac{d_1}{a})(x + \frac{d_2}{a})$ where d_1 and d_2 are two numbers whose product is $a \times c$ and whose sum is b.
  b) Factor a into two numbers, a_1 and a_2, so that $a_1 \times \frac{d_1}{a}$ and $a_2 \times \frac{d_2}{a}$ are two integers. For instance, the process of factoring $4x^2 - 4x - 3$:

i. First, find two numbers whose product is –12 and sum is –4. The two numbers are –6 and 2.

ii. $4 \times (-3) = -12 \quad 4x^2 - 4x - 3 = 4(x + \frac{2}{4})(x - \frac{6}{4})$.
Simplify into $4(x + \frac{1}{2})(x - \frac{3}{2})$.

iii. $4\left(x + \frac{1}{2}\right)\left(x - \frac{3}{2}\right) = \left(2x + 2 \times \frac{1}{2}\right)\left(2x - 2 \times \frac{3}{2}\right) = (2x + 1)(2x - 3)$

Perfect Square of Trinomial

A **trinomial** is an expression with three unlike terms such as $x^2 + 2x + 3$. **Perfect square formulas** are some of the most important formulas in algebra that are worth remembering:

$$x^2 + 2xy + y^2 = (x + y)^2$$

$$x^2 - 2xy + y^2 = (x - y)^2$$

A quadratic equation can be solved with by creating a perfect square using the perfect square formula. A perfect square has the form $a^2 + 2ab + b^2$ where a and b can be any algebraic expression or integer.

Example: Solve for x if $x^2 - 2x - 2 = 0$.
Solution: $x^2 - 2x - 2 = 0$
$x^2 - 2x = 2$ add 1 to both sides to make a perfect square on the left
$x^2 - 2x + 1 = 2 + 1$
$(x - 1)^2 = 3$ take the square root on both sides
$x - 1 = \pm\sqrt{3}$
$x = 1 \pm \sqrt{3}$

Problem Solving Skills

Easy

1. If $2x + 1 = y$, then $6x + 4 = ?$
   a) $y + 3$
   b) $3y + 3$
   c) $3y + 1$
   d) $2y + 3$

Answer: (c)

$6x + 4 = 3(2x + 1) + 1 = 3y + 1$

2. If $c = 5$, which of the following is the equivalent to $cx^2 + cx + c$?
   a) $(5x^3 + 5)$
   b) $5(x + 1)^2$
   c) $(x^2 + 1)$
   d) $5(x^2 + x + 1)$

Answer: (d)

Replace c with value 5.

$5x^2 + 5x + 5 = 5(x^2 + x + 1)$

Medium

3. If x and y are positive integers and $x^2 - y^2 = 5$, what is the value of x?
   a) 1
   b) 2
   c) 3
   d) 4

Answer: (c)

$x^2 - y^2 = (x - y)(x + y) = 5$

$5 = 1 \times 5$
$x - y = 1$
$x + y = 5$
$2x = 6$
$x = 3$

4. If $x^2 + y^2 = 128$ and $xy = 36$, find the value of $(x - y)^2 =$?
   a) 56
   b) 92
   c) 108
   d) 200

Answer: (a)

$(x - y)^2 = x^2 + y^2 - 2xy$

$128 - 2 \times 36 = 56$

5. If $x^2 - y^2 = 55$ and $x + y = 11$, find the value of y.
   a) 1
   b) 3
   c) 5
   d) 7

Answer: (b)

$x^2 - y^2 = (x - y)(x + y)$
$55 = (x - y) \times 11$
$x - y = 5$
$x + y = 11$
$y = 3$

6. If $xy = 5$ and $x - y = 3$, then $x^2y - xy^2 =$?
   a) 3
   b) 5
   c) 10
   d) 15

Answer: (d)

Factor out the common factors.
$x^2y - xy^2 = xy(x - y) = 5 \times 3 = 15$

7. If $x^2 - y^2 = 15$, and $x - y = 3$, what is the value of $x + y$?
   a) 1
   b) 3
   c) 5
   d) 10

Answer: (c)

$x^2 - y^2 = (x - y)(x + y)$

$3(x + y) = 15$
$x + y = 5$

Hard

$$x^2 - y^2 < 7$$
$$x + y > 4$$
$$x > y$$

8. If x and y are positive integers, according to inequalities above, what is the value of y?
   a) 5
   b) 4
   c) 3
   d) 2

Answer: (d)

$x^2 - y^2 = (x - y)(x + y) < 7$

Since $(x + y) > 4$, $x > y$, and both x and y are positive integers, $(x - y)$ must equal 1.
If $(x - y)$ equals 1, then $(x + y)$ must equal either 5 or 6 so that $x^2 - y^2 < 7$.
Therefore,
case 1: $x - y = 1$, $x + y = 6$,
$x = 3.5$ (no! not an integer)
case 2: $x - y = 1$, $x + y = 5$,
$x = 3$ (ok! positive integer)

Solve for y.
$y = x - 1 = 3 - 1 = 2$

9. A car rental company calculates the price of renting a car by adding the fixed rental fee with an additional charge for every 10 miles traveled. If the charge to rent a car and drive 50 miles is $100 and the charge to rent a car and drive 200 miles is $160, what would be the price, in dollars, to rent a car and travel 400 miles?
   a) 200
   b) 240
   c) 280
   d) 320

Answer: (b)

Let initial charge be \$$x$, and the fee for every 10 miles be \$$y$.
$x + 5y = 100$
$x + 20y = 160$
$15y = 60$
Solving these equations, we get $y = 4$ and $x = 80$.
For traveling 400 miles, the total charge is $80 + 40 \times 4 = 240$.

IV. FUNCTIONS

Concept Overviews

Functions

A function is a set of data that has a single output for each input. Functions describe the relationship between an input and its output.

Here are some of the common words associated with input and output:

- **Input:**
  - x-value
  - **independent variable**
  - **domain** – the possible value(s) of the function's input
  - For a real function, input values could be restricted because of the nature of the function itself. For instance, x cannot be equal to zero when $f(x) = \frac{1}{x}$ because $f(x)$ would become undefined. Apply the following rules when checking possible values of x:
    1) The denominator cannot be zero.
    2) Values inside a square root or an even radical must be nonnegative.

    Example 1: What value(s) of x are not possible for the function $f(x) = \frac{2}{x-3}$?
    Answer: Apply rule 1), the denominator cannot be zero, therefore x cannot be 3.

    Example 2: What are the possible values of x when the function $f(x) = \sqrt{x+3}$?
    Answer: Apply rule 2), the values inside a square root must be nonnegative.
    $x + 3 \geqq 0$
    $x \geqq -3$
    x could be any number greater than or equal to -3.

- **Output:**
  - y-value
  - **dependent variable**
  - **range** – the possible value(s) that the function's output can take on

    Example: Determine the domain and range of the function $y = x^2$
    Answer: Domain: all real numbers
    Range: all numbers greater than or equal to 0

Graphs of Functions

- Every point (x, y) on the graph of $y = f(x)$ satisfies $y = f(x)$.
- **Vertical Line Test:** A test to determine whether the graph is a graph of a function. If any vertical line intersects the graph at more than one point, then the graph is not a graph of a function.

Domain: All possible inputs to a function (otherwise known as the independent variable or, frequently, the x variable).

For a real function,

- The value inside a square root must be greater or equal to zero.
- Denominators CANNOT be zero.

Range: All possible outputs of a function (otherwise known as the dependent variable or, frequently, $f(x)$ or y). Be careful of square root functions and absolute value functions.

Examples: Find the domain and range for each of the following functions:

a) $f(x) = \frac{5}{x-3}$
Domain: $\{x \mid -\infty < x < 3 \ \cup 3 < x < \infty\}$
Range: all real numbers

b) $f(x) = \sqrt{16 - x^2}$
$16 - x^2 \geq 0$
$x^2 - 16 \leq 0$
$(x-4)(x+4) \leq 0$
$-4 \leq x \leq 4$
Domain: $\{x \mid -4 \leq x \leq 4\}$
Range: $0 \leq f(x) \leq 4$

c) $f(x) = \frac{\sqrt{x-5}}{x-12}$
$x - 5 \geq 0$
$x \geq 5$
Domain: $\{x \mid 5 \leq x < 12 \ \cup 12 < x < \infty\}$
Range: all real numbers

d) $f(x) = 3|x-4| - 2$
Domain: all real numbers
Range: $f(x) \geq -2$

Function Properties: For two functions f and g,

$$(f+g)(x) = f(x) + g(x)$$
$$(f-g)(x) = f(x) - g(x)$$
$$(f \cdot g)(x) = f(x) \times g(x)$$
$$\frac{f}{g}(x) = \frac{f(x)}{g(x)} \quad where\ g(x) \neq 0$$
$$(f \circ g)(x) = f(g(x))$$

Examples:

If $f(x) = x^2 - 4$ and $g(x) = x + 2$, evaluate the following:

a. $(f + g)(x)$
Solution: $(f + g)(x) = x^2 - 4 + x + 2 = x^2 + x - 2$

b. $(f - g)(x)$
Solution: $(f - g)(x) = x^2 - 4 - x - 2 = x^2 - x - 6$

c. $(f \cdot g)(x)$
Solution: $(f \cdot g)(x) = (x^2 - 4)(x + 2) = x^3 - 4x + 2x^2 - 8$
$= x^3 + 2x^2 - 4x - 8$

d. $\left(\frac{f}{g}\right)(x)$
Solution: $\left(\frac{f}{g}\right)(x) = \frac{x^2-4}{x+2} = x - 2$

Composition of Functions

When the results of a function *g(x)* are plugged into a function *f(x)* to create a new function, the result is called the composition of *f(x)* and *g(x)*. The notation used for the composition of functions is

$$(f \circ g)(x) = f(g(x))$$

Example: If $f(x) = x^2 - 4$ and $g(x) = x + 2$, evaluate $(f \circ g)(x)$.
Solution: $(f \circ g)(x) = f(g(x)) = (x + 2)^2 - 4 = x^2 + 4x + 4 - 4 = x^2 + 4x$

Problem Solving Skills

Easy

1. If $f(x) = \frac{x+3}{x}$ and $g(x) = x^2 - 10$, what is the difference between *f(x)* and *g(x)* when $x = 3$?

Answer: 3

Substitute 3 for x in both functions. The difference between f(3) and g(3) is f(3) – g(3).
$\frac{3+3}{3} - [(3)^2 - 10] = 2 - (-1) = 3$

2. If $f(x) = 2x - 1$ and $g(x) = \sqrt{x^2 - 8}$, what is the value of *f(g(3))*?
   a) 1
   b) 3
   c) 5
   d) 7

Answer: (a)

Substitute 3 for x in the function g(x) first.
$g(3) = \sqrt{3^2 - 8} = \sqrt{1} = 1$
$f(g(3)) = f(1) = 2(1) - 1 = 1$

3. If $f(x) = \sqrt{x^2 + \frac{1}{2}}$ for all real values of x, which of the following is NOT a possible value of $f(x)$?
   a) 0
   b) 1
   c) $\frac{2}{3}$
   d) 5

Answer: (a)

Since $x^2 \geq 0$, $x^2 + \frac{1}{2} \geq \frac{1}{2}$
$\sqrt{x^2 + \frac{1}{2}} \geq \sqrt{\frac{1}{2}}$

4. If $f(x) = x^{-1} + x + x^2$, at which of the following values of x is $f(x)$ undefined?
   a) −1
   b) 0
   c) 1
   d) 2

Answer: (b)

$f(x)$ is generally undefined when a term is divided by 0.
$x^{-1} + x^2 = \frac{1}{x} + x^2 + x$
So when $x = 0$, $\frac{1}{0}$ is undefined.

5. The number of water lilies in a pond has doubled every four years since t = 0. This relation is given by $y = (x)2^{t/4}$, where t is in number of years, y is the number of water lilies in the pond at time t, and x is the original number of water lilies. If there were 600 water lilies in this pond 8 years after t = 0, then what was the original number of water lilies?
   a) 100
   b) 150
   c) 180
   d) 200

Answer: (b)

Plug in t = 8 and y = 600 in the function.

$600 = (x) \times 2^{(8/4)} = x \times 2^2 = 4x$
$x = 150$

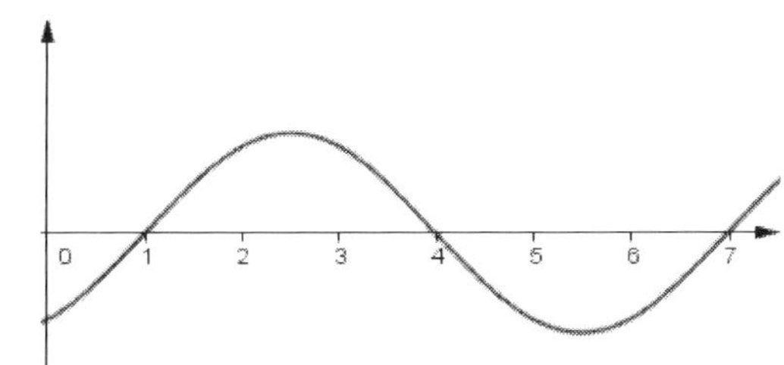

6. According to the graph above of the function f, what are the values of x where $f(x)$ is negative?
   a) $1 < x < 4$
   b) $0 < x < 1$ or $4 < x < 7$
   c) $x < 1$ or $x > 7$
   d) $1 < x < 4$ or $7 < x$

Answer: (b)

There are two regions which have negative values of $f(x)$, which are $0 < x < 1$ and $4 < x < 7$.

7. The amount of money, in dollars, earned from a school fundraiser by selling x cookies is given by $A(x) = 1.5x - 80$. How many cookies must the event sell in order to raise 220 dollars?

Answer: 200

Set $A(x)$ equal to 220.
$1.5x - 80 = 220$
$x = 200$

8. If $g(x) = 5x - 10$, then at what value of x does the graph of $g(x)$ cross the x-axis?
   a) - 6
   b) -3
   c) 0
   d) 2

Answer: (d)

The value of x where g(x) crosses the x-axis is the value of x where g(x) is equal to 0.

$0 = 5t - 10$
$t = 2$

$$p(x) = \frac{17}{200}x^2 - 8x + c$$

9. The function above calculates the profit, in dollars, from growing and selling x units of corn. c is a constant. If 200 units were sold for a total profit of $1,400, what is the value of c?
   a) -400
   b) -200
   c) 200
   d) 400

Answer: (a)

Plug in the values of x and y to solve for c.

$1400 = \frac{17}{200} \times 200^2 - 8 \times 200 + c$
$c = -400$

x	1	2	3	4
y	1	4	7	9

10. The table above represents a relationship between x and y. Which of the following linear equations describes the relationship?
   a) $y = 4x - 1$
   b) $y = 3x + 1$
   c) $y = 3x - 2$
   d) $y = -3x + 4$

Answer: (c)

The slope of the linear equation is $\frac{4-1}{2-1} = 3$.
Point-slope-form: $y - 1 = 3(x - 1)$
$y = 3x - 2$

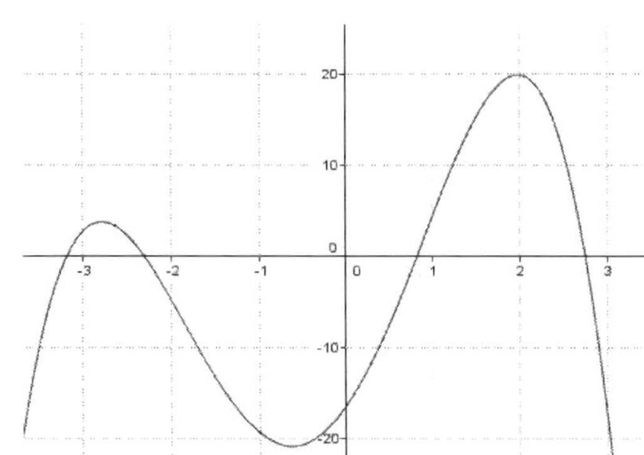

11. The figure above shows the graph of $y = f(x)$. For what value of x in this interval does the function f have its highest value between $x = -3$ to $x = 3$?
   a) -1
   b) 0
   c) 1
   d) 2

Answer: (d)

Maximum value is the value of y at the highest point, which occurs when x = 2.

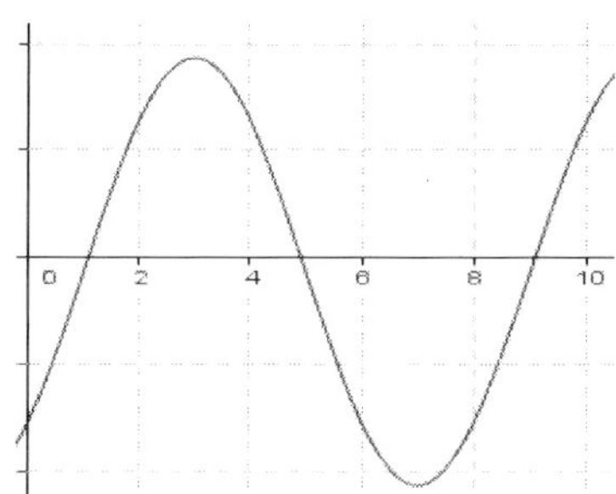

12. According to the graph above of the function f, what are the values of x where $f(x)$ is negative?
    a) $1 < x < 5$ or $9 < x < 10$
    b) $x < 1$ or $5 < x < 9$
    c) $x < 1$ or $x > 9$
    d) $1 < x < 5$ or $9 < x$

Answer: (b)

The function is negative when the value of y is less than 0, which occurs when $x < 1$ and $4 < x < 9$ as seen from the graph.

x	1	2	3	4	5
$f(x)$	5	8	y	14	17

13. The table above defines a linear function. What is the value of y?

Answer: 11

Slope $= \frac{8-5}{2-1} = \frac{y-8}{3-2}$
$3 = y - 8$
$y = 11$

14. Which of the following graphs is a graph of a function?

    a)

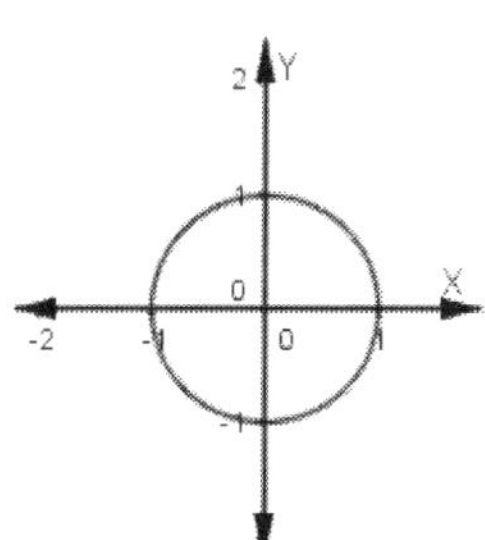

    b)

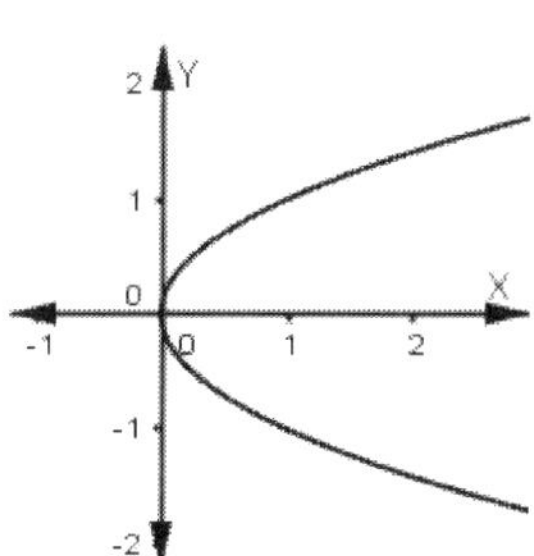

Answer: (d)

Apply Vertical Line Test. A function has at most one intersection with any vertical line.

c)

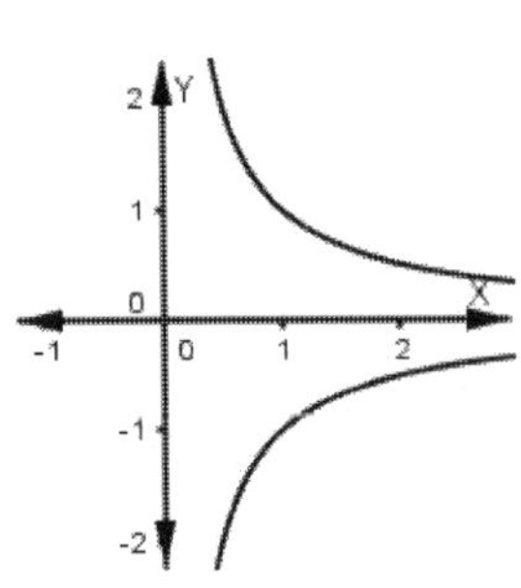

d)

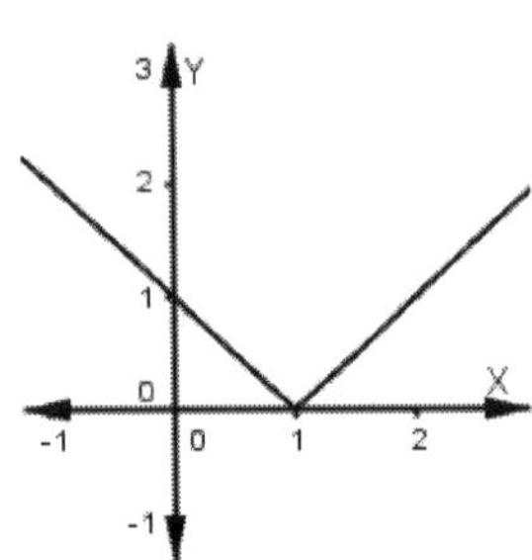

Medium

$$p(t) = 1000 \times (2)^{\frac{t}{3}}$$

15. The growth of certain kind of bacterial is observed and its population growth, P, t days from the first observation, is modeled by the function above. By how much does the bacterial population increase from $t = 3$ to $t = 9$?
    a) 2,000
    b) 4,000
    c) 5,000
    d) 6,000

Answer: (d)

Plug in the two different values of t and find their difference.
$p(9) - p(3) = 8{,}000 - 2{,}000 = 6{,}000$

16. The total cost, in dollars, of manufacturing x units of Sponge Phones is given by the function
$$m(x) = \frac{5000x - 400}{ax}$$
where a is a constant. If the total cost of 10 units is \$2480, what is the value of a?

Answer: 2

$$2480 = \frac{5000 \times 10 - 400}{a \times 10}$$

$$a = \frac{5000 \times 10 - 400}{2480 \times 10} = 2$$

17. Let the function f be defined by $f(x) = 2x - 1$. If $2f(a+1) = 10$, what is the value of $f(2a)$?

Answer: 7

Substitute x with (a + 1).

$10 = 2 \times (2a + 2 - 1)$
$2a = 5 - 1 = 4$
$a = 2$
$f(2a) = f(4) = 2 \times 4 - 1 = 7$

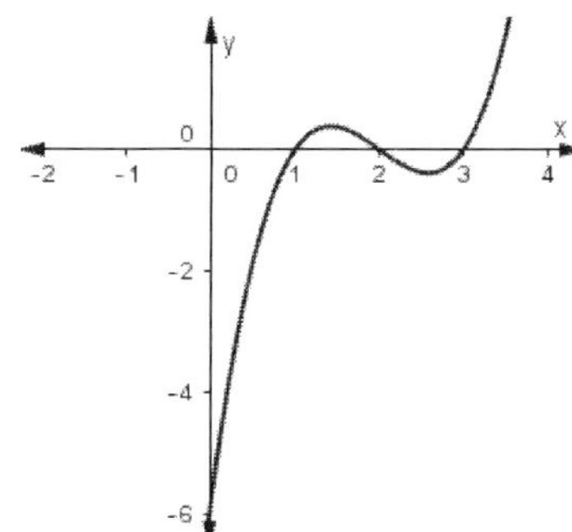

18. The graph of $y = f(x)$ is shown above. If $f(3) = a$, which of the following could be the value of $f(a)$?
    a) −2
    b) −4
    c) −6
    d) 2

Answer: (c)

As seen from the graph above, $f(3) = 0$, hence $a = 0$.
$f(a) = f(0) = -6$ (from graph above)

$$f(x) = \sqrt{x^2 - 1}$$

19. Which of the following values of x makes $f(x)$ undefined?
    a) −2
    b) 0
    c) 2
    d) 1

Answer: (b)

The value under the square root must be greater than or equal to zero.

20. At what value(s) of x does the function $f(x) = x^2 - 9$ cross the x-axis?
    a) 0 only
    b) 3 only
    c) –3 only
    d) –3 and 3

Answer: (d)

"$f(x)$ crosses the x-axis" means $f(x) = 0$.

$x^2 - 9 = 0$, $x = \pm 3$

21. $f(x)$ is graphed in the figure above. For what values of x does $f(x)$ have a negative slope?
    a) $x > -1$
    b) $-1 < x < 1$
    c) $x > 1$
    d) $0 < x$

Answer: (c)

A line with a negative slope descends from left to right. According to the graph above, only when $x > 1$ does the line have a negative slope.

22. The number of births in a local hospital in 1885, the year it was founded, was 15. After 1885, the number of births has doubled every 15 years. The number of births in the hospital can be found by the equation $N = 150\times 2^{t/15}$ where N is the number of births and t is the number of years since 1885. In what year would the annual birthrate in the hospital reach 3840?

Answer: 2005

Set N equal to 3840 to find t.

$3840 = 15 \times 2^{t/15}$

$\frac{3840}{15} = 2^{\frac{t}{15}} = 256 = 2^8$

$\frac{t}{15} = 8$

$t = 120$

$1885 + 120 = 2005$

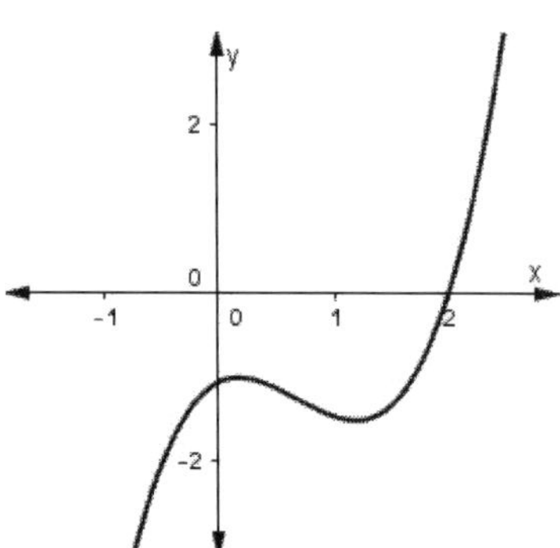

23. The figure above shows the graph of $g(x)$. At what value(s) of x does $g(x)$ equal to 0?
   a) 0
   b) -1
   c) 2
   d) -2

Answer: (c)

When g(x) is equal to 0, the graph of the function intersects the x-axis.
The value of x is 2 when the graph intercepts x-axis.

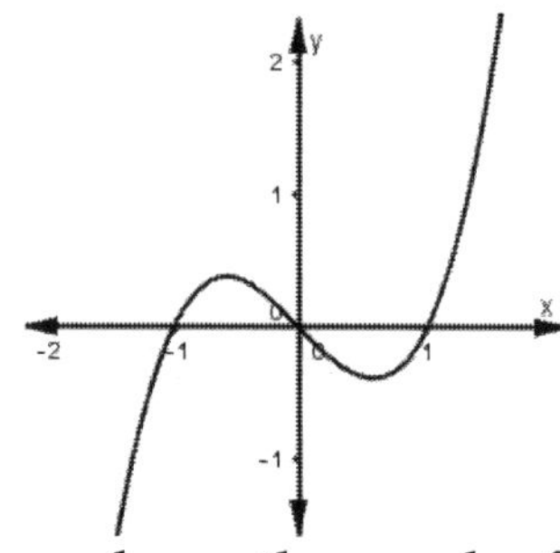

24. The figure above shows the graph of $y = f(x)$. If the function g is defined by $g(x) = f\left(\frac{x}{3}\right) - 2$, what is the value of $g(3)$?
   a) −2
   b) −1
   c) 0
   d) 1

Answer: (a)

$g(3) = f(\frac{3}{3}) - 2 = f(1) - 2$

From the graph above, $f(1) = 0$

$g(3) = 0 - 2 = -2$

25. The maximum height of a rock thrown upward with an initial velocity of v feet per second is $h + \frac{v^2}{64}$ feet, where h is the initial height, in feet. If the rock is thrown upward with velocity of 16 feet per second from a height of 10 feet, what is the maximum height, in feet, of the trajectory?

Answer: 14

Plug h and v into the function.

$10 + \frac{16^2}{64} = 14$ *feet*

x	0	1	2	4
$f(x)$	−5	−3	−1	3

26. The table above shows input values as x and the output values of the linear function f(x). Which of the following is the expression for $f(x)$?

a) $f(x) = \frac{1}{2}x - 5$

b) $f(x) = -\frac{1}{2}x - 5$

c) $f(x) = 2x - 5$

d) $f(x) = -2x - 5$

Answer: (c)

$f(x) - y_o = m(x - x_0)$

m (*the slope*) $= \frac{-3-(-5)}{1-0} = 2$

$f(x) + 5 = 2(x - 0)$

$f(x) = 2x - 5$

x	1	2	3	4	5
$f(x)$	−2	1	6	13	22

27. Some pairs of input and output values of the function f are shown above. The function h is defined by $h(x) = f(2x - 1)$. What is the value of $h(3)$?

Answer: 22

$h(3) = f(2 \times 3 - 1) = f(5) = 22$

28. If $f(x) = x^2 - 1$ and $g(x) = \frac{1}{x}$, write the expression $f(g(x))$ in terms of x.

a) $\frac{(1+x)(1-x)}{x^2}$

b) $\frac{(1+x)}{x^2}$

c) $\frac{(1-x)}{x^2}$

d) $\frac{1}{x^2}$

Answer: (a)

$f(g(x)) = \left(\frac{1}{x}\right)^2 - 1$

$= \frac{1-x^2}{x^2}$

$= \frac{(1+x)(1-x)}{x^2}$

29. The domain of the function $y = \frac{x-2}{(x-1)(x+3)}$ consists of all real numbers except?

a) $x \neq 1$

b) $x \neq 2$

c) $x \neq 1$, $x \neq 2$, and $x \neq -3$

d) $x \neq 1$ and $x \neq -3$

Answer: (d)

This function is defined everywhere except when the denominator is equal to zero.

30. The graph of $h(x)$ is a line. If $h(-2) = 7$ and $h(4) = 3$, then an equation of $h(x)$ is
    a) $\frac{2}{3}x - \frac{17}{3}$
    b) $-\frac{2}{3}x + \frac{17}{3}$
    c) $\frac{2}{3}x + \frac{17}{3}$
    d) $-\frac{3}{2}x + \frac{17}{3}$

Answer: (b)

Either use the substitution method or find the slope of the line.

Slope $= \frac{3-7}{4-(-2)} = \frac{-4}{6} = -\frac{2}{3}$

y-intercept: $7 = -\frac{2}{3} \times (-2) + b$

$b = \frac{3}{17}$

31. If $f\left(\frac{3x}{x-4}\right) = x^2 + x + 1$, what is the value of $f(5)$?
    a) 18
    b) 55
    c) 100
    d) 111

Answer: (d)

$\frac{3x}{x-4} = 5,\ x = 10$

$f(5) = x^2 + x + 1$

$= 100 + 10 + 1$

$= 111$

Hard

Questions 32 – 33 refer to the following information:
Boyle's law says that when all other factors are constant, the pressure of a gas decreases as the volume of that gas increases and vice versa. Therefore, the relationship of the pressure and volume of a gas, according to Boyle's law, is inversely proportional when the temperature remains unchanged.

32. According to Boyle's law, which of the following graphs represents the relationship between the pressure and volume of a gas if temperature is constant?

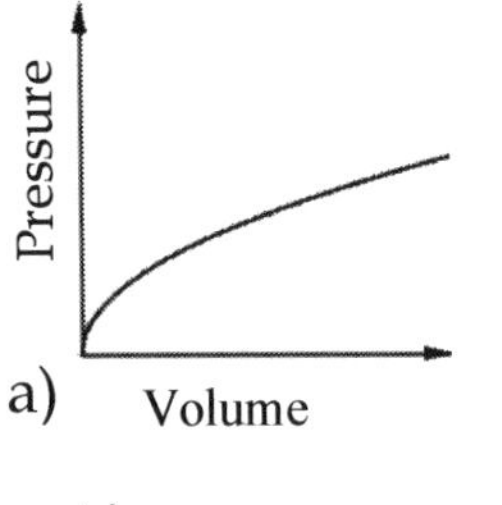

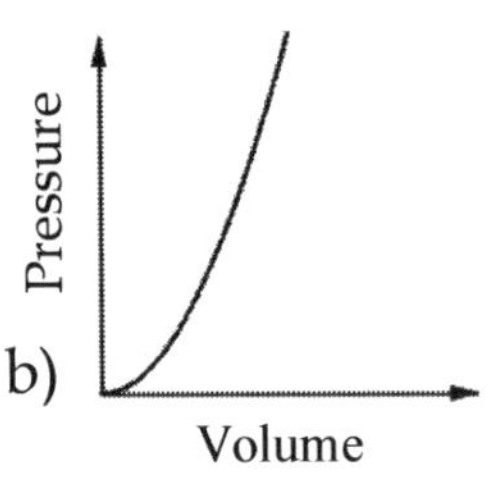

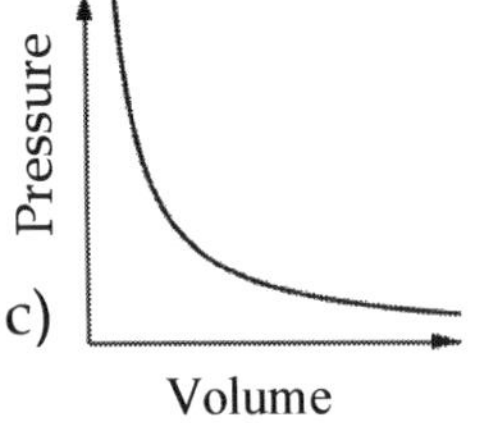

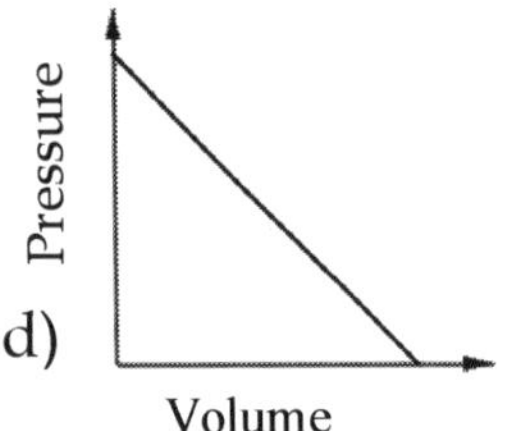

Answer: (c)

The relationship of the pressure and the volume of a gas is inversely proportional.

Graph c) represents the inversely proportional relationship: $PV = k$.

33. Assume that a gas has a volume of 20 liters and a pressure of 5 atmospheres initially. After some force is applied, the pressure becomes 8 atmospheres. According to Boyle's law, what is the final volume, in liters, of this gas? (Atmosphere (atm) is a unit of pressure.)
    a) 24.5
    b) 18.5
    c) 15.5
    d) 12.5

Answer: (d)

As the pressure increases, the volume of the gas decreases proportionately.

$P_1V_1 = P_2V_2$

$20 \times 5 = 8 \times V_2$

$V_2 = 12.5\ liters$

34. Which of the following is the graph of $y = |-3x+3|$?

a) 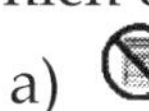

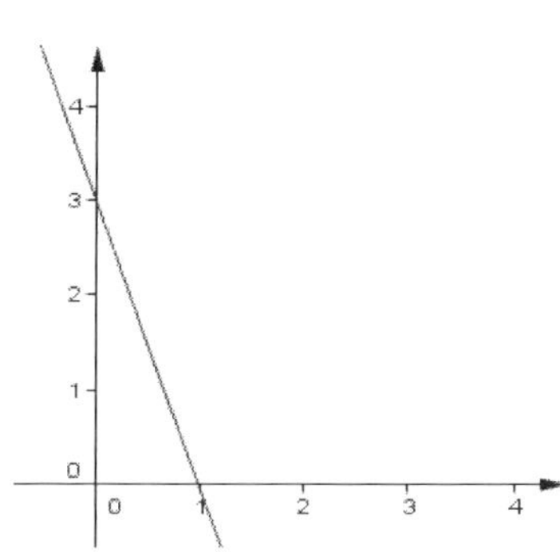

b)

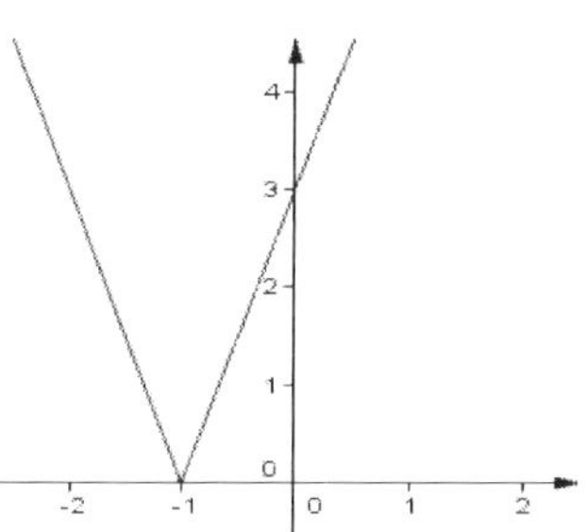

c)

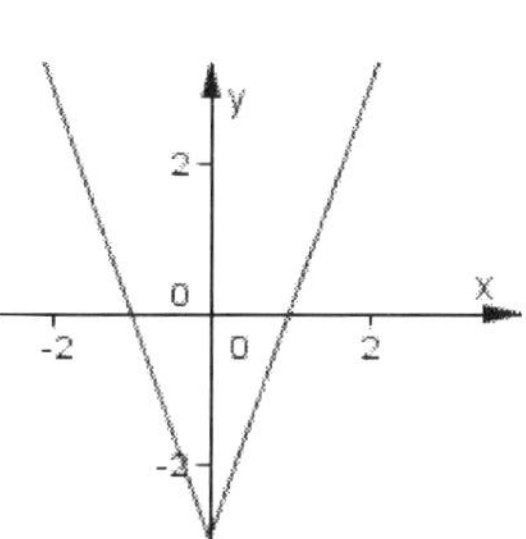

d)

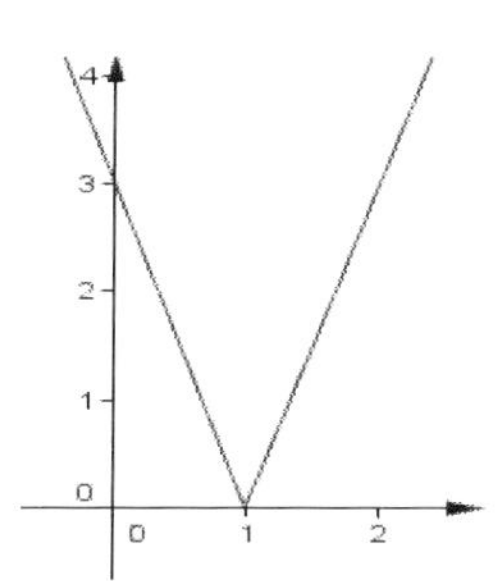

Answer: (d)

After taking the absolute value of (-3x + 3), any negative values on the graph will flip across the x-axis and become positive values.

The graph of y = -3x + 3 is shown below:

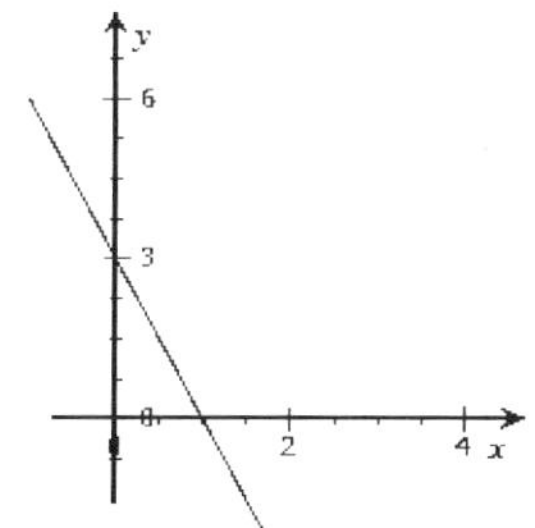

After flipping all negative values to positive values, the graph of y = |-3x + 3| will look like graph (d).

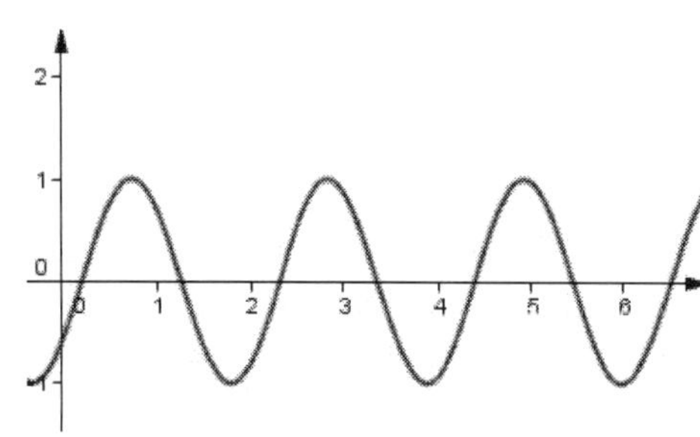

35. According to the graph shown above, how many distinct positive values of x are there on the graph when $y = 0.5$?
   a) 4
   b) 5
   c) 6
   d) 7

Answer: (d)

Draw a horizontal line $y = 0.5$ to find how many interceptions with the graph.
From the graph above, there are seven interceptions with line $y = 0.5$.

36. Let the function g be defined by: $g(x) = 2x + 1$. If $\frac{1}{3}g(x^2) = 1$, what could be the value of x?
   a) 0
   b) 1
   c) 2
   d) 3

Answer: (b)

Replace x with x^2 and solve the equation.

$\frac{1}{3}g(x^2) = 1$
$g(x^2) = 3$
$2(x^2) + 1 = 3$
$x^2 = 1$
$x = \pm 1$

37. Let the function f be defined by $f(x) = x^2 + 28$. If $f(3y) = 2f(y)$, what is the one possible value of y?
   a) -1
   b) 1
   c) 2
   d) -3

Answer: (c)

$f(3y) = (3y)^2 + 28 = 2f(y) = 2(y^2 + 28)$
$9y^2 + 28 = 2y^2 + 56$
$7y^2 = 28$
$y^2 = 4$
$y = \pm 2$

38. The monthly cost of renting an apartment increases every year by 5%. John paid $600 per month this year on his rental. What is the monthly cost for John's rental n years from now?
   a) 600×0.05^n
   b) $600 \times 1.05 \times n$
   c) 600×1.05^n
   d) $600^n \times 1.05$

Answer: (c)

Increasing every year by 5% is to multiply $(1 + \frac{5}{100})$ for each additional year.
$C(n) = (1.05)^n \times 600$
$= 600 \times (1.05)^n$

39. The value of one particular copy machine decreases by 15 percent each year. If a new machine was purchased at $20,000, how many years from the date of purchase will the value of this machine be approaching to $12,200?
   a) One
   b) Two
   c) Three
   d) Four

Answer: (c)

The price is decreasing by 15 percent each year, so the value of next year is 85% of the value of this year.

$12{,}200 = 20{,}000 \times (\frac{85}{100})^n$
$0.61 = (0.85)^n \rightarrow n = 3$

40. If $f(x) = \frac{x-1}{x+2}$ and $f(g(x)) = \frac{1}{x}$, then which of the following could be $g(x)$?
   a) $\frac{2+x}{1-x}$
   b) $\frac{x+2}{x-1}$
   c) $(x+1)(x+2)$
   d) $\frac{x-2}{x-1}$

Answer: (b)

$f(g(x)) = \frac{g(x)-1}{g(x)+2} = \frac{1}{x}$
$[g(x)-1]x = g(x)+2$
$g(x) \times x - x = g(x) + 2$
$g(x)(x-1) = 2 + x$
$g(x) = \frac{x+2}{x-1}$

41. The table below shows some coordinate pairs on the graph of $g(x)$. Which of the following could be $g(x)$?

x	$g(x)$
-1	0
0	3
1	0
2	3

   a) $(x^2+1)(2x+2)$
   b) $(x^2-1)(2x-3)$
   c) $(x+1)(x+3)$
   d) $(x+1)(x-3)$

Answer: (b)

Only the equation $g(x) = (x^2-1)(2x-3)$ *satisfies every point in the table.*

42. If $f(x) = x + 7$ and $f(g(2)) = 3$, which of the following functions could be $g(x)$?
   a) $x - 6$
   b) $x + 6$
   c) $3x - 1$
   d) $2x - 1$

Answer: (a)

$f(g(2)) = g(2) + 7 = 3$
$g(2) = -4$
Only (a) satisfies this condition.

43. If $f(x+1) = x^2 - 1$, then $f(x) = ?$
   a) $x^2 - 2x + 1$
   b) $x^2 + 2x + 1$
   c) $x^2 - 2x$
   d) $x^2 + 2x$

Answer: (d)

$f(x+1) = x^2 - 1$
$f(x) = f((x+1)-1)$
$= (x-1)^2 - 1$
$= x^2 - 2x + 1 - 1$
$= x^2 - 2x$

Questions 44 – 45 refer to the following information:

According to the combined ideal gas law, if the amount of gas stays constant, the relationship between pressure, volume, and temperature is as follows:

$$\frac{PV}{T} = constant$$

P is the pressure measured in atmospheres (atm), V is the volume measured in liters (L), and T is the temperature measured in Kelvin (K).

The relationship between Kelvin and Celsius is as follows:

$$K = 273 + °\text{C}$$

K is the temperature in Kelvin and °C is the temperature in Celsius.

The relationship between Celsius and Fahrenheit is as follows:

$$°\text{C} = (°\text{F} - 32) \times \frac{5}{9}$$

Where °C is the temperature in Celsius and °F is the temperature in Fahrenheit.

44. What will be the final volume, in liters, if the pressure of 6-liter sample of an ideal gas is changed from 1 atm to 3 atm and the temperature is changed from 273 K to 400 K? (Round your answer to the nearest tenth.)

Answer: 2.9

$\frac{PV}{T} = constant$

$\frac{P_1V_1}{T_1} = constant = \frac{P_2V_2}{T_2}$

$\frac{1 \times 6}{273} = \frac{3 \times V_2}{400}$

$v_2 = 2.9\ liters$

45. If the initial volume of a gas is 6 liters and the pressure of 1 atm, what will be the approximate new volume, in liters, when the temperature is changed from 32 °F to 212 °F and the pressure remains unchanged? (Round your answer to the nearest tenth.)

Answer: 8.2

$T_1 = (32 - 32) \times \frac{5}{9} = 0\ °\text{C} = 273 + 0 = 273\ K$

$T_2 = (212 - 32) \times \frac{5}{9} = 100\ °\text{C} = 273 + 100 = 373\ K$

$\frac{1 \times 6}{273} = \frac{1 \times V_2}{373}$

$V_2 = 8.2\ liters$

Questions 46 – 47 refer to the following information:

A new machine in a manufacturing factory is depreciated approximately 10% for the first 5 years and 5% for the next 10 years. If this machine costs \$10,000 brand new, the following equations are used to model its value for the first 15 years:

$$\begin{cases} V_t = \$10{,}000 \times r_1^t & when\ 0 < t \le 5 \\ V_t = V_5 \times r_2^{t-5} & when\ 5 < t \le 15 \end{cases}$$

V_t is the value of the machine at time t, the number of years after purchasing.

46. What is the value of $r_1 + r_2$?

Answer: 1.85

The machine depreciates 10% each year for the first 5 years:
$V_t = 10{,}000 \times (1 - 0.1)^t$
$r_1 = 0.9$
The machine depreciates 5% each year for the next 10 years:
$V_t = V_5 \times (1 - 0.05)^{t-5}$
$r_2 = 0.95$
$r_1 + r_2 = 0.9 + 0.95 = 1.85$

47. After how many years will a brand new machine be worth less than \$5,000?

Answer: 9

After the first five years:
$V_5 = 10{,}000 \times (0.9)^5 = 5{,}904.9$

$5{,}904.9 \times (0.95)^{t-5} < 5{,}000$
$0.95^{t-5} < 0.85$
With calculator, the first whole number value of t that satisfies the above inequality is 9.
After 9 years, the value of the machine will be less than \$5,000

V. Complex Numbers

Concept Overviews

A **complex number** is a number of the form $a + bi$, where a and b are real numbers and i is the imaginary unit.

$i = \sqrt{-1}$
$i^2 = -1$
$i^3 = -i$
$i^4 = 1$

When two complex numbers are equal, their real parts are equal and their imaginary parts are also equal. For example, if $a + bi = c + di$, it must be true that $a = c$ and $b = d$.

Example: $3x + yi = 2x + 2 + 3i$
$3x = 2x + 2 \rightarrow x = 2$
$yi = 3i \rightarrow y = 3$

The expressions $a + bi$ and $a - bi$ are called **complex conjugates**. Multiplying a complex number by its complex conjugate will give you a real number.

$$(a + bi) \times (a - bi) = a^2 + b^2$$

Example: $(3 + 4i) \times (3 - 4i) = 3^2 + 4^2 = 25$

Rationalizing the Complex Number

We can rationalize a fraction involving a complex number, such as $\frac{1}{1+2i}$, by making the denominator a real number. **Complex conjugates** are used to simplify the fraction when the denominator is a complex number.

Example: $\frac{1}{1+2i} = \frac{1}{1+2i} \times \frac{1-2i}{1-2i} = \frac{1(1-2i)}{1^2+2^2} = \frac{1-2i}{5} = \frac{1}{5} - \frac{2}{5}i$

Operations on Complex Numbers

Let $z_1 = a + bi$ and $z_2 = c + di$. Then,

$z_1 + z_2 = (a + c) + (b + d)i$
$z_1 - z_2 = (a - c) + (b - d)i$
$z_1 \times z_2 = (a + bi) \times (c + di) = (ac - bd) + (ad + bc)i$
$\frac{z_1}{z_2} = \frac{a+bi}{c+di} = \frac{a+bi}{c+di} \times \frac{c-di}{c-di} = \frac{ac+bd}{c^2+d^2} + \frac{bc-ad}{c^2+d^2}i$ where $z_2 \neq 0$

Example: If $z = 3 - 2i$, what is the value of z^2?

$$z^2 = (3 - 2i)(3 - 2i) = 3^2 - 2^2 - 6i - 6i = 5 - 12i$$

Example: Write $\frac{i}{2-i}$ as a standard form complex number.

$$\frac{i}{2-i} = \frac{i}{2-i} \times \frac{2+i}{2+i} = \frac{2i-1}{2^2-i^2} = \frac{2i-1}{4-(-1)} \quad -\frac{1}{5} + \frac{2}{5}i$$

Example: Find $(1 + i)^8$.

$$(1+i)^2 = 1 - 1 + 2i = 2i$$
$$(1+i)^8 = [(1+i)^2]^4 = (2i)^4 = 2^4 = 16$$

Powers of *i* have a repeating pattern:

$i = i = \sqrt{-1} \rightarrow i^{4n+1} = i$
$i^2 = -1 \rightarrow i^{4n+2} = -1$
$i^3 = -i \rightarrow i^{4n+3} = -i$
$i^4 = 1 \rightarrow i^{4n} = 1$

Example: $i^{2012} + i^{2013} + i^{2015} = ?$

$$i^{2012} = i^{4(503)} = 1$$
$$i^{2013} = i^{4(503)+1} = i$$
$$i^{2015} = i^{4(503)+3} = -i$$
$$i^{2012} + i^{2013} + i^{2015} = 1$$

Complex numbers can be represented as a two-dimensional complex plane where the **horizontal axis** is **real component** and the **vertical axis** is the **imaginary component**. In the following figure, the complex number ***a* + *bi*** can be identified with the *point* ***(a, b)*** in the complex plane.

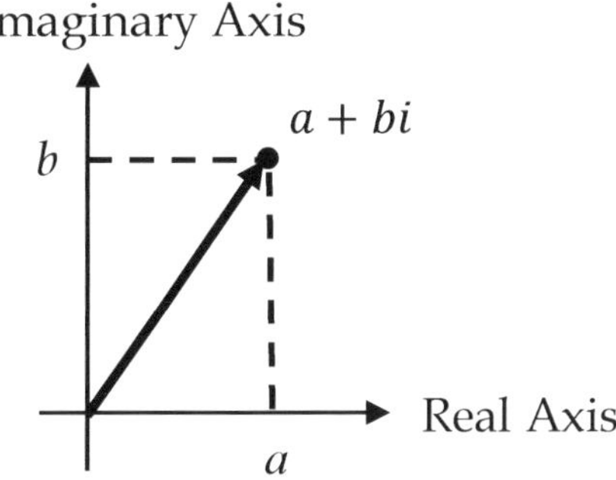

The Complex Plane

The magnitude of $a + bi$, denoted by $|a + bi|$, is equal to $\sqrt{a^2 + b^2}$.

Example: What is $|4 + 3i|$?

$$|4 + 3i| = \sqrt{4^2 + 3^2} = \sqrt{25} = 5$$

Problem Solving Skills

Easy

1. What is the magnitude of $4 + 3i$?
   a) 4
   b) 5
   c) 6
   d) 7

Answer: (b)

$|4 + 3i| = \sqrt{4^2 + 3^2} = 5$

2. If $i = \sqrt{-1}$ and n is a positive integer, which of the following statements is FALSE?
   a) $i^{4n} = 1$
   b) $i^{4n+1} = -i$
   c) $i^{4n+2} = -1$
   d) $i^{n+4} = i^n$

Answer: (b)

If you don't remember the pattern, you can try plugging in n = 0 into each of the choices.

$i = \sqrt{-1} \rightarrow i^{4n+1} = i$
$i^2 = -1 \rightarrow i^{4n+2} = -1$
$i^3 = -i \rightarrow i^{4n+3} = -i$
$i^4 = 1 \rightarrow i^{4n} = 1$

3. $(3 - \sqrt{-4} + (5 - 2\sqrt{-9})) =$
   a) $8i$
   b) 8
   c) $8 - 8i$
   d) $8 + 8i$

Answer: (c)

$(3 - \sqrt{-4} + (5 - 2\sqrt{-9}))$
$= 3 - 2\sqrt{-1} + 5 - 6\sqrt{-1}$
$= 8 - 8i$

4. $(2 - 5i) - (5 + 2i) =$
   a) 0
   b) $10i$
   c) $3 + 7i$
   d) $-3 - 7i$

Answer: (d)

$(2 - 5i) - (5 + 2i)$
$= (2 - 5) + (-5 - 2)i$
$= -3 - 7i$

5. If $i^n = 1$, what could n be?
   a) 7
   b) 8
   c) 9
   d) 10

Answer: (b)

n must be a multiple of 4.

6. $5i^{11} + 6i^{12} + 7i^{13} + 8i^{14} =?$
   a) -2
   b) $-2 + 2i$
   c) $-4i$
   d) $2 - 2i$

Answer: (b)

$5i^{11} + 6i^{12} + 7i^{13} + 8i^{14}$
$= 5i^3 + 6 + 7i + 8i^2$
$= -5i + 6 + 7i - 8 = -2 + 2i$

7. $i^{24} + i^{25} + i^{26} + i^{27} = ?$
   a) 1
   b) i
   c) 0
   d) $-i$

Answer: (c)

$i = \sqrt{-1} \rightarrow i^{4n+1} = i$
$i^2 = -1 \rightarrow i^{4n+2} = -1$
$i^3 = -i \rightarrow i^{4n+3} = -i$
$i^4 = 1 \rightarrow i^{4n} = 1$
$i^{24} + i^{25} + i^{26} + i^{27}$
$= 1 + i - 1 - i = 0$

Medium

8. Which of the following is the fraction $\frac{1}{2-i}$ equivalent to?
   a) $-2i$
   b) $2 + i$
   c) $\frac{2-i}{3}$
   d) $\frac{2+i}{5}$

Answer: (d)

Rationalize the denominator.

$$\frac{1}{2-i} \times \frac{2+i}{2+i} = \frac{2+i}{4-i^2} = \frac{2+i}{5}$$

9. Which of the following is the equivalent of $\frac{3-2i}{4+3i}$?
   a) $\frac{12-4i}{7}$
   b) $\frac{6+17i}{25}$
   c) $\frac{6-10i}{7}$
   d) $\frac{6-17i}{25}$

Answer: (d)

Rationalize the denominator.

$$\frac{3-2i}{4+3i} \times \frac{4-3i}{4-3i} = \frac{(3-2i)(4-3i)}{16+9} = \frac{6-17i}{25}$$

10. In $a + bi$ form, the reciprocal of $2 + 5i$ is
    a) $\frac{2}{29} - \frac{5}{29}i$
    b) $\frac{-2}{21} + \frac{5}{21}i$
    c) $\frac{1}{29} + \frac{5}{29}i$
    d) $\frac{2}{21} - \frac{5}{21}i$

Answer: (a)

The reciprocal of $(2 + 5i)$ *is* $\frac{1}{2+5i}$.
Rationalize the denominator.

$$\frac{1}{2+5i} \times \frac{2-5i}{2-5i} = \frac{2-5i}{4+25} = \frac{2-5i}{29}$$

11. What is the value of $|4 - 3i|$?
    a) 5
    b) $5\sqrt{2}$
    c) $2\sqrt{5}$
    d) $4 - 3i$

Answer: (a)

$|4 - 3i| = \sqrt{4^2 + 3^2} = \sqrt{25} = 5$

12. If $a - bi = \frac{2+i}{1-i}$ which of the following is true?
    a) $a = 1, b = 3$
    b) $a = -\frac{1}{2}, b = -\frac{3}{2}$
    c) $a = \frac{3}{2}, b = \frac{1}{2}$
    d) $a = \frac{1}{2}, b = -\frac{3}{2}$

Answer: (d)

Rationalize the denominator.
$\frac{2+i}{1-i} \times \frac{1+i}{1+i} = \frac{1+3i}{1+1} = \frac{1}{2} + \frac{3}{2}i$
$a - bi = \frac{1}{2} + \frac{3}{2}i$
$a = \frac{1}{2}$ *and* $b = -\frac{3}{2}$

13. If $a + bi = \frac{2+i}{1+i}$, what is the value of $a + b$?

a) $a = 1, b = 3$
b) $a = -\frac{1}{2}, b = -\frac{3}{2}$
c) $a = \frac{3}{2}, b = -\frac{1}{2}$
d) $a = \frac{1}{2}, b = -\frac{3}{2}$

Answer: (c)

Rationalize the denominator.
$\frac{2+i}{1+i} = \frac{(2+i)(1-i)}{(1+i)(1-i)} = \frac{3-i}{2} = \frac{3}{2} - \frac{1}{2}i$
$= a + bi$
$a = \frac{3}{2}$ *and* $b = -\frac{1}{2}$

Hard

14. If $3 - 2i$ is a root of $2x^2 + ax + b = 0$, then the value of b is

a) 7.5
b) -7.5
c) 26
d) It cannot be determined.

Answer: (c)

The product of the roots is $\frac{b}{2}$. *The sum of the roots is* $-\frac{b}{a}$.
$(3 - 2i)(3 + 2i) = 13 = \frac{b}{2}$
$b = 26$

15. What is the value of $|\frac{3+i}{i-3}|$?

a) i
b) $-i$
c) 1
d) $2i$

Answer: (c)

$\left|\frac{3+i}{i-3}\right| = \left|\frac{3+i}{-3+i}\right|$
$= \left|\frac{\sqrt{3^2+1^2}}{\sqrt{(-3)^2+1^2}}\right| = \left|\frac{\sqrt{10}}{\sqrt{10}}\right| = 1$

16. In the equation below, x and y are real numbers and $i = \sqrt{-1}$. Which of the following ordered pair could be the solution for this equation?

$$3xi + 2i^6 = 6i + 4i^{13} + 5y$$

a) $(\frac{10}{3}, -\frac{2}{5})$
b) $(-\frac{2}{5}, -\frac{10}{3})$
c) $(\frac{10}{3}, \frac{2}{5})$
d) $(-\frac{2}{5}, \frac{10}{3})$

Answer: (a)

$3xi + 2i^6 = 6i + 4i^{13} + 5y$
$3xi - 2 = 6i + 4i + 5y$
$3xi - 2 = 10i + 5y$
$-2 + (3x - 10)i = 5y + 0i$
$5y = -2$ *and* $3x - 10 = 0$
$y = -\frac{2}{5}$ *and* $x = \frac{10}{3}$

17. If $f(x) = 4x^3 - 3x^2 + 2x - 3$, then $f(i)=$

a) 2
b) -2
c) $-2i$
d) $2i$

Answer: (c)

$f(x) = 4x^3 - 3x^2 + 2x - 3$
$f(i) = 4i^3 - 3i^2 + 2i - 3$
$= -4i + 3 + 2i - 3$
$= -2i$

18. If $x = i - 1$, then $3x^2 + x + 1 =$

a) $-12 - i$
b) $12 - i$
c) $5i$
d) $-5i$

Answer: (d)

$3x^2 + x + 1 = 3(-2i) + i - 1 + 1$
$= -5i$

19. If $x = 2i$ is a solution to the equation $3x^3 + 2kx = 0$, what is the value of k?
    a) 6
    b) $-\frac{3}{2}$
    c) -6
    d) $\frac{3}{2}$

Answer: (a)

Substitute x with 2i into the equation.
$3x^3 + 2kx = 3(2i)^3 + 2k(2i) = 0$
$3(-8i) + 4ki = (-24 + 4k)i = 0$
$-24 + 4k = 0$
$k = 6$

$$(1 - i)(3 + i) = a + bi$$

20. In the equation above, a and b are two real numbers. What is the value of $a + b$?

Answer: 2

$(1 - i)(3 + i) = 4 - 2i = a + bi$
$a = 4$ *and* $b = -2$
$a + b = 2$

VI. Quadratic Functions and Equations

Concept Overviews

Quadratic functions are functions of the form $(x) = ax^2 + bx + c$, where $a \neq 0$.

Important Properties of Quadratic Functions

- The vertex of a quadratic function is located at coordinate $(\frac{-b}{2a}, \frac{-b^2+4ac}{4a})$.
- The axis of symmetric of $f(x)$ is $= -\frac{b}{2a}$.
- If $a > 0$, the quadratic function opens upwards and has a minimum value at the vertex.
- If $a < 0$, the quadratic function opens downwards and has a maximum value at the vertex.
- The domain of a quadratic function is $(-\infty, \infty)$.
- The range of a quadratic function is
  - $\left(\frac{-b^2+4ac}{4a}, \infty\right)$ when $a > 0$.
  - $\left(-\infty, \frac{-b^2+4ac}{4a}\right)$ when $a < 0$.

Quadratic Equations
A quadratic equation is an equation where the greatest exponent of the variable is 2. It can be converted into standard form, which is expressed as $ax^2 + bx + c = 0$, where a, b, and c are real number coefficients, $a \neq 0$, and x is the variable.

Zero-Product Rule: If the product of two or more terms is zero, at least one of the terms has to be zero. For instance, $(x - 1)(x - 2) = 0$, so either $(x - 1) = 0 \rightarrow x = 1$ or $(x - 2) = 0 \rightarrow x = 2$. Both 1 and 2 are the two roots of x.

Solving a Quadratic Equation Method 1: Factoring

$x^2 - 3x + 2 = 0$
$(x - 1)(x - 2) = 0$ *(trinomial factoring)*
$x = 1$ *or* 2 *(zero-product rule)*

Solving a Quadratic Equation Method 2: Complete the Square

$x^2 + 4x - 5 = 0$
$x^2 + 4x = 5$
$x^2 + 4x + 2^2 = 5 + 2^2$ *(add 2^2 on both side to make left hand side a perfect square)*
$(x + 2)^2 = 9$
$x + 2 = \pm 3$
$x = -2 \pm 3$
$x = 1$ *or* -5

Solving a Quadratic Equation Method 3: Quadratic Formula $x = \frac{-b \pm \sqrt{b^2-4ac}}{2a}$

$2x^2 - 7x + 3 = 0$

$$x = \frac{-(-7) \pm \sqrt{(-7)^2 - 4 \times (2) \times (3)}}{2 \times 2} = \frac{7 \pm \sqrt{49 - 24}}{4} = \frac{7 \pm 5}{4}$$

$$x = 3 \text{ or } \frac{1}{2}$$

The Discriminant of Quadratic Equations: For a quadratic equation in standard form ($ax^2 + bx + c = 0$), the discriminant Δ is equal to $b^2 - 4ac$. The discriminant gives information about the roots.

- If $\Delta > 0$, then this quadratic equation has two real roots.
- If $\Delta = 0$, then this quadratic equation has one real double root (i.e., two roots have the same real value.)
- If $\Delta < 0$, then this quadratic equation has two complex roots with imaginary parts.

Important Properties of Quadratic Equations

- The sum of two roots of a quadratic equation written in the form $ax^2 + bx + c = 0$ is $\frac{-b}{a}$.
- The product of two roots of a quadratic equationwriiten in the form $ax^2 + bx + c = 0$ is $\frac{c}{a}$.
- If $a > 0$ and $\Delta < 0$, the graph will go upwards and no interception with x-axis, then $ax^2 + bx + c$ is always greater than 0.
- If $a < 0$ and $\Delta < 0$, the graph will go downwards and no interception with x-axis, then $ax^2 + bx + c$ is always less than 0.

Problem Solving Skills

Easy

1. How many points does the graph of function, $f(x) = x^2 - 1$, cross the x-axis?
   a) 0
   b) 1
   c) 2
   d) 3

Answer: (c)

The graph of $f(x)$ intersects the x-axis when $f(x) = 0$.

$0 = x^2 - 1$
$x = \pm 1$

2. If $x^2 - 64 = 0$, which of the following could be a value of x?
   a) -4
   b) -8
   c) 2
   d) 4

Answer: (b)

$x^2 - 64 = 0$
$x^2 = 64$
$x = \pm 8$

3. If $x^2 = 16$ and $2y^3 = -16$, which of the following could be true?
   I. $x = 4$
   II. $y = 2$
   III. $x + y = 2$
   a) I only
   b) II only
   c) 1 and III only
   d) I, II, and III

Answer: (c)

Solve for x first.

$x^2 = 16, \quad x = \pm 4$
$2y^3 = -16$
$y^3 = -8, \quad y = -2$
Only I and III are correct.

4. What are the solutions of x for which $(x - 1)(x + 2) = 0$?
   a) –1
   b) –2
   c) 1 and –2
   d) –1 and 2

Answer: (c)

$(x - 1)(x + 2) = 0$
$x - 1 = 0, \; x = 1$ *or*
$x + 2 = 0, \; x = -2$

5. Equation $(x + 2)(x + a) = x^2 + 4x + b$ where a and b are constants. If the equation is true for all values of x, what is the value of b?
   a) 8
   b) 6
   c) 4
   d) 2

Answer: (c)

This is an identity equation question. The two expressions have the same coefficients for corresponding terms.
$(x + 2)(x + a) = x^2 + (2 + a)x + 2a$
By comparison: $2 + a = 4$ *and* $2a = b$
$a = 2$ *and* $b = 4$

6. If $x < 2$ and $a(x - 2)(x - 3) = 0$, what is the value of a?
   a) 3
   b) 2
   c) 1
   d) 0

Answer: (d)

Solve for x by zero-product rule.
$a(x - 2)(x - 3) = 0$
One of the terms a, (x− 2), and (x − 3) must be equal to zero.
Given that $x < 2$*, only a can be equal to zero.*

7. In the xy-coordinate system, $(k, 7)$ is one of the points of intersection of the graphs $y = 2x^2 - 3$ and $y = -x^2 + m$, where m and k are constants. What is the value of m?
   a) 6
   b) 8
   c) 10
   d) 12

Answer: (d)

Plug in the values for x and y into the equation.
$2(k)^2 - 3 = 7$
$k = \pm\sqrt{5}$
$7 = -(\pm\sqrt{5})^2 + m$
$7 = -5 + m; \; m = 12$

8. If $x - 2$ is a factor of $x^2 - ax - 8$, what is the value of a ?
   a) 2
   b) 4
   c) -4
   d) -2

Answer: (d)

$x^2 - ax - 8 = 0$
$(x - 2)(x + 4) = 0$
$x^2 + 2x - 8 = 0$
$a = -2$

Medium

9. If $x(x - 4) = -4$, what is the value of $x^2 + 3x - 5$?
   a) 3
   b) 5
   c) 1
   d) 0

Answer: (b)

$x^2 - 4x + 4 = 0$
$(x - 2)^2 = 0$
$x = 2$
$x^2 + 3x - 5 = 2^2 + 3 \times 2 - 5 = 5$

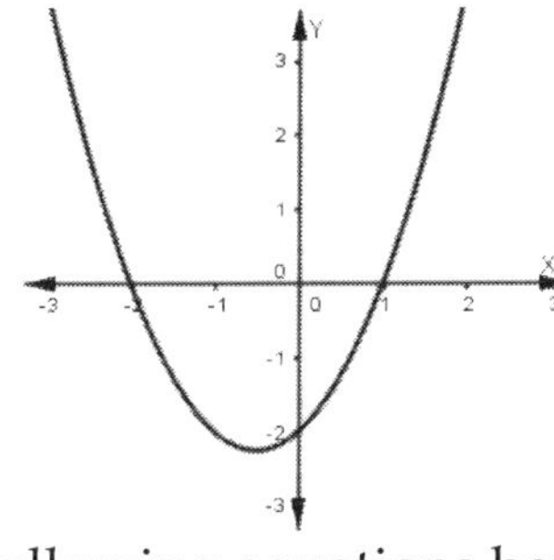

10. Which of the following equations best describes the curve in the figure above?
   a) $y = x^2 - 2$
   b) $y = x^2 + 2$
   c) $y = x^2 + x + 2$
   d) $y = x^2 + x - 2$

Answer: (d)

From the graph above, there are two roots, −2 and 1.

$y = (x + 2)(x - 1) = x^2 + x - 2$

11. If the function f is defined by $f(x) = ax^2 + bx + c$, where $a < 0$, $b > 0$, and $c > 0$, which of the following could be the graph of $f(x)$?
   a)

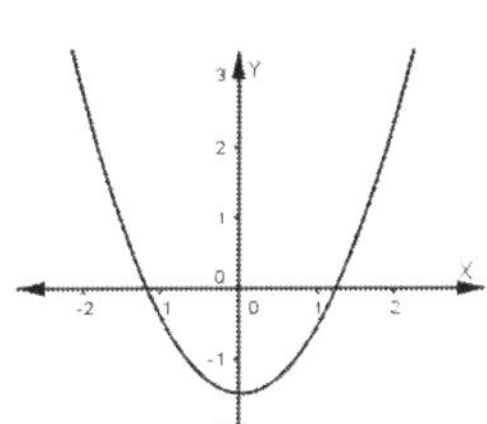

   b)

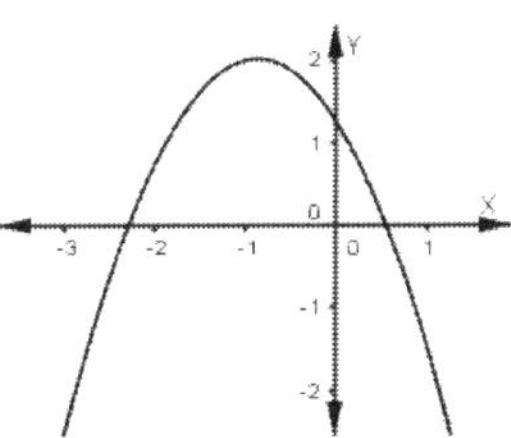

   c)

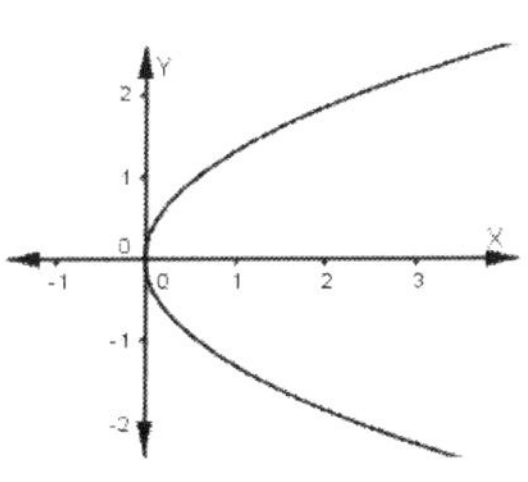

Answer: (d)

The leading coefficient of a quadratic function −1 means the curve goes downwards; a positive constant c means y-intercept is positive. The value of b is positive, so x-coordinate of the maximum point is positive. Only (d) meets all these conditions.

d)

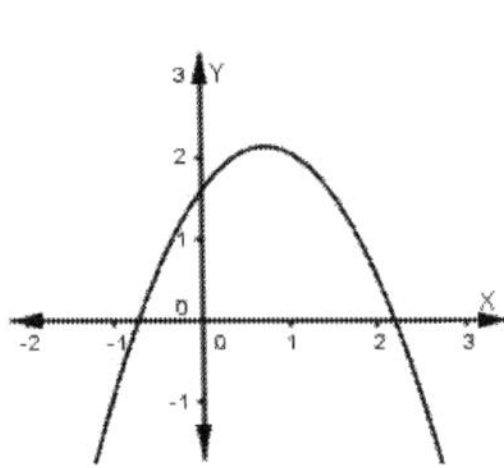

12. Which of the following could be a graph of the equation $y = ax^2 + bx + c$, where $b^2 - 4ac = 0$?

a)

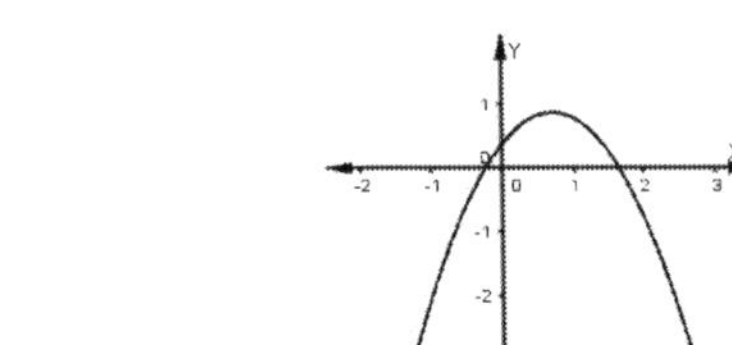

b)

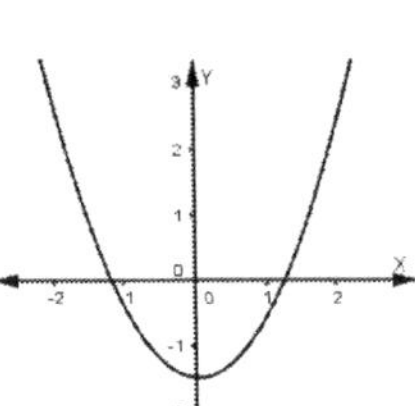

c)

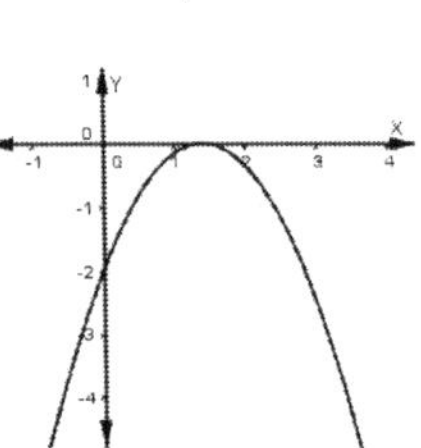

d)

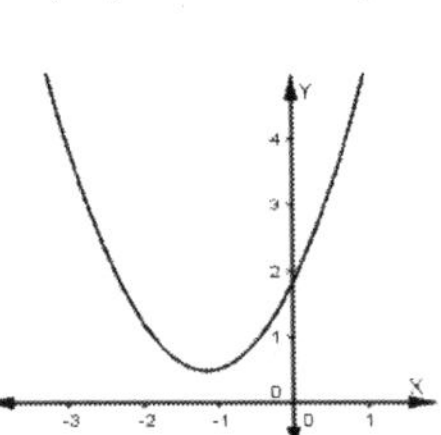

Answer: (c)

The discriminant, $b^2 - 4ac$, of a quadratic equation reveals the type of its roots.

- *When $b^2 - 4ac = 0$, the quadratic equation two equal, real roots.*
- *When $b^2 - 4ac > 0$, the quadratic equation has two unequal, real roots.*
- *When $b^2 - 4ac < 0$, the quadratic equation has no real roots.*

13. At what points the graph of $y = x^2 + 2x - 8$ cuts the x-axis?

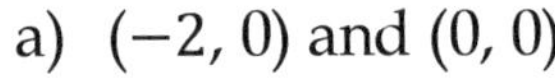

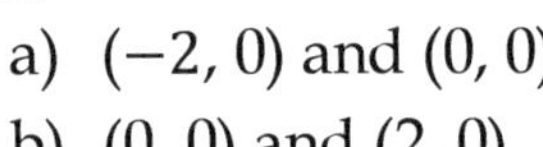

a) $(-2, 0)$ and $(0, 0)$
b) $(0, 0)$ and $(2, 0)$
c) $(2, 0)$ and $(-4, 0)$
d) $(4, 0)$ and $(2, 0)$

Answer: (c)

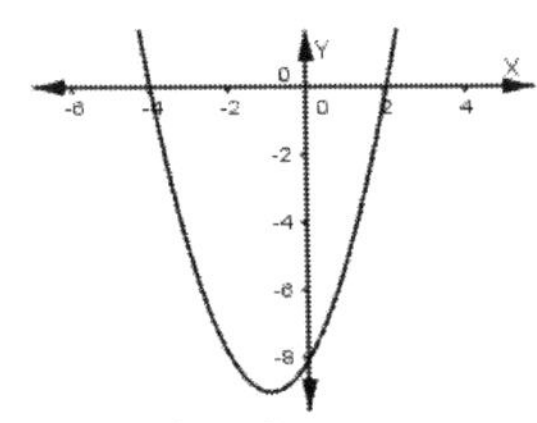

$x^2 + 2x - 8 = 0$
$(x - 2)(x + 4) = 0$
The graph intersects the x-axis at $(2, 0)$ and $(-4, 0)$.

14. A baseball is hit and flies into a field at a trajectory defined by the equation $d = -1.2t^2 + 100$, where t is the number of seconds after the impact and d is the horizontal distance from the home plate to the outfield fence. How many seconds have passed if the ball is 50 meters away from the outfield fence?

Answer: 6.45

$50 = -1.2t^2 + 100$
$t = 6.45$

Hard

15. At a particular time, the speed (velocity) of a car is equal to the slope of the tangent line of the curve in the position-time graph. Which of the following position-time graphs represents the motion of a car when its speed (velocity) is constant?

a)

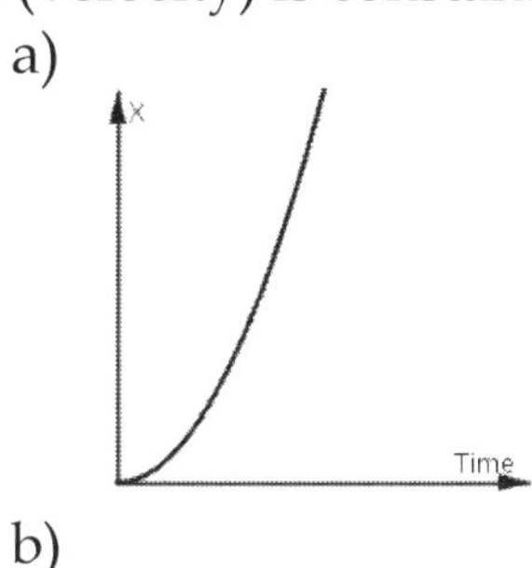

b)

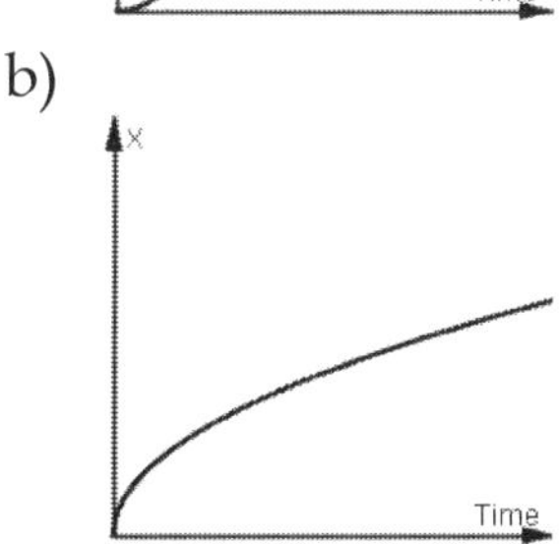

c)

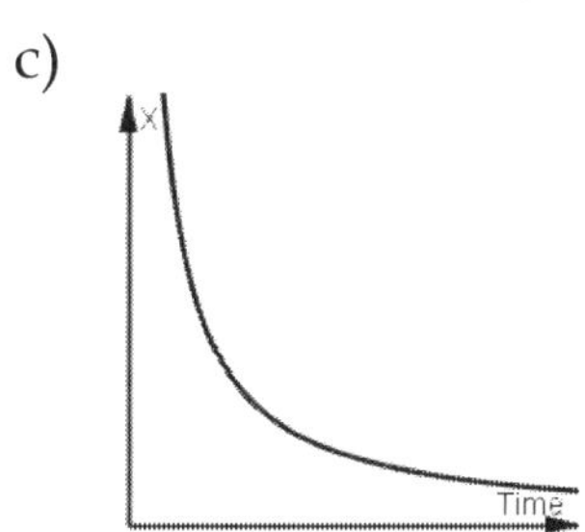

d)

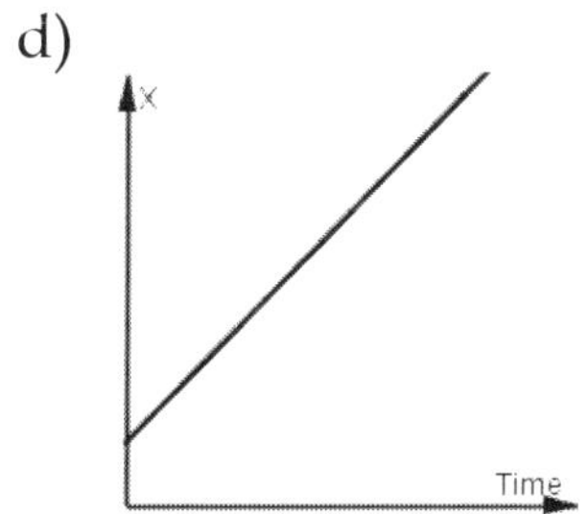

Answer: (d)

Only answer d) presents a straight line with the constant slope

$$h(t) = -5t^2 + at + b$$

16. At time $t = 0$, a ball was thrown upward from the top of a building. Before the ball hit the ground, its height $h(t)$, in feet, at the time t seconds is given by the function above. a and b are constants. If the ball reached its maximum height of 125 feet at time $t = 3$, what could be the height of the building?

Answer: 80

The height of the building is equal to the height of the ball when t equals 0.
The maximum height occurs when $t = \frac{-a}{2 \times (-5)} = 3$, *solve for a,* $a = 30$
$125 = -5(3)^2 + 30(3) + b$
$b = 80$
$h(0) = b = 80$ *feet*

17. If $h(x) = 6 + \frac{x^2}{4}$ and $h(2m) = 5m$, what is one possible value of m?

Answer: 2, 3

Substitute 2m for x solve for m.
$h(2m) = 6 + \frac{(2m)^2}{4} = 5m$
$6 + m^2 = 5m$
$m^2 - 5m + 6 = 0$
$(m - 2)(m - 3) = 0$
$m = 2$, *or* 3

18. In the xy-coordinate plane, the graph of $x = -y^2 + 5$ intersects the line at $(4, a)$ and $(1, b)$, what is the greatest possible slope of the line?

Answer: 1

Plug in the values of x and y.
$4 = -a^2 + 5 \rightarrow a = \pm 1$
$1 = -b^2 + 5 \rightarrow b = \pm 2$
Slope $= \frac{a-b}{4-1}$
The greatest possible slope of the line $= \frac{1-(-2)}{3} = 1$

19. In the xy-coordinate plane, the graph of $y = x^2 + 1$ intersects the line m at $(a, 2)$ and $(b, 5)$. What is the greatest possible slope of m?

Answer: 3

Plug in the values of x and y.
$2 = a^2 + 1 \rightarrow a = \pm 1$
$5 = b^2 + 1 \rightarrow b = \pm 2$
Slope $= \frac{5-2}{b-a} = \frac{5-2}{2-1} = 3$
The greatest possible slope of m is 3.

20. What is the minimum value of x in the equation $f(x) = x^2 + 4x + 2$?
 a) 7.75
 b) 2.25
 c) 0
 d) -2

Answer: (d)

The vertex of a quadratic function is $(\frac{-b}{2a}, \frac{-b^2+4ac}{4a})$.
If $a > 0$, $f(x)$ *opens upwards and has a minimum value at the vertex. If* $a < 0$, $f(x)$ *opens downwards and has a maximum value at the vertex.*
The equation $f(x) = x^2 + 4x + 2$ *has a minimum value of x equal to* $\frac{-b}{2a} = \frac{-4}{2} = -2$.

21. The axis of symmetry for $f(x) = x^2 + 3x - 2$ is $x = ?$
   a) 3
   b) -1
   c) 1
   d) -1.5

Answer: (d)

The axis of symmetry is equal to $-\frac{b}{2a}$.

$x = -\frac{3}{2} = -1.5$

22. If the value of $f(x) = x^2 - 5x - 2k$ is always positive for any x, which of the following could be the value of k?
   a) -2
   b) -3
   c) -4
   d) 3

Answer: (c)

If $f(x)$ is always positive, then $x^2 - 5x - 2k = 0$ has no real roots.

Discriminant, $b^2 - 4ac < 0$

$25 + 8k < 0$

$k < -3.125$

23. If the ratio of the two roots of the equation $x^2 - kx + 8 = 0$ is $1 : 2$, find all the possible values of k.
   a) $\{2, 3\}$
   b) $\{3, 6\}$
   c) $\{-2, 2\}$
   d) $\{-6, 6\}$

Answer: (d)

The sum of two roots of $ax^2 + bx + c = 0$: $-\frac{b}{a}$

The product of two roots of $ax^2 + bx + c = 0$: $\frac{c}{a}$

Let the two roots be r and 2r.

$r \times 2r = 2r^2 = \frac{8}{1} \quad r = \pm 2$

$r + 2r = 3r = \pm 6 = \frac{k}{1}$

24. What is the range of the quadratic function $f(x) = x^2 - 10x + 23$?
   a) $y \geq -2$
   b) $y \leq -2$
   c) $x \geq 5$
   d) $x \leq 5$

Answer: (a)

The vertex of a quadratic function is $(\frac{-b}{2a}, \frac{-b^2+4ac}{4a})$, *where* $a \neq 0$.

$f(x) = x^2 - 10x + 23$ *has a minimum at* $\frac{-b^2+4ac}{4a} = -2$, *since* $a > 0$.

25. In the xy-plane, the point $(-1, 2)$ is the minimum of the quadratic function $f(x) = x^2 + ax + b$. What is the value of $|a - 2b|$?

Answer: 4

The vextex of the quadratic function $f(x) = x^2 + ax + b$ *is* $(-\frac{a}{2}, f\left(-\frac{a}{2}\right))$

$-\frac{a}{2} = -1$

$a = 2$

$2 = (-1)^2 + 2(-1) + b$

$b = 3$

$|a - 2b| = |2 - 2 \times 3| = 4$

VII. Polynomials

Concept Overviews

Polynomial Factoring

The **common factors** of two or more polynomials are nonnegative numbers or polynomials other than 1 that can divide evenly into each. For instance, the common factors of $2x^5, 4x^4, 6x^2, 2x$ are $2, x$, and $2x$.

One way to see if polynomials can be factored is to factor "in pairs." Split the expression into pairs of terms and try to factor the pairs separately.

Example: Factor $x^3 - 7x^2 - 2x + 14$.
Solution: Group into pairs:
$x^3 - 7x^2 - 2x + 14 = (x^3 - 7x^2) - (2x - 14)$
Take out the common factor from each pair:
$x^3 - 7x^2 - 2x + 14 = (x^3 - 7x^2) - (2x - 14)$
$= x^2(x - 7) - 2(x - 7) = (x - 7)(x^2 - 2)$

An expression in the form of the difference of two squares can always be factored as such:

$$x^2 - y^2 = (x + y)(x - y)$$

Example: Factor $x^2 - 1$.
Solution: $x^2 - 1 = x^2 - 1^2 = (x + 1)(x - 1)$.

Example: Factor $x^4 - 16$.
Solution: $x^4 - 16 = [(x^2)^2 - 4^2] = (x^2 + 4)(x^2 - 4) = (x^2 + 4)(x + 2)(x - 2)$

To factor a trinomial, or a polynomial of the form $ax^2 + bx + c$, we split the cases up into two:

1. Where b and c are integers: First, by FOIL, we know that
$$(x + m)(x + n) = x^2 + (m + n)x + mn$$
Therefore, by backwards logic, in order to factor $x^2 + bx + c$, numbers m and n must be found such that $m + n = b$ and $mn = c$.

2. Where a, b, and c are integers and $a \neq 1$: Set $ax^2 + bx + c$ equal to $a(x + \frac{d_1}{a})(x + \frac{d_2}{a})$ where d_1 and d_2 are two numbers whose product is $a \times c$ and whose sum is b. Factor a into two numbers, a_1 and a_2, so that $a_1 \times \frac{d_1}{a}$ and $a_2 \times \frac{d_2}{a}$ are two integers.

   Example: Factor $4x^2 - 4x - 3$.
   Solution: First, find two numbers whose product is -12 and sum is -4. The two numbers are -6 and 2.

$$4x^2 - 4x - 3 = 4\left(x + \frac{2}{4}\right)\left(x - \frac{6}{4}\right) = 4\left(x + \frac{1}{2}\right)\left(x - \frac{3}{2}\right)$$
$$4\left(x + \frac{1}{2}\right)\left(x - \frac{3}{2}\right) = \left(2x + 2 \times \frac{1}{2}\right)\left(2x - 2 \times \frac{3}{2}\right) = (2x + 1)(2x - 3)$$

A perfect square trinomial is the result of multiplying a binomial by itself. It would be worth remembering the following formulas:

$$x^2 + 2xy + y^2 = (x + y)^2$$
$$x^2 - 2xy + y^2 = (x - y)^2$$

Any Polynomial $P(x)$ can always be written into the following form:

$$P(x) = (x - r)Q(x) + P(r)$$

Where $Q(x)$ is the quotient, $(x - r)$ is the divisor, and $P(r)$ is the remainder.

Example: If $P(x) = x^{10} + 3x^5 - 2x + 4$ is divided by $(x - 1)(x + 1)$, what is the remainder?

Solution: We can solve this problem by using long division but it will be very tedious. If we rewrite the equation as

$$P(x) = (x + 1)(x - 1)Q(x) + a(x - 1) + b$$

then the problem will become easier to solve.

$x^{10} + 3x^5 - 2x + 4 = (x + 1)(x - 1)Q(x) + a(x - 1) + b$

If $x = 1$, then $1 + 3 - 2 + 4 = 0 + a \times 0 + b \rightarrow b = 6$

If $x = -1$, then $(-1)^{10} + 3(-1)^5 - 2(-1) + 4 = 0 + a(-1 - 1) + 6 \rightarrow a = 1$

So the remainder of $\frac{x^{10} + 3x^5 - 2x + 4}{(x+1)(x-1)}$ is $(x - 1) + 6 = x + 5$.

The **factor theorem** states that if $x - r$ is a factor of $P(x)$, then $P(r) = 0$. Also, r is an x-intercept of $P(x)$.

Example: If $P(x) = x^7 + kx + 1$ has the factor $x + 1$, what is the value of k?

Solution: Since $P(x)$ has the factor $x + 1$, $P(-1) = 0$

$(-1)^7 + k(-1) + 1 = 0$

$k = 0$

The **remainder theorem** states that if polynomial $P(x)$ is divided by $x - r$, the remainder will be $P(r)$.

Example: If $P(x) = x^{100} + 2$ is divided by $x + 1$, what is the remainder?

Solution: The remainder of $\frac{P(x)}{x+1}$ is $P(-1) = (-1)^{100} + 2 = 3$

Sums and Products of the Roots of Polynomials

If a real polynomial $P(x) = a_n x^n + a_{n-1}x^{n-1} + \cdots + a_1 x + a_0$ has n roots, then

$$P(x) = a_n x^n + a_{n-1}x^{n-1} + \cdots + a_1 x + a_0 = a_n(x - r_n)(x - r_{n-1}) \ldots (x - r_1)$$

Sum of all roots: $r_n + r_{n-1} + r_{n-2} \ldots + r_2 + r_1 = -\frac{a_{n-1}}{a_n}$

Product of all roots: $r_n \times r_{n-1} \times r_{n-2} \ldots \times r_2 \times r_1 = (-1)^n \frac{a_0}{a_n}$

Example: What is the sum and product of all roots of the following polynomial:

$$P(x) = x^8 + 7x^7 + 5x^3 - 3x + 1$$

Solution: Sum of all roots: $= \frac{-7}{1} = -7$

Product of all roots: $(-1)^8 \frac{1}{1} = 1$

Example: If $f(x) = x^2 - 3x - 2$ has two roots at r_1 and r_2, what is the value of $\frac{1}{r_1} + \frac{1}{r_2}$?

Solution: $\frac{1}{r_1} + \frac{1}{r_2} = \frac{r_1 + r_2}{r_1 r_2}$

Sum of all roots: $r_1 + r_2 = 3$

Product of all roots: $r_1 r_2 = -2$

$\frac{1}{r_1} + \frac{1}{r_2} = \frac{r_2 + r_1}{r_1 r_2} = -\frac{3}{2}$

Problem Solving Skills

Easy

1. What is the remainder when $2x^4 - 3x^3 + 4x^2 - 5x + 6$ is divided by $x - 3$?
   a) 108
   b) 96
   c) 87
   d) 75

Answer: (a)

The remainder theorem states that if polynomial $P(x)$ is divided by $x - r$, its remainder is $P(r)$.
$P(3) = 2 \times 3^4 - 3 \times 3^3 + 4 \times 3^2 - 5(3) + 6 = 108$

2. If $(x + 1)$ is a factor of $3x^6 + kx^5 - 4x^3 + 1$, what is the value of k?
   a) 8
   b) 6
   c) 5
   d) 3

Answer: (a)

$P(-1) = 3 \times (-1)^6 + k \times (-1)^5 - 4 \times (-1)^3 + 1 = 0$
$k = 8$

3. If $3x + 6$ is a divisor of $3x^3 + 5x^2 - 4x + d$ with a remainder of *0*, what is the value of *d*?
   a) 8
   b) 4
   c) -4
   d) -8

Answer: (c)

$3x + 6 = 0, \ x = -2$
$P(-2) = 3 \times (-2)^3 + 5 \times (-2)^2 - 4 \times (-2) + d = 0$
$d = -4$

4. If $(x+2)$ is a factor of $x^6 - 3x^4 + 2x^3 - x + d$, what is the value of *d*?
   a) 14
   b) −14
   c) −2
   d) 2

Answer: (c)

$P(-2) = (-2)^6 - 3 \times (-2)^4 + 2 \times (-2)^3 - (-2) + d = 0$
$d = -2$

5. If $x - 2$ divides $2x^3 - 4k^3x^2 + 16x - 32$ with a remainder of 0, what is the value of *k*?
   a) −2.2
   b) −0.33
   c) 1
   d) 2

Answer: (c)

$P(2) = 2(2)^3 - 4k^3(2)^2 + 16 \times 2 - 32 = 0$
$2^4 - 2^4k^3 = 0$
$k^3 = 1 \rightarrow k = 1$

Medium

6. If two roots of the equation $2x^3 - mx^2 + nx - m = 0$ are 3 and 5, what is the third root?
   a) $-\frac{4}{7}$
   b) $-\frac{4}{7}$
   c) 1
   d) $\frac{4}{7}$

Answer: (d)

If polynomial $P(x) = a_n x^n + a_{n-1}x^{n-1} + \cdots + a_1 x + a_0$ *has n roots, then*
Sum of all roots: $-\frac{a_{n-1}}{a_n}$
Product of all roots: $r_n \times r_{n-1} \times r_{n-2} \ldots \times r_2 \times r_1 = (-1)^n \frac{a_0}{a_n}$
Let r be the third root, then
$3 + 5 + r = -\frac{-m}{2}$
$8 + r = \frac{m}{2}$
$3 \times 5 \times r = (-1)^3 \frac{-m}{2}$
$8 + r = 15r \rightarrow r = \frac{4}{7}$

7. If the $f(x) = x^5 + bx^4 + cx^3 + dx^2 + ex + k$, $f(-1) = 0$, and $f(3) = 0$, then $f(x)$ is divisible by
   a) $x - 1$
   b) $x + 3$
   c) $x^2 + 3x + 2$
   d) $x^2 - 2x - 3$

Answer: (d)

f(x) should be divisible by $(x+1), (x-3),$ *and* $(x^2 - 2x - 3)$.

8. If −2 and 4 are both zeros of the polynomial *f(x)*, then a factor of *f(x)* could be
   a) $x - 2$
   b) $x^2 - 2x - 8$
   c) $x^2 + 2x + 8$
   d) $x + 4$

Answer: (b)

f(x) should be divisible by $(x+2),\ (x-4),$ *and* $(x^2 - 2x - 8)$.

9. Which of the following is the sum of the roots of $6x^3 + 4x^2 - 3x = 0$?
   a) $-\frac{1}{2}$
   b) $\frac{1}{2}$
   c) $-\frac{2}{3}$
   d) $\frac{2}{3}$

Answer: (c)

Sum of all roots: $-\frac{a_{n-1}}{a_n}$
The sum of all roots of $6x^3 + 4x^2 - 3x = 0$ *is* $-\frac{4}{6} = -\frac{2}{3}$.

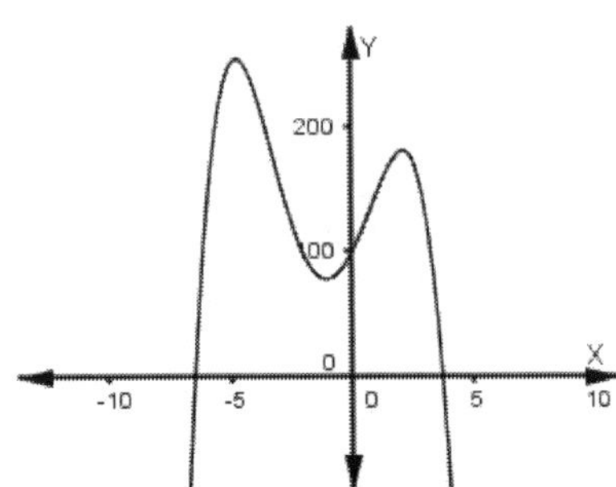

10. The graph above represents the function $y = -x^4 - 5x^3 + 14x^2 + 40x + c$. Which of the following could be the value of c?
    a) -100
    b) -7
    c) 3
    d) 100

Answer: (d)

c is the y-intercept which is equal to 100.

Questions 11 – 12 refer to the following information:

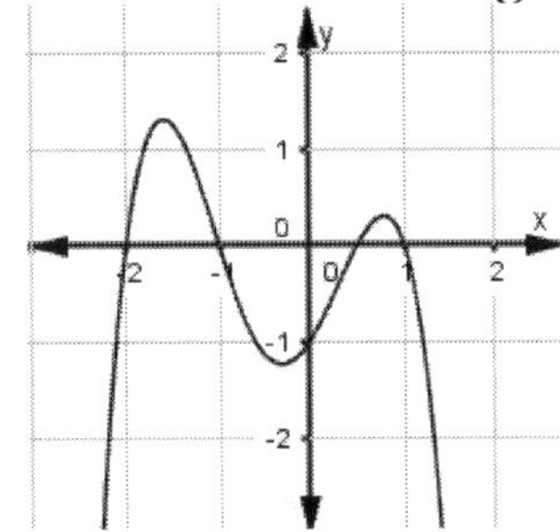

The function $f(x) = -x^4 - \frac{3}{2}x^3 + 2x^2 + \frac{3}{2}x - 1$ is graphed in the xy-plane above.

11. If c is a constant such that the equation $f(x) = c$ has four real solutions, which of the following could NOT be the value of c?
    a) 1
    b) 0
    c) $-\frac{1}{2}$
    d) -1

Answer: (a)

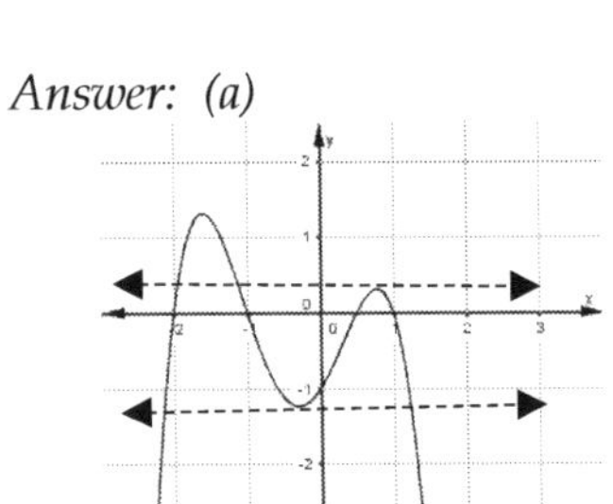

According to the graph above, there will be four intersection points when the value of c is roughly between -1.3 *and* 0.3.

12. How many real solutions are there if $f(x) = x$?
    a) 1
    b) 2
    c) 3
    d) 4

Answer: (b)

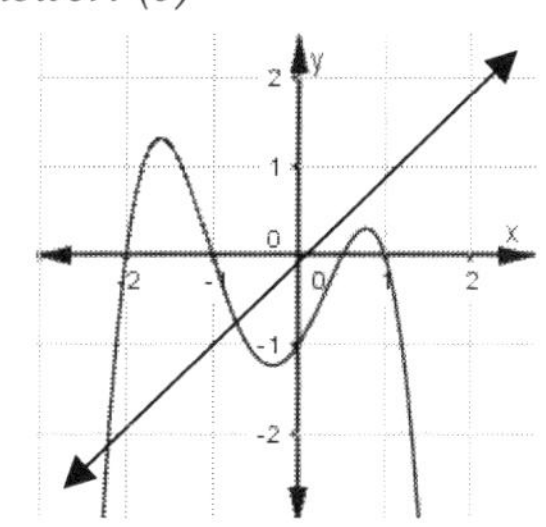

According to the graph above, there are two intersection points between the lines $f(x) = x$ and $f(x) = -x^4 - \frac{3}{2}x^3 + 2x^2 + \frac{3}{2}x - 1$.

13. The length of a rectangular piece of cardboard is 15 inches longer than its width. If a 5-inch square is cut from each corner of the cardboard, and the remaining piece is folded up to form a box, the volume of the box is 2,250 cubic inches. Find the sum of the length and the width, in inches, of the original cardboard.

Answer: 65

If the width of the cardboard is x inches, the length of the carboard is $15 + x$ inches.
After 5-inch square is cut from each corner and the cardboard is folded to form a box, the width will be $x - 10$, the length will be $x + 5$, and the height will be 5 inches. The volume of the box is given, so
$(x - 10)(x + 5)(5) = 2250.$
$x^2 - 5x - 50 = 450$
$x^2 - 5x - 500 = 0$
$(x + 20)(x - 25) = 0$
$x = 25$ *inches*
25 + (25 + 15) = 65

Hard

14. A polynomial *P(x)* has a remainder of 4 when divided by $(x + 1)$ and a remainder of 7 when divided by $(x - 2)$. What will be the remainder when *P(x)* is divided by $(x + 1)(x - 2)$?
    a) $x + 5$
    b) $x + 7$
    c) $x - 4$
    d) $x - 2$

Answer: (a)

Polynomial $P(x)$ can always be written into the following form:
$P(x) = (x - r)Q(x) + P(r)$
P(x) can be factored into the following three forms:
(1) $P(x) = (x + 1)Q(x) + 4$
(2) $P(x) = (x - 2)Q(x) + 7$
(3) $P(x) = (x + 1)(x - 2)Q(x) + ax + b$
Plugging in r = -1, 2 and setting both (1) and (2) equal to (3):
$P(-1) = 4 = -a + b$
$P(2) = 7 = 2a + b$
$a = 1, \quad b = 5$
The remainder is $x + 5$.

15. If i is a root of $3x^4 - 2x^3 + 5x^2 + 4x - 15 = 0$, what is the product of all real roots of the equation?
   a) 0
   b) -3
   c) -5
   d) 5

Answer: (c)

Product of all roots: $(-1)^n \frac{a_0}{a_n}$

$(-1)^4 \times \frac{-15}{3} = -5$

$= i(-i) \times Product\ of\ Real\ Roots$

$Therefore,$

$Product\ of\ Real\ Roots = -5$

$Product\ of\ All\ Roots = -5$

16. The graph of $2y^4 - x^2 + 11 = 0$ is symmetric with respect to which of the following?

   I. the x-axis
   II. the y-axis
   III. the origin

   a) only I
   b) only II
   c) only III
   d) I, II, and II

Answer: (d)

The following rules determine symmetry:

$f(-x) = f(x)$*: symmetric with respect to y-axis*

$f(-y) = f(y)$*: symmetric with respect to x-axis*

$f(-x, -y) = f(x, y)$*: symmetric with respect to origin*

17. Which of the following is the equation of the polynomial with roots at 0 and $3 - \sqrt{2}$?
   a) $x^3 + 6x^2 - 9x = 0$
   b) $x^3 - 6x^2 - 7x = 0$
   c) $x^3 + 6x^2 + 7x = 0$
   d) $x^3 - 6x^2 + 7x = 0$

Answer: (d)

The equation should also have a root at $3 + \sqrt{2}$*, because all of the answer choices have rational coefficients. Therefore the polynomial is* $x[x - (3 - \sqrt{2})][x - (3 + \sqrt{2})] = x[(x - 3) + \sqrt{2}][(x - 3) - \sqrt{2}] = x[(x - 3)^2 - (\sqrt{2})^2] = x(x^2 - 6x + 7) = x^3 - 6x^2 + 7x = 0$

Questions 18 – 19 refer to the following information:

In chemistry, a chemical reaction proceeds at a rate dependent on the concentration of its reactant. For reactant A, the rate of a reaction is defined as:

$$Rate = k\,[A]^n$$

k is a constant and $[A]$ is the concentration of A. The order of reaction of a reactant A is the exponent n to which its concentration term in the rate equation is raised.

18. When n is equal to -1, It is called an order (-1) with respect to reactant A. Which of the following graphs depicts an order (-1) with respect to concentration A and reaction rate?

Answer: (c)

$Rate = k[A]^{-1}$
$Rate \times [A] = k$
When $n = -1$, the rate of the reaction is inversely proportional to the concentration A.
Only graph c) represents the inversely proportional relationship.

a)
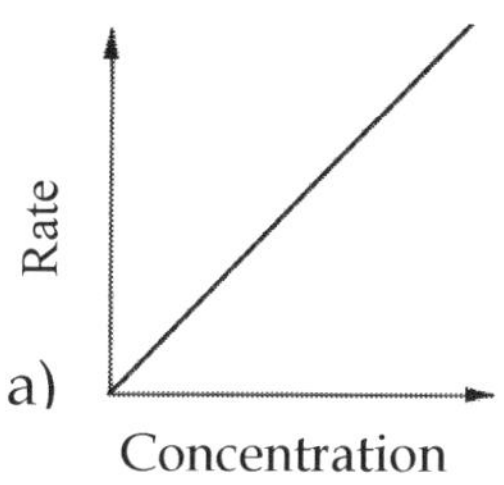

b)
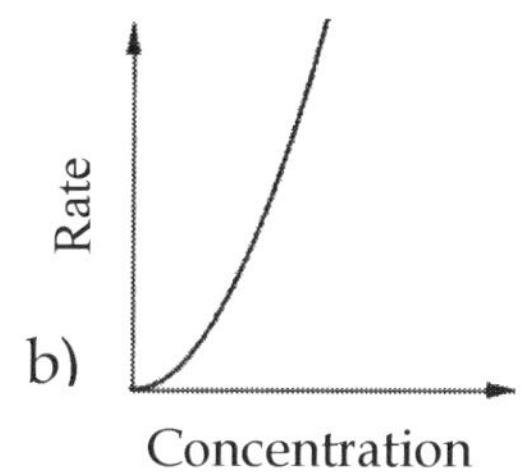

c)
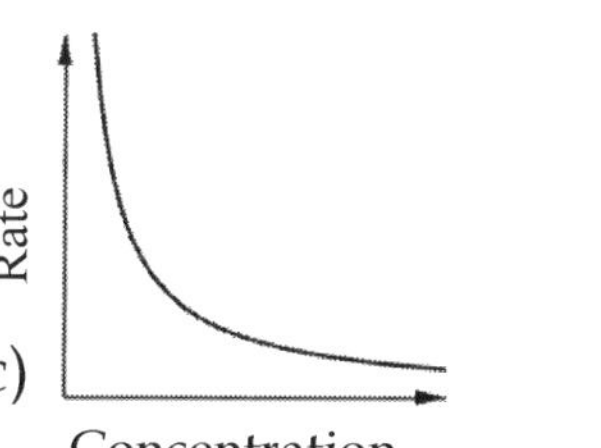

d)
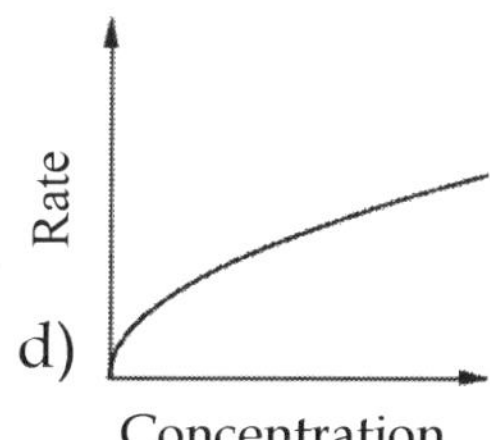

19. If the graph below shows the reaction rate versus the concentration of reactant A, what is the most likely order of reactant A?

Answer: (c)

The graph is an exponential function with exponent less than 1 and greater than zero.
Only c) is the possible choice.

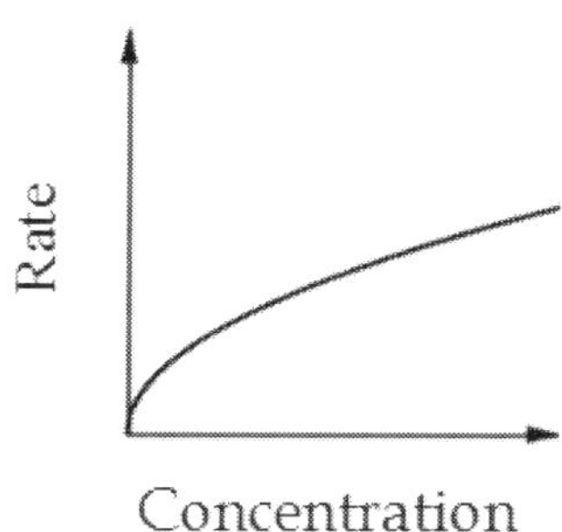

a) 1st order
b) 2nd order
c) $\frac{1}{2}$ order
d) 0th order

VIII. Powers and Roots

A. Exponent Operations

Concept Overviews

Raising a number to the nth power is the product of multiplying n copies of that number. The number being raised to a power is denoted as the **base.** The **power** is also called the **exponent**, and is expressed as a small number written on the top right of the base number.

Example: "y to the 4th power" may be written as y^4. The base number is y and the exponent is 4. This denotes 4 copies of y being multiplied together. $y^4 = y \times y \times y \times y$.

Multiplying and Dividing Numbers with Exponents

- **Same Base**: Keep the same base and add the exponents when multiplying. Keep the same base but subtract the exponents when dividing.

Examples:

$$x^4 \times x^3 = x^{4+3} = x \qquad x^4 \div x^3 = x^{4-3} = x^1$$

- "$x^3 \times x^2$" denotes $(x \times x \times x)$ being multiplied by $(x \times x)$. There are 5 copies of x being multiplied together, which means that $x^3 \times x^2 = x \times x \times x \times x \times x = x^5$.

- Same exponent but different base: Keep the same exponent but combine the bases.

Examples:

$$x^3 \times y^3 = (x \times y)^3 \qquad x^3 \div y^3 = \left(\frac{x}{y}\right)^3$$

- "$\frac{x^5}{x^2}$" is equal to 5 copies of x divided by 2 copies of x. This is equal to only 3 copies of x multiplied together, which is also x^3.

$$\frac{x^5}{x^2} = x^{5-2} = x^3$$

Raising One Power to Another (Raising an Exponent to Another Exponent): To raise an exponent to another exponent, multiply their exponents.

Example:

$$(x^4)^3 = x^{4\times3}$$

Basic Exponent Rules to Be Remembered

- $x^a x^b = x^{a+b}$
- $(x^a)^b = x^{ab}$
- $x^a y^a = (xy)^a$
- $\frac{x^a}{x^b} = x^{a-b}$
- $x^0 = \frac{x^a}{x^a} = x^{a-a} = 1$
- $x^{-a} = \frac{x^0}{x^a} = \frac{1}{x^a}$

Multiplying a Decimal Number by 10^n: If n is a positive integer, then this operation will move the decimal point n places to the right. If n is a negative integer, then this operation will move the decimal point $|n|$ places to the left.

Problem Solving Skills

Easy

1. Which of the following is equal to 0.00126691?
   a) 1.26691×10^{-3}
   b) 1.26691×10^{-2}
   c) 1.26691×10^{-1}
   d) 12.6691×10^{-2}

Answer: (a)

1.26691 multiplied by 10^{-3} will move its decimal point 3 places to the left.

$1.26691 \times 10^{-3} = 0.00126691$

2. If $n > 0$, what is the value of $4^n + 4^n + 4^n + 4^n$?
   a) $4^{(n+4)}$
   b) $4^{(n+1)}$
   c) $4^{(4n+1)}$
   d) $4^{(4n+3)}$

Answer: (b)

$4^n + 4^n + 4^n + 4^n = 4 \times 4^n = 4^{(n+1)}$

3. If $xyz \neq 0$, then $\frac{x^2y^4z^8}{x^6y^4z^2} = ?$
   a) xyz
   b) $\frac{z^3}{x^3}$
   c) $\frac{z^4}{x^3}$
   d) $\frac{x^4}{z^6}$

Answer: (d)

Apply exponent rules.

$\frac{x^2y^4z^6}{x^6y^4z^2} = \left(\frac{x^2}{x^6}\right)\left(\frac{y^4}{y^4}\right)\left(\frac{z^8}{z^2}\right) = \frac{z^6}{x^4}$

4. If $a^x \cdot a^4 = a^{16}$ and $(a^3)^y = a^{12}$, what is the value of $x + y$?
   a) 17
   b) 16
   c) 15
   d) 13

Answer: (b)

$a^x \cdot a^4 = a^{(x+4)} = a^{16}$

$(a^3)^y = a^{3y} = a^{12}$

$x = 12$

$y = 4$

$x + y = 16$

5. If x, y and z are different positive integers and $2^x \times 2^y \times 2^z = 64$, then $x + y + z$?
   a) 12
   b) 3
   c) 4
   d) 6

Answer: (d)

$2^x \times 2^y \times 2^z = 2^{(x+y+z)} = 64 = 2^6$

$x + y + z = 6$

6. If x and y are positive integers and $5^2x + 5^2y = 100$, what is the value of $x + y$?
   a) 1
   b) 2
   c) 4
   d) 8

Answer: (c)

$5^2x + 5^2y = 25(x + y) = 100$

$x + y = 4$

7. Positive integers x, y, and z satisfy the equations $x^{-\frac{1}{2}} = \frac{1}{2}$ and $y^z = 8$, $z > y$, what is the value of $x + y + z$?
   a) 5
   b) 7
   c) 9
   d) 11

Answer: (c)

$x^{-\frac{1}{2}} = \frac{1}{2}$, $x = (\frac{1}{2})^{-2} = 2^2 = 4$
$8 = 2^3 = y^z$
$y = 2$ and $z = 3$
$x + y + z = 2 + 3 + 4 = 9$

8. If x is a positive integer, then $(5 \times 10^{-x}) + (2 \times 10^{-x})$ must be equal to?
   a) $\frac{10}{10^x}$
   b) $\frac{1}{10^x}$
   c) $\frac{7}{10^{-x}}$
   d) $\frac{7}{10^x}$

Answer: (d)

$(5 \times 10^{-x}) + (2 \times 10^{-x}) = 7 \times 10^{-x}$
$7 \times 10^{-x} = \frac{7}{10^x}$

9. If m is a positive number, which of the following is equal to $m^3 \times m^{-3}$?
   a) 0
   b) 1
   c) m^{-6}
   d) m

Answer: (b)

Except the number 0, any numbers raised to the power of 0 is equal to 1.
$m^3 \times m^{-3} = m^0 = 1$

Medium

10. If $8 = a^y$, then $8a^2 =$?
   a) a^{y+1}
   b) a^{y+2}
   c) $8a^y$
   d) a^{8y}

Answer: (b)

$8a^2 = a^y \times a^2 = a^{y+2}$

11. If $7 = m^x$, then $7m^2$=?
   a) m^{2x}
   b) m^{7x}
   c) m^{x+2}
   d) m^{x+7}

Answer: (c)

$7m = m^x \times m^2 = m^{(x+2)}$

12. If $81 = a^x$, where a and x are both positive integers and $x > a$, what is the value of x^a?
   a) 16
   b) 27
   c) 64
   d) 81

Answer: (c)

$a = 3$ and $x = 4$

$4^3 = 64$

13. If $3^{7x+6} = 27^{3x}$, what is the value of x? ⦸
   a) 1
   b) 2
   c) 3
   d) 4

Answer: (c)

When solving the equation, convert both sides to the same base.

$3^{7x+6} = 27^{3x} = [(3)^3]^{3x} = 3^{9x}$

$7x + 6 = 9x \rightarrow x = 3$

14. If $2^{x+1} = 8$, then what is the value of x? ⦸
   a) 0
   b) 1
   c) 2
   d) 3

Answer: (c)

Change both sides of equation to the same base 2.

$2^{(x+1)} = 2^3$

$x + 1 = 3 \rightarrow x = 2$

15. $(-2x^2y^6)^3$ =? ⦸
   a) $4x^5y^9$
   b) $-8x^6y^{18}$
   c) $4x^6y^{18}$
   d) $8x^6y^{18}$

Answer: (b)

Raise power for each term inside the parentheses and apply the $(x^a)^b = x^{ab}$ rule.

$(-2x^2y^6)^3 = (-2)^3 (x^2)^3 (y6)^3 = -8x^6 y^{18}$

16. If $x > 0$, then $(9^x)(27^x)$ =? ⦸
   a) 3^{9x}
   b) 3^{8x}
   c) 3^{6x}
   d) 3^{5x}

Answer: (d)

Convert to the same base before performing multiplication.

$(9^x)(27^x) = (3^2)^x(3^3)^x$

$= 3^{2x} \times 3^{3x} = 3^{5x}$

17. If $3^4 = x$, which of the following expressions is equal to 3^{10}? ⦸
   a) $3x^2$
   b) $9x^2$
   c) $27x^2$
   d) x

Answer: (b)

$3^{10} = 3^2 \times (3^4)^2 = 9x^2$

18. $10^{xy} = 1{,}000$, where x and y are positive integers and $x > y$, what is one possible value of x?

a) 3
b) 4
c) 5
d) 7

Answer: (a)

Change both sides of equation to the same base 10.
$10^{xy} = 10^3 \rightarrow xy = 3$
Since both x and y are positive integers, both x and y can only be equal to 1 or 3.
$x > y$
$x = 3$

19. If x is a positive integer and $3^{2x} + 3^{(2x+1)} = y$, what is $3^{(2x+2)}$ in terms of y?

a) $\frac{y-1}{3}$
b) $4y$
c) $9y$
d) $\frac{9}{4}y$

Answer: (d)

$3^{2x} + 3^{(2x+1)} = 4 \times 3^{2x}$
$4 \times 3^{2x} = y$
$3^{2x} = \frac{y}{4}$
$3^{(2x+2)} = 9 \times 3^{2x} = 9 \times \frac{y}{4} = \frac{9y}{4}$

20. If x and y are positive integers and $9(3^x) = 3^y$, what is x in terms of y?

a) $y - 2$
b) y^2
c) $3y$
d) $y - 1$

Answer: (a)

Given that $9(3^x) = 3^y$, *then*
$3^2 \times 3^x = 3^y$.
$3^{2+x} = 3^y$
$2 + x = y$
$x = y - 2$

21. If $y = 2^{\frac{1}{4}}$, which of the following expressions is equal to 2^2?

a) 8
b) y^8
c) $8y^4$
d) $8y^8$

Answer: (b)

$2^2 = (2^{\frac{1}{4}})^8 = y^8$

22. $\frac{2}{(x+y)^{-\frac{2}{3}}} = (x+y)^{-\frac{1}{3}}$, which of the following must be true?

a) $x = 0$
b) $\sqrt{x+y} = 2$
c) $x + y = \frac{1}{2}$
d) $x + y = 1$

Answer: (c)

$\frac{2}{(x+y)^{-\frac{2}{3}}} = (x+y)^{-\frac{1}{3}}$

$2 = (x+y)^{-\frac{2}{3}}(x+y)^{-\frac{1}{3}}$
$= (x+y)^{-1}$
$x + y = \frac{1}{2}$

Questions 23 – 24 refer to the following information:

Compound interest is the interest added to the principal of a deposit so that the interest earned also earns interest continuously. A formula for calculating annual compound interest is as follows:

$$A = P\left(1 + \frac{r}{100}\right)^t$$

A is the amount of money, in dollars, generated after t years by a principal amount P in a bank account that pays an annual interest rate of r%, compounded annually.

23. If Bill deposits $1,000 in his bank account today with an annual interest rate of 3% compounded annually, what will be the amount of money in his bank account after 5 years? (Round your answer to the nearest dollar and ignore the dollar sign when gridding your response.)

Answer: 1159

$A = 1{,}000(1 + 0.03)^5 = \$1{,}159$

24. What is the fewest whole number of years that he will have $2000 or more in the bank?

Answer: 24

$1{,}000(1 + 0.03)^t \geq 2{,}000$

$1.03^t \geq 2$

With calculator, the first whole number value of t that satisfies above inequality is 24. Therefore, the fewest number of years required for him to accrue $2,000 is 24.

Hard

25. a, b, x, and y are positive numbers. If $x^{-\frac{2}{3}} = a^{-4}$ and $y^{\frac{2}{3}} = b^4$, what is $xy^{-\frac{1}{3}}$ in terms of a and b?
    a) ab
    b) $a^{-1}b^{-1}$
    c) a^2b^2
    d) $a^{-2}b^{-2}$

Answer: (d)

$x^{-\frac{2}{3}} = a^{-4}$

$x = (a^{-4})^{-\frac{3}{2}} = a^6$

$y^{\frac{2}{3}} = b^4$

$y = (b^4)^{\frac{3}{2}} = b^6$

$xy^{-\frac{1}{3}} = (a^6b^6)^{-\frac{1}{3}} = a^{-2}b^{-2}$

B. Roots and Radical Operations

Concept Overviews

Taking the Square Root

Taking the **square root** of a number is the inverse operation of squaring the number. The square root of a number is a value that can be multiplied by itself to give the original number.

Examples:

$$\sqrt{y} \times \sqrt{y} = y \quad \text{and} \quad \sqrt{4} \times \sqrt{4} = 4$$

A square root of a variable represents the variable's exponent being divided by 2.

Examples:

$$\sqrt{x} = x^{\frac{1}{2}} \quad \text{and} \quad \sqrt{x^4} = x^{\frac{4}{2}} = x^2$$

Taking n^{th} Root of a Number

Taking n^{th} **"root" (or "radical")** of a number is the inverse operation of taking the nth power of the number. The nth root of a number is a value that can be multiplied n copies of that value to give the original number.

Examples:

$$\sqrt[3]{8} = 2 \text{ while } 2^3 = 8 \quad \text{and} \quad 3^4 = 81 \text{ while } \sqrt[4]{81} = 3$$

In general, $\sqrt[n]{x} = x^{\frac{1}{n}}$ and $\sqrt[n]{x^m} = x^{\frac{m}{n}}$.

Examples:

$$\sqrt[3]{8} = 8^{\frac{1}{3}} = \sqrt[3]{2^3} = 2^{\frac{3}{3}} = 2 \quad \text{and} \quad \sqrt[3]{5^2} = 5^{\frac{2}{3}}$$

Multiplying and Dividing Radicals

When multiplying or dividing two variables **with the same radical**, multiply or divide two variables and keep the original radical.

Examples:

$$\sqrt{x} \times \sqrt{y} = \sqrt{xy} \quad \text{and} \quad \frac{\sqrt{x}}{\sqrt{y}} = \sqrt{\frac{x}{y}}$$

When multiplying or dividing two radicals **with same variable**, add or subtract their exponents.

Examples:

$$\sqrt{x} \times \sqrt[3]{x} = x^{\frac{1}{2}} \times x^{\frac{1}{3}} = x^{\frac{1}{2}+\frac{1}{3}} = x^{\frac{5}{6}}$$

$$\frac{\sqrt{x}}{\sqrt[3]{x}} = \frac{x^{\frac{1}{2}}}{x^{\frac{1}{3}}} = x^{\frac{1}{2}-\frac{1}{3}} = x^{\frac{1}{6}} = \sqrt[6]{x}$$

Only numbers with the same radicals can be combined through multiplication or division. The product of two radicals is equal to the radical of the product. The quotient of two radicals is equal to the radical of the quotient.

Examples:

$$\sqrt{2} \times \sqrt{6} = \sqrt{2 \times 6} = \sqrt{12} \qquad \frac{\sqrt{6}}{\sqrt{2}} = \sqrt{\frac{6}{2}} = \sqrt{3}$$

Adding and Subtracting Radicals
Adding and Subtracting Radicals only apply when both the root and the base are the same (when the terms are like terms).

Example:

$$2\sqrt{3} + 3\sqrt{3} = 5\sqrt{3}$$

Consider $\sqrt{3}$ as a unit. 2 units plus 3 units of $\sqrt{3}$ is equal to 5 units of $\sqrt{3}$. Therefore simply add the coefficients of like terms.

Simplify a Square Root
To simplify a square root, factor out all perfect squares and place its square root outside.

Example:

$$\sqrt{18} = \sqrt{3^2 \times 2} = 3\sqrt{2}$$

Similar steps apply to different radicals. To simplify a cube root, factor out cubes (factors with an exponent of 3) and place its cube root (base) outside.

Example:

$$\sqrt[3]{54} = \sqrt[3]{3^3 \times 2} = 3\sqrt[3]{2}$$

Rationalize a Denominator with a Square Root: multiply the top and bottom of the fraction by the square root in the denominator to get a rational denominator.

Example:

$$\frac{\sqrt{12}}{\sqrt{2}} = \frac{\sqrt{12} \times \sqrt{2}}{\sqrt{2} \times \sqrt{2}} = \frac{\sqrt{24}}{2} = \frac{\sqrt{2^2 \times 6}}{2} = \frac{2\sqrt{6}}{2} = \sqrt{6}$$

Problem Solving Skills

Easy

1. If $x^{\frac{1}{4}} = \sqrt{3}$, then what is the value of x^2?
   a) 81
   b) 72
   c) 36
   d) 27

Answer: (a)

$(x^{\frac{1}{4}})^8 = x^2$
$(\sqrt{3})^8 = 81$

2. If $\sqrt{x} = 2$ then $x + 4 =$?
   a) 2
   b) 4
   c) 8
   d) 80

Answer: (c)

Square both sides of the radical equation.
$\sqrt{x} = 2$
$(\sqrt{x})^2 = 2^2$
$x = 4$
$x + 4 = 8$

3. If $x^{\frac{1}{3}} = 2$, what is the value of x?
   a) 2
   b) 4
   c) 6
   d) 8

Answer: (d)

$x^{\frac{1}{3}} = 2$
$x = 2^3 = 8$

Medium

4. If $x > 0$ and $x^y x^{\frac{1}{2}} = x^{\frac{3}{8}}$, what is the value of y?
   a) $\frac{1}{2}$
   b) $\frac{1}{3}$
   c) $\frac{1}{4}$
   d) $-\frac{1}{8}$

Answer: (d)

$x^y x^{\frac{1}{2}} = x^{(y+\frac{1}{2})} = x^{\frac{3}{8}}$

$y + \frac{1}{2} = \frac{3}{8}$
$y = -\frac{1}{8}$

5. If $x^{\frac{3}{2}} = \frac{1}{27}$, then what does x equal?
   a) −9
   b) −3
   c) $\frac{1}{9}$
   d) $-\frac{1}{9}$

Answer: (c)

Tips:
$x^{\frac{3}{2}} = \frac{1}{27}$
$x = (\frac{1}{27})^{\frac{2}{3}}$
$\frac{1}{27} = 3^{-3}$
$x = (3^{-3})^{\frac{2}{3}} = 3^{-2} = \frac{1}{9}$

6. If $12\sqrt{12} = x\sqrt{y}$ where x and y are positive integers and $x > y$, which of the following could be the value of xy?
   a) 32
   b) 48
   c) 72
   d) 102

Answer: (c)

$12\sqrt{12} = 12 \times 2\sqrt{3} = 24\sqrt{3}$
$x = 24$ and $y = 3$
$xy = 24 \times 3 = 72$

7. If $\sqrt{3x} = \sqrt{18}$ what is the value of x?
   a) 2
   b) 3
   c) 4
   d) 6

Answer: (d)

$\sqrt{18} = \sqrt{3 \times 6}$

$x = 6$

8. If x is a positive integer, what is the least value of x for which $\sqrt{\frac{7x}{3}}$ is an integer?
   a) 3
   b) 7
   c) 9
   d) 21

Answer: (d)

For $\sqrt{\frac{7x}{3}}$ being an integer, $7x$ must be a product of 3 and a perfect square number. The least value of $7x$ is 3×7^2 therefore $x = 3 \times 7 = 21$. Another way to solve this question is trial and error. Plug in the values from the choices and find the one that gives $x = 21$.

9. If x and y are both positive real numbers and if $x^4 = y$, what is x in term of y?
   a) y^4
   b) y
   c) $y^{\frac{1}{4}}$
   d) $y^{\frac{1}{2}}$

Answer: (c)

Take 4th root of both sides.

$x = y^{\frac{1}{4}}$

10. If x and y are positive integers and $(x^{1/6}y^{1/6})^3 = 8$, what is the value of xy?
    a) 8
    b) 32
    c) 64
    d) 128

Answer: (c)

$(x^{1/6}y^{1/6})^3 = (xy)^{\frac{1}{2}}$

$(xy)^{\frac{1}{2}} = 8$
$xy = 64$

Hard

11. If $x^2 > 9$, which of the following must be true?
    a) $x > 3$
    b) $x < 3$
    c) $x < -3$
    d) $x > 3$ or $x < -3$

Answer: (d)

$x^2 > 9$
$x^2 - 9 > 0$
$(x-3)(x+3) > 0$
The terms $(x-3)$ and $(x+3)$ must be both positive or both negative for the term $(x-3)(x+3)$ to be greater than 0.
$x > 3$ or $x < -3$

12. If $x^{\frac{y}{2}} = 81$, where x and y are positive integers, $x < 81$, and $x > y$, what is the value of $x + y$?
    a) 9
    b) 13
    c) 15
    d) 16

Answer: (b)

$x^{\frac{y}{2}} = 81 = 3^4 = 9^2$

$x > y$
$x^{\frac{y}{2}} = 9^2$
$x = 9$ *and* $y = 4$
$x + y = 13$

13. If $2 \times 2^x + 2^x + 2^x = 2^5$, what is the value of x?
    a) 0
    b) 1
    c) 2
    d) 3

Answer: (d)

$2 \times 2^x = 2^x + 2^x$

$2^x + 2^x + 2^x + 2^x$
$= 4 \times 2^x = 2^5$
$2^{x+2} = 2^5$
$x = 3$

14. If $9^y = \frac{27^{y-1}}{27}$, what is y =?
    a) 6
    b) 5
    c) 3
    d) 1

Answer: (a)

Change both sides of equation to the same base.

$9^y = 3^{2y}$
$27^{(y-2)} = 3^{3(y-2)}$
$2y = 3y - 6$
$y = 6$

Chapter 4 Additional Topics in Math

I. Lines and Angles

A. Angle Relationships

Concept Overview

Lines, Rays, and Line Segments

- A **line** is a straight path that travels forever in both directions.

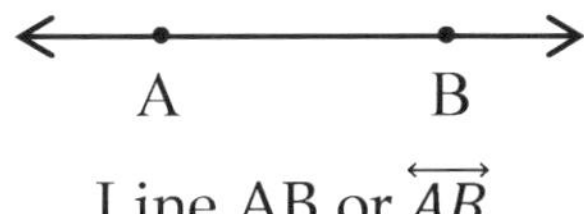

Line AB or $\overleftrightarrow{AB}$

- A **ray** is a straight path that has one endpoint and travels forever in the other direction. $\overrightarrow{AB}$ is not equal to $\overrightarrow{BA}$.

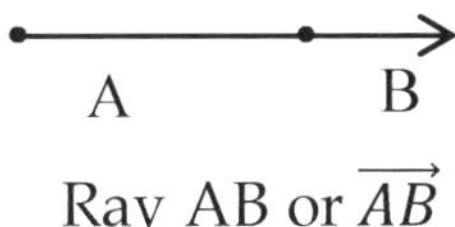

Ray AB or $\overrightarrow{AB}$

- A **line segment** is a segment of a line with two endpoints.

A B

Segment AB or $\overline{AB}$

Angles

An **angle** is formed when two rays extend from the same point, called a vertex.

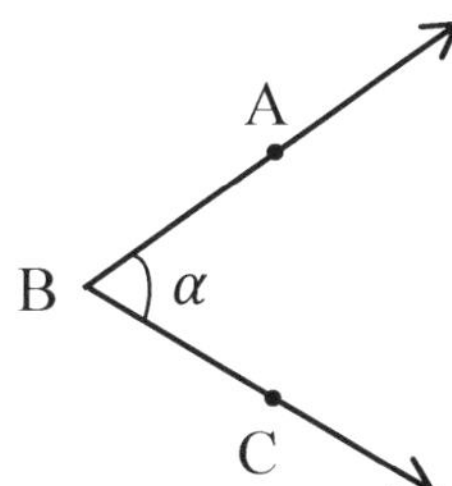

Angle ∠ABC with vertex B

There are three ways of naming this angle.

- By the vertex if there are no other angles at this vertex: ∠B
- By three points that define the angle: $\angle ABC$ or $\angle CBA$ (The vertex B is always in the middle.)
- By a symbol representing the angle itself: $\angle\alpha$

If more than one angle share the same vertex, only the first two methods can be used for naming the angles. For the graph shown below, ∠1 and ∠2 are **adjacent angles**. ∠1 can be denoted as ∠BAD or ∠DAB while ∠2 can be denoted as ∠CAD or ∠DAC.

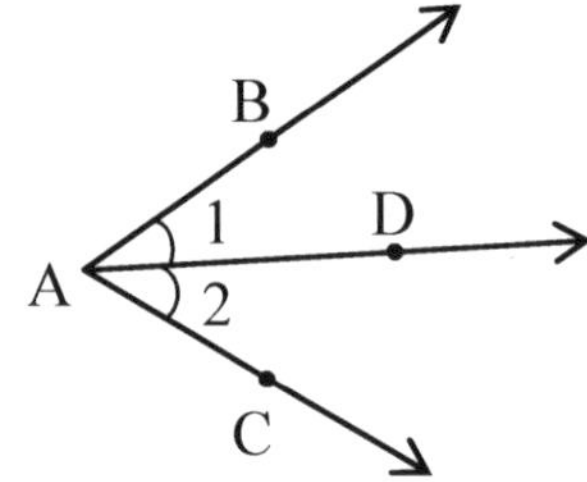

A **degree** is a unit measure of an angle. A full circle is 360 degrees which is denoted as 360°.
- $m\angle ABC$ denotes the degree of the angle ∠ABC.

Angles can be classified according to the measure of their degree.
- An **acute angle** is an angle that has degree less than 90°.
- A **right angle** is an angle that has degree equal to 90°.
- An **obtuse angle** is an angle that has degree greater than 90° and less than 180°.
- A **straight line** can be said to be an angle which is equal to 180°.

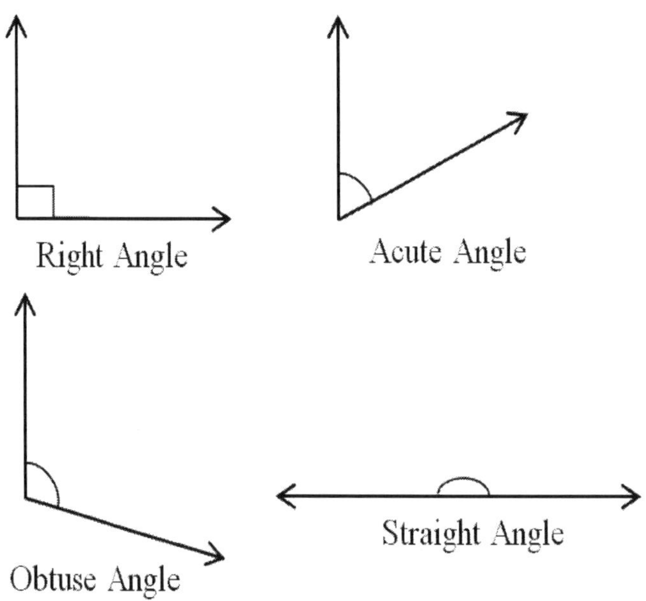

Angles classified by their degree measure

Lines and Angles
If two angles placed adjacently make a straight angle, these two angles are **supplementary angles**. The sum of two supplementary angles is 180°.

Example: In the figures below, $m\angle 1 + m\angle 2 = 180^o$ and $m\angle A + m\angle B = 180^o$.

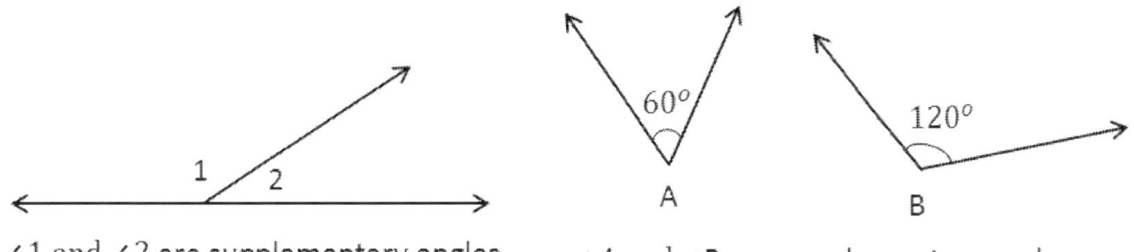

∠1 and ∠2 are supplementary angles. ∠A and ∠B are supplementary angles.

If two angles placed adjacently make a right angle, these two angles are **complementary angles**. The sum of two complementary angles is 90°.

Examples: In the figures below, $m\angle 1 + m\angle 2 = 90°$ and $m\angle A + m\angle B = 90°$.

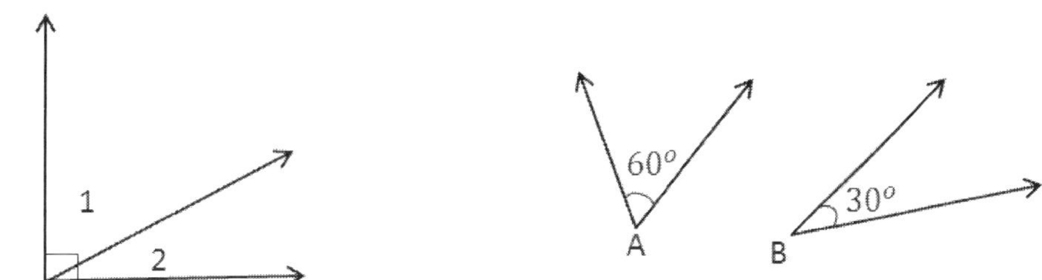

∠1 and ∠2 are complimentary angles. ∠A and ∠B are complimentary angles.

If two angles have the same measure, they are **congruent**.

Vertical Angles Are Congruent

In the figure below, ∠1 and ∠3 are vertical angles, and ∠2 and ∠4 are vertical angles. Thus, $m\angle 1 = m\angle 3$ and $m\angle 2 = m\angle 4$.

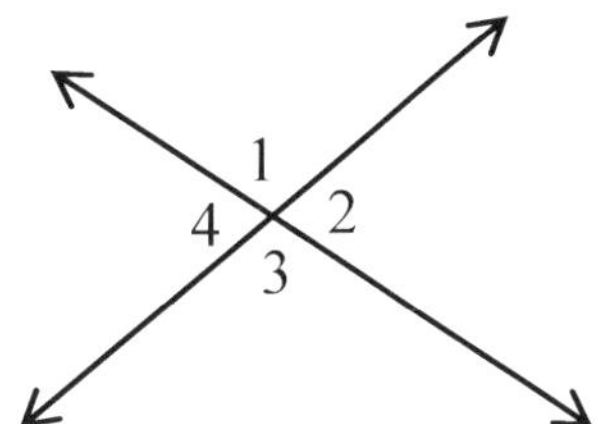

Problem Solving Skills

Easy

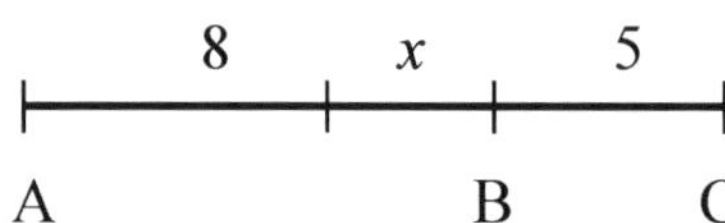

1. In the diagram above, line segment $\overline{AC}$ has a length of 17. What is the length of the line segment between the midpoint of segment $\overline{AB}$ and endpoint C?
   a) 11
   b) 9
   c) 7
   d) 5

Answer: (a)

$8 + x + 5 = 17$
$x = 4$
Half of the length of $\overline{AB}$ *is 6.*
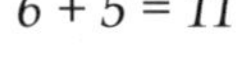
$6 + 5 = 11$

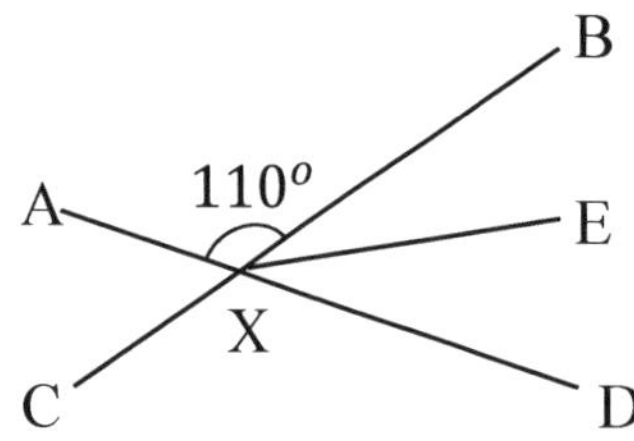

Note: Figure not drawn to scale.

2. Two line segments $\overline{AD}$ and $\overline{BC}$ intersect at point X as shown in the figure above. If $\overline{XE}$ bisects angle ∠BXD, what is $m\angle EXD$?
   a) 30
   b) 35
   c) 55
   d) 60

Answer: (b)

$m\angle BXD = 180 - 110 = 70^o$

$m\angle EXD = \frac{1}{2} \times m\angle BXD = 35^o$

3. A line contains Points A, B, and C from left to the right. If the length of line segment BC is twice the length of AB, and the length of line segment AC is 60, what is the length of line segment BC?
   a) 10
   b) 20
   c) 30
   d) 40

Answer: (d)

$\overline{BC}$ *is* $\frac{2}{3}$ *of the entire line.*

$2 : 3 = \overline{BC} : \overline{AC} = \overline{BC} : 60$
$\overline{BC} = 40$

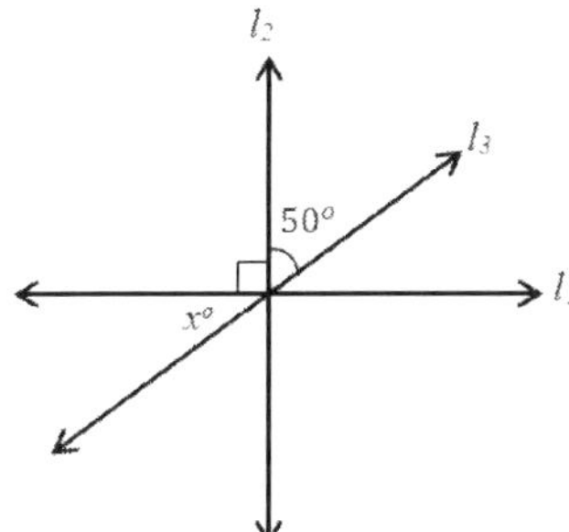

4. In the figure above, l_1 and l_2 are perpendicular to each other and l_3 intersects l_1 and l_2. What is the value of degree x?
   a) 50
   b) 60
   c) 40
   d) 30

Answer: (c)

$x = 180^o - 90^o - 50^o = 40^o$

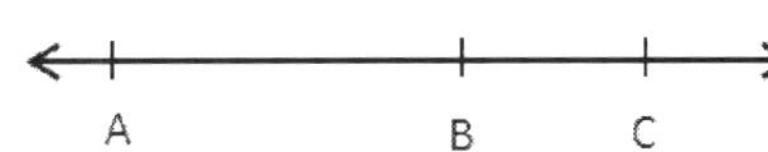

5. According to figure above, the intersection of $\overrightarrow{AB}$ and $\overleftarrow{CB}$ is
   a) $\overline{BC}$
   b) $\overline{BA}$
   c) $\overline{AC}$
   d) $\overrightarrow{AC}$

Answer: (c)

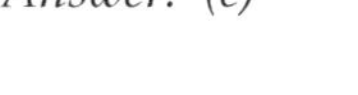

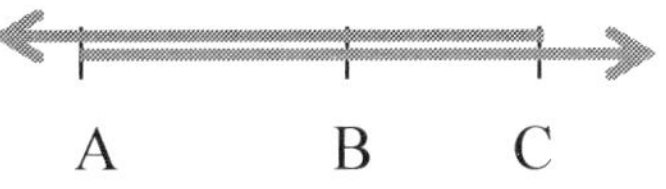

The intersection of the two rays is line segment $\overline{AC}$.

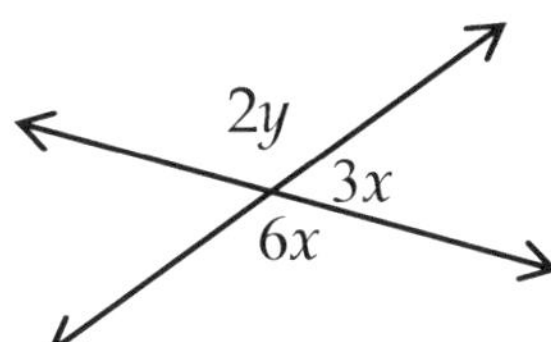

6. In the figure above, what is the value of $x + y$?
   a) 60
   b) 75
   c) 80
   d) 100

Answer: (c)

$3x + 6x = 180^\circ$ and $2y = 6x$
$9x = 180$
$x = 20^\circ$
$2y = 6x = 6 \times 20 = 120$
$y = 60^\circ$
$x + y = 60 + 20 = 80^\circ$

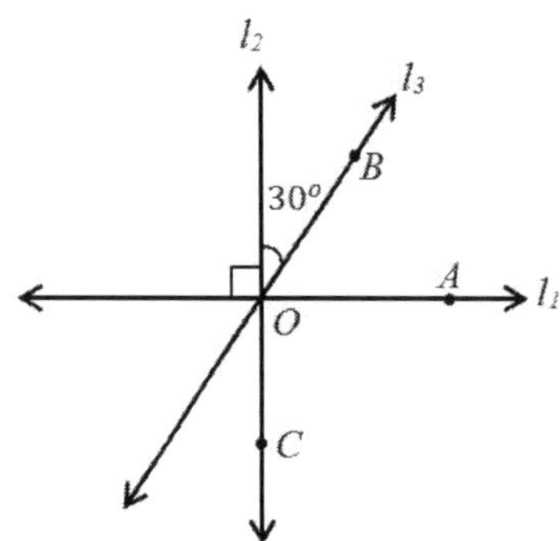

7. In the figure above, lines l_1, l_2 and l_3 intersect at point O and l_1 is perpendicular to l_2. What is the value of $m\angle BOC$?
   a) 75
   b) 90
   c) 120
   d) 150

Answer: (d)

$m\angle BOC = 180 - 30 = 150°$

8. A bicycle wheel makes a full turn every 2 seconds. How many degrees does a point on this wheel turn in 10 seconds?
   a) 36°
   b) 180°
   c) 360°
   d) 1800°

Answer: (d)

The wheel turns 5 times in 10 seconds.

$5 \times 360° = 1800°$

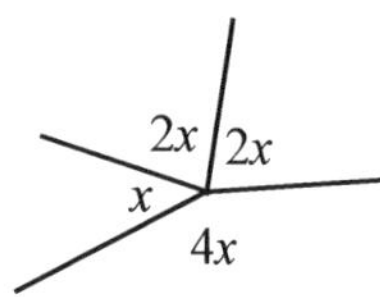

9. In the figure above, four line segments intercept at a point. How many degrees is x?

Answer: 40

$360° = x + 4x + 2x + 2x$
$360° = 9x$
$x = 40°$

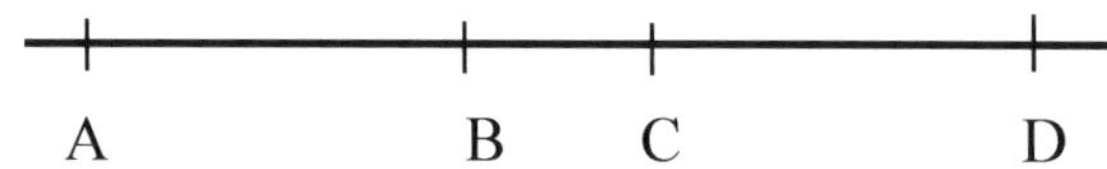

10. In the figure above, AC = 9, AB = 2BC, and AB = CD. What does AD equal?
   a) 12
   b) 14
   c) 15
   d) 16

Answer: (c)

The length of $\overline{AC}$ plus $\overline{CD}$ is equal to the length of $\overline{AD}$.
$\overline{AB} = \frac{2}{3} \times 9 = 6$
$\overline{CD} = 6$
$AD = AC + CD = 9 + 6 = 15$

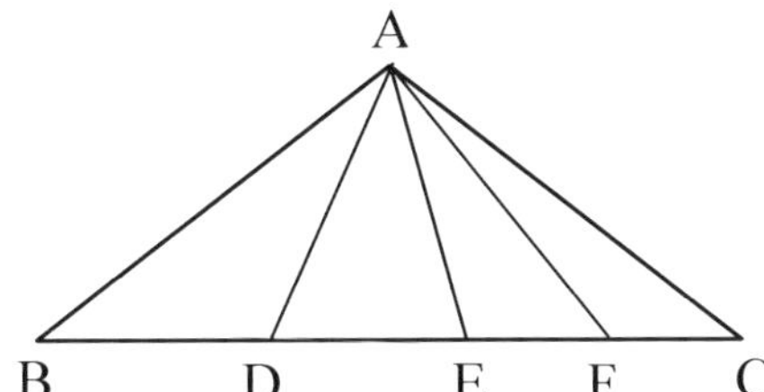

11. In the figure above, if segment AD bisects $\angle BAE$, segment AF bisects $\angle EAC$, and $m\angle BAC = 106^\circ$, what is the value of $m\angle DAF$ in degrees?
    a) 30°
    b) 40°
    c) 45°
    d) 53°

Answer: (d)

Since segment AD and segment AF bisects $\angle BAE$ and $\angle EAC$ respectively, $\angle DAF$ will be half of $\angle BAC$

$\angle DAF = \frac{106^\circ}{2} = 53^\circ$

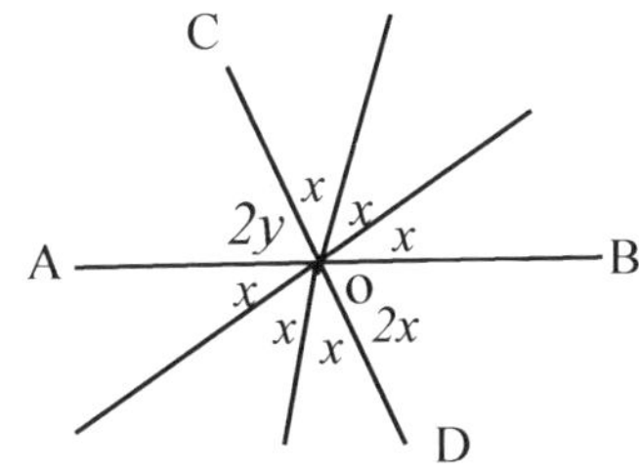

Note: Figure not drawn to scale.

12. In the figure above, segments AB and CD intercept at point O, what is the value of y?
    a) 45°
    b) 40°
    c) 36°
    d) 30°

Answer: (c)

$5x = 180^o$ *and* $2y + 3x = 180^o$

$x = 36^o$

$y = 36^o$

Medium

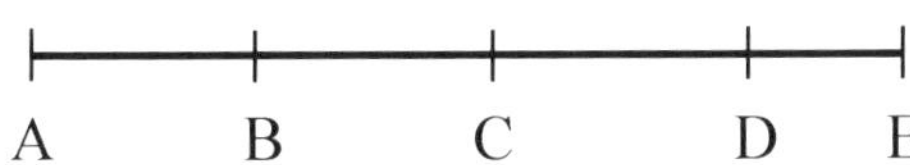

13. In the figure above, C is the midpoint of AE, B is the midpoint of AC, and CD = 2DE. If DE =3, what is the length of AB?

Answer: 4.5

If DE = 3, then CD = 6.

$AC = DE + CD = 3 + 6 = 9$

$AB = \frac{1}{2} \times AC = 4.5$

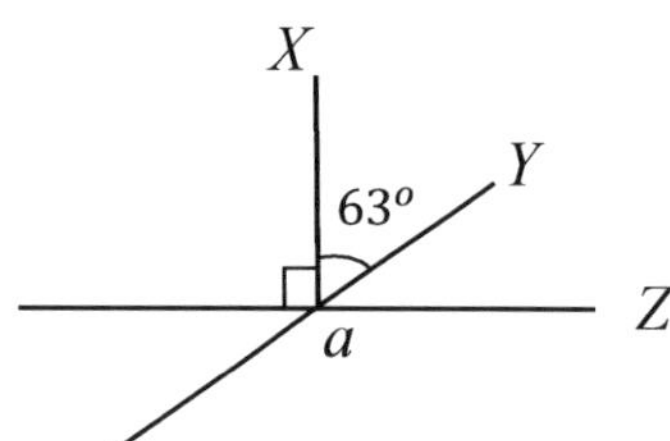

14. What is the value of a in the figure above?

Answer: 153

$a + (90 - 63)° = 180°$
$a = 153°$

15. Points A, B, C, D, E lie on a line from left to right. The length of AC is 4, the length of BE is 6 and the length of BC is 3. What is the length of AE?
    a) 10
    b) 9
    c) 8
    d) 7

Answer: (d)

$AE = AC + BE - BC$
$4 + 6 - 3 = 7$

16. Five points A, B, C, D, and E, lie on a line. Point B is the midpoint of AC and point D is the midpoint of BC. If AC is 12 and DE is 2, what is the sum of the possible lengths of segment AE?

Answer: 18

Point E could be on either the right or the left side of point D with a distance of 2 away from D.
The distance from points A to D is $\frac{12}{2} + \frac{6}{2} = 6 + 3 = 9$.
Thus, $AE = 9 \pm 2$. *AE can be 7 or 11.*
$7 + 11 = 18$

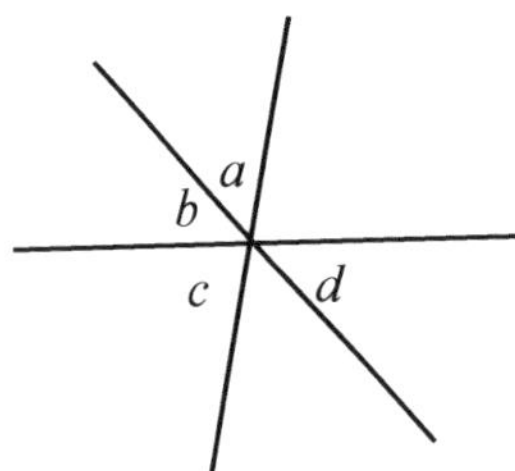

17. In the figure above, three line segments intersect at one point here $a° = d°$ and $c° = 2a°$. What is the value of $b°$?
    a) 30°
    b) 40°
    c) 45°
    d) 50°

Answer: (c)

$a° + b° + c° = 180°$
$a = d = b$, and $c = 2a$
$b° + b° + 2b° = 180°$
$b° = 45°$

B. Parallel Lines and Their Transversals

Concept Overviews

Lines

- Only one distinct line can pass through any two distinct points.
- Two different lines can intersect at most one point.
- If two lines intersect at right angles, they are **perpendicular**.

Two lines on the same plane that never intercept each other are **parallel** lines. If two distinct lines on the same plane are both perpendicular to another line, the two lines must be parallel.

Example: In the following graph, both l_1 and l_2 are perpendicular to l_3. Therefore l_1 is parallel to l_2 (otherwise written as $l_1 \parallel l_2$).

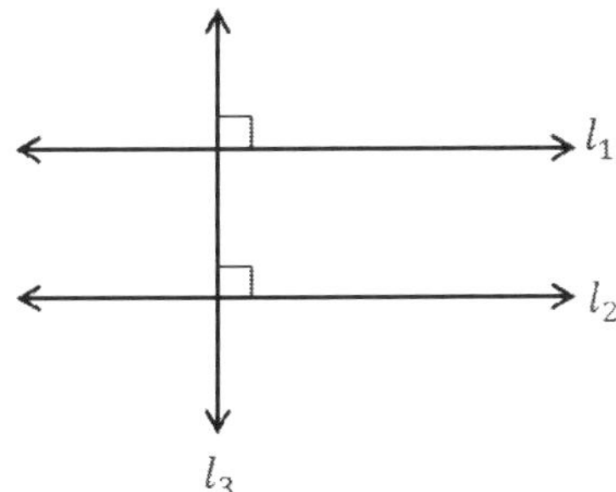

- If two distinct lines on the same plane are parallel to another line, the two lines must be parallel as well.

  Example: In the following graph, if lines l_1 and l_2 are both parallel to line l_3, then l_1 is parallel to l_2.

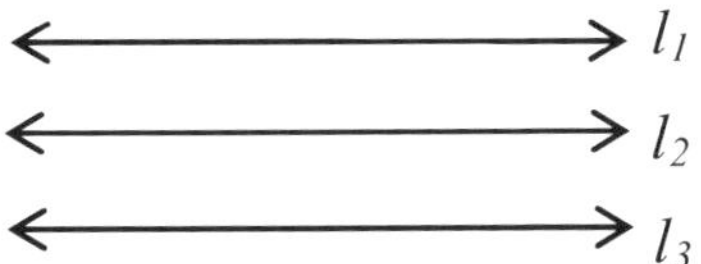

- If a line is perpendicular to a second line, it has to be perpendicular to all lines parallel to the second line as well.

  Example: In the following graph, if $l_1 \parallel l_2$ and l_3 is perpendicular to l_1, then l_3 is also perpendicular to l_2.

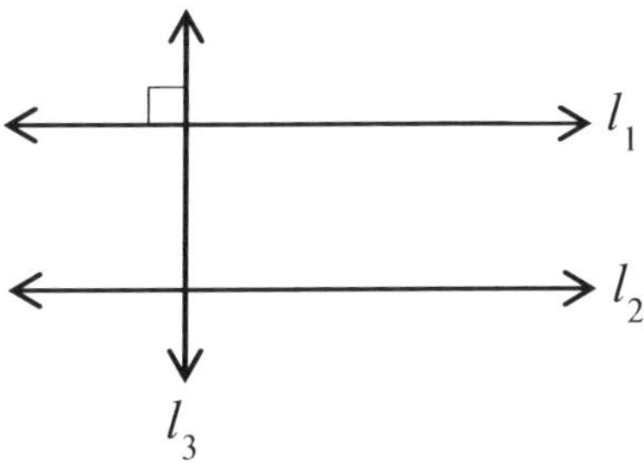

If lines l and m are parallel and line n crosses both lines, line n is a **transversal** of lines l and m. Then the following holds:

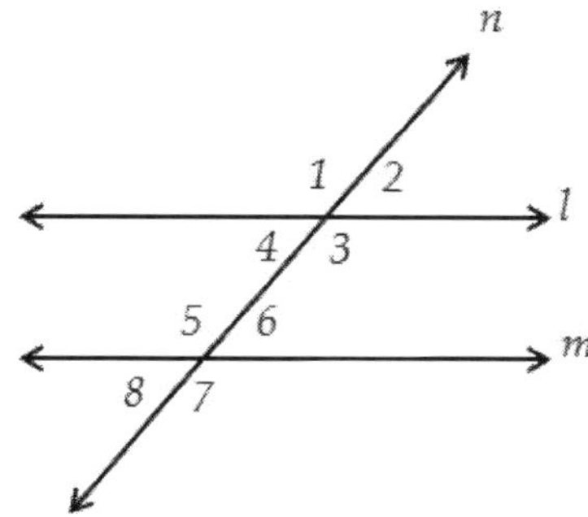

- **Corresponding angles** are congruent: pairs of corresponding angles include $\angle 1$ and $\angle 5$, $\angle 2$ and $\angle 6$, $\angle 4$ and $\angle 8$, and $\angle 3$ and $\angle 7$.
- **Alternate interior angles** are congruent: pairs of alternate interior angles include $\angle 3$ and $\angle 5$, and $\angle 4$ and $\angle 6$.
- **Consecutive interior angles** are supplementary: pairs of consecutive interior angles include $\angle 3$ and $\angle 6$, and $\angle 4$ and $\angle 5$.
- **Alternate exterior angles** are congruent: pairs of alternate exterior angles include $\angle 1$ and $\angle 7$, and $\angle 2$ and $\angle 8$.
- Pairs of **vertical angles** are always congruent, such as $\angle 1$ and $\angle 3$, and $\angle 6$ and $\angle 8$.

Example: From the graph below, if l_1 is parallel to l_2 and $x = 50$, what are the values of a, b, c, and d?

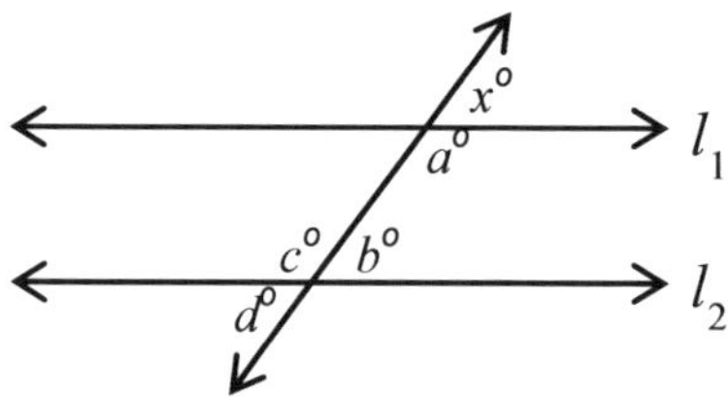

Answer: $b = 50$ (Corresponding angles $\boldsymbol{x}$ and $\boldsymbol{b}$ are congruent.)
$d = 50$ (Alternate exterior angles $\boldsymbol{d}$ and $\boldsymbol{x}$ are congruent.)
$a = 130$ (Consecutive interior angles $\boldsymbol{a}$ and $\boldsymbol{b}$ are supplementary.)
$c = 130$ (Alternate interior angles $\boldsymbol{a}$ and $\boldsymbol{c}$ are congruent.)

Problem Solving Skills

Easy

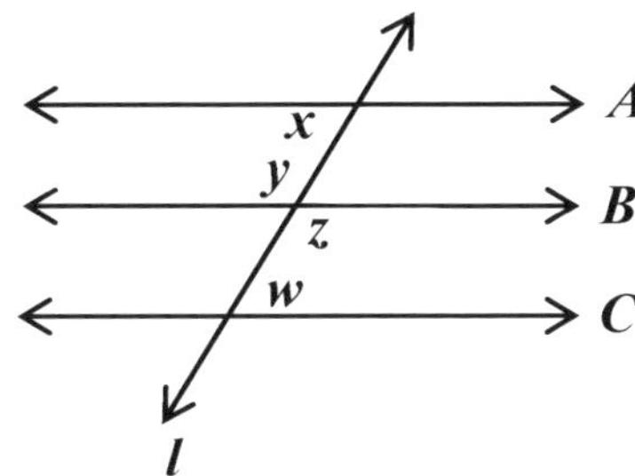

1. In the figure above, lines *A*, *B*, and *C* are parallel to one another. If $x = 65^\circ$, what is the value of *w*, in degrees?

Answer: 65

Alternate interior angles are congruent.
$m\angle x = m\angle w = 65^\circ$

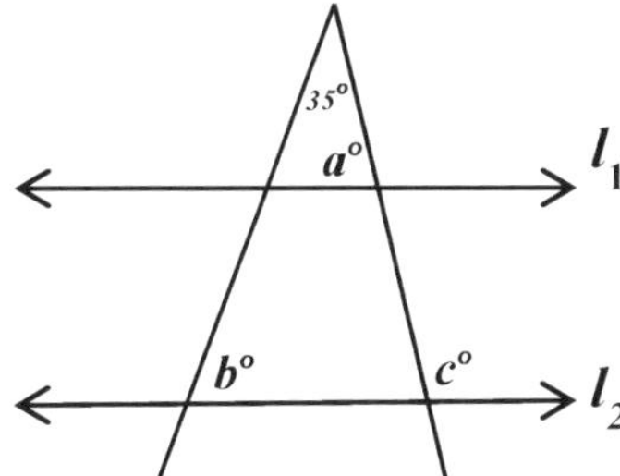

2. In the figure above, if $l_1 \parallel l_2$ and c = 110, what is the value of *b* in degrees?
   a) 70
   b) 75
   c) 80
   d) 85

Answer: (b)

Corresponding angles are congruent.
$a = 180^\circ - c = 70^\circ$
$a + b + 35^\circ = 180^\circ$
$b = 75^\circ$

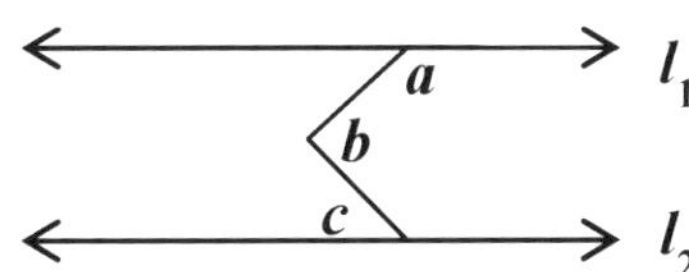

3. In the figure above, $l_1 \parallel l_2$, $a = 130^\circ$, and c = 40°. What is the value of b?
   a) 50°
   b) 60°
   c) 70°
   d) 90°

Answer: (d)

Draw an auxiliary line extending to l_2:

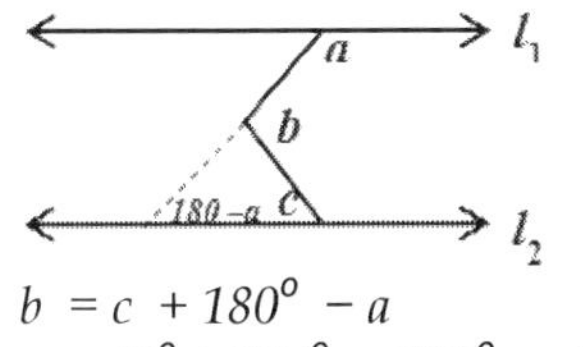

$b = c + 180^\circ - a$
$= 40^\circ + 180^\circ - 130^\circ = 90^\circ$

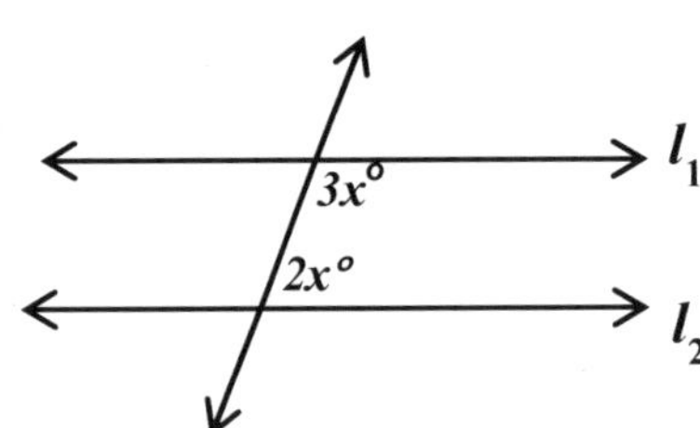

4. In the figure above $l_1 \parallel l_2$, what is the value of x?
   a) 36
   b) 40
   c) 45
   d) 54

Answer: (a)

Consecutive interior angles are supplementary.
$2x + 3x = 180$
$x = 36$

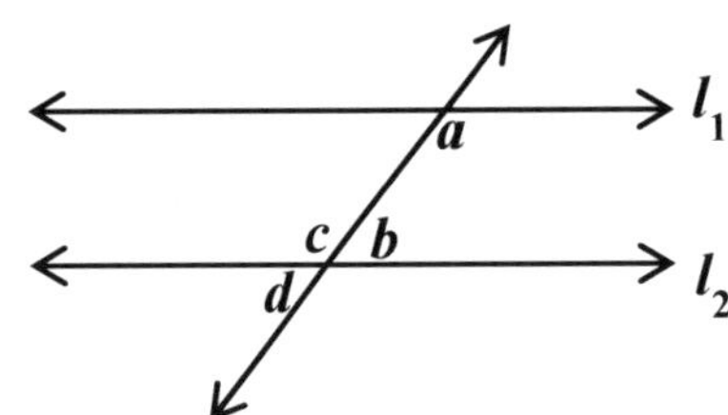

5. If $l_1 \parallel l_2$ in the figure above, what is the value of $\frac{1}{2}(b + a) - (c + d)$?
   a) −90°
   b) 0°
   c) −120°
   d) 90°

Answer: (a)

Consecutive interior angles are supplementary.
$a + b = 180°$
$c + d = 180°$
$\frac{1}{2}(b + a) = 90°$
$90° - 180° = -90°$

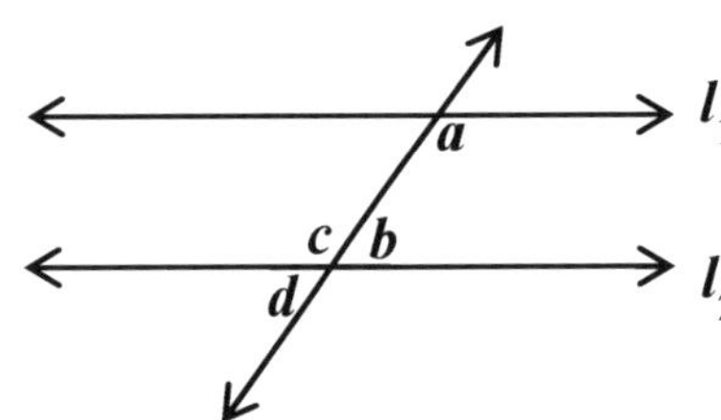

6. In the figure above, $l_1 \parallel l_2$. If angle a is 130°, what is the value of d?
   a) 80°
   b) 75°
   c) 50°
   d) 45°

Answer: (c)

$b = d$
$a + b = 180°$
$d = 180° - 130° = 50°$

Medium

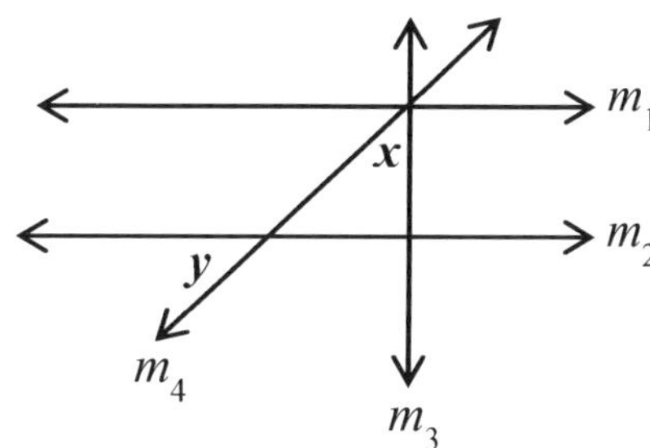

7. In the figure above, if m_1 is parallel to m_2 and m_3 is perpendicular to m_1, what is the sum of x and y, in degrees?
   a) 180°
   b) 120°
   c) 100°
   d) 90°

Answer: (d)

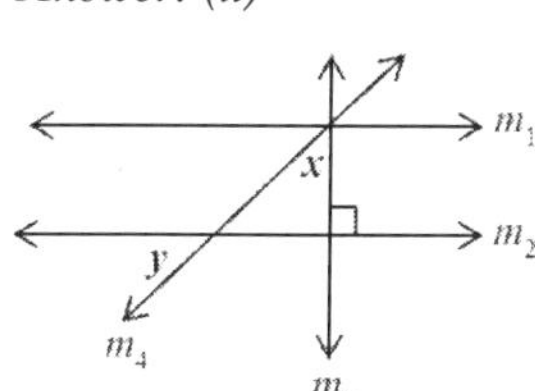

We are given that $m_1 \parallel m_2$, so if $m_1 \perp m_3$, then $m_2 \perp m_3$.
x plus the vertical angle of y equals 90° since $m_2 \perp m_3$.
Thus, $x + y = 90°$

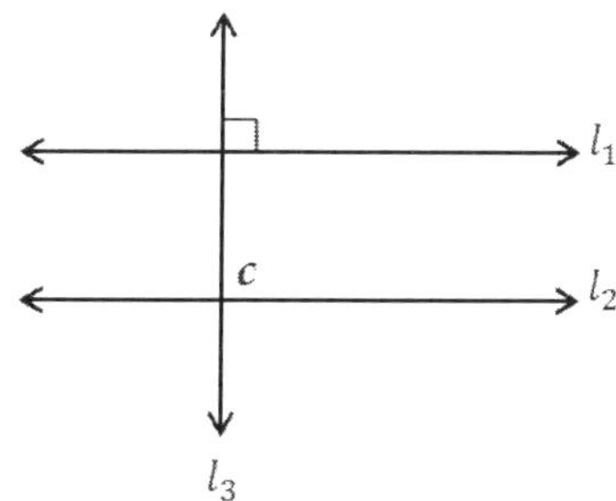

8. In the figure above, $l_1 \parallel l_2$ and $l_3 \perp l_1$. Which of the following must be true?
   a) $c < 90°$
   b) $c > 90°$
   c) $c = 90°$
   d) $l_1 \perp l_2$

Answer: (c)

∠C is the supplementary angle of a right angle.
$c = 90°$

9. In the figure below, $l_1 \parallel l_2$ and $b = 2a + 6$. What is the value of a, in degrees?

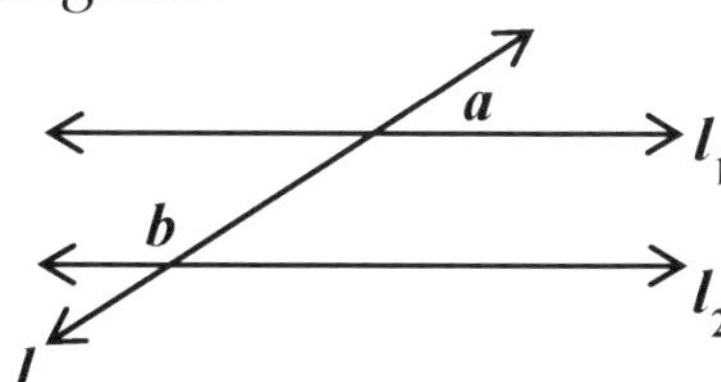

Note: Figure not drawn to scale.

Answer: 58

$a + b = 180°$
$2a + 6 + a = 180°$
$3a = 174$
$a = 58°$

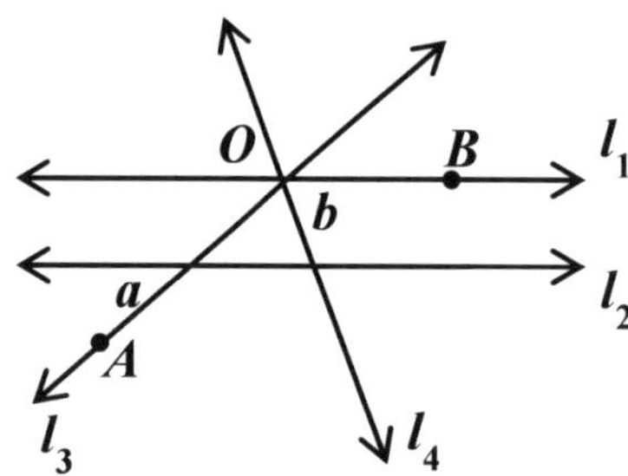

10. In the figure above, $l_1 \parallel l_2$ and l_4 bisects $\angle AOB$. If $3a = 2b$, what is the value of b, in degrees?

Answer: 67.5

$\angle AOB + a = 180^\circ$ and $\angle AOB = 2b$
$2b + a = 3a + a = 180^\circ$
$a = 45^\circ$
$b = \frac{3}{2} \times 45^\circ = 67.5^\circ$

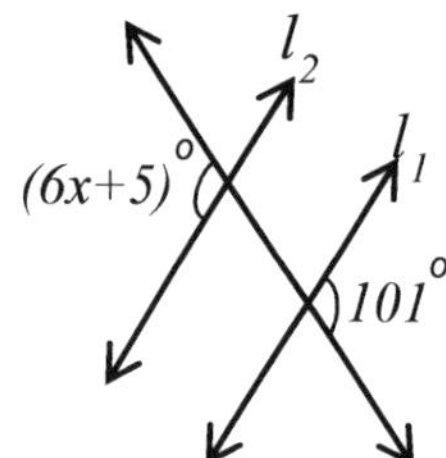

11. In the figure above, $l_1 \parallel l_2$. What is the value of x?
   a) 15
   b) 16
   c) 17
   d) 18

Answer: (b)

$6x + 5 = 101$
$x = 16$

12. In the figure below, $\overline{AB} \parallel \overline{CD}$ and $\overline{CD} \perp \overline{BC}$. What is the value of $x + y$?

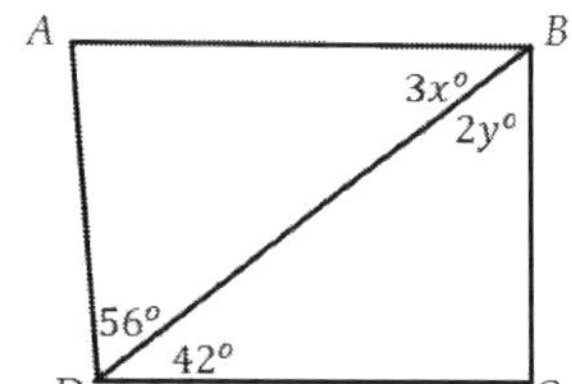

   a) 21
   b) 34
   c) 36
   d) 38

Answer: (d)

$3x = 42$

$x = 14$
$2y + 42 = 90$
$y = 24$
$x + y = 14 + 24 = 38$

II. TRIANGLES

A. INTERIOR AND EXTERIOR ANGLES

CONCEPT OVERVIEWS

Sum of Interior Angles Theorem: The sum of the three interior angles of a triangle is 180°.

Exterior Angle Theorem: The measure of an exterior angle of a triangle is equal to the sum of the measures of the two non-adjacent interior angles of that triangle.

The sum of the three exterior angles of a triangle is equal to 360°. (In fact, the sum of all exterior angles of a convex polygon is equal to 360°.)

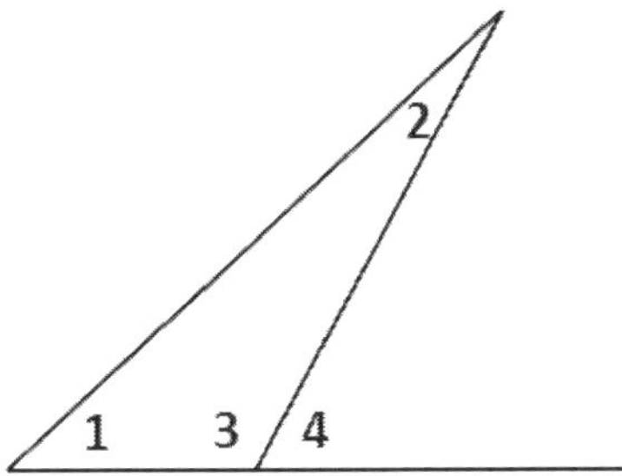

$$m\angle 1 + m\angle 2 + m\angle 3 = 180^\circ \text{ (Sum of Interior Angles Theorem)}$$

$$m\angle 4 = m\angle 1 + m\angle 2 \text{ (Exterior Angle Theorem)}$$

Example: Find the value of x.

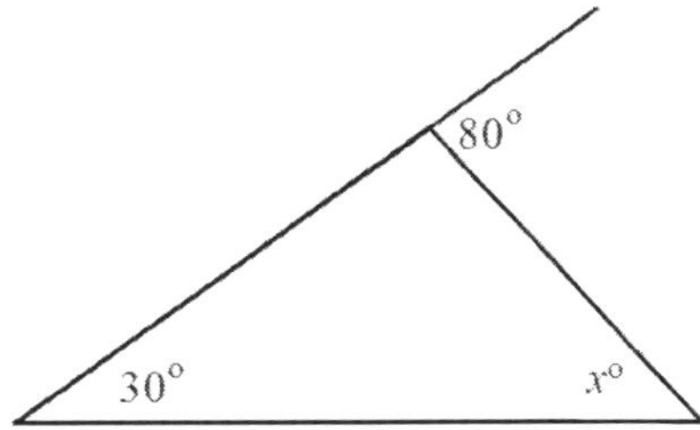

Solution: $80 = 30 + x$

$x = 50$

Problem Solving Skills

Easy

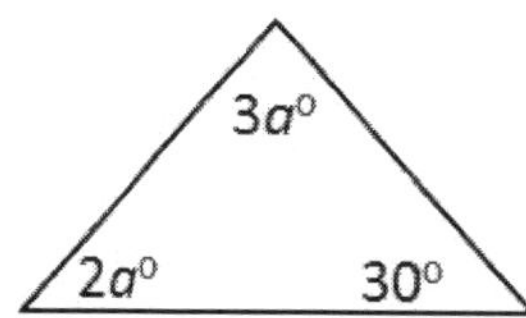

Note: Figure not drawn to scale.

1. Based on the figure above, what is the value of a?
   a) 25
   b) 30
   c) 35
   d) 40

Answer: (b)

Sum of Interior Angles = 180°
$3a + 2a + 30 = 180$
$a = 30$

2. In a triangle, one angle is double the size of another angle. If the measure of the third angle is 30 degrees, what is the measure of the largest angle in degrees?
   a) 70°
   b) 80°
   c) 90°
   d) 100°

Answer: (d)

Let x be one unknown angle and 2x the other unknown angle.
$30 + 2x + x = 180°$
$x = 50°$
The largest angle is $2 \times 50 = 100°$.

3. In the figure below, what is the value of x?

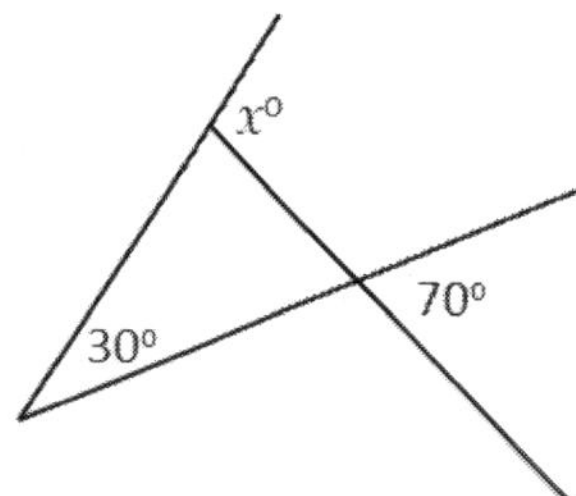

   a) 80
   b) 100
   c) 120
   d) 130

Answer: (b)

$x = 70 + 30 = 100$

4. In the figure below, what is the value of $a + b + c + d$?

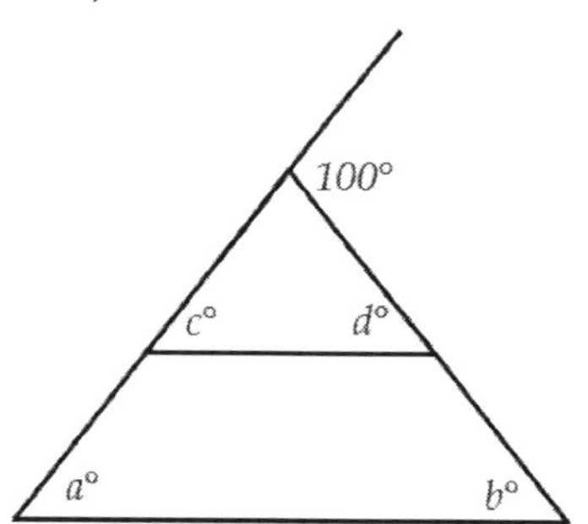

Answer: 200

$100 = c + d = a + b$
$a + b + c + d = 200$

5. In the figure below, $c = 150$. What is the value of $a + b$?

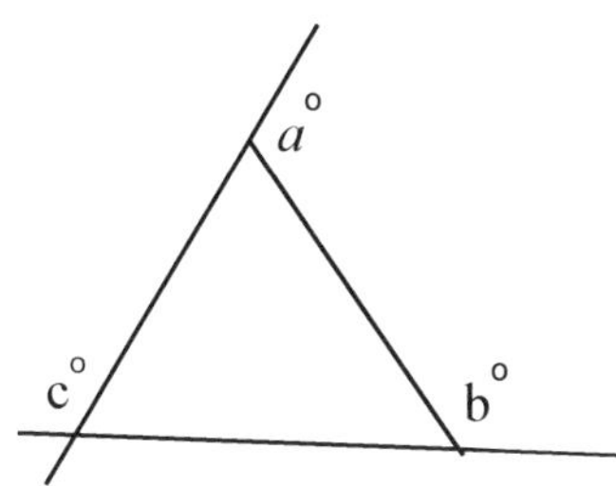

a) 140
b) 180
c) 210
d) 240

Answer: (c)

The sum of any polygon's exterior angles is 360°.
$a + b + c = 360$
$a + b = 360 - c = 210$

6. In the figure below, what is the value of $2a - b$?

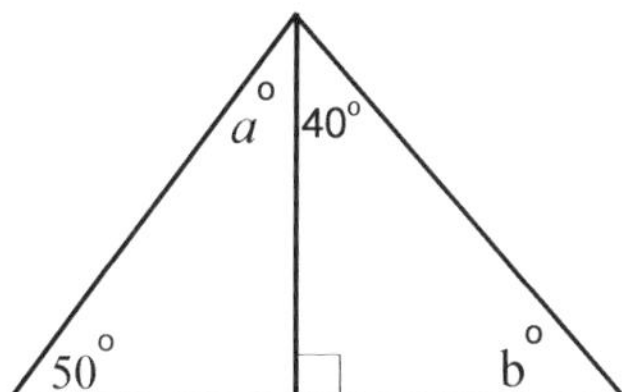

a) 10
b) 15
c) 20
d) 30

Answer: (d)

$a = 40$ *and* $b = 50$
$2a - b = 80 - 50 = 30$

7. In the figure below, if $a = 3c$, and $b = 2a$, what is the value of c?

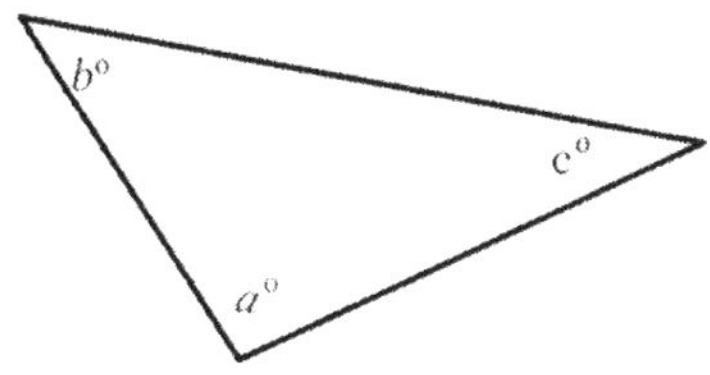

Note: Figure not drawn to scale.

a) 18
b) 20
c) 28
d) 34

Answer: (a)

$a + b + c = 180$
$3c + 6c + c = 180$
$c = 18$

8. In the figure below, what is the value of $a - b$?

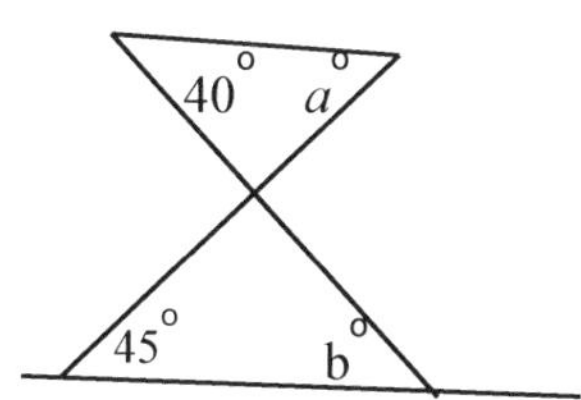

Answer: 5

Since the two triangles share an angle with the same measure (vertical angle theorem), the sum of their other two angles must be equal.
$a + 40 = b + 45$
$a - b = 5$

9. In the figure below, what is the value of a?

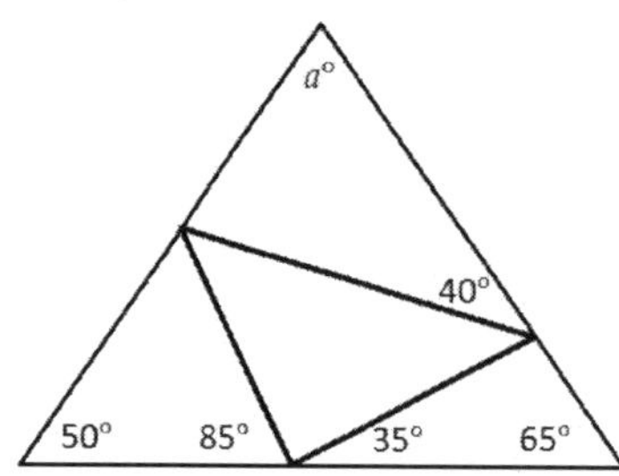

Note: Figure not drawn to scale.

Answer: 65

Look at a in terms of the big triangle.

$a + 65 + 50 = 180$
$a = 65$

10. In the figure below, what is the sum of a, b and c?

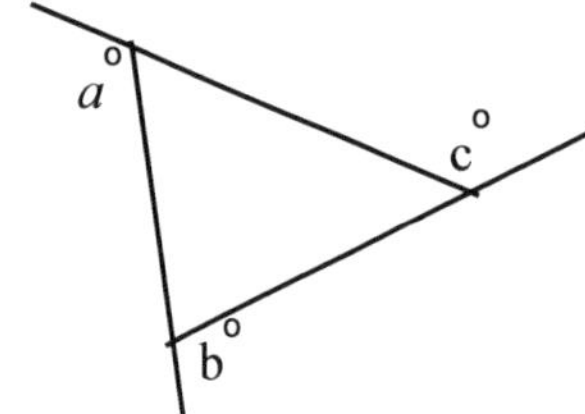

a) 90
b) 180
c) 270
d) 360

Answer: (d)

The sum of any polygon's exterior angles is 360°.

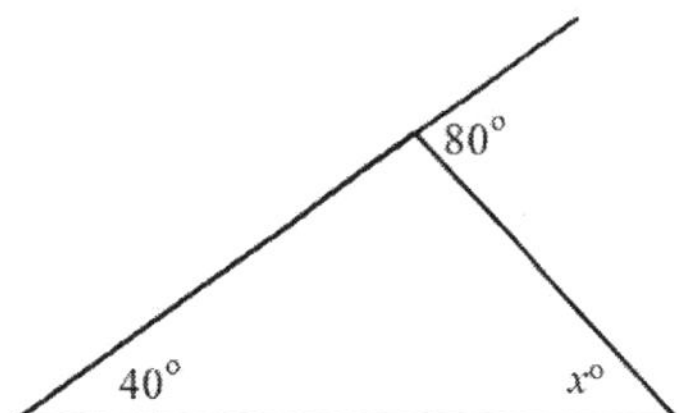

11. In the triangle above, what is the value of x?
a) 30
b) 40
c) 50
d) 60

Answer: (b)

Use the exterior angle theorem.
$80 = 40 + x$
$x = 40$

12. In the figure below, what is the value of x?

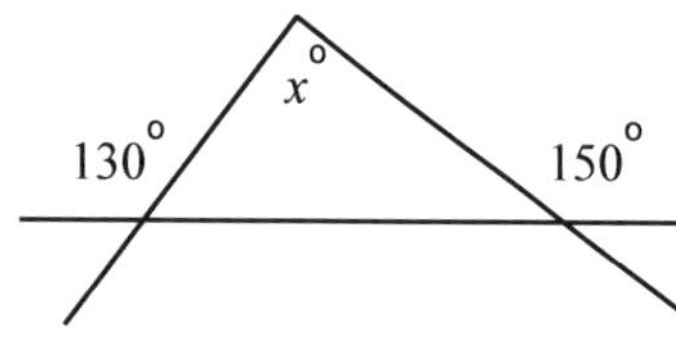

a) 50
b) 70
c) 90
d) 100

Answer: (d)

The three interior angles of the triangle are x°, (180 – 130)°, and (180 – 150)°.

$x + 50 + 30 = 180$
$x = 100$

13. In the figure below, what is the value of $a + 2b$?

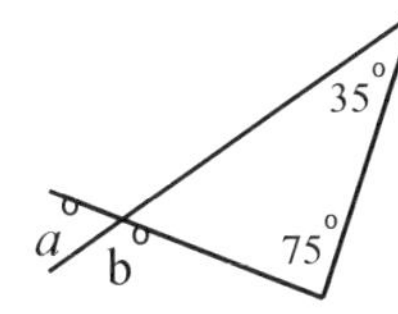

Note: Figure not drawn to scale.

a) 250
b) 260
c) 290
d) 300

Answer: (c)

$b = 35 + 75 = 110$
$a + b = 180$
$a + b + b = a + 2b = 180 + 110 = 290$

Medium

14. In the figure below shows ΔABC and its exterior angle ∠DAC. What is the value of a?

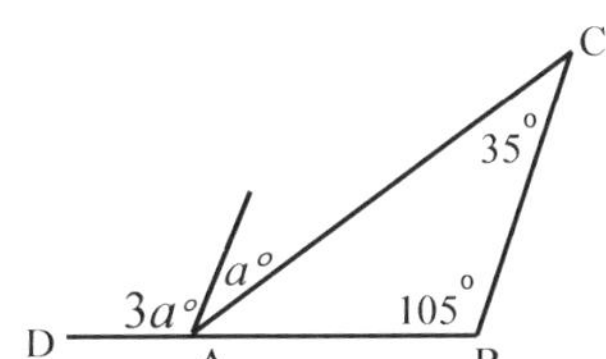

Answer: 35

$3a + a = 35 + 105 = 140$
$4a = 140$
$a = 35$

15. The three interior angle measures of a triangle have the ratio 3 : 4 : 5. What is the sum of the measures, in degrees, of the smallest and largest angles?

a) 100°
b) 110°
c) 120°
d) 140°

Answer: (c)

We can define the measures of the three angles to be 3x, 4x, and 5x.
$3x + 4x + 5x = 180^\circ$
$x = 15^\circ$
$3x + 5x = 8x = 8 \times 15 = 120^\circ$

16. The three angles of a triangle have measures x°, $2x^\circ$, and $4y^\circ$, where $x > 56$. If x and y are integers, what is one possible value of y?

Answer: 1 or 2

$x + 2x + 4y = 180$
$4y = 180 - 3x$
$4y < 180 - 3 \times 56$
$4y < 12$
$y < 3$
$y = 1, 2$

17. In the figure below, what is the value of x?

Answer: 56

Use the exterior angle theorem.
$81 = x + 25$
$x = 56$

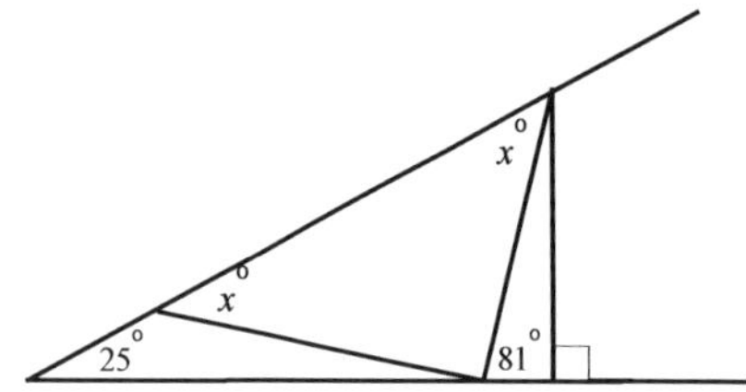

Note: Figure not drawn to scale.

18. In the figure below, what is the value of a?

Answer: (d)

$10a + 2a + 10 = 5a + 8a$
$a = 10$

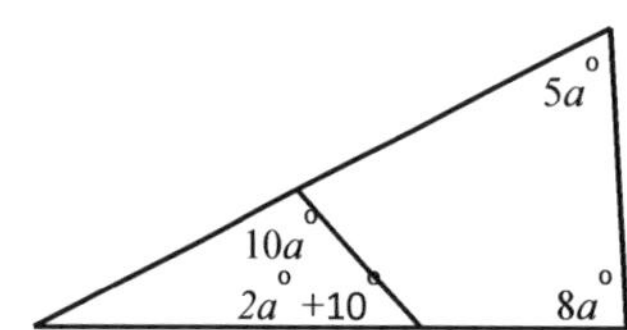

Note: Figure not drawn to scale.

a) 25
b) 20
c) 15
d) 10

19. In the figure below, what is the value of $a + b$?

Answer: 255

Use the exterior angle theorem.

$a = 75 + (180 - b)$
$a + b = 75 + 180 = 255$

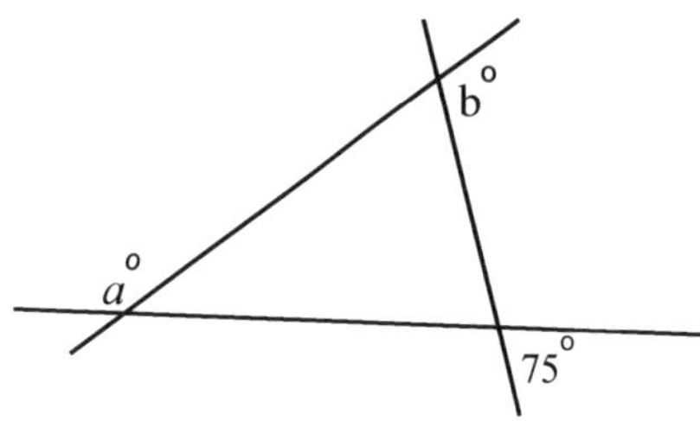

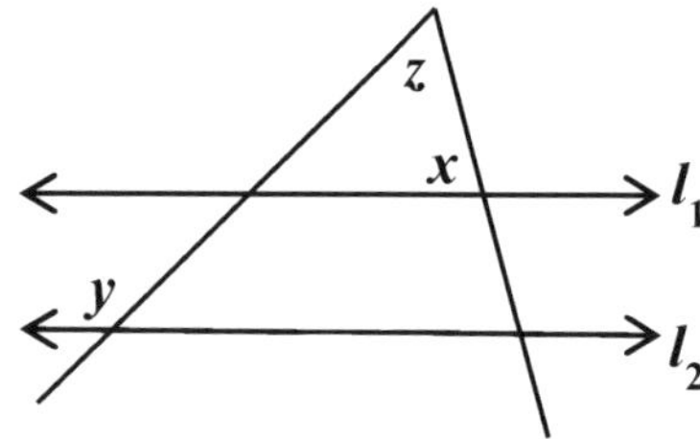

20. In the figure above, if $l_1 \parallel l_2$, what does z equal in terms of x and y?
a) $180° - x - y$
b) $180° - y + x$
c) $y - x$
d) $x - y$

Answer: (c)

$y = x + z$ *(exterior angle theorem and corresponding angles)*
$z = y - x$

Hard

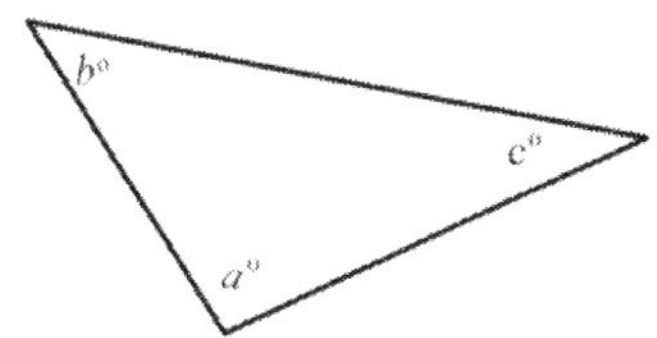

Note: Figure not drawn to scale.

21. In the triangle above, $a + b = 100$, and $b + c = 150$. What is the value of b?
    a) 40
    b) 50
    c) 70
    d) 80

Answer: (c)

$a + b + c = 180$
$a + b = 100$
$c = 80$
$b + c = 150$
$b = 70$

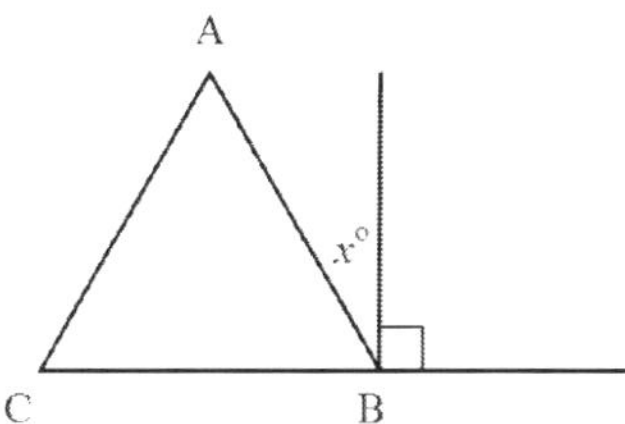

22. In the figure above, ΔABC is an isosceles triangle and $m\angle A = 60^o$. What is the value of x?

Answer: 30

Use the exterior angle theorem.
$90 + x = 60 + 60$
$x = 30$

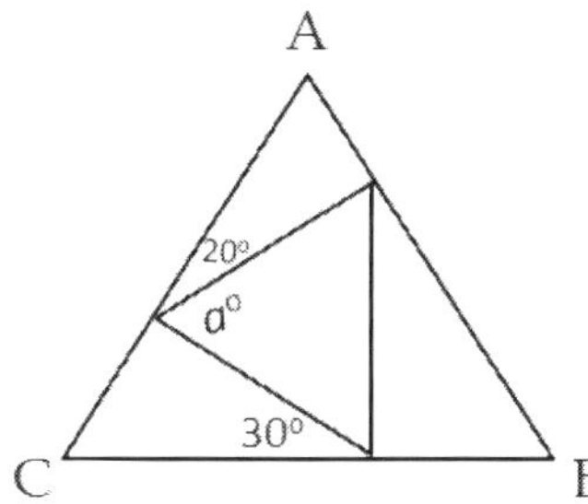

Note: Figure not drawn to scale.

23. In the figure above, ΔABC is an equilateral triangle. What is the value of a?
    a) 70°
    b) 60°
    c) 50°
    d) 40°

Answer: (a)

ΔABC is an equilateral triangle, so
$m\angle A = m\angle B = m\angle C = 60^o$
$20 + a = 30 + 60$
$a = 70$

24. In the figure below, what is $b - a$?

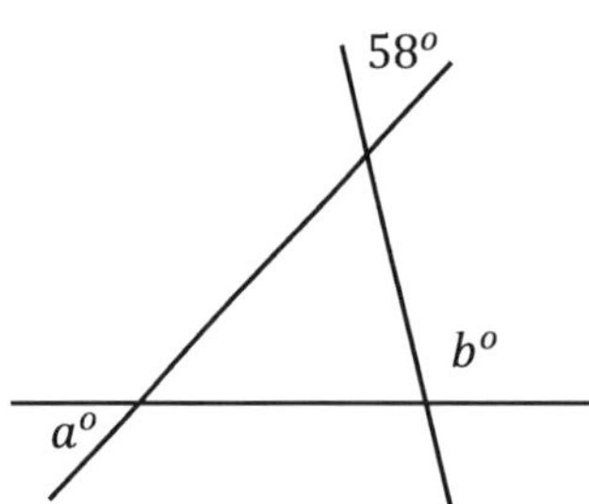

Answer: 58

Use the vertical angle theorem and the exterior angle theorem.

$b = a + 58$
$b - a = 58$

25. In the figure below, what is $a + b - c - d$?

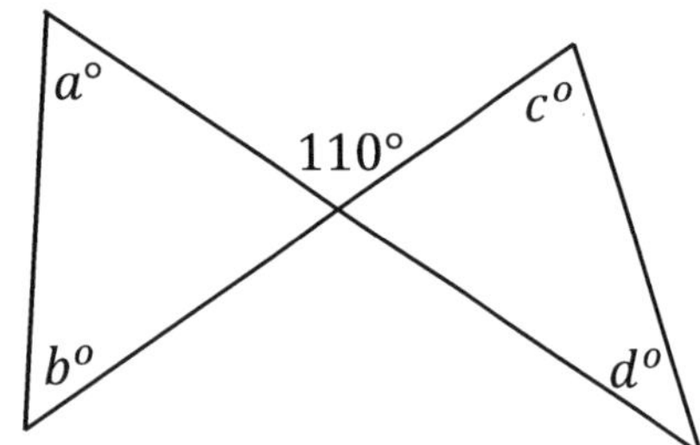

Note: Figure not drawn to scale.

Answer: 0

Use the exterior angle theorem.
$110 = a + b = c + d$
$a + b - (c + d) = 0$

26. In the figure below, what is the value of a?

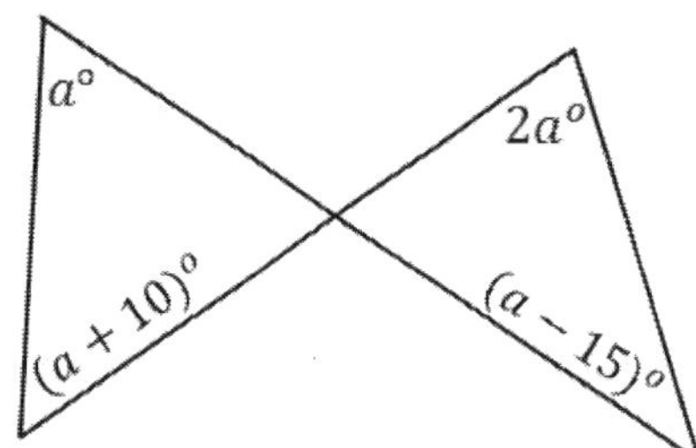

Note: Figure not drawn to scale.

Answer: 25

Use the exterior angle theorem.

$a + a + 10 = 2a + a - 15$
$a = 25$

B. Special Triangles

Concept Overviews

An **equilateral triangle** is a triangle with three equal sides and three equal interior angles measuring 60°.

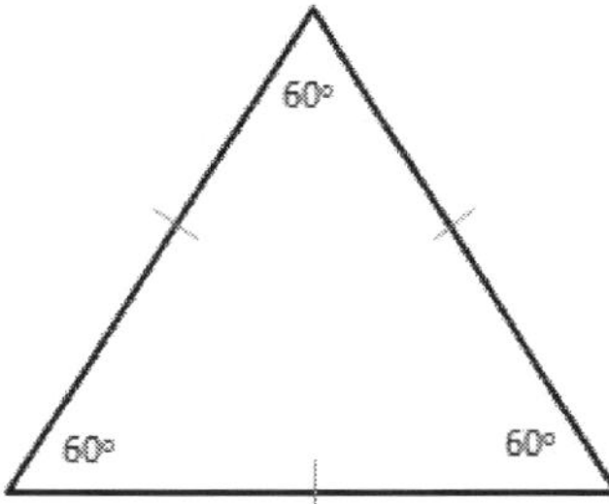

An **isosceles triangle** is a triangle with two equal sides and congruent corresponding base angles. If two sides of a triangle are equal in length, their opposite angles must be congruent as well.

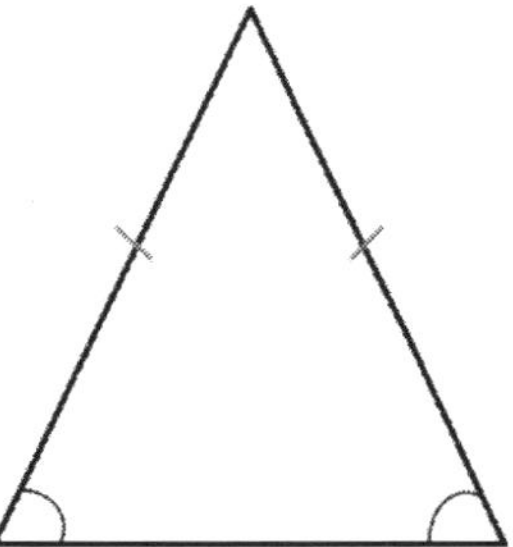

NOTE: The height of an isosceles triangle always bisects the triangle, creating two equal right triangles.

A **right triangle** is a triangle with a 90° angle. The two perpendicular sides are called legs and the side opposite the right angle is called the hypotenuse.

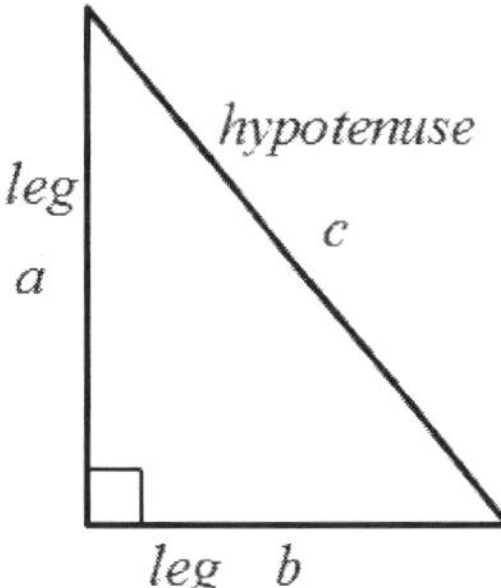

Pythagorean theorem for right triangles: $a^2 + b^2 = c^2$

Special Right Triangles: Two special right triangles you need to get familiar with: 45°-45°-90° and 30°-60°-90° right triangles.

- The ratio of the sides of a 45-45-90 right triangle is $1 : 1 : \sqrt{2}$.
- The ratio of the sides of a 30-60-90 right triangles is $1 : \sqrt{3} : 2$.

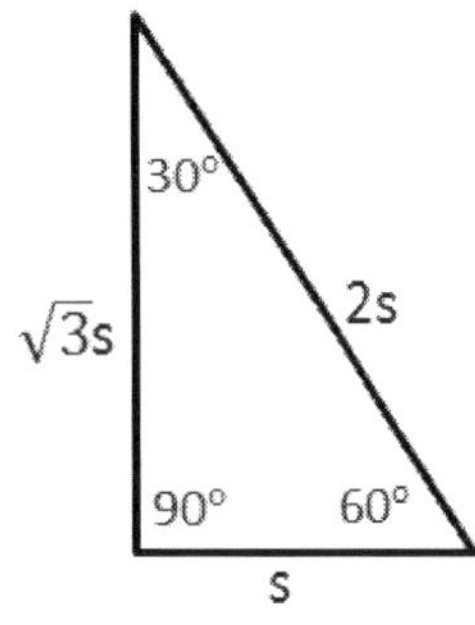

30-60-90 right triangle

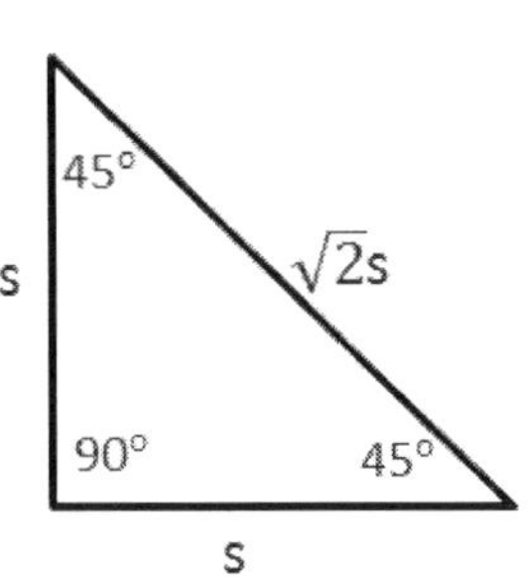

45-45-90 right triangle

Example: Find the values of x and y.

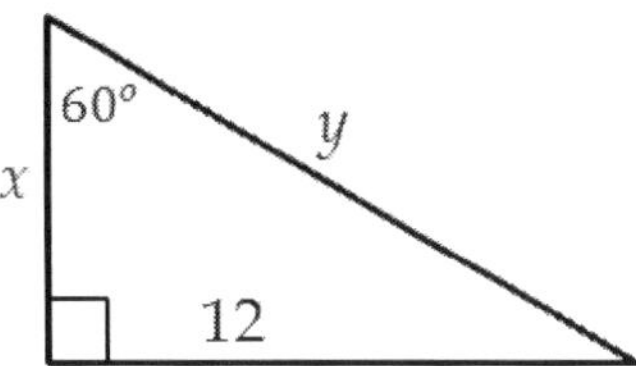

Answer: This is a 30-60-90 special right triangle. The ratio of sides is $1 : \sqrt{3} : 2$.

$$\frac{1}{x} = \frac{\sqrt{3}}{12} = \frac{2}{y}$$

Therefore, $x = 4\sqrt{3}$ and $y = 8\sqrt{3}$.

Problem Solving Skills

Easy

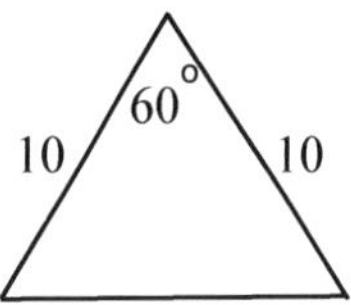

1. What is the length of the third side in the triangle above?
   a) 8
   b) 9
   c) 10
   d) 12

Answer: (c)

Isosceles triangle with base angles of 60° is an equilateral triangle.

The two angles at the base must be equal, so this triangle must be an equilateral triangle. This means that the third side has length 10.

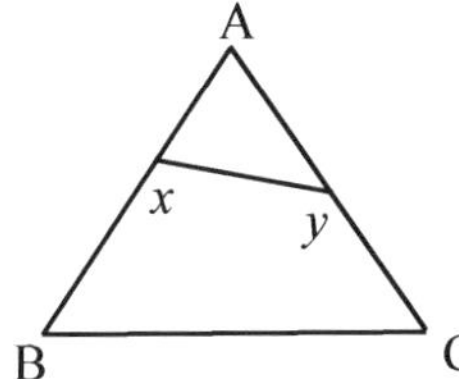

2. In the figure above, ΔABC is an equilateral triangle. What is the value of $x + y$ in degrees?

Answer: 240

The sum of the interior angles of a quadrilateral triangle is 360°.
$60^\circ + 60^\circ + x + y = 360^\circ$
$x + y = 240^\circ$

3. A 24-foot-long ladder is placed against a building to form a triangle with the sides of the building and ground. If the angle between ladder and ground is 60°, how far is the bottom of the ladder to the base of the building?
   a) 10
   b) $10\sqrt{3}$
   c) 12
   d) $12\sqrt{3}$

Answer: (c)

Since the building makes a 90° angle with the ground, the triangle must be a 30–60–90 special right triangle. The ladder itself is the hypotenuse and the bottom of the ladder to the base of the building is across from the 30° angle. Therefore, the distance between the bottom of the ladder and the base of the building is one half of the length of the ladder.

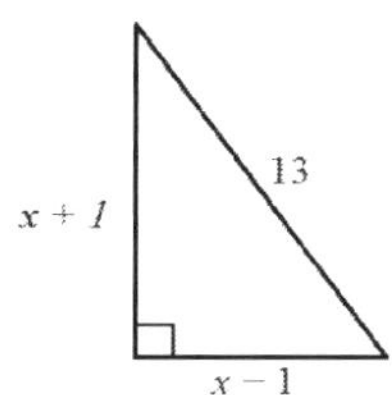

4. In the figure shown above, we assume that $x > 1$. What is the value of $2x^2 + 1$?
   a) 166
   b) 167
   c) 168
   d) 169

Answer: (c)

Use the Pythagorean theorem.
$(x - 1)^2 + (x + 1)^2 = 13^2$
$x^2 - 2x + 1 + x^2 + 2x + 1 = 169$
$2x^2 + 1 = 168$

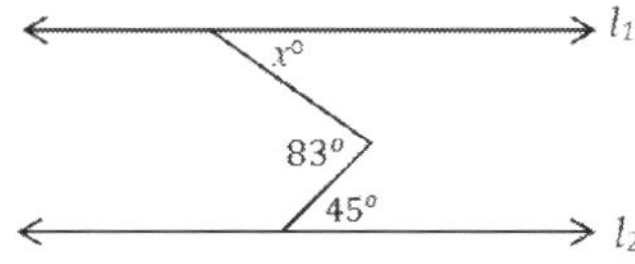

5. In the figure above, lines l_1 and l_2 are parallel. What is the value of x?
   a) 110
   b) 95
   c) 85
   d) 38

Answer: (d)

Use the exterior angle theorem.
$83 = 45 +$
$x = 83 - 45 = 38$

Note: Figure not drawn to scale.

6. In the figure above, which of the following CANNOT be the value of x?
   a) 100
   b) 110
   c) 115
   d) 120

Answer: (a)

As an exterior angle, x is equal to (180 – 75) plus a small interior angle. Therefore, x > 105. x cannot be 100.

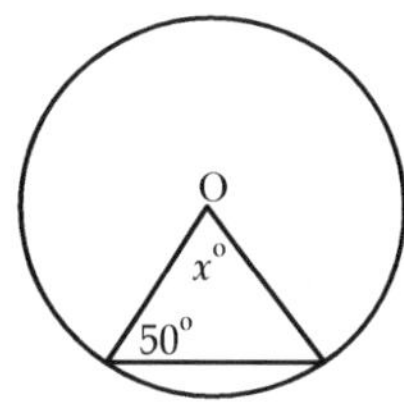

7. In the figure above, point O is the center of the circle. Whit is the value of x?
   a) 85
   b) 80
   c) 60
   d) 55

Answer: (b)

Two of the legs of the triangle are the radii of the circle. This triangle is an isosceles triangle with equal base angles.
$180 - 50 - 50 = x \rightarrow x = 80$

8. A square and an equilateral triangle have equal perimeter. If the square has an area of 36 square feet, what is the length of one side of the triangle, in feet?
   a) 4
   b) 6
   c) 8
   d) 10

Answer: (c)

The length of a side of the square: $\sqrt{36} = 6$. *The perimeter of this square is* $4 \times 6 = 24$.
Let x be the length of one side of the triangle. The perimeter of the triangle is 3x.
$3x = 24 \rightarrow x = 8$

9. The perimeter of ΔABC is equal to the perimeter of ΔXYZ, which are shown below. If ΔABC is equilateral, what is the value of x?

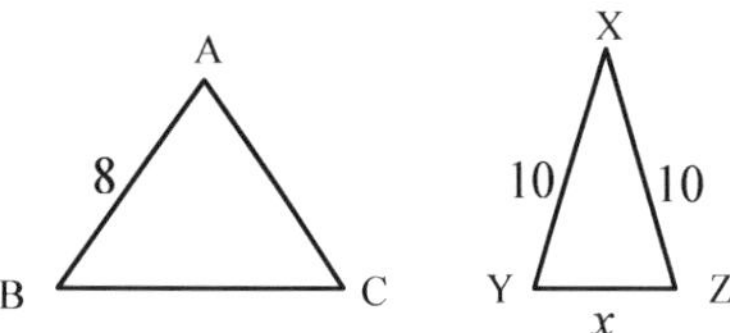

   a) 4
   b) 5
   c) 6
   d) 8

Answer: (a)

The perimeter of ΔABC:
$10 + 10 + x = 3 \times 8$
$x = 4$

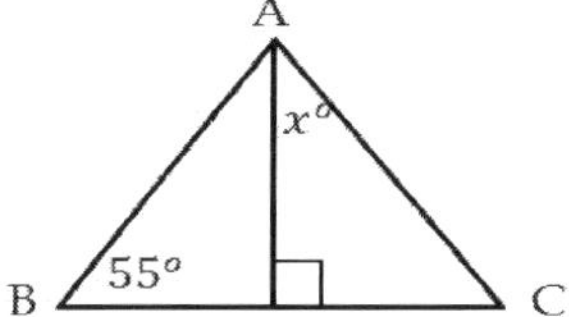

10. If AB = AC in the figure above, what is the value of x, in degrees?
    a) 30°
    b) 35°
    c) 40°
    d) 45°

Answer: (b)

ΔABC is an isosceles triangle.

$m\angle C = 55°$
$x = 180 - 90 - 55$
$x = 35$

11. The area of equilateral triangle ΔXYZ is 4 times the area of equilateral triangle ΔABC. If the perimeter of ΔABC is 12, what is the length of one side of ΔXYZ?
    a) 6
    b) 8
    c) 10
    d) 12

Answer: (b)

The ratios of perimeters: $\sqrt{4}$: 1
The perimeter of ΔXYZ:
$\sqrt{4} \times 12 = 24$.
Side length of ΔXYZ: $\frac{24}{3} = 8$

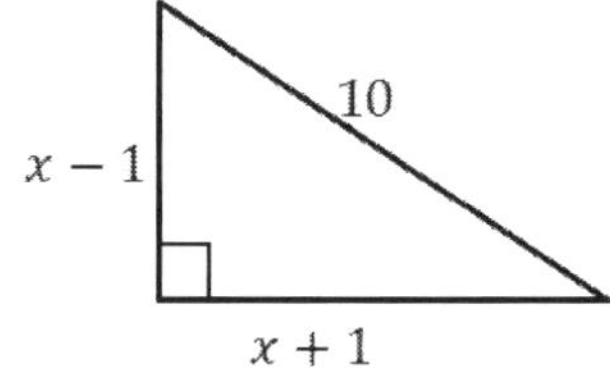

12. The figure above is a right triangle. If $x > 1$, what is the value of x?
    a) 6
    b) 7
    c) 8
    d) 9

Answer: (b)

Use the Pythagorean theorem.
$(x-1)^2 + (x+1)^2 = 10^2$
$x^2 - 2x + 1 + x^2 + 2x + 1 = 100$
$2x^2 + 2 = 100$
$x^2 = 49$
$x = 7$

13. In the figure above, the perimeter of the triangle is $12 + 6\sqrt{2}$. What is the value of a?
    a) 3
    b) 6
    c) $3\sqrt{2}$
    d) $6\sqrt{2}$

Answer: (b)

The length of the hypotenuse is $\sqrt{a^2 + a^2} = a\sqrt{2}$.
Perimeter of triangle:
$a + a + a\sqrt{2} = 12 + 6\sqrt{2}$
$a = 6$

Medium

14. An isosceles right triangle has a hypotenuse with a length of $6\sqrt{2}$. What is the area of this triangle?
    a) 12
    b) 15
    c) 18
    d) $12\sqrt{3}$

Answer: (c)

An isosceles right triangle is a 45−45−90 triangle.

Length of Leg $= 6\sqrt{2} \times \frac{\sqrt{2}}{2} = 6$

Area of Triangle $= \frac{1}{2} \times 6 \times 6 = 18$

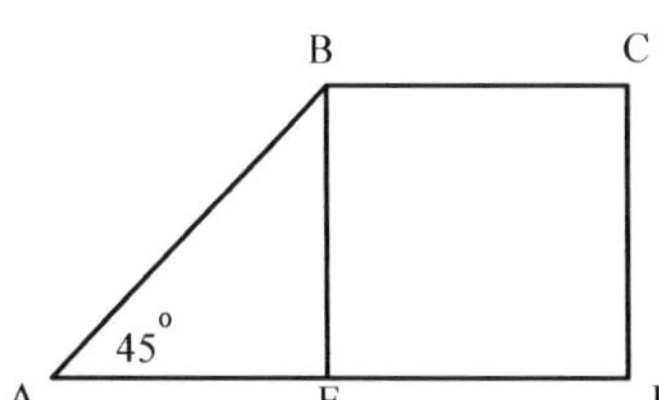

15. In the figure above, BCDE is a square and its area is 64. The points A, E and D are on the same line. What is the length of $\overline{AB}$?
    a) 8
    b) $8\sqrt{2}$
    c) $8\sqrt{3}$
    d) 10

Answer: (b)

ΔAEB is a 45−45−90 right triangle.

$\overline{BE} = \sqrt{64} = 8$

$\overline{AB} = \sqrt{2} \times 8$

16. In the figure below, if $\overline{AB} = 8\sqrt{2}$, what is the area of ΔABD?

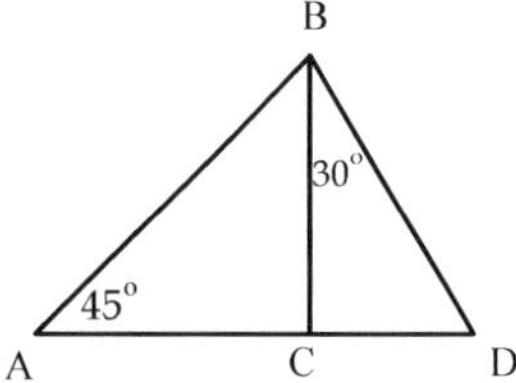

    a) 32
    b) 64
    c) $32\sqrt{3}$
    d) $32(1 + \frac{1}{\sqrt{3}})$

Answer: (d)

We have two special right triangles here.

$\overline{AC} = \frac{8\sqrt{2}}{\sqrt{2}} = 8 = \overline{BC}$

$\frac{\overline{BC}}{\overline{CD}} = \frac{\sqrt{3}}{1} = \frac{8}{\overline{CD}}$

$\overline{CD} = \frac{8}{\sqrt{3}}$

Area of ΔABD $= \frac{1}{2}(AC + CD) \times BC$

$= \frac{1}{2}(8 + \frac{8}{\sqrt{3}}) \times 8 = 32(1 + \frac{1}{\sqrt{3}})$

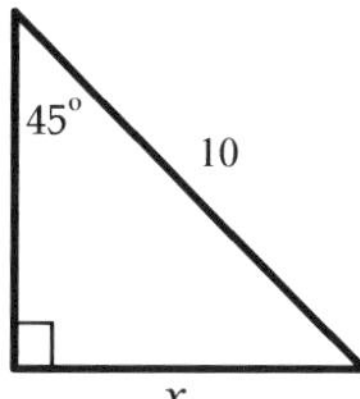

17. What is the value of x in the figure above? 
    a) 5
    b) $5\sqrt{3}$
    c) 8
    d) $5\sqrt{2}$

Answer: (d)

This is a 45−45−90 right triangle.
Length of Leg = Hypotenuse × $\frac{\sqrt{2}}{2}$
$x = 10 \times \frac{\sqrt{2}}{2} = 5\sqrt{2}$

18. In the figure below, the vertices of a square, an equilateral triangle, and a regular hexagon intersect at one point. What is the value of a + b + c?

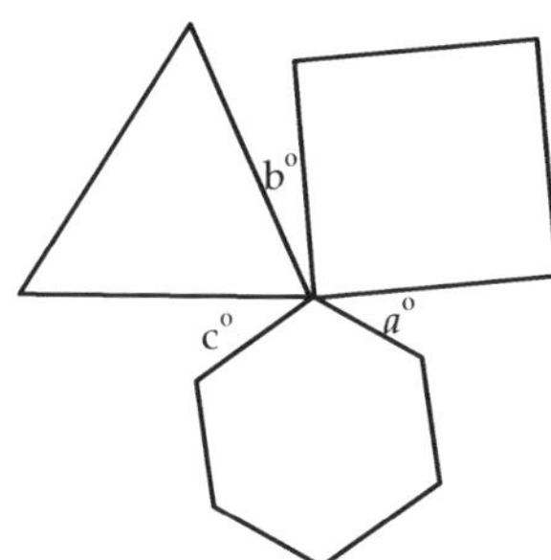

    a) 60
    b) 90
    c) 100
    d) 110

Answer: (b)

Each interior angle of a square is 90°, each interior angle of an equilateral triangle is 60°, and each interior angle of a regular hexagon is 120°.

$a + b + c + 90° + 60° + 120° = 360°$
$a + b + c = 90°$

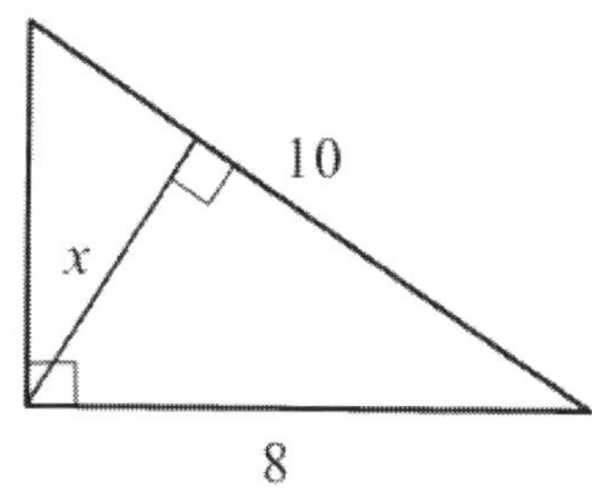

Note: Figure not drawn to scale..

19. In the right triangle above, what is the length of x?

Answer: 4.8

Use the Pythagorean theorem.
Length of Unknown Leg =
$\sqrt{10^2 - 8^2} = 6$
Area of Triangle $= \frac{1}{2}(8 \times 6) = \frac{1}{2}(10 \times x)$
$x = 4.8$

Note: Figure not drawn to scale..

20. The figure above shows a quadrilateral ABCD and its exterior angle ∠CDE. What is the value of x, in degrees?

Answer: 105

Find the interior angle ∠ADC first.

$\angle ADC = 360^o - 130^o - 60^o - 95^o = 75^o$

$x = 180 - 75 = 105$

21. In the figure below, AB = 2. What is the length of AD?

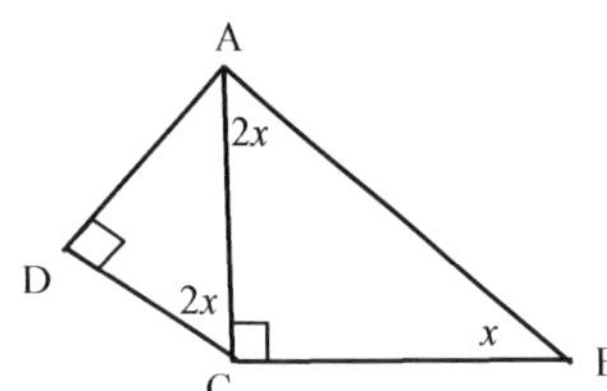

Note: Figure not drawn to scale.

a) $\sqrt{3}$
b) 1
c) $\frac{1}{2}$
d) $\frac{\sqrt{3}}{2}$

Answer: (d)

$2x + x = 90^o$

$x = 30^o$

These are two special 30−60−90 right triangles.

$AB = 2$

$AC = \frac{1}{2} \times 2 = 1$

$AD = \frac{\sqrt{3}}{2} \times AC = \frac{\sqrt{3}}{2}$

Hard

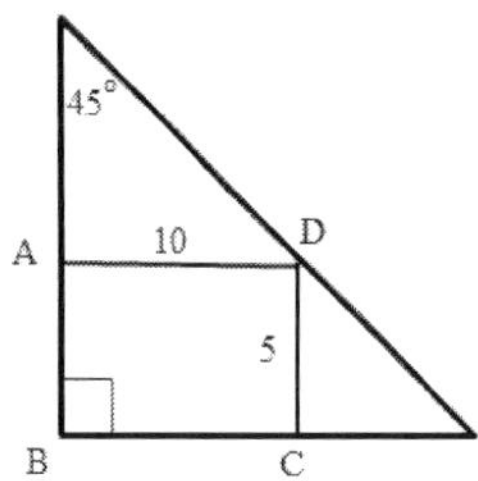

22. In the figure above, if ABCD is a rectangle, what is the length of the big triangle's hypotenuse?

a) 15
b) 20
c) $15\sqrt{2}$
d) $15\sqrt{3}$

Answer: (c)

The length of the isosceles right triangle hypotenuse is $\sqrt{2}$ times the length of its leg.
The hypotenuse is formed by two isosceles right triangles. Find the sum of their hypotenuses.

$\sqrt{2} \times 5 + \sqrt{2} \times 10 = 15\sqrt{2}$

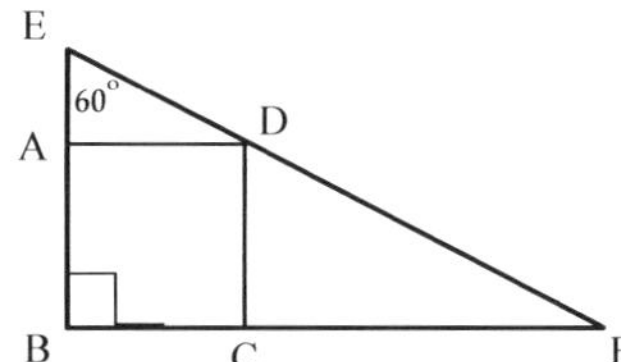

23. In the figure above, if ABCD is a square with area of 16, what is the area of triangle BEF?
    a) 12
    b) 18
    c) $16(1 + \frac{2\sqrt{3}}{3})$
    d) $16\sqrt{3}$

Answer: (c)

Each of these triangles is a 30–60–90 triangle.

The Area of Large Triangle $= \frac{1}{2} \times \overline{BE} \times \overline{BF}$

Side of Square $= \sqrt{16} = 4$

$\overline{BE}$ *(faces 30° angle)* $= 4 + \frac{4}{\sqrt{3}}$

$\overline{BF}$ *(faces 60° angle)* $= 4 + 4\sqrt{3}$

Area $= \frac{1}{2} \times (4 + 4\sqrt{3})(4 + \frac{4}{\sqrt{3}}) = 16(1 + \frac{2\sqrt{3}}{3})$

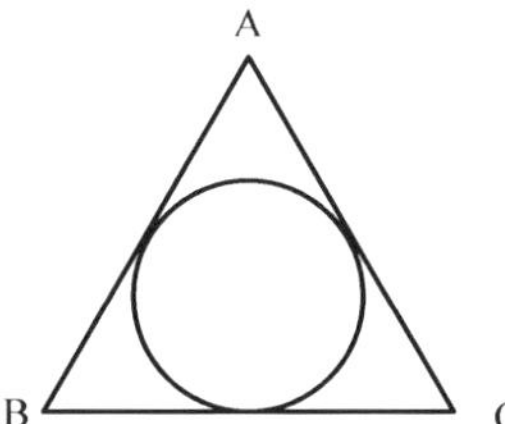

24. In the figure above. ΔABC is an equilateral triangle with side of length 8. What is the radius of a circle that is inscribed inside of ΔABC?

Answer: 2.30 or 2.31

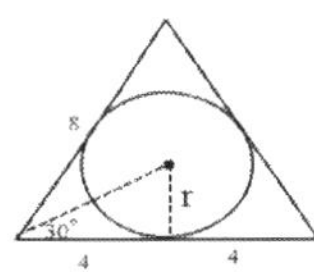

The inner triangle is a 30-60-90 special right triangle. The ratio of its sides is $2 : \sqrt{3} : 1$

$\frac{r}{4} = \frac{1}{\sqrt{3}}$

$r = \frac{4}{\sqrt{3}} = \frac{4\sqrt{3}}{3} = 2.3091$

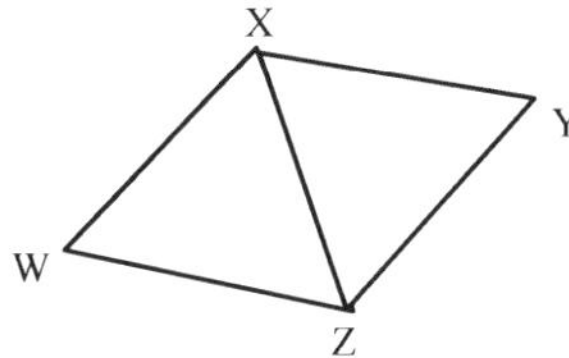

25. If the five line segments in the figure above are all congruent, what is the ratio of the length of WY (not shown) to the length of XZ?

Answer: 1.73

Draw a line connecting W and Y

WY and XZ will bisect each other and form four 30−60−90 triangles.

The ratio of the length of WY to length of XZ is $\sqrt{3} : 1$

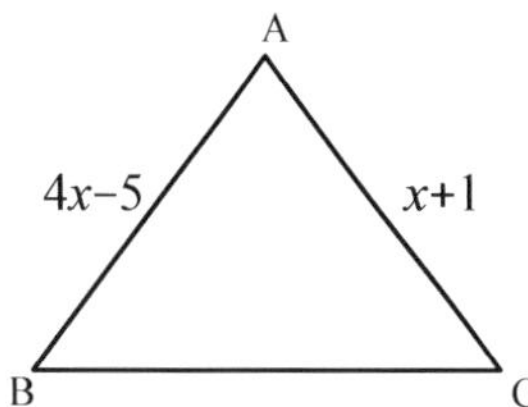

26. In the figure above, if **Δ**ABC is an equilateral triangle, what is the perimeter of **Δ**ABC?
    a) 6
    b) 9
    c) 12
    d) 15

Answer: (b)

All sides are equal in length.

$4x - 5 = x + 1$
$x = 2$
Perimeter $= 3 \times (2 + 1) = 9$

27. In the figure below, ΔABC is an isosceles triangle where $m\angle B = m\angle C$ and **Δ**DEF is an equilateral triangle. If the measure of $\angle ABC$ is 55° and the measure of $\angle BDE$ is 75°, what is the measure of $\angle DFA$?

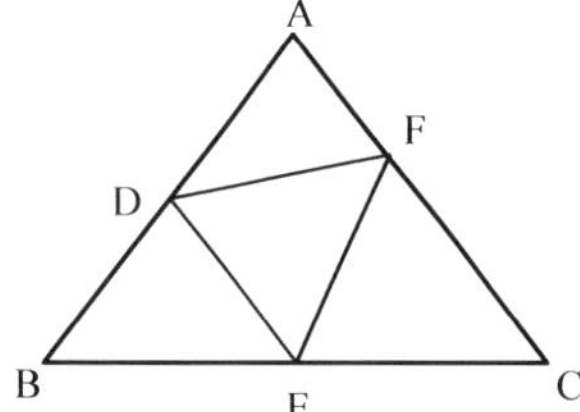

    a) 40°
    b) 55°
    c) 60°
    d) 65°

Answer: (d)

ΔDEF is an equilateral triangle, so $m\angle FDE = 60^\circ$.

$m\angle BDE + m\angle FDE + m\angle FDA = 180^\circ$
$180^\circ - 75^\circ - 60^\circ = m\angle FDA = 45^\circ$
$m\angle DFA + m\angle FDA + m\angle A = 180^\circ$

ΔABC is an isosceles Δ where $m\angle B = m\angle C$.

$m\angle A = 180^\circ - 2 \times \angle B = 180^\circ - 2 \times 55^\circ = 70^\circ$
$m\angle DFA + 45^\circ + 70^\circ = 180^\circ$
$m\angle DFA = 65^\circ$

C. Similar Triangles

Concept Overviews

When two triangles are similar, their corresponding angles are congruent and their corresponding sides are proportional.

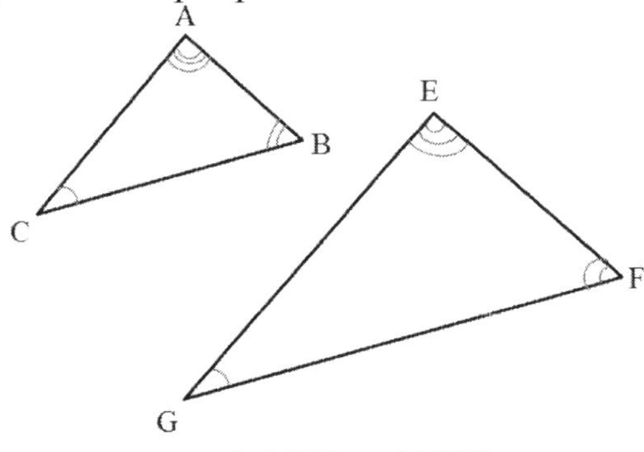

$$\Delta ABC \sim \Delta EFG$$
$$m\angle A = m\angle E, m\angle B = m\angle F, m\angle C = m\angle G$$
$$\frac{AB}{EF} = \frac{AC}{EG} = \frac{BC}{FG}$$

Similarity Theorems

- **SSS (Side-Side-Side) Similarity Theorem**: If the ratios of all three pairs of corresponding sides are equal, then the triangles are similar.
- **AA (Angle-Angle) Similarity Theorem**: If two angles of the first triangle are congruent to two angles of the second triangle, then the triangles are similar.
- **SAS (Side-Angle-Side) Similarity Theorem**: If the ratios of two pairs of corresponding sides are equal, and their included angles are congruent, then the triangles are similar.

Example: Find the length of $\overline{QS}$.

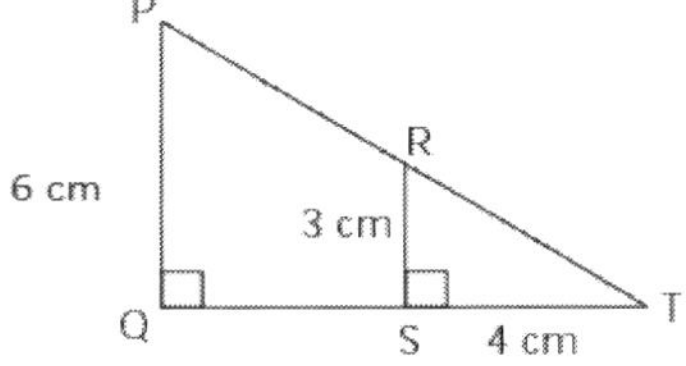

Answer: $\Delta RTS \sim \Delta PTQ$ by the AA (Angle-Angle) Similarity Theorem.

Therefore,

$$\frac{TS}{TQ} = \frac{RS}{PQ}$$

$$\frac{4}{TQ} = \frac{3}{6}$$

$$\overline{TQ} = 8$$

$$\overline{QS} = 8 - 4 = 4$$

Problem Solving Skills

Easy

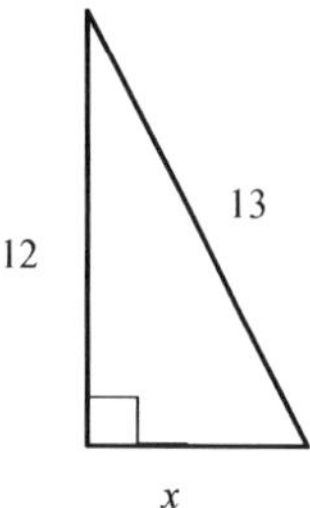

1. In the right triangle above, what is the value of x?

Answer: 5

Use the Pythagorean theorem.
$x^2 + 12^2 = 13^2$
$x = 5$

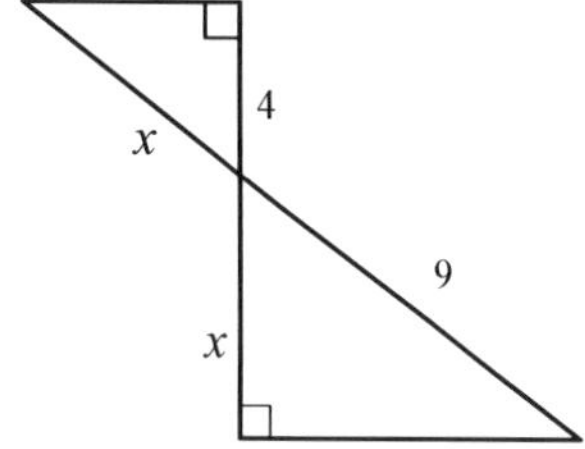

2. In the figure above, what is the value of x?
    a) 9
    b) 8
    c) 6
    d) $3\sqrt{5}$

Answer: (c)

The two triangles are similar by the AA Similarity Theorem.
$\frac{x}{9} = \frac{4}{x}$
$x^2 = 36$
$x = 6$

3. In the figure below, EB = 3, DC = 5, and BC = 4. What is the value of AB?

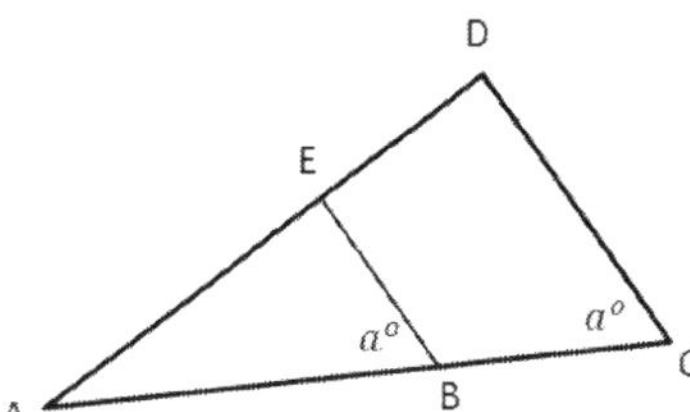

    a) 4
    b) 5
    c) 6
    d) 8

Answer: (c)

Since ∠B and ∠C have the same angle degree, $\overline{EB} \parallel \overline{DC}$. Thus, ΔABE is similar to ΔACD.
$$\frac{AB}{AC} = \frac{EB}{DC} = \frac{AB}{AB+BC} = \frac{3}{5}$$
$$\frac{AB}{AB+4} = \frac{3}{5}$$

$AB = 6$

Medium

4. The lengths of the sides of a right triangle are consecutive even integers, and the length of the shortest side is x. Which of the following equations could be used to find x? 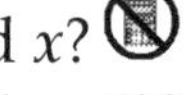
   a) $x^2 + (x + 1)^2 = (x + 2)^2$
   b) $x^2 + (x + 2)^2 = (x + 4)^2$
   c) $x + x + 2 = x + 4$
   d) $x^2 = (x + 2)(x + 4)$

Answer: (b)

Consecutive even integers can be written as x, x + 2, and x + 4. The longest side, x + 4, is the hypotenuse.
Apply the Pythagorean theorem.
$x^2 + (x + 2)^2 = (x + 4)^2$

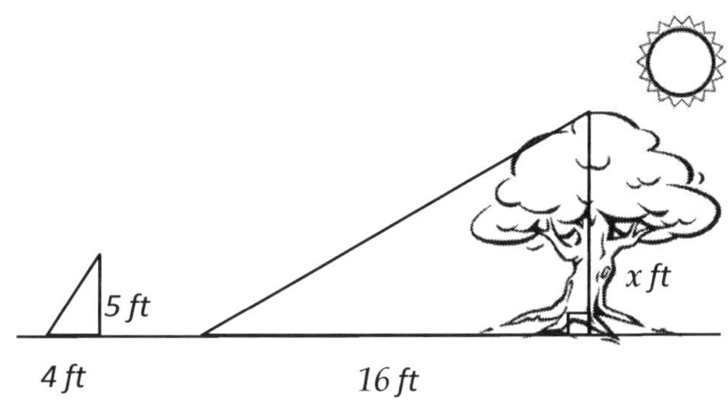

5. At a certain time of day, a tree casts a 16-foot shadow and a 5-foot stick casts a 4-foot shadow. What is the height, in feet, of the tree?

Answer: 20

The corresponding sides of two similar triangles are proportional.
$\frac{5}{4} = \frac{x}{16}$
$x = 20\ ft$

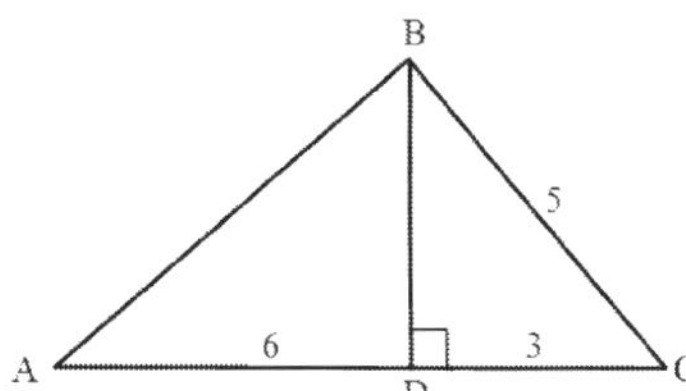

6. In the figure above, what is the length of AB?
   a) 4
   b) 7
   c) $\sqrt{52}$
   d) $\sqrt{65}$

Answer: (c)

The two right triangles share a common edge $\overline{BD}$.
$BD = \sqrt{5^2 - 3^2} = 4$
$AB = \sqrt{4^2 + 6^2} = \sqrt{52}$

7. In the figure below, points D is the mid-point of $\overline{AB}$ and point E is the mid-point of $\overline{AC}$. If AB = 10, AC = 12, and DE = 7, what is the perimeter of quadrilateral DBCE?

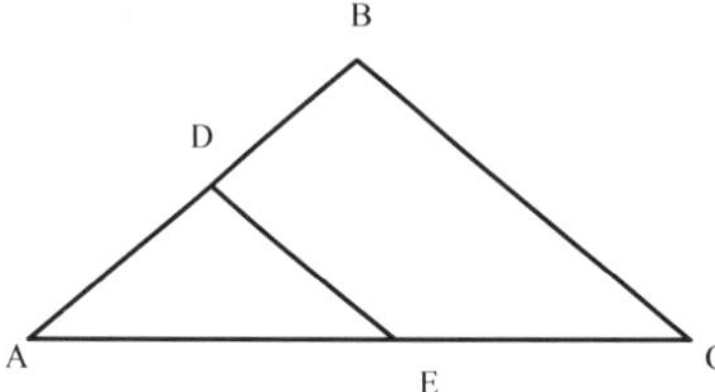

a) 29
b) 30
c) 31
d) 32

Answer: (d)

Point D is the mid-point of $\overline{AB}$ and point E is the mid-point of $\overline{AC}$, so

$\frac{AD}{AB} = \frac{AE}{AC} = \frac{1}{2}$

Therefore, $\Delta ADE \sim \Delta ABC$ by SAS Similarity theorem

$AB = 10$

$DB = 5$

$\frac{1}{2} = \frac{DE}{BC}$

$DE = 7$

$BC = 14$

$EC = \frac{1}{2}AC = 6$

Perimeter of DBCE $= 5 + 7 + 14 + 6 = 32$

8. Jon walks 10 meters away from a wall outside his school building as shown in the figure below. At the point he stands, he notices that his shadow reaches to the same spot as the shadow of the school. If Jon is 1.6 meters tall and his shadow is 2.5 meters long, how high is the school building, in meters?

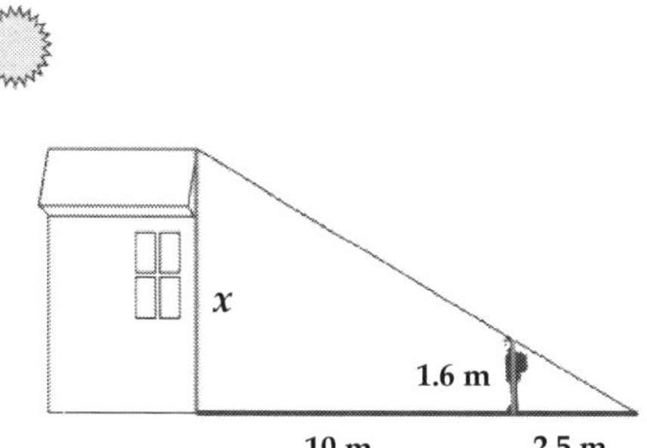

Answer: 8

Let the height of the school building be x.

The two triangles are similar, therefore their corresponding sides are proportional.

$\frac{2.5}{10 + 2.5} = \frac{1.6}{x}$

$x = 8\,m$

9. A girl who is 160 centimeters tall stands 360 centimeters away from a lamp post at night. If her shadow is 90 centimeters long, how high, in centimeters, is the lamp post?

Answer: 800

The two triangles are similar, so their corresponding sides are proportional.

Let the height of the lamp post be x.

$\frac{160}{x} = \frac{90}{90 + 360}$

$x = 800\,cm$

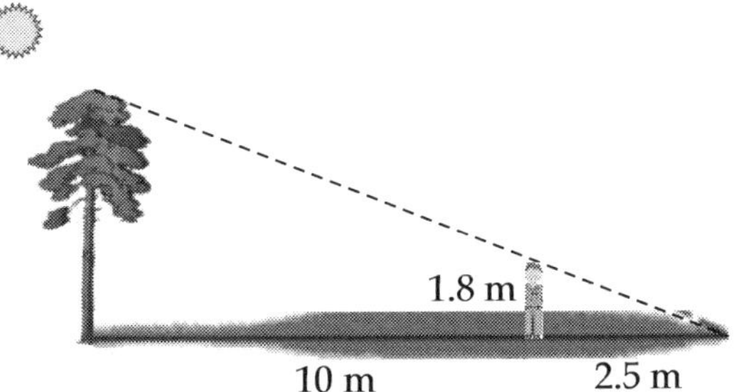

10. Sam walked 10 meters away from the base of a tree as shown in the figure above. At the point he was standing, he noticed that his shadow reached the same spot on the ground as the shadow of the tree. If Sam is 1.8 meters tall and his shadow is 2.5 meters long, how high is the tree, in meters?

Answer: 9

Let the height of the tree be x. The two triangles are similar, therefore their corresponding sides are proportional.

$\frac{2.5}{10+2.5} = \frac{1.8}{x}$

$x = 9\ m$

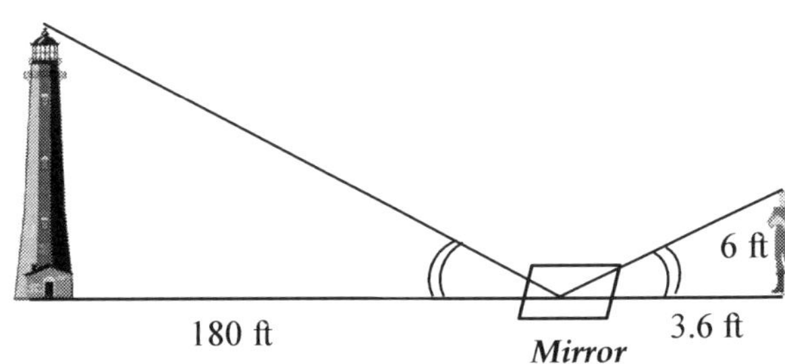

11. John places a mirror on the ground 180 feet from the base of a lighthouse. He walks backward until he can see the top of the lighthouse in the middle of the mirror. At that point, John's eyes are 6 feet above the ground and he is 3.6 feet from the mirror. Find the height, in feet, of the lighthouse.

Answer: 300

The two triangles are similar, therefore their corresponding sides are proportional.

$\frac{x}{180} = \frac{6}{3.6}$

$x = 300\ feet$

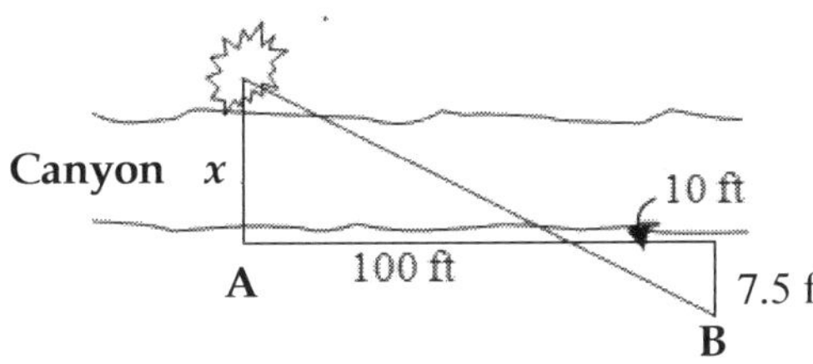

12. A bush fire is sighted on the other side of a canyon at points *A* and *B* as shown in the figure above. Find the width, in feet, of the canyon.

Answer: 75

The two triangles are similar, therefore their corresponding sides are proportional.

$\frac{x}{100} = \frac{7.5}{10}$

$x = 75\ feet$

Hard

13. In the two squares in the figure above, if the area of smaller square is one half of the big square, what is the ratio of x to y?
    a) 1
    b) $\sqrt{2}$
    c) $\sqrt{3}$
    d) $\frac{1}{2}$

Answer: (a)

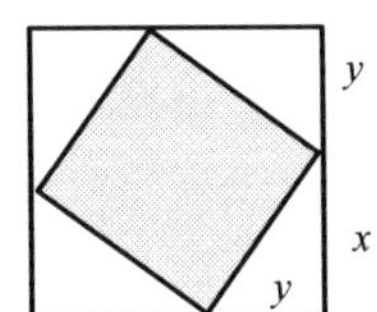

Area of Big Square = $(x + y)^2$
Area of Gray Square = $(\sqrt{x^2 + y^2}\,)^2$

$x^2 + y^2 = \frac{1}{2}(x + y)^2$
$x^2 + y^2 = \frac{1}{2}(x^2 + y^2 + 2xy)$

Divide by y^2 *on both sides.*
$(\frac{x}{y})^2 + 1 = \frac{1}{2}(\frac{x}{y})^2 + \frac{1}{2} + \frac{x}{y}$
$\frac{1}{2}(\frac{x}{y})^2 - \frac{x}{y} + \frac{1}{2} = 0$
$\frac{x}{y} = 1$

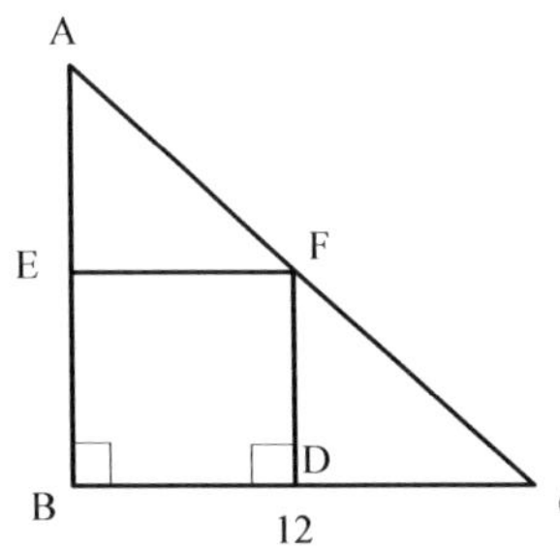

14. In isosceles right triangle ΔABC above, $EF \parallel BC$ and length of $\overline{AF}$ is half of the length of $\overline{AC}$. What is the area of the rectangular region?
    a) 16
    b) 25
    c) 36
    d) 64

Answer: (c)

$AB = BC$
$EF = BD = \frac{1}{2}BC = 6$
$BE = \frac{1}{2}AB = 6$
Area $= 6 \times 6 = 36$

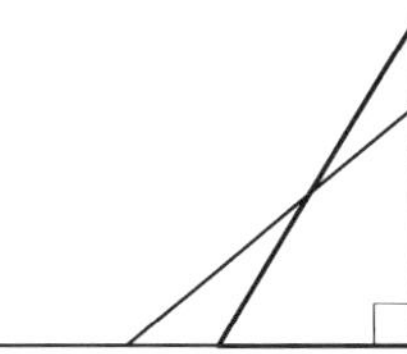

15. In the figure above, a 20-foot-long ladder is placed against a building which is perpendicular to the ground. After the ladder slides down 4 feet vertically, the bottom of the ladder is now 16 feet away from the base of the building, what is the original distance of the bottom of the ladder from the base of the building, in feet?
    a) 12
    b) 14
    c) 16
    d) 18

Answer: (a)

After slipping, the height becomes $\sqrt{20^2 - 16^2} = 12$.

Before slipping, the height was $12 + 4 = 16$.

The bottom of the ladder was originally $\sqrt{20^2 - 16^2} = 12$ *feet away from the base.*

16. The graph below is a right triangle. Find the area of this right triangle?

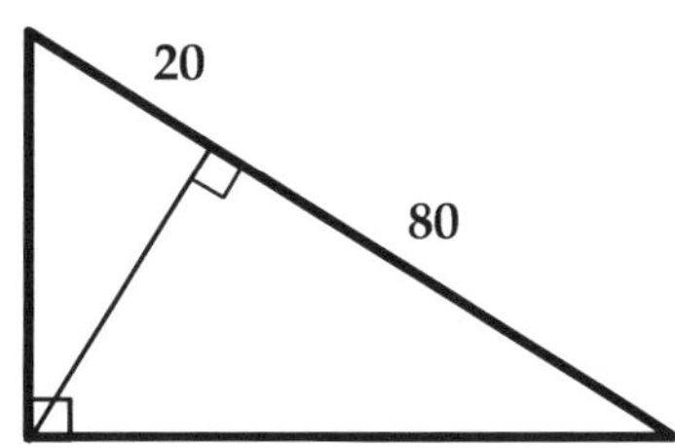

Answer: 2000

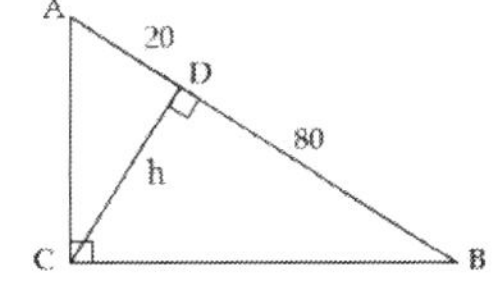

$\angle A + \angle ACD = \angle DCB + \angle ACD = 90°$

$\angle A = \angle DCB$

$\angle ADC = \angle CDB = 90°$

$\Delta ADC \sim \Delta CDB$

$\frac{CD}{AD} = \frac{BD}{CD} = \frac{h}{20} = \frac{80}{h}$

$h^2 = 20 \times 80 = 1600$

$h = 40$

$Area = \frac{1}{2}(20 + 80)(40) = 2000$

D. AREA OF A TRIANGLE

CONCEPT OVERVIEWS

Area of a Triangle

$$\textit{Area of a Triangle} = \frac{\textbf{Base} \times \textbf{Height}}{\textbf{2}}$$

The **height** of a triangle is the perpendicular distance from the **base** to the opposite vertex.

Some different triangles with different bases and heights are shown below:

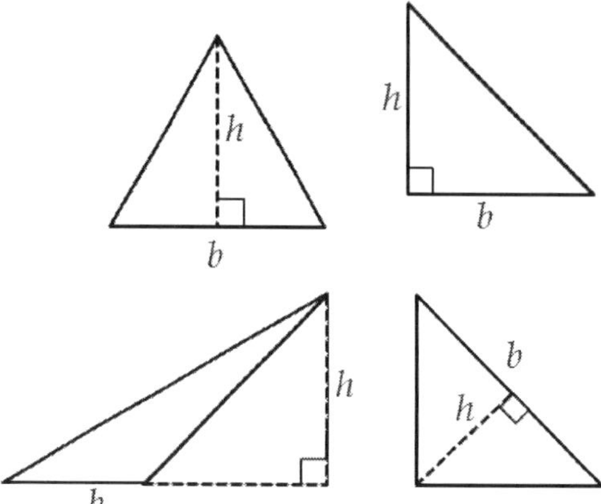

Area of an Equilateral Triangle $= \frac{\sqrt{3}}{4} s^2$, where s is the length of a side.

Example: Find the area of this triangle.

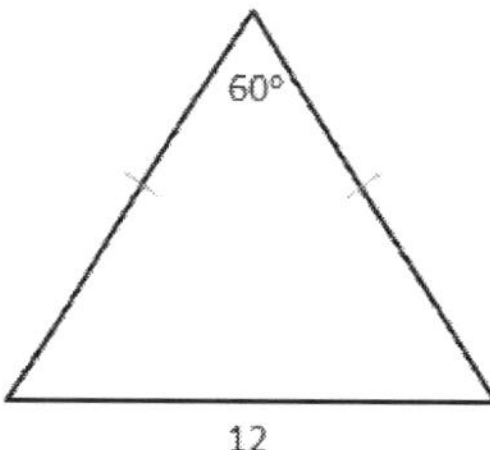

Solution: This is an equilateral triangle with equal side length of 12.
The easy way to solve this problem is to apply the formula for finding the area of an equilateral.

$$A = \frac{\sqrt{3}}{4} s^2 = \frac{\sqrt{3}}{4} (12)^2 = 36\sqrt{3}$$

If the ratio of the corresponding sides of two similar triangles is $a : b$, then the ratio of their areas is $a^2 : b^2$.

Example: Find the area of triangle B if the triangles A and B are similar.

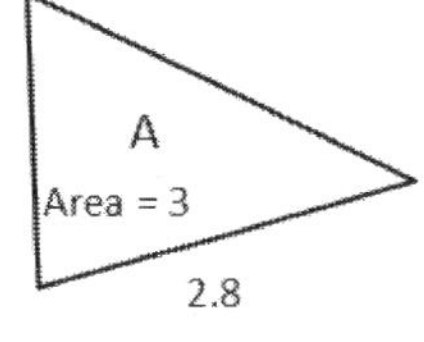

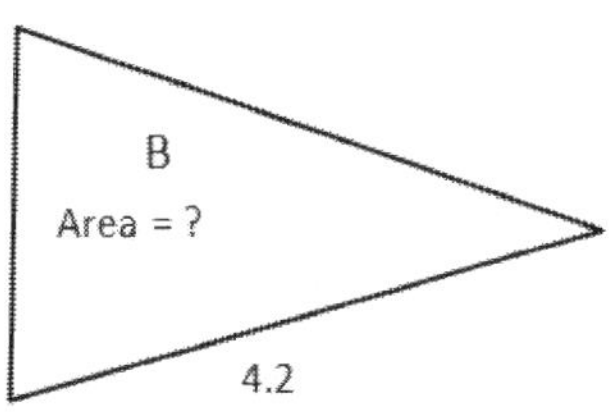

Solution: In two similar triangles, the ratio of their areas is equal to the square of the ratio of their sides.
Let the area of B be x.

Set up the proportion: $\left(\frac{2.8}{4.2}\right)^2 = \frac{3}{x}$

$\frac{0.44}{1} = \frac{3}{x}$

Cross multiply: $0.44x = 3$

$x = 6.82$

Problem Solving Skills

Easy

1. ΔABC is an equilateral triangle with side length of 10. What is the area of ΔABC?
   a) 100
   b) 50
   c) $25\sqrt{2}$
   d) $25\sqrt{3}$

Answer: (d)

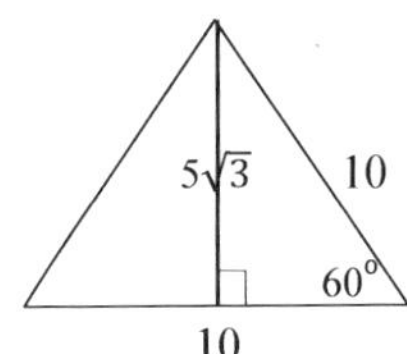

30-60-90 special right triangle
$\frac{1}{2} \times 10 \times 5\sqrt{3} = 25\sqrt{3}$ *Or*
$A = \frac{\sqrt{3}}{4}s^2 = \frac{\sqrt{3}}{4} \times 100 = 25\sqrt{3}$

2. An isosceles triangle has one side of length 40 and one side of length 50. What is the smallest possible value that the perimeter of the triangle could be?

Answer: 130

An isosceles triangle must have two sides with the same length. The third side has a length of either 40 or 50.
The smallest perimeter can be 40 + 40 + 50 = 130.

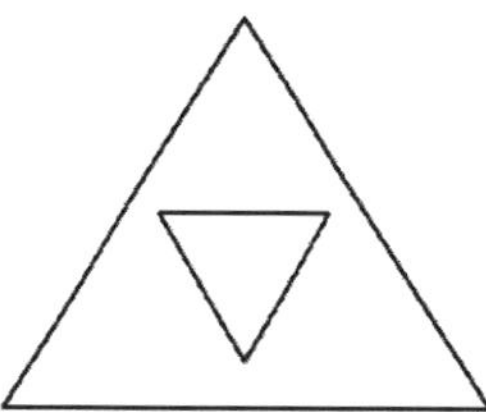

3. Two equilateral triangles are shown above with the ratio of their side lengths equal to $\frac{1}{3}$. What is the ratio of their areas?
   a) $\frac{1}{3}$
   b) $\frac{1}{\sqrt{3}}$
   c) $\frac{1}{6}$
   d) $\frac{1}{9}$

Answer: (d)

The ratio of two triangles' areas is equal to the square of the ratio of their sides.

$(\frac{1}{3})^2 = \frac{1}{9}$

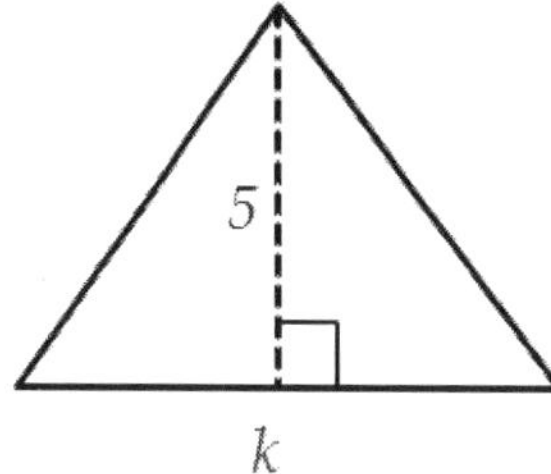

4. In the figure above, if the area of the triangle is 20, what is the value of k?

Answer: 8

$20 = \frac{1}{2} \times 5 \times k$
$k = 8$

Medium

5. In the figure below, the area of the shaded region is 26 square units. What is the height of the smaller triangle?

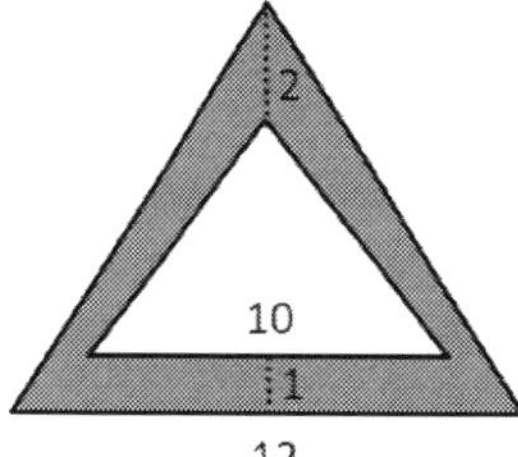

Answer: 8

If h is the height of smaller triangle, then the height of the big triangle is $h + 3$.
Area of Big Δ – Area of Small Δ = 26
$\frac{1}{2}(h + 3) \times 12 - \frac{1}{2}h \times 10 = 26$
$6h + 18 - 5h = 26$
$h = 8$

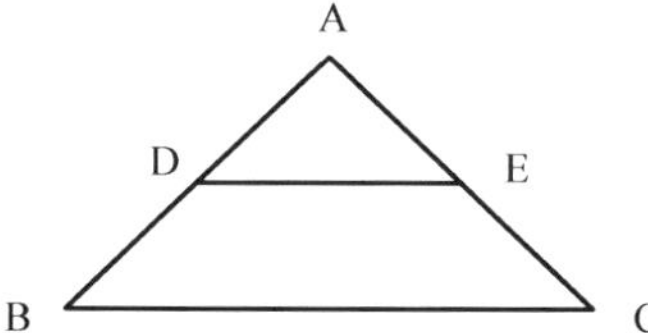

6. In ΔABC above, D and E are the midpoints of $\overline{AB}$ and $\overline{AC}$ respectively, and the area of ΔABC is 48. What is the area of **Δ**ADE?
   a) 10
   b) 11
   c) 12
   d) 16
   e) 24

Answer: (c)

Since DE∥BC, $\Delta ABC \sim \Delta ADE$.
$DE : BC = 1 : 2$
The ratio of the areas of ΔABC to ΔADE is 4 : 1.
$4 : 1 = 48 : x$
$4x = 48$
$x = 12$

7. The figure below shows four squares with sides of length 4, 6, 9, and L. Line l_1 hits the upper left corner of each square. What is the value of L?

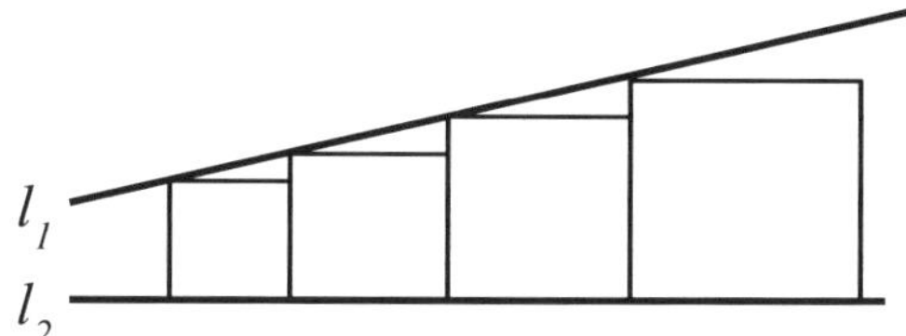

Answer: 13.5

There are 3 similar triangles between l_1 and the first 3 squares. Their heights have the same ratio of as the ratio of the sides of the squares.
The first triangle has height $6 - 4 = 2$. We will use x to denote the height of triangle 2 and y to denote the height of triangle 3.
$4 : 6 : 9 = 2 : x : y$
$y = 4.5$
L = Length of 3rd Square + y = 9 + 4.5 = 13.5

8. In the figure below, triangles A and B are isosceles right triangles and C is a square. If the area of A is 8 and the area of B is 18, what is the area of C?

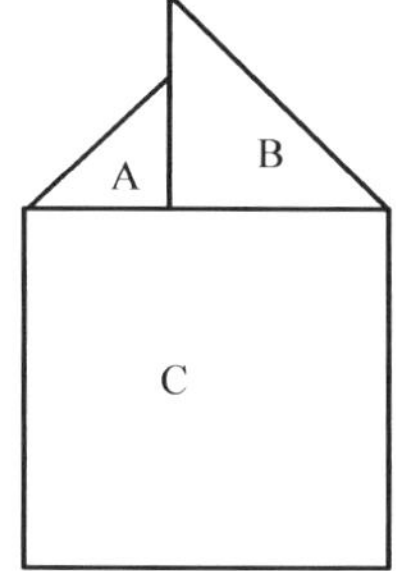

   a) 64
   b) 81
   c) 100
   d) 144

Answer: (c)

The area of each of the right isosceles triangles is $\frac{1}{2} \times$ (length of leg)^2.
Let x be the length of triangle A's legs
$\frac{1}{2}x^2 = 8$
$x = 4$
Let y be the length of triangle B's legs
$\frac{1}{2}y^2 = 18$
$y = 6$
Thus, the square C has a side of 10 and its area is 100.

E. Triangle Inequality Theorem

Concept Overviews

The bigger side of a triangle is always opposite the bigger angle and the smaller side is always opposite the smaller angle.

Example: List the angles from largest to smallest based on the following triangle:

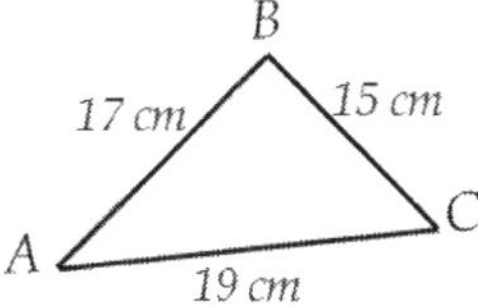

Answer: $\angle B > \angle C > \angle A$

Triangle Inequality Theorem: The length of one side of a triangle is always less than the sum of the lengths of the other two sides but greater than their difference.

Example: Which of the following could be the length of $\overline{YZ}$?

a) 3
b) 4
c) 10
d) 12

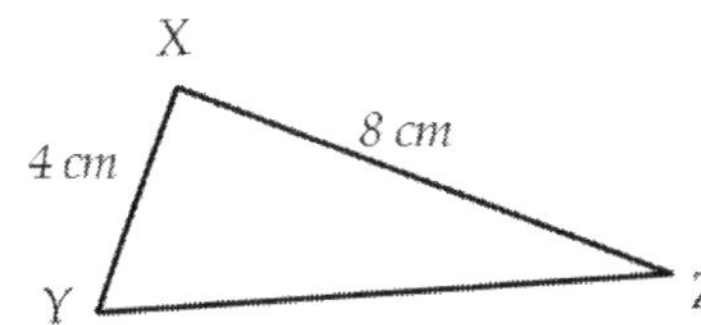

Answer: The difference of the lengths of any two sides of a triangle is less than the length of the third side in the triangle. The sum of the lengths of any two sides of a triangle is greater than the length of the third side of the triangle.

$8 - 4 < \overline{YZ} < 8 + 4$

$4 < \overline{YZ} < 12$

Only (c) satisfies these conditions.

Problem Solving Skills

Easy

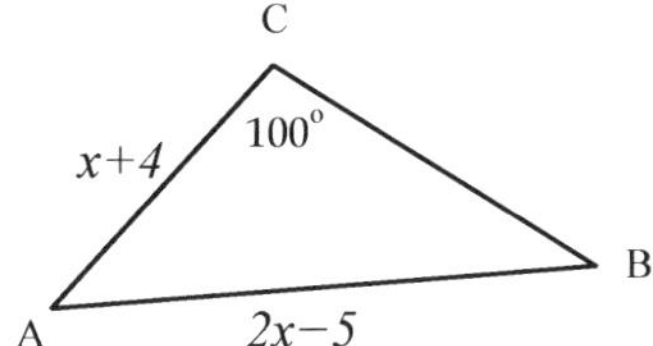

1. In ΔBC above, which of the following must be true? 
   a) $x < 18$
   b) $x > 18$
   c) $x < 9$
   d) $x > 9$

Answer: (d)

∠C is the biggest angle so that $\overline{AB}$ must be the longest side.
$2x - 5 > x + 4$
$x > 9$

2. If one triangle has two sides that have lengths of 3 and 8, which of the following CANNOT be the length of the third side of the triangle?
   a) 5
   b) 6
   c) 8
   d) 9

Answer: (a)

The length of the 3rd side should be smaller than the sum of the lengths of the other two sides and greater than their difference.
$8 - 3 < x < 8 + 3$
$5 < x < 11$

3. A triangle has a perimeter of 27. The medium-length side is 3 more than the length of the shortest side, and the longest side is twice the length of the shortest side. Find the length of the shortest side?
   a) 5
   b) 6
   c) 7
   d) 8

Answer: (b)

Let the length of the shortest side be x.

$27 = x + x + 3 + 2x$
$x = 6$

4. Which of the following cannot be the lengths of the three sides of a triangle?
   a) 6, 4, and 3
   b) 6, 3, and 5
   c) 6, 5, and 11
   d) 6, 6, and 10

Answer: (c)

Let the lengths of the two sides other than the side with length 6 be x and y, where $x > y$.
$x - y < 6 < x + y$
Only (c) violates above condition.

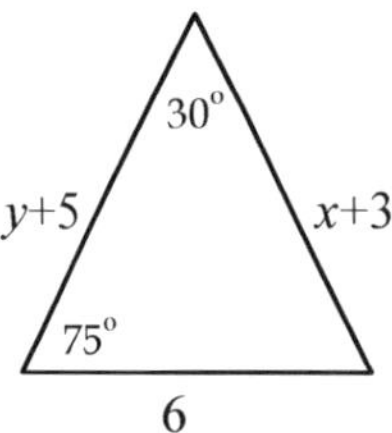

Note: Figure not drawn to scale.

5. In the triangle above, which of the following must be true?
   a) $x = y$
   b) $x = 6$
   c) $x < y$
   d) $x = y + 2$

Answer: (d)

The degree of the 3rd interior angle is $180^\circ - 30^\circ - 75^\circ = 75^\circ$.
Since this triangle has two angles that are 75°, it is an isosceles triangle.
$y + 5 = x + 3$
$x = y + 2$

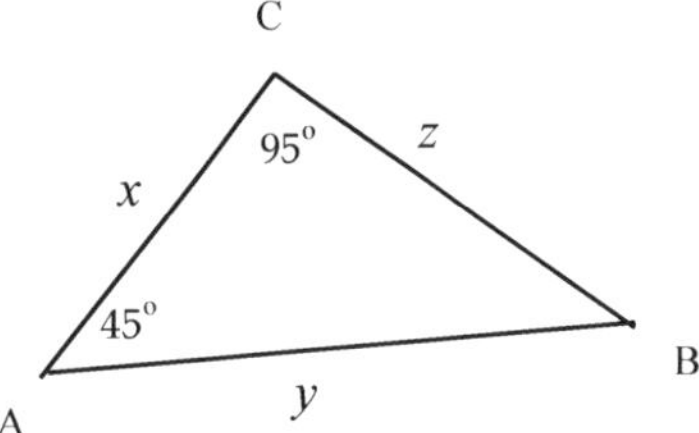

6. Which of the following must be true about x, y, and z in the figure above?
   a) $x < z < y$
   b) $z < x < y$
   c) $x < y < z$
   d) $z < y < x$

Answer: (a)

The bigger angle is always facing the bigger side.
$m\angle C > m\angle A > m\angle B$
$y > z > x$

7. An isosceles triangle has one side that has length 6. All of the following could be the lengths of the other two sides EXCEPT?
   a) 4, 4
   b) 6, 3
   c) 6, 10
   d) 6, 12

Answer: (d)

Case 1:length of three sides: 6, 6, x
$6 - 6 < x < 6 + 6$
$0 < x < 12$
Case 2 length of three sides: 6, x, x
$6 - x < x < 6 + x$
$x > 3$
(a), (b), and (c) all satisfy either case 1 or case 2.

8. In ΔABC below, $\angle ACB$ is 91°. Which of the following segments has the longest length?

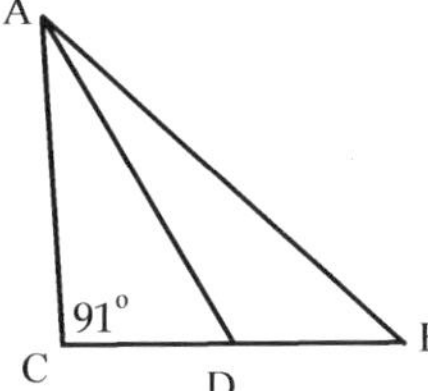

a) Segment AD
b) Segment AC
c) Segment CB
d) Segment AB

Answer: (d)

In a triangle, bigger angles will always face bigger sides. No angle in ΔABC will have degree greater than 91, so the side facing $\angle ACB$ will be largest.
$\angle ADB > \angle ACD$ (by exterior angle theorem)
$AB > AD > AC$ and CD

Medium

9. What is one possible integer length of $\overline{AC}$ if $\angle A > \angle B > \angle C$?

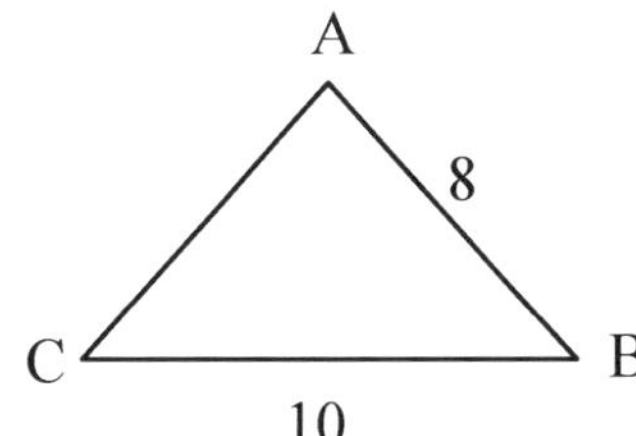

Note: Figure not drawn to scale.

Answer: 9

The Longest side of a triangle is opposite the largest angle. The shortest side of a triangle is opposite the smallest angle. Since $\angle A > \angle B > \angle C$, $\overline{BC} > \overline{AC} > \overline{AB}$, and so $10 > \overline{AC} > 8$. The only possible integer is 9.

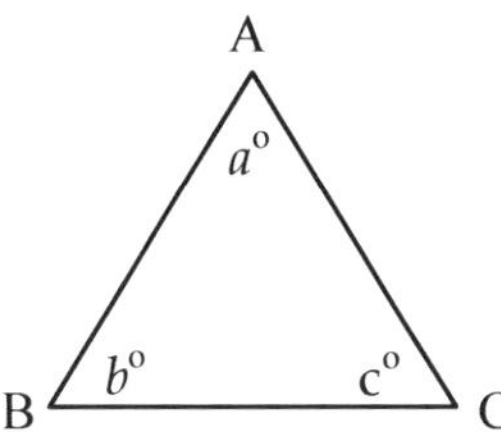

Note: Figure not drawn to scale.

10. The triangle above is isosceles and $a > b$. Which of the following must be FALSE?

a) AB = BC
b) BC = AC
c) AC = AB
d) $a = c$

Answer: (b)

If $a > b$, then $BC > AC$.

Hard

11. If the lengths of the sides of a certain triangle are x, y, and z, which of the following statements could be true?

    a) $x = y + z + 1$
    b) $x = y - z - 1$
    c) $x = 2y + z$
    d) $x = z + \frac{1}{2}y$

Answer: (d)

$y - z < x < y + z$

Only (d) meets the above conditions.

12. The lengths of two sides of a triangle are $(x + 1)$ and $(x + 3)$, where x is a positive number. Which of the following ranges includes all the possible values of the third side?

    a) $(0, x)$
    b) $(0, 2x)$
    c) $(2, 2x)$
    d) $(2, 2x + 4)$

Answer: (d)

$(x + 3) - (x + 1) < y < (x + 3) + (x + 1)$

$2 < y < 2x + 4$

III. Polygons and Quadrilaterals

A. Polygons

Concept Overviews

A **polygon** is a plane figure composed of three or more line segments that are connected at both ends.

- **Convex Polygon:** All interior angles of the polygon are less than 180°.

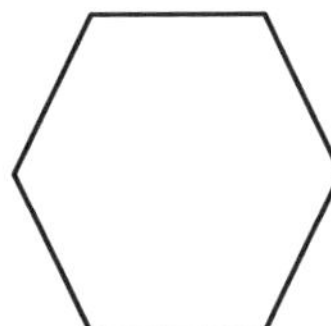

A Convex Hexagon

- **Concave Polygon:** One or more interior angles are greater than 180°.

A Concave Heptagon

Sum of Interior Angles of a Polygon

Since an n-sided polygon can be divided into $(n - 2)$ triangles without overlapping and the sum of the interior angles of each triangle is 180°, the sum of the interior angles of a polygon is equal to $\mathbf{(n - 2) \times 180°}$

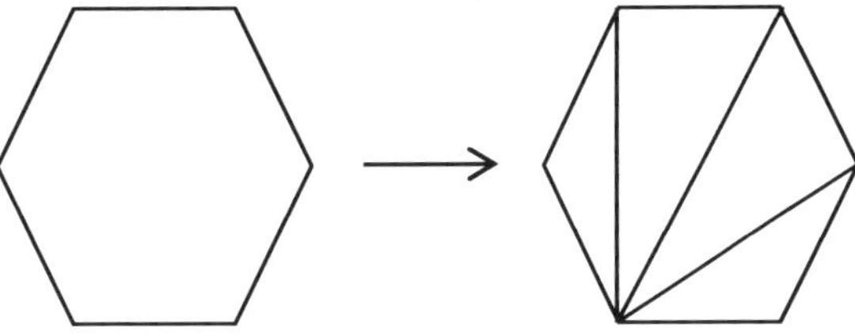

- A **regular polygon** is a polygon where all sides are equal in length and all angles have the same degree measure.
- Each interior angle of a regular polygon is $(\frac{(n-2) \times 180}{n})^{o}$.

Sum of Exterior Angles of a Polygon

For an n-sided polygon, the sum of its exterior angles is equal to

$$n \times 180° - (n - 2) \times 180° = 360°.$$

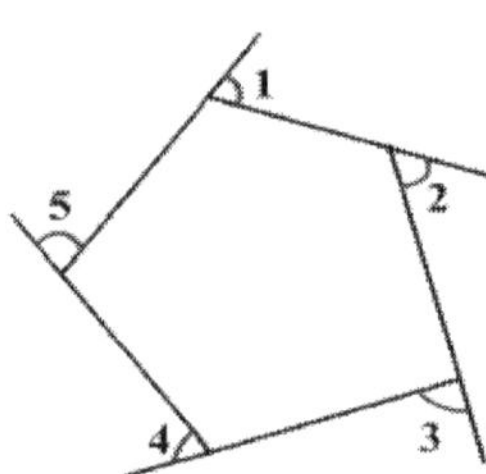

The 5 exterior angles of a pentagon sum to 360°.

Example: Find the measure of each interior angle of a regular heptagon as shown below and find the measure of x.

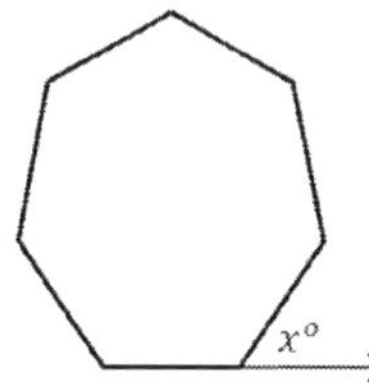

Answer: When $n = 7$, the measure of each interior angle is $\frac{(7-2)\times 180^o}{7} = 128.6^o$.
$x = 180 - 128.6 = 51.4$

Problem Solving Skills

Easy

1. Point A is a vertex of a 10-sided polygon. When all possible diagonals are drawn from point A to any other vertex of the polygon, how many triangles are formed?
   a) 10
   b) 9
   c) 8
   d) 7

Answer: (c)

There are always (n – 2) non-overlapping triangles formed by drawing all the possible non-intersecting diagonals in an n-sided polygon.
10 − 2 = 8 triangles

Medium

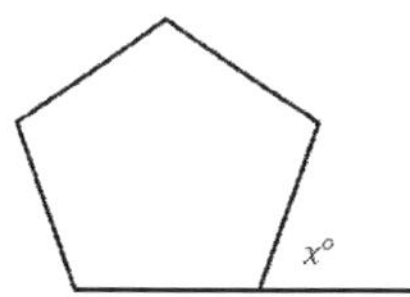

2. In the regular pentagon shown above, what is the value of x?
   a) 120
   b) 90
   c) 80
   d) 72

Answer: (d)

The sum of the interior angles of a regular pentagon is $\frac{(5-2)\times 180}{5} = 108^o$.
$x = 180 - 108 = 72$

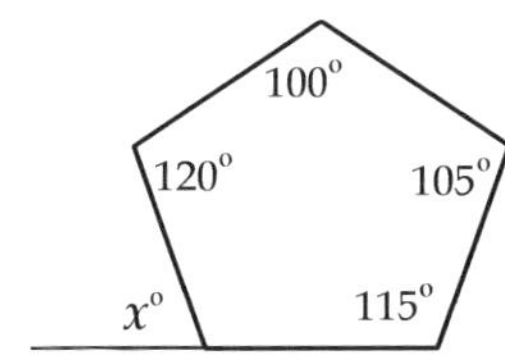

Note: Figure not drawn to scale.

3. The figure shown above is composed of five straight line segments, what is the value of x?

Answer: 80

The sum of all interior angles of a pentagon is $(5-3) \times 180 = 540^{\circ}$.
$540 = 120 + 100 + 105 + 115 + (180 - x)$
$x = 80$

4. The figure shown below is a regular octagon with center O. What is the value of a?

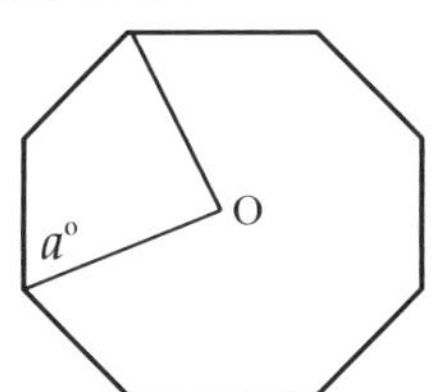

a) 90
b) 72.5
c) 70
d) 67.5

Answer: (d)

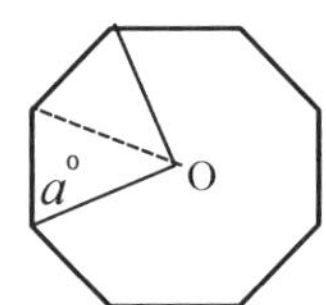

There are two congruent isosceles triangles shown above. The measure of a is one half of an interior angle.
The interior angle of a regular octagon is $\frac{(8-2) \times 180}{8}$ degrees.
$a = \frac{6 \times 180}{8} \times \frac{1}{2} = 67.5$

5. What is the area of the figure below?

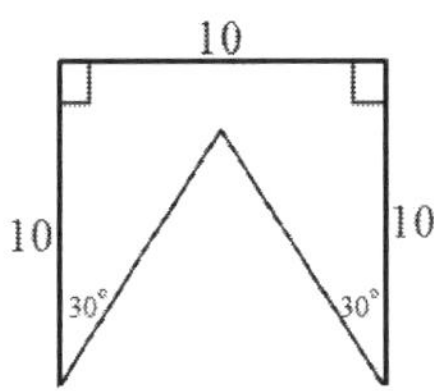

Answer: 56.6 or 56.7

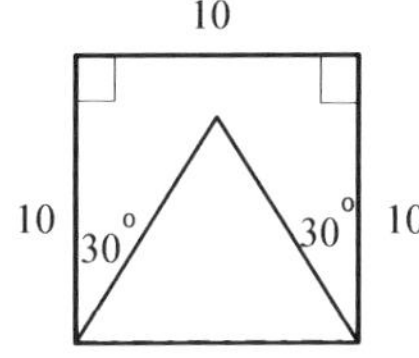

The triangle above has 60° - 60° - 60° interior angles, which makes it an equilateral triangle with side length 10. To find the area, find the area of the square and subtract the area of the triangle.

$10 \times 10 - \frac{\sqrt{3}}{4} \times 10 \times 10 = 56.7$

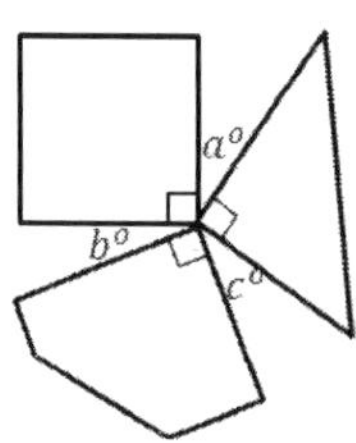

6. The figure above shows a right triangle, a square, and a pentagon. Each polygon has a 90° angle that intersects at the same point. What is the value of a + b + c?
   a) 60
   b) 90
   c) 120
   d) 150

Answer: (b)

$a + b + c + 270 = 360$
$a + b + c = 90$

7. In the figure below, what is the value of *a*?

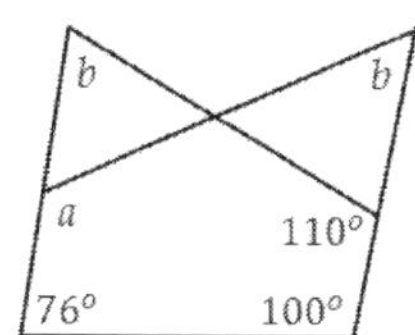

Answer: 110

Use the two quadrilaterals to set up an equation.
$b + 110 + 100 + 76$
$= b + a + 76 + 100$
$a = 110^{\circ}$

Hard

8. In the figure below, what is the value of $a + b + c$?

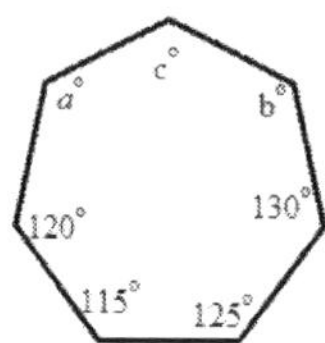

Note: Figure not drawn to scale.

Answer: 410
he sum of all interior angles is equal to 180 × (7 − 2).
$180 \times (7 - 2) = 900 = a + b + c + 130 + 125 + 120 + 115$
$a + b + c = 410$

9. If the perimeter of the figure below is 30, what is the sum of x and y?

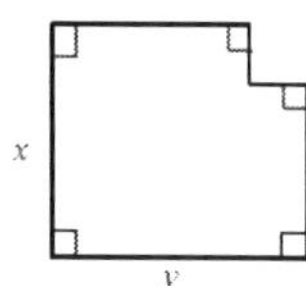

Answer: 15
The perimeter of the figure should be the same as the perimeter of the rectangle: $2(x + y) = 30$
$x + y = 15$

10. In the figure below, a regular polygon is inscribed in a circle O. If O is the center of the circle, what is the value of *a*?

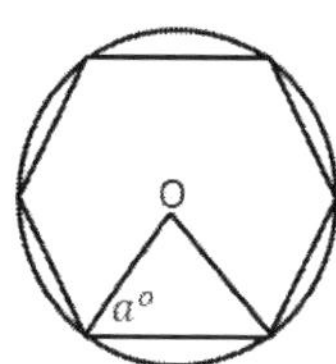

Answer: 60

The measurement of a is half of an interior angle of the regular polygon.
$a = \frac{1}{2} \times (\frac{6-2}{6} \times 180) = 60$

B. Parallelograms

Concept Overviews

The Properties of a Parallelogram

A **parallelogram** is a special type of quadrilateral where both pairs of opposite sides are parallel. Parallelograms have the following properties:

1. Opposite sides are equal in length and parallel.

$$\overleftrightarrow{AB} \parallel \overleftrightarrow{DC} \text{ and } \overleftrightarrow{AD} \parallel \overleftrightarrow{BC}$$
$$\overline{AB} = \overline{DC} \text{ and } \overline{AD} = \overline{BC}$$

2. Opposite angles are congruent.

3. Consecutive angles are supplementary.

$$\angle A \cong \angle C \text{ and } \angle B \cong \angle D$$

$m\angle A + m\angle B = 180^\circ$ $m\angle A + m\angle D = 180^\circ$

$m\angle D + m\angle C = 180^\circ$ $m\angle B + m\angle C = 180^\circ$

4. A diagonal of any parallelogram makes two congruent triangles.

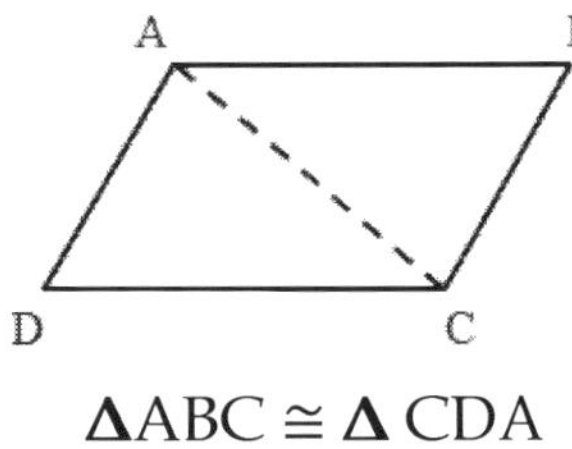

$$\Delta ABC \cong \Delta CDA$$

5. The diagonals of any parallelogram bisect each other.

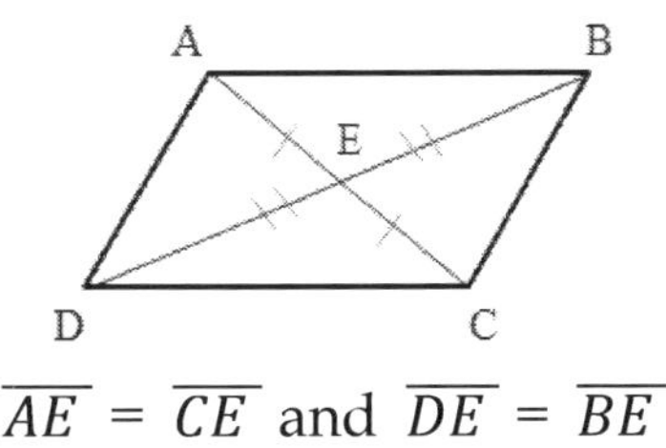

$$\overline{AE} = \overline{CE} \text{ and } \overline{DE} = \overline{BE}$$

Special Parallelograms

- A **rhombus** is a parallelogram with four equal sides. Rhombuses have the following properties in addition to the properties of parallelograms:
  - o Diagonals are perpendicular.

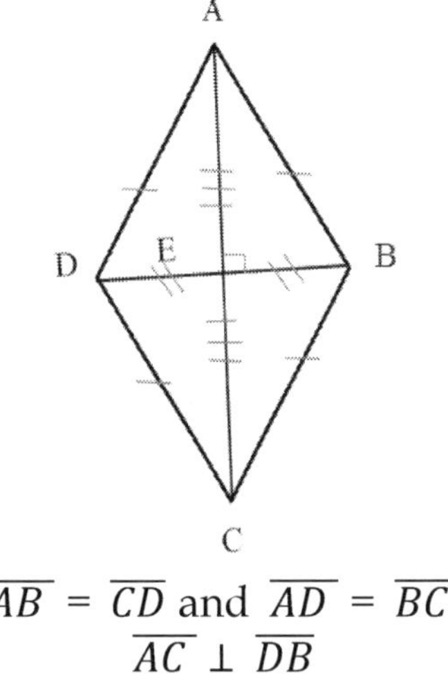

$\overline{AB} = \overline{CD}$ and $\overline{AD} = \overline{BC}$
$\overline{AC} \perp \overline{DB}$

- A **rectangle** is a parallelogram with four right angles. Rectangles have the following properties in addition to the properties of parallelograms:
  - o Diagonals are equal in length.

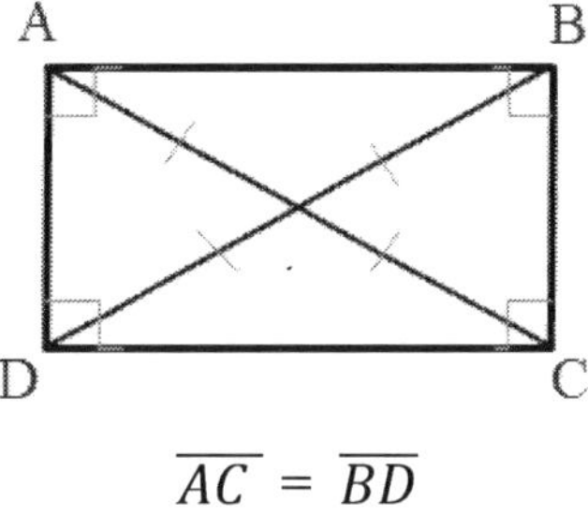

$\overline{AC} = \overline{BD}$

- A **square** is a regular quadrilateral with four equal sides and four right angles. Squares have all the properties of parallelograms, rhombuses, and rectangles, since they are a special case of all three.
  - o Diagonals are equal.
  - o Diagonals are perpendicular.

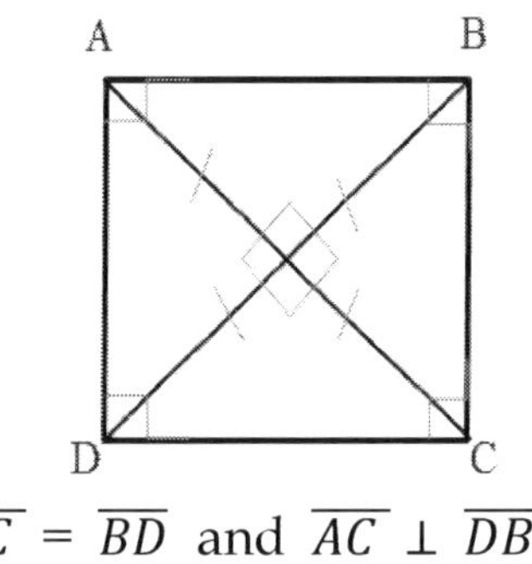

$\overline{AC} = \overline{BD}$ and $\overline{AC} \perp \overline{DB}$

Problem Solving Skills

Easy

1. If the perimeter of an equilateral triangle equals the perimeter of a square, what is the ratio of the length of a side of the square to the length of a side of the triangle?
   a) 1 : 1
   b) 2 : 3
   c) 3 : 4
   d) 4 : 3

Answer: (c)

Let the length of the side of the triangle be x and the length of the side of the square be y.

$3x = 4y$
$y : x = 3 : 4$

2. A circle is tangent to two sides of a parallelogram ABCD as shown in the figure below. If the circle has an area of 25π, what is the area of the parallelogram ABCD?

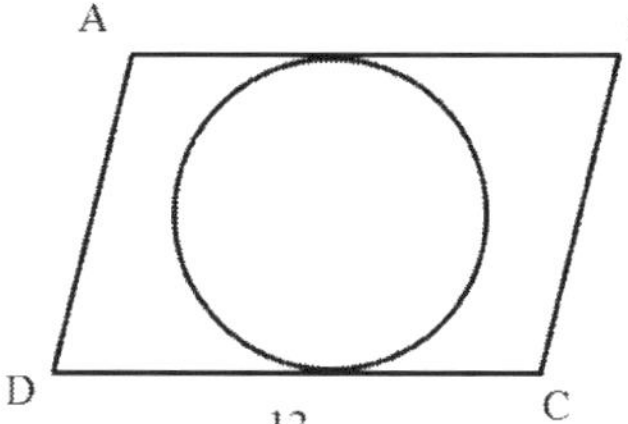

Answer: 120

The area of the parallelogram ABCD is equal to its base multiplied by its height.
Base × Height = 12 × Diameter of Circle
$\pi r^2 = 25\pi$
$r = 5$
$d = 2r = 10$
Area of Parallelogram $= 12 \times 10 = 120$

3. A rectangular box is 24 inches long, 18 inches wide, and 12 inches high. What is the least number of cubic boxes that can be stored perfectly in this box?
   a) 12
   b) 18
   c) 24
   d) 36

Answer: (c)

Cubic boxes' length, width, and height have the same length, so the number of cubic boxes must be a common factor of 24, 18, and 12. To find the minimum number of boxes, we need to find the GCF (greatest common factor) of these three numbers.
The GCF of 24, 18 and 12 is 6, so there are $\frac{24}{6} \times \frac{18}{6} \times \frac{12}{6}$ *cubic boxes.*
$\frac{24}{6} \times \frac{18}{6} \times \frac{12}{6} = 24$

4. The perimeter of square X is 5 times the perimeter of square Y. If the area of square Y is 36, then what is the length of the side of square X?
   a) 18
   b) 24
   c) 28
   d) 30

Answer: (d)

Side of X : Side of Y = 5 : 1
Area of X : Area of Y = 25 : 1
Area of X = 25 × 36 = 900
Side of X $= \sqrt{900} = 30$

5. In a square ABCD above, vertices A, B, C, and D are the centers of 4 equal circles with radius 1. Find the area of the shaded region?
   a) π
   b) $4 - \frac{1}{2}\pi$
   c) $4 - \pi$
   d) $2 + \pi$

Answer: (c)

Area of Shaded Region = Area of Square – 4 × Area of Quarter Circle

Area $= 2 \times 2 - 4 \times \frac{\pi(1)^2}{4} = 4 - \pi$

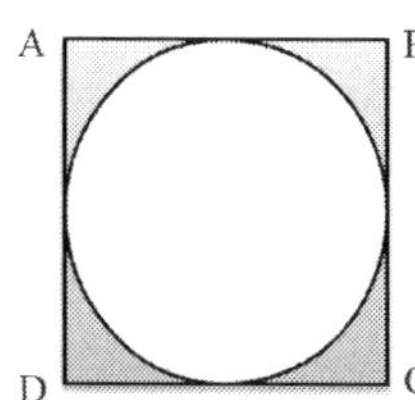

6. In square ABCD above, if the radius of the circle is 4, what is the area of the shaded region?
   a) $64 - 16\pi$
   b) $32 - 2\pi$
   c) $64 - 2\pi$
   d) $32 - 4\pi$

Answer: (a)

Shaded Area = Area of Square – Area of Circle
Length $= 4 \times 2 = 8$
$8 \times 8 - (\pi \times 4^2) = 64 - 16\pi$

Medium

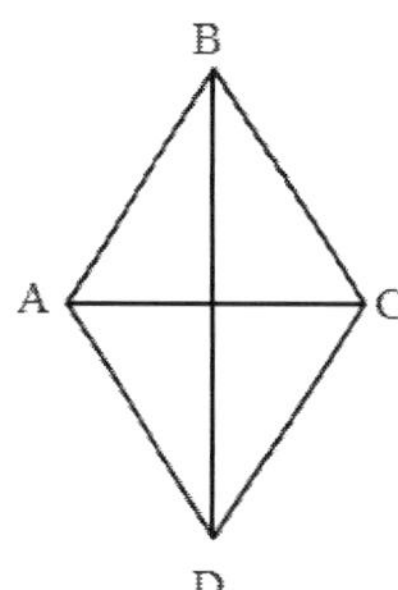

7. In the figure above, segments BD and AC are the diagonals of rhombus ABCD. If BD = 10 and AC = 8, what is the area of ΔACD?
   a) 10
   b) 20
   c) 30
   d) 40

Answer:(b)

Area of $\Delta ACD = \frac{1}{2} AC \times \frac{1}{2} BD$
$\frac{1}{2} \times 8 \times \frac{1}{2} \times 10 = 20$

8. In quadrilateral ABCD, $m\angle A = m\angle B = 128°$, and $m\angle D$ is $10°$ less than 5 times of $m\angle C$. Find $m\angle D$.

Answer: 85

$A + B + C + D = 360°$
$128° + 128° + 5x - 10° + x = 360°$
$x = 19°$
$5x - 10° = 85°$

9. The figure below shows a square and a right triangle. What is the area of the shaded region?

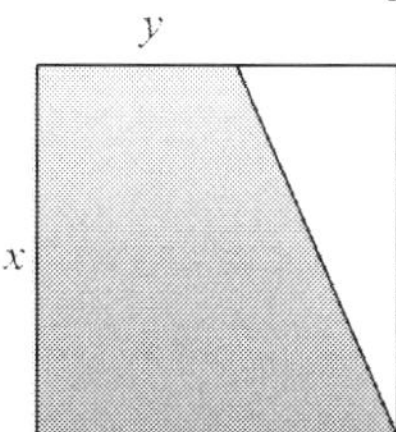

a) $\frac{x(x+y)}{2}$
b) $\frac{x2 + y2}{2}$
c) xy
d) $x(x+y)$

Answer: (a)

Area of Square $= x^2$
Area of Triangle $= \frac{1}{2} \times x \times (x - y)$
Shaded Area = Area of Square − Area of Triangle
$= x^2 - \frac{1}{2}x^2 + \frac{1}{2}xy$
$= \frac{1}{2}x^2 + \frac{1}{2}xy = \frac{1}{2}x(x+y)$

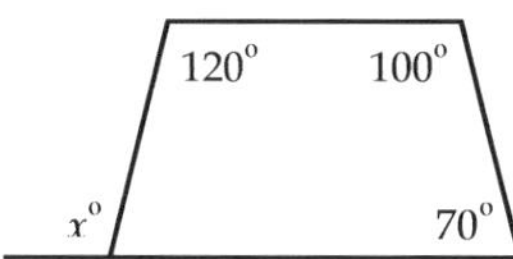

Note: Figure not drawn to scale.

10. What is the value of x in the figure above?
a) 70
b) 100
c) 105
d) 110

Answer: (d)

The sum of the interior angles of a quadrilateral is equal to 360°.
$120 + 100 + 70 + (180 - x) = 360$
$x = 110$

11. The area of a rectangle is 2400 square meters. If the length of one side of the rectangle is 80 meters, what is the perimeter of the rectangle, in meters?

Answer: 220

$2400 = 80x$
$x = 30$; Perimeter $= (30 + 80) \times 2$ $= 220$ meters

Hard

12. The figure below shows an arrangement of 14 squares, each with side length of x inches. The perimeter of the figure is P inches and the area of the figure is A square inches. If $7P = A$, what is the value of x?

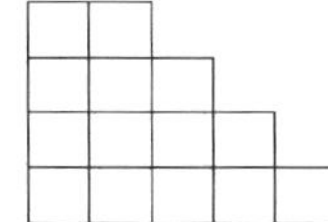

Answer: 9

Let the length of the side of a small square be x. The perimeter P is equal to 18x and its area is equal to 14 × x².
$7P = A$
$7 \times 18x = 14x^2$
$x = 9$

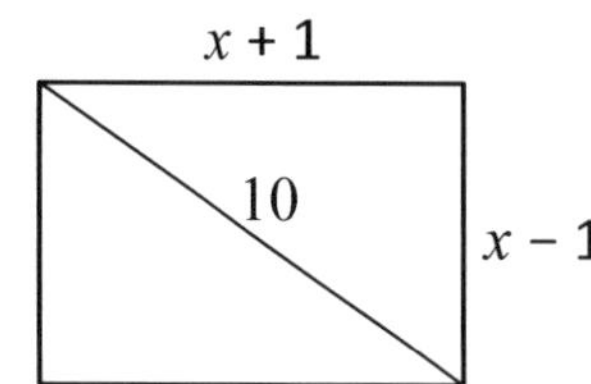

13. The figure above is a rectangle. What is the value of x?
    a) 5
    b) 6
    c) $5\sqrt{2}$
    d) 7

Answer: (d)

Use the Pythagorean theorem.
$(x - 1)^2 + (x + 1)^2 = 10^2$
$x^2 - 2x + 1 + x^2 + 2x + 1 = 100$
$2x^2 + 2 = 100$
$x^2 = 49$
$x = 7$

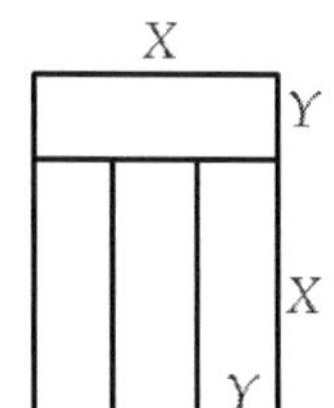

14. The unit above is composed of four congruent rectangular tiles which are each X inches long and Y inches wide. If this pattern unit will be used repeatedly to fully cover a square which has a side of 24Y inches, how many of rectangular tiles with dimension X×Y will be used?
    a) 192
    b) 144
    c) 122
    d) 96

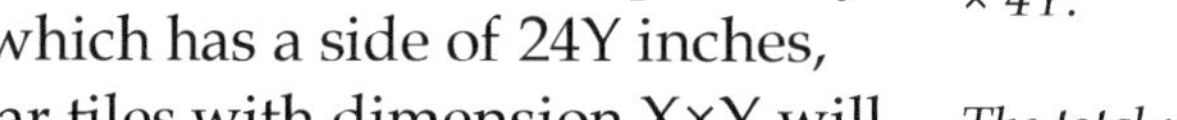

Answer: (a)

X is equal to 3Y, so the unit is 3Y × 4Y.

The total number of units needed is $\frac{24}{3} \times \frac{24}{4} = 48$*. The total number of rectangular tiles used is* $48 \times 4 = 192$.

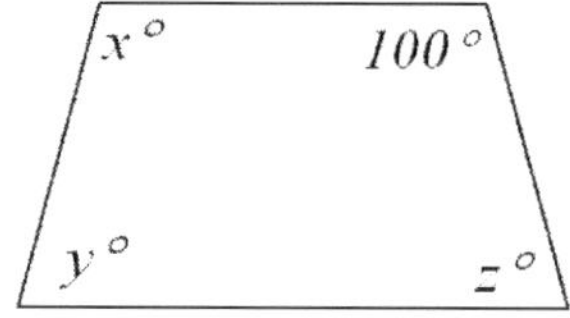

Note: Figure not drawn to scale.

15. In the quadrilateral above, if $x > 90$, which of the following is one possible value of $y + z$?
    a) 240
    b) 200
    c) 180
    d) 100

Answer: (d)

The sum of the interior angles of a quadrilateral is equal to 360°.
$360 = 100 + x + y + z$
$x + y + z = 260$
$x > 90 \longrightarrow y + z < 170$
$x < 180 \longrightarrow y + z > 80$
$80 < z + y < 170$

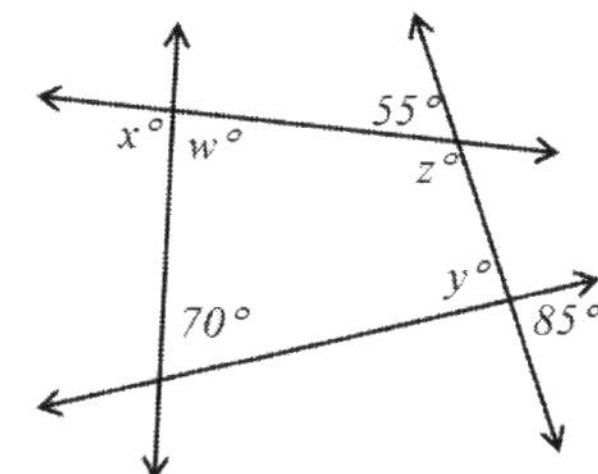

Note: Figure not drawn to scale.

16. In the figure above, what is the value of x?

Answer: 100

$70 + w + z + y = 360$
$z = 180 - 55 = 125$
$y = 85$
$w = 360 - 70 - 125 - 85 = 80$
$x = 180 - 80 = 100$

17. One of the angles of a rhombus is 120°. If the shorter diagonal has length 2, what is the area of the rhombus?
    a) 2
    b) $\sqrt{3}$
    c) 3
    d) $2\sqrt{3}$

Answer: (d)

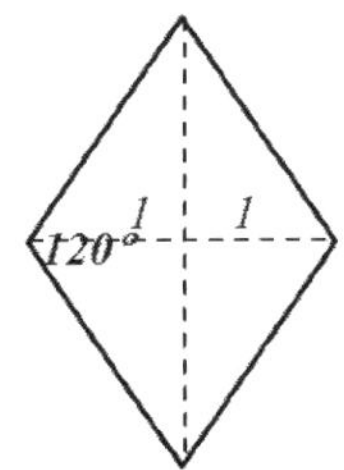

Four 30–60–90 triangles are formed by the diagonals of the rhombus. The longer diagonal is therefore of length $2\sqrt{3}$.

Area of Rhombus $= \frac{1}{2} \times 2 \times 2\sqrt{3} = 2\sqrt{3}$

C. Area of Polygons

Concept Overviews

Area of a Parallelogram: Base × Height

$A = b \times h$

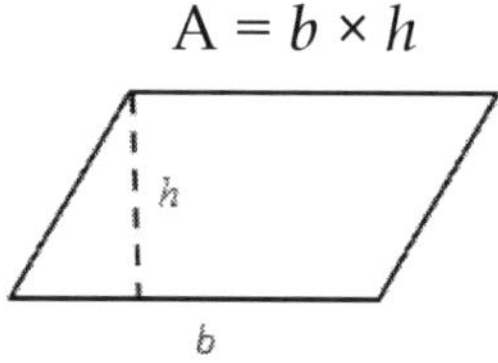

Area of a Rectangle: Length × Width

$A = l \times w$

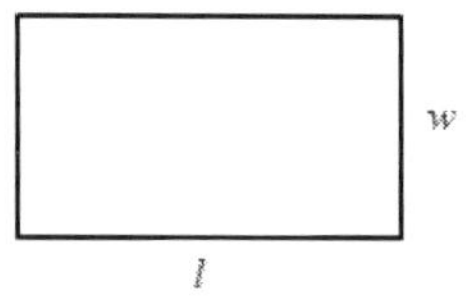

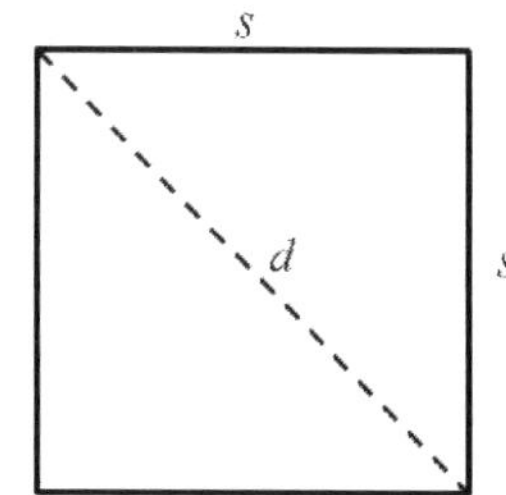

Area of a Square:
- Side × Side = (Side)^2
- $\frac{1}{2}$ × (Diagonal)^2

$A = s^2 = \frac{1}{2}d^2$

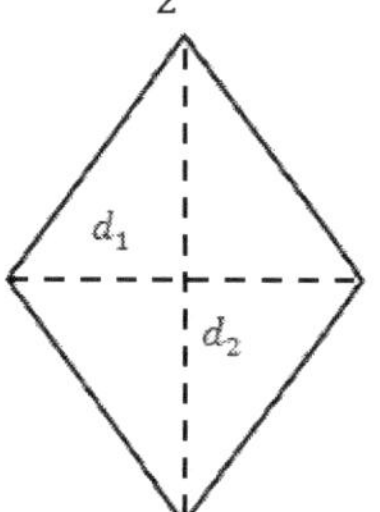

Area of a Rhombus: $\frac{1}{2}$ × Diagonal 1 × Diagonal 2

$A = \frac{1}{2} \times d_1 \times d_2$

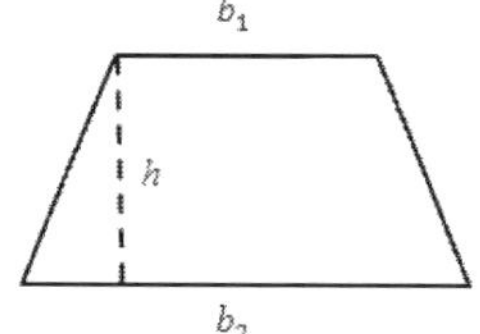

Area of a Trapezoid: $\frac{1}{2}$ × (Base 1 + Base 2) × Height

$A = \frac{1}{2} \times (b_1 + b_2) \times h$

Problem Solving Skills

Easy

1. A rectangular frame with a 1-inch margin is placed around a rectangular picture with dimensions of 8 inches by 10 inches. What is the area of the frame itself in square inches?
   a) 40
   b) 44
   c) 48
   d) 52

Answer: (a)

Area WITH Frame and Picture = (8 + 2) × (10 + 2) = 120

Area of Picture = 10 × 8 = 80
Area of Frame = 120 − 80 = 40

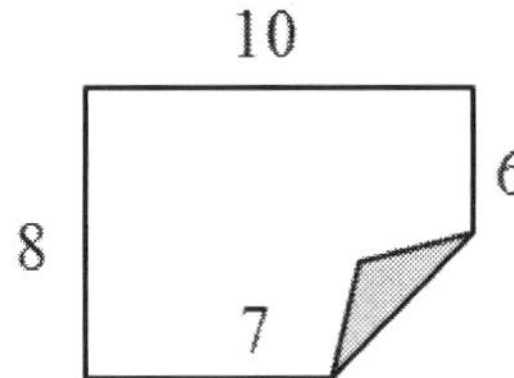

2. The figure above was originally a rectangle. What is the area of the figure after one corner was folded over as shown above?
   a) 70
   b) 72
   c) 75
   d) 77

Answer: (d)

Area of Original Rectangle − Area of Folded Triangle =
$8 \times 10 - \frac{1}{2}(2 \times 3) = 77$

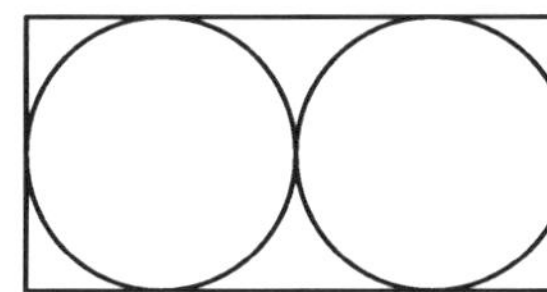

3. In the figure above, two congruent circles are inscribed in a rectangle. If the area of one circle is 9π, what is the area of the rectangle?
   a) 24
   b) 27
   c) 36
   d) 72

Answer: (d)

The length of the rectangle is 4r and its width is 2r.
$\pi r^2 = 9\pi$
$r = 3$
Area of Rectangle = $4r \times 2r = 72$

4. If no wallpaper is wasted, how many square feet of wall paper is needed to cover a rectangular wall that is 5 yards by 7 yards (1 yard = 3 feet)?
   a) 35 square feet
   b) 105 square feet
   c) 300 square feet
   d) 315 square feet

Answer: (d)

$3 \times 5 \times 3 \times 7 = 315$ *square feet*

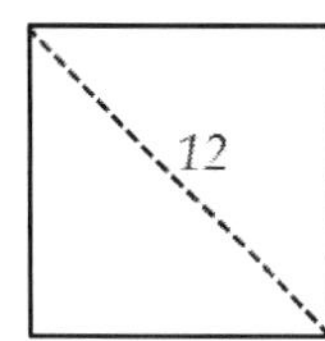

5. What is the area of the square above?
   a) 64
   b) 72
   c) 100
   d) 144

Answer: (b)

Area of Square $= \frac{1}{2}$ *(Diagonal)*^{2}

$\frac{1}{2} \times 12^2 = 72$

Medium

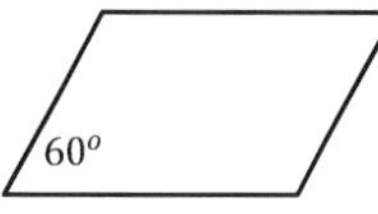

6. If the parallelogram above has side lengths all equal to 12, what is the area of this parallelogram?
   a) 72
   b) $72\sqrt{2}$
   c) $72\sqrt{3}$
   d) 144

Answer: (c)

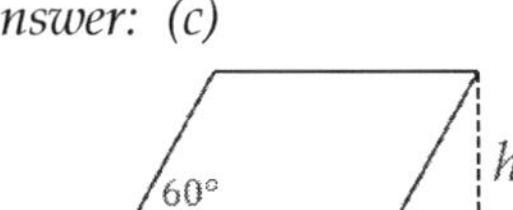

Area = Base × Height $= 12 \times 12 \times \frac{\sqrt{3}}{2} = 72\sqrt{3}$

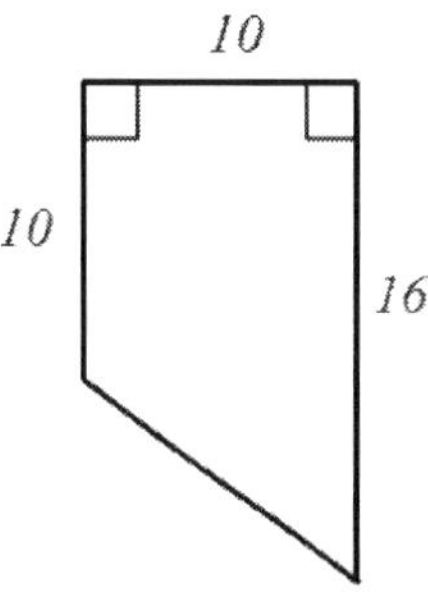

7. What is the area of above quadrilateral?

Answer: 130

Area = Area of Missing Triangle + Area of Rectangle $= 10 \times 10 + \frac{1}{2} \times 6 \times 10 = 130$

8. In rectangle WXYZ, point A is the midpoint of XY. If the area of **Δ**WXA is 2, what is the area of rectangle WXYZ?

Answer: 8

Area of $\Delta WXA = 2 = \frac{1}{2}$ *Base × Height* $= \frac{1}{4}$ *Area of Rectangle*

Area of Rectangle $= 4 \times 2 = 8$

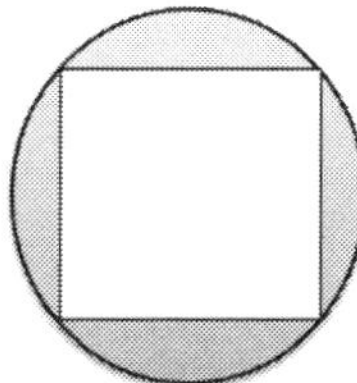

9. A square is inscribed inside a circle as shown in the figure above. If the radius of the circle is 2, what is the area of the shaded region?

Answer: 4.56 or 4.57

Area of Shaded Region = Area of Circle – Area of Square
Area of Circle = $\pi(2)^2 = 4\pi$
Area of Square = $\frac{1}{2}$ *(Diagonal of Square)*^{2} $= \frac{1}{2}$ *(Diameter of Circle)*^{2}
$= \frac{1}{2}(4)^2 = 8$
Area of Shaded Region = $4\pi - 8 = 4.566$

Hard

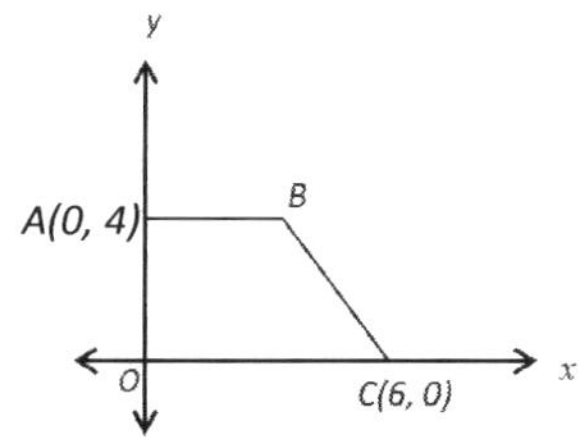

10. In the xy-coordinate plane, AB is parallel to the x-axis. If AO = AB, what is the area of quadrilateral ABCO?
    a) 12
    b) 16
    c) 18
    d) 20

Answer: (d)

This is a trapezoid whose area is equal to $\frac{1}{2}(AB + OC) \times OA$.
Area = $\frac{1}{2}(4 + 6) \times 4 = 20$

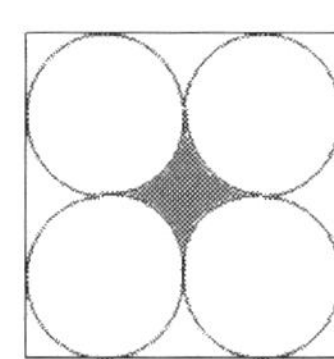

11. If 4 congruent circles of radius 1 are tangent to the sides of a square as shown in the figure above, what is the area of the shaded region?
    a) $1 + \pi$
    b) $2 + \pi$
    c) $4 - \pi$
    d) $6 - \pi$

Answer: (c)

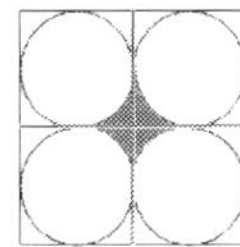

Area of Shaded Region = $\frac{1}{4}$ *(Area of Square – 4 × Area of Circle)*
Area of Square = $4 \times 4 = 16$
$16 - 4 \times \pi(1)^2 = 16 - 4\pi$
Area of Shaded Region = $\frac{1}{4}(16 - 4\pi) = 4 - \pi$

IV. CIRCLE

CONCEPT OVERVIEWS

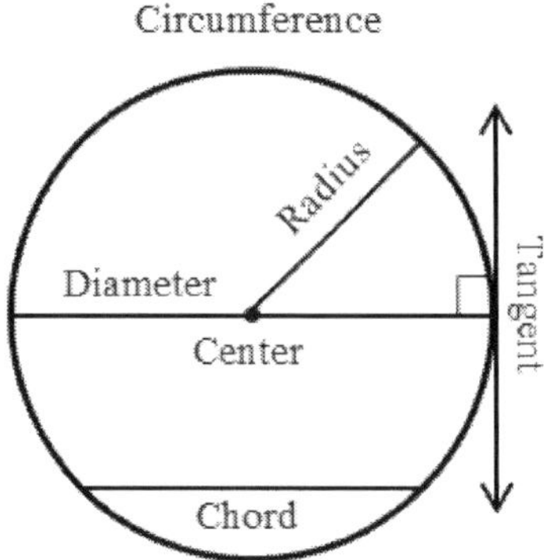

Segments of a Circle

The **radius** is a line segment that connects the center of a circle with any point on the circle. The lengths of all the radii of a circle are equal. A **chord** is a line segment that connects any two points on a circle. The **diameter** is a chord that passes through the center of the circle. The diameter is the longest chord in the circle and has length equal to twice the radius. A **tangent** line is a line that intersects the circle at exactly one point. A radius that touches the point of the tangent is perpendicular to the tangent line.

A radius that is perpendicular to a chord bisects the chord:

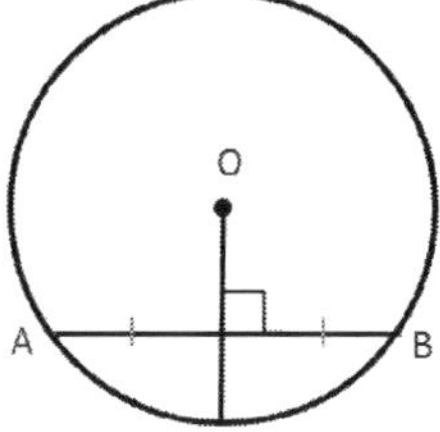

Arc Length and Circumference of the Circle

An **arc** is a curved segment of the circle. Connecting two endpoints of the arc to the center of the circle forms a **central angle**. An arc with a central angle less than 180° is called **minor arc** while an arc with a central angle greater than 180° is called **major arc**. A diameter divides its circle into two equal arcs of 180° known as **semicircles**.

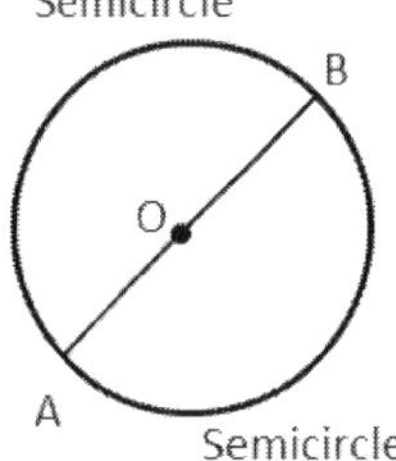

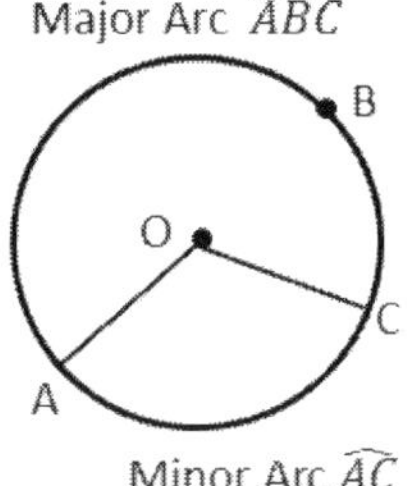

Circumference of a Circle

The **circumference** of a circle is equal to $2\pi r$, where r is the radius of the circle.

Example: Find the circumference of the circle below.

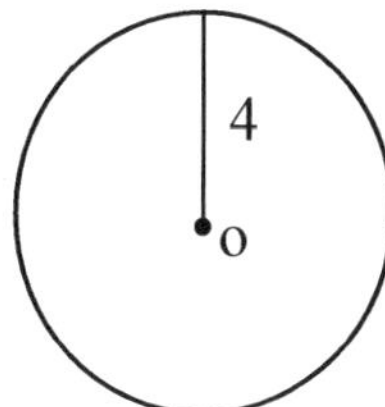

Answer: $r = 4$

$2\pi r = 2\pi \times 4 = 8\pi$

Length of an Arc

A whole circle has 360°. An arc with a central angle of θ is $\frac{\theta}{360}$ of a whole circle, so the length of the arc is equal to : $\frac{\theta}{360} \times 2\pi r$

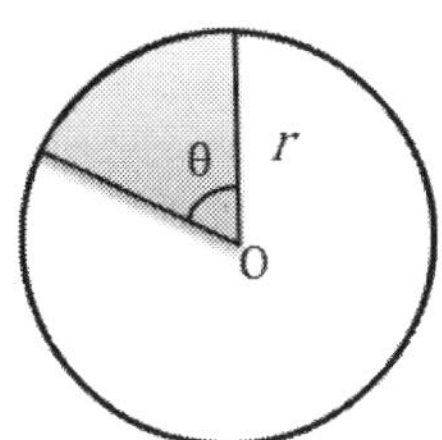

Example: Find the length of arc AB in the figure below.

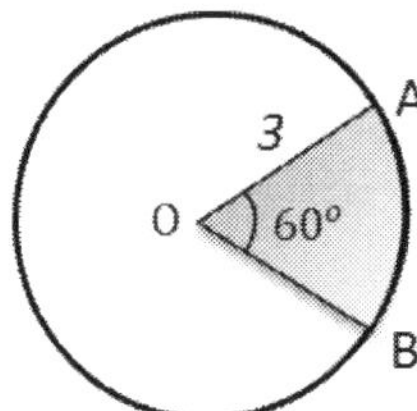

Answer: $r = 3$, so the length of arc $AB = \frac{\theta}{360} \times 2\pi r = \frac{60}{360} \times 2\pi(3) = \pi$.

Area of a Circle

The area of a circle is πr^2, where r is the radius of the circle.

Example: Find the area of the circle below.

Answer: $r = 5$

$\pi r^2 = \pi \times 5^2 = 25\pi$

Area of a Sector

A **sector** with a central angle of θ is $\frac{\theta}{360}$ of a whole circle, so the area of the sector is $\frac{\theta}{360}\pi r^2$.

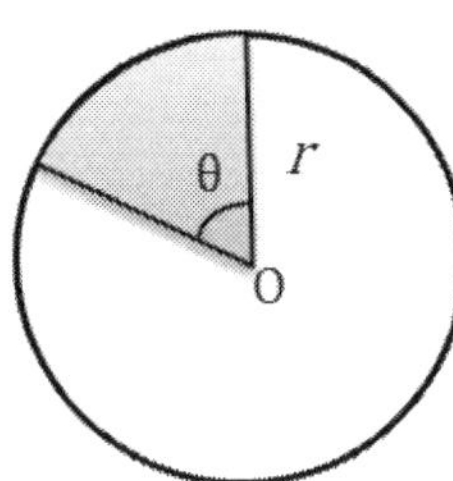

Example: Find the area of sector with the central angle 60° in the figure below.

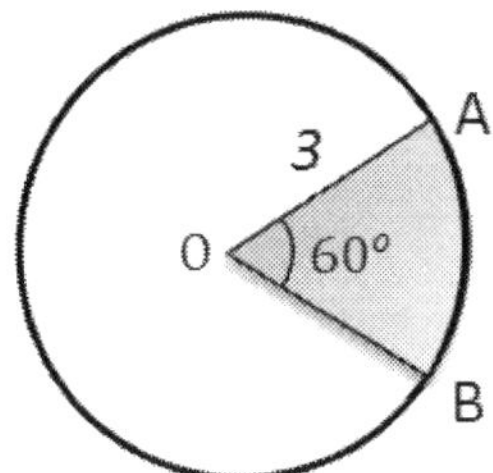

Answer: $\frac{\theta}{360}\pi r^2 = \frac{60}{360}\pi(3)^2 = \frac{3}{2}\pi$

Inscribed Angles and Central Angles

An **inscribed angle** is formed from two chords of a circle meeting at a point on the circle. If an inscribed angle and a central angle carve the same arc on the circle, then

$$\text{Inscribed Angle} = \frac{1}{2} \times \text{Central Angle}$$

- When a chord is a diameter, the inscribed angle is 90°.

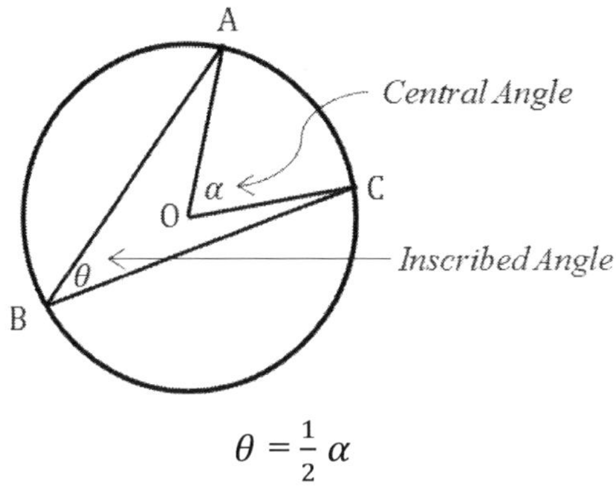

$$\theta = \frac{1}{2}\alpha$$

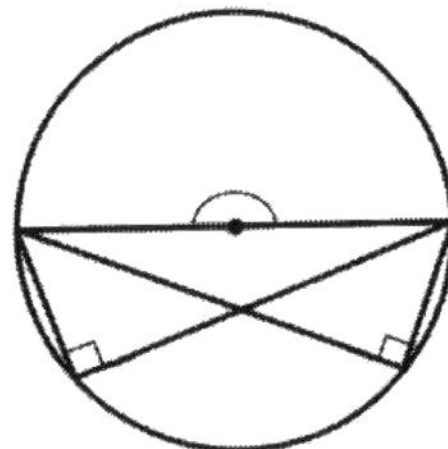

The inscribed angle that carves the same arc as a diameter has degree 90 while the central angle of the diameter is 180°.

Two Tangents to a Circle

Given any point outside a circle, there are two unique lines that intersect this point and also lie **tangent** to the circle. These two lines will each contain a line segment created by the point outside the circle and the point of tangency. The two line segments will have equal length.

A line tangent to the circle is always perpendicular to the radius that touches the point of tangency.

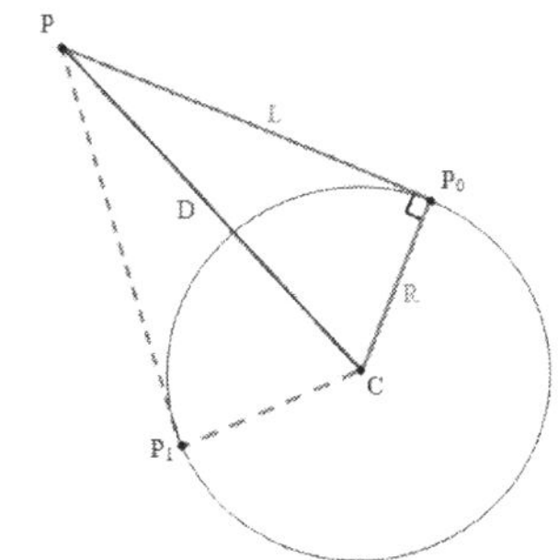

$$\overline{PP_0} = \overline{PP_1}\ ;\ \overleftrightarrow{CP_0} \perp \overline{PP_0}\ ;\ \overleftrightarrow{CP_1} \perp \overline{PP_1}$$

Example: Find the area of ΔABO if line AB is tangent to the circle below.

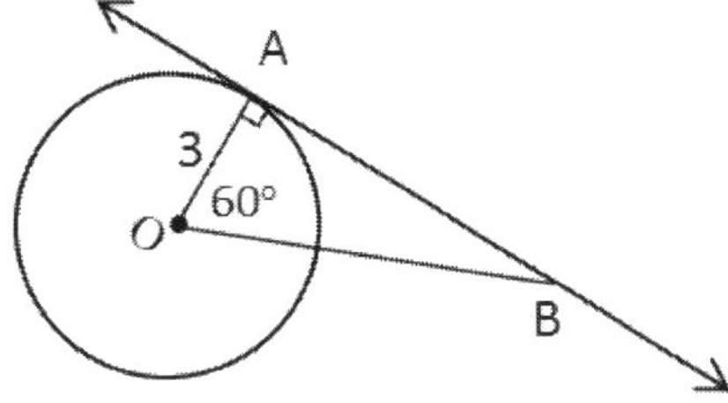

Answer: ∠BAO is a right angle since radius OA is perpendicular to the tangent line.

Given that ∠AOB = 60°, then ∠ABO = 30° and ΔABO is a 30-60-90 right triangle. The ratio of the sides must be $1 : \sqrt{3} : 2$.

$\overline{OA} : \overline{AB} : \overline{OB} = 1 : \sqrt{3} : 2$

$\overline{OB} = 6$ and $\overline{AB} = 3\sqrt{3}$

The area of ΔABO is $\frac{1}{2}(\overline{OA})(\overline{AB}) = \frac{1}{2}(3)(3\sqrt{3}) = \frac{9\sqrt{3}}{2} = 4.5\sqrt{3}$.

Problem Solving Skills

Easy

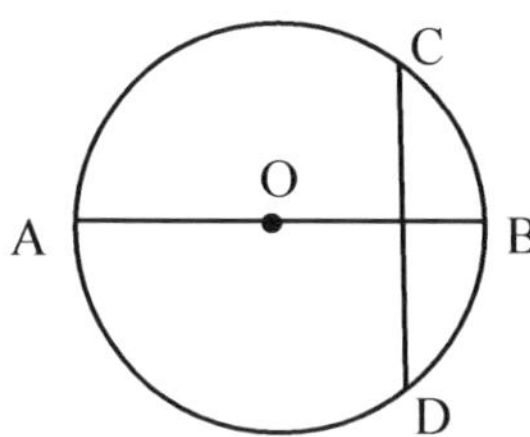

1. The figure above shows a circle with center O. Lines AB and CD are perpendicular and AB passes through point O. If the length of AB is 10 and length of CD is 8, what is the distance of O to line CD?
   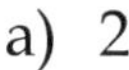
   a) 2
   b) 3
   c) 4
   d) 5

Answer: (b)

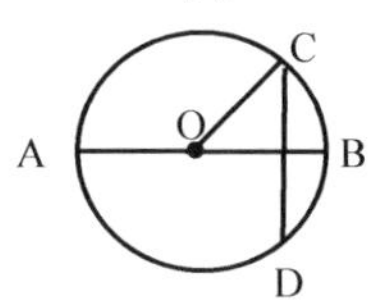

Distance $= \sqrt{\overline{OC}^2 - \left(\frac{CD}{2}\right)^2}$
$= \sqrt{5^2 - 4^2} = 3$

2. The diameter of a semi-circle is 4. What is its perimeter?
   a) $2\pi + 2$
   b) $2\pi + 4$
   c) $2\pi + 6$
   d) $\pi + 2$

Answer: (b)

The perimeter of semicircle is the sum of half of the circumference of a circle plus the length of the diameter.
Perimeter $= \frac{1}{2}(2\pi r) + 2r$
$= \frac{1}{2} \times 2\pi \times 2 + 2 \times 2 = 2\pi + 4$

3. In the figure below, the two circles are tangent at point P and OQ = 9. If the area of the circle with center O is four times the area of the circle with center Q, what is the length of OP?

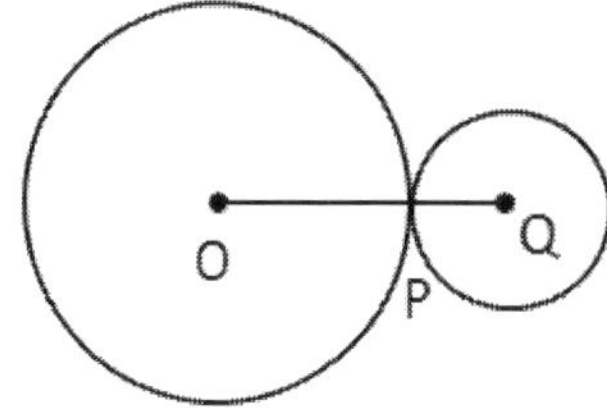

   a) 2
   b) 4
   c) 6
   d) 8

Answer: (c)

Since the area of circle O is four times the area of circle Q, the radius of circle O is $\sqrt{4}$ times of the radius of circle Q.

If $PQ = r$, $OP = 2r$, then $r + 2r = 9$.

$r = 3 = PQ$
$OP = 9 - 3 = 6$

4. A chord of a circle is 2 inches away from the center of the circle at its closest point. If the circle has a 3-inch radius, what is the length of this chord, in inches?
   a) 1
   b) $\sqrt{5}$
   c) 2
   d) $2\sqrt{5}$

Answer: (d)

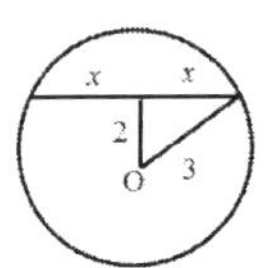

$x = \sqrt{3^2 - 2^2} = \sqrt{5}$
Length of Chord $= 2\sqrt{5}$ *inches*

5. Point O is the center of the circle in the figure below. If angle $\angle PQO = 65^\circ$, what is the measure of the center angle $\angle POQ$?

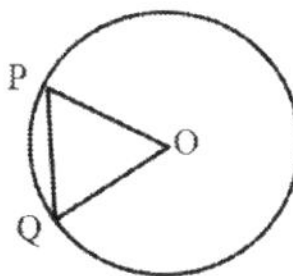

   a) 40°
   b) 50°
   c) 60°
   d) 70°

Answer: (b)

Triangle PQO is an isosceles triangle with $\angle O = 50^\circ$.
$2 \times m\angle PQO + m\angle POQ = 180^\circ$
$m\angle PQO = 65^\circ$
$m\angle POQ = 180 - 2 \times 65 = 50^\circ$

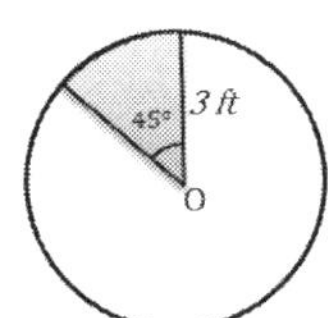

6. In the figure above, the circle has a center O and radius of 3 ft. What is the area of the shaded portion, in square feet?
   a) $\frac{3}{4}\pi$
   b) $\frac{9}{8}\pi$
   c) $\frac{11}{8}\pi$
   d) 1.5π

Answer: (b)

The area of the shaded portion is $\frac{45}{360}$ *of the area of the whole circle.*

Shaded Area $= \frac{45}{360} \times \pi \times 3^2 = \frac{9}{8}\pi$

7. In the figure below, circle O is composed of a shaded region and an un-shaded region. If the area of the shaded region is 80π and the radius of the circle is 10, what is the length of arc AB (un-shaded region)?

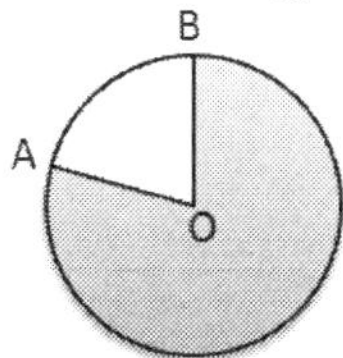

   a) 2π
   b) 4π
   c) 6π
   d) 8π

Answer: (b)

$$\frac{\text{Area of Shaded Region}}{\text{Area of Circle}} = \frac{\text{Arc Length}}{\text{Circumference}}$$

$$\frac{80\pi}{10^2\pi} = \frac{x}{2\pi(10)}$$

$x = 16\pi$

x is the arc of the shaded region, so we subtract it from the total circumference.
$AB = 20\pi - 16\pi = 4\pi$

8. In the figure below, points A and B lie on circle O. If $\angle AOB = y^o$, what is the value of x in term of y?

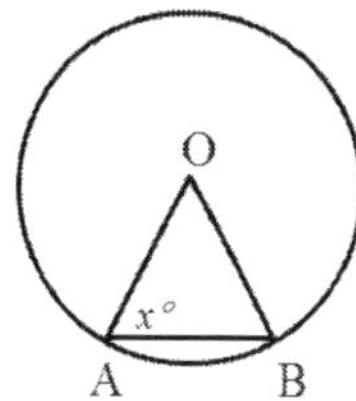

a) y
b) $90 - y$
c) $180 - y$
d) $90 - \frac{1}{2}y$

Answer: (d)

ΔOAB is an isosceles Δ.

$2 \times x + y = 180$
$x = \frac{1}{2}(180 - y) = 90 - \frac{1}{2}y$

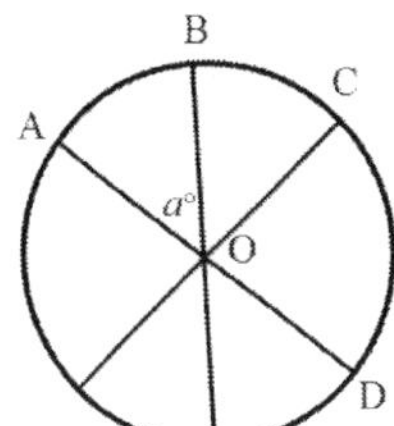

<u>Note:</u> Figure not drawn to scale.

9. In the figure above, O is the center of the circle, $\widehat{AB} = \widehat{BC}$, and $\widehat{AC} = \widehat{CD}$. What is the value of a, in degrees?

Answer: 45

$\widehat{AB}$ is half of $\widehat{AC}$ so it is $\frac{1}{4}$ of $\widehat{AD}$.
$a = \frac{1}{4} \times 180^o$
$a = 45^o$

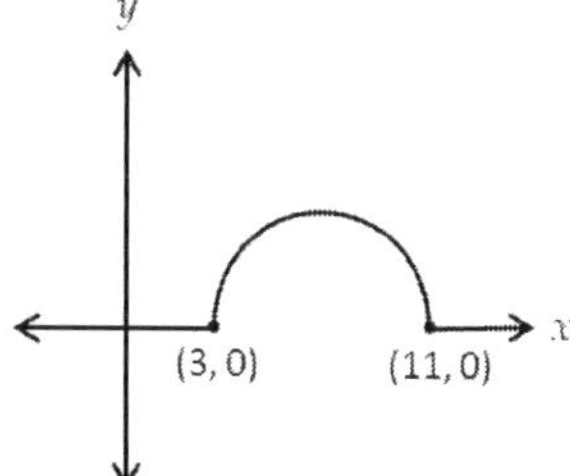

10. In the figure above, what is the sum of the x and y coordinates of the highest point on the above semicircle?
    a) 6
    b) 8
    c) 9
    d) 11

Answer: (d)

The highest point is at the middle of semicircle.

y-Coordinate = Radius = $\frac{11 - 3}{2} = 4$
x-Coordinate = $\frac{1}{2}(3 + 11) = 7$
x-Coordinate + y-Coordinate = 11

11. In the circle below, Hexagon ABCDEF is equilateral. What is the ratio of the length of arc ABCD to the length of arc AFE?

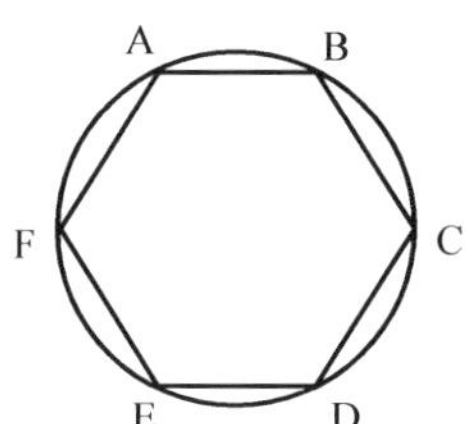

a) 1 to 2
b) 2 to 3
c) 3 to 2
d) 4 to 5

Answer: (c)

The arc ABCD is 3 times the arc AB and arc AFE is 2 times the arc AB (since the polygon is regular).

ABCD : AFE = 3 : 2

12. The area of circle A is 9 times the area of circle B. What is the ratio of the diameter of circle A to the diameter of circle B?
a) 9 : 1
b) 6 : 1
c) 3 : 1
d) 3 : 2

Answer: (c)

The ratio of the diameter of two circles is the square root of the ratio of their areas.

Ratio = $\sqrt{9} : \sqrt{1} = 3 : 1$

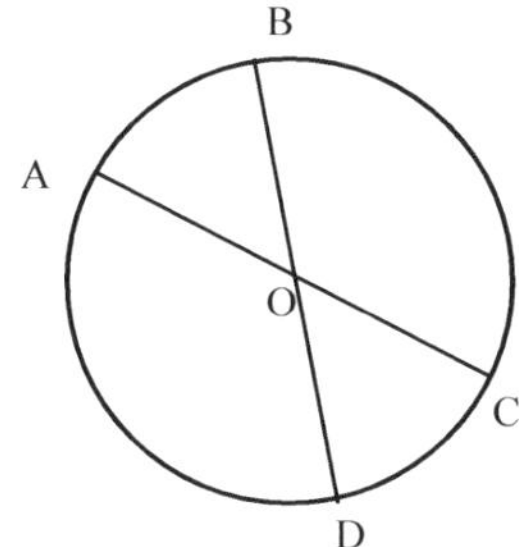

13. In the figure above, point O is the center of the circle and segments BD and AC are diameters. If $\overline{OA} = 5$ and $m\angle AOB < 60^\circ$. Which of the following statements is true?
a) $\overline{OC} = 5$
b) $\overline{CD} > 5$
c) $\overline{OD} < 5$
d) $\overline{CD} = 5$

Answer: (a)

CD should be less than the radius because $m\angle AOB < 60^\circ$ *and* $m\angle COD < 60^\circ$

OC is a radius with length 5.

14. What is the difference, in degrees, between an arc that is $\frac{3}{8}$ of a circle and an arc that is $\frac{1}{3}$ of a circle?
a) 20°
b) 18°
c) 15°
d) 12°

Answer: (c)

$(\frac{3}{8} - \frac{1}{3}) \times 360^\circ = 15^\circ$

15. Segment $\overline{AB}$ is the diameter of a circle with center O. Another point C lies on circle O. If AC = 6 and BC = 8, what is the area of circle O?
    a) 25π
    b) 50π
    c) 100π
    d) 200π

Answer: (a)

ΔABC is a right triangle.

$AB^2 = AC^2 + BC^2$
$AB = \sqrt{6^2 + 8^2} = 10$
$Radius = \frac{1}{2}(10) = 5$
$Area = \pi \times 5^2 = 25\pi$

16. One circle has a radius of 3 and another circle has a radius of 2. What is the ratio of the area of the larger circle to the area of the smaller circle?
    a) $3:2$
    b) $9:4$
    c) $3:1$
    d) $4:1$

Answer: (b)

The ratio of the areas of two circles is equal to the square of the ratio of their radius.

$3^2 : 2^2 = 9 : 4$

Medium

17. A circle with center at coordinates (4, 5) touches the y-axis at only one point. What is the radius of the circle?

Answer: 4

The circle is tangent to the y−axis, since otherwise it would touch the axis at zero or two points (try drawing it out to see). Its radius is the distance from the center to the y-axis which is 4.

18. An old clock has 2 different sizes of gears. The area of the bigger gear is 4 times the area of the smaller gear. The gears are attached so they must move together. How many revolutions must the smaller gear make for each revolution of the bigger gear?

Answer: 2

The amount of 'perimeter' that travels through a point when two gears rotate together must be the same for both gears. However, since one gear is smaller than the other, the amount of angle it rotates is much larger than the bigger gear (the bigger gear rotates less for the same amount of perimeter). The ratio of the rates of revolution is the inverse of the ratio of the radii. Let S be the rate of revolution for the smaller gear and B be the rate of revolution of the larger gear.
Ratio of Revolution = Ratio of $\sqrt{Area}$
$S : B = \sqrt{4} : 1 = 2 : 1$

19. In the figure below, rectangle ABOC is drawn in circle O. If OB = 3 and OC = 4, what is the area of the shaded region?

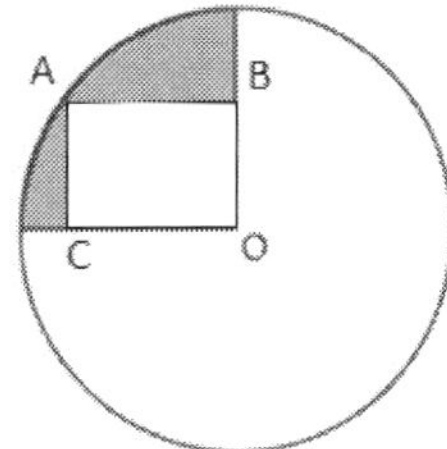

a) $6\pi - 3$
b) $\frac{25\pi}{4} - 12$
c) $25\pi - 12$
d) $\frac{25\pi}{4} - 3$

Answer: (b)

OA is the radius of the circle and the shaded area is the area of the quarter circle minus the area of the rectangle.
Radius = $\sqrt{OB^2 + OC^2}$= $\sqrt{3^2 + 4^2}$= 5
Shaded Area = Area of $\frac{1}{4}$ *Circle – Area of Rectangle =*
$\frac{1}{4}(\pi \times 5^2) - 4 \times 3$
$= \frac{1}{4} \times 25\pi) - 12$
$= \frac{25\pi}{4} - 12$

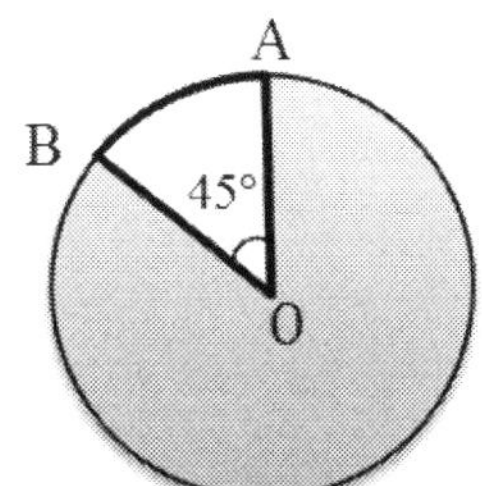

20. The circle above has an area of 16π. What is the perimeter of the shaded region?
a) $8 - \frac{1}{3}\pi$
b) $8 + 7\pi$
c) $8 + \frac{2}{3}\pi$
d) $8 + \frac{1}{3}\pi$

Answer: (b)

The perimeter of the shaded region is equal to the arc length plus twice the radius.
Perimeter = Arc Length + 2 × Radius
To find the radius, we solve:
$\pi r^2 = 16\pi \rightarrow r = 4$
Arc Length of Shaded Region =
$\frac{2 \times \pi r \times (360^o - 45^o)}{360^o} = 7\pi$
Perimeter of Shaded Region = $7\pi + 8$

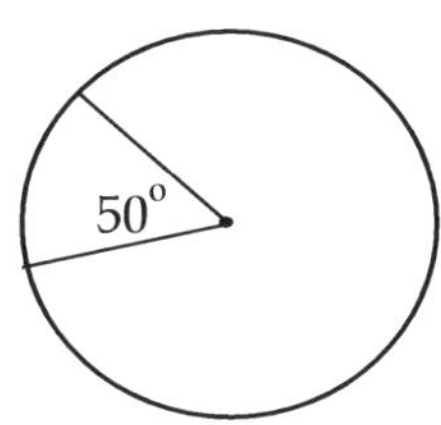

21. In the figure above, a piece with a 50° center angle has been cut out of an 18-ounce pie. How many ounces was the piece of pie that was cut out?

Answer: 2.5

Weight of Pie : 360° = Weight of Piece : 50°
$18 : 360^o = x : 50^o$
$\frac{18}{360} = \frac{x}{50} \rightarrow x = 2.5$ *ounces*

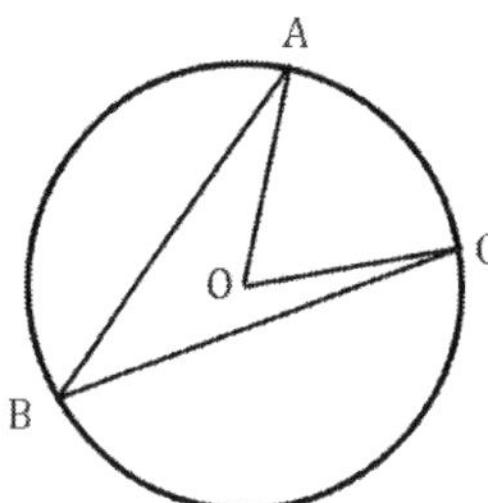

22. In the figure above, if $\widehat{AC}$ has arc length equal to $\frac{1}{6}$ of the circumference of the circle, what is the value of $m\angle ABC$, in degrees?

Answer: 30

$m\angle ABC = \frac{1}{2} m\angle AOC = \frac{1}{2} \times \frac{1}{6} \times 360^o = 30^o$

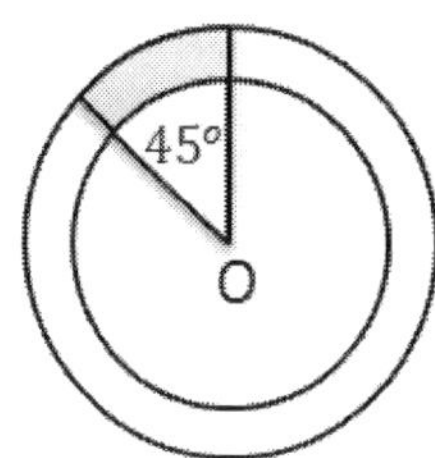

23. In the figure above, O is the center of the two circles. If the bigger circle has a radius of 5 and the smaller circle has a radius of 4, what is the area of shaded region?
   a) 2π
   b) π
   c) $\frac{9}{8}\pi$
   d) $\frac{1}{2}\pi$

Answer: (c)

$Area = \frac{45}{360}(\pi \times 5^2 - \pi \times 4^2) = \frac{9}{8}\pi$

24. In the figure above, a circle O with diameter $\overline{AC}$ has an area of 16π. What is the length of segment $\overline{AB}$?
   a) 4
   b) 6
   c) $6\sqrt{2}$
   d) $4\sqrt{2}$

Answer: (d)

ΔOAB is a 45−45−90 special right triangle.

Radius = OA = $\sqrt{16}$= 4 = OB

AB = $\sqrt{OA^2 + OB^2}$ = $4\sqrt{2}$

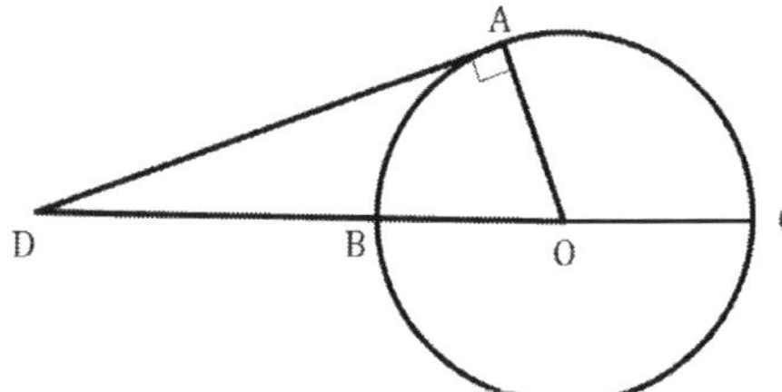

25. Point O is the center of the circle in the figure above. If DA = 12 and DB = 8, what is the area of the circle?

Answer: 78.5

Use the Pythagorean theorem.
$DA^2 + OA^2 = OD^2$
$12^2 + r^2 = (8 + r)^2$
$= 64 + 16r + r^2$
$r = 5$
$Area = \pi \times 5^2 = 78.54$

Hard

26. Circle A has an area of 4π and circle B has an area of 9π. If the circles intersect at only one point, what is the sum of all possible distances from the center of circle A to the center of circle B?

Answer: 6

There are only two possible distances. The larger distance is the sum of the two radii and the smaller distance is the difference of the two radii.
Radius of Big Circle = 3
Radius of Small Circle = 2
$x = 3 - 2$ *or* $3 + 2$
$x = 1, 5$
$1 + 5 = 6$

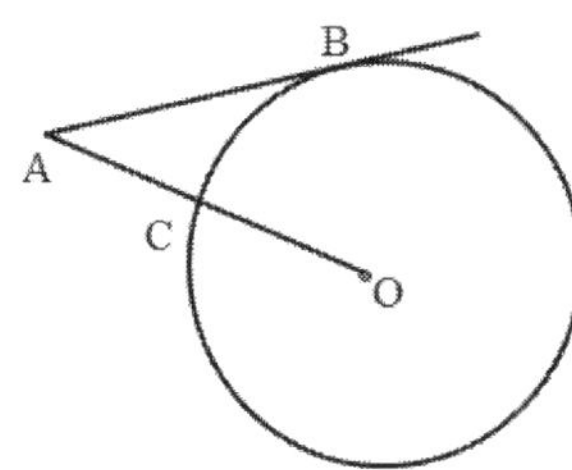

27. In the diagram above, AB is tangent to circle O at point B. AB = 2AC and the radius has length 3. What is the length of $\overline{AO}$?

Answer: 5

ΔOAB is a right triangle with hypotenuse $\overline{OA}$, *so use the Pythagorean theorem.*
$OB = OC = 3$
$AC = x \qquad AB = 2x$
$AO = 3 + x$
$(2x)^2 + 3^2 = (3 + x)^2$
$4x^2 + 9 = x^2 + 6x + 9$
$3x^2 = 6x$
$x = 2$
$AO = 5$

28. In the figure below, AB is tangent to circle O, $\overline{AB} = 8$, and $\overline{AC} = 4$. What is the area of ΔOAB?

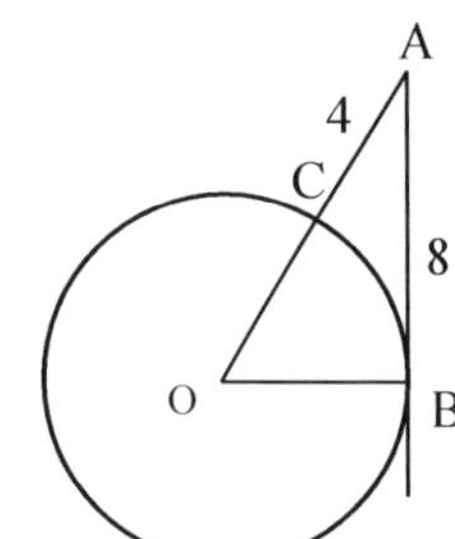

Note: Figure not drawn to scale.

Answer: 24

ΔABO is a right triangle with hypotenuse $\overline{AO}$, so use the Pythagorean theorem to find OB. OB and OC are radii and let their length be r.

$8^2 + r^2 = (4 + r)^2$
$64 + r^2 = 16 + 8r + r^2$
$48 = 8r$
$r = 6$
Area of $\Delta OAB = \frac{1}{2} \times 6 \times 8 = 24$

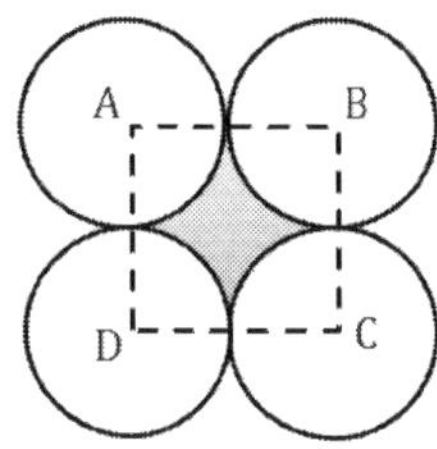

29. The figure above consists of four congruent, tangent circles with radius 1. What is the area of the shaded region?

Answer: .858

Area of Shaded Region = Area of Square – 4 × Area of a Quarter-Circle

$2^2 - \pi \times 1^2 = 4 - \pi = 0.8584$

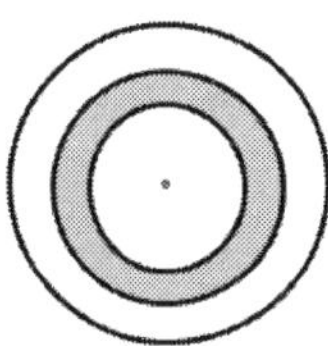

30. The figure above consists of three circles that share the same center. The circles have radii of 2, 3, and 4 respectively. What is the probability that a randomly chosen point will be in the shaded region?

a) $\frac{3}{16}$
b) $\frac{1}{4\pi}$
c) $\frac{5}{16}$
d) $\frac{7}{16}$

Answer: (c)

The probability that a randomly chosen point will be in the shaded area is equal to $\frac{\text{Area of Shaded Region}}{\text{Total Area}}$

Area of Shaded Region = Area of Medium Circle – Area of Small Circle
$\pi \times 3^2 - \pi \times 2^2 = 5\pi$
Total Area $= \pi \times 4^2 = 16\pi$
Probability $= \frac{5\pi}{16\pi} = \frac{5}{16}$

31. In the figure below, circle O is tangent to a square at points A and B. If the area of ΔABC is 8, what is the area of the circle?

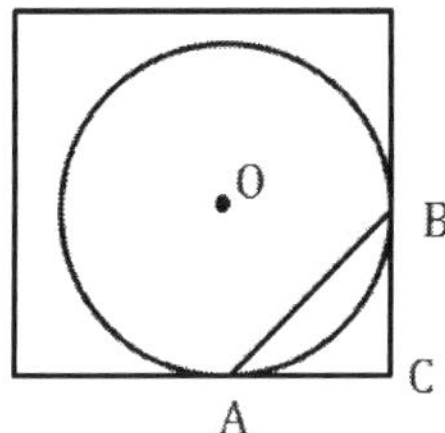

a) 4π
b) 6π
c) $6\pi\sqrt{2}$
d) 16π

Answer: (d)

Since CB = CA, ΔABC is an isosceles right triangle.
Area of $\Delta ABC = \frac{1}{2} \times AC^2 = 8$
$AC = 4$
Since OB is a radius of the circle and it is equal to AC, the radius of the circle has length 4.
Area of Circle $= \pi \times 4^2 = 16\pi$

32. In the figure below, point O is the center of the circle, line segments PQ and PR are tangent to the circle at points Q and R, respectively, and the segments intersect at point P as shown. If the radius of the circle is 6 and the length of PQ is $6\sqrt{3}$, what is the area of minor sector $\widehat{RQ}$?

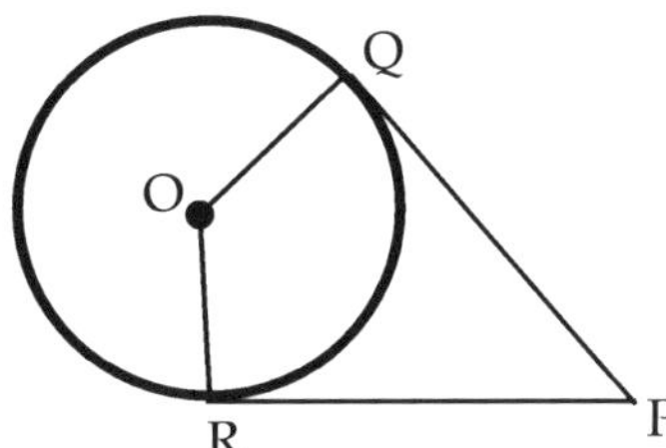

Answer: 12

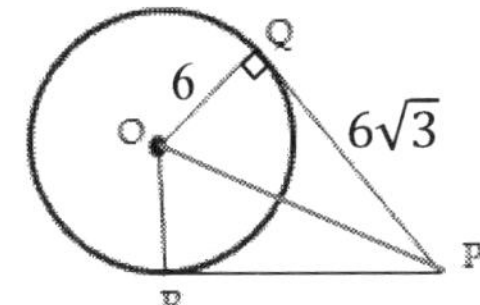

In the right triangle ΔOPQ, *the ratio of* $\frac{QP}{QO} = \sqrt{3}$, *therefore* $\angle QOP = 60^o$ *and* $\angle QOR = 120^o$

The area of the minor sector $\widehat{RQ} = \frac{120}{360} \times \pi \times 6^2 = 12$

33. Find the radius of the circle given by the equation $x^2 + y^2 + 4x + 4y - 1 = 0$.

Answer: 3

Rewrite the equation in standard form.
$x^2 + 4x + 4 + y^2 + 4y + 4 = 1 + 8$
$(x + 2)^2 + (y + 2)^2 = 3^2$
The center of the circle is $(-2, -2)$ *and the radius is 3.*

34. Find the area of the circle given by the equation $x^2 + y^2 + 4x + 4y - 1 = 0$. (Round your answer to the nearest tenth.)

Answer: 28.3

Rewrite the equation in standard form.
$x^2 + 4x + 4 + y^2 + 4y + 4 = 1 + 8$
$(x + 2)^2 + (y + 2)^2 = 3^2$
The center of the circle is $(-2, -2)$ *and the radius is 3.*
The area of the circle is
$\pi r^2 = 9\pi = 28.3.$

V. Volumes and Surface Areas

Concept Overviews

Cubes

Surface area: $6a^2$
Volume: a^3

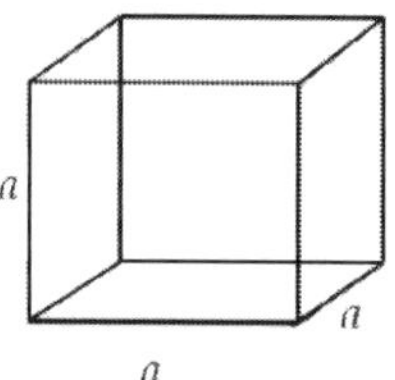

Rectangular Prisms

Surface area: $2(w \times h + l \times w + l \times h)$
Volume: $l \times w \times h$
Diagonal of a rectangular prism: $d = \sqrt{h^2 + l^2 + w^2}$

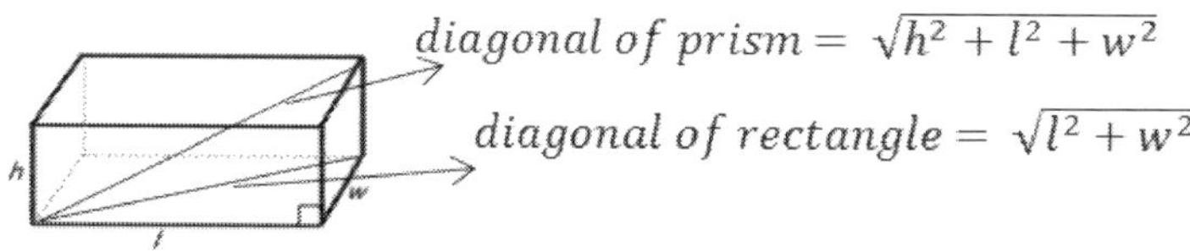

Cylinders

Surface area: $2\pi r^2 + 2\pi rh$
Volume: $\pi r^2 h$

Cones

Volume: $\frac{1}{3}$ (Area of Base) × (Height) = $\frac{1}{3}\pi r^2 h$

Pyramid

Volume: $\frac{1}{3}$ (Area of Base) × (Height) = $\frac{1}{3} l \times w \times h$

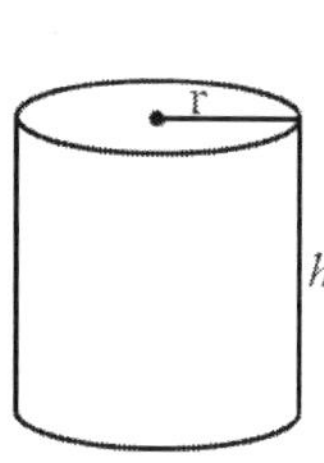

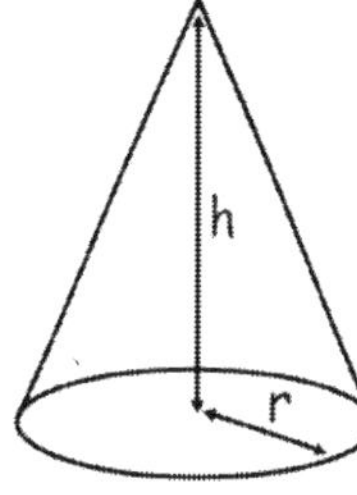

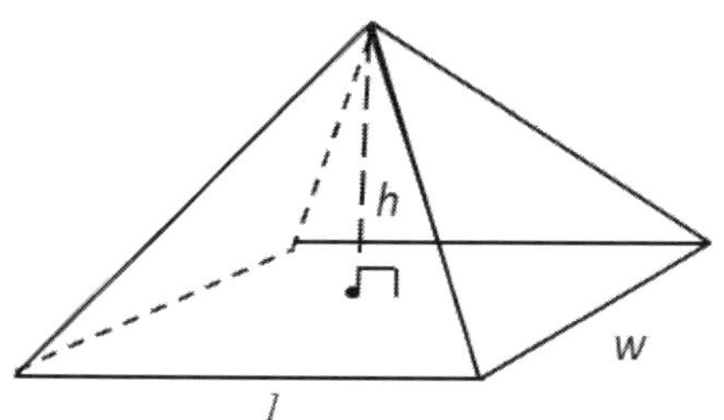

Problem Solving Skills

Easy

1. A rectangular storage room has a volume of 9375 cubic feet. If its length is 75 feet and its height is 5 feet, what is the width of the room?

Answer: 25

Volume = Length × Height × Width
9375 = 75 × 5 × Width
Width = 25 feet

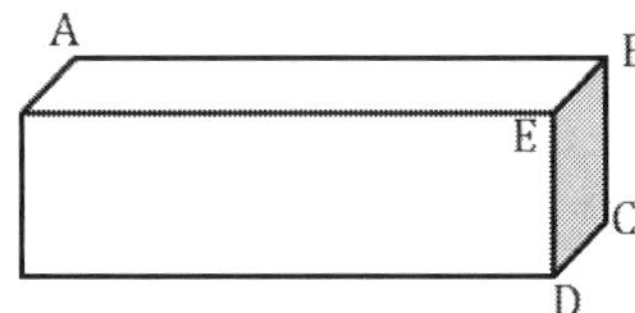

2. In the rectangular solid above, the area of BCDE is 10 and $\overline{AB}$ = 12. What is the volume of this solid?
   a) 120
   b) 180
   c) 240
   d) 90

Answer: (a)

Volume = Area of Base × Height = 10 × 12 = 120

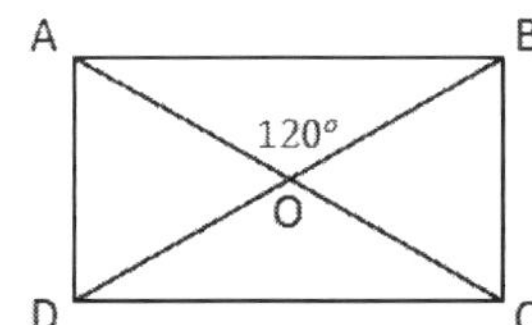

3. In the figure above, ABCD is a rectangle. If the two diagonals of ABCD intersect at point O, what is the measure of ∠OAD?
   a) 30°
   b) 60°
   c) 90°
   d) 120°

Answer: (b)

ΔADO is an isosceles triangle.

$m\angle AOD = 180^{\circ} - 120^{\circ} = 60^{\circ}$
$m\angle OAD = \frac{180^{\circ} - 60^{\circ}}{2} = 60^{\circ}$

Medium

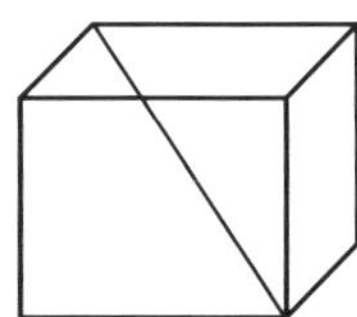

4. The cube shown above has side length a. What is the length of its diagonal as drawn?
   a) a
   b) $2a$
   c) $\sqrt{2}a$
   d) $\sqrt{3}a$

Answer: (d)

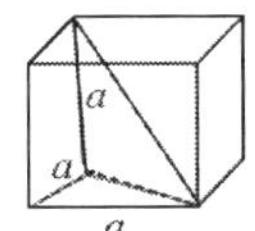

Diagonal = $\sqrt{a^2 + a^2 + a^2} = \sqrt{3}a$

5. A truck has a container with dimensions 40 × 12 × 8 feet. How many cubic boxes with side length of 2 feet can fit into the container?

Answer: 480

Total Number of Boxes = $\frac{40}{2} \times \frac{12}{2} \times \frac{8}{2}$ *= 480 boxes*

6. A rectangular box has dimensions 36 × 14 × 18. If this rectangular box can contain 84 smaller identical rectangular boxes without wasting any space, which of the following could be the dimensions of these smaller boxes?
   a) 2 × 5 × 6
   b) 2 × 6 × 9
   c) 3 × 5 × 6
   d) 7 × 6 × 12

Answer: (b)

The number 5 is not a factor of 14, 36 or 18, therefore answers (a), (c), (d) are not possible. Only (b)'s dimensions can store 84 rectangular boxes.
$\frac{14}{2} \times \frac{36}{6} \times \frac{18}{9} = 84$

7. What is the volume of a cube if its total surface area is 96 square units?

Answer: 64

Let a be the length of one side of the cube.
Surface Area $= 6 \times a^2 = 96$
$a = 4$
Volume $= a^3 = 4^3 = 64$

8. In the rectangular solid above, the total surface area is 40. Face A has an area 4 and face B has an area 8. What is the volume of the rectangular solid?

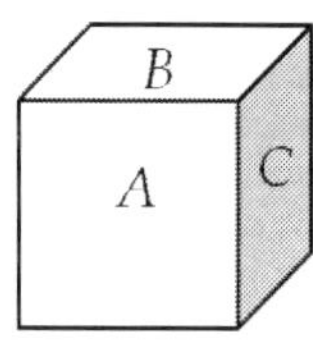

Answer: 16

Area of Face C $= \frac{1}{2} \times 40 -$ *Area of Face A* $-$ *Area of Face B* $= 20 - 4 - 8 = 8$
Letting the lengths of the three different sides be x, y, and z respectively, then the volume of the solid is $x \times y \times z$.
Area of Face A $= x \times y = 4$
Area of Face B $= y \times z = 8$
Area of Face C $= x \times z = 8$
$(xy) \times (yz) \times (zx) = 4 \times 8 \times 8$
$(xyz)^2 = 256$
$xyz = \sqrt{4 \times 8 \times 8} = 16$

9. The cube shown below has edges of length 3. If $\overline{CB} = \overline{AD} = 1$, what is the length of $\overline{AB}$?

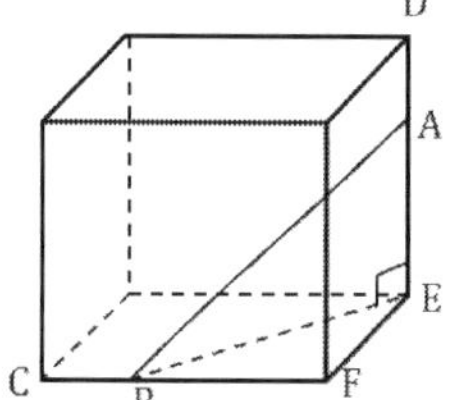

Answer: 4.12

$BF = 2$
$EF = 3$
$EA = 2$
$AB = \sqrt{EA^2 + EB^2} = \sqrt{EA^2 + BF^2 + EF^2}$
$AB = \sqrt{2^2 + 2^2 + 3^2} = \sqrt{17} = 4.123$

10. If the volume of a cube is 27, what is the length of the longest diagonal of the cube?

Answer: 5.19 or 5.20

Let a be the length of one side.
Length of Longest Diagonal =
$\sqrt{a^2 + a^2 + a^2} = \sqrt{3} \times a.$
$a = \sqrt[3]{27} = 3$
$3 \times \sqrt{3} = 3\sqrt{3} = 5.196$

Questions 11 – 12 refer to the following information:
Density describes how compact or concentrated a material is. It is defined as the ratio between mass and volume, or mass per unit volume. The formula to calculate the density is:

$$Density = \frac{Mass}{Volume}$$

11. The kilobar of gold is 1,000 grams in mass. If the density of the gold bar is 19.3 grams per cm^3, what would be the volume of the kilobar, in cm^3? (Round your answer to the nearest tenth)

Answer: 51.8

$Density = \frac{Mass}{Volume}$
$19.3 = \frac{1000}{Volume}$
$Volume = \frac{1000}{19.3} = 51.8\ cm^3$

12. If a cylinder gold block has a diameter of 2 centimeters and height of 10 centimeters, what would be its mass, in grams? (Round your answer to the nearest whole number)

Answer: 606

$volume = \pi r^2 h = \pi \times 1^2 \times 10$
$mass = 19.3 \times 10\pi = 606.3$

Hard

13. In the figure above, a circular cylinder has radius 3 and height 5. What is the volume of the smallest rectangular box that can store this circular cylinder inside?
    a) 120
    b) 150
    c) 180
    d) 200

Answer: (c)

The smallest rectangular box that can contain this cylinder should have both its width and length equal to the diameter of the cylinder, and its height equal to the height of the cylinder.
Volume of Rectangle =
$(2 \times r)^2 \times h$
$6^2 \times 5 = 180$

14. The square pyramid shown below has volume $\frac{128}{3}$ and height 8. What is the length of YZ?

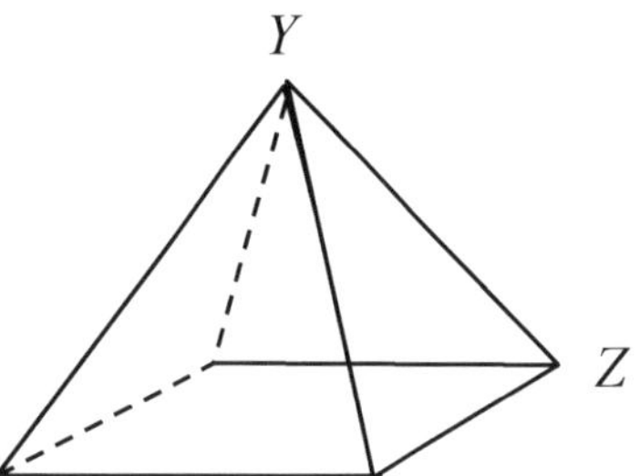

a) $8\sqrt{2}$
b) $8\sqrt{6}$
c) $6\sqrt{2}$
d) 8

Answer: (c)

If center of the square base is O, then ΔYOZ is a right triangle.

Volume $= \frac{1}{3} \times$ *Area of Base* $\times$ *Height*

$= \frac{128}{3}$

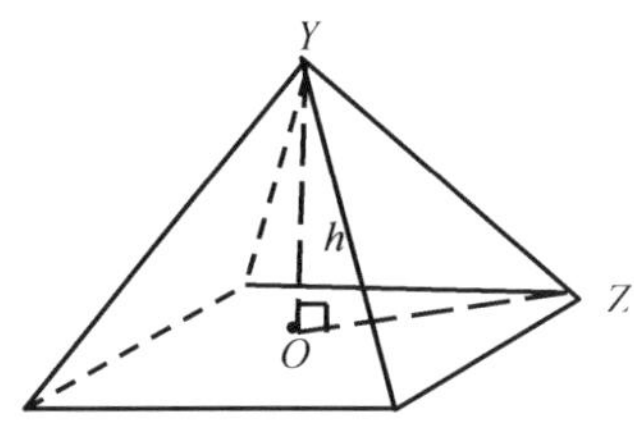

Let x be the length one side of the square.

$\frac{1}{3}x^2 \times 8 = \frac{128}{3} \quad \rightarrow \quad = 4$

Length of the Diagonal of the Square $= 4\sqrt{2}$

$YZ = \sqrt{\left(\frac{Diagonal}{2}\right)^2 + Height}$

$YZ = \sqrt{(2\sqrt{2})^2 + 8^2} = \sqrt{72} = 6\sqrt{2}$

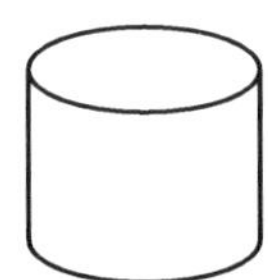

15. The right circular cylinder above has radius r and height h. Which of the following can represent the volume of the biggest rectangular box that is completely inscribed inside the cylinder?

a) $r \times h$
b) $2 \times r^2 \times h$
c) $2 \times r^2 \times h^2$
d) $\frac{(2r + h)^2}{2}$

Answer: (b)

The diagonal of the base of the rectangular box must be equal to diameter of the cylinder in order to be inscribed inside the cylinder. The biggest rectangular box inside the cylinder must have a square of base.

Area of Base $= \frac{1}{2} \times Diagonal^2$

$= 2r^2$

Volume of Box $= 2r^2 \times h$

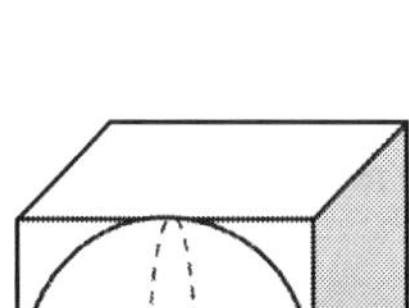

16. In the figure above, a cube has a volume of 27 cubic units. What is the length of the diameter of a sphere that is inscribed in the cube?

Answer: 3

Length of Side of Cube = Diameter of Sphere

Length of Side of Cube $= \sqrt[3]{27} = 3$

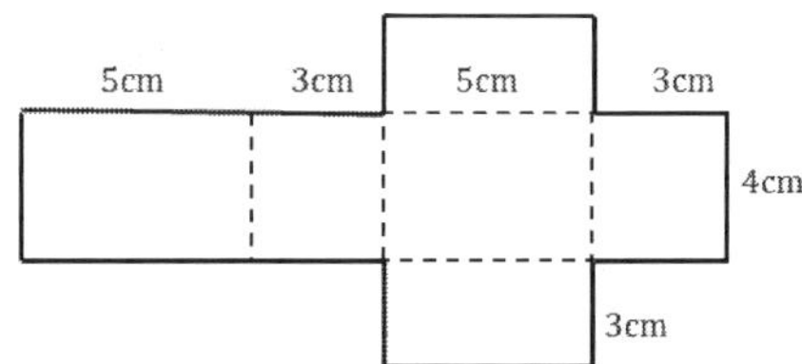

17. If the figure above is folded along the dashed lines, a rectangular box will be formed. What is the volume of the box in cubic centimeters?
    a) 45
    b) 60
    c) 72
    d) 81

Answer: (b)

After folding, the height of the box will be 3 cm, the length will be 5 cm, and the width will be 4cm.
Volume = 3 cm × 4 cm × 5 cm = 60 cm^3

18. If each edge of a rectangular solid has a length that is an integer greater than one, which of the following could be the volume of the solid, in cubic units?
    a) 9
    b) 12
    c) 15
    d) 21

Answer: (b)

The volume should be the product of at least 3 integers greater than one.
Only 12 has more than 3 factors greater than 1.
12 = 2 × 2 × 3

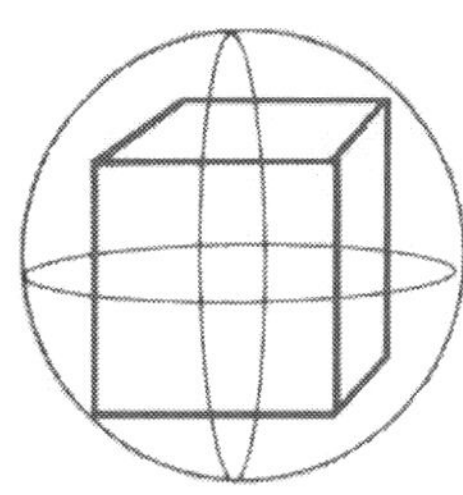

19. A cube is inscribed in a sphere as shown in the figure above. Each vertex of the cube touches the sphere. If the diameter of this sphere is $3\sqrt{3}$, what is the volume of the cube?
    a) 8
    b) 27
    c) 36
    d) 48

Answer: (b)

Let x be the length of one side of the cube.
Diameter of Sphere = Diagonal of Cube
Diagonal of Cube =
$\sqrt{x^2 + x^2 + x^2} = x\sqrt{3}$
$\sqrt{x^2 + x^2 + x^2} = 3\sqrt{3}$
$x\sqrt{3} = 3\sqrt{3}$
$x = 3$
Volume of Cube $= 3^3 = 27$

VI. COORDINATE GEOMETRY

Concept Overviews

The Distance between Two Points

To find the distance between two points A and B on a Cartesian plane, draw a right triangle with a line connecting the two points as the hypotenuse. Use the Pythagorean theorem to find the distance between two points. The distance between the points (x_1, y_1) and (x_2, y_2) is given by the **distance formula**:

$$Distance = \sqrt{(x_2 - x_1)^2 + (y_2 - y_1)^2}$$

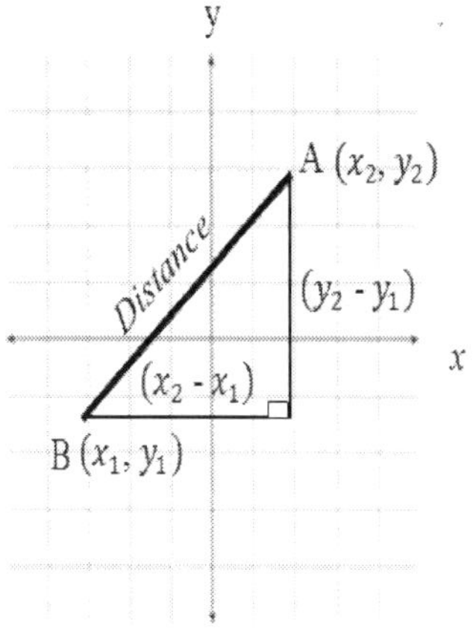

y
A (x_2, y_2)
Distance
$(y_2 - y_1)$
x
$(x_2 - x_1)$
B (x_1, y_1)

Example: Find the distance between the points (2, 2) and (-2, 5).
Answer: Plug the coordinates into the distance formula:

$$d = \sqrt{(x_2 - x_1)^2 + (y_2 - y_1)^2} = \sqrt{(-2 - 2)^2 + (5 - 2)^2} = \sqrt{25} = 5$$

The distance between the two points is 5.

The Midpoint between Two Points

The midpoint of a line segment is the average of the two end points, (x_1, y_1) and (x_2, y_2). The **midpoint formula** is:

$$M(x, y) = \left(\frac{x_1 + x_2}{2}, \frac{y_1 + y_2}{2}\right)$$

Example: Find the midpoint between (3, –2) and (-3, 4).
Answer: Plug the two points into the midpoint formula:

$$M\,(x, y) = \left(\frac{x_1 + x_2}{2}, \frac{y_1 + y_2}{2}\right) = \left(\frac{3 + (-3)}{2}, \frac{(-2) + 4}{2}\right) = (0, 1)$$

The midpoint between the two points is (0, 1).

The Slope between Two Points

The slope m of a line segment connecting two points is found by:

$$m = \frac{Rise}{Run} = \frac{y_2 - y_1}{x_2 - x_1}$$

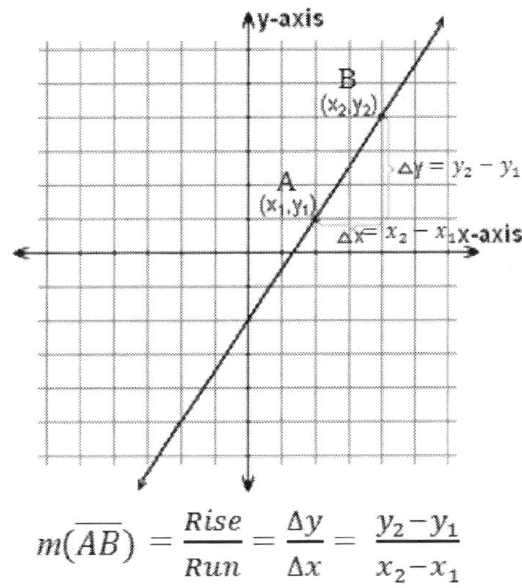

$$m(\overline{AB}) = \frac{Rise}{Run} = \frac{\Delta y}{\Delta x} = \frac{y_2 - y_1}{x_2 - x_1}$$

- If $m > 0$, the line passing the two points slopes upward from left to right.
- If $m < 0$, the line passing the two points slopes downward from left to right.
- If $m = 0$, the line is horizontal.
- If the line is a vertical line, its slope is undefined.

Example: Find the slope of the line formed by the two points (3, 5) and (2, 1).
Answer: $m = \frac{Rise}{Run} = \frac{\Delta y}{\Delta x} = \frac{1-5}{2-3} = 4$

The slope between the two points is 4, so the line passing the two points slopes upwards from left to right.

Equations of Lines

- **Slope-intercept Form:** The slope-intercept form of a line is written as $y = mx + b$, where m is the slope of the line and b is the y-intercept of the line.

- **Standard Form:** The standard form of a line is written as $ax + by = c$, where the slope of the line is $-\frac{a}{b}$.

Example: Find the slope of the line from the equation $4x - 2y + 2 = 0$.
Answer: Change the equation to any of the forms listed above.

Convert to slope-intercept form:
$2y = 4x + 2$
$y = 2x + 1$
$m = 2$
The slope is 2. (The graph slopes upward from left to right.)

Convert to the standard form:
$4x - 2y = -2$
$m = -\frac{a}{b} = -\frac{4}{-2} = 2$

Equations of Circles

A circle is the set of all points on a plane that are a fixed distance from a point, its center. The fixed distance is the radius of the circle. Any equation that can be written in the form of $(x-h)^2+(y-k)^2=r^2$ is a graph of the circle with radius r and center at point (h,k).

Example: Find the center and radius of the circle given by the equation

$$(x-2)^2+(y+1)^2=4.$$

Answer: According to the standard equation of a circle, the center of this circle is $(2,-1)$ and the radius is 2.

Example: Find the center and radius of the circle given by the equation $x^2+y^2-4x+2y=20$.

Answer: Rewrite the original equation into the standard equation of a circle:

$x^2+y^2-4x+2y=20$

$(x^2-4x+2^2)+(y^2+2y+1^2)=20+2^2+1^2=25$

$(x-2)^2+(y+1)^2=5^2$

The center of the circle is $(2,-1)$ and the radius is 5.

Graph Translations

A **translation** of a graph moves the graph horizontally or vertically. If $y=f(x)$ is a graph on a xy-coordinate system and c is a positive constant number, then

- $y=f(x)+c$ will shift the graph of $y=f(x)$ up c units.
- $y=f(x)-c$ will shift the graph of $y=f(x)$ down c units.
- $y=f(x-c)$ will shift the graph of $y=f(x)$ to the right c units.
- $y=f(x+c)$ will shift the graph of $y=f(x)$ to the left c units.

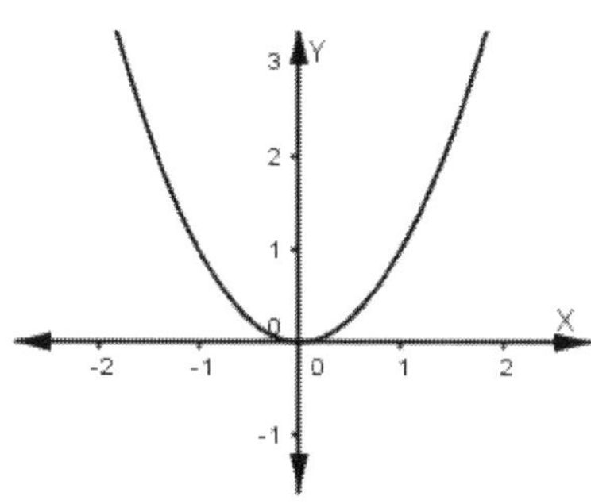

Example: If the figure above shows the graph of a quadratic function $f(x)$, then what would the graphs of $f(x+1)$, $f(x-1)$, $f(x)+1$, and $f(x)-1$ look like?

Answer: f(x + 1) shows the graph shifted to the left 1 unit.

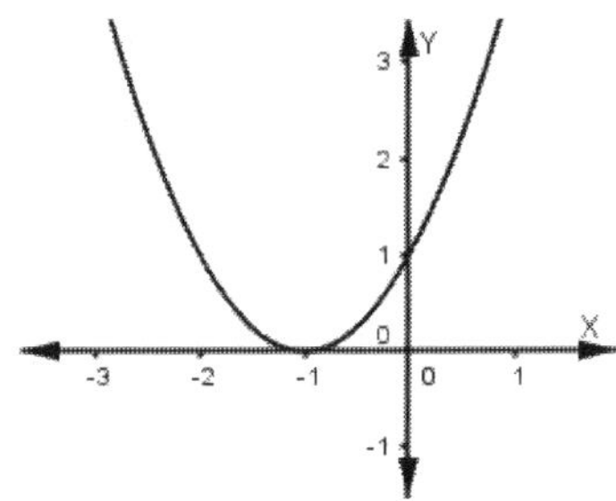

f(x − 1) shows the graph shifted to the right 1 unit.

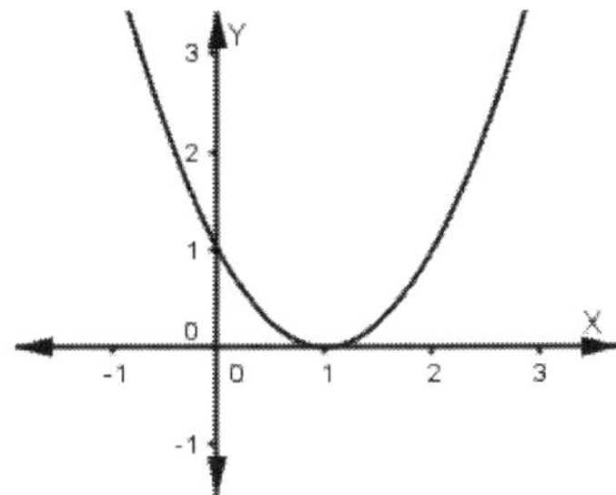

f(x) + 1 shows the graph shifted up 1 unit.

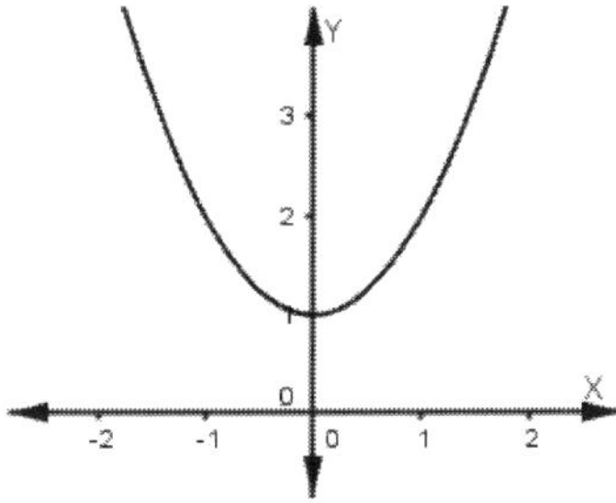

f(x) − 1 shows the graph shifted down 1 unit.

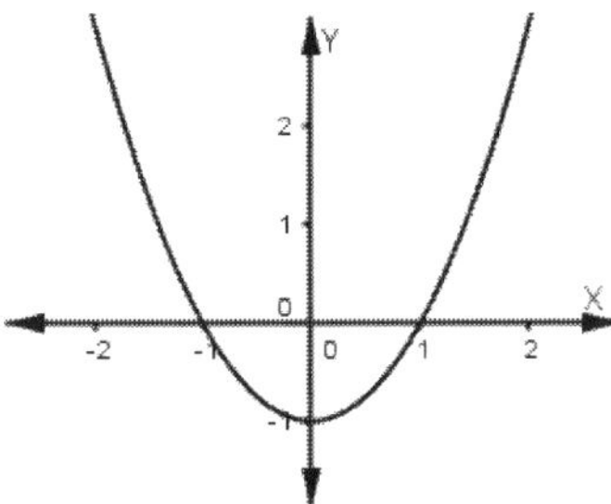

Graph Reflections

The **reflection** of a graph looks like a mirror image. The **line of reflection** (the **line of symmetry**) is line across which the graph is reflected. The part of the graph that intersects the line of reflection will stay the same.

If $y = f(x)$ is a graph on a xy-coordinate system, then:

- $y = -f(x)$ will show $y = f(x)$ reflected about the *x-axis*, that is, for every point (x, y) will be replaced with a new point at $(x, -y)$.
- $y = f(-x)$ will show $y = f(x)$ reflected about the *y-axis*, that is, for every point (x, y) will be replaced with a new point at $(-x, y)$.
- $y = -f(-x)$ will show $y = f(x)$ reflected about the origin, that is, every point (x, y) will be replaced with a new point at $(-x, -y)$.

If a graph is **symmetric** across a line l, then if you fold an image of the graph at line l, the two parts of the graph will match up perfectly.

Example 1: Sketch a graph that is symmetric about the x-axis.
Answer: If a graph is symmetric about the x-axis, then for a point (x, y), there will also be a point $(x, -y)$ on the graph.

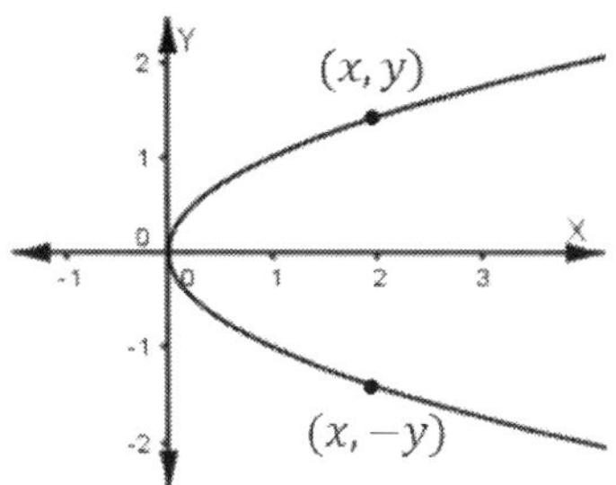

Example 2: Sketch a graph that is symmetric about the y-axis.
Answer: If a graph is symmetric about the y-axis, then for a point (x, y), there will also be a point $(-x, y)$ on the graph.

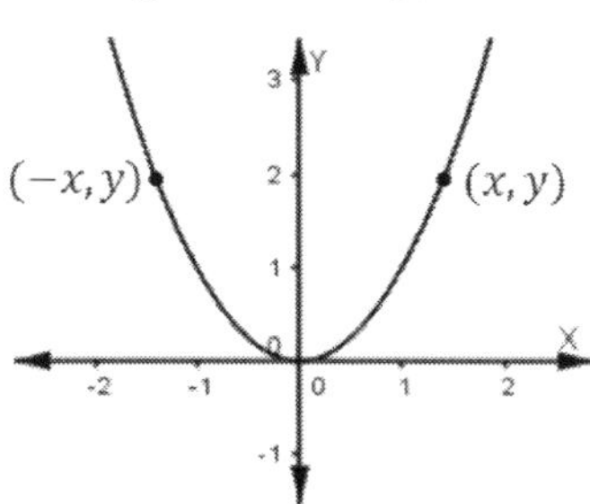

Example 3: Sketch a graph that is symmetric about the origin.
Answer: If a graph is reflected (symmetric) about the origin, then for a point of (x, y), there will also be a point $(-x, -y)$ on the graph.

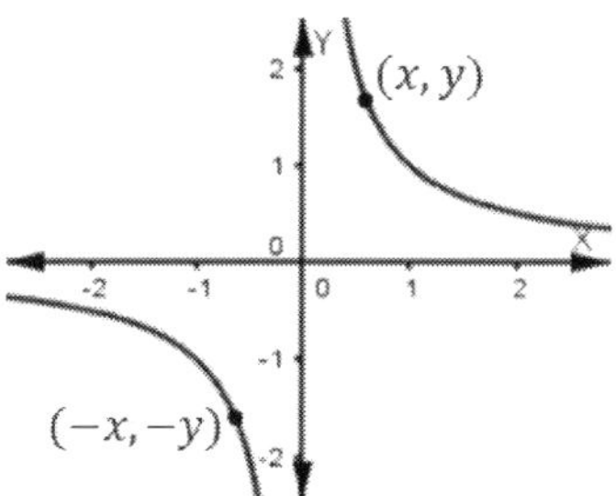

Problem Solving Skills

Easy

1. In the figure below, $\overline{AC} = 2\overline{AB}$ and the coordinates of A are (−4, *b*). What is the value of *b*?

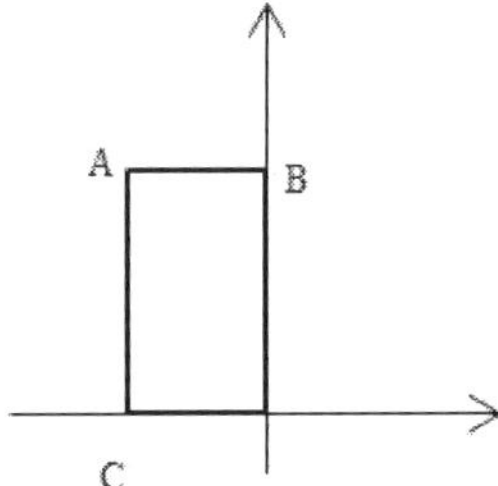

Answer: 8

b is the y-coordinate which, since $\overline{AC} = 2\overline{AB}$, is double the x-coordinate in length and extends in the positive direction.

$2 \times |-4| = 8$

2. In the figure below, a circle with center A is tangent to the *x*-axis and the *y*-axis on the *xy*-coordinate plane. If the coordinates of the center A are (−2, 2), what are the coordinates of point C?

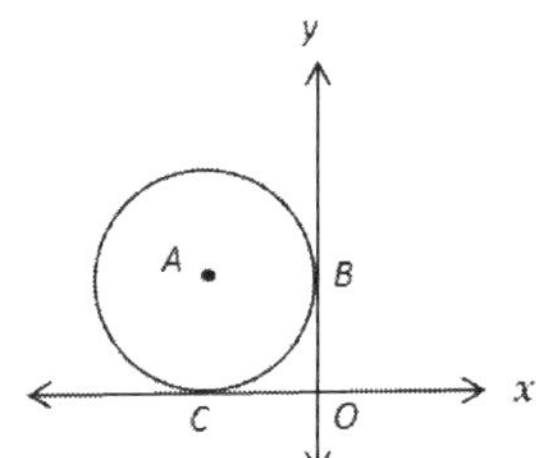

a) (−2, 0)
b) (−4, 0)
c) (2, 0)
d) (−2, 2)

Answer: (a)

AC = AB

The coordinates of B: (0, 2)
The coordinates of C: (−2, 0)

3. The following are coordinates of points on the *xy*-plane. Which of these points is nearest to the origin?

a) (0, −2)
b) (2 , 1)
c) (−1, 0)
d) (−1, −1)

Answer: (c)

Distance to the Origin = $\sqrt{(x-0)^2 + (y-0)^2} = \sqrt{x^2 + y^2}$
(c) has the shortest distance of 1 from the origin.

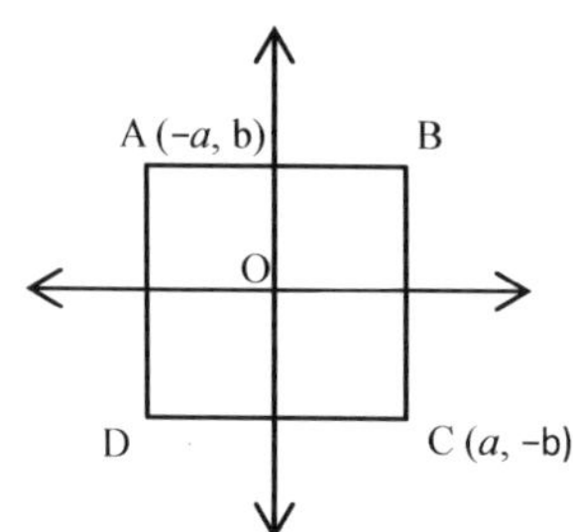

4. In the figure above, rectangle ABCD lies on the xy-coordinate plane. If the origin is located at the center of rectangle, which of the following could be the coordinates of point D?
   a) $(-a, b)$
   b) $(-a, -b)$
   c) $(-b, -a)$
   d) (b, a)

Answer: (b)

D is located in the quadrant III which has negative x and y coordinates.

$(-a, -b)$

5. In the figure below, if the two segments have the same length, what is the value of a?

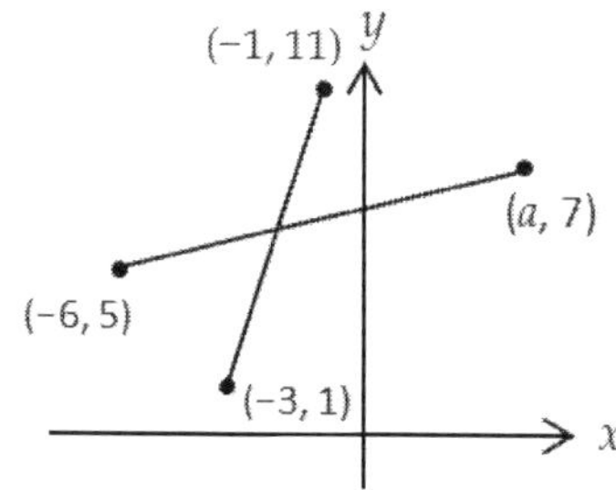

Answer: 4

$(a + 6)^2 + (7 - 5)^2$
$= (-1 + 3)^2 + (11 - 1)^2$
$a = 4$

6. Which of the following letters is symmetric with respect to at least two different lines?
   a) T
   b) S
   c) I
   d) A

Answer: (c)

"I" has both horizontal and vertical symmetry.

7. What is the perimeter of ΔXYZ if vertex X is located at coordinates (1, 2), vertex Y is located at coordinates (1, 5), and vertex Z is located at coordinates (5, 5) in the xy-coordinate system?
   a) 6
   b) 8
   c) 9
   d) 12

Answer: (d)

Use the distance formula to find the length of each side.

Perimeter $= 3 + 4 + \sqrt{(5-1)^2 + (5-2)^2} = 12$

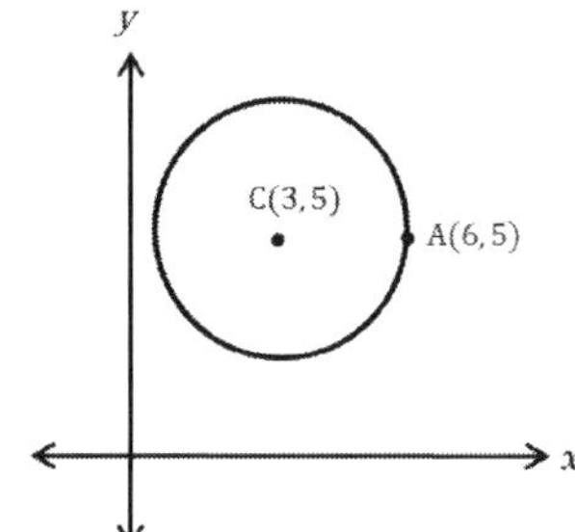

8. In the figure above, what is the circumference of the circle with center C?
   a) 4π
   b) 5π
   c) 6π
   d) 7π

Answer: (c)

Radius = $\overline{CA}$ = $\sqrt{(6-3)^2 + (5-5)^2} = 3$

Circumference = $2\pi r = 6\pi$

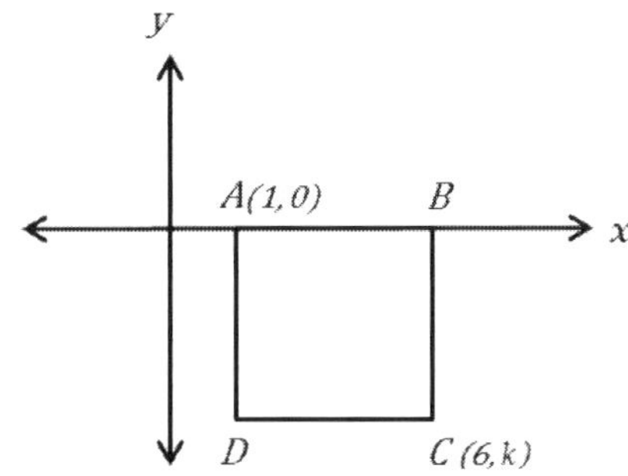

9. In the figure above, ABCD is a square. If the coordinates of A are (1, 0) and the coordinates of C are (6, *k*), what is the value of *k*?
   a) 2
   b) −2
   c) −4
   d) −5

Answer: (d)

Length of Side of Square =
$6 - 1 = 5$
$5 = 0 - k$
$k = -5$

10. If the figure above is rotated clockwise 90° about point O, which of the following will be the result?
   a) 
   b) 
   c) 
   d)

Answer: (d)

The arrow will point down and to the left after a clockwise 90° rotation.

11. The figure above shows the graph of a quadratic function f that has a vertex point of (2, 3) in the xy-coordinate system. If $f(a) = f(4)$, which of the following could be the value of a?
    a) –2
    b) –1
    c) 0
    d) 1

Answer: (c)

The curve shown is symmetric to the line $x = 2$, a vertical line. Thus, two points are equal if their x-coordinate is equidistance from the line $x = 2$. The x-coordinate 4 is 2 away from $x = 2$, and so is the x-coordinate of 0. Thus, $f(4)$ should be equal to $f(0)$.

12. Which of the following graphics is symmetric with respect to at least two different lines?
    a) 
    b) 
    c) 
    d) 

Answer: (d)

(d) is the only graphic that has more than two different symmetric lines.

Medium

13. What is the perimeter of a triangle that has vertices (–2, 0), (4, 0), and (1, 4) on the xy-coordinates plane?
    a) 16
    b) 14
    c) $6 + 2\sqrt{6}$
    d) 10

Answer: (a)

Without using the distance formula, we can tell that the points (–2, 0) and (4, 0) are 6 units apart. Use the distance formula to find the lengths for the other two sides.
Perimeter =
$6 + \sqrt{(-2-1)^2 + (0-4)^2} + \sqrt{(4-1)^2 + (0-4)^2}$
$= 6 + 5 + 5 = 16$

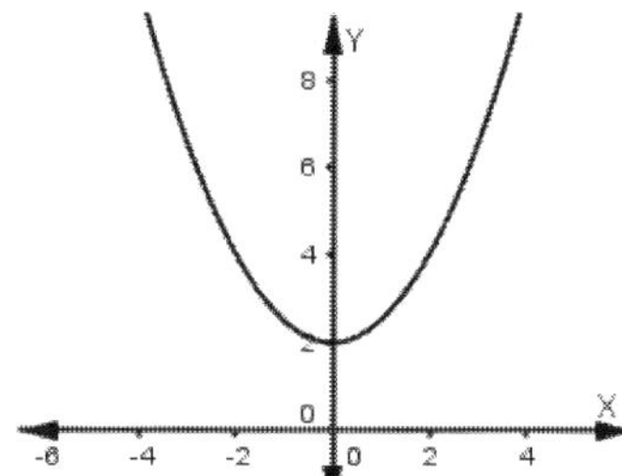

14. The figure above is a parabola of the equation $y = ax^2 + 2$, where a is a constant. If graphed on the same axes, which of the following describes the graph of $y = 2ax^2 + 2$ as compared to the graph above?
    a) The new graph will move to the right.
    b) The new graph will move to the left.
    c) The new graph will be narrower.
    d) The new graph will be the same.

Answer: (c)

The larger the coefficient of x^2, the larger the y-coordinate will be for a point at the same x-coordinate. Therefore, the new graph will be narrower. Plug the two functions into your calculator for an easy way to solve this problem.

15. Which of the following is the equation of a parabola whose vertex is at (–3, –4)?
    a) $y = x^2 - 4$
    b) $y = (x - 3)^2 + 4$
    c) $y = (x - 4)^2 - 3$
    d) $y = (x + 4)^2 - 3$

Answer: (d)

The equation of a parabola with vertex (h, k) is $y = (x - h)^2 + k$.

$(h, k) = (-3, -4)$
$y = (x + 3)^2 - 4$

16. On a number line, what is the sum, in a fraction, of all possible coordinates of a point P, if the distance from P to $\frac{1}{3}$ is twice the distance from P to $\frac{1}{2}$?

Answer: $\frac{10}{9}$ or 1.11

$|P - \frac{1}{3}| = 2 \times |(P - \frac{1}{2})|$
$P - \frac{1}{3} = 2(P - \frac{1}{2}) \rightarrow P = \frac{2}{3}$
$P - \frac{1}{3} = -2(P - \frac{1}{2}) \rightarrow P = \frac{4}{9}$
$\frac{2}{3} + \frac{4}{9} = \frac{10}{9}$

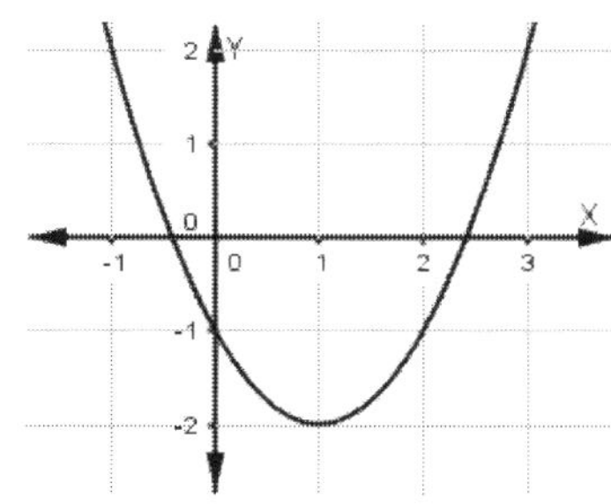

17. What is the equation for the parabola shown above?
    a) $y = (x - 1)^2 - 2$
    b) $y = (x + 1)^2 - 2$
    c) $y = (x - 1)^2 + 2$
    d) $y = (x + 1)^2 + 2$

Answer: (a)

The equation of a parabola with vertex (h, k) is $y = (x - h)^2 + k$.
$(h, k) = (1, -2)$
$y = (x - 1)^2 - 2$

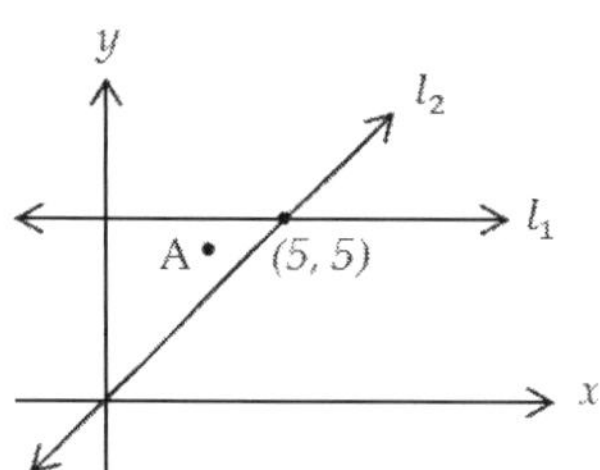

18. In the xy-coordinate plane, line l_1 is parallel to the x-axis and line l_2 passes through the origin. Which of the following points could be the coordinates of point A?
    a) (-1, 1)
    b) (1, -3)
    c) (4, 2)
    d) (3, 4)

Answer: (d)

Point A has all positive coordinates and its y coordinate is greater than its x coordinate but less than 5.

19. In the figure below, two circles with centers A and B are tangent to each other and both tangent to the x-axis in the xy-coordinate system. If circle A has a radius of 1 and circle B has a radius of 4, what is the slope of the segment that connects both centers?

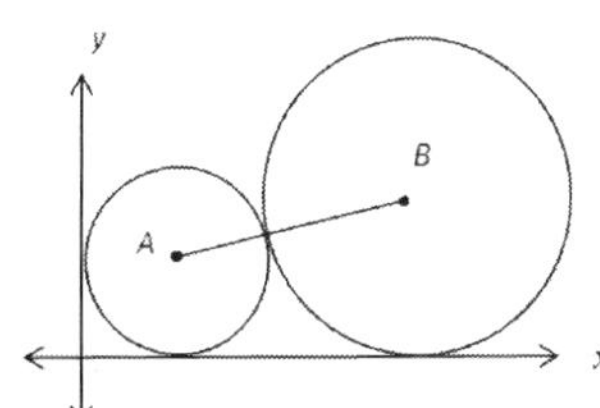

Note: Figure not drawn to scale.

Answer: $\frac{3}{4}$ *or .75*

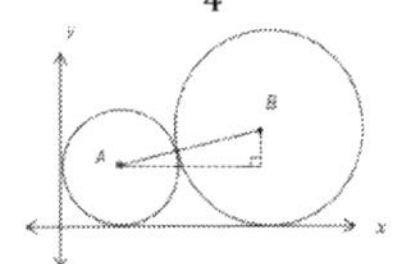

Slope = $\frac{Rise}{Run}$
Rise = Difference of Radii = 4−1= 3
AB = 4 + 1 = 5
The triangle is a right triangle, so we use the Pythagorean theorem to solve for the run.
$Run^2 + Rise^2 = 5^2$
Run = $\sqrt{5^2 - 3^2}$ = 4 *and Slope* = $\frac{3}{4}$

20. Find the equation of a circle that has a diameter with the endpoints given by the points (3, 5) and (−1, 1).
    a) $(x-1)^2 + (y-3)^2 = 8$
    b) $(x+1)^2 + (y+3)^2 = 8$
    c) $(x-1)^2 + (y-3)^2 = 4$
    d) $(x+1)^2 + (y-3)^2 = 8$

Answer: (a)

Center: $\left(\frac{3-1}{2}, \frac{5+1}{2}\right) = (1, 3)$
Radius: $\sqrt{(3-1)^2 + (5-3)^2} = \sqrt{8}$
Equation: $(x-1)^2 + (y-3)^2 = 8$

21. If the center of circle $x^2 + y^2 - 4x - 6y + 8 = 0$ is (h, k) and the radius is r, then $h + k + r = ?$

Answer: 9

$x^2 + y^2 - 4x - 6y - 3 = 0$
$(x-2)^2 + (y-3)^2 = 3 + 4 + 9$
$(x-2)^2 + (y-3)^2 = 4^2$
$h + k + r = 2 + 3 + 4 = 9$

22. On the xy-plane, what is the equation of the line that is a reflection the line $y = -2x - 1$ across the x-axis?
    a) $y = -2x + 1$
    b) $y = -2x - 1$
    c) $y = 2x - 1$
    d) $y = 2x + 1$

Answer: (d)

A reflection across the x-axis flips all y-coordinates from y to −y and keeps the x-coordinates unchanged.
$-y = -2x - 1$
$y = 2x + 1$

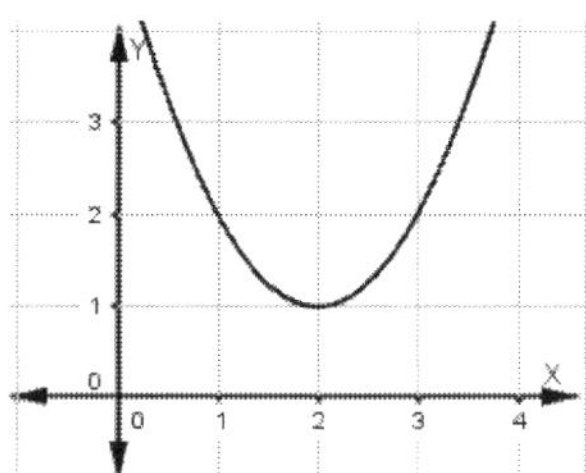

23. The graph of $f(x)$ is shown in the figure above. Which of the following is the graph of $f(x + 1)$?

    a)

    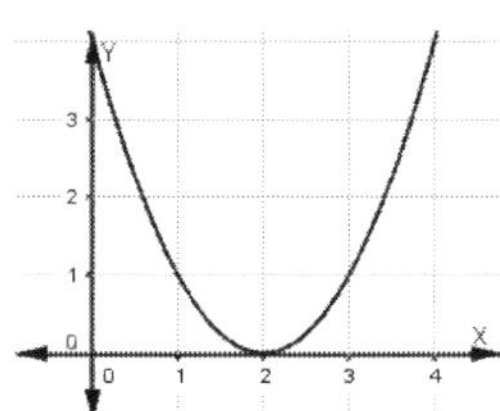

    b)

    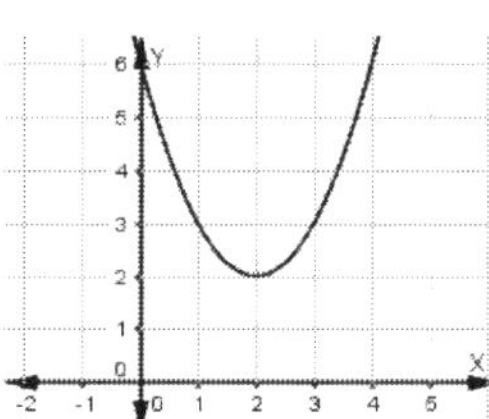

    c)

    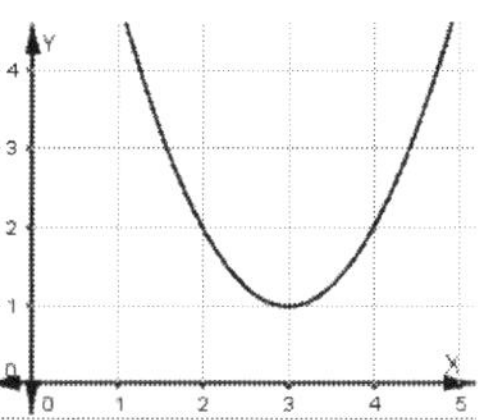

    d)

    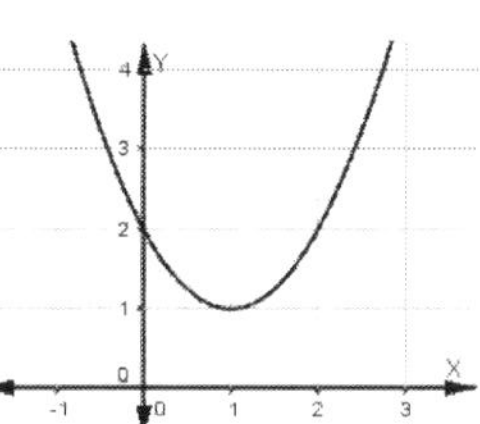

Answer: (d)

The graph of $f(x + 1)$ is a graph of $f(x)$ shifted 1 unit to the left. The vertex point of the graph of (d) is located at $x = 1$ which means the original graph shifted 1 unit to the left (from 2 to 1 along the x-coordinate.)

24. The dimensions of the rectangular storage box shown on the above left are 2 feet by 2 feet by 1 foot. What is the maximum number of Lego blocks (shown on the right) that can fit inside the storage box if each Lego block has dimensions 4 inches by 4 inches by 1 inch?

Answer: 432

2 feet by 2 feet by 1 foot = 24 inches by 24 inches by 12 inches

$\frac{24}{4} \times \frac{24}{4} \times \frac{12}{1} = 432$ *Legos*

25. The equation of line p is $y = -x + 2$. If the dotted line q is the reflection of line p over the y-axis, what is the slope of line q?
    a) -2
    b) 1
    c) $-\frac{1}{2}$
    d) $\frac{1}{2}$

Answer: (b)

If you reflect a line over the y-axis, the slope of the new line will have the opposite sign of the slope of the old line.
The slope of p is −1, so the slope of q is 1.

26. In the xy-coordinate plane, line m is the reflection of line l about the x-axis. Which of the following could be the sum of the slopes of lines m and l?
    a) 1
    b) −1
    c) 0
    d) $-\frac{1}{2}$

Answer: (c)

The reflection about x−axis will change all negative slopes to their positives and vice versa. Therefore, the sum of any such pairs of slopes must be zero.

27. In a rectangular coordinate system, the center of a circle has coordinates $(3, y)$. The circle is tangent to both the x-axis and y-axis. What is a possible value of y?

Answer: 3

The circle is tangent to both the x-axis and y−axis, so the coordinates of $|x|$ *and* $|y|$ *should be the same.* $y = \pm 3$

28. In the xy-plane, line r passes through the origin and is perpendicular to line t and intersects at the point $(4, 2)$. What is the slope of line t?
    a) −1
    b) −2
    c) 1
    d) 2

Answer: (b)

The product of the slopes of two perpendicular lines must be −1.
Slope of r $= \frac{2-0}{4-0} = \frac{1}{2}$
Slope of t $= -2$

Hard

29. In the xy-coordinate plane, point A has coordinates $(x, -5)$ and point B has coordinates $(3, 7)$. If $\overline{AB} = 13$ and x is a positive value, what is the value of x?

Answer: 8

Use the distance formula.

$\sqrt{(x-3)^2 + (-5-7)^2} = 13$

$(x-3)^2 + 12^2 = 13^2$

$(x-3)^2 = 25$

$x-3 = \pm 5 \rightarrow x = -2, 8$

30. In the figure below, if the area of parallelogram OABC is 20, what is the value of x?

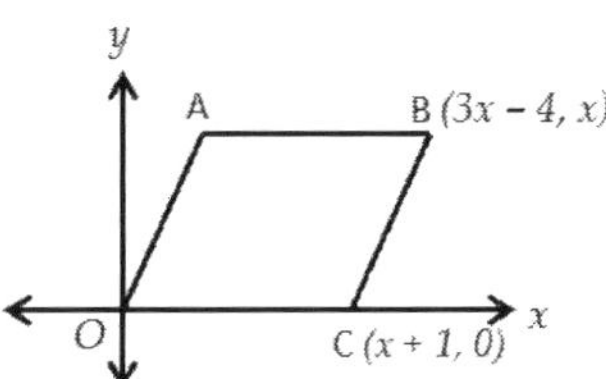

Answer: 4

Area of OABC = Base × Height =
$(x + 1) \times (x) = 20$
$x^2 + x - 20 = 0$
$(x + 5)(x - 4) = 0$
$x = 4$ *or* $x = -5$

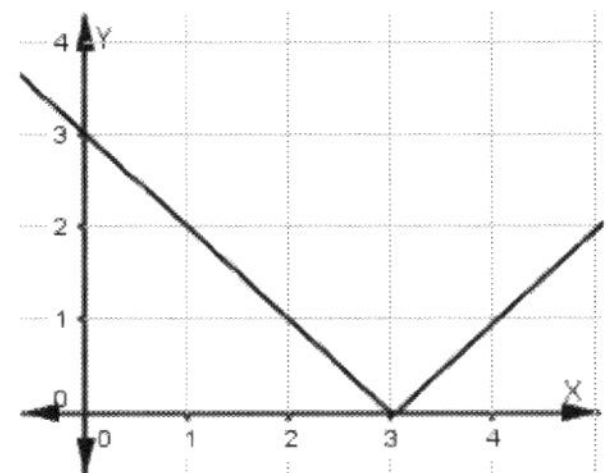

31. The graph of $y = f(x)$ is shown above. Which of the following could be the graph of $y = f(x + 1)$?

a)

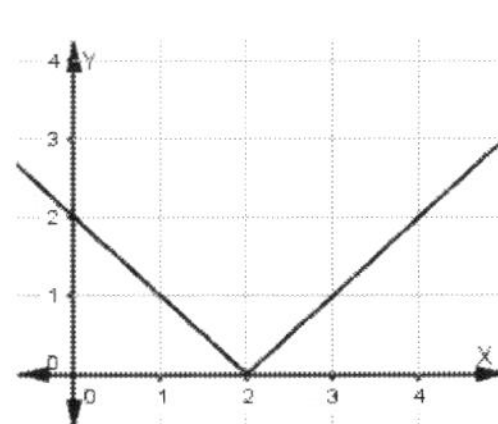

b)

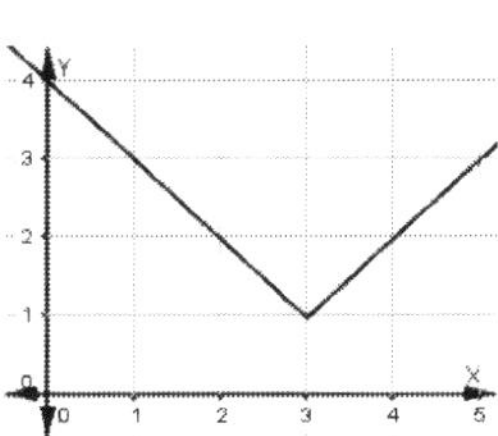

c)

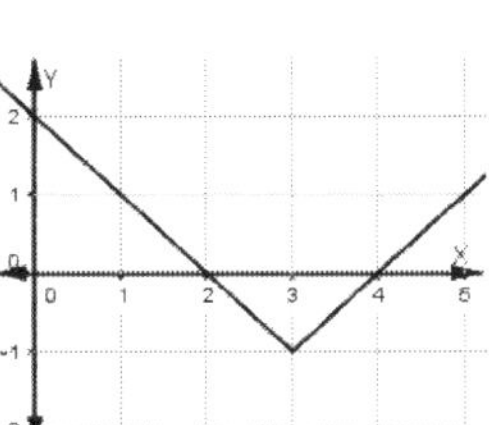

d)

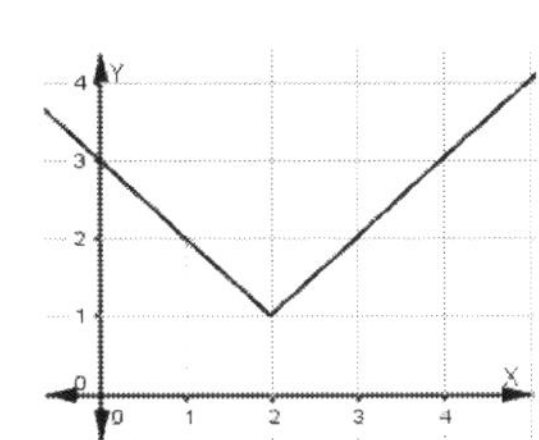

Answer: (a)

The graph of $y = f(x+1)$ *is the graph of* $y = f(x)$ *shifted to the left one unit with respect to the x-axis.*

VII. Trigonometric Functions and Their Inverses

Concept Overviews

Right Triangle Trigonometry

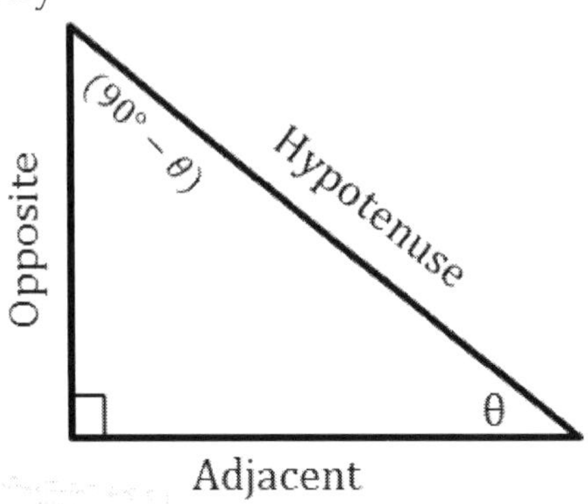

SOH CAH TOA

$$sin(\theta) = \frac{Opposite}{Hypotenuse} = cos(90° - \theta)$$

$$cos(\theta) = \frac{Adjacent}{Hypotenuse} = sin(90° - \theta)$$

$$tan(\theta) = \frac{Opposite}{Adjacent} = cot(90° - \theta)$$

Pythagorean Theorem: $Hypotenuse^2 = Adjacent^2 + Opposite^2$

Example: If $0 < \theta < 90°$ and $sin(\theta) = \frac{3}{5}$, what are the values of $cos(\theta)$ and $tan(\theta)$?

Solution: If $sin(\theta) = \frac{3}{5}$, we can represent $sin(\theta)$ as the following triangle:

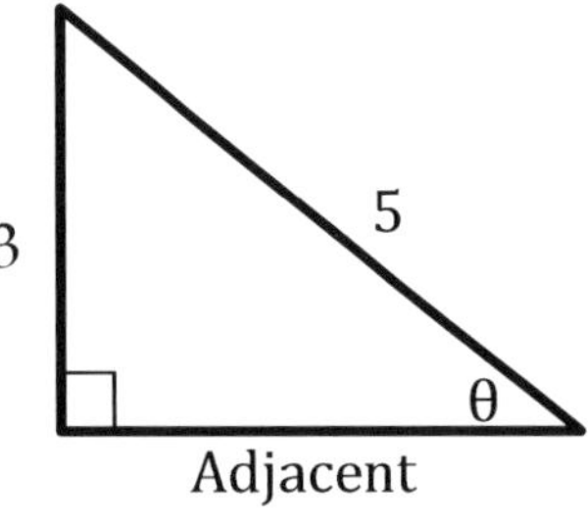

According to the Pythagorean theorem, the length of the adjacent side is $\sqrt{5^2 - 3^2} = 4$. Therefore, $cos(\theta) = \frac{4}{5}$ and $tan(\theta) = \frac{3}{4}$

Example: Solve the right triangle as shown below.

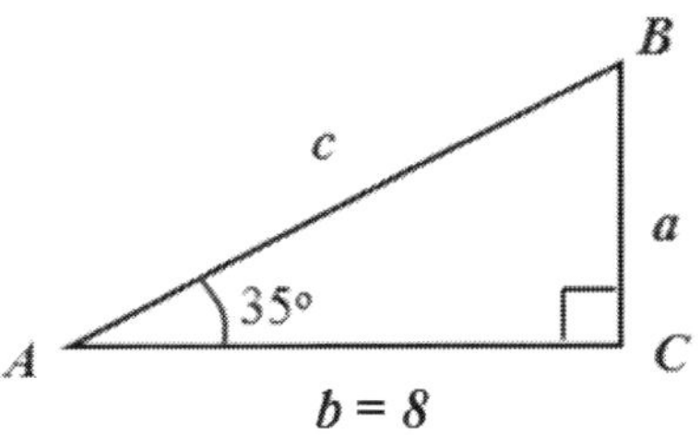

Solution: $\cos(35°) = 0.8192 = \frac{b}{c} = \frac{8}{c}$ c = 9.77

$\tan(35°) = 0.7002 = \frac{a}{b} = \frac{a}{8}$ $a = 5.60$

$\angle B = 90° - 35° = 55°$

Example: What is the height of the tree according to the following figure?

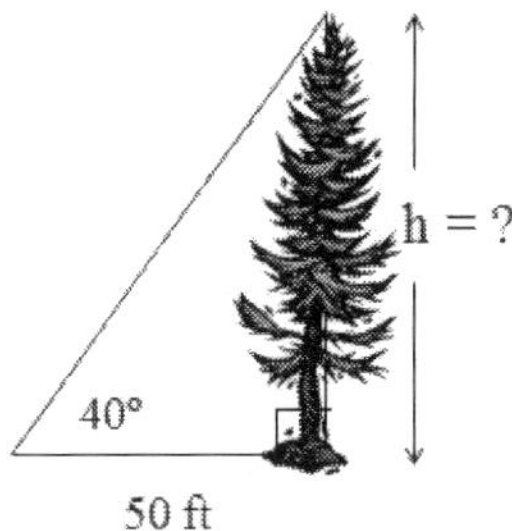

Solution: $tan(40°) = \frac{h}{50}$

$h = 50 \times tan(40°) = 50 \times 0.8391 = 41.95$ ft.

A unit circle is a circle with a radius of 1 centered at the origin on the coordinate plane as shown in the figure below.

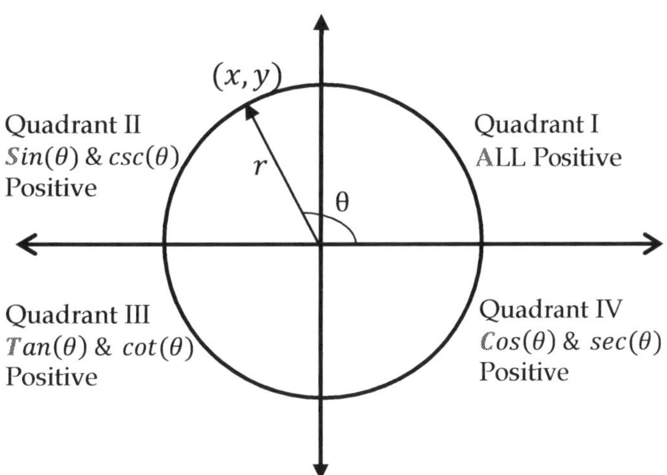

Use the mnemonic "All Students Take Calculus!"

$sin(\theta) = \frac{y}{r}$ $cos(\theta) = \frac{x}{r}$ $tan(\theta) = \frac{y}{x}$

$csc(\theta) = \frac{r}{y}$ $sec(\theta) = \frac{r}{x}$ $cot(\theta) = \frac{x}{y}$

There are two **special right triangles** that you need to remember:

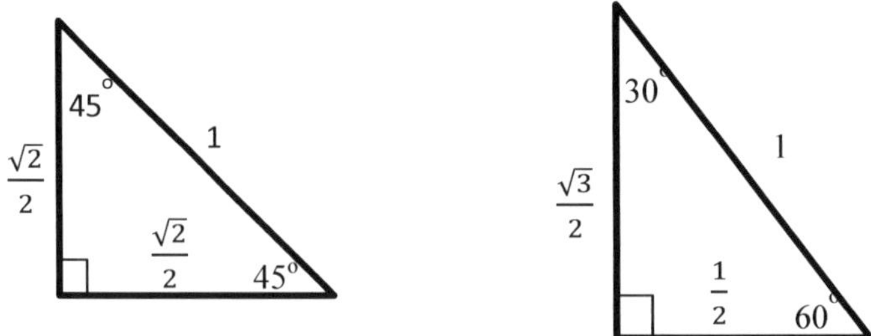

Some important angles, $0°, 30°, 45°, 60°$, and $90°$, and their sine, cosine, and tangent values are summarized below:

θ	$sin(\theta)$	$cos(\theta)$	$tan(\theta)$
0°	0	1	0
30°	$\frac{1}{2}$	$\frac{\sqrt{3}}{2}$	$\frac{\sqrt{3}}{3}$
45°	$\frac{\sqrt{2}}{2}$	$\frac{\sqrt{2}}{2}$	1
60°	$\frac{\sqrt{3}}{2}$	$\frac{1}{2}$	$\sqrt{3}$
90°	1	0	undefined

A **cofunction** is a trigonometric function whose value for the complement of a given angle is equal to the value of a trigonometric function of the angle itself. Pairs of cofunctions are sine and cosine, tangent and cotangent, and secant and cosecant.

$$sin(\theta) = \cos(90° - \theta) \qquad \cos(\theta) = sin(90° - \theta)$$
$$tan(\theta) = cot(90° - \theta) \qquad cot(\theta) = tan(90° - \theta)$$
$$\sec(\theta) = \csc(90° - \theta) \qquad \csc(\theta) = \sec(90° - \theta)$$

Example: Find the values of θ.

a. $\sin(13°) = \cos(\theta)$
Solution: $\theta = 90 - 13 = 77°$

b. $\sin(\theta) = \cos(65°)$
Solution: $\theta = 90 - 65 = 25°$

c. $\sin(\theta - 57°) = \cos(\theta)$
Solution: $\theta = 90 - 57 = 33°$

Example: One angle measures x, where $sin(x) = \frac{2}{3}$. What is $cos(90° - x)$?

Solution: $\cos(90° - x) = \sin(x) = \frac{2}{3}$

A reference angle of an angle θ is the smallest angle, β, formed by the terminal side of the angle θ and the x-axis (either the positive or negative x-axis).

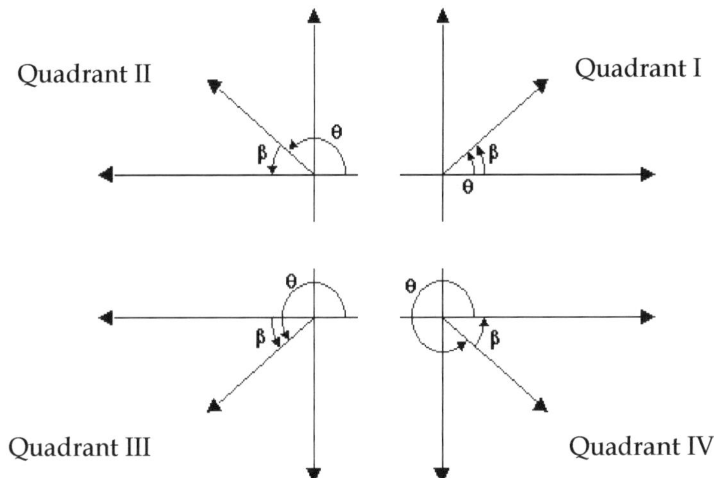

All simple trigonometric functions of θ are equal to ± 1 multiplying the function value of its corresponding β, depending on the Quadrant where θ is located:

$$\sin(\theta) = \pm\sin(\beta)$$
$$\cos(\theta) = \pm\cos(\beta)$$
$$\tan(\theta) = \pm\tan(\beta)$$

Example: What are the values of $sin(150°)$, $cos(150°)$, and $tan(150°)$?

Solution: 150° is located in Quadrant II and has a reference angle of 30°, so

$sin(150°) = sin(30°) = \frac{1}{2}$ (sin(θ) is positive in Quadrant II.)

$cos(150°) = -cos(30°) = \frac{\sqrt{3}}{2}$ (cos(θ) is negative in Quadrant II.)

$tan(150°) = -tan(30°) = \frac{\sqrt{3}}{3}$ (tan(θ) is negative in Quadrant II.)

Example: What are the values of $sin(-45°)$, $cos(-45°)$, and $tan(-45°)$?

Solution: The reference angle of $-45°$ is $45°$, so

$sin(-45°) = -sin(45°) = -\frac{\sqrt{2}}{2}$ (sin(θ) is negative in Quadrant IV.)

$\cos(-45°) = cos(45°) = \frac{\sqrt{2}}{2}$ (cos(θ) is positive in Quadrant IV.)

$tan(-45°) = -tan(45°) = -1$ (tan(θ) is negative in Quadrant IV.)

Domain, Range, and Period of Trigonometry Functions (sine, cosine, and tangent)

Function	Domain	Range	Period
$sin(\theta)$	All real numbers	$-1 \le sin(\theta) \le 1$	2π
$cos(\theta)$	All real numbers	$-1 \le cos(\theta) \le 1$	2π
$tan(\theta)$	All real except $n\pi + \frac{\pi}{2}$	All real numbers	π

Graphs of Trigonometry Functions (sine, cosine, and tangent)

$sin(\theta)$

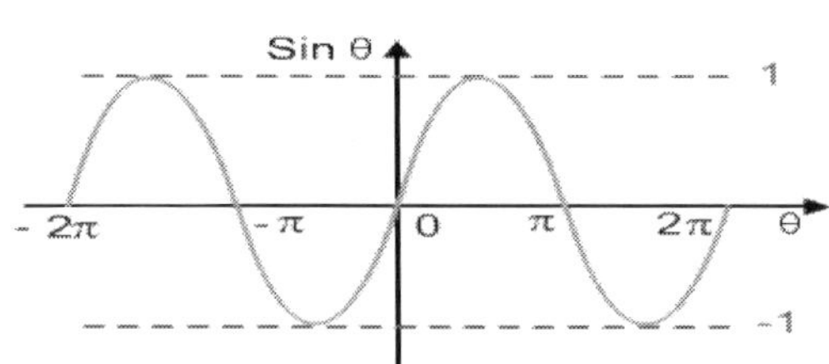

$cos(\theta)$

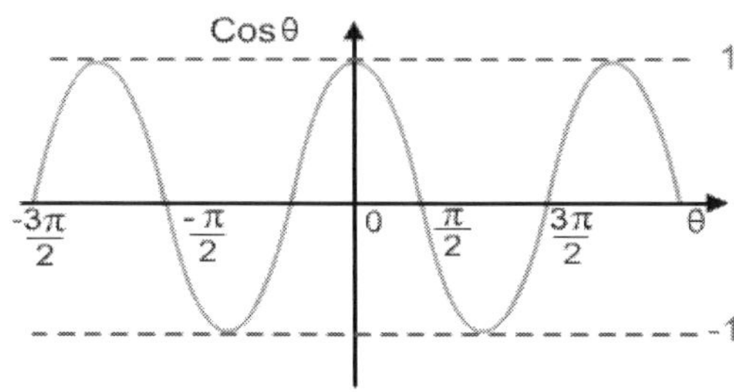

$tan(\theta)$

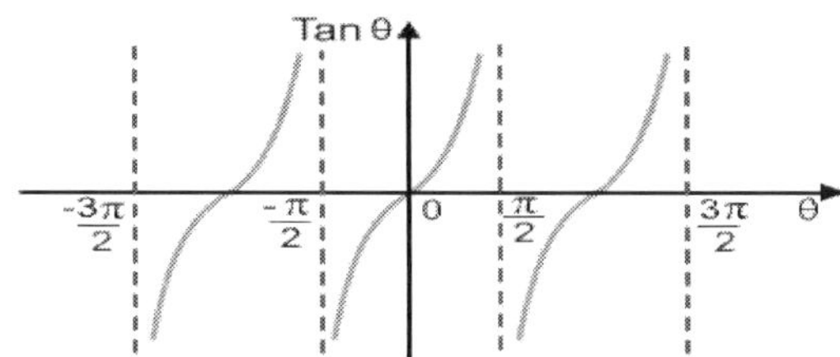

Radians and **degrees** are two units for measuring angles. A full circle has a total angle of 360 degrees or 2π radians.

The formulas to convert between degrees and radians are:

$$\text{Degrees} = \frac{180}{\pi} \times \text{Radians}$$

$$\text{Radians} = \frac{\pi}{180} \times \text{Degrees}$$

Example: What is the angle 225° in radians?
Solution: Radians $= \frac{\pi}{180} \times 225 = \frac{5}{4}\pi$

Example: Convert 2.36 radians to degrees.
Solution: Degrees $= \frac{180}{\pi} \times 2.36 = 135°$

The **arc length** is the distance along the curve which subtends the central angle θ in a circle.

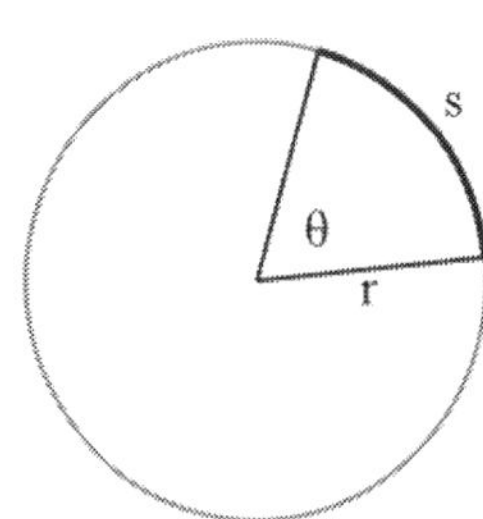

If the central angle is in degrees, the formula to find the arc length s is:

$$s = \frac{\theta}{360} \times 2\pi r$$

If the central angle is in radians, the formula to find the arc length is:

$$s = \theta r$$

Example: How long is the arc subtended by an angle of $\frac{3\pi}{5}$ radians on a circle with a radius of 3 inches?

Solution: $s = \theta r = \frac{3\pi}{5} \times 3 = \frac{9\pi}{5}$ inches

Example: The minute hand of a clock rotates 100° since midnight. If the hand is 12 centimeters long, what is the length of the arc it travels?

Solution: $l = \frac{\theta}{360} \times 2\pi r = \frac{100}{360} \times 2\pi(12) = 20.9$ cm

Problem Solving Skills

Easy

1. If $0 < \theta < 90°$ and $cos(\theta) = \frac{5}{13}$, what is the value of $sin(\theta)$?

   a) $\frac{12}{13}$
   b) $\frac{5}{13}$
   c) $\frac{4}{5}$
   d) $\frac{5}{12}$

Answer: (a)

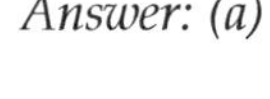

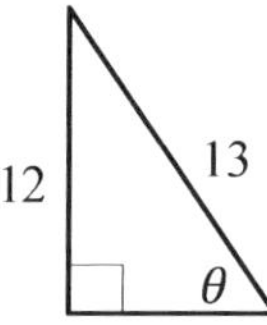

$\sin(\theta) = \frac{12}{13}$

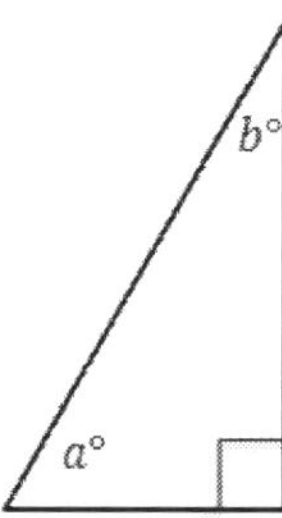

2. In the triangle above, the cosine of $b°$ is $\frac{12}{13}$. What is the cosine of $a°$?

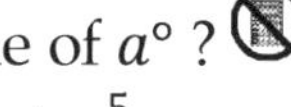

   a) $\frac{5}{13}$
   b) $\frac{5}{12}$
   c) $\frac{13}{12}$
   d) $\frac{13}{5}$

Answer: (a)

Use the value of cos (b°) and the Pythagorean theorem to find the ratio of lengths of sides of the right triangle. $\cos(a°) = \frac{5}{13}$

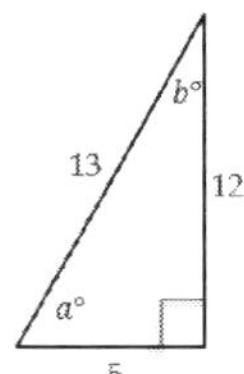

3. A seven feet long ladder leans against a wall and makes an angle of 60° with the ground. How high up the wall does the ladder reach?
   a) $\frac{2\sqrt{3}}{7}$
   b) $\frac{7\sqrt{3}}{2}$
   c) $\frac{\sqrt{3}}{14}$
   d) $7\sqrt{3}$

Answer: (b)

$\sin(60°) = \frac{Height}{7}$

$Height = 7 \times \frac{\sqrt{3}}{2} = \frac{7\sqrt{3}}{2}$

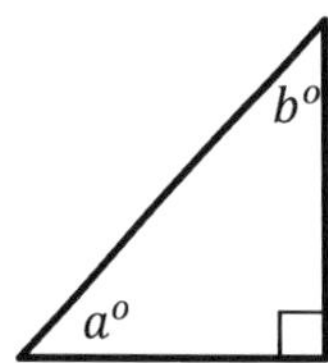

4. In the triangle above, the sine of $b°$ is 0.8. What is the cosine of $a°$?
   a) 0.8
   b) 0.6
   c) 0.4
   d) 0.2

Answer: (a)

Use the value of sine(b°) and the Pythagorean theorem to find the ratio of lengths of sides of the right triangle.

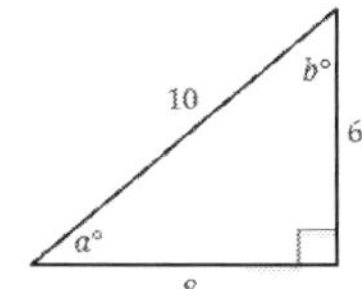

$\cos(a°) = \sin(90° - a°) = 0.8$

$Or \cos(a°) = \frac{8}{10} = 0.8$

5. If $\sin(\frac{\pi}{2} - x) = 0.35$, what is $\cos x$?
   a) 0.35
   b) 0.43
   c) 0.45
   d) 0.53

Answer: (a)

$sin(\theta) = cos(90° - \theta)$

$cos(\theta) = sin(90° - \theta)$

6. If $\sin(x - \frac{\pi}{2}) = 0.2$, what is $\cos x$?
   a) 0.8
   b) 0.98
   c) -0.2
   d) 0.2

Answer: (c)

$\cos x = \sin\left(\frac{\pi}{2} - x\right)$

$= -\sin\left(x - \frac{\pi}{2}\right) = -0.2$

7. If $(\theta - 60°) = \cos(25°)$, what is the measure of θ?
   a) 96°
   b) 100°
   c) 125°
   d) 136°

Answer: (c)

$sin(\theta) = cos(90° - \theta)$

$cos(\theta) = sin(90° - \theta)$

$\theta - 60 + 25 = 90$

$\theta = 125$

8. If $a + b = 90°$, which of the following must be true?
   a) $\cos a = \cos b$
   b) $\sin a = \sin b$
   c) $\sin a = \cos b$
   d) $\sin a = -\cos b$

Answer: (c)

$\sin(\theta) = \cos(90° - \theta)$
$\cos(\theta) = \sin(90° - \theta)$

9. If $0° \le A \le 90°$, $0° \le B \le 90°$, and $\sin A = \cos B$, which of the following must be true?
   a) $A - B = 90$
   b) $A = B$
   c) $A = 90 - B$
   d) $A = B - 45$

Answer: (c)

$\sin(\theta) = \cos(90° - \theta)$
$\cos(\theta) = \sin(90° - \theta)$

10. 45° is equivalent to an angle measure of
   a) $\frac{1}{4}$ radians
   b) $\frac{\pi}{4}$ radians
   c) $\frac{\pi}{3}$ radians
   d) $\frac{\pi}{2}$ radians

Answer: (b)

$$Radians = \frac{\pi}{180} \times 45 = \frac{\pi}{4}$$

11. How many degrees are in 1.65 radians?
   a) 94.54
   b) 78.56
   c) 10.88
   d) 0.029

Answer: (a)

$$Degrees = \frac{180}{\pi} \times 1.65 = 94.54$$

12. 75° is equivalent to an angle measure of?
   a) $\frac{5\pi}{12}$ radians
   b) $\frac{1}{12\pi}$ radians
   c) $\frac{5\pi}{6}$ radians
   d) $\frac{2\pi}{3}$ radians

Answer: (a)

$$Radians = \frac{\pi}{180} \times 75 = \frac{5\pi}{12}$$

13. Find the degree measure for $\frac{3\pi}{4}$.

Answer: 135

$$Degrees = \frac{180}{\pi} \times \frac{3\pi}{4} = 135$$

14. Which of the following trigonometric functions is (are) positive in the third Quadrant?
   a) $\sin(x)$
   b) $\cos(x)$
   c) $\tan(x)$
   d) All of the above

Answer: (c)

Use the mnemonic "All Students Take Calculus!!"

Medium

15. Which of the following cofunctions is (are) true?
    a) $\sin(90° - x) = \cos x$
    b) $\cos(90° - x) = \sin x$
    c) $\tan(90° - x) = \cot x$
    d) All of the above

Answer: (d)

The value of a trigonometric function of an angle is equal to the value of the cofunction of the complement of that angle.

16. In triangle ABC, the measure of $\angle C$ is $90°$, $AB = 15$, and $BC = 12$. Triangle XYZ is similar to triangle ABC, where vertices $X, Y,$ and Z correspond to vertices A, B, and C, respectively. If each side of triangle XYZ is $\frac{1}{3}$ the length of the corresponding side of triangle ABC, what is the value of $\sin X$?

Answer: $\frac{4}{5}$ *Or 0.8*

$\sin X = \frac{YZ}{XY} = \frac{4}{5}$

17. If $sin(\theta) = m$ and $0 < \theta < 90°$, what is the value of $cos(\theta)$?
    a) $\frac{m}{\sqrt{1-m^2}}$
    b) $\frac{1}{\sqrt{1-m^2}}$
    c) $\frac{\sqrt{1-m^2}}{m}$
    d) $\sqrt{1-m^2}$

Answer: (d)

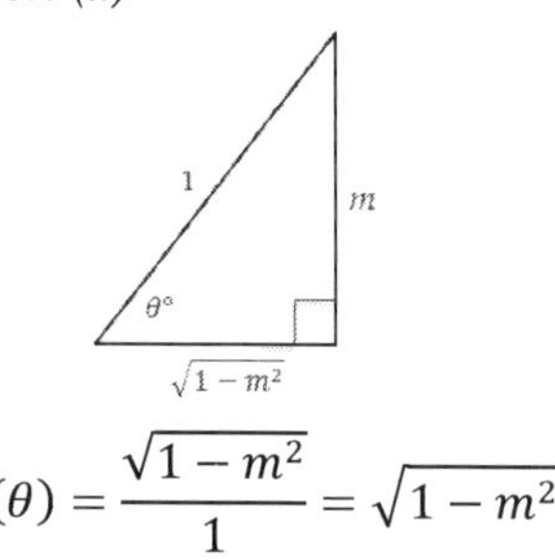

$$\cos(\theta) = \frac{\sqrt{1-m^2}}{1} = \sqrt{1-m^2}$$

18. If $sin(\theta) = n$ and $0 < \theta < 90°$, what is the value of $tan(\theta)$?
    a) $\frac{1}{n^2}$
    b) $\frac{n}{\sqrt{1-n^2}}$
    c) $\frac{1-n^2}{n}$
    d) $\frac{n}{1-n^2}$

Answer: (b)

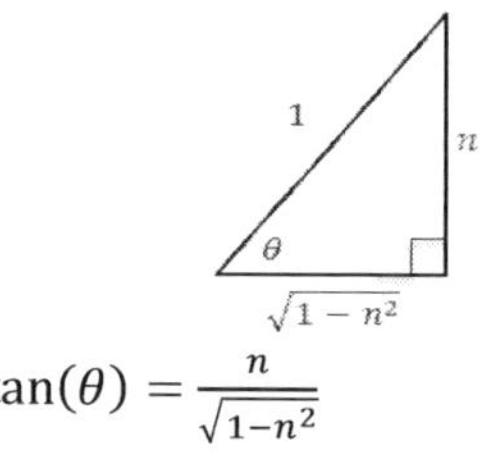

$$\tan(\theta) = \frac{n}{\sqrt{1-n^2}}$$

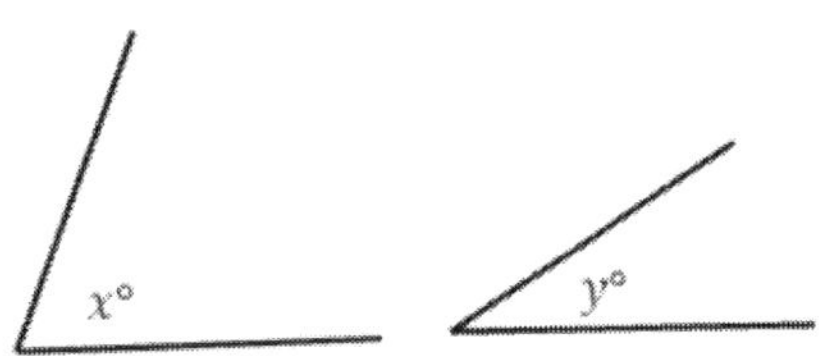

Note: Figures not drawn to scale.

19. The angles shown above are acute, and $\sin(x^o) = \cos(y^o)$. If $x = 3k - 11$ and $y = 2k - 9$, what is the value of k?
    a) 12
    b) 22
    c) 23.5
    d) 27.5

Answer: (b)

$(3k - 11) + (2k - 9) = 90$
$k = 22$

20. A ramp is 60 meters long and set at a 25° angle of inclination. If you walk up to the top of the ramp, how high off the ground will you be?
    a) 25.357 meters
    b) 26.561 meters
    c) 27.91 meters
    d) 28.13 meters

Answer: (a)

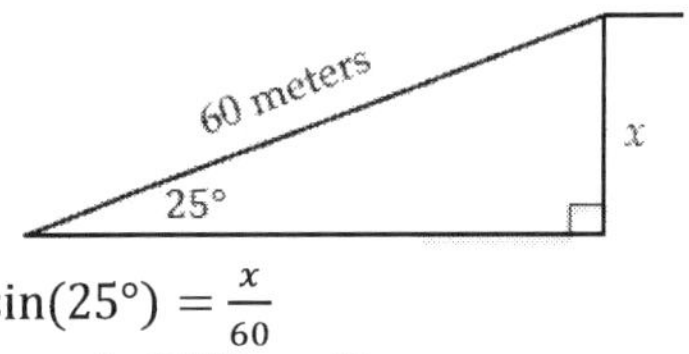

$\sin(25°) = \frac{x}{60}$
$x = \sin(25°) \times 60$
$x = 25.357$

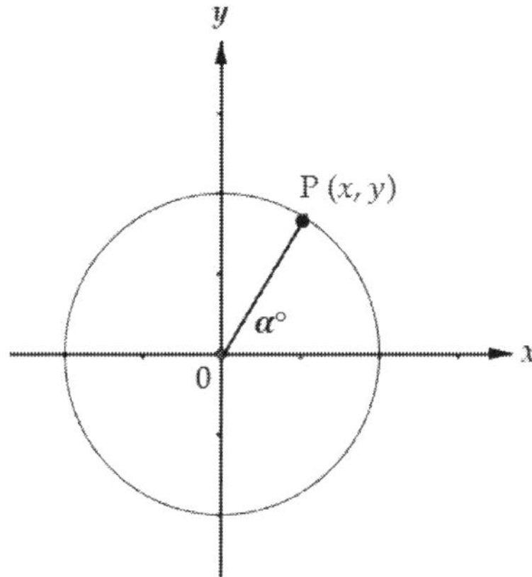

Note: Figure not drawn to scale.

21. On the unit circle above, if the values of sine and cosine of the angle $\alpha°$ are equal, what is the sum $x + y$?
    a) $2\sqrt{2}$
    b) $\sqrt{2}$
    c) $\frac{\sqrt{2}}{2}$
    d) $\frac{\sqrt{2}}{3}$

Answer: (b)

In the first Quadrant, the values of sine and cosine are only equal at $\alpha = 45$. *Here,* $\cos(\alpha°) = \sin(\alpha°) = \frac{\sqrt{2}}{2}$, *so* $x = y = \frac{\sqrt{2}}{2}$ *and* $x + y = \sqrt{2}$.

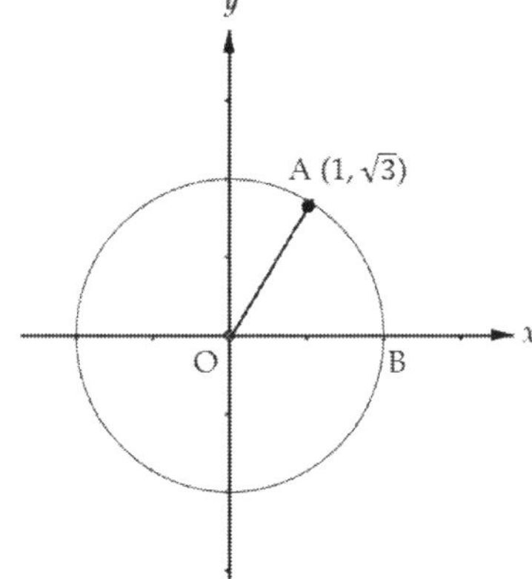

22. On the circle O in the xy-plane above, the measure of $\angle AOB$ is $\frac{\pi}{a}$ radians. What is the value of a?
    a) 4
    b) 3
    c) 2
    d) 1

Answer: (b)

$\overline{OA} = 2$

$sin\frac{\pi}{a} = \frac{\sqrt{3}}{2}$

$\frac{\pi}{a} = \frac{\pi}{3} \rightarrow a = 3$

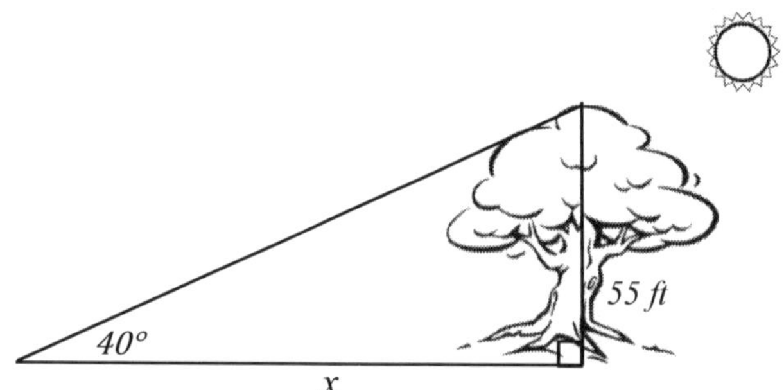

23. When the Sun is 40° above the horizon, how long is the shadow cast by a tree 55 feet tall? (Round your answer to the nearest tenth.)

Answer: 65.5

$tan(40°) = \frac{55}{x}$

$x = \frac{55}{tan40°} = \frac{55}{0.8391} = 65.5$

24. If an angle θ measured counter-clockwise from the positive x-axis terminates in the third Quadrant, which of the following is true?
    a) Both of $\sin(\theta)$ and $\cos(\theta)$ are negative.
    b) Both of $\sin(\theta)$ and $\cos(\theta)$ are positive.
    c) $\sin(\theta)$ is negative and $\cos(\theta)$ is positive.
    d) $\sin(\theta)$ is positive and $\cos(\theta)$ is negative.

Answer: (a)

Use the mnemonic "All Students Take Calculus!!"

25. A ferris wheel with diameter of 52 feet revolves $\frac{9\pi}{2}$ radians every five minutes. What is the total distance a seat on the rim of the wheel travels in five minutes? (Round your answer to the nearest whole number.)

Answer: 368

Find the length of the arc.

$l = r\theta = \frac{52}{2} \times \frac{9\pi}{2} = 368$

26. A shaft, pivoted at one end, spins through $\frac{4\pi}{3}$ radians. If the shaft is 15 centimeters long, what is the distance (in cm) that the shaft travels?
    a) 5π
    b) 10π
    c) 15π
    d) 20π

Answer: (d)

Find the length of the arc.

$l = r\theta = 15 \times \frac{4\pi}{3} = 20\pi$

27. An hour hand of a clock rotates through $\frac{9\pi}{7}$ radians clockwise. If the hour hand is 4 inches long, what is the length of the arc that the tip of the hour hand moves through?
    a) 5π inches
    b) 5.14π inches
    c) 6.17π inches
    d) 8.78π inches

Answer: (b)

$l = \theta r = \frac{9\pi}{7} \times 4$

$= \frac{36\pi}{7} = 5.14\pi \text{ inches}$

28. How many degrees does the minute hand of a clock turn every 20 minutes?

Answer: 120

Minute hands turn 360° *every hour.*

$\frac{60\ min}{360^o} = \frac{20\ min}{x} \rightarrow x = 120^o$

29. In the triangle below, if $\sin(b°) = 0.8$ and the BC = 12, what is the perimeter of the triangle?

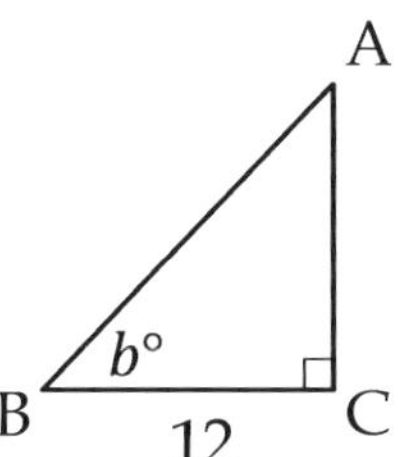

Note: Figure not drawn to scale.

Answer: 48

Use the Pythagorean theorem to find the lengths of sides of the right triangle.

$cos(b^o) = \sqrt{1 - 0.8^2} = 0.6$

$cos(b^o) = 0.6 = \frac{12}{AB}$

$AB = 20$

$AC = AB \times sin(b^o) = 20 \times 0.8 = 16$

$12 + 16 + 20 = 48$

30. The graph of $y = 3\cos(2x) + 3$ intersects the y–axis at what value of y?

Answer: 6

The graph of $y = 3\cos(2x) + 3$ *intersects the* $y-$ *axis at* $x = 0$.

$y = 3\cos(2 \times 0) + 3 = 3\cos(0) + 3 = 3 \times 1 + 3 = 6$

31. In a triangle, one angle measures $x°$, where $sin(x°) = \frac{2}{5}$. What is $cos(90° - x°)$?

Answer: $\frac{2}{5}$ *or* 0.4

$\cos(90^o - x^o) = \sin(x^o) = \frac{2}{5}$

32. In the xy-plane below, O is the center of the circle with a radius of 2, and the measure of $\angle\theta$ is $\frac{\pi}{3}$ radians. What is the value of $x + y$? (Round your answer to the nearest tenth.)

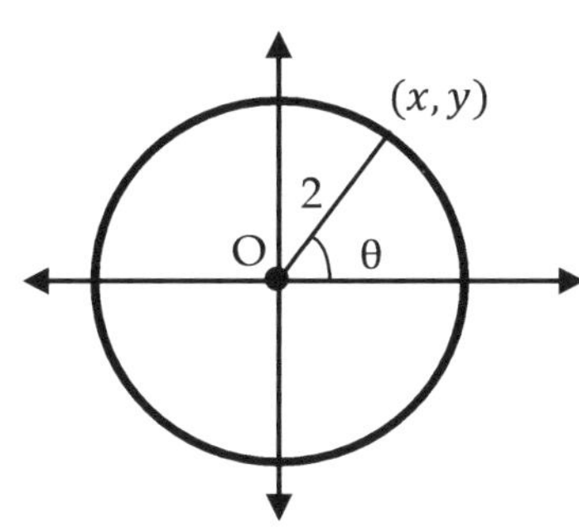

Answer: 2.7

$x = rcos(\theta) = 2 \times \cos\left(\frac{\pi}{3}\right) = 1$

$y = rsin(\theta) = 2 \times \sin\left(\frac{\pi}{3}\right) = 1.7$

$x + y = 2.7$

33. In the figure below, the circle has center O and radius 3. If the area of the minor sector $\widehat{AB}$ is between 5 and 10, what is one possible integer value of arc length s?

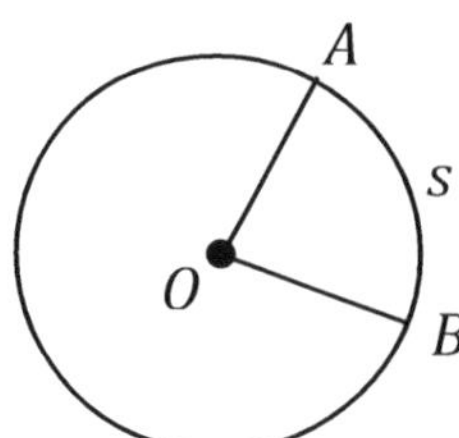

Answer: 4, 5 or 6

Area of the Sector $= \frac{1}{2}r^2\theta$

$5 < \frac{1}{2}3^2\theta < 10$

$\frac{10}{9} < \theta < \frac{20}{9}$

$1.1 < \theta < 2.2$

$s = r\theta$

$3.3 < s < 6.6$

$s = 4, 5 \text{ or } 6$

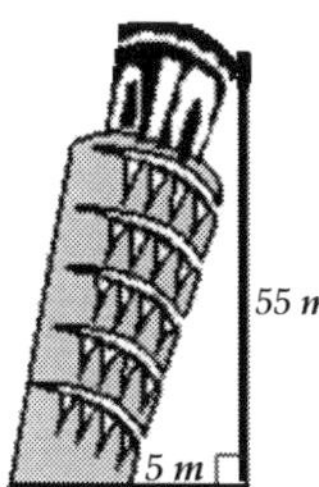

34. If the Leaning Tower of Pisa is 55 meters tall and the top edge of the tower leans 5 meters out from the bottom edge, what is *sine* of the angle created between the ground and the tower?
   a) 1
   b) 0.091
   c) 0.993
   d) 0.996

Answer: (d)

Use the Pythogoream Theorm to find the hypotenuse.

Hypotenuse $= \sqrt{55^2 + 5^2} = 55.23\ m$

$sin(\theta) = \frac{55}{55.23} = 0.996$

Hard

35. Every morning before breakfast, Jacques jogs 2.5 miles at 10 degrees north of east and then 1.5 miles at 18 degrees in the same direction. How many miles east from his starting point will he end up?
   a) 4 miles
   b) 3.89 miles
   c) 3.5 miles
   d) 3.43 miles

Answer: (b)

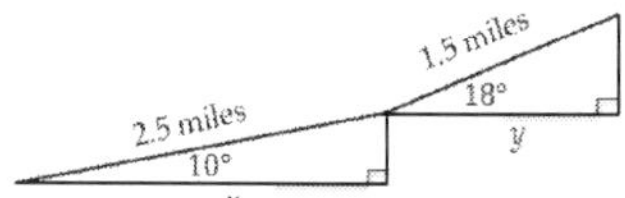

Find the sum of x and y.

$x = \cos(10°) \times 2.5 = 2.46$

$y = \cos(18°) \times 1.5 = 1.43$

$x + y = 2.46 + 1.43 = 3.89\ miles$

36. Which of the following trigonometric function(s) has (have) no end behavior (asymptotes)?

I. $\sin(x)$
II. $\cos(x)$
III. $\tan(x)$

a) I only
b) I and II only
c) III only
d) I, II, and III

Answer: (b)

For the six standard trig functions, only sine and cosine functions have no end behavior (asymptotes) because they are continuously cycling. The other four have asymptotes that approach negative and positive infinity.

37. As angle x increases from 0 to 2π radians, in which Quadrant(s) does $\tan(x)$ increase?

a) The first and third Quadrants only
b) The second and fourth Quadrants only
c) All four Quadrants
d) None of the above

Answer: (c)

The graph of $\tan(x)$ *shows the function increases in all of four Quadrants.*

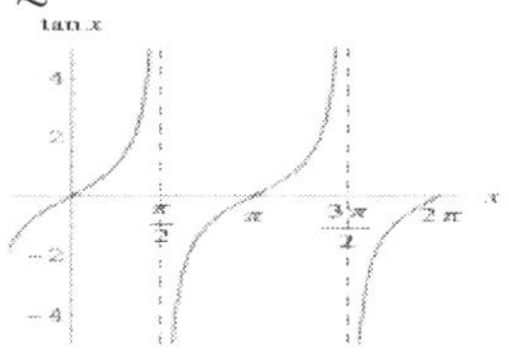

38. What is the measure in radians of the smallest positive angle x that will give the maximum value for $y = 3 - \cos(2x)$?

a) 0
b) $\frac{\pi}{2}$
c) π
d) $\frac{3\pi}{2}$

Answer: (b)

y is maximized when $\cos(2x)$ *has the value* -1*, since its coefficient is negative and the lowest value of cosine is* -1.

When $2x = \pi$, $\cos(2x) = -1$. *Therefore,* $x = \frac{\pi}{2}$.

39. Which of the following must be FALSE?

I. $\sin(-\theta) = -\sin(\theta)$
II. $\cos(-\theta) = -\cos(\theta)$
III. $\tan(-\theta) = -\tan(\theta)$

a) I only
b) II only
c) I and III only
d) I, II, and III

Answer: (b)

The following are always true:
$\cos(-\theta) = \cos(\theta)$
$\sin(-\theta) = -\sin(\theta)$
$\tan(-\theta) = -\tan(\theta)$

Chapter 5 Ten SAT Math Mock Tests

SAT Math Mock Test No. 1

SECTION 3 

Math Test – NO Calculator **25 MINUTES, 20 QUESTIONS**

Directions:

For questions 1-15, solve each problem, choose the best answer from the choices provided, and fill in the corresponding circle on your answer sheet. **For questions 16-20**, solve the problem and enter your answer in the grid on the answer sheet. Please refer to the directions before question 16 on how to enter your answers in the grid. You may use any available space in your test booklet for scratch work.

Notes:

1. **No calculator** is allowed for this section. All numbers used are real numbers.
2. Figures that accompany problems in this test are intended to provide information useful in solving the problems. They are drawn as accurately as possible EXCEPT when it is stated in a specific problem that the figure is not drawn to scale. All figures lie in a plane unless otherwise indicated.
3. Unless otherwise specified, the domain of any function *f(x)* assumed to be the set of all real numbers *x* for which *f(x)* is a real number.

References:

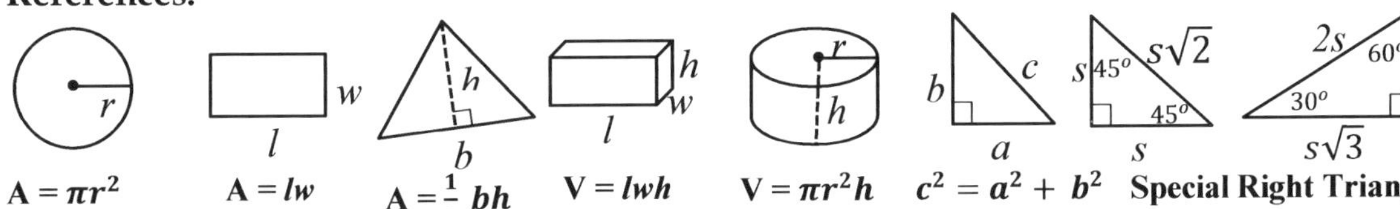

$A = \pi r^2$, $C = 2\pi r$ $A = lw$ $A = \frac{1}{2}bh$ $V = lwh$ $V = \pi r^2 h$ $c^2 = a^2 + b^2$ **Special Right Triangles**

The number of degrees of arc in a circle is 360; the number of radians of arc in a circle is 2π.
The sum of the degree measures of the angles in a triangle is 180.

1. If $3x - 1 = 3$, then $12x$ =?
   a) 4
   b) 8
   c) 12
   d) 16

2. If $x > 1$ and $a(x + 3)(x - 1) = 0$, what is the value of a?
   a) 3
   b) 2
   c) 1
   d) 0

3. If $2x + 6y = 12$, then $\frac{1}{3}x + y$ =?
   a) 2
   b) 3
   c) 4
   d) 6

4. If $\frac{3\sqrt{x} + y}{\sqrt{x} + 1} = 3$ then y = ?
   a) 1
   b) 3
   c) 5
   d) 8

Questions 5 – 6 refer to the following information:

In chemistry, a chemical reaction proceeds at a rate dependent on the concentration of its reactant. For reactant A, the rate of a reaction is defined as:

$$Rate = k\,[A]^n$$

k is a constant and $[A]$ is the concentration of A. The order of reaction of a reactant A is the exponent n to which its concentration term in the rate equation is raised.

5. When n is equal to 2, A is called a 2nd order reactant. Which of the following graphs depicts a 2nd order of reactant with respect to concentration and reaction rate?

a) 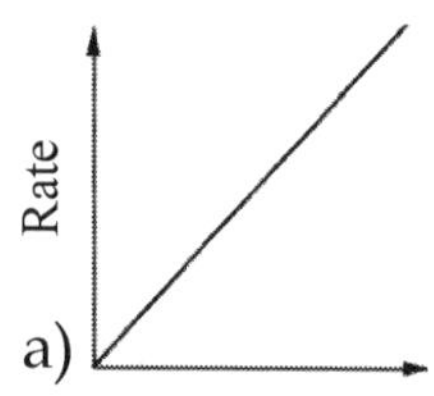

b) 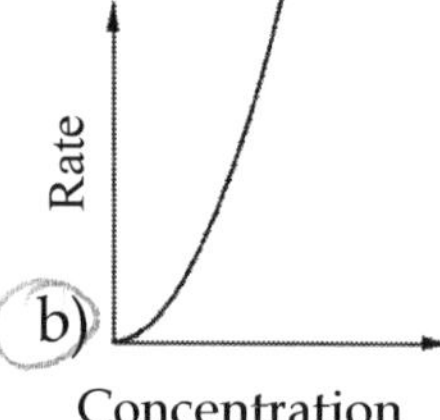

c) 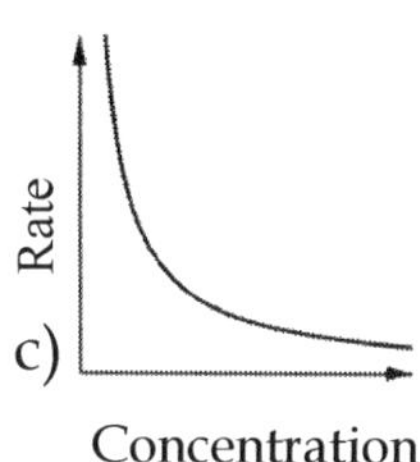

d) 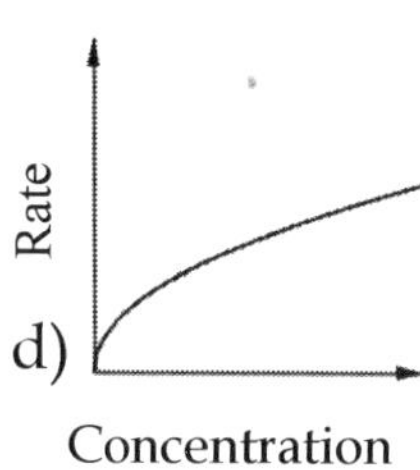

6. If the graph below shows the reaction rate versus the concentration of reactant A, what is the most likely order of reactant A?

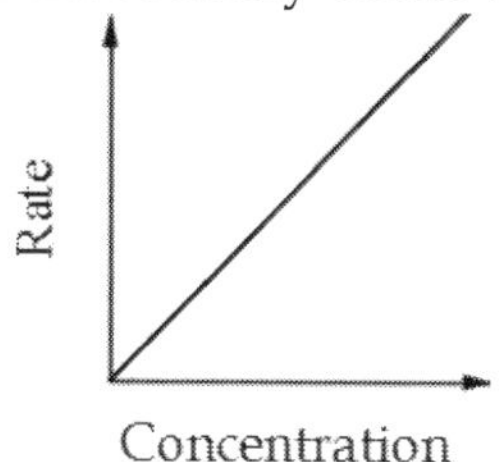

   a) 1st order
   b) 2nd order
   c) 3rd order
   d) 0th order

7. In the xy-plane, line r passes through the origin and is perpendicular to line t and intersects at the point (2, 2). What is the slope of line t?
   a) −1
   b) −2
   c) 1
   d) 2

8. If $x = 2(4z^2 + 2z - 3)$ and $y = 2z$, what is x in terms of y?
   a) $2y^2 - 2y - 6$
   b) $4y^2 + 2y - 3$
   c) $2y^2 + 2y - 6$
   d) $2y^2 + y + 6$

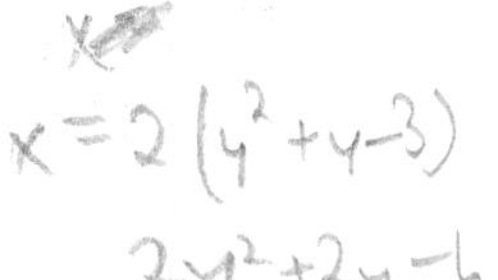

9. If $\frac{4+x-y}{3} = 7$, find the value of $x - y$.
   a) 9
   b) 13
   c) 15
   d) 17

10. How old was William c years ago if a years later he will b years old (given that $b > a + c$)?
   a) $a + b$
   b) $a + b + c$
   c) $a - b - c$
   d) $b - a - c$

11. Which of the following numbers could NOT be the remainder when a positive integer is divided by 5?
   a) 6
   b) 5
   c) 3
   d) 0

Questions 12 – 13 refer to the following information:

Jenny has a summer job at an ice cream shop. She needs to order a few boxes of small cups and a few boxes of large cups. The storage room can hold up to 20 boxes. Each box of small cups costs \$25 and each box of large cups costs \$40. A maximum of \$600 is budgeted for cups.

12. If x represents the number of boxes of small cups and y represents the number of boxes of large cups that Jenny can order, which of the following systems of equations represents the number of each

she could order?

a) $\begin{cases} x \geq 0 \\ y \geq 0 \\ x + y \leq 20 \\ 25x + 40y \leq 600 \end{cases}$

b) $\begin{cases} x \geq 0 \\ y \geq 0 \\ x + y < 20 \\ 25x + 40y < 600 \end{cases}$

c) $\begin{cases} x \geq 0 \\ y \geq 0 \\ x + y > 20 \\ 25x + 40y > 600 \end{cases}$

d) $\begin{cases} x \geq 0 \\ y \geq 0 \\ x + y \geq 20 \\ 25x + 40y \leq 600 \end{cases}$

13. Which of the following graphs represents the number of boxes of each type of cup she could order?

a)

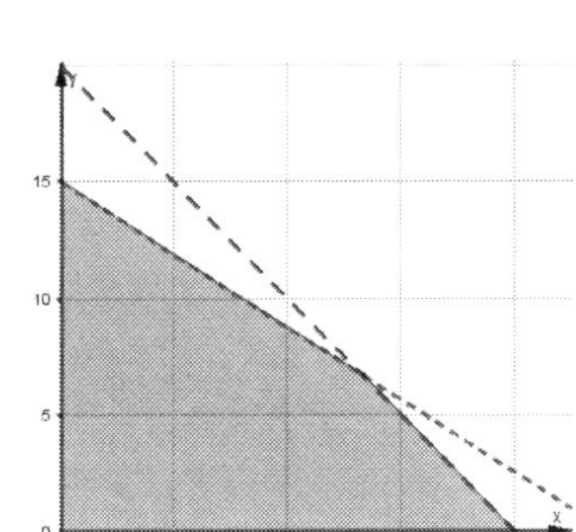

b)

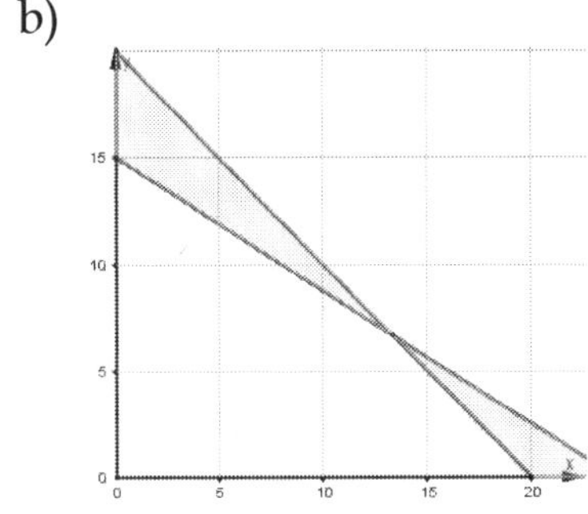

c)

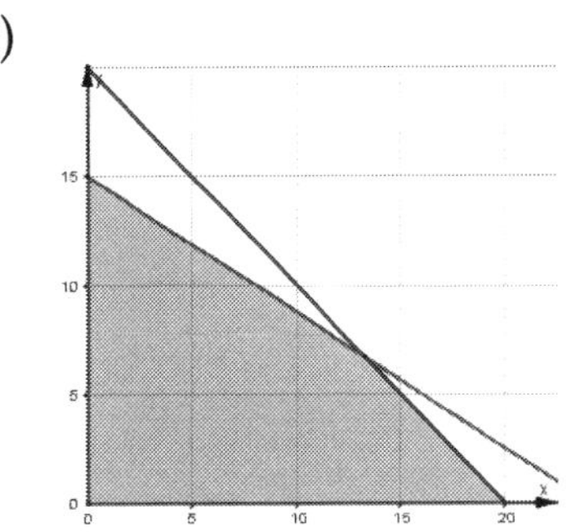

d)

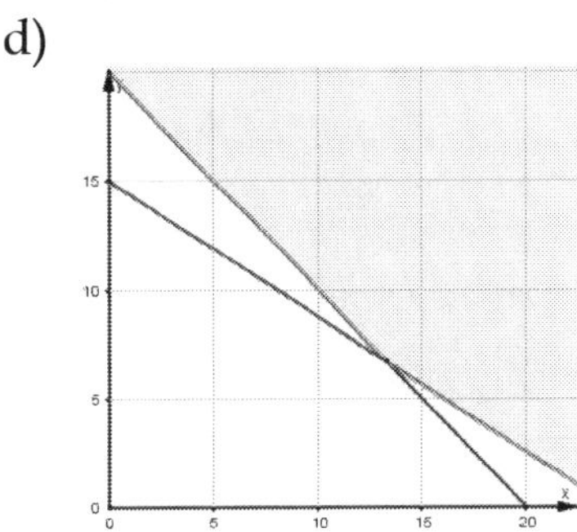

14. The expressway from Maya's house to her college is 2 miles longer than the local route. When she drives by the local route and returns by the expressway, the round trip is 18 miles. How many miles does Maya have to drive if she goes to school through the local route?

a) 8
b) 9
c) 10
d) 11

15. Set X has x elements and set Y has y elements. If they have exactly w elements in common, how many elements are in set X or set Y but not in both set X and Y?

a) $x + y$
b) $x + y - w$
c) $x + y - 2w$
d) $x + y + 2w$

Directions:

For questions 16-20, solve the problem and enter your answer in the grid, as described below, on the answer sheet.

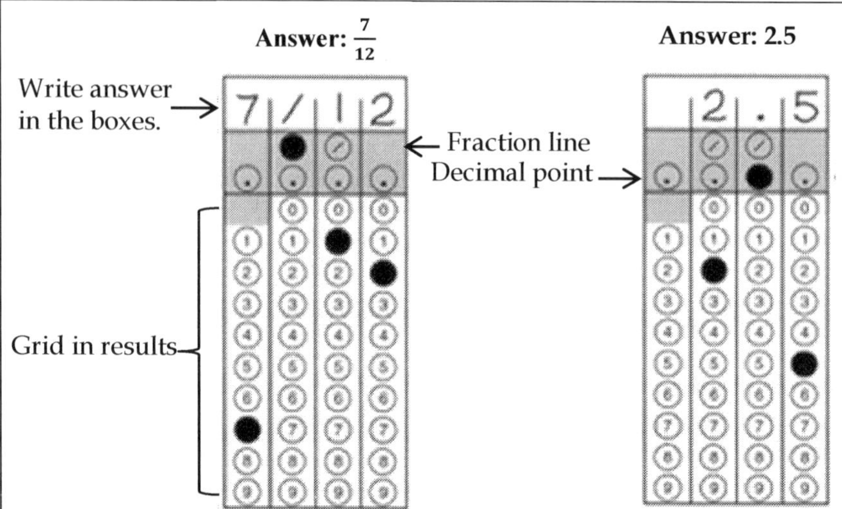

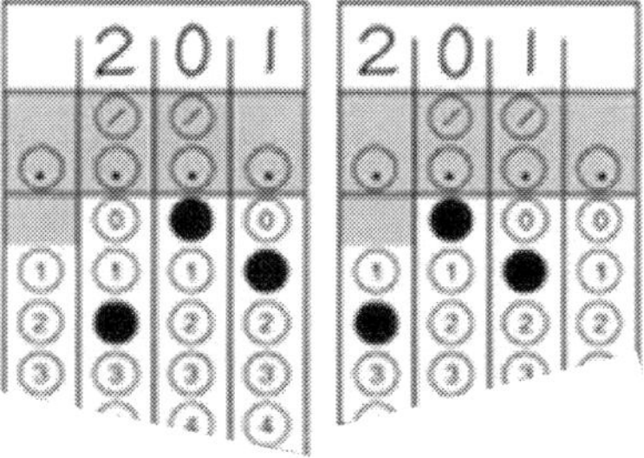

Note: You may start your answers in any column, space permitting. Columns not needed should be left blank.

- Mark no more than one circle in any column.
- Because the answer sheet will be machine-scored. **You will receive credit only if the circles are filled in correctly.**
- Although not required, it is suggested that you write your answer in the boxes at the top of the columns to help you fill in the circles accurately.
- Some problems may have more than one correct answer. In such case, grid only one answer.
- No question has a negative answer.
- **Mixed numbers** such as $3\frac{1}{2}$ must be gridded as 3.5 or $\frac{7}{2}$. (If 31/2 is gridded, it will be interpreted as $\frac{31}{2}$, not $3\frac{1}{2}$.)

- **Decimal Answer**: If you obtain a decimal answer with more digits than the grid can accommodate, it may be either rounded or truncated, but it must fill the entire grid. The acceptable ways to grid $\frac{2}{3}$ are:

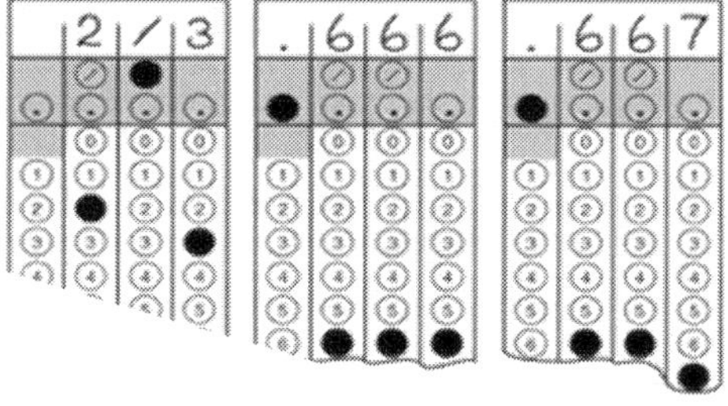

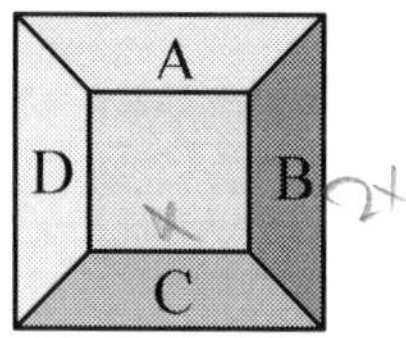

16. The figure above shows a top view of a container with a square-shaped opening and which is divided into 5 smaller compartments. The side of the overall square is double the length of the side of the center square and the areas of compartments A, B, C, and D are all equal. If a baseball is thrown into the box at random, what is the probability that the baseball is found in the center compartment?

17. If $x = 7 + (6 \times 5^3 + 1)$, what is the value of x?

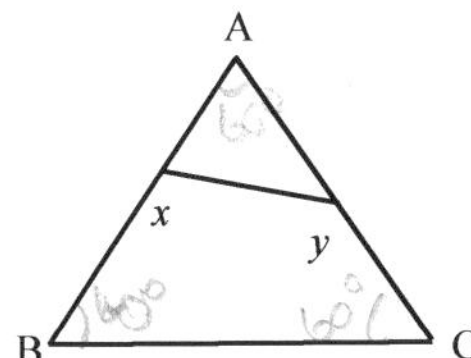

18. In the figure above, ΔABC is an equilateral triangle. What is the value of $x + y$ in degrees?

19. John's weigh is $\frac{3}{5}$ of Peter's weight. If John were to gain 8 pounds, he would weigh $\frac{2}{3}$ of Peter's weight. What is Peter's weight in pounds?

20. The price of a pizza at the pizza store includes:
    i. The basic charge
    ii. An additional charge for each topping

If the price of a 1-topping pizza is \$16 and the price of a 3-topping pizza is \$20, what is the price of a 5-topping pizza?

SECTION 4 

Math Test – Calculator **55 MINUTES, 38 QUESTIONS**

Directions:

For questions 1-30, solve each problem, choose the best answer from the choices provided, and fill in the corresponding circle on your answer sheet. **For questions 31-38**, solve the problem and enter your answer in the grid on the answer sheet. Please refer to the directions before question 31 on how to enter your answers in the grid. You may use any available space in your test booklet for scratch work.

Notes:

1. Acceptable calculators are allowed for this section. All numbers used are real numbers.
2. Figures that accompany problems in this test are intended to provide information useful in solving the problems. They are drawn as accurately as possible EXCEPT when it is stated in a specific problem that the figure is not drawn to scale. All figures lie in a plane unless otherwise indicated.
3. Unless otherwise specified, the domain of any function *f(x)* assumed to be the set of all real numbers *x* for which *f(x)* is a real number.

References:

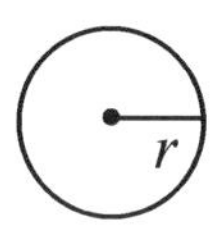

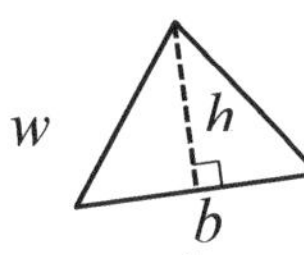

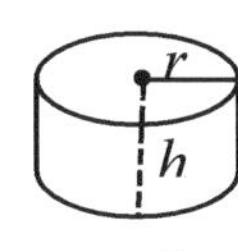

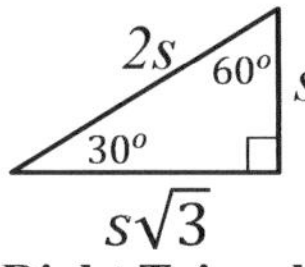

$A = \pi r^2$, $C = 2\pi r$ $A = lw$ $A = \frac{1}{2}bh$ $V = lwh$ $V = \pi r^2 h$ $c^2 = a^2 + b^2$ **Special Right Triangles**

The number of degrees of arc in a circle is 360; the number of radians of arc in a circle is 2π.
The sum of the degree measures of the angles in a triangle is 180.

1. If $a^x \cdot a^4 = a^{12}$ and $(a^4)^y = a^{12}$, what is the value of $x + 2y$?
   a) 7
   b) 8
   c) 11
   d) 14

2. A jaguar can run at speeds up to 70 miles per hour. About how many miles can a jaguar run in 10 seconds?
   a) 0.1
   b) 0.2
   c) 0.3
   d) 0

3. The function $f(x) = 18x - 60$ represents the net profit, in dollars, of selling x plastic dinosaurs at Mega Toy Central. What is the total profit if Mega Toy Central sells 20 plastic dinosaurs?
   a) \$300
   b) \$250
   c) \$200
   d) \$155

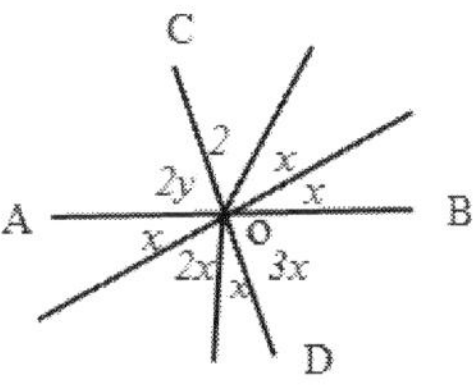

4. In the figure above, segments AB and CD intercept at point O, what is the value of y?
   a) 22.5°
   b) 25°
   c) 34°
   d) 38.6°

5. A restaurant offers a choice of one side dish when a main course is ordered. Customers can choose from a list of 3 different main courses and 4 different side dishes. How many different combinations are there of one main course and one side dish?
   a) 7
   b) 12
   c) 16
   d) 2

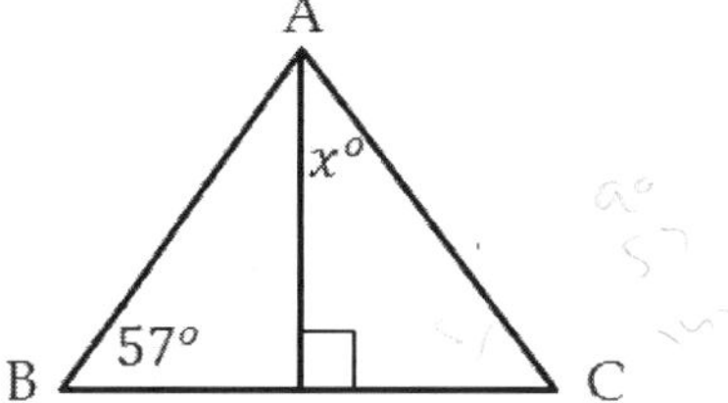

6. If AB = AC in the figure above, what is the value of x, in degrees?
   a) 33°
   b) 35°
   c) 40°
   d) 43°

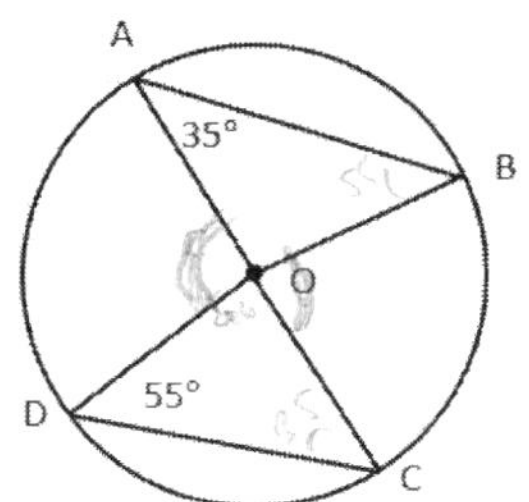

Note: Figure not drawn to scale.

7. In the graph shown above, what is the value of m∠AOD + m∠BOC?
   a) 180
   b) 150
   c) 110
   d) 100

Questions 8 – 9 refer to the following information:

Percent error is useful for determining the precision of a calculation. Percent error close to zero means the calculation is very close to the target value. The formula to measure percent error is:

$$Percent\ Error = \frac{Measured\ Data - Actual\ Data}{Actual\ Data} \times 100\%$$

8. The density of water at 4°C is known to be 1.00 g/mL. If Anny experimentally found the density of water be 0.9875 g/mL, what would be her percent error?
   a) 1.25%
   b) −1.25%
   c) 2.5%
   d) −2.5%

9. Chason got his lab report back with "10.0% error" written in red on it. If he had examined the boiling point of an unknown liquid to be 85 °C, what could be the actual boiling point for his unknown liquid?
   a) 93.5 °C
   b) 88.0 °C
   c) 77.3 °C
   d) 75.1 °C

10. If there are 8 points in a plane, no three of which are collinear, how many distinct lines can be formed by connecting two of these points?
   a) 15
   b) 21
   c) 28
   d) 49

11. The table below, describing number of students who passed or failed the Algebra I final exam, is partially filled in. Based on the information in the table, how many females have failed?

Algebra I Final Exam Results			
	Pass	*Fail*	*Total*
Male	*120*		
Female			*140*
Total	*220*		*300*

a) 35
b) 40
c) 45
d) 50

12. Class A has X students and class B has Y students. The average of the test scores of class A is 85, and the average of the test scores of class B is 90. When the scores of class A and B are combined, the average score is 88. What is the ratio of X to Y?
    a) $\frac{1}{2}$
    b) $\frac{1}{3}$
    c) $\frac{1}{4}$
    d) $\frac{2}{3}$

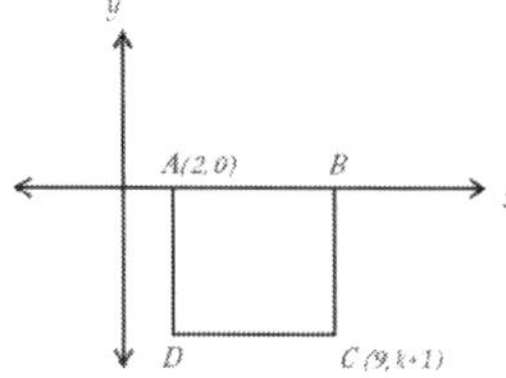

13. In the figure above, $ABCD$ is a square. If the coordinates of A are (2, 0) and the coordinates of C are $(9, k+1)$, what is the value of k?
    a) 6
    b) 7
    c) −6
    d) −8

14. If a supermarket has brand A juice smoothie on sale every 7 days and has brand B juice smoothie on sale every 5 days. Within a year (365 days), how many times does this supermarket have both brands of juice smoothie on sale on the same day?
    a) 9
    b) 10
    c) 11
    d) 12

15. Of the following, which is the closest approximation of the cost per ticket when one purchases 8 tickets?

Bus Ticket Price	
Number of Bus Tickets	*Price*
1	*7.5*
Book of 6	*40*
Book of 12	*75*

    a) \$6.67
    b) \$6.70
    c) \$6.80
    d) \$6.90

16. Based on Mrs. Johnson's grading policies, if a student answers 90 to 100 percent of the questions correctly in a math test, she/he will receive a letter grade of A. If there are 50 questions on the final exam, what is the minimum number of questions the student would need to answer correctly to receive a grade of A?
    a) 36
    b) 40
    c) 42
    d) 45

17. If x, y and z are three different prime numbers and $m = x^2 \times y \times z^3$, how many positive factors, excluding 1 and m itself, does m have?
    a) 6
    b) 12
    c) 18
    d) 22

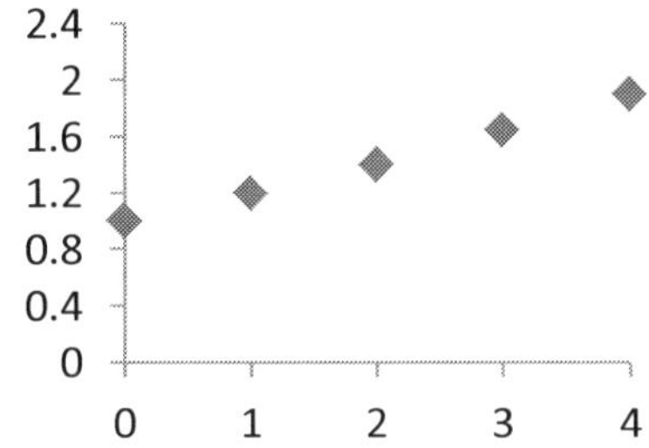

18. Which of the lines described by the following equations best fits those points above?

a) $y = 0.2x - 1$
b) $y = 0.2x + 1$
c) $y = -0.2x - 1$
d) $y = -0.2x + 1$

19. In the figure below, what is the sum of a, b, c, d, e, f?

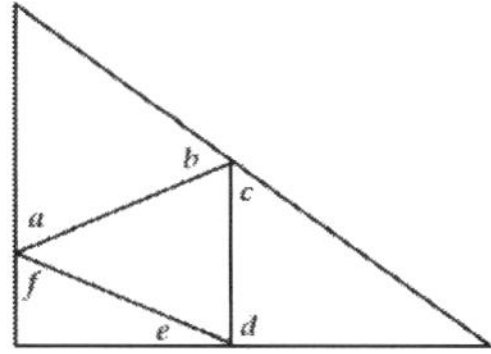

a) 360
b) 300
c) 240
d) 180

20. A rectangular frame with a 1-inch margin is placed around a rectangular picture with dimensions of 6 inches by 8 inches. What is the area of the frame itself in square inches?
a) 80
b) 48
c) 32
d) 24

21. Segment $\overline{AB}$ is the diameter of a circle with center O. Another point C lies on circle O. If AC = 3 and BC = 4, what is the area of circle O?
a) 6.25π
b) 12.5π
c) 25π
d) 35π

22. In all except one of the following, at least one of the coordinates of the ordered pair, when squared, is equal to the reciprocal of the other coordinate. For which ordered pair does this not hold true?
a) $(1, 1)$
b) $(-1, 1)$
c) $(2, \frac{-1}{4})$
d) $(4, \frac{-1}{2})$

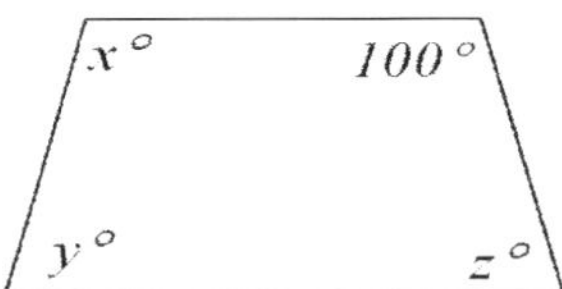

Note: Figure not drawn to scale.

23. In the quadrilateral above, if $x > 110$, which of the following is one possible value of $y + z$?
a) 200
b) 180
c) 150
d) 130

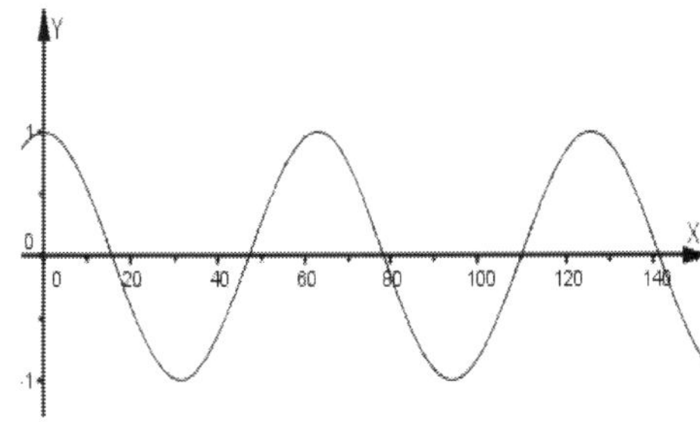

24. According to the graph shown above, how many distinct positive values of x are there on the graph when $y = -0.5$?
a) 4
b) 5
c) 6
d) 7

Questions 25 – 26 refer to the following information:

The fluid dynamics continuity model states that the rate at which mass enters a system is equal to the rate at which mass leaves the system. The rate of mass at any cross section in a pipe is the product of the cross sectional area and the speed of the fluid.

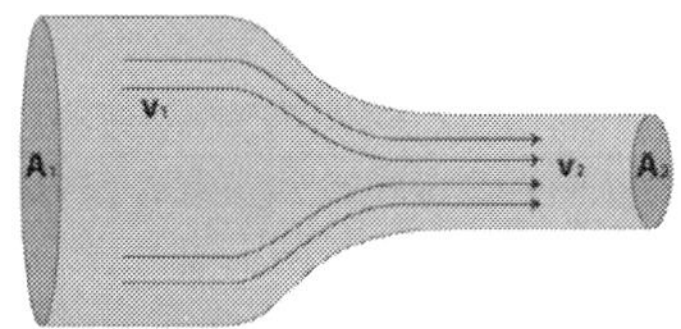

25. If water runs through a pipe with cross sectional area 0.3 m^2 at a speed of 5 m/s, calculate the speed of the water in the pipe when the pipe tapers off to a cross sectional area of 0.2 m^2.
    a) 3.3 m/s
    b) 7.5 m/s
    c) 9.0 m/s
    d) 10.0 m/s

26. If water enters a certain type of garden hose with a diameter of 1.5 cm at a speed of 4 m/s, calculate the speed of water when it travels to the nozzle, which has diameter 0.5 cm.
    a) 36 m/s
    b) 24 m/s
    c) 12 m/s
    d) 4 m/s

27. Every student at Oak Tree High School is required to study at least one language among Spanish, French, and Chinese, but no one may study more than two. If 150 students study Spanish, 110 study French, 90 study Chinese, and 40 study two languages, how many students are there at Oak Tree High School?
    a) 430
    b) 390
    c) 350
    d) 310

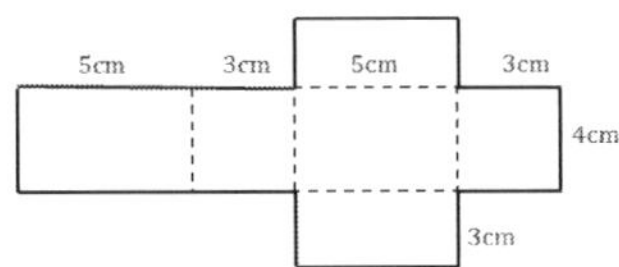

28. If the figure above is folded along the dashed lines, a rectangular box will be formed. What is the surface area of the box in square centimeters?
    a) 47
    b) 60
    c) 94
    d) 120

Questions 29 – 30 refer to the following information:

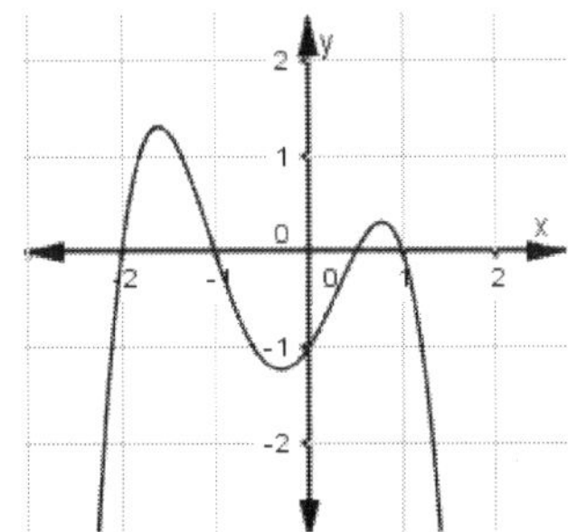

The function $f(x) = -x^4 - \frac{3}{2}x^3 + 2x^2 + \frac{3}{2}x - 1$ is graphed in the xy-plane above.

29. If c is a constant such that the equation $f(x) = c$ has four real solutions, which of the following could NOT be the value of c?
    a) 1
    b) 0
    c) $-\frac{1}{2}$
    d) -1

30. How many real solutions are there if $f(x) = x$?
    a) 1
    b) 2
    c) 3
    d) 4

Directions:

For questions 31-38, solve the problem and enter your answer in the grid, as described below, on the answer sheet.

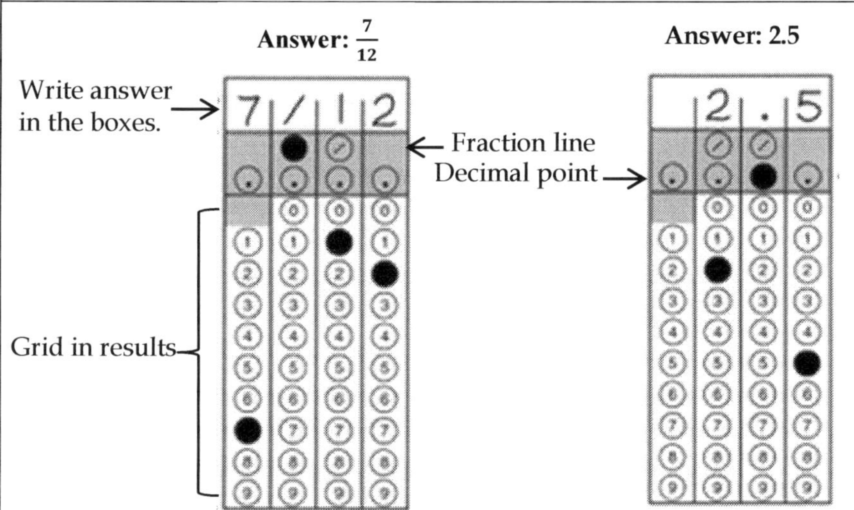

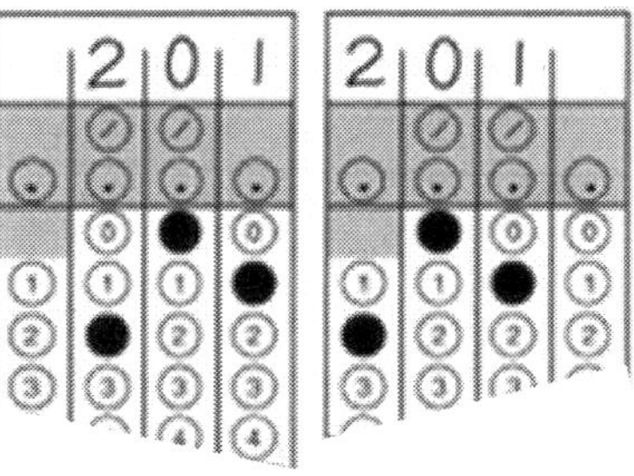

Note: You may start your answers in any column, space permitting. Columns not needed should be left blank.

- Mark no more than one circle in any column.
- Because the answer sheet will be machine-scored. **You will receive credit only if the circles are filled in correctly.**
- Although not required, it is suggested that you write your answer in the boxes at the top of the columns to help you fill in the circles accurately.
- Some problems may have more than one correct answer. In such case, grid only one answer.
- No question has a negative answer.
- **Mixed numbers** such as $3\frac{1}{2}$ must be gridded as 3.5 or $\frac{7}{2}$. (If 3 1 / 2 is gridded, it will be interpreted as $\frac{31}{2}$, not $3\frac{1}{2}$.)
- **Decimal Answer**: If you obtain a decimal answer with more digits than the grid can accommodate, it may be either rounded or truncated, but it must fill the entire grid. The acceptable ways to grid $\frac{2}{3}$ are:

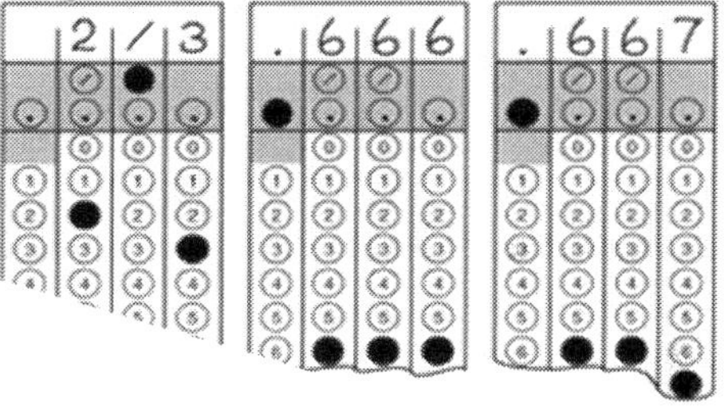

31. In the figure below, what is the value of x?

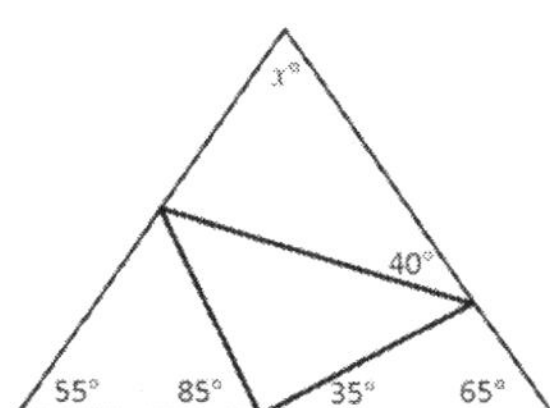

Note: Figure not drawn to scale.

32. Each term in a sequence of numbers is greater than the term before it and the difference between any two consecutive terms is constant. If the 15th and 20th terms in the sequence are 6 and 16, respectively, what is the 300th term?

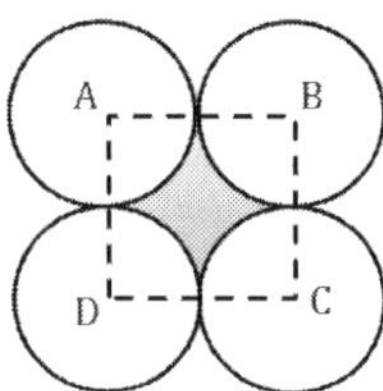

33. The figure above consists of four congruent, tangent circles with radius 2. What is the area of the shaded region? (Round your answer to the nearest hundredth)

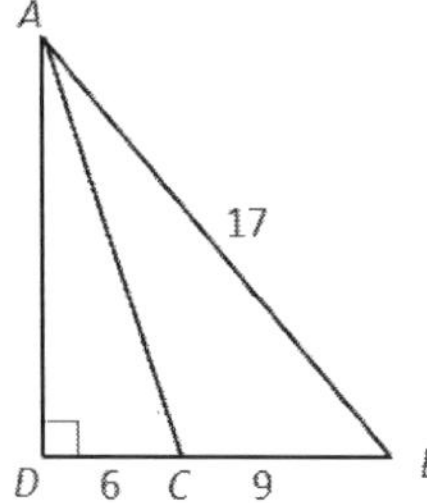

34. In the right triangle as shown above, what is the length of $\overline{AC}$

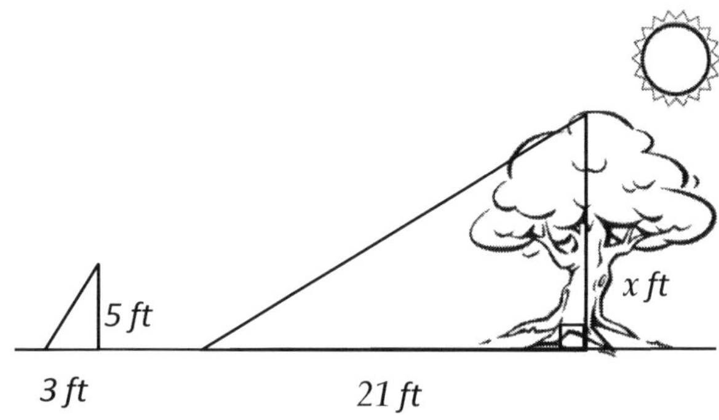

35. At a certain time of day, a tree casts a 21-foot shadow and a 5-foot stick casts a 3-foot shadow. What is the height, in feet, of the tree?

Questions 36 – 37 refer to the following information:

According to the combined ideal gas law, if the amount of gas stays constant, the relationship between pressure, volume, and temperature is as follows:

$$\frac{PV}{T} = constant$$

P is the pressure measured in atmospheres (atm), V is the volume measured in liters (L), and T is the temperature measured in Kelvin (K).

The relationship between Kelvin and Celsius is as follows:

$$K = 273 + ^\circ\text{C}$$

K is the temperature in Kelvin and °C is the temperature in Celsius.

The relationship between Celsius and Fahrenheit is as follows:

$$^\circ\text{C} = (^\circ\text{F} - 32) \times \frac{5}{9}$$

Where °C is the temperature in Celsius and °F is the temperature in Fahrenheit.

36. What will be the final volume, in liters, if the pressure of 10-liter sample of an ideal gas is changed from 2 atm to 3 atm and the temperature is changed from 273 K to 300 K? (Round your answer to the nearest tenth.)

37. If the initial volume of a gas is 10 liters and the pressure of 2 atm, what will be the approximate new volume, in liters, when the temperature is changed from 32 °F to 212 °F and the pressure remains unchanged? (Round your answer to the nearest tenth.)

38. If $a + bi = \frac{2+i}{1-i}$, what is the value of $a + b$?

SAT MATH MOCK TEST No. 1 ANSWER KEYS

Section 3									
1. D	2. D	3. A	4. B	5. B	6. A	7. A	8. C	9. D	10. D
11. B	12. A	13. C	14. A	15. C	16. $\frac{1}{4}$	17. 758	18. 240	19. 120	20. 24

Section 4									
1. D	2. B	3. A	4. D	5. B	6. A	7. A	8. B	9. C	10. C
11. D	12. D	13. B	14. D	15. D	16. D	17. D	18. B	19. A	20. C
21. A	22. C	23. D	24. B	25. B	26. A	27. D	28. C	29. A	30. B
31. 60	32. 576	33. 3.43	34. 10	35. 35	36. 7.3	37. 13.7	38. 2		

SECTION 3

1. *Answer: (d)*
   $3x - 1 = 3$
   $3x = 4,\ \ 12x = 4 \times 4 = 16$

2. *Answer: (d)*
   Solve by zero-product rule.
   $a(x - 1)(x + 3) = 0$
   One of the terms a, (x − 1), and (x + 3) must be equal to zero.
   Given that x > 1, only a can be equal to zero.

3. *Answer: (a)*
   $2x + 6y = 12$
   $\frac{1}{6}\ (2x + 6y) = \frac{1}{6} \times 12$
   $\frac{1}{3}x + y = 2$

4. *Answer: (b)*
   $3\sqrt{x} + y = 3\sqrt{x} + 3$
   $y = 3$

5. *Answer: (b)*
   When n = 2, the graph will be a parabola curve.

6. *Answer: (a)*
   A linear line represents a 1st order reaction.

7. *Answer: (a)*
   The product of the slopes of two perpendicular lines must be −1.
   Slope of r $= \frac{2-0}{2-0} = 1$
   Slope of t $= -1$

8. *Answer: (c)*
   Write z in terms of y.
   $z = \frac{1}{2}y$
   $x = 2[4(\frac{1}{2}y)^2 + 2(\frac{1}{2}y) - 3)]$
   $x = 2(y^2 + y - 3)$
   $= 2y^2 + 2y - 6$

9. *Answer: (d)*
   $4 + x - y = 21$
   $x - y = 17$

10. *Answer: (d)*
    Find the current age first, and then subtract c. Let x be the current age.
    $x + a = b$
    $x = b - a$
    Current Age $= b - a$
    William's Age c Years Ago $= b - a - c$

11. *Answer: (b)*
    The remainder of a number divided by 5 must be less than 5.

12. *Answer: (a)*
    The number of boxes must be greater or equal than zero.
    The storage room can hold up to 20 boxes and the maximum of $600 can be spent, therefore the answer is a).
    $$\begin{cases} x \geq 0 \\ y \geq 0 \\ x + y \leq 20 \\ 25x + 40y \leq 600 \end{cases}$$

13. *Answer: (c)*
    Only answer c) depicts the correct system of equations of the previous question.

$$\begin{cases} x \ge 0 \\ y \ge 0 \\ x + y \le 20 \\ 25x + 40y \le 600 \end{cases}$$

14. *Answer: (a)*
Let the expressway be x miles between Maya's house and her college. The local route would be x– 2 miles, which means that the round trip would be x + (x – 2) = 18
$x = 10$
$10 - 2 = 8$

15. *Answer: (c)*
There are (x – w) members belong to X only and (y – w) members belong to Y only.
$(x - w) + (y - w) = x + y - 2w$

16. *Answer:* $\frac{1}{4}$ *or .25*
Find the ratio of the total area to the central square area.
If the total area is 1, the small square area in the middle will be $\frac{1}{4}$.
Probability $= \frac{\frac{1}{4}}{1} = \frac{1}{4}$

17. *Answer: 758*
Apply PEMDAS.
$x = 7 + (6 \times 125 + 1) = 7 + (750 + 1) = 7 + 751 = 758$

18. *Answer: 240*
The sum of the interior angles of a quadrilateral triangle is 360°.
$60^\circ + 60^\circ + x + y = 360^\circ$
$x + y = 240^\circ$

19. *Answer: 120*
If Peter's weight is x, then John's weight is $\frac{3}{5}x$.
$\frac{3}{5}x + 8 = \frac{2}{3}x$
$\frac{1}{15}x = 8$
$x = 120$ *pounds*

20. *Answer: 24*
Let the initial charge be x dollars and the charge for one topping be y dollars.
$x + y = 16$ (1)
$x + 3y = 20$ (2)
Subtract (1) from (2).
$2y = 20 - 16 = 4, \ y = 2$
$x = 14$
The price for 5-topping: $x + 5y = 14 + 5 \times 2 = 24$

SECTION 4

1. *Answer: (d)*
$a^x \cdot a^4 = a^{(x+4)} = a^{12}$
$(a^4)^y = a^{4y} = a^{12}$
$x = 8; y = 3$
$x + 2y = 14$

2. *Answer: (b)*
1 hour = 3600 seconds
70 miles : 3600 seconds = x miles : 10 seconds
$3600x = 70 \times 10$
$x = \frac{700}{3600} \sim 0.2$ *miles*

3. *Answer: (a)*
Substitute x with 20.
$f(20) = 18 \times 20 - 60 = 300$

4. *Answer: (d)*
$7x = 180^o$ *and* $2y + 4x = 180^o$
$x = 25.7^o$
$y = 38.6^o$

5. *Answer: (b)*
Because the customer is ordering a main course AND a side dish, use the multiplication Principle.
Total number of choices: $3 \times 4 = 12$

6. *Answer: (a)*
ΔABC is an isosceles triangle.
$m\angle C = 57^o$
$x = 180 - 90 - 57$
$x = 33$

7. *Answer: (a)*
$m\angle AOD + m\angle BOC = 360 - m\angle DOC - m\angle AOB$
$m\angle AOB = 180 - 2 \times 35 = 110$
$m\angle DOC = 180 - 2 \times 55 = 70$
$m\angle AOD + m\angle BOC = 360 - 110 - 70 = 180$

8. *Answer: (b)*
$Percent\ Error = \frac{0.9875-1}{1} \times 100\%$
$= -1.25\%$

9. *Answer: (c)*
$10\% = \frac{85-x}{x} \times 100\%$
$850 = 11x$
$x = 77.3\ ℃$

10. *Answer: (c)*
This is combination. The number of ways to select m objects from n objects ($n \geq m$), where order does not matter:
$$C_m^n = \frac{n!}{m!(n-m)!}$$
To choose any two points among the 8 points:
$C_2^8 = 28$

11. *Answer: (b)*
The number of students passing = The number of males passing + The number of females passing
220 = 120 + The number of females passing
The number of females passing = 100
Total number of females = The number of females passing + The number of females failing
The number of females failing: 140 – 100 = 40

12. *Answer: (d)*
We want to find $\frac{X}{Y}$.
Average: $\frac{\text{Sum of Terms}}{\text{Number of Terms}}$
$\frac{85X+90Y}{X+Y} = 88$ *(cross multiply)*
$85X + 90Y = 88 \times (X + Y)$
$85X + 90Y = 88X + 88Y$
$2Y = 3X$
$\frac{X}{Y} = \frac{2}{3}$

13. *Answer: (d)*
Length of Side of Square = 9 – 2 = 7
$7 = 0 - (k+1)$
$-k = 8$
$k = -8$

14. *Answer: (b)*
The LCM of 7 and 5 is 35.
Every 35 days, A and B will be on sale on the same day.
$\frac{365}{35} = 10.4$

15. *Answer: (d)*
$\frac{\$40+2\times7.5}{8 \text{ tickets}} = \$6.875$ *per ticket*

16. *Answer: (d)*
$90\% = \frac{\text{Correct Answers}}{\text{Total Questions}}$
$\frac{x}{50} = \frac{90}{100}$ *(cross multiply)*
$x = \frac{90\times50}{100} = 45$

17. *Answer: (d)*
$m = x^2 \times y \times z^3$
The total number of factors including 1 and m is (2 + 1) × (1 + 1) × (3 + 1) = 24
Excluding 1 and m = 24 – 2 = 22

18. *Answer: (b)*
Slope = $\frac{Rise}{Run} = 0.2$
y-intercept = 1
$y = 0.2x + 1$

19. *Answer: (a)*
a + b + c + d + e + f + sum of the three interior angles of triangle = 3 × 180
Sum of three interior angles of triangle $= 180^o$
$a + b + c + d + e + f = 540 - 180 = 360$

20. *Answer: (c)*
Area WITH Frame and Picture = (6 + 2) × (8 + 2) = 80
Area of Picture = 6 × 8 = 48
Area of Frame = 80 – 48 = 32

21. *Answer: (a)*
ΔABC is a right triangle.
$AB^2 = AC^2 + BC^2$
$AB = \sqrt{3^2 + 4^2} = 5$
Radius = $\frac{1}{2}(5) = \frac{5}{2}$
Area = $\pi \times \frac{5^2}{2^2} = \frac{25}{4}\pi = 6.25\pi$

22. *Answer: (c)*
a) $1^2 = \frac{1}{1}$
b) $(-1)^2 = \frac{1}{1}$
c) $2^2 \neq \frac{1}{\frac{-1}{4}}$
d) $(\frac{-1}{2})^2 = \frac{1}{4}$

23. *Answer: (d)*
The sum of the interior angles of a quadrilateral is equal to 360°.
$360 = 100 + x + y + z$
$x + y + z = 260$
$x > 110 \longrightarrow y + z < 150$
$x < 180 \longrightarrow y + z > 80$
$80 < z + y < 150$

24. *Answer: (b)*
Draw a horizontal line y = −0.5 to find how many interceptions with the graph.
From the graph above, there are 5 interceptions with line y = −0.5.

25. *Answer: (b)*
$A_1V_1 = A_2V_2$
$0.3 \times 5 = 0.2 \times V_2$
$V_2 = 7.5\ m/s$

26. *Answer: (a)*
$A_1V_1 = A_2V_2$
$\pi\left(\frac{1.5}{2}\right)^2 \times 4 = \pi\left(\frac{0.5}{2}\right)^2 \times V_2$
$V_2 = 36\ m/s$

27. *Answer: (d)*
Total number of students is equal to the number of students who study one langue only plus number of students who study two languages.
If number of students who only study Spanish is a, only study French is b and only study Chinese is c.
The number of students who study Spanish and another langue is 150 – a
The number of students who study French and another language is 110 – b
The number of students who study Chinese and another language is 90 – c
However, we count French/Spanish and Spanish/French twice. Therefore
(150 – a) + (110 – b) + (90 – c) = 40 × 2
a + b + c = 150 + 110 + 90 – 80 = 270
So the total number of students in high school is 270 + 40 = 310

28. *Answer: (c)*
After folding, the height of the box will be 3 cm, the length will be 5 cm, and the width will be 4cm.
Surface Area = (3 × 4 + 4 × 5 + 5 × 3) × 2 = 94 cm²

29. *Answer: (a)*

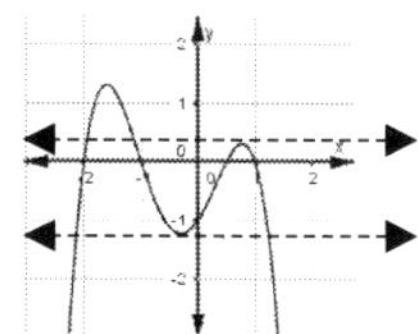

According to the graph above, there will be four intersection points when the value of c is roughly between -1.3 *and* 0.3.

30. *Answer: (b)*

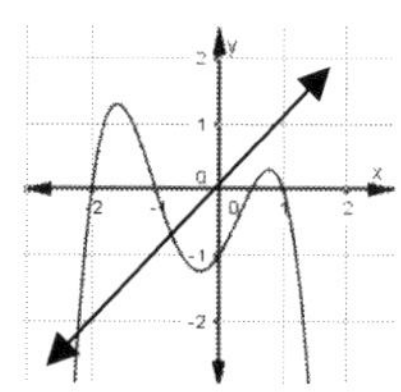

According to the graph above, there are two intersection points between the lines $f(x) = x$ *and* $f(x) = -x^4 - \frac{3}{2}x^3 + 2x^2 + \frac{3}{2}x - 1$.

31. *Answer: 60*
Look at x in terms of the big triangle.
x + 65 + 55 = 180 → x = 60

32. *Answer: 576*
Because the difference between any two consecutive terms is constant = $\frac{16-6}{20-15} = 2$
15th term: 6
300th term: 15th term + (300 – 15) × 2
= 6 + 285 × 2 = 576

33. *Answer: 3.43*
Area of Shaded Region = Area of Square – 4 × Area of a Quarter-Circle
$4^2 - \pi \times 2^2 = 16 - 4\pi = 3.43$

34. *Answer: 10*
$\overline{AD}^2 = (17^2 - (6+9)^2) = 64 \rightarrow \overline{AD} = 8$
$\overline{AC}^2 = 8^2 + 6^2 \rightarrow \overline{AC} = 10$

35. *Answer: 35*
The corresponding sides of two similar triangles are proportional.
$\frac{5}{3} = \frac{x}{21}$
$x = 35\ ft$

36. *Answer: 7.3*
$\frac{PV}{T} = constant$
$\frac{P_1V_1}{T_1} = constant = \frac{P_2V_2}{T_2}$
$\frac{2 \times 10}{273} = \frac{3 \times V_2}{300}$
$v_2 = 7.3\ liters$

37. *Answer: 13.7*
$T_1 = (32 - 32) \times \frac{5}{9} = 0\ ^\circ C = 273 + 0 = 273\ K$
$T_2 = (212 - 32) \times \frac{5}{9} = 100\ ^\circ C = 273 + 100 = 373\ K$
$\frac{2 \times 10}{273} = \frac{2 \times V_2}{373} \rightarrow V_2 = 13.7\ liters$

38. *Answer: 2*
Rationalize the denominator
$\frac{2+i}{1-i} = \frac{(2+i)(1+i)}{(1-i)(1+i)} = \frac{2+2i+i-1}{1+1} = \frac{1+3i}{2} = \frac{1}{2} + \frac{3}{2}i$
$= a + bi$
$a = \frac{1}{2}, b = \frac{3}{2} \rightarrow a + b = 2$

SAT Math Mock Test No. 2

SECTION 3 

Math Test — NO Calculator 25 MINUTES, 20 QUESTIONS

Directions:
For questions 1-15, solve each problem, choose the best answer from the choices provided, and fill in the corresponding circle on your answer sheet. **For questions 16-20**, solve the problem and enter your answer in the grid on the answer sheet. Please refer to the directions before question 16 on how to enter your answers in the grid. You may use any available space in your test booklet for scratch work.

Notes:

4. **No calculator** is allowed for this section. All numbers used are real numbers.
5. Figures that accompany problems in this test are intended to provide information useful in solving the problems. They are drawn as accurately as possible EXCEPT when it is stated in a specific problem that the figure is not drawn to scale. All figures lie in a plane unless otherwise indicated.
6. Unless otherwise specified, the domain of any function *f(x)* assumed to be the set of all real numbers *x* for which *f(x)* is a real number.

References:

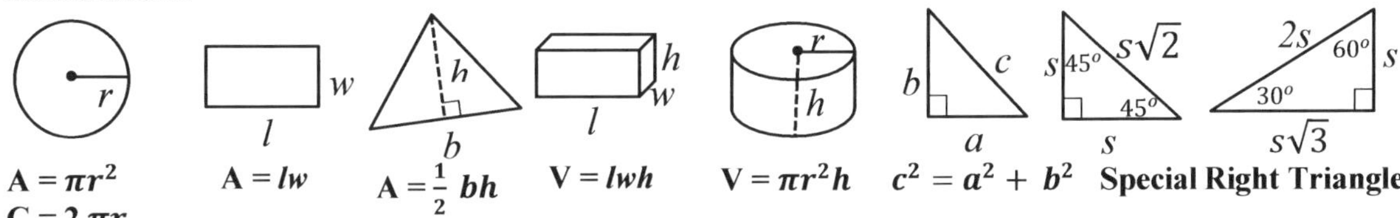

$A = \pi r^2$ $C = 2\pi r$ $A = lw$ $A = \frac{1}{2}bh$ $V = lwh$ $V = \pi r^2 h$ $c^2 = a^2 + b^2$ **Special Right Triangles**

The number of degrees of arc in a circle is 360; the number of radians of arc in a circle is 2π.
The sum of the degree measures of the angles in a triangle is 180.

1. If x is less than 0 and y is greater than zero, which of the following must be greater than 0?
   a) $y - x$
   b) $\frac{y}{x}$
   c) xy
   d) $x - y$

2. If $\frac{2}{x} + x = 4 + \frac{1}{2}$, then x can be equal to which of the following?
   a) 1
   b) 2
   c) 3
   d) 4

3. The amount of money, in dollars, earned from a school fundraiser by selling x cookies is given by $A(x) = 2x - 90$. How many cookies must the event sell in order to raise 250 dollars?
   a) 150
   b) 170
   c) 175
   d) 180

4. If x is a positive integer, then $3 \times 10^{-x} + 10^{-x}$ must be equal to?
   a) $\frac{1}{10^x}$
   b) $\frac{2}{10^x}$
   c) $\frac{3}{10^{-x}}$
   d) $\frac{4}{10^x}$

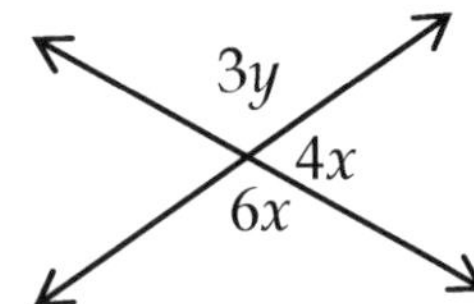

5. In the figure above, what is the value of $2x + y$?
   a) 60
   b) 72
   c) 85
   d) 100

6. Which two lines are perpendicular to each other?
   a) $y = x - 2;\ x = 1$
   b) $y = x + 2;\ x = 1$
   c) $y = -x - 1;\ x = 1$
   d) $y = -5;\ x = 1$

7. If k is a constant and $2x + 5 = 3kx + 5$ for all values of x, what is the value of k?
   a) 3
   b) 2
   c) 1
   d) $\frac{2}{3}$

8. If $3 = m^x$, then $9m^2$=?
   a) m^{2x}
   b) m^{3x}
   c) m^{2x+2}
   d) m^{2x+3}

9. At a particular time, the speed (velocity) of a car is equal to the slope of the tangent line of the curve in the position-time graph. Which of the following position-time graphs represents the motion of a car when its speed (velocity) is increasing?
   a)

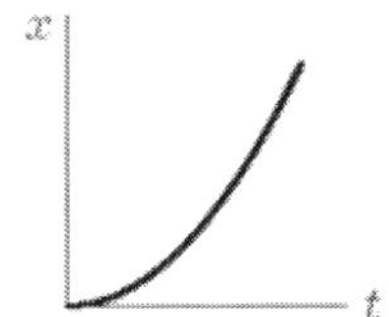

   b)

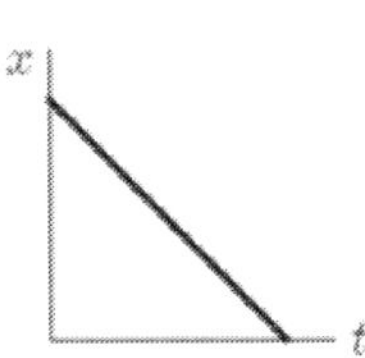

   c)

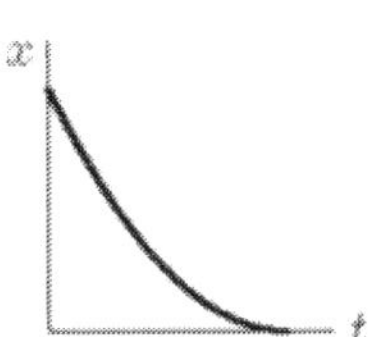

   d)

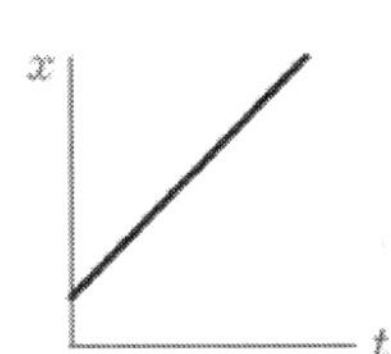

10. One circle has the area of 3 and another circle has the area of 4. What is the ratio of the diameter of the smaller circle to the diameter of the larger circle?
    a) $3:2$
    b) $9:4$
    c) $\sqrt{3}:2$
    d) $2:\sqrt{3}$

11. If $x - y = 7$, $y = 2z + 4$, and $z = 1$, what is the value of x?
    a) −13
    b) 13
    c) 11
    d) 12

12. A number a is multiplied by $\frac{1}{4}$. The product is then multiplied by 9, which results in 27. What is the value of a?
    a) 3
    b) 6
    c) 9
    d) 12

13. If $a = \frac{3}{5}xy$, what is the value of y when $x = 3$ and $a = 18$?
   a) 10
   b) 20
   c) 35
   d) 40

14. If $3x + 1 = a$, then $6x + 1$?
   a) $a + 3$
   b) $a - 3$
   c) $2a - 1$
   d) $2a + 1$

15. A school choir consists of one row of singers, half of which are boys and the other half girls. Which of the following must be true?
   a) The first person and the last person have different genders.
   b) There are two girls next to each other.
   c) If the last two are girls, there are at least two adjacent boys.
   d) If there are two adjacent boys, there are also two adjacent girls.

Directions:

For questions 16-20, solve the problem and enter your answer in the grid, as described below, on the answer sheet.

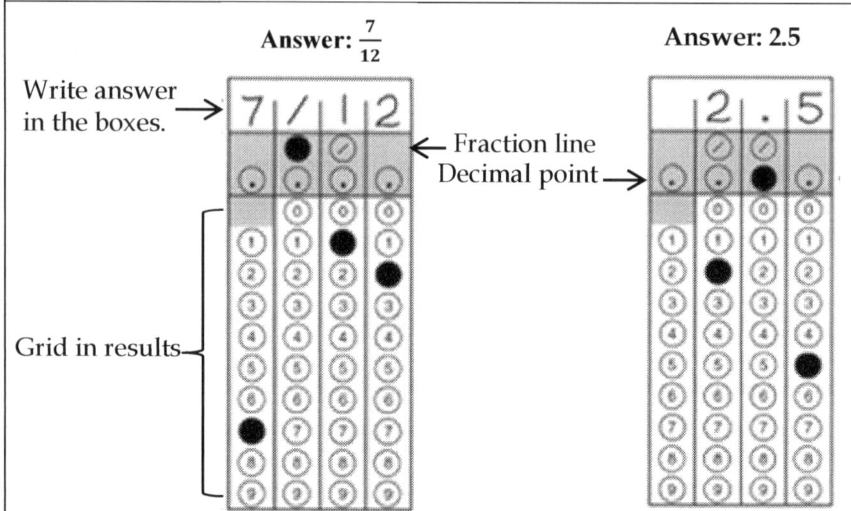

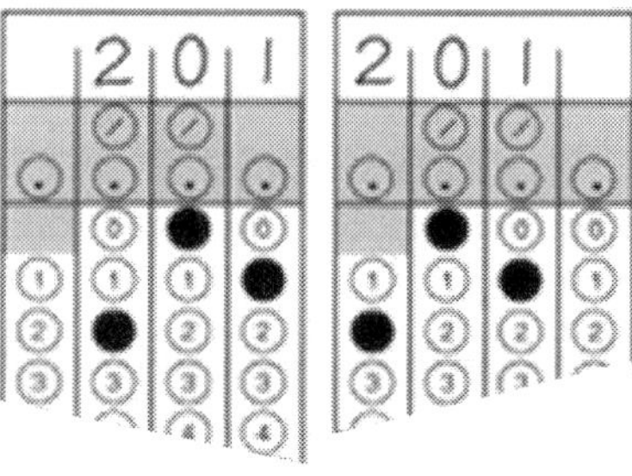

Note: You may start your answers in any column, space permitting. Columns not needed should be left blank.

- Mark no more than one circle in any column.
- Because the answer sheet will be machine-scored. **You will receive credit only if the circles are filled in correctly.**
- Although not required, it is suggested that you write your answer in the boxes at the top of the columns to help you fill in the circles accurately.
- Some problems may have more than one correct answer. In such case, grid only one answer.
- No question has a negative answer.
- **Mixed numbers** such as $3\frac{1}{2}$ must be gridded as 3.5 or $\frac{7}{2}$. (If 31/2 is gridded, it will be interpreted as $\frac{31}{2}$, not $3\frac{1}{2}$.)
- **Decimal Answer**: If you obtain a decimal answer with more digits than the grid can accommodate, it may be either rounded or truncated, but it must fill the entire grid. The acceptable ways to grid $\frac{2}{3}$ are:

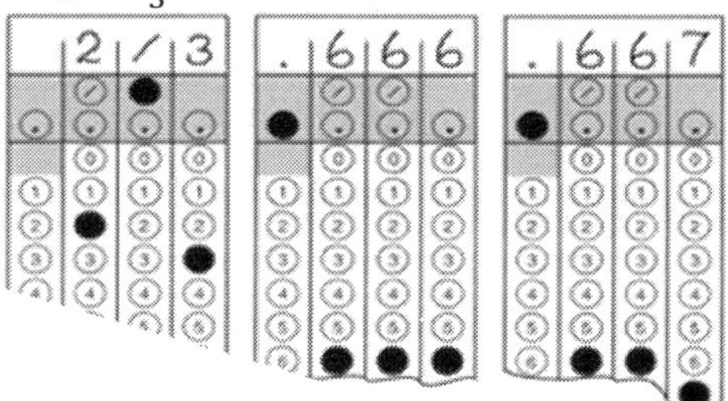

16. When a number is tripled and then reduced by 15, the result is 300. What is the number?

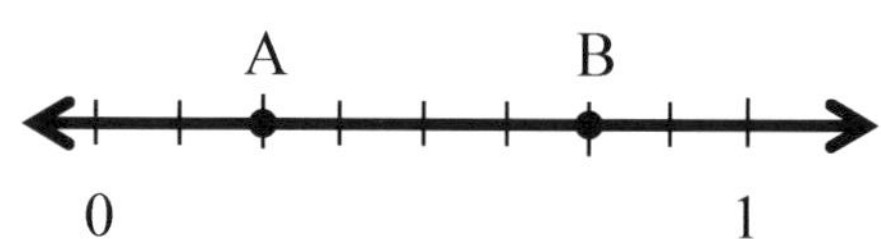

17. The number line is equally spaced as shown above. What is the value of $|A - 2B|$?

18. If $g(x) = 4x - 12$, then at what value of x does the graph of $g(x)$ cross the x-axis?

19. If $6x + 2 = 5$, what is the value of $6x - 2$?

20. What is the hundredths digit in the number 123.987?

SECTION 4

Math Test – Calculator **55 MINUTES, 38 QUESTIONS**

Directions:

For questions 1-30, solve each problem, choose the best answer from the choices provided, and fill in the corresponding circle on your answer sheet. **For questions 31-38**, solve the problem and enter your answer in the grid on the answer sheet. Please refer to the directions before question 31 on how to enter your answers in the grid. You may use any available space in your test booklet for scratch work.

Notes:

1. Acceptable calculators are allowed for this section. All numbers used are real numbers.
2. Figures that accompany problems in this test are intended to provide information useful in solving the problems. They are drawn as accurately as possible EXCEPT when it is stated in a specific problem that the figure is not drawn to scale. All figures lie in a plane unless otherwise indicated.
3. Unless otherwise specified, the domain of any function *f(x)* assumed to be the set of all real numbers *x* for which *f(x)* is a real number.

References:

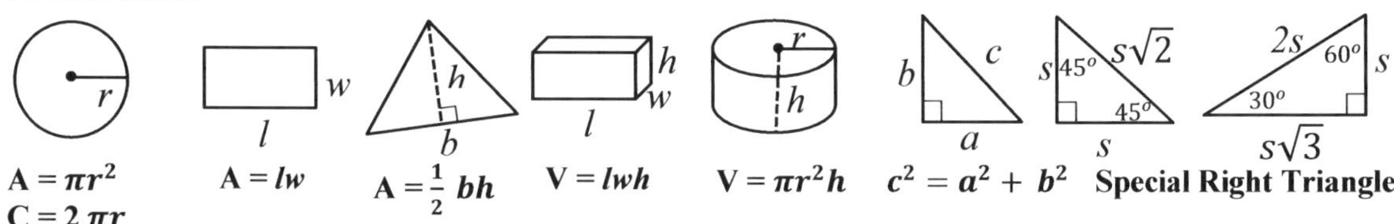

$A = \pi r^2$ $C = 2\pi r$ $A = lw$ $A = \frac{1}{2}bh$ $V = lwh$ $V = \pi r^2 h$ $c^2 = a^2 + b^2$ **Special Right Triangles**

The number of degrees of arc in a circle is 360; the number of radians of arc in a circle is 2π.
The sum of the degree measures of the angles in a triangle is 180.

1. If one soft drink costs \$0.60 and one burger cost \$2.5, which of the following represents the cost, in dollars, of S soft drinks and B burgers?
   a) S × B
   b) .6S × B
   c) 2.5(B + S)
   d) 2.5B + 0.6S

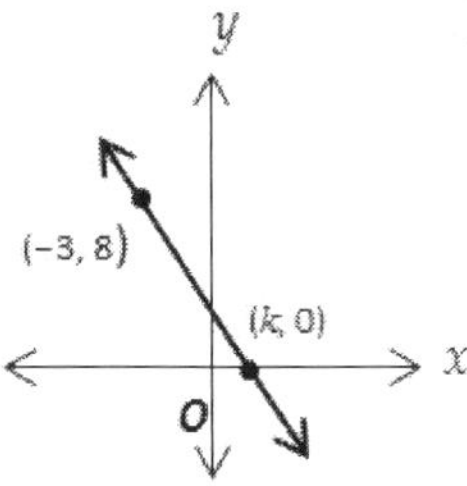

2. In the figure above, the slope of the line through points (–3, 8) and (*k*, 0) is −2. What is the value of *k*?
   a) 4
   b) 3
   c) 2
   d) 1

3. If 20 percent of x is 50, what is x percent of 40?
   a) 50
   b) 100
   c) 150
   d) 200

4. The chart below shows the results of a swimming race. If all the students started at the same time, who finished third?

Swimming Race Results	
Student	*Time (in seconds)*
Grant	*52.17*
Robert	*52.71*
Larry	*53.81*
Adam	*53.02*
Chris	*54.01*

   a) Grant
   b) Robert
   c) Larry
   d) Adam

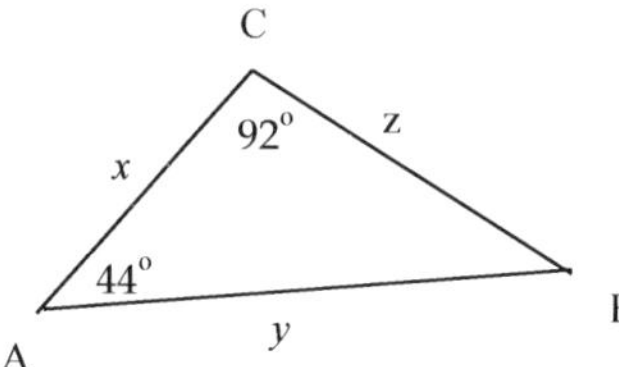

5. Which of the following must be true about x, y, and z in the figure above?
   a) $x < z < y$
   b) $z = x < y$
   c) $x < y < z$
   d) $z < y < x$

6. ΔABC is an equilateral triangle with side length of 8. What is the area of ΔABC?
   a) 64
   b) 32
   c) $16\sqrt{3}$
   d) $16\sqrt{2}$

7. The ratio of three interior angle measures in a triangle is 2:3:4. What is the measure, in degrees, of the largest angle in this triangle?
   a) 80°
   b) 90°
   c) 100°
   d) 120°

8. If $z = \frac{3x^4}{y^2}$, what happens to the value of z when both x and y are tripled?
   a) z is multiplied by 27.
   b) z is multiplied by 9.
   c) z is multiplied by 8.
   d) z is doubled.

$$\sqrt{x+1} = x - 2$$

9. For all values of x greater than 2, the equation above is equivalent to which of the following?
   a) $x = x^2$
   b) $x = x^2 - 1$
   c) $x = x^2 - 4x - 3$
   d) $x = x^2 - 4x + 3$

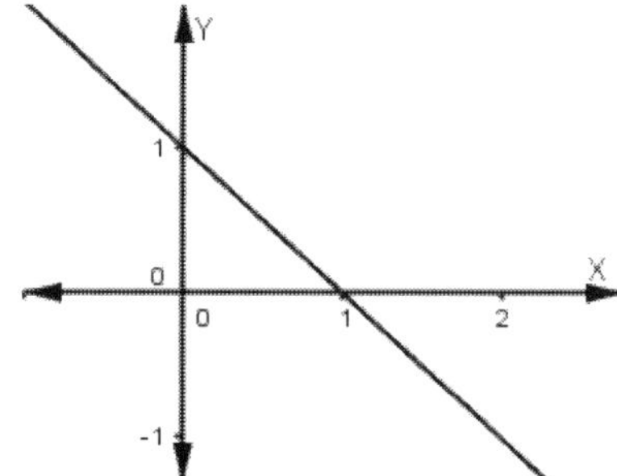

10. The figure above shows the graph of the line $y = mx + b$, where m and b are constants. Which of the following best represents the graph of the line $y = -2mx - b$?

a)

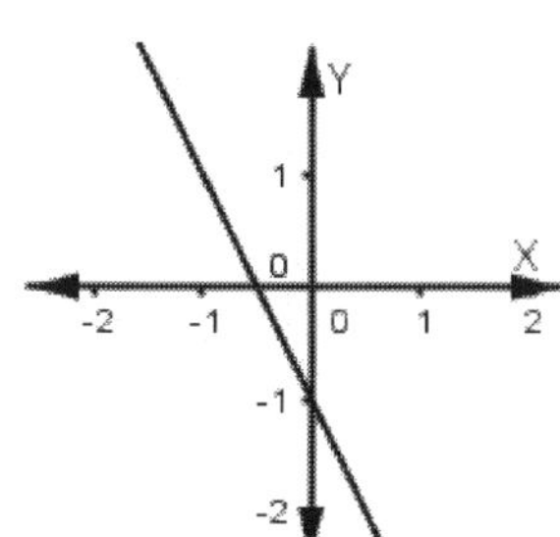

b)

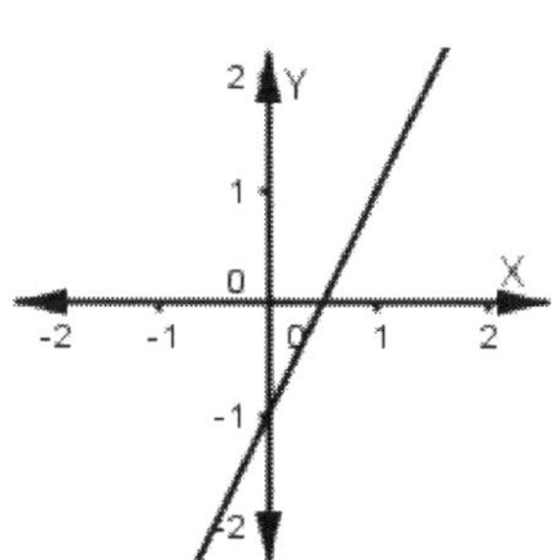

c)

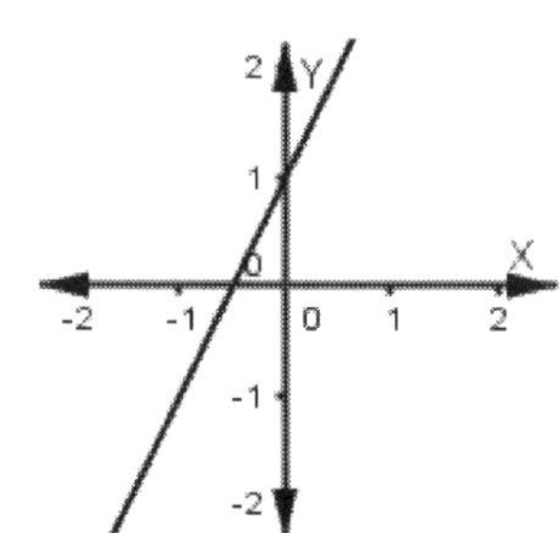

d)

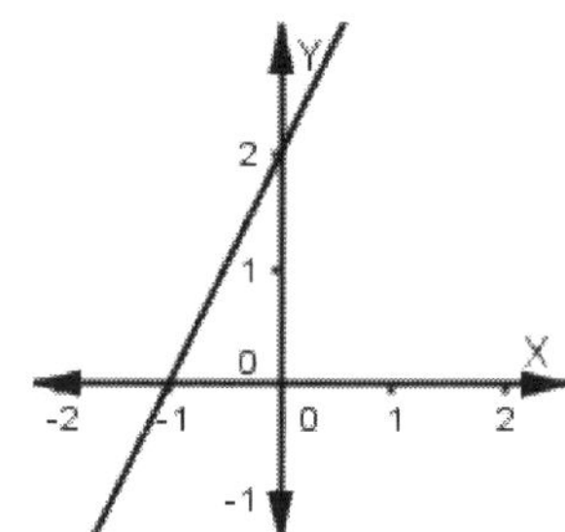

11. Vehicle A ran 15 miles an hour for 4 hours. The total distance A traveled was twice the distance of Vehicle B after Vehicle B traveled 10 miles an hour for X hours. What is X?
    a) 3
    b) 4
    c) 4.5
    d) 5

Number of Hours of TV Watched

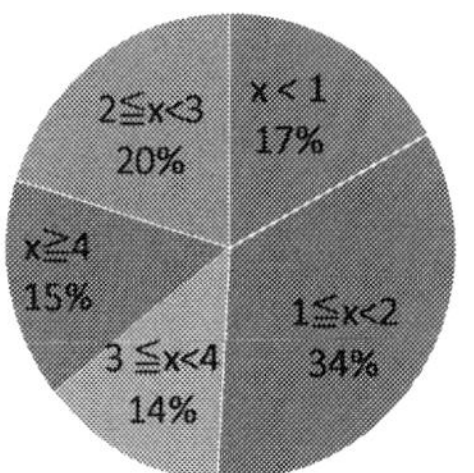

12. The graph above shows breakdown of the average number of hours of TV watched per day. 1000 people were surveyed, and all but 160 people surveyed responded to the question. If x is the number of hours spent, about how many respondents watch TV for more than 3 hours a day?
    a) 210
    b) 221
    c) 243
    d) 255

13. If the function f is defined by $f(x) = ax^2 + bx + c$, where a > 0, and $c > 0$, which of the following could be the graph of $f(x)$?
    a)

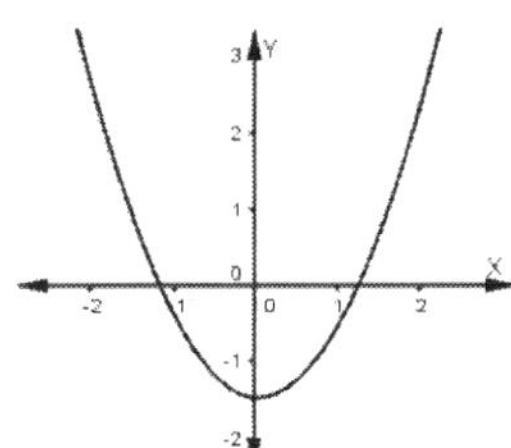

    b)

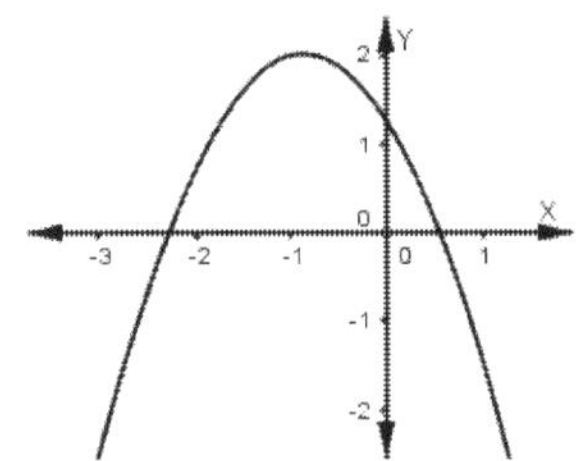

c)

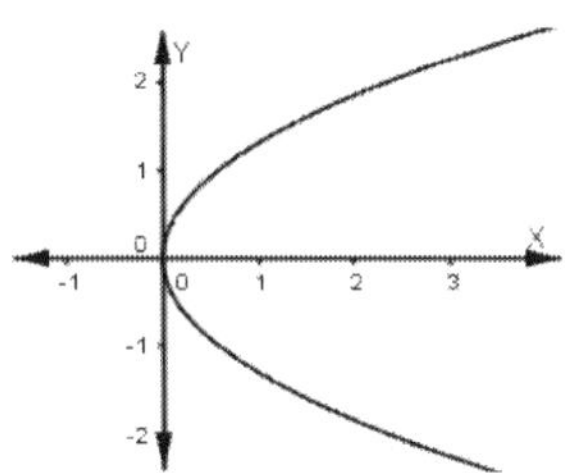

d)

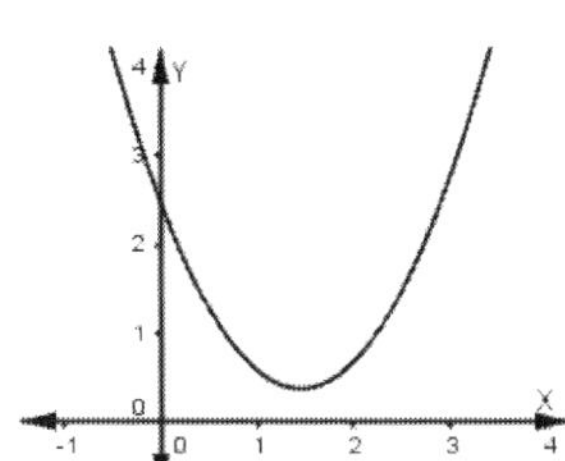

Questions 14 – 15 refer to the following information:

In our Solar System, it takes the Earth 365 days (one Earth year) to orbit the Sun. The orbital period of a planet correlates with its distance from the Sun. According to Kepler's law, the square of the orbital period is proportional to the cube of the average distance of the planet from the Sun.

$$\frac{(Orbital\ Period\ of\ Planet)^2}{(Distance\ of\ Planet\ to\ the\ Sun)^3} = constant$$

14. Jupiter is the largest planet in the Solar System and the fifth planet from the Sun. If Jupiter is 5.2 times farther from the Sun than Earth is, What is Jupiter's orbital period, in Earth years?
    a) 5.2
    b) 9.0
    c) 11.9
    d) 27.9

15. Mars is the fourth planet from the Sun and has all the four seasons that Earth has. If Mars takes 687 Earth days to revolve around the Sun, what is the ratio of the average distance between Mars and the Sun to the average distance between Earth and the Sun?
    a) 0.54
    b) 1.52
    c) 20.95
    d) 77.86

16. In the figure below, points A and B lie on circle O. If $\angle AOB = 30^o$, what is the value of x?

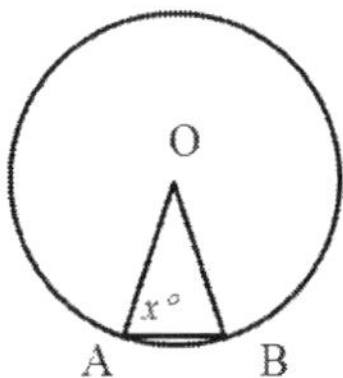

    a) 60
    b) 65
    c) 70
    d) 75

17. The fruits provided in the student lounge contain pears, apples, and oranges. The ratio of the numbers of pears to apples is 3 : 5 and the ratio of the numbers of apples to oranges is 3 : 5. Find the ratio of the numbers of pears to oranges?
    a) 9 : 25
    b) 25 : 9
    c) 3 : 5
    d) 5 : 3

18. In the figure below, what is the value of $a - b$?

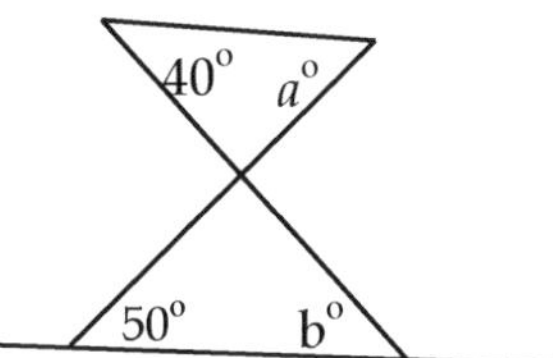

    a) 10
    b) 15
    c) 20
    d) 25

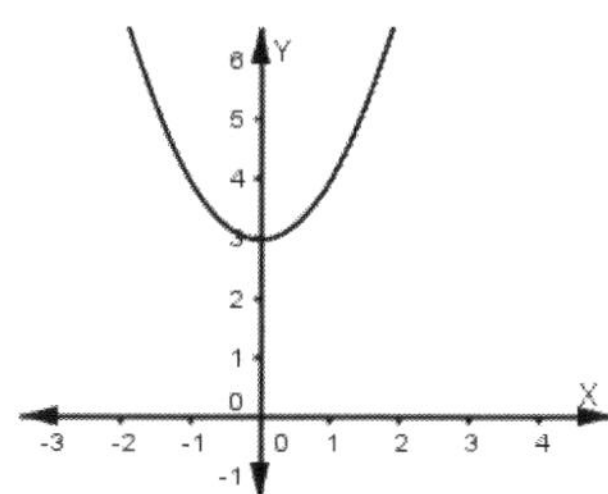

19. The figure above is a parabola of the equation $y = ax^2 + 3$, where a is a constant. If graphed on the same axes, which of the following describes the graph of $y = \frac{a}{2}x^2 + 3$ as compared to the graph above?
    a) The new graph will move to the right.
    b) The new graph will move to the left.
    c) The new graph will be narrower.
    d) The new graph will be wider.

20. Which of the following is the graph of a linear function with a positive slope and a negative y-intercept?
    a)

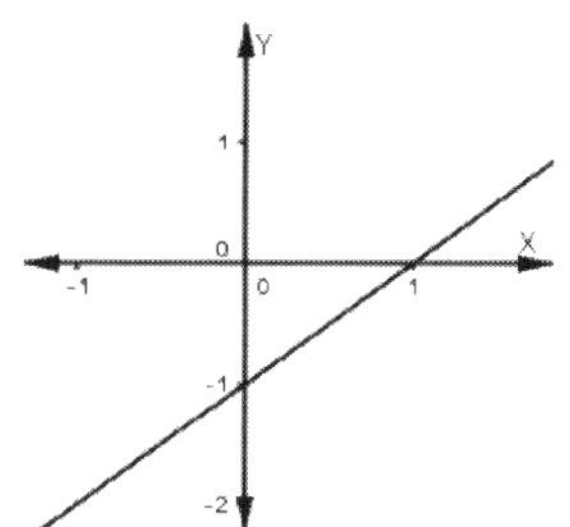

    b)

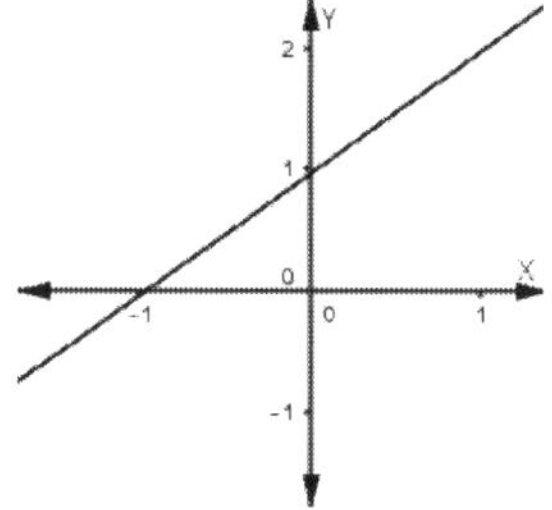

    c)

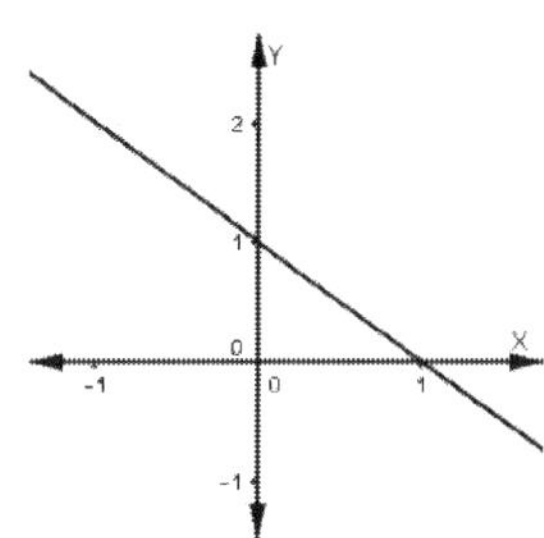

    d)

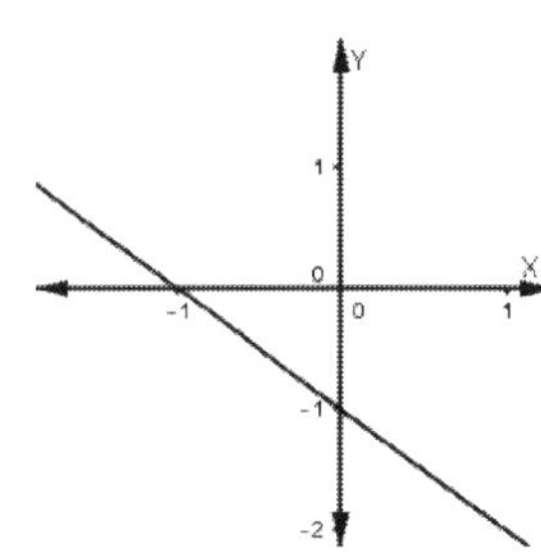

21. \$18,000 in winnings for a tennis tournament was distributed in the ratio of 6:2:1 to the first-, second-, and third-place finishers, respectively. How much money did the first place finisher receive?
    a) \$12,000
    b) \$15,000
    c) \$10,000
    d) \$8,000

Questions 22 – 23 refer to the following information:

According to research, 90 percent of 20 to 36 month-old children in the United States need to have received measles vaccination in order to achieve herd immunity. In 2013, California did not meet the vaccination goal and Colorado, Ohio, and West Virginia had 86 percent of 20 to 36 month-olds received the vaccination.

22. If the total number of 20 to 36 month-olds in California in 2013 is 1.41 million, which of the following is NOT the possible number of 20 to 36 month-olds who have received the measles vaccination in California in 2013?
    a) 1.24 million
    b) 1.25 million
    c) 1.26 million
    d) 1.27 million

23. If the total number of 20 to 36 month-olds in Colorado in 2013 is 0.155 million, how many of 20 to 36 month-olds in Colorado have received the measles vaccination in 2013?
    a) 167,800
    b) 156,500
    c) 141,200
    d) 133,300

24. A bike traveled 80 miles in 5 hours. At this rate, how many miles would the bike travels in 6 hours?
    a) 64
    b) 90
    c) 96
    d) 100

25. $\frac{1}{5}$ of 80 is equal to what percent of 200?
    a) 5 %
    b) 8 %
    c) 10 %
    d) 16 %

26. If 40 percent of 40 percent of a number is 64.96, what is the number?
    a) 0.205
    b) 35.4
    c) 406
    d) 203

$$2x,\ y,\ 2y$$

27. If the average (arithmetic mean) of the three numbers above is $3x$ and $x \neq 0$, what is y in terms of x?
    a) $2x$
    b) $3x$
    c) $\frac{5x}{2}$
    d) $\frac{7x}{3}$

x	1	2	3	4	5
$f(x)$	−2	1	6	13	22

28. Some pairs of input and output values of the function f are shown above. The function h is defined by $h(x) = f(2x + 1)$. What is the value of $h(1)$?
    a) −2
    b) 1
    c) 6
    d) 13

29. The price of a certain stock was x dollars on January 1, 2013. The price decreased by 10% in January, increased by 30% in February, decreased by 20% in March, and increased by 25% in April. In terms of x, what was the price of the stock at the end of April?
    a) $0.91x$
    b) $1.1x$
    c) $1.17x$
    d) $1.21x$

30. If N has a remainder of 2 when divided by 3, 4, 5, or 6 and N is a three-digit number, what is the largest possible value for N?
    a) 360
    b) 362
    c) 720
    d) 722

Directions:

For questions 31-38, solve the problem and enter your answer in the grid, as described below, on the answer sheet.

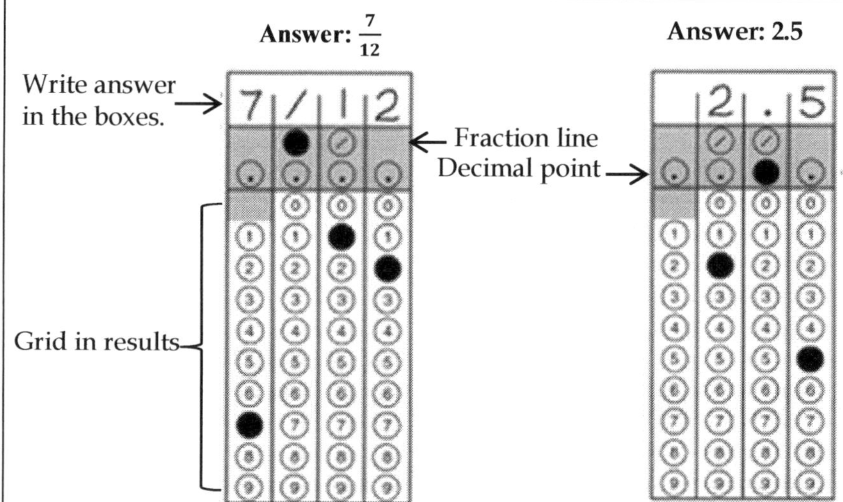

Answer: 201
Either position is correct.

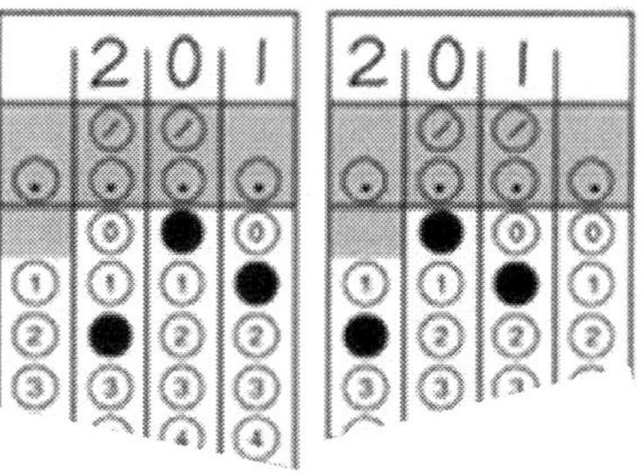

Note: You may start your answers in any column, space permitting. Columns not needed should be left blank.

- Mark no more than one circle in any column.
- Because the answer sheet will be machine-scored. **You will receive credit only if the circles are filled in correctly.**
- Although not required, it is suggested that you write your answer in the boxes at the top of the columns to help you fill in the circles accurately.
- Some problems may have more than one correct answer. In such case, grid only one answer.
- No question has a negative answer.
- **Mixed numbers** such as $3\frac{1}{2}$ must be gridded as 3.5 or $\frac{7}{2}$. (If 31/2 is gridded, it will be interpreted as $\frac{31}{2}$, not $3\frac{1}{2}$.)
- **Decimal Answer**: If you obtain a decimal answer with more digits than the grid can accommodate, it may be either rounded or truncated, but it must fill the entire grid. The acceptable ways to grid $\frac{2}{3}$ are:

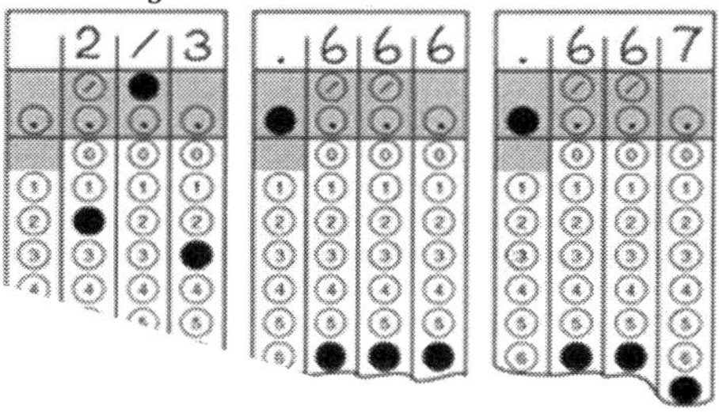

y
A
B $(3x - 4, x)$
O
C $(x + 1, 0)$
x

31. In the figure above, if the area of parallelogram OABC is 42, what is the value of x?

32. The maximum height of a rock thrown upward with an initial velocity of v feet per second is $h + \frac{v^2}{64}$ feet, where h is the initial height, in feet. If the rock is thrown upward with velocity of 32 feet per second from a height of 20 feet, what is the maximum height, in feet, of the trajectory?

33. A sack contains red, blue, and yellow marbles. The ratio of red marbles to blue marbles to yellow marbles is 3 : 4 : 8. If there are 24 yellow marbles in the sack, how many total marbles are in the sack?

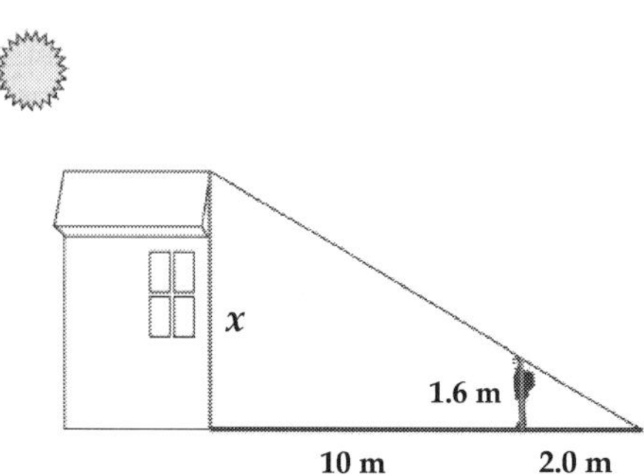

34. Jon walks 10 meters away from a wall outside his school building as shown in the figure above. At the point he stands, he notices that his shadow reaches to the same spot as the shadow of the school. If Jon is 1.6 meters tall and his shadow is 2 meters long, how high is the school building, in meters?

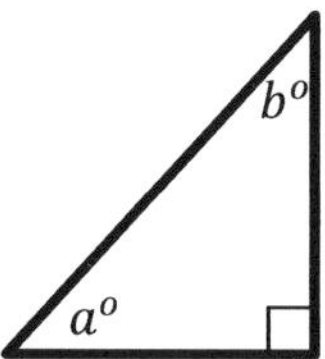

35. In the triangle above, the sine of $a°$ is 0.6. What is the sine of $b°$? (Round your answer to the nearest tenth.)

Questions 36 – 37 refer to the following information:

Compound interest is interest added to the principal of a deposit so that the added interest also earns interest from then on. A formula for calculating annual compound interest is as follows:

$$A = P\left(1 + \frac{r}{100}\right)^t$$

Where A is the amount of money, in dollars, generated after t years by a P dollars deposit in a bank account that pays an annual interest rate of $r\%$, compounded annually.

36. If Bill deposits $1,000 in his bank account today with an annual interest rate of 5% compounded annually, what will be the amount of money in his bank account after 5 years? (Round your answer to the nearest dollar and ignore the dollar sign when gridding your response.)

37. What is the least amount of years in whole number, that his money in the bank account will become more than or equal to $3000?

38. If $a + bi = \frac{1+i}{2-i}$, what is the value of $a + b =$?

SAT MATH MOCK TEST No. 2 ANSWER KEYS

Section 3									
1. A	2. D	3. B	4. D	5. B	6. D	7. D	8. C	9. A	10. C
11. B	12. D	13. A	14. C	15. C	16. 105	17. $\frac{5}{4}$	18. 3	19. 1	20. 8

Section 4									
1. D	2. D	3. B	4. D	5. B	6. C	7. A	8. B	9. D	10. B
11. A	12. C	13. D	14. C	15. B	16. D	17. A	18. A	19. D	20. A
21. A	22. D	23. D	24. C	25. B	26. C	27. D	28. C	29. C	30. D
31. 6	32. 36	33. 4.5	34. 9.6	35. 0.8	36. 1276	37. 23	38. $\frac{4}{5}$		

SECTION 3

1. *Answer: (a)*
   $(-)\times(-) \rightarrow$ *positive*
   $y - x = y + -x \rightarrow$ *positive*

2. *Answer: (d)*
   Compare both sides of the equation and find the corresponding terms.
   $x = 4$

3. *Answer: (b)*
   Set A(x) equal to 200.
   $2x - 90 = 250$
   $x = 170$

4. *Answer: (d)*
   $(3 \times 10^{-x})+(1 \times 10^{-x}) = 4 \times 10^{-x}$
   $4 \times 10^{-x} = \frac{4}{10^x}$

5. *Answer: (b)*
   $4x + 6x = 180°$ *and* $3y = 6x$
   $10x = 180$
   $x = 18°$
   $3y = 6x = 6 \times 18 = 108$
   $y = 36°$
   $2x + y = 36 + 36 = 72°$

6. *Answer: (d)*
   The value of the y coordinate is constant for a horizontal line.

7. *Answer: (d)*
   Because the equation is true for all values of x, the two expressions have the same coefficients for corresponding terms.
   $3k = 2, \quad k = \frac{2}{3}$

8. *Answer: (c)*
   $9m = 3^2 \times m^2 = m^{2x} \times m^2 = m^{(2x+2)}$

9. *Answer: (a)*
   Only answer a) presents a curve with the slope of its tangent line increasing.

10. *Answer: (c)*
    The ratio of the diameter of two circles is equal to the square root of their ratio of area.
    $\sqrt{3} : \sqrt{4} = \sqrt{3} : 2$

11. *Answer: (b)*
    $y = 2z + 4 = 2 \times 1 + 4 = 6$
    $x - y = 7, \quad x - 6 = 7, \quad x = 13$

12. *Answer: (d)*
    $a \times \frac{1}{4} \times 9 = 27$
    $a = 12$

13. *Answer: (a)*
    Plug x = 3 and a = 18 into the equation.
    $a = \frac{3}{5}xy, \quad 18 = \frac{3}{5} \times 3 \times y$
    $y = \frac{18 \times 5}{3 \times 3} = 10$

14. *Answer: (c)*
    $3x = a - 1$
    $6x = 2 \times (3x) = 2 \times (a - 1) = 2a - 2$
    $6x + 1 = 2a - 2 + 1 = 2a - 1$

15. *Answer: (c)*
There are no rules about how to arrange boys and girls, so (a) and (b) are incorrect.
If there is one girl at each end, then two boys must be adjacent. Therefore, (d) is wrong.
If the last two seated are girls, then two boys must be adjacent. (c) is correct.

16. *Answer: 105*
$3a - 15 = 300$
$a = 105$

17. *Answer:* $\frac{5}{4}$ *or* 1.25
Since the line is equally spaced between 0 and 1, A equals $\frac{2}{8}$ *and B equals* $\frac{6}{8}$.
$A - 2B = \frac{2}{8} - 2 \times \frac{6}{8} = -\frac{10}{8} = -\frac{5}{4}$
$|A - 2B| = \frac{5}{4}$

18. *Answer: 3*
The value of x where g(x) crosses the x-axis is the value of x where g(x) is equal to 0.
$0 = 4x - 12$
$x = 3$

19. *Answer: 1*
$6x + 2 - 4 = 5 - 4$
$6x - 2 = 1$

20. *Answer: 8*
Thousands digit: 1
Hundreds digit: 2
Units digit: 3
Tenths digit: 9
Hundredths digit: 8
Thousandths digit: 7

SECTION 4

1. *Answer: (d)*
$Total = 2.5 \times B + 0.6 \times S$

2. *Answer: (d)*
$Slope = \frac{Rise}{Run} = \frac{0-8}{k-(-3)} = -2$
$-2k = -2, \quad k = 1$

3. *Answer: (b)*
Translate "20 percent of x is 50" into an algebraic equation: $\frac{20}{100} \times x = 50$
$x = \frac{100 \times 50}{20} = 250$
"x percent of 40" $= 40 \times \frac{250}{100} = 100$

4. *Answer: (d)*
Adam has the 3rd shortest time listed.

5. *Answer: (b)*
$m\angle B = 180 - 92 - 44 = 44$
The bigger angle is always facing the bigger side.
$m\angle C > m\angle A = m\angle B$
$y > z = x$

6. *Answer: (c)*

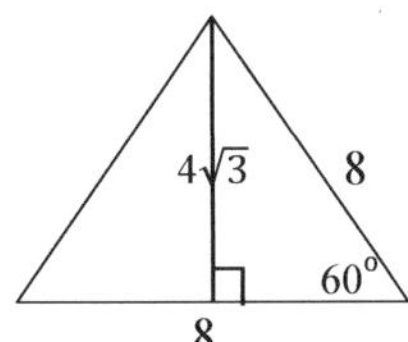

30-60-90 special right triangle
$\frac{1}{2} \times 8 \times 4\sqrt{3} = 16\sqrt{3}$

7. *Answer: (a)*
We can define the measures of the three angles to be x, 2x and 3x.
$2x + 3x + 4x = 180°$
$x = 20°$
The largest angle is $4x = 80°$

8. *Answer: (b)*
$\frac{3(3x)^4}{(3y)^2} = 3^2 \left(\frac{3x^4}{y^2}\right) = 9 \times z$

9. *Answer: (d)*
Square both sides of the equation.
$(\sqrt{x+1})^2 = (x - 2)^2$
$x + 1 = x^2 - 4x + 4$
$x = x^2 - 4x + 3$

10. *Answer: (b)*
From the graph, slope equals −1 and y-intercept is 1.
$m = -1, \quad b = 1$
$y = -2mx - b = 2x - 1$ *(with positive slope and negative y-intercept)*

11. *Answer: (a)*
Total Distance A Traveled = Rate × Time
= 15 miles/hour × 4 hours = 60 miles
Total Distance B Traveled
= 10 miles/hour × x hours = $\frac{1}{2}$ *× 60 miles = 30 miles*
$x = \frac{30 \text{ miles}}{10 \text{ miles/hour}} = 3$ *hours*

12. *Answer: (c)*
Watching TV for more than 3 hours a day includes those who answered with $3 \leqq x < 4$ and $4 \leqq x$, which make up 29% (14% + 15%) of those who answered.
Total Respondents = 1000 – 160 = 840 people
840 × 29% = 243 people

13. *Answer: (d)*
The positive leading coefficient of a quadratic function means the curve goes upwards; a positive constant c means y-intercept is positive. Only (d) meets all these conditions.

14. *Answer: (c)*
$$\frac{(Jupiter's\ Period)^2}{(Earth's\ Period)^2} = \frac{(5.2 \times Earth's\ Distance)^3}{(Earth's\ Distance)^3}$$
$$\frac{(Jupiter's\ Period)^2}{1^2} = \frac{(5.2)^3}{1^3}$$
$$Jupiter's\ Period = \sqrt{140.6} = 11.86\ Earth\ years$$

15. *Answer: (b)*
$$\frac{687}{365} = 1.88\ Earth\ years$$
$$\frac{1.88^2}{1^2} = \frac{(Mars'\ Distance)^3}{1^3}$$
$$\frac{Mars'Distance}{Earth's\ Distance} = \sqrt[3]{1.88^2} = 1.52$$

16. *Answer: (d)*
ΔOAB is an isosceles Δ.
$2 \times x + 30 = 180$
$x = \frac{1}{2}(180 - 30) = 75$

17. *Answer: (a)*
Use the same ratio number to compare
Pear : Apple = 3 : 5 = 9 : 15
Pear: Orange = 3 : 5 = 15 : 25
Apple : Orange = 9 : 25

18. *Answer: (a)*
Since the two triangles share an angle with the same measure (vertical angles), the sum of their other two angles must be equal.
$a + 40 = b + 50$
$a - b = 10$

19. *Answer: (d)*
The smaller the coefficient of x^2, the smaller the y-coordinate will be for a point at the same x-coordinate. Therefore, the new graph will be wider. Plug the two functions into your calculator for an easy way to solve this problem.

20. *Answer: (a)*
A line with a positive slope increases from left to right. (a) has a positive slope and a negative y-intercept.

21. *Answer: (a)*
1st place will have $\frac{6}{6+2+1} \times 18000 = \$12{,}000$

22. *Answer: (d)*
The measles vaccination percentage in California is less than 90%.
The number of 20 to 36 month-olds who had received measles vaccination in California need to be less than 1.41 million × 0.9 = 1.269 million.

23. *Answer: (d)*
0.155 million × 0.86 = .1333 million = 133,300

24. *Answer: (c)*
This is a ratio problem.
$\frac{80}{5} = \frac{x}{6}$ *(cross multiply)*
$x = 96$

25. *Answer: (b)*
$\frac{1}{5}\ of\ 80 \rightarrow \frac{1}{5} \times 80 = 16$
$16 = \frac{x}{100} \times 200$
$16 = 2x, \quad x = 8$
Therefore, $\frac{1}{5} \times 80 = 16$*, which is equal to* $200 \times 8\% = 16$

26. *Answer: (c)*
This can be translated into 0.4 × 0.4 × A = 64.96.
$A = \frac{64.96}{0.4 \times 0.4} = 406$

27. *Answer: (d)*
$3x = \frac{2x+y+2y}{3}$
$9x = 2x + 3y$
$7x = 3y$
$y = \frac{7x}{3}$

28. *Answer: (c)*
$h(1) = f(2 \times 1 + 1) = f(3) = 6$

29. *Answer: (c)*
In April, the price of the stock is $x \times (1 - 0.1) \times (1 + 0.3) \times (1 - 0.2) \times (1 + 0.25) = 1.17x$

30. *Answer: (d)*
The LCM of 3, 4, 5 and 6 is 360. The multiple of 360 that is three–digit value is 360 and 720.
The largest possible value for N *is 360 × 2 + 2 = 722*

31. *Answer: 6*
Area of OABC = Base × Height = (x + 1) × (x) = 42
$x^2 + x - 42 = 0$
$(x + 7)(x - 6) = 0$
x = 6 or x = −7(x must be positive)

32. *Answer: 36*
Plug h and v into the function.
$20 + \frac{32^2}{64} = 36$ *feet*

33. *Answer: 45*
Total : Yellow = (3 + 4 + 8) : 8 = 15 : 8
There are 24 yellow marbles.
15 : 8 = Total Marbles : 24
8 × Total Marbles = 24 × 15
Total Marbles = 45

34. *Answer: 9.6*
Let the height of the school building be x.
The two triangles are similar, therefore their corresponding sides are proportional.
$\frac{2}{10 + 2} = \frac{1.6}{x}$
$x = 9.6\ m$

35. *Answer: 0.8*

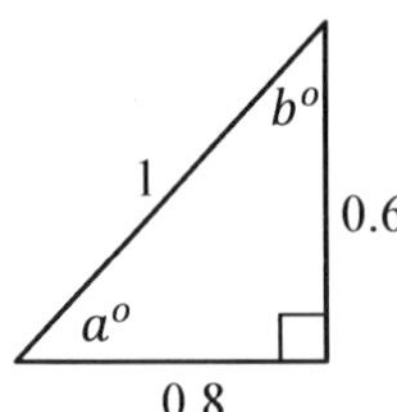

$\sin(b^\circ) = \frac{0.8}{1} = 0.8$
or
$a^o + b^o = 90^o$
$sin(b^o) = cos(a^0) = \sqrt{1 - sin(a^o)^2} =$
$\sqrt{1 - 0.6^2} = 0.8$

36. *Answer: 1276*
$A = 1{,}000(1 + 0.05)^5 = \$1{,}276$

37. *Answer: 23*
$1{,}000(1 + 0.05)^t \geq 3{,}000$
$1.05^t \geq 3$
With calculator, the first whole number value of t that satisfies above inequality is 23.
Therefore, the fewest number of years required for him to accrue $3000 is 23.

38. *Answer:* $\frac{4}{5}$ *or* 0.8
Rationalize the denominator.
$\frac{2+i}{2+i} \times \frac{1+i}{2-i} = \frac{1+3i}{1+4} = \frac{1}{5} + \frac{3}{5}i$
$a + bi = \frac{1}{5} + \frac{3}{5}i$
$a = \frac{1}{5}\ ; \quad b = +\frac{3}{5}$
$a + b = \frac{4}{5} = 0.8$

SAT Math Mock Test No. 3

SECTION 3 

Math Test — NO Calculator 25 MINUTES, 20 QUESTIONS

Directions:

For questions 1-15, solve each problem, choose the best answer from the choices provided, and fill in the corresponding circle on your answer sheet. **For questions 16-20**, solve the problem and enter your answer in the grid on the answer sheet. Please refer to the directions before question 16 on how to enter your answers in the grid. You may use any available space in your test booklet for scratch work.

Notes:

1. **No calculator** is allowed for this section. All numbers used are real numbers.
2. Figures that accompany problems in this test are intended to provide information useful in solving the problems. They are drawn as accurately as possible EXCEPT when it is stated in a specific problem that the figure is not drawn to scale. All figures lie in a plane unless otherwise indicated.
3. Unless otherwise specified, the domain of any function *f(x)* assumed to be the set of all real numbers *x* for which *f(x)* is a real number.

References:

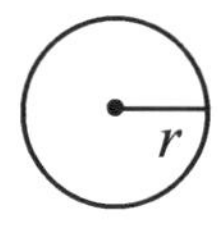

$A = \pi r^2$, $C = 2\pi r$ | $A = lw$ | $A = \frac{1}{2}bh$ | $V = lwh$ | $V = \pi r^2 h$ | $c^2 = a^2 + b^2$ | **Special Right Triangles** (s, s, $s\sqrt{2}$, 45°, 45°; s, $s\sqrt{3}$, $2s$, 30°, 60°)

The number of degrees of arc in a circle is 360; the number of radians of arc in a circle is 2π.
The sum of the degree measures of the angles in a triangle is 180.

1. If *a, b,* and *c* are consecutive positive integers such that $a < b < c$ and $a + b + c$ is a multiple of 6, then which of the following must be true?
   a) a is an even integer
   b) b is an odd integer
   c) c is a multiple of 3
   d) a is an odd integer

2. If $c = 3$, which of the following is the equivalent to $cx2 + cx + c$?
   a) $(3x^3 + 5)$
   b) $3(x + 1)^2$
   c) $(x^2 + 1)$
   d) $3(x^2 + x + 1)$

3. If $a^2 + 11 = b^3$, and $3a = 12$, which of the following could be the value of *b*?
   a) 3
   b) 2
   c) 0
   d) −3

4. Mr. Jones has taught math for 5 years less than half as long as Miss Carter. If Mr. Jones has taught Math for m years, which of the following indicates the number of years that Miss Carter has taught?
   a) $2m + 5$
   b) $m + 5$
   c) $2m - 5$
   d) $2(m + 5)$

5. A litter of milk can fill up 3 large cups or 5 small cups. If there are 6 large cups and 15 small cups, about how many litters of milk will be needed to fill up all the cups?
   a) 3
   b) 4
   c) 5
   d) 6

6. If w, x and y are positive integers such that the value of $x + y$ is even and the value of $(x + y)^2 + 4x + w$ is odd, which of the following must be true?
   a) y is even.
   b) w is odd.
   c) If w is even, then x is even.
   d) If w is even, then x is odd.

7. Let <I, J> be defined as any integer greater than I but less than J, such as <–3, 3> = { –2, –1, 0, 1, 2, }. Which of the following has the same elements as the intersection of <–1, 4> and <1, 6>?
   a) <–2, 2>
   b) <–1, 3>
   c) <–3, 2>
   d) <1, 4>

8. If the lengths of the sides of a certain triangle are x, y, and z, which of the following statements could be true?
   a) $x = y + z + 1$
   b) $x = y - z - 1$
   c) $x = z + \frac{1}{2}y$
   d) $x = y - 2z$

9. The area of circle A is 4 times the area of circle B. What is the ratio of the diameter of circle A to the diameter of circle B?
   a) 2 : 1
   b) 3 : 1
   c) 4 : 1
   d) 1 : 2

10. Which of the following CANNOT affect the value of the median in a set of nonzero unique numbers with more than two elements?
   a) Decrease each number by 3
   b) Increase the largest number only
   c) Increase the smallest number only
   d) Decrease the largest number only

11. If $0 < xy$ and $y > 0$, which of the following statements must be true?

    $x < 0$
    $x < y$
    $x > 0$

   a) I only
   b) III only
   c) I and II
   d) II and III

12. In the xy-coordinate plane, line m is the reflection of line l about the y-axis. Which of the following could be the sum of the slopes of lines m and l?
    a) 1
    b) −1
    c) 0
    d) $\frac{1}{2}$

13. On the xy-plane, what is the equation of the line that is a reflection the line $y = -2x - 1$ across the y-axis?
    a) $y = -2x + 1$
    b) $y = -2x - 1$
    c) $y = 2x - 1$
    d) $y = 2x \div 1$

14. Ken, Justin, and Tiff have read a total of 100 books from the library. Justin read 3 times as many books as Ken and Tiff read 2 times as many as Justin. How many books did Ken read?
    a) 12
    b) 10
    c) 9
    d) 8

15. If $x^2 - y^2 = 24$, and $x - y = 4$, what is the value of $x + 2y$?
    a) 1
    b) 3
    c) 5
    d) 7

Directions:

For questions 16-20, solve the problem and enter your answer in the grid, as described below, on the answer sheet.

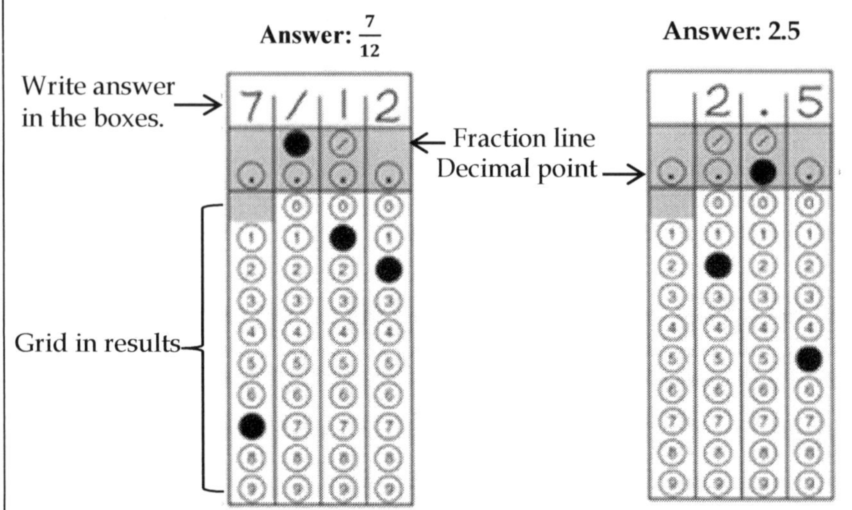

Answer: 201
Either position is correct.

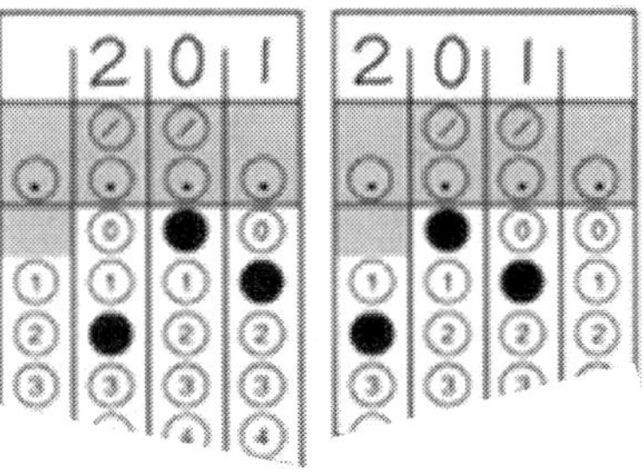

Note: You may start your answers in any column, space permitting. Columns not needed should be left blank.

- Mark no more than one circle in any column.
- Because the answer sheet will be machine-scored. **You will receive credit only if the circles are filled in correctly.**
- Although not required, it is suggested that you write your answer in the boxes at the top of the columns to help you fill in the circles accurately.
- Some problems may have more than one correct answer. In such case, grid only one answer.
- No question has a negative answer.
- **Mixed numbers** such as $3\frac{1}{2}$ must be gridded as 3.5 or $\frac{7}{2}$. (If 3 1 / 2 is gridded, it will be interpreted as $\frac{31}{2}$, not $3\frac{1}{2}$.)

- **Decimal Answer**: If you obtain a decimal answer with more digits than the grid can accommodate, it may be either rounded or truncated, but it must fill the entire grid. The acceptable ways to grid $\frac{2}{3}$ are:

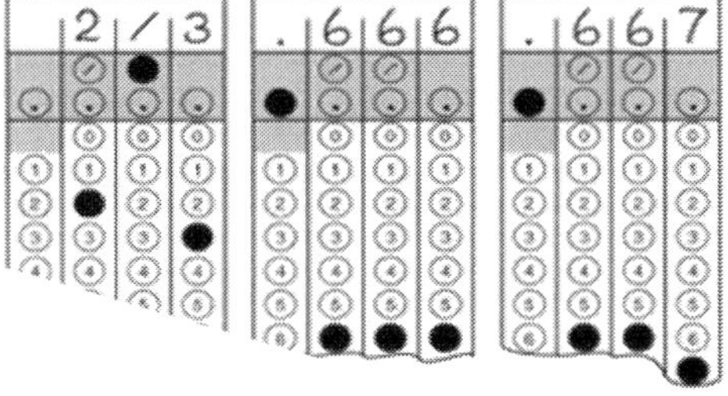

16. For every 20 cars sold by a dealer, 6 of them were red. What is the probability, in fraction, that a car sold that is selected at random would be red?

17. When twice a number is reduced by 10, the result is 200. What is the number?

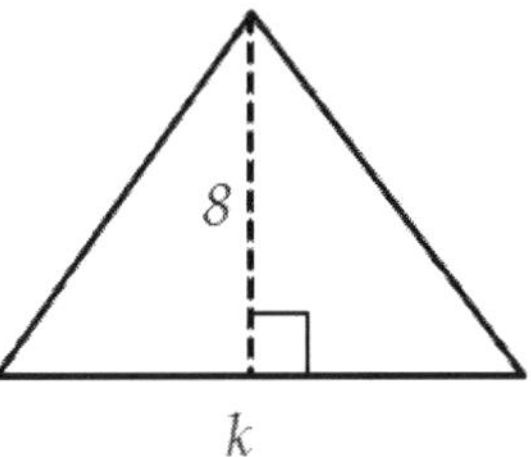

18. In the figure above, if the area of the triangle is 40, what is the value of k?

19. For every 15 cars sold by a dealer, 3 of them were red. What is the probability that a car sold that is selected at random would be red?

20. An isosceles triangle has one side of length 20 and one side of length 30. What is the largest possible value that the perimeter of the triangle could be?

SECTION 4

Math Test – Calculator **55 MINUTES, 38 QUESTIONS**

Directions:

For questions 1-30, solve each problem, choose the best answer from the choices provided, and fill in the corresponding circle on your answer sheet. **For questions 31-38**, solve the problem and enter your answer in the grid on the answer sheet. Please refer to the directions before question 31 on how to enter your answers in the grid. You may use any available space in your test booklet for scratch work.

Notes:

1. Acceptable calculators are allowed for this section. All numbers used are real numbers.
2. Figures that accompany problems in this test are intended to provide information useful in solving the problems. They are drawn as accurately as possible EXCEPT when it is stated in a specific problem that the figure is not drawn to scale. All figures lie in a plane unless otherwise indicated.
3. Unless otherwise specified, the domain of any function *f(x)* assumed to be the set of all real numbers *x* for which *f(x)* is a real number.

References:

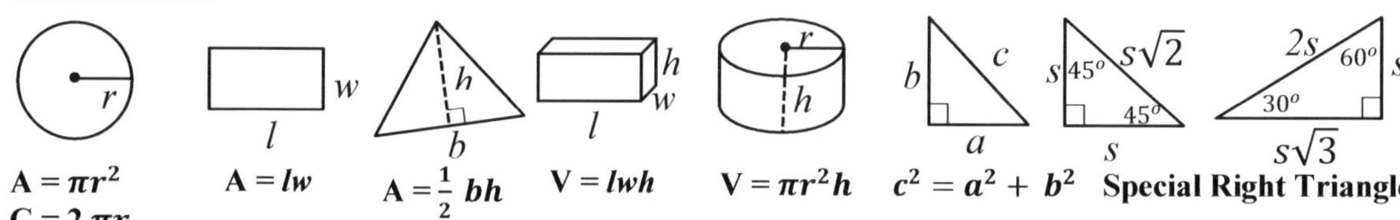

$A = \pi r^2$ $C = 2\pi r$ $A = lw$ $A = \frac{1}{2}bh$ $V = lwh$ $V = \pi r^2 h$ $c^2 = a^2 + b^2$ **Special Right Triangles**

The number of degrees of arc in a circle is 360; the number of radians of arc in a circle is 2π. The sum of the degree measures of the angles in a triangle is 180.

1. A parking lot charges \$6.00 maintenance fee per day to use its parking space. In addition, there is a charge of \$2.5 per hour. Which of the following represents the total charge, in dollars, to park a car in the parking lot for m hours in one day?
   a) $6m + 2.5$
   b) $(6 + 2.5)m$
   c) $6 + 2.5 + m$
   d) $6 + 2.5m$

2. If x, y and z represent consecutive positive odd integers. Which of the following is true?
   a) $x + y + z$ = even integer
   b) $x + y$ = odd integer
   c) $\frac{z-x}{2} = 2$
   d) $\frac{x+y+z}{2}$ is an even integer

3. If $x = \frac{2}{3}yz$, what is the value of y when $z = 6$ and $x = 20$?
   a) 2
   b) 4
   c) 5
   d) 10

4. Worker A can install a toy in 12 minutes. Worker B takes 10 minutes to install the same toy. In 6 hours, how many more

toys can be installed by worker B than by worker A?

a) 4
b) 5
c) 6
d) 8

5. If $x = \frac{1}{5}yz$, what is the value of y when $z = 15$ and $x = 60$?

a) 8
b) 10
c) 20
d) 25

Add 5 to x;
Divide this sum by 3;
Subtract 1 from this quotient;
Square this difference

6. Which of the following results after performing the operations above?

$\frac{x+1}{3}$
b) $\frac{x-2}{9}$
c) $\frac{(x+2)^2}{3}$
d) $\frac{(x+2)^2}{9}$

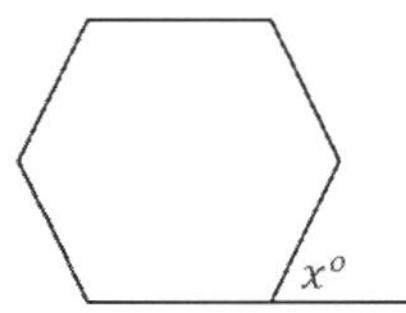

7. In the regular hexagon shown above, what is the value of x?

a) 120
b) 108
c) 72
d) 60

8. Bob needs four 36″ pieces of duct tape to protect each window in his house during hurricane season. There are 12 windows in the house. Bob had an m-foot roll of duct tape when he started. If no tape was wasted, which of the following represents the number of feet of duct tape left after he finished taping all of his windows?

a) $m - 76$
b) $m - 144$
c) $m - 216$
d) $m - 12 \times 144$

9. Kim spent 3 hours installing 600 square feet of solar panels. At this rate, how many hours will she require to install 4800 square feet of solar panels?

a) 15
b) 18
c) 24
d) 25

10. The square of the sum of x and 2 is equal to y. If y is the square of the difference of x and 3, what is the value of x?

a) 2
b) $\frac{1}{2}$
c) $-\frac{1}{2}$
d) $-\frac{1}{4}$

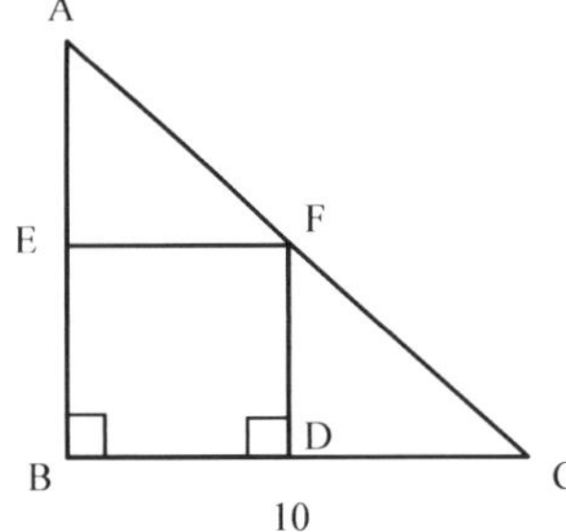

11. In isosceles right triangle ΔABC above, EF∥BC and length of $\overline{AF}$ is half of the length of $\overline{AC}$. What is the area of the rectangular region?

a) 16
b) 25
c) 36
d) 64

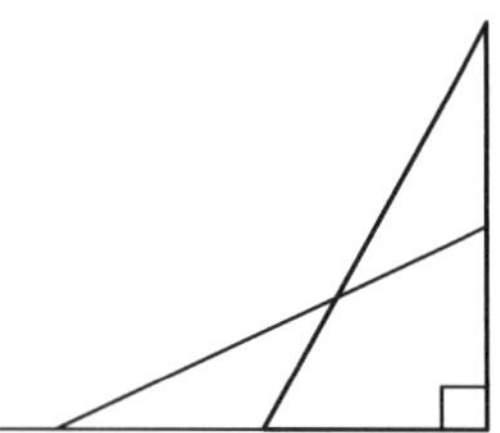

12. In the figure above, a 26-foot-long ladder is placed against a building which is perpendicular to the ground. After the ladder slides down 14 feet vertically, the bottom of the ladder is now 24 feet away from the base of the building, what is the original distance of the bottom of the ladder from the base of the building, in feet?
    a) 10
    b) 13
    c) 20
    d) 24

13. If a and b are both positive integers and $\frac{a}{3} = \frac{8}{b}$, how many pairs of (a, b) is possible?
    a) 12
    b) 10
    c) 8
    d) 6

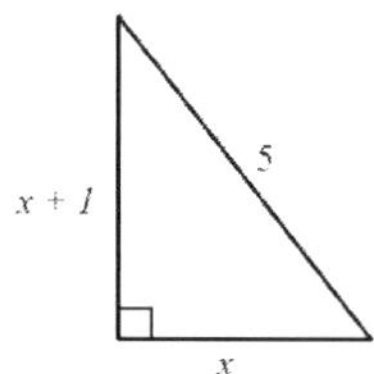

14. The figure above is a right triangle. If $x > 0$, what is the value of x?
    a) 2
    b) 3
    c) 3.5
    d) 4

15. According to the graph below, how many employees have salary less than or equal to $60,000?

    a) 300
    b) 550
    c) 250
    d) 100

16. On a certain test, the highest possible score is 100 and the lowest is 0. If the average score of 5 students is 86, what is the lowest possible score of the fifth student?
    a) 0
    b) 10
    c) 20
    d) 30

Questions 17 – 18 refer to the following information:

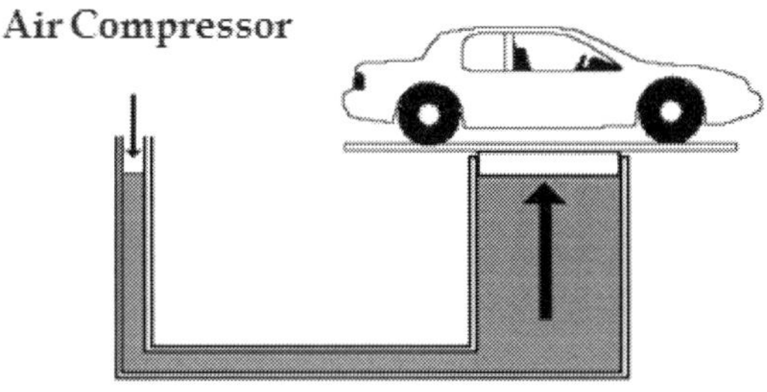

The hydraulics system in the figure above uses liquids to create pressure and lift heavy objects. The pressure from one end of the hydraulics system (the air compressor) will always be equal to the pressure on the other end (the car). Pressure is defined as force divided by the cross sectional area:

$$Pressure = \frac{Force}{Area}$$

17. The cross sectional area of the cylinder underneath the car is 600 cm^2 and the cross sectional area of the cylinder at the end with the air compressor is 6 cm^2. If a car is lifted by a force of 2,400 kg, what force should be exerted by the air compressor?
   a) 32 kg
   b) 28 kg
   c) 24 kg
   d) 20 kg

18. In order to lift a car by a force of 2,400kg, a 3 kg force is applied at the air compressor end. Find the ratio of the radii of the cylinder at the car end to the air compressor end.
   a) 28.3
   b) 24.5
   c) 9.26
   d) 5.3

19. If the area of an equilateral triangle equals the area of a square multiplied by$\sqrt{3}$, what is the ratio of the length of a side of the triangle to the length of a side of the square?
   a) 2 : 1
   b) 2 : 3
   c) 1 : 2
   d) 4 : 3

20. If $x \neq 0$ and x is inversely proportional to y, which of the following is directly proportional to $\frac{1}{x^2}$?
   a) $\frac{1}{y^2}$
   b) $-\frac{1}{y^2}$
   c) y^2
   d) $-y^2$

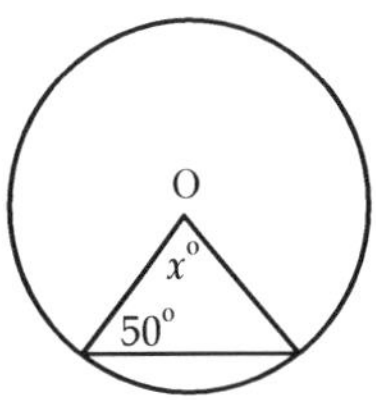

21. In the figure above, point O is the center of the circle. Whit is the value of x?
   a) 40
   b) 50
   c) 60
   d) 80

22. The perimeter of square X is 4 times the perimeter of square Y. If the area of square Y is 25, then what is the length of the side of square X?
   a) 10
   b) 20
   c) 24
   d) 25

23. If 2,500 = 100(2x + 5), then x =
   a) $\frac{1}{10}$
   b) 1
   c) 10
   d) 100

24. How many different positive three-digit integers begin with an even digit and end with an odd digit?
   a) 100
   b) 120
   c) 200
   d) 120

25. Given the set of integers that are greater than 0 and less than 1000, how many of the integers are multiples of either 2 or 5?
   a) 900
   b) 898
   c) 600
   d) 599

26. The daily cost of phone services in a business building is $.25 per hour from 9 AM through 9 PM, and $.06 per hour at any other hours of the day. Which of the following expressions represents the cost, in dollars, of the phone service starting from 9 AM and lasting for 20 hours a day over 30 days?
    a) $30 \times 11(.25) + 30(20 - 11)(.6)$
    b) $30 \times 12(.25) + 30(20 - 12)(.6)$
    c) $30 \times 13(.25) + 30(20 - 13)$
    d) $30 \times 12(.25) + 30(.6)$

Questions 27 – 28 refer to the following information:

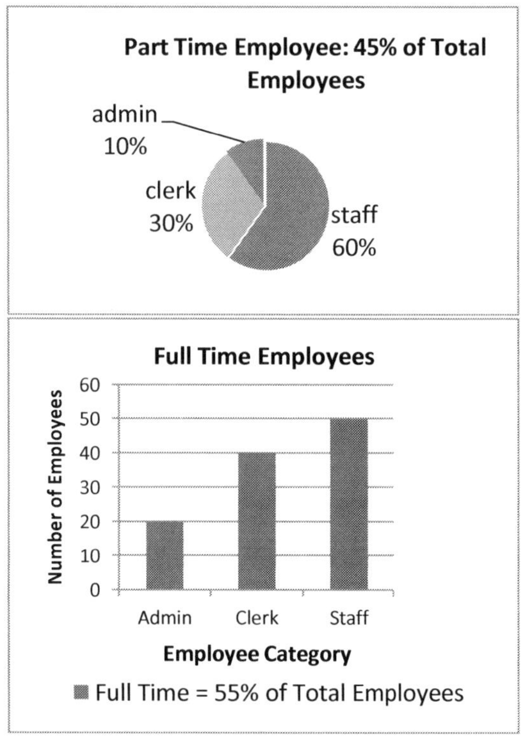

27. According to the graphs above, the total number of full-time employees is how many more than the total number of part-time employees at Oak Town High School?
    a) 20
    b) 40
    c) 50
    d) 60

28. According to the graphs above, how many part-time staff members are at Oak Town High School?
    a) 80
    b) 72
    c) 64
    d) 54

29. The nth term of a sequence has a value of $3n - 1$. The 290th term is how much greater than the 243th term?
    a) 150
    b) 147
    c) 144
    d) 141

30. For $b > a$, the product of 4 and $(b - a)$ is equal to the average of a and b. If b is 63, what is a?
    a) 42
    b) 45
    c) 49
    d) 50

Directions:

For questions 31-38, solve the problem and enter your answer in the grid, as described below, on the answer sheet.

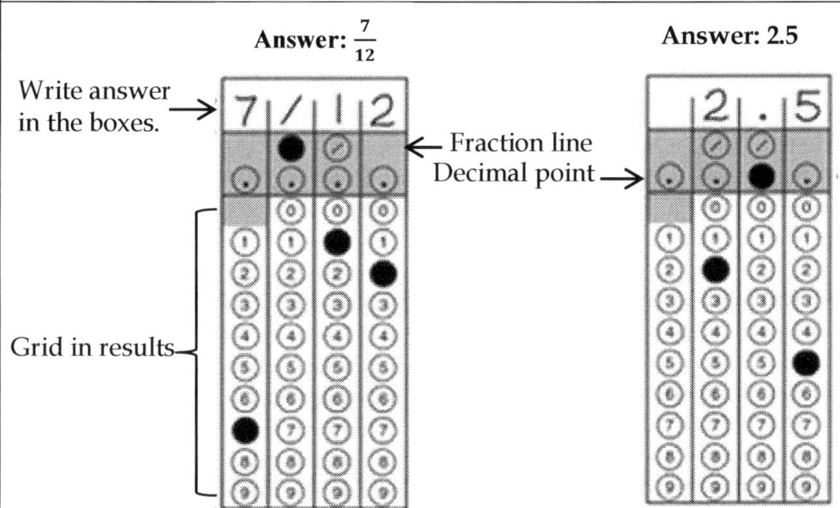

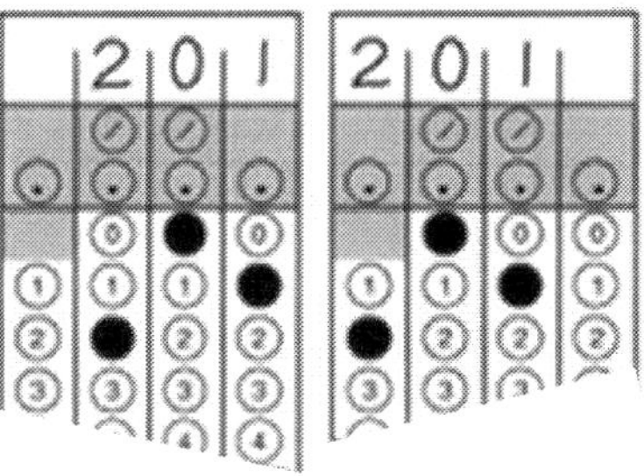

Note: You may start your answers in any column, space permitting. Columns not needed should be left blank.

- Mark no more than one circle in any column.
- Because the answer sheet will be machine-scored. **You will receive credit only if the circles are filled in correctly.**
- Although not required, it is suggested that you write your answer in the boxes at the top of the columns to help you fill in the circles accurately.
- Some problems may have more than one correct answer. In such case, grid only one answer.
- No question has a negative answer.
- **Mixed numbers** such as $3\frac{1}{2}$ must be gridded as 3.5 or $\frac{7}{2}$. (If 31/2 is gridded, it will be interpreted as $\frac{31}{2}$, not $3\frac{1}{2}$.)
- **Decimal Answer**: If you obtain a decimal answer with more digits than the grid can accommodate, it may be either rounded or truncated, but it must fill the entire grid. The acceptable ways to grid $\frac{2}{3}$ are:

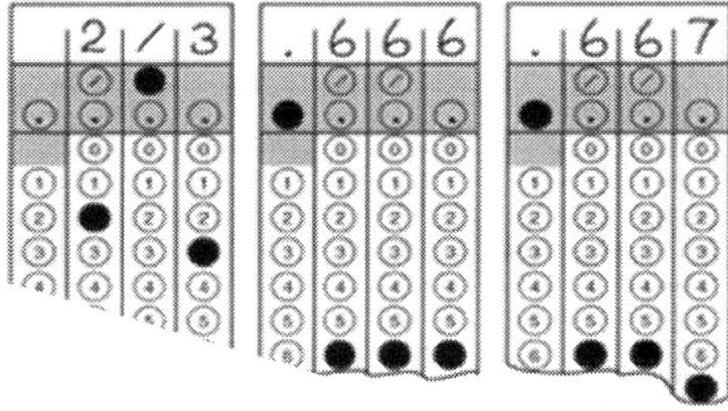

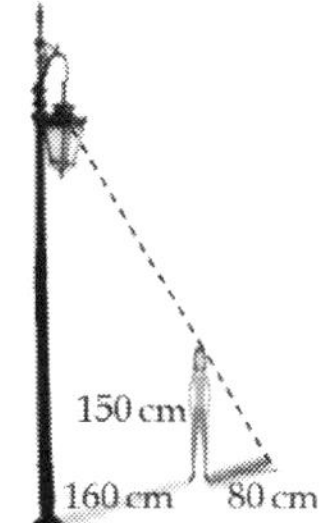

31. A girl who is 150 centimeters tall stands 160 centimeters away from a lamp post at night. If her shadow is 80 centimeters long, how high, in centimeters, is the lamp post?

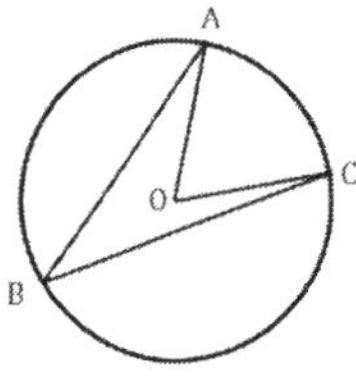

32. In the figure above, if $\widehat{AC}$ has arc length equal to $\frac{1}{5}$ of the circumference of the circle, what is the value of $m\angle ABC$ in degrees?

33. A circle with center at coordinates (4, 5) touches the x-axis at only one point. What is the radius of the circle?

34. A smartphone costs $15 more than five times the cost of a basic cell phone. If the smartphone and the basic phone together cost $615, how much more does the smartphone cost than the basic phone?

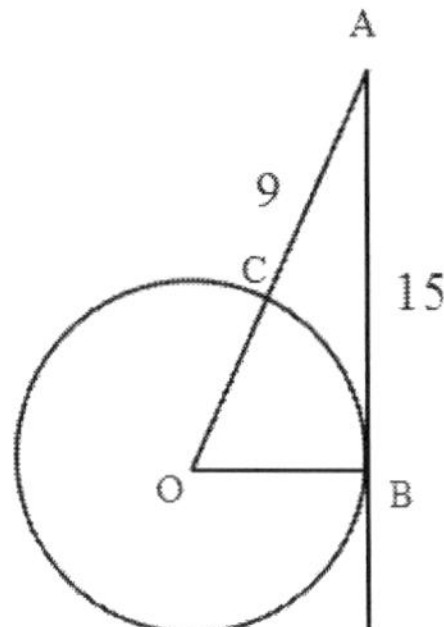

35. In the figure above, AB is tangent to circle O, $\overline{AB} = 15$, and $\overline{AC} = 9$. What is the area of ΔOAB?

Questions 36 – 37 refer to the following information:

Planetary Data of Solar System

Planet	*Distance from the Sun (billions meters)*	*Orbital Period (Earth years)*
Mercury	*57.9*	*0.241*
Earth	*149.6*	*1.0*
Mars	*227.9*	*1.88*
Saturn	*1,427*	*29.5*
Uranus	*2,870*	*84.0*
Neptune	*Y*	*165*
Planet X	*30,000*	*X*

The chart above shows our Solar System's planetary data applied to the Kepler's Third Law, which states that the square of the period of any planet is proportional to the cube of its distance from the Sun. For any planets in the Solar System, the square of the orbital period divided by the cube of its distance from the Sun should be a constant.

36. If Neptune has a period of 165 Earth years, find its distance from the Sun, in billions of meters? (Round your answer to the nearest whole number.)

37. If Planet X is 30,000 billion meters away from the Sun, what is its orbital period, in Earth years? (Round your answer to the nearest whole number.)

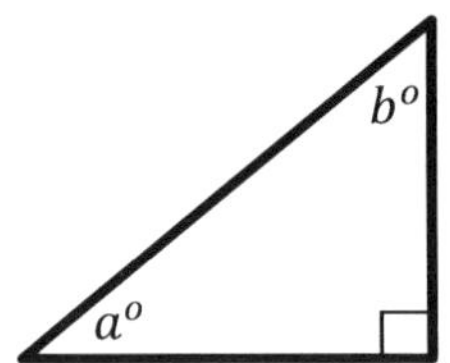

38. In the triangle above, the sine of $a°$ is 0.6. What is the tangent of $b°$? (Round your answer to the nearest hundredth.)

SAT MATH MOCK TEST No. 3 ANSWER KEYS

Section 3									
1. D	2. D	3. A	4. D	5. C	6. B	7. D	8. C	9. A	10. B
11. B	12. C	13. C	14. B	15. D	16. 0.3	17. 105	18. 10	19. 0.2	20. 80

Section 4									
1. D	2. C	3. C	4. C	5. C	6. D	7. D	8. B	9. C	10. B
11. B	12. A	13. C	14. B	15. B	16. D	17. C	18. A	19. A	20. C
21. D	22. B	23. C	24. C	25. D	26. B	27. A	28. D	29. D	30. C
31. 450	32. 36	33. 5	34. 415	35. 60	36. 4500	37. 2840	38. 1.33		

SECTION 3

1. *Answer: (d)*
   If a, b and c are consecutive positive integers, then $b = a + 1$ *and* $c = a + 2$
   $a + b + c = a + a + 1 + a + 2 = 3a + 3 = 6n$
   $a + 1 = 2n$
   Since 2n is an even integer, a is an odd integer.

2. *Answer: (d)*
   Replace c with value 3.
   $3x^2 + 3x + 3 = 3(x^2 + x + 1)$

3. *Answer: (a)*
   $3a = 12, \ a = 4$
   $4^2 + 11 = b^3$
   $27 = b^3 = 3^3$
   $b = 3$

4. *Answer: (d)*
   If Miss Carter has taught x years, then
   $m = \frac{1}{2}x - 5.$
   $m + 5 = \frac{1}{2}x$
   $x = 2(m + 5)$

5. *Answer: (c)*
   6 large cups need 2 litters and15 small cups need 3 litters.
   The amount of milk needed:
   $3 + 2 = 5$ *litters*

6. *Answer: (b)*
   Since $(x + y)$ *is even,* $(x+y)^2 + 4x$ *is an even integer.*
   If $(x + y)^2 + 4x + w$ *is odd, then w must be odd.*

7. *Answer: (d)*
   Intersection of $<-1, 4>$ *and* $<1, 6> = \{0, 1, 2, 3\} \cap \{2, 3, 4, 5\} = \{2, 3\}$
   (d) $<1, 4>$ *has the same elements of {2, 3}.*

8. *Answer: (c)*
   $y - z < x < y + z$
   Only (c) meets the above conditions.

9. *Answer: (a)*
   The ratio of the diameter of two circles is the square root of the ratio of their areas.
   Ratio $= \sqrt{4} : \sqrt{1} = 2 : 1$

10. *Answer: (b)*
    The median of an odd-numbered set is the number in the middle when all numbers in the set have been sorted in numerical order. In an even-numbered set, it is the average of the two middle elements.
    We can change the median by:
    Changing the value of the median
    Changing order of numbers so that we have a new median
    Choices (a) change all values so the median will be changed. Choice (c) and (d) could result in a new median if the number changed becomes the new median. Choice (b) increases the element that is already the largest, and we know that there are more than 2 elements, so the median does not get changed.

11. *Answer: (b)*
    $xy > 0 \rightarrow$ *both x and y must have the same sign.*
    (Both are positive or both are negative.)
    If $y > 0$, *then* $x > 0$.

12. *Answer: (c)*
    The reflection about y-axis will change all negative slopes to their positives and vice versa. Therefore, the sum of any such pairs of slopes must be zero.

13. *Answer: (c)*
A reflection across the y-axis flips all y-coordinates from x to –x and keeps the y-coordinates unchanged.
$y = -2(-x) - 1$
$y = 2x - 1$

14. *Answer: (b)*
Let k be the number of books Ken read, j be the number of books Justin read, and t be the number of books Tiff read.
$j = 3k$
$t = 3j = 2(3k) = 6k$
Given that $k + j + t = 100$
Substitute for j and t:
$k + 3k + 6k = 100$
$10k = 100$
$k = 10$

15. *Answer: (d)*
$x^2 - y^2 = (x - y)(x + y)$
$4(x + y) = 24,$
$x + y = 6$
$x - y = 4$
Solve above system equations:
$x = 5$ *and* $y = 1$
$x + 2y = 7$

16. *Answer:* $\frac{3}{10}$ *or* .3
$\frac{6}{20} = \frac{3}{10}$

17. *Answer: 105*
$2a - 10 = 200$
$a = 105$

18. *Answer: 10*
$40 = \frac{1}{2} \times 8 \times k$
$k = 10$

19. *Answer:* $\frac{1}{5}$ *or* .2
$\frac{3}{15} = \frac{1}{5}$

20. *Answer: 80*
An isosceles triangle must have two sides with the same length. The third side has a length of either 20 or 30.
The largest perimeter can be 20 + 30 + 30 = 80.

SECTION 4

1. *Answer: (d)*
Parking m hours costs \$2.5 × m plus \$6 maintenance fee per day, so the total charge would be 6 + 2.5m.

2. *Answer: (c)*
Consecutive positive odd integers can be written in the form 2n+1, 2n+3, 2n+5
$x=2n+1$
$y=2n+3$
$z=2n+5$
$x + y = 4n + 4$ *(even)*
$x + y + z = 6n + 9$ *(odd)*
$\frac{z-x}{2} = 2$
$z - y = 2$
$\frac{x+y+z}{2} = \frac{6n+9}{2} = 3n + \frac{9}{2}$
$\frac{x+y}{2} = \frac{2n+1+2n+3}{2} = 2n+2$ *(even)*
Shortcuts: Pick easy numbers to plug in.
Let $x = 1$, $y = 3$, $z = 5$, *then*
$\frac{z-x}{2} = 2$

3. *Answer: (c)*
If $x = 20$ *and* $z = 6$, *then* $20 = \frac{2}{3}(y)(6)$.
$4y = 20$
$y = 5$

4. *Answer: (c)*
Worker A can finish $6 \times \frac{60}{12} = 30$ *toys in 6 hours.*
Worker B can finish $6 \times \frac{60}{10} = 36$ *toys in 6 hours.*
36 – 30 = 6 toys

5. *Answer: (c)*
If $x = 60$ *and* $z = 15$, *then* $60 = \frac{1}{5}(y)(15)$.
$60 = 3y$
$y = 20$

6. *Answer: (d)*
Add 5 to x → $x + 5$
Divide the sum by 3 → $\frac{(x+5)}{3}$
Subtract 1 from the quotient → $\frac{x+5}{3} - 1 = \frac{x+2}{3}$
Square the difference → $(\frac{x+2}{3})^2 = \frac{(x+2)^2}{9}$

7. *Answer: (d)*
The sum of the interior angles of a regular hexagon is $\frac{(6-2) \times 180}{6} = 120^o$.
$x = 180 - 120 = 60$

8. *Answer: (b)*
Every window needs 4 pieces of tape and each piece of tape is 36 inches long, so $36 \times 4 = 144$ *inches needed for each window.*
Twelve windows, in total, would need
12×144 *inches of tape.*
12 × 144 inches = 144 feet
(m – 144) feet left after the use.

9. *Answer: (c)*
$\frac{3\ hours}{600\ sq\ ft} = \frac{x\ hours}{4800\ sq\ ft}$
$x = \frac{3 \times 4800}{600} = 24$ *hours*

10. *Answer: (b)*
$(x + 2)^2 = y$ and $y = (x - 3)^2$
$(x + 2)^2 = (x - 3)^2$
$x^2 + 4x + 4 = x^2 - 6x + 9$
$10x = 5,\ x = \frac{1}{2}$

11. *Answer: (b)*
AB = BC
$EF = BD = \frac{1}{2} BC = 5$
$BE = \frac{1}{2} AB = 5$
Area = 5 × 5 = 25

12. *Answer: (a)*
After slipping, the height becomes $\sqrt{26^2 - 24^2} = 10$.
Before slipping, the height was
10 + 14 = 24.
The bottom of the ladder was originally
$\sqrt{26^2 - 24^2} = 10$ *feet away from the base.*

13. *Answer: (c)*
$\frac{a}{3} = \frac{8}{b}$
$ab = 24$
The number of possible pairs of (a, b) is equal to the number of factors of 24.
$24 = 3^1 \times 2^3$
24 has (1 + 1) × (3 + 1) = 8 factors.

14. *Answer: (b)*
Use the Pythagorean theorem.
$x^2 + (x + 1)^2 = 5^2$
$x^2 + x^2 + 2x + 1 = 25$
$2x^2 + 2x = 24$
$x^2 + x = 12$
$(x + 4)(x - 3) = 0$
$x = 3$

15. *Answer: (b)*
According to the bar graph, there are 100 + 150 + 300 =550 employees with a salary of $60,000 or less.

16. *Answer: (d)*
The lowest possible score is equal to the lowest score a student can get if each of other four students got the highest possible score (otherwise we can always increase another student's score and decrease the lowest score). Thus, each of other four students must get 100.
Total Score = 5 × 86 = 430
Lowest Possible Score = 430 – 400 = 30

17. *Answer: (c)*
$\frac{Force_1}{Area_1} = \frac{Force_2}{Area_2}$
$\frac{2400}{600} = \frac{x}{6}$
$x = 24\ kg$

18. *Answer: (a)*
$\frac{Force_1}{Area_1} = \frac{Force_2}{Area_2}$
$\frac{2400}{\pi r_1^2} = \frac{3}{\pi r_2^2}$
$\frac{r_1}{r_2} = \sqrt{\left(\frac{2400}{3}\right)} = 28.3$

19. *Answer: (a)*
Let the length of the side of the triangle be x and the length of the side of the square be y.
Area of an equilateral triangle= $\frac{\sqrt{3}}{4} x^2$
Area of a square $= y^2$
$\frac{\sqrt{3}}{4} x^2 = \sqrt{3}\, y^2$
$x^2 = 4y^2$
$x : y = 2 : 1$

20. *Answer: (c)*
If "x is inversely proportional to y", then xy = k.
Raise power of 2 on both sides:
$(xy)^2 = k^2$
$x^2y^2 = k^2 \rightarrow y^2 = k^2 \left(\frac{1}{x^2}\right) \rightarrow \frac{y^2}{\frac{1}{x^2}} = k^2$
So $\frac{1}{x^2}$ *directly proportional to* y^2

21. *Answer: (d)*
Two of the legs of the triangle are the radii of the circle. This triangle is an isosceles triangle with equal base angles.
$180 - 50 - 50 = x$
$x = 80$

22. *Answer: (b)*
Side of X : Side of Y = 4 : 1
Area of X : Area of Y = 16 : 1
Area of X = $25 \times 16 = 400$
Side of X = $\sqrt{400} = 20$

23. *Answer: (c)*
Divide both sides by 100.
$2{,}500 = 100(2x + 5)$
$25 = 2x + 5$
$2x = 20$
$x = 10$

24. *Answer: (c)*
Units digit has 5 choices (1, 3, 5, 7, 9).
Tens digit has 10 choices (0 ~ 9).
Hundreds digit has 4 choices (2, 4, 6, 8).
$5 \times 10 \times 4 = 200$

25. *Answer: (d)*
Between 0 and 1000 (exclude), there are 499 ($\frac{998-2}{2} + 1$*) integers which are multiples of 2.*
Between 0 and 1000 (exclude), there are 199 ($\frac{995-5}{5} + 1$*) integers which are multiples of 5.*
LCM of 2 and 5 is 10.
Between 0 and 1000 (exclude), there are 99 ($\frac{990-10}{10} + 1$*) integers which are multiples of 10*
$499 + 199 - 99 = 599$
The number of integers which are multiples of both 2 and 5 is 599.

26. *Answer: (b)*
In order to find the daily price, add the cost from the rush hours, which is 12 (hours) × (.25), and the cost from the additional hours, which is (20 – 12)(hours) × (.6).
Multiply the daily cost by 30 to find the total cost for 30 days.

27. *Answer: (a)*
Number of Full Time Employees = 20 + 40 + 50 =110 employees.
Full time employees comprise of 55% of the total.
0.55 × Number of Employees = 110.
Number of Employees = 200.
Part Time Employees = 200 × 0.45= 90.
Full Time Employees – Part Time Employees = 110 – 90 = 20 employees

28. *Answer: (d)*
Number of Part time staff = number of Part Time Employees × 0.6 = 90 × 0.6 = 54.

29. *Answer: (d)*
*The difference of two consecutive terms is 3. There are 47 consecutive terms between the 243*th *and the 290*th *terms.*
$3 \times 47 = 141$

30. *Answer: (c)*
$\frac{63 + a}{2} = 4 \times (63 - a).$
$63 + a = 8(63 - a)$
$63 + a = 8 \times 63 - 8a$
$9a = 7 \times 63$
$a = 49$

31. *Answer: 450*
The two triangles are similar, so their corresponding sides are proportional.
Let the height of the lamp post be x.
$\frac{150}{x} = \frac{80}{80 + 160}$
$x = 450\ cm$

32. *Answer: 36*
$m\angle ABC = \frac{1}{2} m\angle AOC = \frac{1}{2} \times \frac{1}{5} \times 360^o = 36^o$

33. *Answer: 5*
The circle is tangent to the x−axis, since otherwise it would touch the axis at zero or two points (try drawing it out to see). Its radius is the distance from the center to the x-axis which is 5.

34. *Answer : 415*
Let the price of a basic phone be x, then the price of a smartphone is 5x + 15. Solve the equation: x + (5x + 15) = 615, and get x = 100. Therefore, a basic phone costs $100 while a smartphone costs 5 × 100 + 15 = $515.
$515 - 100 = 415$

35. *Answer: 60*
ΔABO *is a right triangle with hypotenuse* $\overline{AO}$*, so use the Pythagorean theorem to find OB.*
OB and OC are radii and let their length be r.
$15^2 + r^2 = (9 + r)^2$
$225 + r^2 = 81 + 18r + r^2$
$144 = 18r$
$r = 8$
Area of $\Delta OAB = \frac{1}{2} \times 8 \times 15 = 60$

36. *Answer: 4500*

Kepler's Third Law states:

$$\frac{(Orbital\ Period)^2}{(Distance\ from\ the\ Sun)^3} = constant$$

$$\frac{165^2}{(Distance\ from\ the\ Sun)^3} = \frac{1^2}{149.6^3}$$

$$Distance = 4500\ billion\ meters$$

37. *Answer: 2840*

$$\frac{(Orbital\ Period)^2}{30000^3} = \frac{1^2}{149.6^3}$$

$$Orbital\ Period = 2840\ Earth\ years$$

38. *Answer: 1.33*

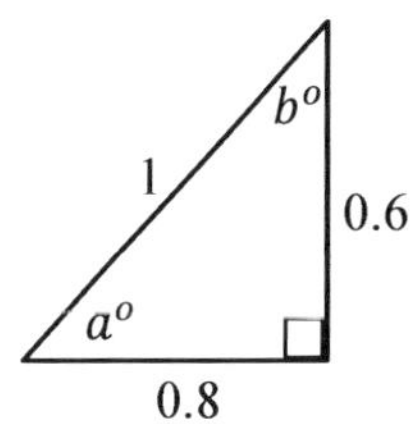

$\tan(b^o) = \frac{0.8}{0.6} = 1.33$

or

$a^o + b^o = 90^o$

$\sin(b^o) = \cos(a^0) = \sqrt{1 - \sin(a^o)^2} = \sqrt{1 - 0.6^2} = 0.8$

$\tan(b^o) = \frac{\sin(b^O)}{\cos(b^O)} = \frac{0.8}{0.6} = \frac{4}{3} = 1.33$

SAT Math Mock Test No. 4

SECTION 3 

Math Test – NO Calculator **25 MINUTES, 20 QUESTIONS**

Directions:

For questions 1-15, solve each problem, choose the best answer from the choices provided, and fill in the corresponding circle on your answer sheet. **For questions 16-20**, solve the problem and enter your answer in the grid on the answer sheet. Please refer to the directions before question 16 on how to enter your answers in the grid. You may use any available space in your test booklet for scratch work.

Notes:

1. **No calculator** is allowed for this section. All numbers used are real numbers.
2. Figures that accompany problems in this test are intended to provide information useful in solving the problems. They are drawn as accurately as possible EXCEPT when it is stated in a specific problem that the figure is not drawn to scale. All figures lie in a plane unless otherwise indicated.
3. Unless otherwise specified, the domain of any function *f(x)* assumed to be the set of all real numbers *x* for which *f(x)* is a real number.

References:

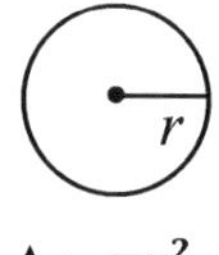

$A = \pi r^2$
$C = 2\pi r$

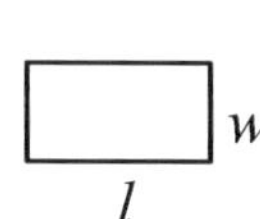

$A = lw$

$A = \frac{1}{2}bh$

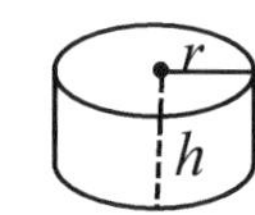

$V = lwh$

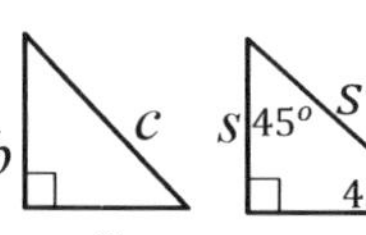

$V = \pi r^2 h$

b c a

$c^2 = a^2 + b^2$

s 45° $s\sqrt{2}$ 45° s

2s 60° s 30° $s\sqrt{3}$

Special Right Triangles

The number of degrees of arc in a circle is 360; the number of radians of arc in a circle is 2π.
The sum of the degree measures of the angles in a triangle is 180.

1. If $x = -2$ is a solution of the equation $x^2 = -x + c$ where c is a constant, what is another value of x that satisfies the equation?
   a) 1
   b) 2
   c) 3
   d) 4

2. Sean was assigned a login password to his library account. He was told that his password consists of 3 two-digit numbers that have to satisfy the following three conditions:

   One number is an even number.
   One number is a prime number.
   One number is a multiple of 5.

   If each number can only satisfy one of the conditions above, then which of the following could be his login password?
   a) 14−29−45
   b) 20−16−13
   c) 12−25−49
   d) 15−21−26

3. In the figure below, what is the value of x?

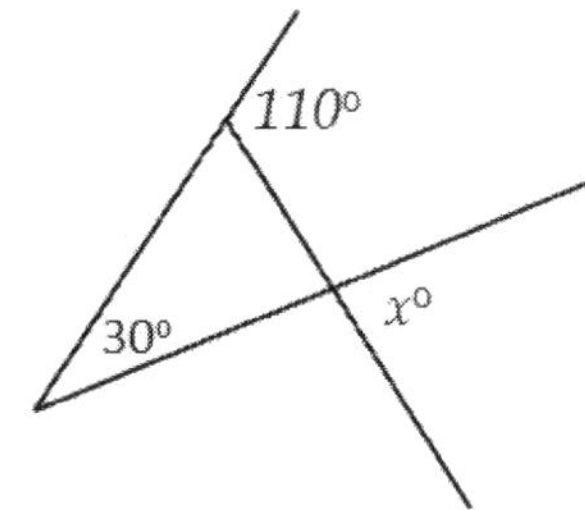

a) 30
b) 80
c) 90
d) 100

4. If $a = \left|\frac{1}{x+4}\right|$ and $b = \frac{1}{y+2}$, what is the value of $a + b$ when $x = -5$ and $y = -3$?
a) $\frac{1}{2}$
b) $-\frac{1}{2}$
c) $\frac{1}{4}$
d) 0

5. If $y^2 = x\sqrt{7}$ and $x \neq 0$, what does x^2 equal in terms of y?
a) $\frac{y}{7}$
b) $7y^4$
c) $\frac{49}{y^2}$
d) $\frac{y^4}{7}$

6. If 4 more than twice a number is equal to 20. What is 2 more than 4 times the number?
a) 12
b) 34
c) 26
d) 32

7. a, b, x, and y are positive numbers. If $x^{-2/3} = a^{-2}$ and $y^{2/3} = b^4$, what is $(xy)^{-1/3}$ in terms of a and b?
a) ab
b) $a^{-1}b^{-2}$
c) a^2b^2
d) $a^{-2}b^{-2}$

8. a, b, x, and y are positive numbers. If $x^{-2/3} = a^{-6}$ and $y^{2/3} = b^6$, what is $(xy)^{-\frac{1}{3}}$ in terms of a and b?
a) ab
b) $a^{-3}b^{-3}$
c) a^2b^2
d) $a^{-2}b^{-2}$

9. In Bridgetown High School, each class period is 1 hour and 25 minutes long, each break in between periods is 5 minutes long and lunch (between 2nd and 3rd period) is 45 minutes long. If 4th period is to end at 2:00, what time should the school day begin?
a) 7:00
b) 7:15
c) 7:25
d) 7:45

10. If $x \neq 0$ and x is inversely proportional to y, which of the following is directly proportional to $\frac{1}{x}$?
a) $\frac{1}{y}$
b) $-\frac{1}{y}$
c) y^2
d) $-y^2$

11. If $\frac{5}{q} = \frac{3}{9}$, what is the value of q?
a) 12
b) 13
c) 15
d) 16

12. If $x - y = 1$, $y = 2z + 1$, and $z = 5$ what is the value of x?
    a) –14
    b) –12
    c) 10
    d) 12

13. What is the y-intercept of the linear equation $5y - x = 10$?
    a) -4
    b) -2
    c) 0
    d) 2

14. A box contains red, blue and green pens. If one pen is chosen at random, the probability that a red pen will be chosen is three times the probability for a blue pen and four times the probability for a green pen. If there are 24 red pens in the box, how many pens are in the box?
    a) 38
    b) 44
    c) 48
    d) 60

15. If $a + 3b = 2b$, which of the following must equal $6a + 6b$?
    a) 0
    b) 1
    c) b
    d) $2b$

Directions:

For questions 16-20, solve the problem and enter your answer in the grid, as described below, on the answer sheet.

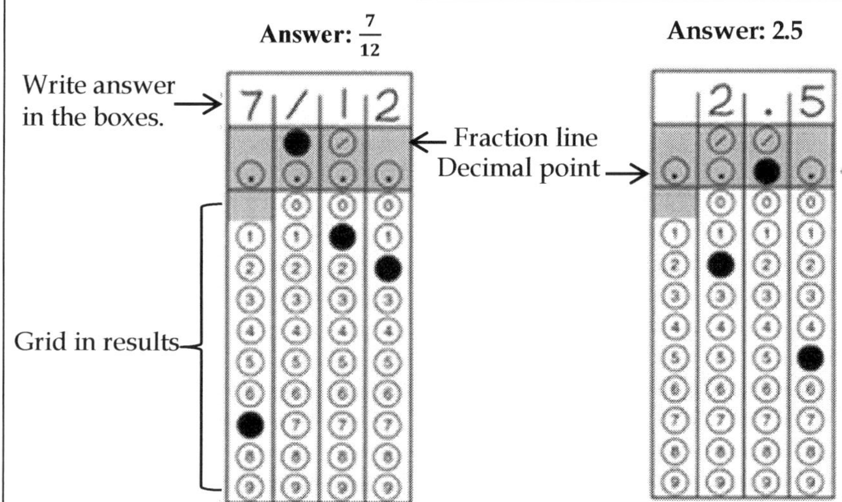

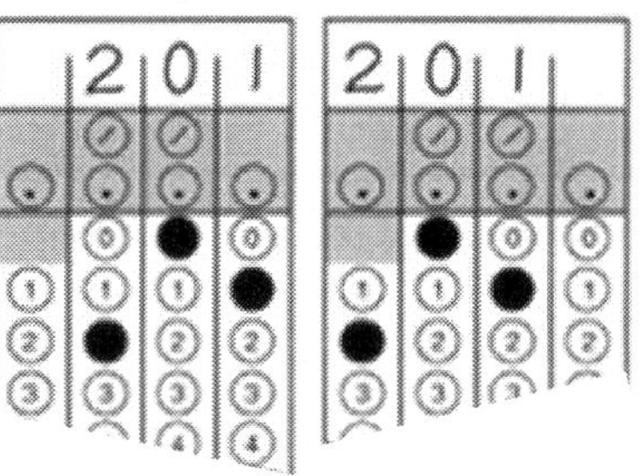

Note: You may start your answers in any column, space permitting. Columns not needed should be left blank.

- Mark no more than one circle in any column.
- Because the answer sheet will be machine-scored. **You will receive credit only if the circles are filled in correctly.**
- Although not required, it is suggested that you write your answer in the boxes at the top of the columns to help you fill in the circles accurately.
- Some problems may have more than one correct answer. In such case, grid only one answer.
- No question has a negative answer.
- **Mixed numbers** such as $3\frac{1}{2}$ must be gridded as 3.5 or $\frac{7}{2}$. (If 3 1 / 2 is gridded, it will be interpreted as $\frac{31}{2}$, not $3\frac{1}{2}$.)
- **Decimal Answer**: If you obtain a decimal answer with more digits than the grid can accommodate, it may be either rounded or truncated, but it must fill the entire grid. The acceptable ways to grid $\frac{2}{3}$ are:

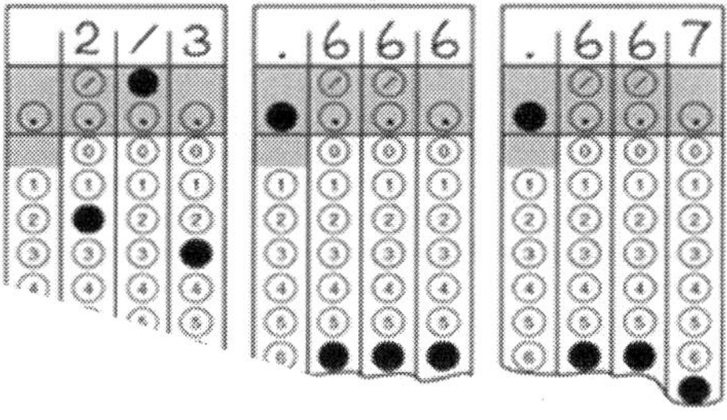

16. In the figure below, what is the value of $2a + 2b - c - d$?

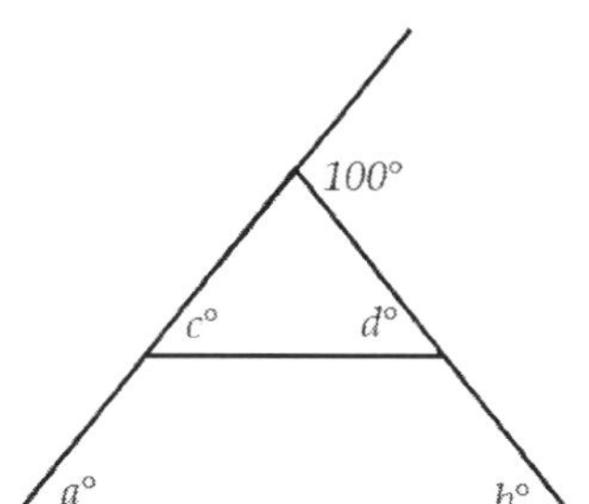

17. The three angles of a triangle have measures $x°$, $2(x+1)°$ and $4y°$, where $x > 55$. If x and y are integers greater than zero, what is one possible value of y?

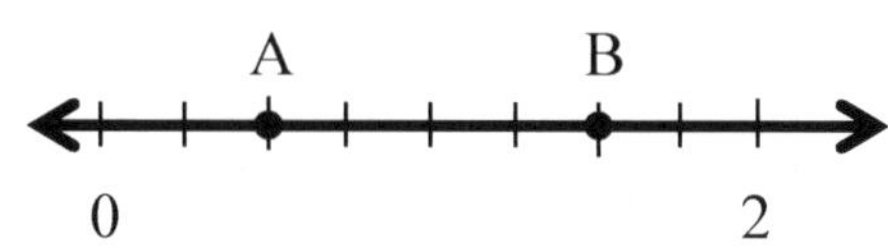

18. The number line is equally spaced as shown above. What is the value of $|A - B|$?

19. A rectangular storage room has a volume of 7350 cubic feet. If its length is 70 feet and its height is 5 feet, what is the width of the room?

20. If $7x = 28$ and $xy = 8$, what is the value of y?

SECTION 4

Math Test – Calculator **55 MINUTES, 38 QUESTIONS**

Directions:

For questions 1-30, solve each problem, choose the best answer from the choices provided, and fill in the corresponding circle on your answer sheet. **For questions 31-38**, solve the problem and enter your answer in the grid on the answer sheet. Please refer to the directions before question 31 on how to enter your answers in the grid. You may use any available space in your test booklet for scratch work.

Notes:

1. Acceptable calculators are allowed for this section. All numbers used are real numbers.
2. Figures that accompany problems in this test are intended to provide information useful in solving the problems. They are drawn as accurately as possible EXCEPT when it is stated in a specific problem that the figure is not drawn to scale. All figures lie in a plane unless otherwise indicated.
3. Unless otherwise specified, the domain of any function *f(x)* assumed to be the set of all real numbers *x* for which *f(x)* is a real number.

References:

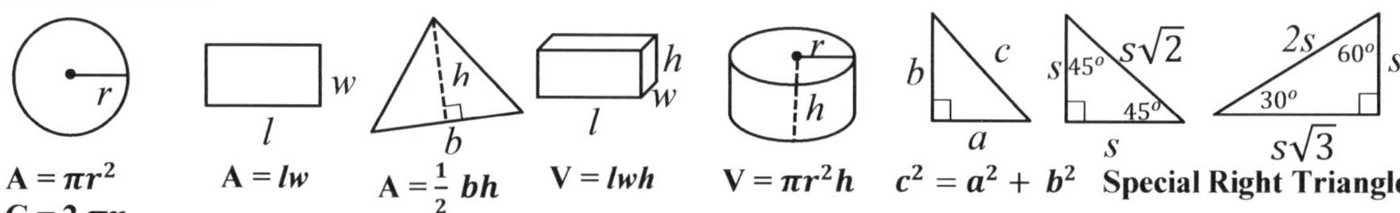

$A = \pi r^2$ $C = 2\pi r$ $A = lw$ $A = \frac{1}{2}bh$ $V = lwh$ $V = \pi r^2 h$ $c^2 = a^2 + b^2$ **Special Right Triangles**

The number of degrees of arc in a circle is 360; the number of radians of arc in a circle is 2π.
The sum of the degree measures of the angles in a triangle is 180.

1. If $n > 0$, what is the value of $4^n + 4^n + 10 \times 4^n + 4^{n+1}$?
   a) 4^{4n}
   b) $4^{(n+4)}$
   c) $4^{(n+1)}$
   d) $4^{(n+2)}$

2. Bob receives a basic weekly salary of \$200 plus a 10% commission on his sales. In a week in which his sales amounted to \$4000, the ratio of his basic salary to his commission was
   a) 2 : 1
   b) 1 : 2
   c) 2 : 3
   d) 3 : 2

3. For a certain type of heater, the increase in gas bills is directly proportional to the temperature setting (in Fahrenheit). If the gas bills increased by \$20 when the temperature setting is increased by 5 degrees Fahrenheit, by how much will expenses increase when the temperature setting is increased by 9 degrees Fahrenheit?
   a) \$30
   b) \$36
   c) \$40
   d) \$45

4. In square ABCD above, if the radius of the circle is 5, what is the area of the shaded region?
   a) $100 - 25\pi$
   b) $50 - 25\pi$
   c) $50 - 12.5\pi$
   d) $64 - 16\pi$

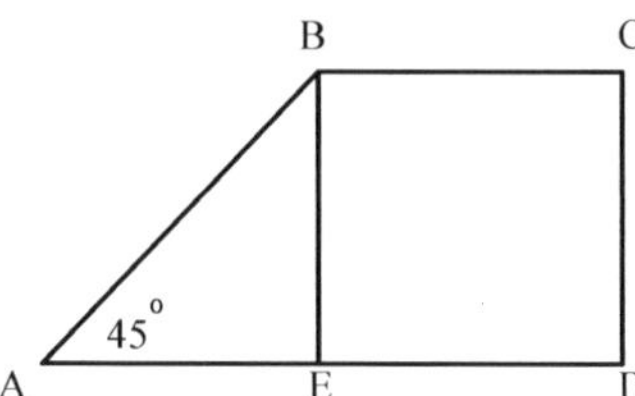

5. In the figure above, BCDE is a square and its area is 16. The points A, E and D are on the same line. What is the length of $\overline{AB}$?
   a) 4
   b) $4\sqrt{2}$
   c) $4\sqrt{3}$
   d) 6

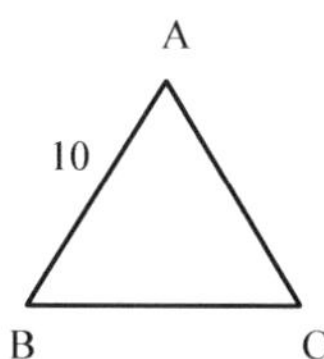

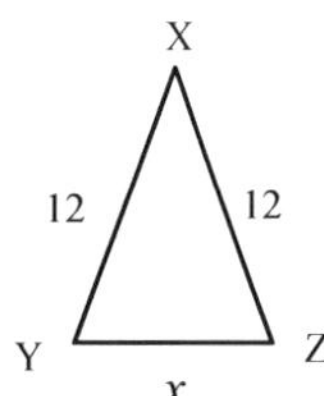

6. The perimeter of ΔABC is equal to the perimeter of ΔXYZ, which are shown above. If ΔABC is equilateral, what is the value of x?
   a) 4
   b) 5
   c) 6
   d) 8

7. $x = -9$ and $y = 3$, what is the value of $|\sqrt[3]{xy} - 5y|$?
   a) 12
   b) 18
   c) −12
   d) −18

8. The average score of John's 5 math tests is 80. If the teacher decides not to count his lowest score, which is 60, what will be John's new average score?
   a) 80
   b) 82
   c) 85
   d) 86

9. If $2 \times 2^x + 2^x + 2^x = 2^6$, what is the value of x?
   a) 4
   b) 3
   c) 2
   d) 1

10. The graph below shows a certain brand of TV sales in four different continents. From 2011 to 2012, the total sales in the four continents decreased by what percentage?

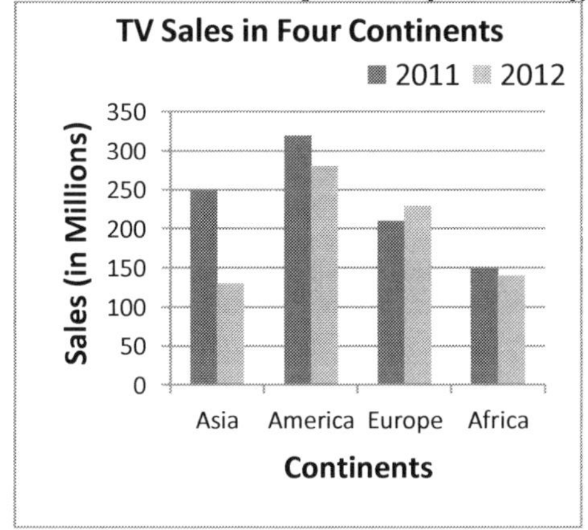

   a) 17
   b) 15
   c) 12
   d) 1

11. If $2x - y$ is equal to 60% of $5y$, what is the value of $\frac{y}{x}$?
    a) $\frac{1}{4}$
    b) $\frac{1}{3}$
    c) $\frac{1}{2}$
    d) $\frac{2}{3}$

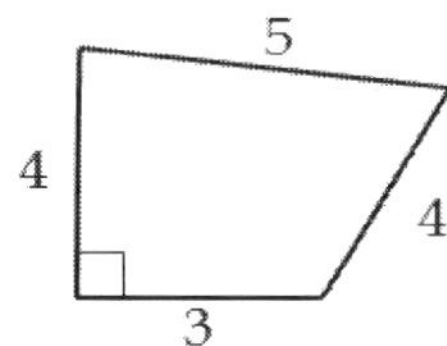

12. What is the area of quadrilateral as shown above?
    a) 12
    b) $6 + \sqrt{21}$
    c) $6 + 2\sqrt{21}$
    d) $6 + 4\sqrt{21}$

x	-2	-1	2	3
y	-7	-4	5	8

13. Which of the following equations satisfies the relationship between x and y in the table above?
    a) $y = x + 6$
    b) $y = -3x + 1$
    c) $y = 3x + 1$
    d) $y = 3x - 1$

14. If the function f is defined by $f(x) = ax^2 + bx + c$, where $a > 0$, $b = 0$, and $c < 0$, which of the following could be the graph of $f(x)$?

a)

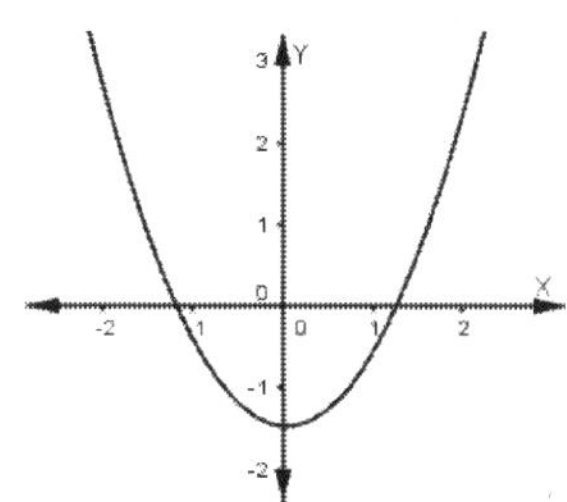

b)

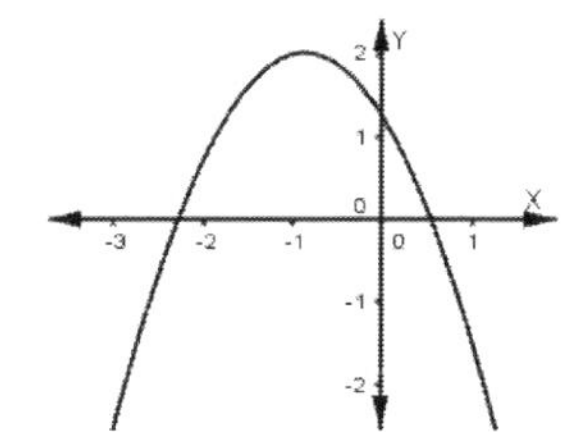

c)

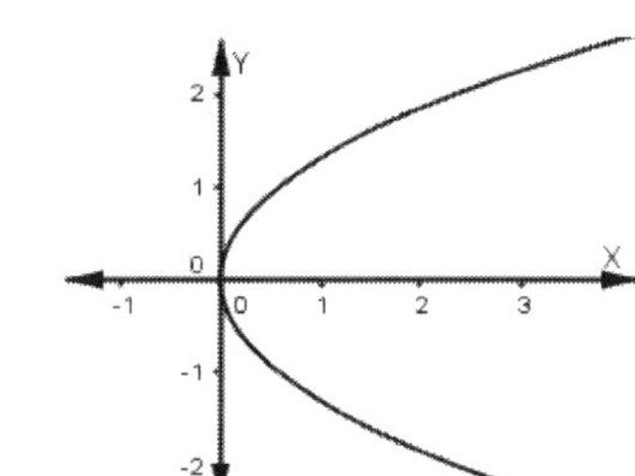

d)

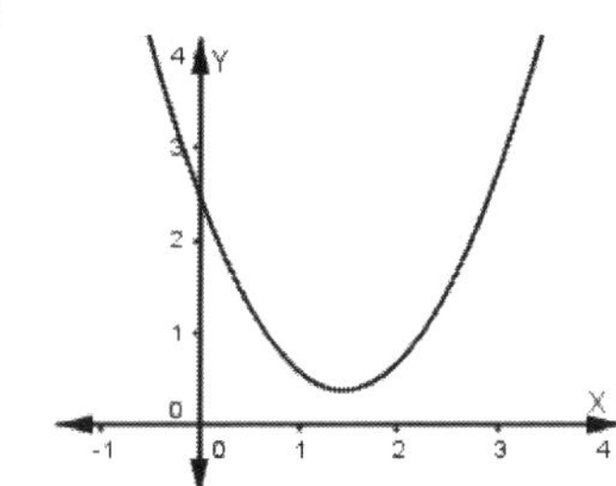

15. We start out with a set of 8 numbers. We subtract 4 from 4 of these numbers. If the average (arithmetic mean) of these eight numbers was 10 originally, what is the new average?
    a) 7
    b) 8
    c) 9
    d) 9.5

16. If $-3 \le x \le 7$ and $-2 \le y \le 3$, which of the following gives the set of all possible values of xy?
    a) $-9 \le xy \le 14$
    b) $0 \le xy \le 21$
    c) $-21 \le xy \le 5$
    d) $-14 \le xy \le 21$

17. If the positive integer n is divided by 7, the remainder is 2. What is the remainder when $4n$ is divided by 7?
    a) 1
    b) 2
    c) 3
    d) 4

18. Which of the following is the expression that represents the statement that the value of the cube of y multiplied by the value of the square root of z, all subtracted from five–sevenths of the square of x equals x?
    a) $\frac{5x^2}{7} - y^3\sqrt{z} = x$
    b) $\frac{5x^2}{7} - y^2\sqrt{z} = x$
    c) $\frac{5x^2}{7} - \sqrt{y^3 z} = x$
    d) $\frac{5}{7}x^2 - y^3 z^2 = x$

19. In the figure below, what is the value of $a - b$?

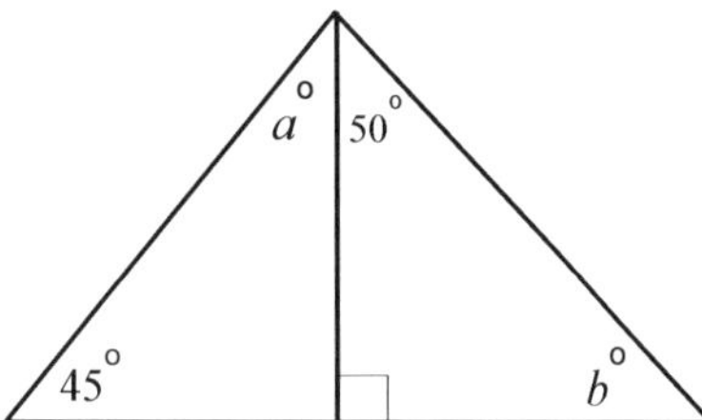

Note: Figure not drawn to scale.
    a) 0
    b) 5
    c) 10
    d) 15

20. A rectangular box has dimensions 36 × 14 × 18. Without wasting any space, which of the following could be the dimensions of the smaller boxes which can be packed into the rectangular box?
    a) 2 × 5 × 6
    b) 7× 9 × 12
    c) 3 × 5 × 6
    d) 4 × 5 × 6

21. Sam drove from home at an average speed of 60 miles per hour to her working place and then returned along the same route at an average speed of 40 miles per hour. If the entire trip took her 2 hours, what is the entire distance, in miles, for the round trip?
    a) 48
    b) 96
    c) 100
    d) 108

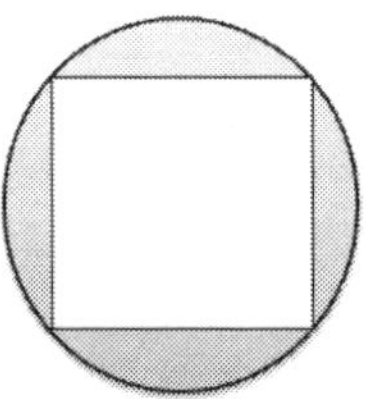

22. A square is inscribed inside a circle as shown in the figure above. If the radius of the circle is 6, what is the area of the shaded region?
    a) 24.5
    b) 40.1
    c) 41.1
    d) 42.2

23. If $x = \sqrt{12} + \sqrt{48}$, what is the value of x^2
    a) 124
    b) 120
    c) 108
    d) 84

Questions 24–25 refer to the following information:

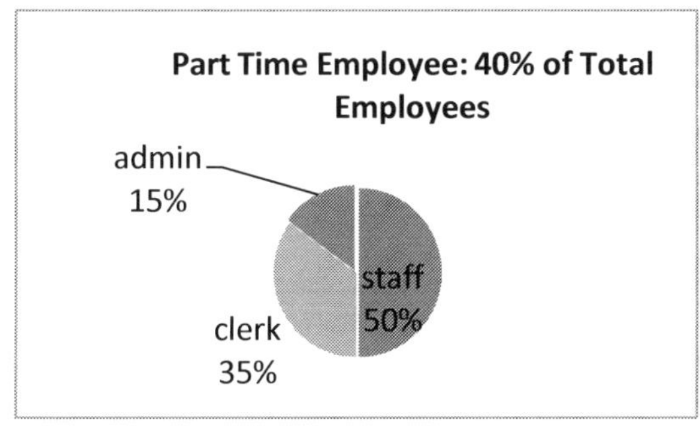

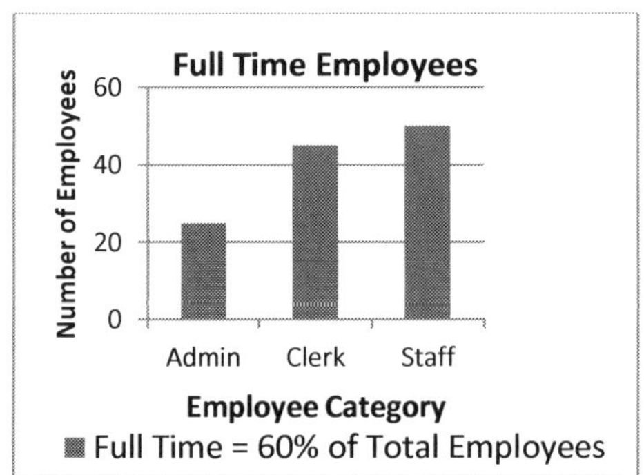

24. According to the graphs above, the total number of full-time employees is how many more than the total number of part-time employees at Oak Town High School?
    a) 20
    b) 40
    c) 50
    d) 60

25. According to the graphs above, how many part-time staff members are at Oak Town High School?
    a) 60
    b) 50
    c) 40
    d) 30

26. In a sequence of numbers, each term after the first term is 3 greater than $\frac{1}{2}$ of the preceding term. If a_o is the first term and $a_o \neq 0$, which of the following represents the ratio of the third term to the second term?
    a) $\frac{a_0+12}{2a_o+6}$
    b) $\frac{a_0+18}{2a_o}$
    c) $\frac{a_0}{2a_0+6}$
    d) $\frac{a_0+18}{2a_0+12}$

27. The number of cats varies inversely with the number of mice. If there are 400 mice when 60 cats are present, how many cats are present when there are 300 mice?
    a) 45
    b) 80
    c) 120
    d) 150

28. Sean needs to finish reading his book in four days. He read $\frac{1}{3}$ of the book on the first day, $\frac{1}{4}$ of the book on the second day, $\frac{1}{5}$ of the book on the third day. If he has 39 pages to finish on the fourth day, how many pages are there in the book?
    a) 120
    b) 130
    c) 180
    d) 200

Questions 29 – 30 refer to the following information:

The function $f(x) = 2x^4 - 13x^3 + 28x^2 - 23x + 6$ is graphed in the xy-plane below.

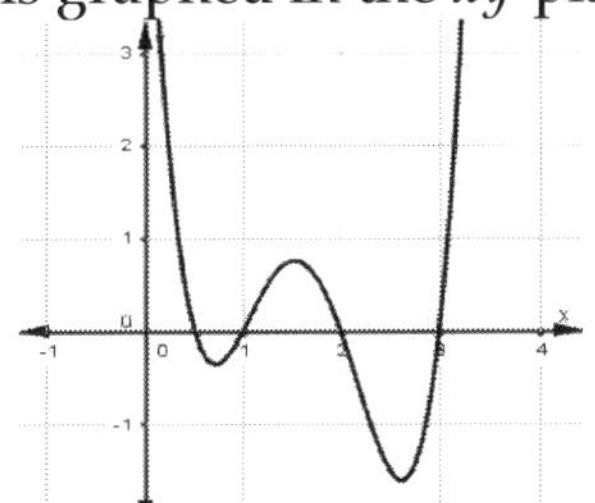

29. If c is a constant such that the equation $f(x) = c$ has four real solutions, which of the following could be the value of c?
    a) 2
    b) 1
    c) 0
    d) −1

30. How many real solutions are there if $f(x) = x$?
    a) 1
    b) 2
    c) 3
    d) 4

Directions:

For questions 31-38, solve the problem and enter your answer in the grid, as described below, on the answer sheet.

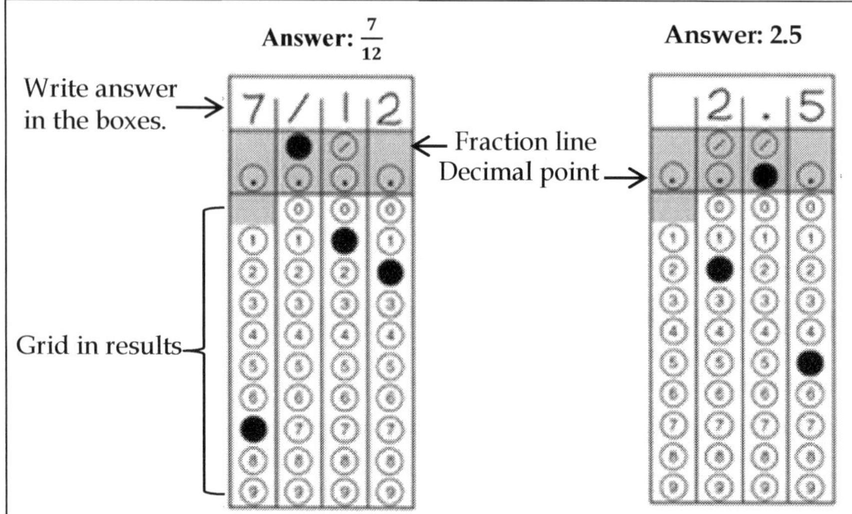

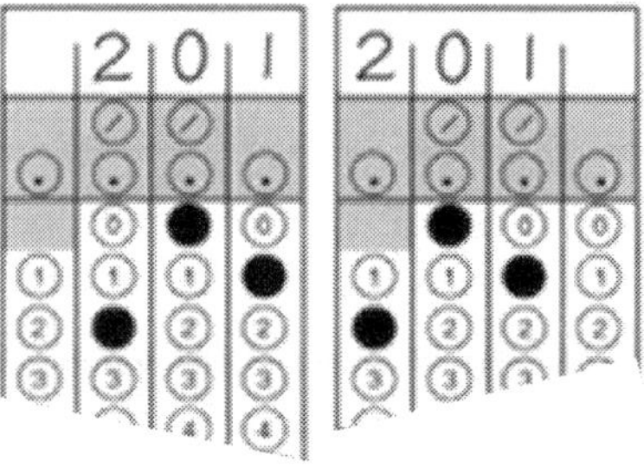

Note: You may start your answers in any column, space permitting. Columns not needed should be left blank.

- Mark no more than one circle in any column.
- Because the answer sheet will be machine-scored. **You will receive credit only if the circles are filled in correctly.**
- Although not required, it is suggested that you write your answer in the boxes at the top of the columns to help you fill in the circles accurately.
- Some problems may have more than one correct answer. In such case, grid only one answer.
- No question has a negative answer.
- **Mixed numbers** such as $3\frac{1}{2}$ must be gridded as 3.5 or $\frac{7}{2}$. (If 3 1 / 2 is gridded, it will be interpreted as $\frac{31}{2}$, not $3\frac{1}{2}$.)

- **Decimal Answer**: If you obtain a decimal answer with more digits than the grid can accommodate, it may be either rounded or truncated, but it must fill the entire grid. The acceptable ways to grid $\frac{2}{3}$ are:

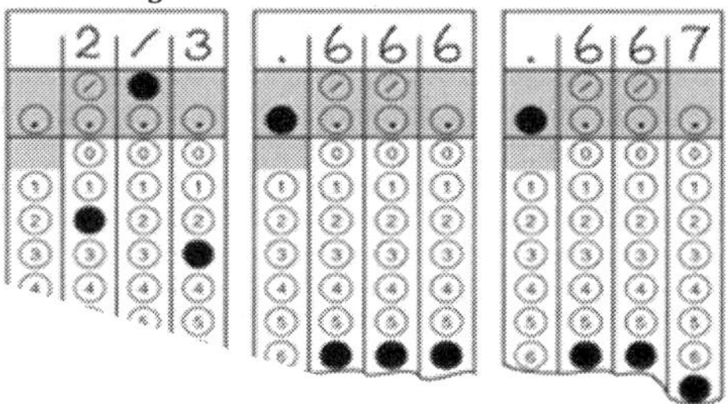

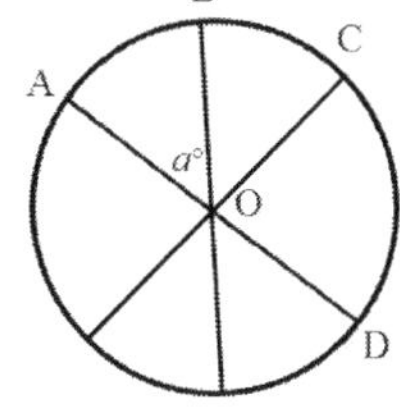

Note: Figure not drawn to scale.

31. In the figure above, O is the center of the circle, $\widehat{AB} = \widehat{BC}$, and $\widehat{AC} = \widehat{CD}$. What is the value of a, in degrees?

x	1	2	3	4	5
$f(x)$	5	7	y	11	13

32. The table above defines a linear function. What is the value of y?

33. One-third of a bottle originally contains grape juice. It is then filled to the top with a fruit juice mix with equal amounts of orange, grape, and apple juices. What fraction of the final mixture is grape juice?

34. If the lengths of the edges of a cube are increased by 20%, the volume of the cube will increase by how many percent? (Round your answer to the nearest tenth)

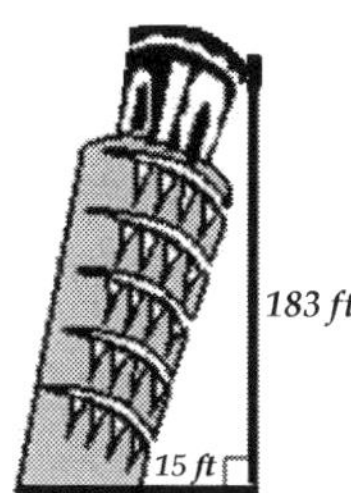

35. If the Leaning Tower of Pisa is 183 feet tall and the top edge of the tower leans 15 feet out from the bottom edge, what is *tangent* of the angle created between the ground and the tower?

Questions 36 – 37 refer to the following information:

A new machine in a manufacturing factory is depreciated approximately 20% for the first 5 years and 8% for the next 10 years. If this machine costs $10,000 brand new, the following equations are used to model its value for the first 15 years:

$$\begin{cases} V_t = \$10{,}000 \times r_1^t & when\ 0 < t \leq 5 \\ V_t = V_5 \times r_2^{t-5} & when\ 5 < t \leq 15 \end{cases}$$

V_t is the value of the machine at time t, the number of years after purchasing.

36. What is the value of $r_1 + r_2$?

37. After how many years will a brand new machine be worth less than $2,000?

38. What is the remainder when $2x^4 - 3x^3 + 4x^2 - 5x + 6$ is divided by $x - 3$?

SAT MATH MOCK TEST No. 4 ANSWER KEYS

Section 3									
1. A	2. A	3. B	4. D	5. D	6. B	7. B	8. B	9. C	10. C
11. C	12. D	13. D	14. A	15. A	16. 100	17. 3	18. 1	19. 21	20. 2

Section 4									
1. D	2. B	3. B	4. A	5. B	6. C	7. B	8. C	9. A	10. A
11. C	12. C	13. D	14. A	15. B	16. D	17. A	18. A	19. B	20. B
21. B	22. C	23. C	24. B	25. C	26. D	27. B	28. C	29. C	30. B
31. 45	32. 9	33. $\frac{5}{9}$	34. 72.8	35. 12.2	36. 1.72	37. 11	38. 108		

SECTION 3

1. *Answer: (a)*
   Plug in $x = -2$
   $(-2)^2 = -(-2) + c$
   $c = 2$
   $x^2 = -x + 2$
   $x^2 + x - 2 = 0$
   $(x + 2)(x - 1) = 0$
   $x = -2$ *or* 1

2. *Answer: (a)*
   Only (a) has one even number, one prime, and one number which is a multiple of 5.

3. *Answer: (b)*
   $x + 30 = 110$ *(exterior angle theorem & vertical angles)*
   $x = 80$

4. *Answer: (d)*
   $a + b = |\frac{1}{-5+4}| + \frac{1}{-3+2}$
   $1 - 1 = 0$

5. *Answer: (d)*
   Divide by $\sqrt{7}$ *on both sides of the equation* $y^2 = x\sqrt{7}$.
   $x = \frac{y^2}{\sqrt{7}}$ *(Then square both sides.)*
   $x^2 = \frac{y^4}{7}$

6. *Answer: (b)*
   Let the number be x.
   $2x + 4 = 20$
   $x = 8$
   $4x + 2 = 32 + 2 = 34$

7. *Answer: (b)*
   $x^{-2/3} = a^{-2}$
   $x = (a^{-2})^{(-3/2)} = a^3$
   $y^{2/3} = b^4$, $y = (b^4)^{(3/2)} = b^6$
   $(xy)^{-1/3} = (a^3b^6)^{(-1/3)} = a^{-1}b^{-2}$

8. *Answer: (b)*
   $x^{-2/3} = a^{-6}$
   $x = (a^{-6})^{(-3/2)} = a^9$
   $y^{2/3} = b^6$, $y = (b^6)^{(3/2)} = b^9$
   $(xy)^{-1/3} = (a^9b^9)^{(-1/3)} = a^{-3}b^{-3}$

9. *Answer: (c)*
   The total time spent in school is 4 periods + lunch + 2 breaks (between periods 1 and 2, and periods 3 and 4).
   Total Time = 4 × (1 hour 25 minutes) + 45 minutes + 2 × 5 minutes= 6 hours 35 minutes
   6 hours 35 minutes before 2:00PM is 7:25 AM.

10. *Answer: (c)*
    If "x is inversely proportional to y", then $xy = k$.
    $xy = k \rightarrow y = k(\frac{1}{x}) \rightarrow \frac{y}{\frac{1}{x}} = k$
    So $\frac{1}{x}$ *is directly proportional to y.*

11. *Answer: (c)*
    Cross multiply.
    $5 \times 9 = 3 \times q$, $q = 15$

12. *Answer: (d)*
    $y = 2z = 2 \times 5 + 1 = 11$
    $x - y = 1$, $x - 11 = 1$, $x = 12$

13. *Answer: (d)*
The y-intercept occurs when $x = 0$.
$5y - 0 = 10$
$y = 2$

14. *Answer: (a)*
Red : Blue : Green $= 1 : \frac{1}{3} : \frac{1}{4}$
$= 12 : 4 : 3 = 24 : 8 : 6$
Total number of pens: $24 + 8 + 6 = 38$

15. *Answer: (a)*
$a + 3b = 2b, \quad a + b = 0$
$6a + 6b = 6(a + b) = 0$

16. *Answer: 100*
$100 = c + d = a + b$
$2(a + b) - c - d = 200 - 100 = 100$

17. *Answer: 3*
$x + 2x + 2 + 4y = 180$
$4y = 178 - 3x$
$4y < 178 - 3 \times 55$
$4y < 13$
$0 < y < 3.25$
$y = 1, 2, \text{ or } 3$

18. *Answer: 1*
Since the line is equally spaced between 0 and 2, A equals $\frac{2}{4}$ *and B equals* $\frac{6}{4}$.
$A - B = \frac{2}{4} - \frac{6}{4} = -\frac{4}{4} = -1$
$|A - B| = 1$

19. *Answer: 21*
Volume = Length × Height × Width
$7350 = 70 \times 5 \times \text{Width}$
Width = 21 feet

20. *Answer: 2*
Solve for x first, then solve for y.
$7x = 28, \ x = 4$
$4y = 8, \ y = 2$

SECTION 4

1. *Answer: (d)*
$4^n + 4^n + 10 \times 4^n + 4 \times 4^n = 16 \times 4^n = 4^{(n+2)}$

2. *Answer: (b)*
Commission $= 10\% \times 4000 = \$400$
Basic Salary : Commission $= 200 : 400 = 1 : 2$

3. *Answer: (b)*
$\$20 : 5^o F = \$x : 9^o F$
$5x = 180$
$x = \$36$

4. *Answer: (a)*
Shaded Area = Area of Square – Area of Circle
Length of the side of square: $5 \times 2 = 10$
Radius of the circle: 5
$10 \times 10 - (\pi \times 5^2) = 100 - 25\pi$

5. *Answer: (b)*
ΔABE is a 45-45-90 right triangle.
$\overline{BE} = \sqrt{16} = 4$
$\overline{AB} = \sqrt{2} \times 4$

6. *Answer: (c)*
The perimeter of ΔABC: $12 + 12 + x = 3 \times 10$
$x = 6$

7. *Answer: (b)*
Plug in the values of x and y.
$|\sqrt[3]{-9 \times 3} - 5 \times 3|$
$= |\sqrt[3]{-27} - 15|$
$= |-3 - 15|$
$= |-18| = 18$

8. *Answer: (c)*
John's original average is 80 for 5 tests.
$5 \times 80 = 400$ *(sum for 5 tests)*
$400 - 60 = 340$ *(sum for 4 tests)*
$\frac{340}{4} = 85$ *(average of 4 tests)*

9. *Answer: (a)*
$2 \times 2^x = 2^x + 2^x$
$2^x + 2^x + 2^x + 2^x = 4 \times 2^x = 2^6$
$2^{x+2} = 2^6$
$x = 4$

10. *Answer: (a)*
Total sales in 2011: $250 + 325 + 210 + 150 = 935$ *TVs.*
Total sales in 2012: $130 + 280 + 230 + 140 = 780$ *TVs.*
Percent Change $= \frac{780-935}{935} = -16.57\% \sim -17\%$

11. *Answer: (c)*
$2x - y = .6 \times 5y$
$2x - y = 3y$
$2x = 4y$
$\frac{y}{x} = \frac{2}{4} = \frac{1}{2}$

12. *Answer: (c)*

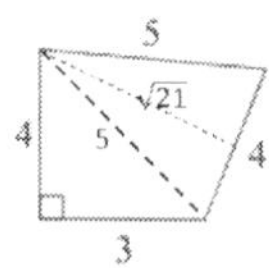

The quadrilateral above includes one right triangle and one isosceles triangle.
Area = ½ (3× 4) + ½ (4 × $\sqrt{21}$) = 6 + $2\sqrt{21}$

13. *Answer: (d)*
$Slope = \frac{Rise}{Run} = \frac{-4-(-7)}{-1-(-2)} = 3$
$y - (-7) = 3(x - (-2))$ *(Point-slope-form)*
$y = 3x - 1$

14. *Answer: (a)*
The leading coefficient of a quadratic function positive means the curve goes upwards; a negative constant c means y-intercept is negative. The value of b is zero, so x-coordinate of the maximum point is located at y-axis. Only (a) meets all these conditions.
Shortcut: By graphing $y = x^2 - 1$ in a graphing calculator, you will get the graph like answer (a).

15. *Answer: (b)*
$Average = \frac{Sum\ of\ Terms}{Number\ of\ Terms}$
$New\ Average = \frac{8\times10-4\times4}{8} = 8$

16. *Answer: (d)*
Try out different combinations of x and y.
$-14 \le xy \le 21$

17. *Answer: (a)*
If the remainder of n divided by 7 is 2, then n can be represented as:
$n = 7 \times q + 2$
$4n = 4 \times 7 \times q + 8$
The remainder of 4n divided by 7 is equal to the remainder of 8 divided by 7 which is 1.
Or simply pick an easy number, such as 9 for n, then $4n = 4 \times 9 = 36$.
36 devided by 7 will have a remaider 1.

18. *Answer: (a)*
Translate to algebraic equation.

19. *Answer: (b)*
$a = 45$ *and* $b = 40$
$a - b = 5$

20. *Answer: (b)*
The number 5 is not a factor of 14, 36 or 18, therefore answers (a), (c), (d) are not possible.
Only (b)'s dimensions could be packed into the rectangular box without wasting space.
$\frac{14}{7} \times \frac{36}{12} \times \frac{18}{9} = 12$

21. *Answer: (b)*
Let one trip have x miles.
$Time = 2 = t_1 + t_2 = \frac{x}{60} + \frac{x}{40}$
$2 = x(\frac{1}{60} + \frac{1}{40})$
$x = 48$
The Round-Trip Distance = 2 × 48 = 96

22. *Answer: (c)*
Area of Shaded Region = Area of Circle – Area of Square
Area of Circle = $\pi (6)^2 = 36\pi$
Area of Square = $\frac{1}{2}$ *(Diagonal of Square)*^{2} = $\frac{1}{2}$ *(Diameter of Circle)*^{2} = $\frac{1}{2}(12)^2 = 72$
Area of Shaded Region = $36\pi - 72 = 41.09$

23. *Answer: (c)*
$(\sqrt{12} + \sqrt{48})^2 = 12 + 48 + 2\sqrt{12 \times 48} = 12 + 48 + 48 = 108$

24. *Answer: (b)*
Number of Full Time Employees = 25 + 45 + 50 =120 employees.
Full time employees comprise of 60% of the total.
0.6 × Number of Employees = 120.
Number of Employees = 200.
Part Time Employees = 200 × 0.4= 80.
Full Time Employees – Part Time Employees = 120 – 80 = 40 employees

25. *Answer: (c)*
Number of Part time staff = number of Part Time Employees × 0.5 = 80 × 0.5 = 40.

26. *Answer: (d)*
$1^{st}\ Term = a_0$
$2^{nd}\ Term = 3 + \frac{1}{2} \times a_0$
$3^{rd}\ Term = 3 + \frac{1}{2}(3 + \frac{1}{2}a_0)$
$= \frac{9}{2} + \frac{1}{4}a_0$
$Ratio = \frac{\frac{9}{2}+\frac{1}{4}a_0}{3+\frac{1}{2}a_0} = \frac{a_0 + 18}{2a_0 + 12}$

27. *Answer: (b)*
"Varying inversely" is inverse proportion.
$A \times B = constant$
$A \times B$ (before) $= A_1 \times B_1$ (after)
$400 \times 60 = 300 \times B_1$
$B_1 = 80$

28. *Answer: (c)*
Find out the last portion of pages and set up ratio equation.
The last portion of pages:
$1 - \frac{1}{3} - \frac{1}{4} - \frac{1}{5} = \frac{13}{60}$
$\frac{13}{60} = \frac{39}{Total\ Pages} = \frac{39}{x}$
Total Pages = 180

29. *Answer: (c)*

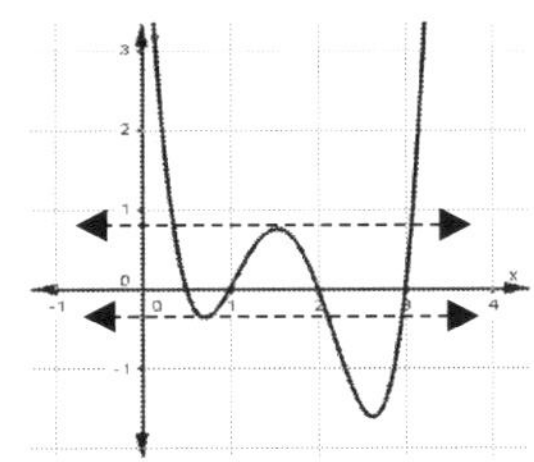

According to the graph above, there will be four intersection points when the value of c is roughly between -0.3 *and* 0.7.

30. *Answer: (b)*

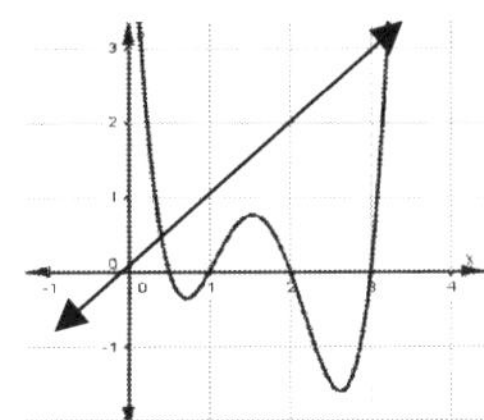

According to the graph above, there are two intersection points between the lines $f(x) = x$ *and* $f(x) = 2x^4 - 13x^3 + 28x^2 - 23x + 6$.

31. *Answer: 45*
$\widehat{AB}$ *is half of* $\widehat{AC}$ *so it is* $\frac{1}{4}$ *of* $\widehat{AD}$.
$a = \frac{1}{4} \times 180$
$a = 45$

32. *Answer: 9*
$Slope = \frac{7-5}{2-1} = \frac{y-7}{3-2}$
$2 = y - 7$
$y = 9$

33. *Answer:* $\frac{5}{9}$ *or .555 or .556*
$\frac{1}{3}$ *of the bottle is originally grape juice. Then* $\frac{2}{3}$ *of the bottle is filled with a mixture that is* $\frac{1}{3}$ *grape juice.*
The fraction that is grape juice is equal to:
$\frac{Amount\ of\ Grape\ Juice}{Amount\ of\ All\ Juice} = \frac{\frac{1}{3}+\frac{2}{3}(\frac{1}{3})}{1} = \frac{5}{9}$

34. *Answer: 72.8*
If the original lengths of the edges of the cube are 1. After increasing by 20%, its lengths become 1.2. The volume of the cube is equal to $(1.2)^3$ *or 1.728. The volume of the cube increases 72.8%.*

35. *Answer: 12.2*
$\tan(\theta) = \frac{183}{15} = 12.2$

36. *Answer: 1.72*
The machine depreciates 20% each year for the first 5 years:
$V_t = 10{,}000 \times (1 - 0.2)^t$
$r_1 = 0.8$
The machine depreciates 8% each year for the next 10 years:
$V_t = V_5 \times (1 - 0.08)^{t-5}$
$r_2 = 0.92$
$r_1 + r_2 = 0.8 + 0.92 = 1.72$

37. *Answer: 11*
After the first five years:
$V_5 = 10{,}000 \times (0.8)^5 = 3276.8$
$3276.8\,(0.92)^{t-5} < 2000$
$0.92^{t-5} < 0.61$
With calculator, the first whole number value of t that satisfies the above inequality is 11.
After 11 years, the value of the machine will be less than $2,000

38. *Answer: 108*
Remainder Theorem: If polynomial $P(x)$ *is divided by* $x - r$*, its remainder is* $P(r)$.
$P(3) = 2 \times 3^4 - 3 \times 3^3 + 4 \times 3^2 - 5(3) + 6 = 108$

SAT Math Mock Test No. 5

SECTION 3

Math Test – NO Calculator **25 MINUTES, 20 QUESTIONS**

Directions:

For questions 1-15, solve each problem, choose the best answer from the choices provided, and fill in the corresponding circle on your answer sheet. **For questions 16-20**, solve the problem and enter your answer in the grid on the answer sheet. Please refer to the directions before question 16 on how to enter your answers in the grid. You may use any available space in your test booklet for scratch work.

Notes:

1. **No calculator** is allowed for this section. All numbers used are real numbers.
2. Figures that accompany problems in this test are intended to provide information useful in solving the problems. They are drawn as accurately as possible EXCEPT when it is stated in a specific problem that the figure is not drawn to scale. All figures lie in a plane unless otherwise indicated.
3. Unless otherwise specified, the domain of any function *f(x)* assumed to be the set of all real numbers *x* for which *f(x)* is a real number.

References:

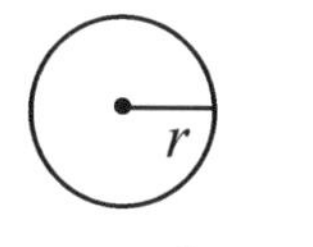

$A = \pi r^2$
$C = 2\pi r$

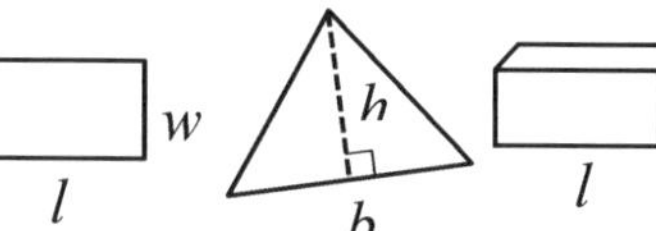

$A = lw$ $A = \frac{1}{2}bh$ $V = lwh$

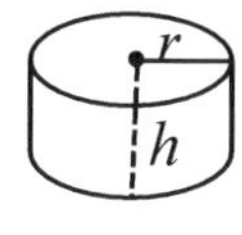

$V = \pi r^2 h$

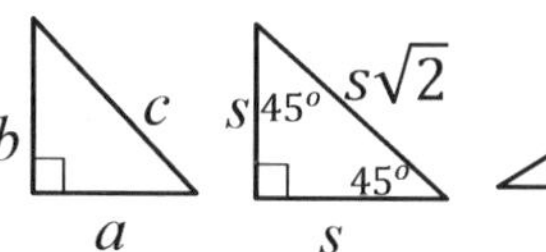

$c^2 = a^2 + b^2$

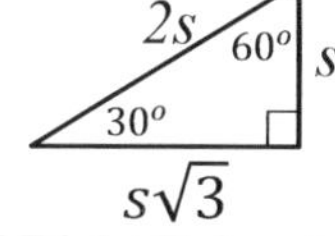

Special Right Triangles

The number of degrees of arc in a circle is 360; the number of radians of arc in a circle is 2π.
The sum of the degree measures of the angles in a triangle is 180.

1. If $3^{a+b} = 81$ and $2^b = 4$, then what is the value of 2^a ?
   a) 1
   b) 2
   c) 4
   d) 8

2. If $3a - 2b = 5$ and $a + 2b = 23$, then $a + b$?
   a) −5
   b) 5
   c) 10
   d) 15

3. If $n > 0$, what is the value of $5 \times 4^n + 4^n + 4^n + 4^n$?
   a) 2^{2n}
   b) $2^{(2n+1)}$
   c) $2^{(2n+2)}$
   d) $2^{(2n+3)}$

4. The lengths of the sides of a right triangle are consecutive even integers, and the length of the longest side is x. What is the value of x?
   a) 2
   b) 6
   c) 8
   d) 10

5. If one triangle has two sides that have lengths of 3 and 7, which of the following CANNOT be the length of the third side of the triangle?
   a) 5
   b) 6
   c) 8
   d) 10

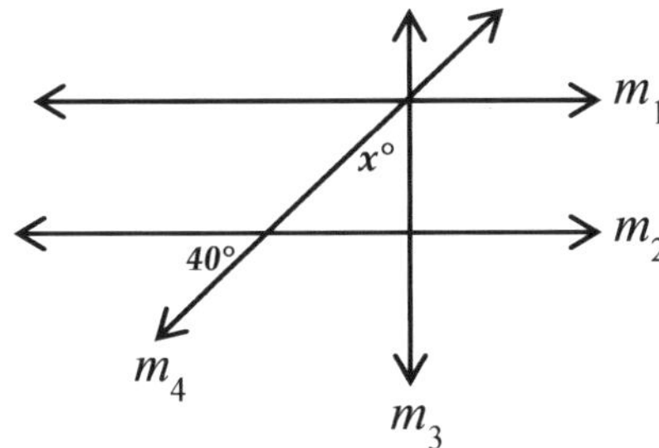

6. In the figure above, if m_1 is parallel to m_2 and m_3 is perpendicular to m_1, what is the value of x, in degrees?
   a) 40
   b) 45
   c) 50
   d) 55

7. For $b > a$, the product of 3 and $(b - a)$ is equal to the average of a and b. If b is 35, what is a?
   a) 21
   b) 25
   c) 30
   d) 35

8. Each of the following is a factor of 72 EXCEPT?
   a) 2
   b) 4
   c) 16
   d) 9

9. If $(3x + 6)(1 - x) = 0$, what are all the possible values of x?
   a) 1 only
   b) −2 only
   c) 0 only
   d) 1 and −2 only

10. If $x^2 - 2x = 8$, which of the following is a possible value of $x^2 - x =$?
   a) 12
   b) 9
   c) −6
   d) −9

11. In the figure below, what is the value of x?

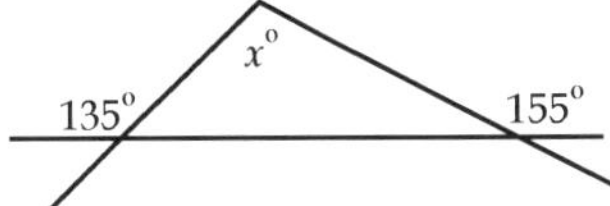

   a) 150
   b) 135
   c) 120
   d) 110

12. If $0 > a > b$, which of the following must be less than $\frac{a}{b}$?
   a) 1
   b) 2
   c) ab
   d) $\frac{a}{2b}$

13. If $g(x) = 3x - 6$, then at what value of x does the graph of $g(x)$ cross the x-axis?
   a) − 6
   b) −3
   c) 0
   d) 2

14. A parking lot charges $3.00 maintenance fee per day to use its parking space. In addition, there is a charge of $1.25 per hour. Which of the following represents the total charge, in dollars, to park a car in the parking lot for m hours in one day?
    a) $3 + 1.25m$
    b) $3m + 1.25$
    c) $(3 + 1.25)m$
    d) $3 + 1.25 + m$

15. Among the 10 colleges Michele applied to, 4 are her top schools. How many admissions would Michele have to receive to guarantee that she can get into at least one of her top schools?
    a) 6
    b) 7
    c) 8
    d) 9

Directions:

For questions 16-20, solve the problem and enter your answer in the grid, as described below, on the answer sheet.

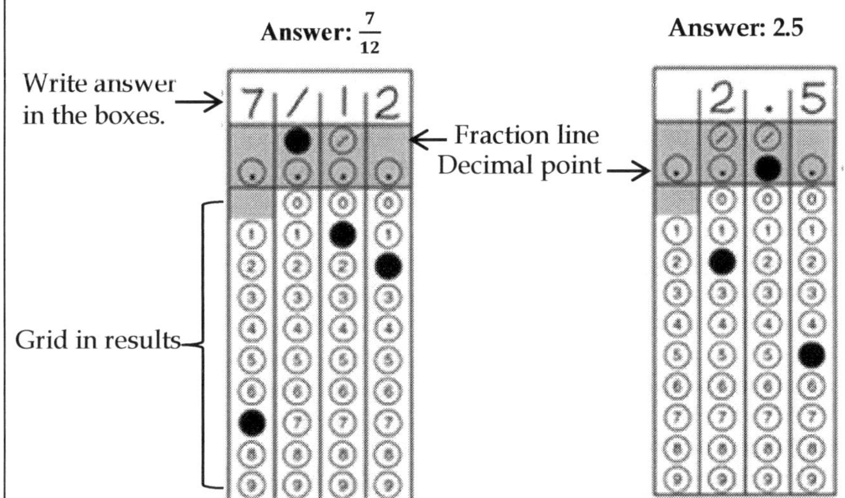

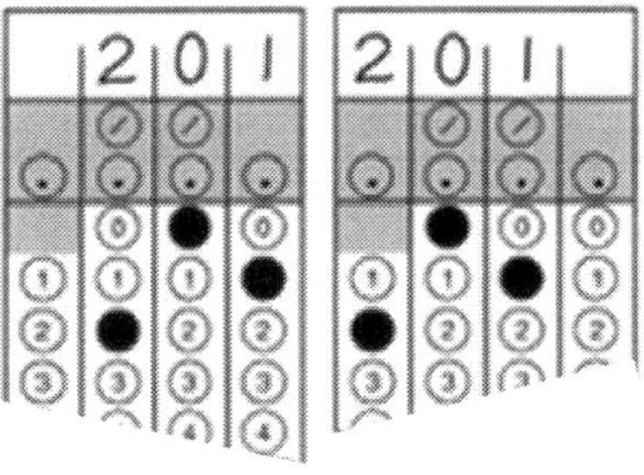

Note: You may start your answers in any column, space permitting. Columns not needed should be left blank.

- Mark no more than one circle in any column.
- Because the answer sheet will be machine-scored. **You will receive credit only if the circles are filled in correctly.**
- Although not required, it is suggested that you write your answer in the boxes at the top of the columns to help you fill in the circles accurately.
- Some problems may have more than one correct answer. In such case, grid only one answer.
- No question has a negative answer.
- **Mixed numbers** such as $3\frac{1}{2}$ must be gridded as 3.5 or $\frac{7}{2}$. (If 31/2 is gridded, it will be interpreted as $\frac{31}{2}$, not $3\frac{1}{2}$.)

- **Decimal Answer**: If you obtain a decimal answer with more digits than the grid can accommodate, it may be either rounded or truncated, but it must fill the entire grid. The acceptable ways to grid $\frac{2}{3}$ are:

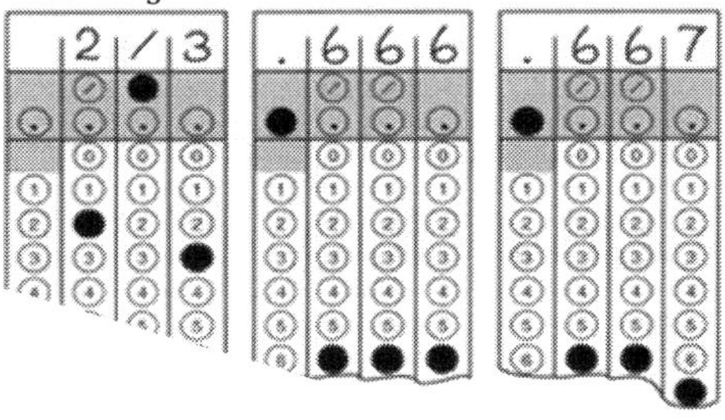

16. If the sum of ten integers is odd, at most how many of these integers could be odd?

17. If $x > 1$ and $\frac{6}{\sqrt{x-1}} = 3$, what is the value of x?

18. There are four points A, B, C, D and E on line l, and another four points W, X, Y, and Z on a different line parallel to line l. How many distinct lines can be drawn that include exactly two of these 9 points?

19. In the figure below shows ΔABC and its exterior angle $\angle$DAC. What is the value of a?

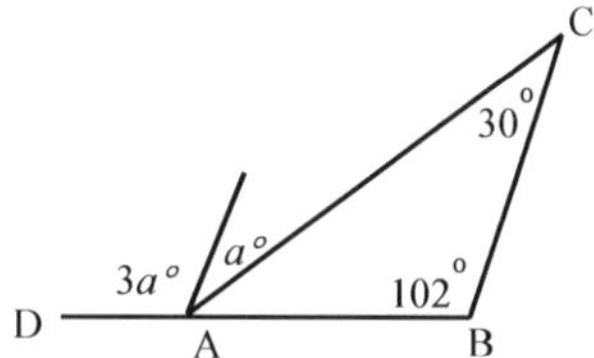

20. Kat has some coins in her purse. Of the coins, 5 are pennies. If she randomly picks one of the coins from her purse, the probability of picking a penny is $\frac{1}{4}$. How many coins are in her purse?

SECTION 4

Math Test – Calculator 55 MINUTES, 38 QUESTIONS

Directions:

For questions 1-30, solve each problem, choose the best answer from the choices provided, and fill in the corresponding circle on your answer sheet. **For questions 31-38**, solve the problem and enter your answer in the grid on the answer sheet. Please refer to the directions before question 31 on how to enter your answers in the grid. You may use any available space in your test booklet for scratch work.

Notes:

1. Acceptable calculators are allowed for this section. All numbers used are real numbers.
2. Figures that accompany problems in this test are intended to provide information useful in solving the problems. They are drawn as accurately as possible EXCEPT when it is stated in a specific problem that the figure is not drawn to scale. All figures lie in a plane unless otherwise indicated.
3. Unless otherwise specified, the domain of any function *f(x)* assumed to be the set of all real numbers *x* for which *f(x)* is a real number.

References:

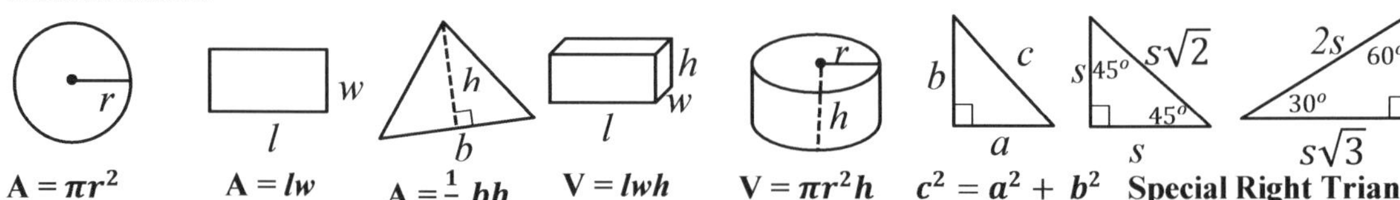

$A = \pi r^2$ $C = 2\pi r$ $A = lw$ $A = \frac{1}{2}bh$ $V = lwh$ $V = \pi r^2 h$ $c^2 = a^2 + b^2$ **Special Right Triangles**

The number of degrees of arc in a circle is 360; the number of radians of arc in a circle is 2π.
The sum of the degree measures of the angles in a triangle is 180.

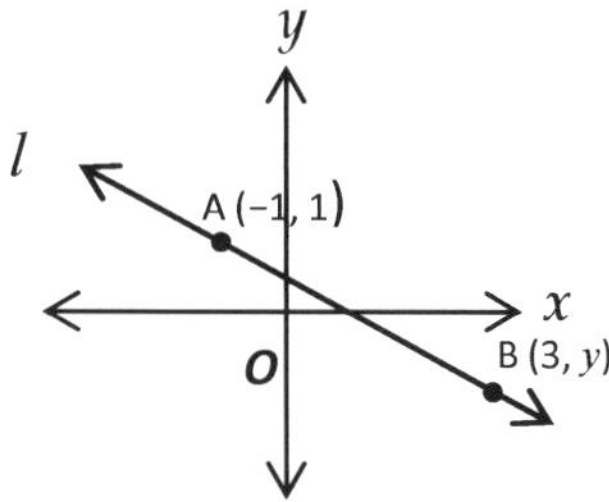

1. In the figure above, the slope of line *l* is $-\frac{1}{2}$. What is the value of *y*?
   a) $\frac{1}{2}$
   b) 1
   c) $-\frac{1}{2}$
   d) −1

2. Which of the following sets of numbers has an average (arithmetic mean) that is less than its median?
   a) {−2, −1, 1}
   b) {−2, −1, 1, 2, 3}
   c) {1, 2, 3, 6}
   d) {1, 2, 3, 4, 5}

3. If 50 pounds of force can stretch a spring 5 inches, how many inches will the spring be stretched by a force of 70 pounds? Assume the force needed to stretch a spring varies directly with its stretch distance.
   a) 10
   b) 9

c) 8
d) 7

4. Mary has the following scores on 7 quizzes in Algebra class: 84, 79, 85, 87, 81, 94, and 87. What is the median score of all of her Algebra quizzes?
   a) 81
   b) 84
   c) 85
   d) 86

5. If 20 % of m is 24, what is 15% of m?
   a) 12
   b) 15
   c) 18
   d) 20

Questions 6 – 7 refer to the following information:

The Doppler effect is the change in frequency of a wave while its source is moving. The Doppler effect formulas shown below are used to calculate the frequency of sound as a result of relative motion between the source and the observer.

If the source is moving toward an observer at rest, the change of observed frequency can be calculated by:

$$f_{observed} = f_{original}\left(\frac{v_{sound}}{v_{sound} - v_{source}}\right)$$

If the observer is moving toward the sound and the source moving closer to the observer, the change of frequency can be calculated by:

$$f_{observed} = f_{original}\left(\frac{v_{sound} + v_{observer}}{v_{sound} - v_{source}}\right)$$

$f_{observed}$ = observed frequency
$f_{original}$ = frequency of the original wave
v_{sound} = speed of the sound
$v_{observer}$ = speed of the observer
v_{source} = speed of the source

6. Standing on the side walk, you observe an ambulance moving toward you. As the ambulance passes by with its siren blaring, you hear the pitch of the siren change. If the ambulance is approaching at the speed of 50 miles/hour and the siren's pitch sounds at a frequency of 340 Hertz, what is the observed frequency, in Hertz? Assume that the speed of sound in air is 760 miles/hour.
   a) 332
   b) 364
   c) 399
   d) 409

7. If you are driving a car at the speed of 50 miles/hour while an ambulance is approaching to you at the speed of 70 miles/hour, what is the observed frequency of the siren, in Hertz? Assume that the ambulance sounds at a frequency of 340 Hertz and the speed of sound in air is 760 miles/hour.
   a) 332
   b) 364
   c) 399
   d) 409

$$p(t) = 1000 \times (3)^{\frac{t}{2}}$$

8. The growth of certain kind of bacterial is observed and its population growth, p, t days from the first observation, is modeled by the function above. By how much does the bacterial population increase from $t = 4$ to $t = 6$?
   a) 18,000
   b) 16,000
   c) 15,000
   d) 14,000

9. If 60 percent of x is 48, then what is 20 percent of x?
   a) 30
   b) 20
   c) 16
   d) 14

10. Let the function f be defined by $f(x) = x^2 + 27$. If $f(3y) = 3f(y)$, what is the one possible value of y?
    a) −1
    b) 1
    c) 2
    d) −3

$$h(t) = -16t^2 + 320t + h_o$$

11. At time $t = 0$, a rocket was launched from a height of h_o feet above the ground. Until the rocket hit the ground, its height, in feet, after t seconds was given by the function h above. For which of the following values of t did the rocket have the same height as it did when $t = 5$
    a) 10
    b) 15
    c) 18
    d) 20

12. If Bill can run $\frac{5}{4}$ as fast as Mitt. Sam can run $\frac{6}{5}$ as fast as Bill. Mitt can run how many times as fast as the average speed of Bill and Sam?
    a) $\frac{8}{11}$
    b) $\frac{9}{11}$
    c) 1
    d) $\frac{11}{9}$

13. How many positive factors does the number 72 have?
    a) 5
    b) 6
    c) 12
    d) 9

14. Linda's purse contains 6 quarters, 3 dimes, 4 nickels, and 5 pennies. If she takes out one coin at random, what is the probability that the coin is worth more than 5 cents?
    a) $\frac{1}{4}$
    b) $\frac{1}{3}$
    c) $\frac{2}{5}$
    d) $\frac{1}{2}$

15. The table below shows the number of students attending Knollwood High School from 2009 through 2013. If the median number of students for the five years was 355, and no two years had the same number of students, what is the most possible value for X?

Old Oak High School Student Population	
Year	*Number of Students*
2009	*X*
2010	*325*
2011	*387*
2012	*376*
2013	*355*

    a) 360
    b) 365
    c) 356
    d) 350

16. The table below gives values of the quadratic function $f(x)$ at selected values of x. Which of the following defines $f(x)$?

x	0	1	2	3
$f(x)$	3	4	7	12

    a) $f(x) = x^2 + 3$
    b) $f(x) = x^2 + 1$
    c) $f(x) = 2x^2 - 3$
    d) $f(x) = 2x^2 + 3$

17. Each term in a sequence of numbers, except for the first term, is 2 less than the square root of the previous term. If the third term of this sequence is 1, what is the first term?
    a) 4
    b) 9
    c) 121
    d) 81

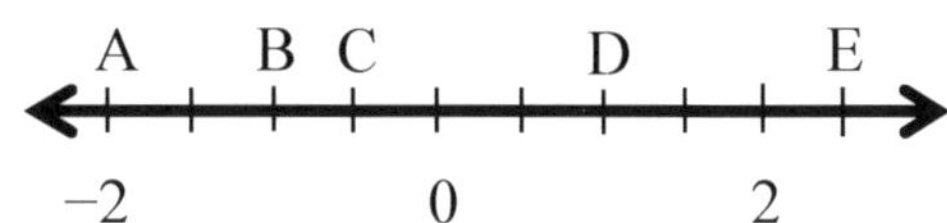

18. On the number line above, A, B, C, D and E are coordinate points. Which of the following is closest in value to |A − 2 × C|?
    a) A
    b) B
    c) C
    d) D

19. In the figure below, the two circles are tangent at point P and OQ = 12. If the area of the circle with center O is nine times the area of the circle with center Q, what is the length of OP?

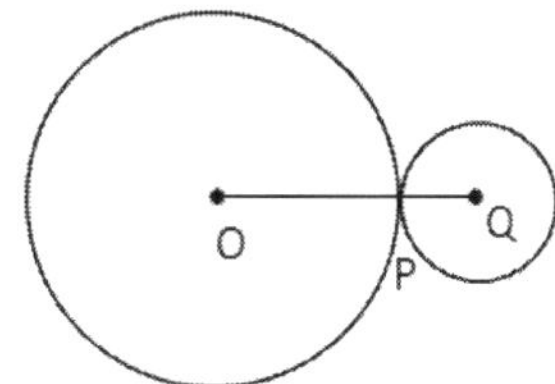

Note: Figure not drawn to scale.
    a) 3
    b) 4
    c) 6
    d) 9

20. If $f(x) = \frac{x^2-15}{x^2-20}$, what is the value of $f(5)$?
    a) 0
    b) 2
    c) 4
    d) 6

21. There are 18 boxes of apples in the storage room. Each box has at least 23 apples, and at most 25 apples. Which of the following could be the total number of apples in the storage room?
    a) 300
    b) 350
    c) 400
    d) 425

22. The kinetic energy of an object is calculated by the following formula:

$$K_e = \frac{1}{2}mv^2$$

where K_e is the kinetic energy, m is the mass, and v is the velocity. If the mass of an object is a constant, which of the following graphs best represents the possible relationship between the kinetic energy (K_e) and the velocity (v) of the object?

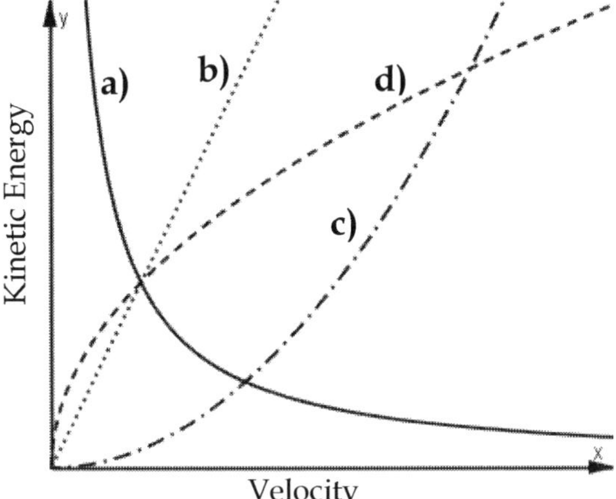

23. Rachel has either blue or black pens in her pencil case. If the ratio of the number of blue pens to the number of black pens is $\frac{1}{5}$, Rachel could have the following number of pens in her pencil case EXCEPT?
    a) 12
    b) 18
    c) 34
    d) 36

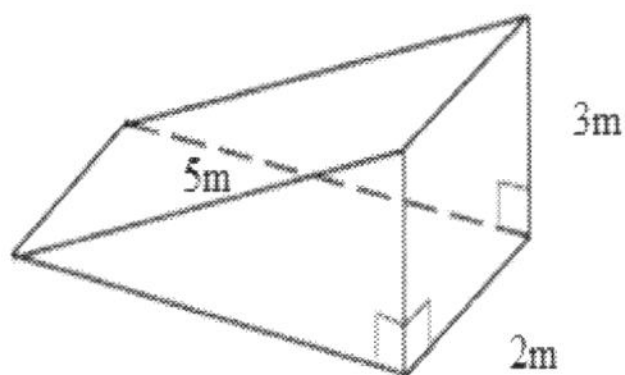

24. Find the surface area in square meter of the half of a rectangular solid as shown above.
    a) 44
    b) 36
    c) 34
    d) 32

Questions 25 – 26 refer to the following information:

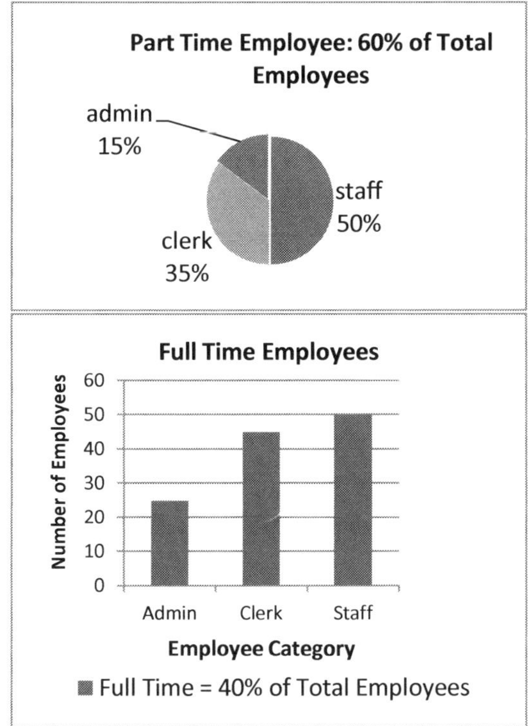

25. According to the graphs above, the total number of part-time employees is how many more than the total number of full-time employees at Oak Town High School?
    a) 20
    b) 40
    c) 50
    d) 60

26. According to the graphs above, how many part-time staff members are at Oak Town High School?
    a) 100
    b) 90
    c) 80
    d) 60

27. If w is a positive number and $w > w^2$, which of the following statements is true?

    $w^2 > w^3$

    $w > \frac{w}{3}$

    $w > w^3$

    a) I, II
    b) II, III
    c) I, II, and III
    d) I only

28. Class A has X students and class B has Y students. The average of the test scores of class A is 81, and the average of the test scores of class B is 86. When the scores of class A and B are combined, the average score is 83. What is the ratio of X to Y?
    a) $\frac{1}{2}$
    b) $\frac{2}{3}$
    c) 1
    d) $\frac{3}{2}$

29. How many positive factors does the number 875 have?
    a) 9
    b) 8
    c) 7
    d) 6

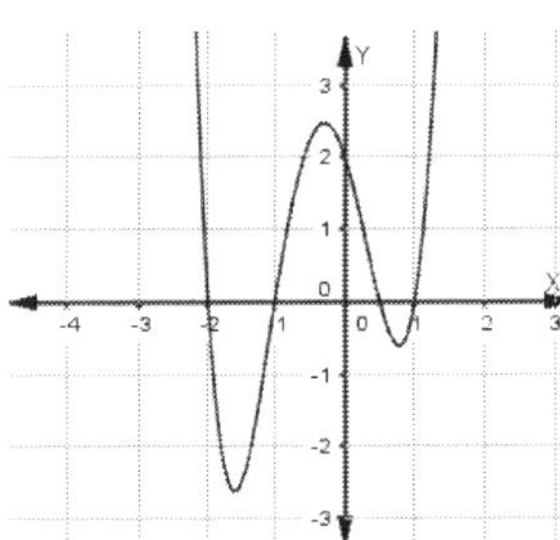

30. The function $f(x) = 2x^4 + 3x^3 - 4x^2 - 3x + 2$ was graphed in the xy-plane above. How many real solutions are there if $f(x) = 3x$?
    a) 1
    b) 2
    c) 3
    d) 4

Directions:

For questions 31-38, solve the problem and enter your answer in the grid, as described below, on the answer sheet.

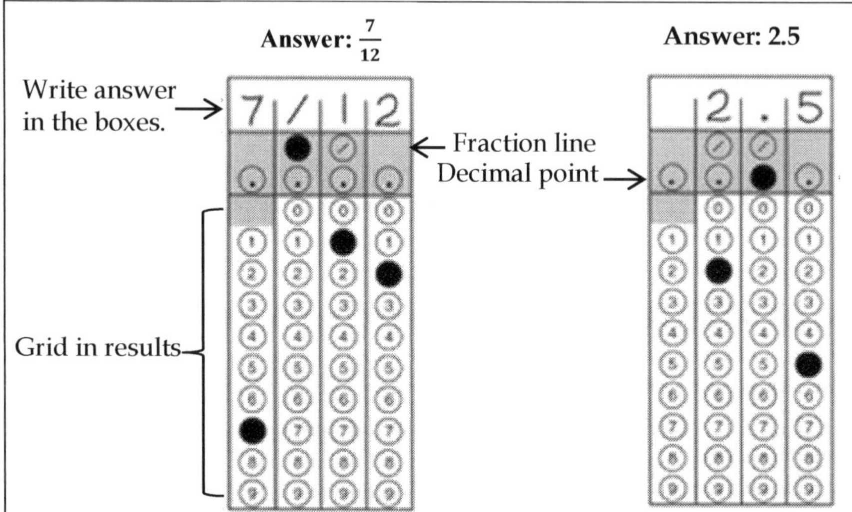

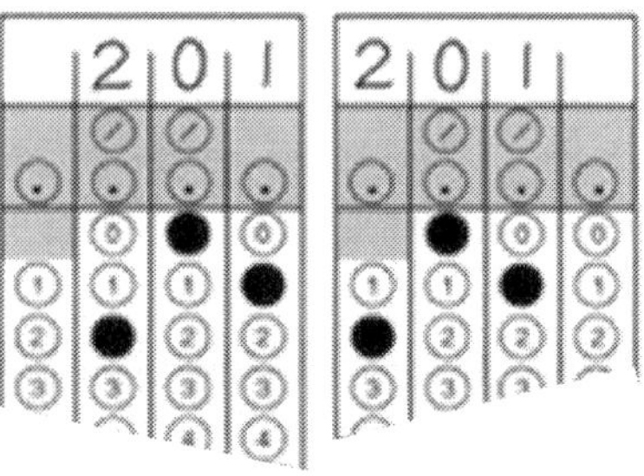

Note: You may start your answers in any column, space permitting. Columns not needed should be left blank.

- Mark no more than one circle in any column.
- Because the answer sheet will be machine-scored. **You will receive credit only if the circles are filled in correctly.**
- Although not required, it is suggested that you write your answer in the boxes at the top of the columns to help you fill in the circles accurately.
- Some problems may have more than one correct answer. In such case, grid only one answer.
- No question has a negative answer.
- **Mixed numbers** such as $3\frac{1}{2}$ must be gridded as 3.5 or $\frac{7}{2}$. (If 3 1/2 is gridded, it will be interpreted as $\frac{31}{2}$, not $3\frac{1}{2}$.)
- **Decimal Answer**: If you obtain a decimal answer with more digits than the grid can accommodate, it may be either rounded or truncated, but it must fill the entire grid. The acceptable ways to grid $\frac{2}{3}$ are:

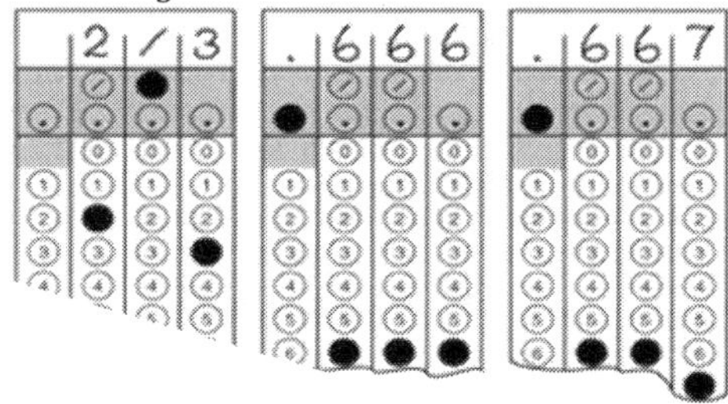

x	1	2	3	4	5
$f(x)$	5	9	y	17	21

31. The table above defines a linear function. What is the value of y?

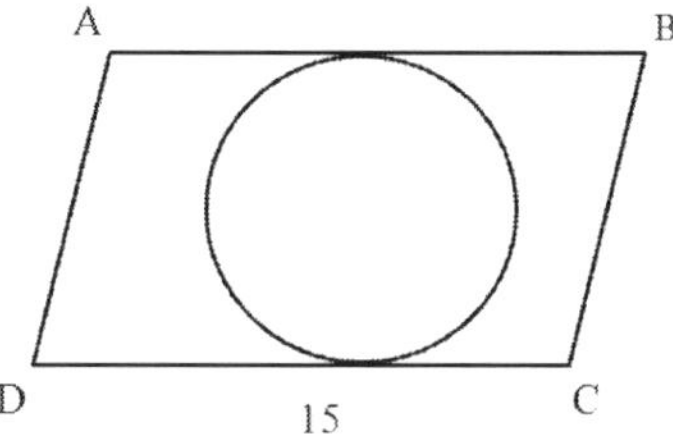

32. A circle is tangent to two sides of a parallelogram ABCD as shown in the figure above. If the circle has an area of 25π, what is the area of the parallelogram ABCD?

33. In a toy factory production line, every 9th toy has their electronic parts checked and every 12th toy will have their safety features checked. In the first 180 toys, what is the probability that a toy will have both its electronic parts and safety features checked?

34. How many combinations of three dishes can be prepared if you have the recipes for 9 dishes?

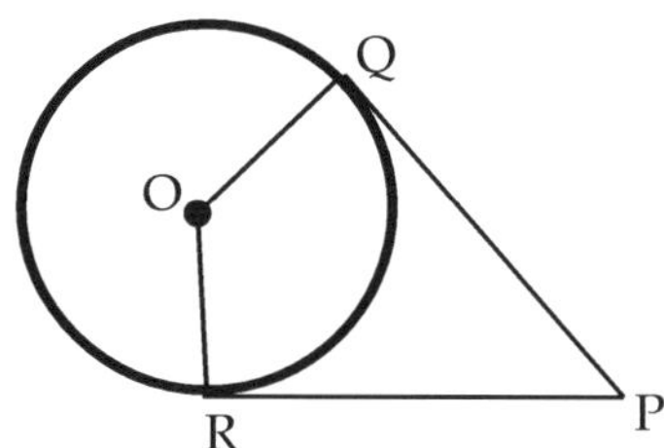

35. In the figure above, point O is the center of the circle, line segments PQ and PR are tangent to the circle at points Q and R, respectively, and the segments intersect at point P as shown. If the radius of the circle is 5 and the length of PQ is $5\sqrt{3}$, what is the area of minor sector $\widehat{RQ}$? (Round your answer to the nearest tenth.)

$$(2-i)(3+2i)=a+bi$$

36. In the equation above, a and b are two real numbers. What is the value of $a+2b$?

37. A ramp is 20 meters long and set at a 30° angle of inclination. If you walk up to the top of the ramp, how high off the ground (in meters) will you be?

38. Find the radius of the circle given by the equation $x^2+y^2-4x+2y=20$.

SAT MATH MOCK TEST No. 5 ANSWER KEYS

Section 3									
1. C	2. D	3. D	4. D	5. D	6. C	7. B	8. D	9. D	10. A
11. D	12. D	13. B	14. A	15. B	16. 9	17. 5	18. 20	19. 33	20. 20

Section 4									
1. D	2. B	3. D	4. C	5. C	6. B	7. C	8. A	9. C	10. D
11. B	12. A	13. C	14. D	15. D	16. A	17. C	18. D	19. D	20. B
21. D	22. C	23. C	24. B	25. D	26. B	27. C	28. D	29. B	30. B
31. 13	32. 150	33. $\frac{1}{36}$	34. 84	35. 26.2	36. 10	37. 10	38. 5		

SECTION 3

1. *Answer: (c)*
   $3^{(a+b)} = 81 = 3^4$
   $a + b = 4$
   $2^b = 4 = 2^2$
   $b = 2$
   $a = 2$
   $2^a = 2^2 = 4$

2. *Answer: (d)*
   It is easier to use the method of elimination for this question.
   $3a - 2b = 5$ (1)
   $a + 2b = 23$ (2)
   Add equations (1) and (2) to eliminate b.
   $(1) + (2) \rightarrow 4a = 28$
   $a = 7$
   $3 \times 7 - 2b = 5$
   $b = 8$
   $a + b = 15$

3. *Answer: (d)*
   $5 \times 4^n + 4^n + 4^n + 4^n = 8 \times 4^n = 2^3 \times 2^{2n} = 2^{2n+3}$

4. *Answer: (d)*
   If x is an even integer, consecutive even integers can be written as x, x − 2, and x − 4.
   Use the Pythagorean theorem.
   $(x-2)^2 + (x-4)^2 = x^2$
   $x^2 - 12x + 20 = 0$
   $(x-2)(x-10) = 0$
   x = 2 (not applicable because length of other sides will be negative) or
   $x = 10$

5. *Answer: (d)*
   The length of the 3rd side should be smaller than the sum of the lengths of the other two sides and greater than their difference.
   $7 - 3 < x < 7 + 3$
   $4 < x < 10$

6. *Answer: (c)*

   We are given that $m_1 \parallel m_2$, so if $m_1 \perp m_3$, then $m_2 \perp m_3$.
   The vertical angles are equal and $m_2 \perp m_3$, thus $x + 40 = 90$.
   $x = 50$

7. *Answer: (b)*
   If b = 35, then $\frac{35+a}{2} = 3 \times (35 - a)$.
   $35 + a = 6(35 - a)$
   $35 + a = 6 \times 35 - 6a$
   $7a = 5 \times 35 \rightarrow a = 25$

8. *Answer: (d)*
   Only 16 is not the factor of 72.

9. *Answer: (d)*
   Solve for x by zero-product rule.
   $(3x + 6)(1 - x) = 0$
   $3x + 6 = 0$ or $1 - x = 0$
   $x = 1$ or -2

10. *Answer: (a)*
Factor $x^2 - 2x - 8$.
$(x - 4)(x + 2) = 0$
$x = 4$ *or* -2
Plug $x = 4$ *and* -2 *into the expression.*
$x^2 - x = (4)^2 - 4 = 12$ *or*
$x^2 - x = (-2)^2 - (-2) = 6$

11. *Answer: (d)*
The three interior angles of the triangle are $x°$, $(180 - 135)°$, *and* $(180 - 155)°$.
$x + 45 + 25 = 180$
$x = 110$

12. *Answer: (d)*
$0 > a > b$
If divided each sides by b, then change direction:
$0 < \frac{a}{b} < 1$.
Only (d) correct. $\frac{a}{2b} < \frac{a}{b}$

13. *Answer: (d)*
The value of x where g(x) crosses the x-axis is the value of x where g(x) is equal to 0.
$0 = 3x - 6$
$x = 2$

14. *Answer: (a)*
Parking m hours costs \$1.25 × m plus \$3 maintenance fee per day, so the total charge would be $3 + 1.25m$.

15. *Answer: (b)*
$10 - 4 = 6$
She applied to 6 schools that are not her top choices. If all 6 of these schools accept Michele, then the 7th school which accepts her must be one of her top schools.
$6 + 1 = 7$

16. *Answer: 9*
Sum of odd number of odd integers is odd. So there are 9 odd integers at most.

17. *Answer: 5*
Apply cross multiplication.
$\frac{6}{\sqrt{x-1}} = \frac{3}{1}$
$\sqrt{x-1} \times 3 = 6$
$\sqrt{x-1} = 2$
$x - 1 = 4$
$x = 5$

18. *Answer: 20*
Each of the five points on line l can be connected to each of the four points on the parallel line.
$5 \times 4 = 20$

19. *Answer: 33*
$3a + a = 30 + 102 = 132$
$4a = 132$
$a = 33$

20. *Answer: 20*
$\frac{5}{\text{Total Coins}} = \frac{1}{4}$
Total Coins = 20

SECTION 4

1. *Answer: (d)*
$slope = \frac{y-1}{3-(-1)} = -\frac{1}{2}$
$y - 1 = -2$
$y = -1$

2. *Answer: (b)*
To find the median, sort all the numbers in the set from least to greatest. If there are odd amount of numbers in a set, then median is the middle number. If there are even amount of numbers in the set, median is the average of the two middle numbers.
Average $= -\frac{2}{3}$ *Median* $= -1$
Average $= 0.6$ *Median* $= 1$
Average $= 3$ *Median* $= 2.5$
Average $= 3$ *Median* $= 3$
Average $= 3.2$ *Median* $= 3$

3. *Answer: (d)*
$\frac{50 \text{ pounds}}{5 \text{ inches}} = \frac{70 \text{ pounds}}{x \text{ inches}}$
$x = 7$ *inches*

4. *Answer: (c)*
Sort the scores in order.
79, 81, 84, 85, 87, 87, 94
The median is 85.

5. *Answer: (c)*
$20\% \times m = 24$
$m = 120$
15% *of* $120 \rightarrow 15\% \times 120$
$15\% \times 120 = 18$

6. *Answer: (b)*
The source is moving toward an observer at rest.

$f_{observed} = f_{original}\left(\frac{v_{sound}}{v_{sound} - v_{source}}\right)$
$v_{observer} = 0\ miles/hour$
$v_{source} = 50\ miles/hour$
$v_{sound} = 760\ miles/hour$
$f_{observed} = 340 \times \left(\frac{760}{760-50}\right)$
$= 364\ Hertz$

7. *Answer: (c)*
The observer is moving toward the sound.
$f_{observed} = f_{original}\left(\frac{v_{sound} + v_{observer}}{v_{sound} - v_{source}}\right)$
$v_{observer} = 50\ miles/hour$
$v_{source} = 70\ miles/hour$
$v_{sound} = 760\ miles/hour$
$f_{observed} = 340 \times \left(\frac{760+50}{760-70}\right)$
$= 399.1$ *Hertz*

8. *Answer: (a)*
Plug in the two different values of t and find their difference.
$p(6) - p(4) = 27{,}000 - 9{,}000 = 18{,}000$

9. *Answer: (c)*
$\frac{60}{100} \times x = 48$
$x = 80$
$80 \times 0.2 = 16$ *(note that 20% = 0.2)*

10. *Answer: (d)*
$f(3y) = (3y)^2 + 27 = 3f(y) = 3(y^2 + 27)$
$9y^2 + 27 = 3y^2 + 3 \times 27$
$6y^2 = 54,\ \ y^2 = 9,\ \ y = \pm 3$

11. *Answer: (b)*
$h(5) = -16(5)^2 + 320(5) + h_o = -16t^2 + 320t + h_o$
divided by 16
$-25 + 100 = -t^2 + 20t$
$t^2 - 20t + 75 = 0$
$(t - 5)(t - 15) = 0$
$t = 5$ *or* 15

12. *Answer: (a)*
Let Mitt can run at speed of x
Bill has speed of $\frac{5}{4}x$
Sam has speed of $\frac{6}{5} \times \frac{5}{4}x = \frac{3}{2}x$
The average speed of Sam and Bill:
$\frac{1}{2} \times (\frac{5}{4} + \frac{3}{2})x = \frac{11x}{8}$
Mitt has $\frac{x}{\frac{11}{8}x} = \frac{8}{11}$ *times as fast as their average speed.*

13. *Answer: (c)*
$72 = 2^3 \times 3^2$
Number of positive factors of 72:
$(3 + 1) \times (2 + 1) = 12$

14. *Answer: (d)*
If the coin is worth more than 5 cents, then the coin must be either a quarter or a dime.
Probability $= \frac{6+3}{6+3+4+5} = \frac{9}{18} = \frac{1}{2}$

15. *Answer: (d)*
If the median number of students for the five years was 355, there should be 2 years with number of students more than 355 and 2 years with number of students less than 355.
X should be less than 355.

16. *Answer: (a)*
Based on the information from the answer choices, assume $f(x) = ax^2 + b$.
Plug in $x = 0$ *and* $x = 1$ *to find a and b.*
$a(0)^2 + b = 3$
$b = 3$
$a(1)^2 + 3 = 4$
$a = 1$
Therefore $f(x) = x^2 + 3$
try $x = 2$
$(2)^2 + 3 = 7$ *(double check)*

17. *Answer: (c)*
If first term is x, then second term is $\sqrt{x} - 2$ *and the third term is* $\sqrt{\sqrt{x} - 2} - 2$.
$\sqrt{\sqrt{x} - 2} - 2. = 1$
$\sqrt{x} - 2 = 3^2$
$\sqrt{x} = 11$
$x = 121$

18. *Answer: (d)*
$A = -2$ *and* $C = -\frac{1}{2}$
$|A - 2 \times C| = |-2 - 2(-\frac{1}{2})|$
$= |-2 + 1| = |-1| = 1$
D has the coordinate of 1.

19. *Answer: (d)*
Since the area of circle O is nine times the area of circle Q, the radius of circle O is $\sqrt{9}$ *times of the radius of circle Q.*
If $PQ = r$, $OP = 3r$, *then* $r + 3r = 12$.
$r = 3 = PQ$
$OP = 12 - 3 = 9$

20. *Answer: (b)*
Plug the number 5 into the function.
$f(5) = \frac{5^2-15}{5^2-20}$
$\frac{10}{5} = 2$

21. *Answer: (d)*
Set up the inequality for the number of apples and then multiply the inequality by 18.
$(23 < x < 25) \times 18$
$414 < 15x < 450$

22. *Answer: (c)*
Since $\frac{1}{2}m$ *is a constant,* $K_e \propto v^2$

23. *Answer: (c)*
The total number of pens is a whole number and a multiple of (1 + 5).
34 is not a multiple of 6.

24. *Answer: (b)*
Surface Area $= 2 \times 3 + 2 \times (\frac{1}{2} \times 3 \times 4) + 4 \times 2 + 5 \times 2 = 36$

25. *Answer: (d)*

Number of Full Time Employees = 25 + 45 + 50 =120 employees.

Full time employees comprise of 40% of the total.
0.4 × Number of Employees = 120.
Number of Employees = 300.
Part Time Employees = 300 × 0.6= 180.
Part Time Employees – Full Time Employees = 180 – 120 = 60 employees

26. *Answer: (b)*
Number of Part time staff = number of Part Time Employees × 0.5 = 180 × 0.5 = 90.

27. *Answer: (c)*
w is a positive number and $w < w^2$.
$w^2 - w > 0$
$w(1 - w) > 0$
$w > 0$ *and* $1 - w > 0$
$-w > -1,\ w < 1$
So $0 < w < 1$.
If $0 < w < 1$, *then any number multiplied by w produces a number smaller than the original number.*
Therefore $w^2 > w^3$, $w^3 > w^4$, *and so on.*
I, II, III are all correct.

28. *Answer: (d)*
We want to find $\frac{X}{Y}$.
Average: $\frac{\text{Sum of Terms}}{\text{Number of Terms}}$
$\frac{81X+86Y}{X+Y} = 83$ *(cross multiply)*
$81X + 86Y = 83 \times (X + Y)$
$81X + 86Y = 83X + 83Y$
$3Y = 2X$
$\frac{X}{Y} = \frac{3}{2}$

29. *Answer: (b)*
$875 = 5^3 \times 7$
Number of positive factors:
$(3 + 1) \times (1 + 1) = 8$

30. *Answer: (b)*
There are two intersections between $y = 3x$ *and* $y = 2x^4 + 3x^3 - 4x^2 - 3x + 2$

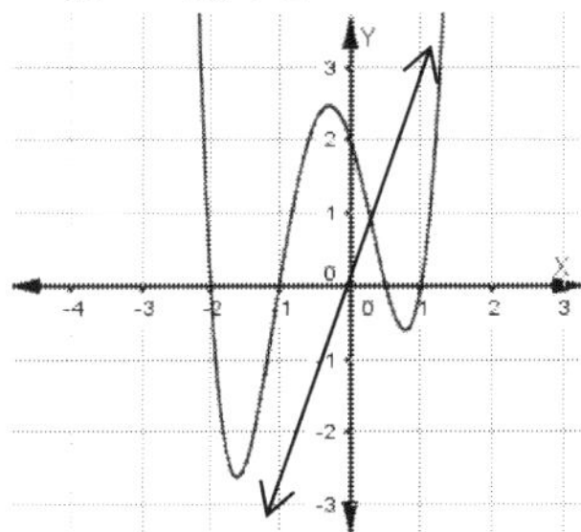

31. *Answer: 13*
Slope $= \frac{9-5}{2-1} = \frac{y-9}{3-2}$
$4 = y - 9$
$y = 13$

32. *Answer: 150*
The area of the parallelogram ABCD is equal to its base multiplied by its height.
Base × Height = 15 × Diameter of Circle
$\pi r^2 = 25\pi$
$r = 5$
$d = 2r = 10$
Area of Parallelogram = 15 × 10 = 150

33. *Answer:* $\frac{1}{36}$
The LCM of 9 and 12 is 36.
The every 36th toy will have both of their electronic parts and safety features checked.
There are 5 such toys (180 divided by 36).
$\frac{5}{180} = \frac{1}{36}$

34. *Answer: 84*
This is combination. The number of ways to select m objects from n objects ($n \geq m$), where order does not matter:

$$(C_m^n = \frac{n!}{m!(n-m)!})$$

To choose 3 from 9: $C_3^9 = \frac{9!}{3! \times 6!} = 84$

35. *Answer: 26.2*

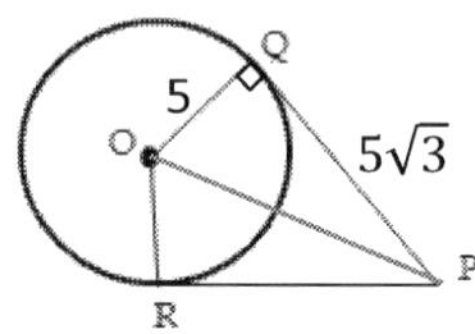

In the right triangle ΔOPQ*, the ratio of* $\frac{QP}{QO} = \sqrt{3}$*, therefore* $\angle QOP = 60^o$ *and* $\angle QOR = 120^o$

The area of the minor sector $\widehat{RQ} = \frac{120}{360} \times \pi \times 5^2 = 26.2$

36. *Answer: 10*
$(2-i)(3+2i) = 6 + 4i - 3i - 2i^2 = 6 + i + 2 = 8 + i$
$a = 8$ *and* $b = 1$
$a + 2b = 10$

37. *Answer: 10*

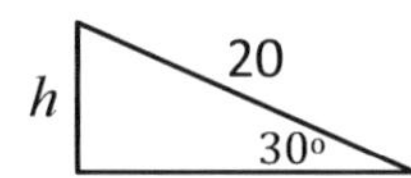

$h = 20 \times sin(30^o)$
$= 20 \times 0.5 = 10$

38. *Answer: 5*
Rewitte to the standard equation for a circle:
$x^2 - 4x + 4 + y^2 + 2y + 1 = 20 + 5$
$(x-2)^2 + (y+1)^2 = 5^2$
The center of the circle is $(2, -1)$ *and the radius is 5.*

SAT Math Mock Test No. 6

SECTION 3 

Math Test – NO Calculator **25 MINUTES, 20 QUESTIONS**

Directions:

For questions 1-15, solve each problem, choose the best answer from the choices provided, and fill in the corresponding circle on your answer sheet. **For questions 16-20**, solve the problem and enter your answer in the grid on the answer sheet. Please refer to the directions before question 16 on how to enter your answers in the grid. You may use any available space in your test booklet for scratch work.

Notes:

1. **No calculator** is allowed for this section. All numbers used are real numbers.
2. Figures that accompany problems in this test are intended to provide information useful in solving the problems. They are drawn as accurately as possible EXCEPT when it is stated in a specific problem that the figure is not drawn to scale. All figures lie in a plane unless otherwise indicated.
3. Unless otherwise specified, the domain of any function *f(x)* assumed to be the set of all real numbers *x* for which *f(x)* is a real number.

References:

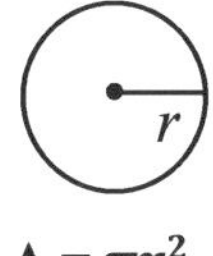

$A = \pi r^2$, $C = 2\pi r$ | $A = lw$ (l, w) | $A = \frac{1}{2}bh$ (b, h) | $V = lwh$ (l, w, h) | $V = \pi r^2 h$ (r, h) | $c^2 = a^2 + b^2$ (a, b, c) | **Special Right Triangles** (s, s, $s\sqrt{2}$, 45°, 45°; s, $2s$, $s\sqrt{3}$, 30°, 60°)

The number of degrees of arc in a circle is 360; the number of radians of arc in a circle is 2π. The sum of the degree measures of the angles in a triangle is 180.

1. If a and b are positive integers, x and y are negative integers, and if $a > b$ and $x > y$ which of the following must be less than zero?

   I. $b - a$
   II. $b \times y$
   III. $a + x$

   a) I only
   b) II only
   c) III only
   d) I and II only

2. If $x = -1$ and $y < 0$, which of the following has the greatest value?
   a) $2xy$
   b) $4x^2y$
   c) $10x^3y$
   d) $10x^4y$

3. The average (arithmetic mean) of 10, 14, and x is 18. What is the value of x?
   a) 25
   b) 26
   c) 27
   d) 30

4. To rent a single movie from a DVD lending machine, Mrs. Kinney was charged \$1 for the first day. For every day afterwards, she must pay a rental fee of \$1 plus a late fee of \$.50. If she paid a total of \$10, how many days did she keep the DVD?
   a) 7
   b) 6
   c) 5
   d) 4

5. By 7 AM, $\frac{1}{4}$ of all students were in school. Half an hour later, 100 more students arrived, raising the attendance to $\frac{3}{4}$ of the total students. How many students are in this school?
   a) 240
   b) 220
   c) 200
   d) 180

6. In the xy-plane, the line with equation $y = 4x - 8$ crosses the x-axis at the point with coordinates (a, b). What is the value of $a + b$?
   a) −3
   b) −2
   c) −1
   d) 2

7. An integer is divided by 2 more than itself. If the fraction is equal to $\frac{3}{4}$, what is the value of this integer?
   a) 2
   b) 5
   c) 6
   d) 8

8. What number decreased by 5 is equal to 21 increased by 3?
   a) 13
   b) 29
   c) 19
   d) 23

9. If $\frac{2x}{3} = \frac{3}{2}$, then x=?
   a) $\frac{2}{3}$
   b) $\frac{3}{2}$
   c) 2
   d) $\frac{9}{4}$

10. If $x^2 > 4$, which of the following must be true?
    a) $x > 4$
    b) $x > 2$
    c) $x < 2$
    d) $x > 2$ or $x < -2$

11. What is the y-intercept of the linear equation $3y - 2x = -12$?
    a) −4
    b) −2
    c) 2
    d) 4

12. Which of the following is an equation you would use to find x if it is given that 10 less than the product of x and 5 is 20?
    a) $5(x - 10) = 20$
    b) $5x - 2 = 20$
    c) $5(x - 2) = 20$
    d) $5x + 10 = 20$

All integers in set X are negative.

13. If the statement above is true, which of the following must also be true?
    a) If an integer is negative, it is in set X.
    b) If an integer is positive, it is in set X.
    c) Not all integers in set X are positive.
    d) Some integers in set X are positive.

14. If $x^2 - y^2 = 24$ and $x + y = 6$, find the value of y.
    a) 1
    b) 3
    c) 5
    d) 7

15. If x and y are positive integers and $(x^{\frac{1}{8}}y^{\frac{1}{8}})^2 = 3$, what is the value of xy?
    a) 9
    b) 27
    c) 64
    d) 81

Directions:

For questions 16-20, solve the problem and enter your answer in the grid, as described below, on the answer sheet.

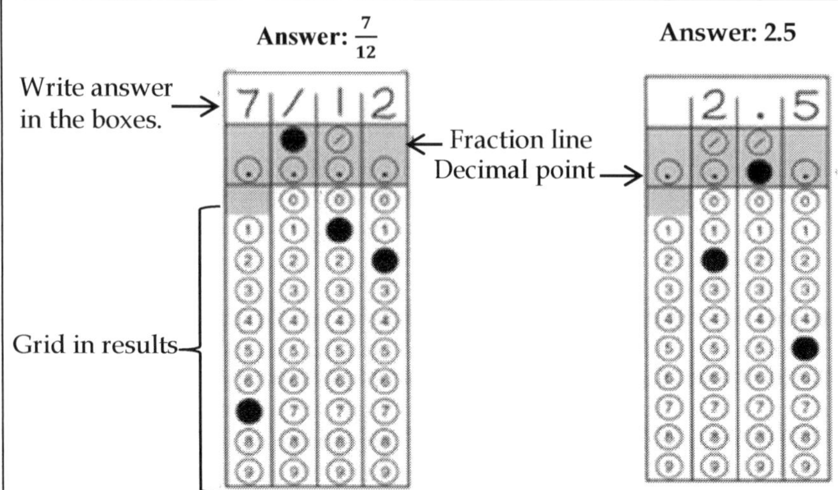

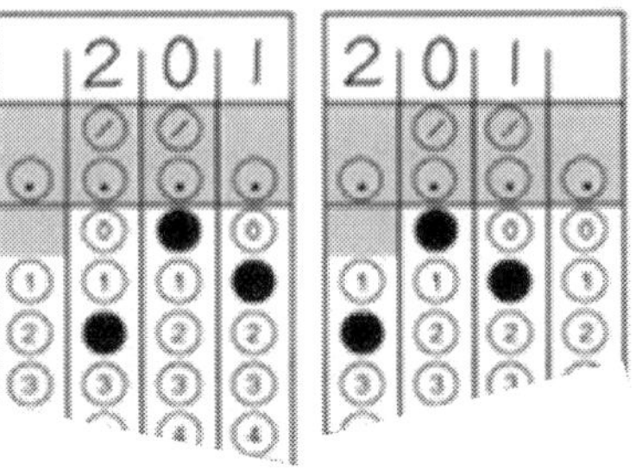

Note: You may start your answers in any column, space permitting. Columns not needed should be left blank.

- Mark no more than one circle in any column.
- Because the answer sheet will be machine-scored. **You will receive credit only if the circles are filled in correctly.**
- Although not required, it is suggested that you write your answer in the boxes at the top of the columns to help you fill in the circles accurately.
- Some problems may have more than one correct answer. In such case, grid only one answer.
- No question has a negative answer.
- **Mixed numbers** such as $3\frac{1}{2}$ must be gridded as 3.5 or $\frac{7}{2}$. (If 3 1 / 2 is gridded, it will be interpreted as $\frac{31}{2}$, not $3\frac{1}{2}$.)
- **Decimal Answer**: If you obtain a decimal answer with more digits than the grid can accommodate, it may be either rounded or truncated, but it must fill the entire grid. The acceptable ways to grid $\frac{2}{3}$ are:

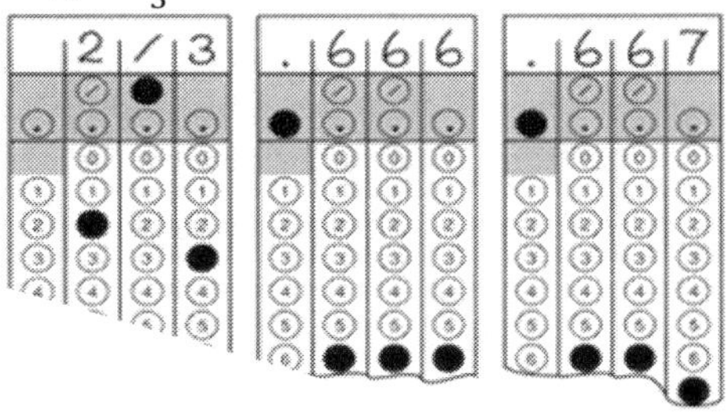

16. If $5x = 4y^2 = 20$, what is the value of xy^2?

17. In a poll, 45 people supported the current city mayor, 22 people were against him, and 8 people had no opinion. What fraction of those polled supported the city mayor?

18. If a certain kind of bird can fly at 2 feet per second, how many feet can it fly in an hour?

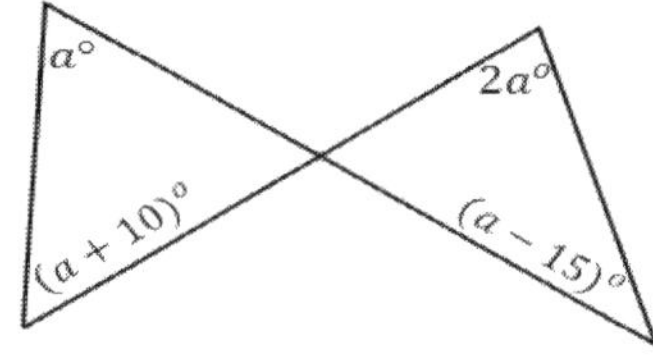

Note: Figure not drawn to scale.

19. In the figure above, what is the value of a?

20. There are $160 cash in John's pocket. John only has 10 and 20 dollar bills. If John has a total of 12 bills, how many 20 dollar bills are in his pocket?

SECTION 4

Math Test — Calculator **55 MINUTES, 38 QUESTIONS**

Directions:

For questions 1-30, solve each problem, choose the best answer from the choices provided, and fill in the corresponding circle on your answer sheet. **For questions 31-38**, solve the problem and enter your answer in the grid on the answer sheet. Please refer to the directions before question 31 on how to enter your answers in the grid. You may use any available space in your test booklet for scratch work.

Notes:

1. Acceptable calculators are allowed for this section. All numbers used are real numbers.
2. Figures that accompany problems in this test are intended to provide information useful in solving the problems. They are drawn as accurately as possible EXCEPT when it is stated in a specific problem that the figure is not drawn to scale. All figures lie in a plane unless otherwise indicated.
3. Unless otherwise specified, the domain of any function *f(x)* assumed to be the set of all real numbers *x* for which *f(x)* is a real number.

References:

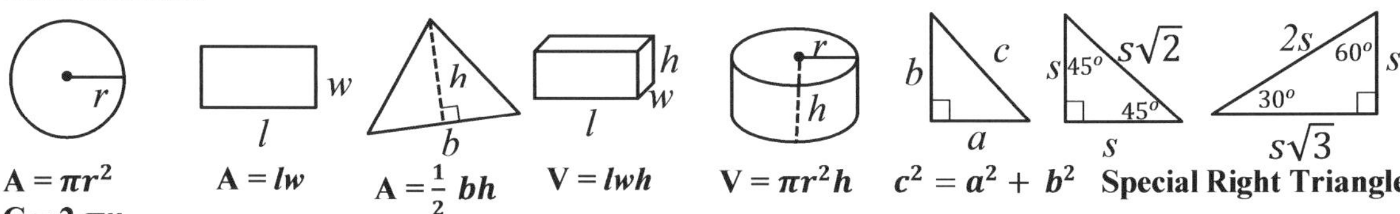

$A = \pi r^2$ $C = 2\pi r$ $A = lw$ $A = \frac{1}{2}bh$ $V = lwh$ $V = \pi r^2 h$ $c^2 = a^2 + b^2$ **Special Right Triangles**

The number of degrees of arc in a circle is 360; the number of radians of arc in a circle is 2π.
The sum of the degree measures of the angles in a triangle is 180.

1. There are 20 high school seniors who are taking the total of 85 AP classes this year. Some of them take 4 APs and the others take 5. How many seniors are taking 5 APs?
   a) 4
   b) 5
   c) 6
   d) 8

2. The area of equilateral triangle ΔXYZ is 9 times the area of equilateral triangle ΔABC. If the perimeter of ΔABC is 6, what is the length of one side of ΔXYZ?
   a) 4
   b) 6
   c) 8
   d) 9

3. If the sum of 4 numbers is between 65 and 67, then the average (arithmetic mean) of the 4 numbers could be which of the following?
   a) 15
   b) 15.2
   c) 15.5
   d) 16.5

4. According to the bar graph below, the total population in all five cities increased by approximately what percent from 2012 to 2013?

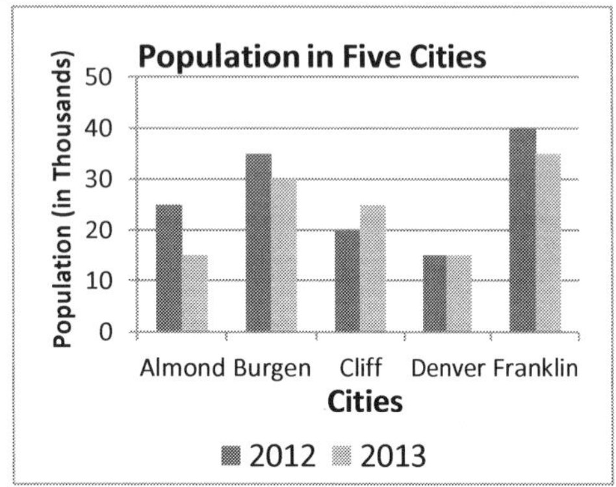

a) 11%
b) 10%
c) −10%
d) −11%

5. A supermarket has brand A juice smoothie on sale every 8 days and has brand B juice smoothie on sale every 5 days. Within a year (365 days), how many times does this supermarket have both brands of juice smoothie on sale on the same day?
a) 9
b) 10
c) 12
d) 24

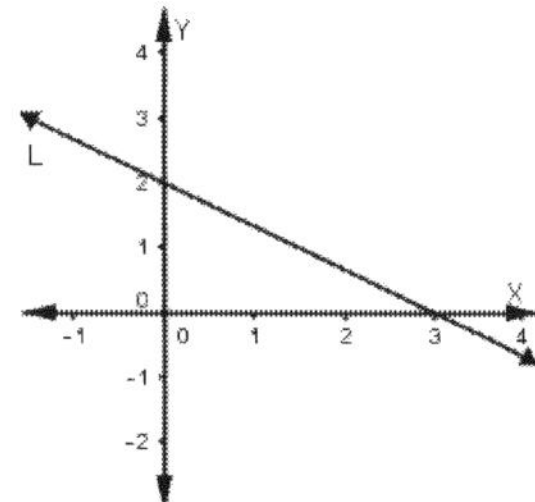

6. What is the equation of line L in the figure above?
a) $y = 3x + 2$
b) $y = -3x + 2$
c) $y = -2x - 3$
d) $y = -\frac{2}{3}x + 2$

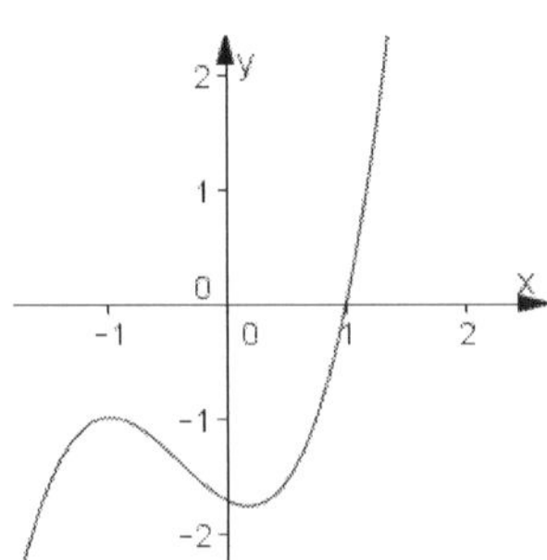

7. The figure above shows the graph of $g(x)$. At what value(s) of x does $g(x)$ equal to 0?
a) 1
b) −1
c) 2
d) −2

8. To make fruit punch, grapefruit juice, orange juice, and lemonade are mixed in with a ratio of 4 : 3 : 1 by volume, respectively. In order to make 4 liters of this drink, how much orange juice, in liters, is needed?
a) 1
b) 1.5
c) 2
d) 2.5

9. How many positive three-digit integers have the hundreds digit equal to the multiple of 3 and the units digit (ones digit) is an even digit?
a) 150
b) 160
c) 162
d) 180

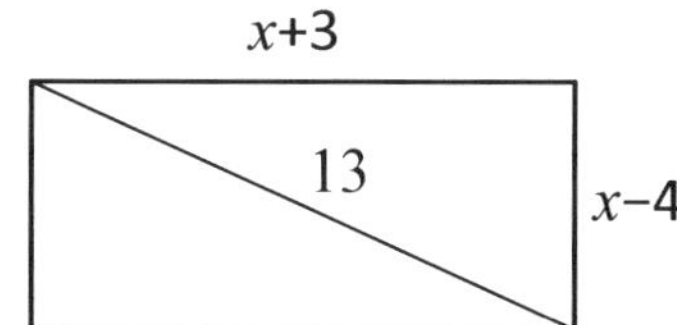

10. The figure above is a rectangle. What is the value of x?
    a) 9
    b) 8
    c) $5\sqrt{2}$
    d) 6

11. A recipe of a cake for 8 people requires 1.2 pounds of flour. Assuming the amount of flour needed is directly proportional to the number of people eating the cake, how many pounds of flour are required to make a big cake for 200 people?
    a) 20
    b) 25
    c) 30
    d) 35

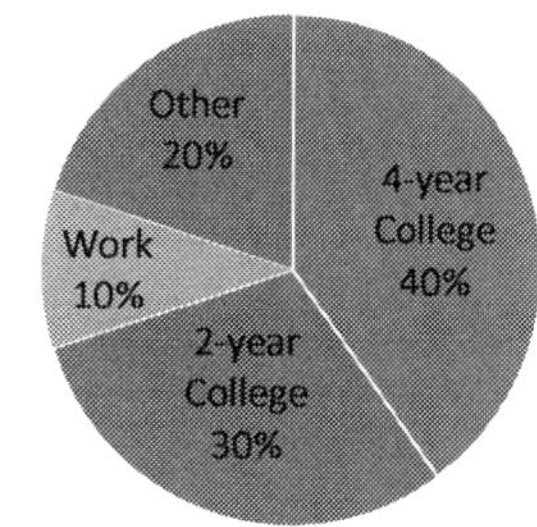

12. In 2012, how many graduates from Paterson High School chose to go to 2 or 4 years of college to continue their education?
    a) 250
    b) 260
    c) 270
    d) 280

13. What is the remainder of 2013^{2014} divided by 10?
    a) 1
    b) 3
    c) 7
    d) 9

14. If $a^x \cdot a^4 = a^{10}$ and $(a^4)^y = a^{12}$, what is the value of $x + y$?
    a) 7
    b) 8
    c) 9
    d) 10

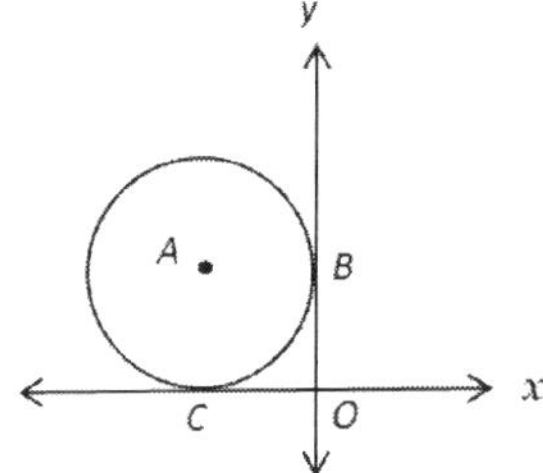

15. In the figure above, a circle with center A is tangent to the x-axis and the y-axis on the xy−coordinate plane. If the coordinates of the center A are (−3, 3), what are the coordinates of point C?
    a) (−2, 0)
    b) (−3, 0)
    c) (2, 0)
    d) (0, − 3)

Questions 16 – 17 refer to the following information:

Boyle's law says that when all other factors are constant, the pressure of a gas decreases as the volume of that gas increases and vice versa. Therefore, the relationship of the pressure and volume of a gas, according to Boyle's law, is inversely proportional when the temperature remains unchanged.

16. According to Boyle's law, which of the following graphs represents the relationship between the pressure and volume of a gas if temperature is constant?

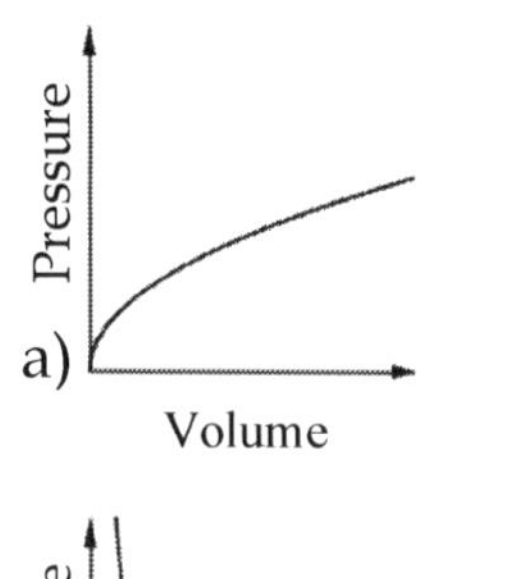
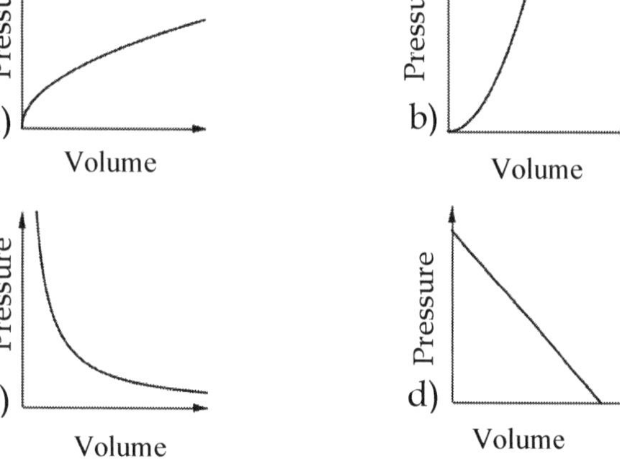

17. Assume that a gas has a volume of 10 liters and a pressure of 2 atmospheres initially. After some force is applied, the pressure becomes 5 atmospheres. According to Boyle's law, what is the final volume, in liters, of this gas? (Atmosphere (atm) is a unit of pressure.)
    a) 25
    b) 10
    c) 5
    d) 4

18. The cost of a long-distance call using phone company A is $1.00 for the first three minutes and $.10 for each additional minute. The same call using the phone company B is charged flat rate at $0.15 per minute for any amount of time. For a call that lasts t minutes, the cost using company A is the same as the cost using the company B, what is the value of t?
    a) 15
    b) 14
    c) 12
    d) 10

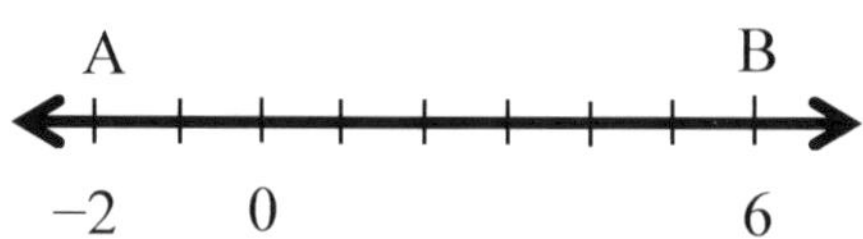

19. In the number line above, if 3 equally spaced points are drawn between A and B and point C is one of those points, which of the following is a possible coordinate for point C?
    a) −1
    b) 1
    c) 2
    d) 3

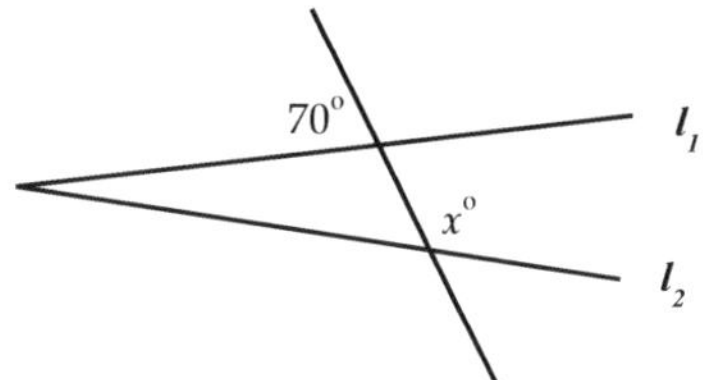

20. In the figure above, which of the following CANNOT be the value of x?
    a) 105
    b) 111
    c) 115
    d) 124

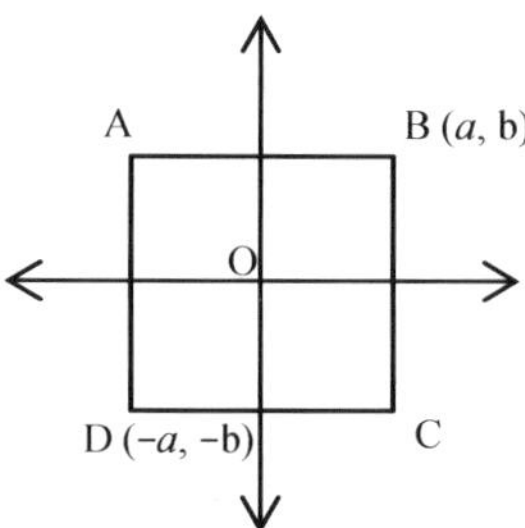

21. In the figure above, rectangle ABCD lies on the xy-coordinate plane. If the origin is located at the center of rectangle, which of the following could be the coordinates of point C?
    a) $(-a, b)$
    b) $(a, -b)$
    c) (a, b)
    d) $(-b, -a)$

22. The fruits provided in the student lounge contain pears, apples, and oranges. The ratio of the numbers of pears to apples is 3 : 4 and the ratio of the numbers of pears to oranges is 5 : 7. Find the ratio of the numbers of apples to oranges?
    a) 20 : 21
    b) 8 : 15
    c) 10 : 3
    d) 15 : 8

23. The kinetic energy of an object is calculated by the following formula:

$$K_e = \frac{1}{2}mv^2$$

where K_e is the kinetic energy, m is the mass, and v is the velocity. If the kinetic energy of an object is a constant, which of the following graphs best represents the possible relationship between the velocity (v) and the mass (m) of the object?

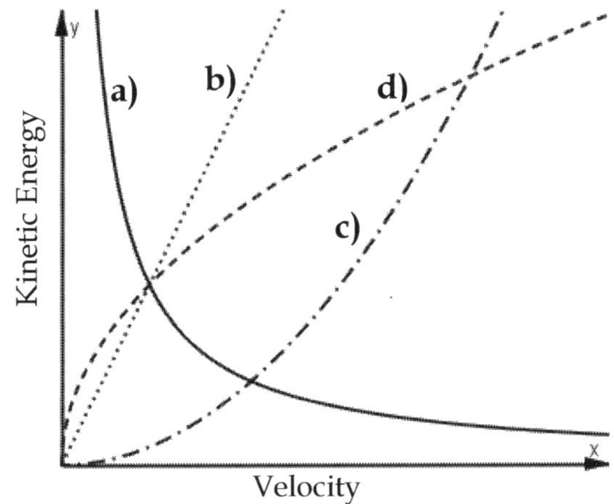

24. What is the difference, in degrees, between an arc that is $\frac{1}{2}$ of a circle and arc that is $\frac{1}{3}$ of a circle?
    a) 40°
    b) 45°
    c) 60°
    d) 50°

25. If x and y are positive integers and $2^{2x} + 2^{(2x+2)} = y$, what is 2^x in terms of y?
    a) $\frac{y}{5}$
    b) $\frac{\sqrt{y}}{\sqrt{5}}$
    c) $\frac{y}{12}$
    d) $\frac{\sqrt{y}}{5}$

$$w, x, y, z$$

26. In the sequence above, if each term after the first is d more than the preceding term, what is the sum of w, x, y, and z in terms of w and d?
    a) $3w + 6d$
    b) $4w + 3d$
    c) $6w + 6d$
    d) $2(2w + 3d)$

27. John's monthly salary increases every year by 4%. If he gets paid $2500 per month this year, what would be his monthly salary in n years from now?
    a) 2500×0.04^n
    b) $2500 \times 1.04 \times n$
    c) 2500×1.04^n
    d) $2500 \times 1.04^{n-1}$

28. February 28, 2014 is Friday, What day of week is February 28, 2034?
    a) Monday
    b) Tuesday
    c) Thursday
    d) Saturday

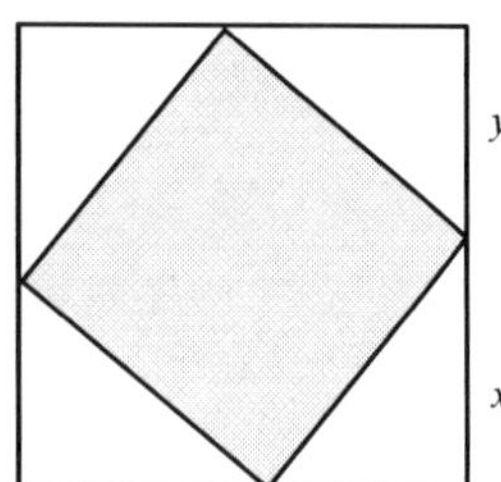

29. In the two squares in the figure above, if the area of smaller square is $\frac{13}{25}$ of the big square, when $x > y$, what is the ratio of x to y?
    a) 1
    b) $\sqrt{2}$
    c) $\sqrt{3}$
    d) $\frac{3}{2}$

30. The term *half-life* is defined as the time it takes for half of a sample of radioactive material to decay. It is constant for any amount of the radioactive material. Initially, there are 100 grams of a radioactive material which has a half-life of two days. Which of the following graphs could model the mass of the radioactive material left as a function of time?

a)

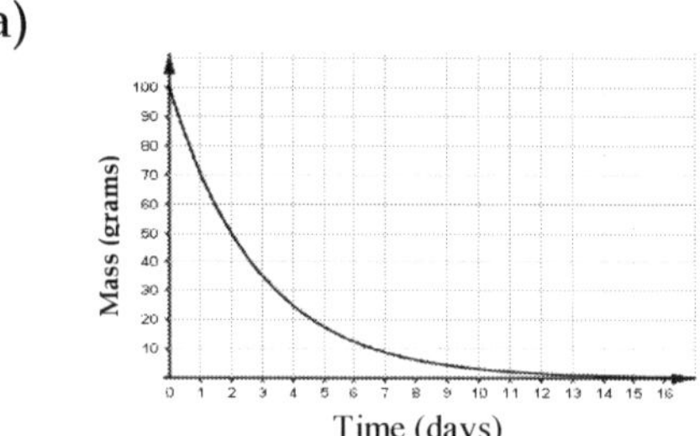

b)

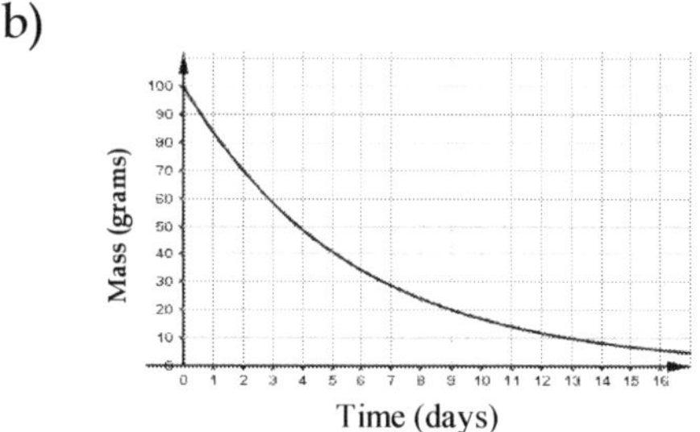

c)

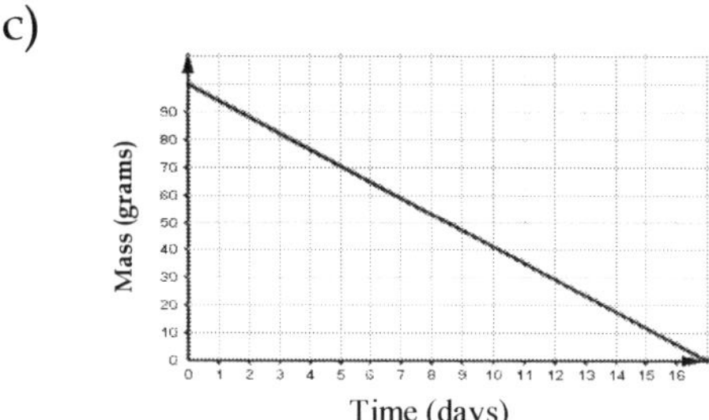

d)

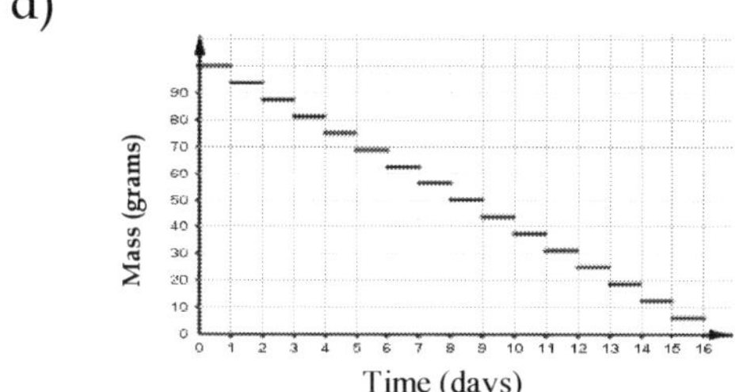

Directions:

For questions 31-38, solve the problem and enter your answer in the grid, as described below, on the answer sheet.

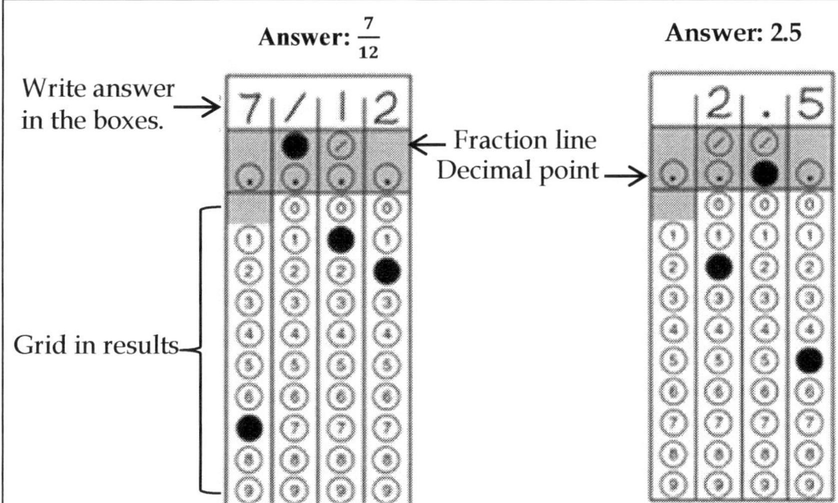

Answer: 201
Either position is correct.

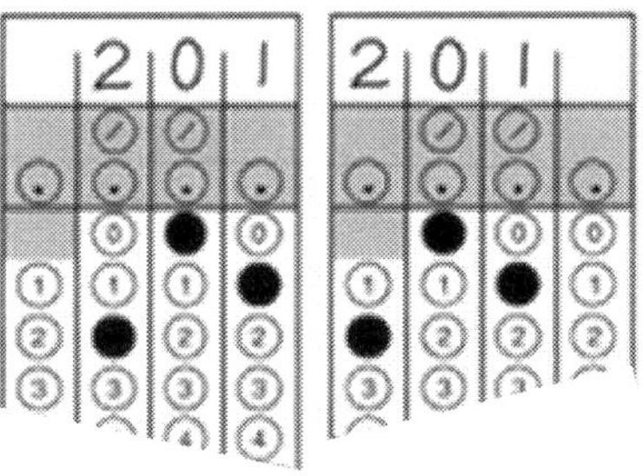

Note: You may start your answers in any column, space permitting. Columns not needed should be left blank.

- Mark no more than one circle in any column.
- Because the answer sheet will be machine-scored. **You will receive credit only if the circles are filled in correctly.**
- Although not required, it is suggested that you write your answer in the boxes at the top of the columns to help you fill in the circles accurately.
- Some problems may have more than one correct answer. In such case, grid only one answer.
- No question has a negative answer.
- **Mixed numbers** such as $3\frac{1}{2}$ must be gridded as 3.5 or $\frac{7}{2}$. (If 31/2 is gridded, it will be interpreted as $\frac{31}{2}$, not $3\frac{1}{2}$.)

- **Decimal Answer**: If you obtain a decimal answer with more digits than the grid can accommodate, it may be either rounded or truncated, but it must fill the entire grid. The acceptable ways to grid $\frac{2}{3}$ are:

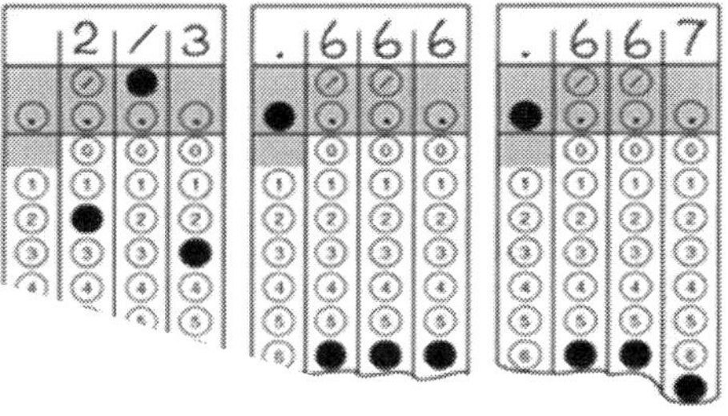

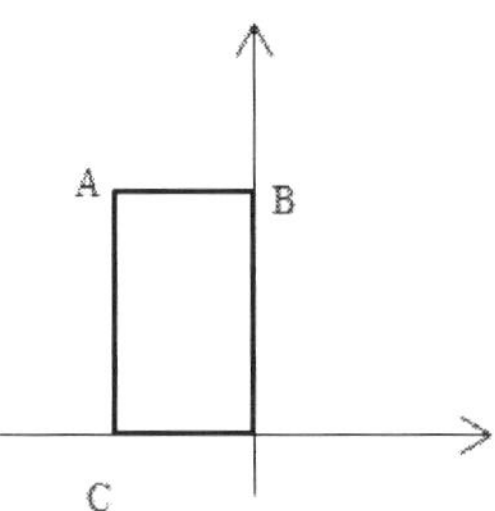

31. In the figure above, $\overline{AC} = 2\overline{AB}$ and the coordinates of A are $(-6, b)$. What is the value of b?

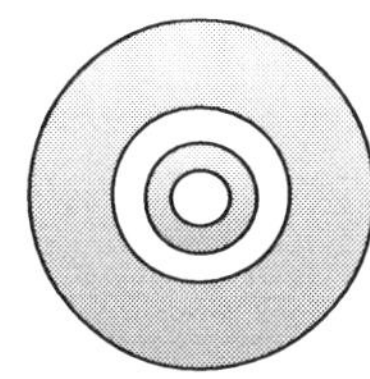

32. The diagram above shows 4 concentric circles, with diameters 2, 4, 6, and 12 respectively. What is the probability that a randomly selected point in the diagram will fall in the shaded region?

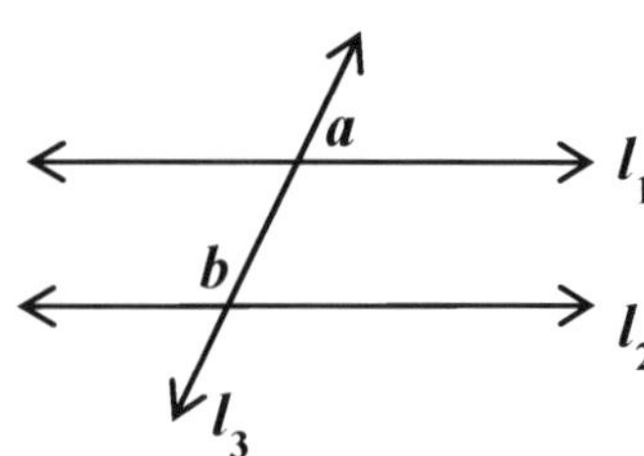

33. In the figure above, $l_1 \parallel l_2$ and $b = 4a - 160$. What is the value of a, in degrees?

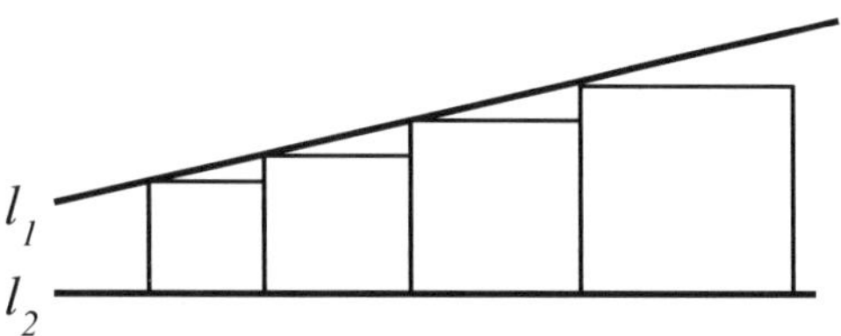

34. The figure above shows four squares with sides of length 2, 3, x, and y. Line l_1 hits the upper left corner of each square. What is the value of y?

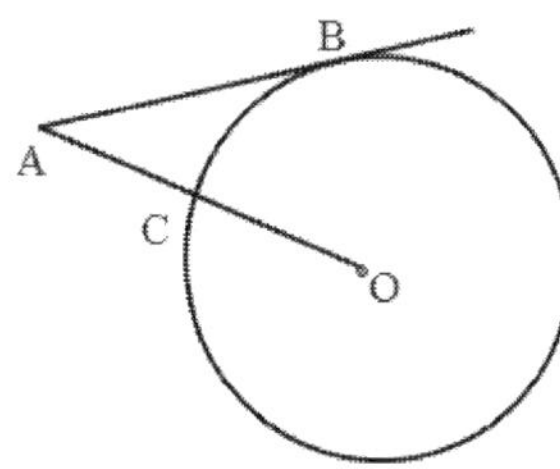

35. In the diagram above, AB is tangent to circle O at point B. AB = 2AC and the radius has length 3. What is the length of $\overline{AO}$?

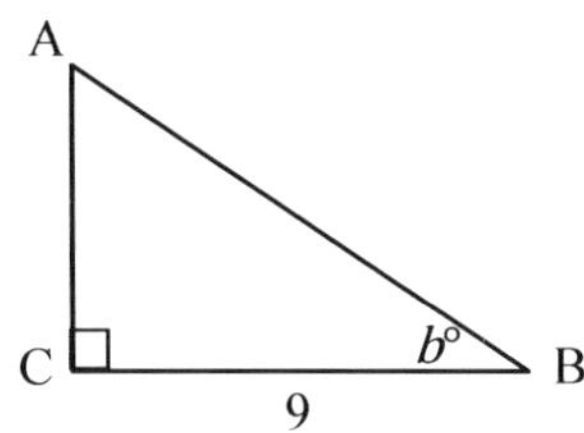

Note: Figure not drawn to scale

36. In the triangle above, if $\sin(b°) = 0.6$ and the BC = 9, what is the perimeter of the triangle?

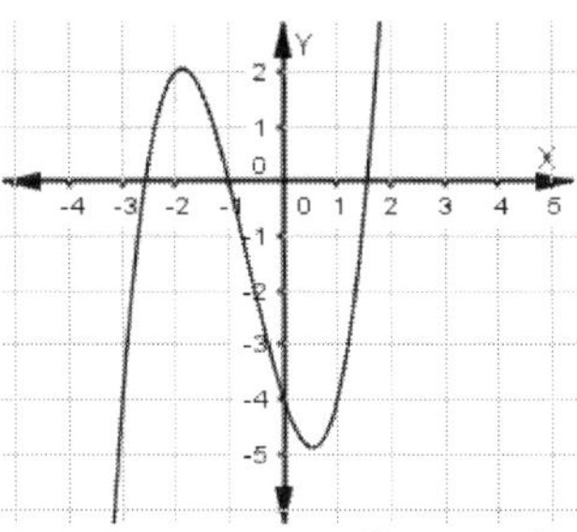

37. The function $f(x) = x^3 + 3x^2 + 3x - 4$ as graphed in the xy-plane above. How many real solutions are there if $f(x) = x$?

38. Find the area of the circle given by the equation $x^2 + y^2 - 4x + 2y = 20$. (Round your answer to the nearest tenth.)

SAT MATH MOCK TEST No. 6 ANSWER KEYS

Section 3									
1. D	2. C	3. D	4. A	5. C	6. D	7. C	8. B	9. D	10. D
11. A	12. C	13. C	14. A	15. D	16. 20	17. $\frac{3}{5}$	18. 7200	19. 25	20. 4

Section 4									
1. B	2. B	3. D	4. D	5. A	6. D	7. A	8. B	9. A	10. A
11. C	12. C	13. D	14. C	15. B	16. C	17. D	18. B	19. C	20. A
21. B	22. A	23. A	24. C	25. B	26. D	27. C	28. B	29. C	30. A
31. 12	32. $\frac{5}{6}$	33. 68	34. 6.75	35. 5	36. 27	37. 3	38. 78.5		

SECTION 3

1. *Answer: (d)*
   $a > b$ so $b - a < 0$
   positive × negative → negative
   $b \times y < 0$

2. *Answer: (c)*
   $(-)\times(-) \rightarrow$ *positive*
   Even powers of real numbers are positive.
   Only (a) , (c) and (c) are positive and (c) has the greatest coefficient.

3. *Answer: (d)*
   The average of these three numbers is 18, so the sum will be 3 × 18 =54.
   $10 + 14 + x = 54$
   $x = 54 - 24 = 30$

4. *Answer: (a)*
   Let n be the number of days that Mrs. Kinney kept the DVD.
   $1 + 1 \times (n - 1) + 0.5(n - 1) = 10 \quad \rightarrow \quad n = 7$

5. *Answer: (c)*
   Let m be the total number of students in the school.
   ($\frac{1}{4} \times m$) students arrive by 7 AM and 100 students arrive half an hour later. The total number of students that have arrived would be
   $\frac{1}{4} \times m + 100 = \frac{3}{4} \times m.$
   $m = 200$ *students*

6. *Answer: (d)*
   The line intersects the x-axis when y = 0.
   $0 = 4x - 8 \quad \rightarrow \quad x = 2$
   $a = 2; b = 0 \quad$ *so* $a + b = 2$

7. *Answer: (c)*
   $\frac{x}{x+2} = \frac{3}{4}$
   $4x = 3(x + 2) \quad \rightarrow \quad x = 6$

8. *Answer: (b)*
   $x - 5 = 21 + 3 \quad \rightarrow \quad x = 29$

9. *Answer: (d)*
   Use cross multiplication to solve fraction equations.
   $\frac{2x}{3} = \frac{3}{2}$
   $2 \times 2x = 3 \times 3$
   $4x = 9$ *(divide both sides by 4)*
   $x = \frac{9}{4}$

10. *Answer: (d)*
    $x^2 > 2$
    $x^2 - 2 > 0$
    $(x - 2)(x + 2) > 0$
    The terms (x − 2) and (x + 2) must be both positive or both negative for (x – 2)(x + 2) to be greater than 0.
    $x > 2$ *or* $x < -2$

11. *Answer: (a)*
    The y-intercept occurs when x = 0.
    $3y - 0 = -12 \quad \rightarrow \quad y = -4$

12. *Answer: (c)*
    10 less than the product of x and 5 → $5x - 10$
    $5x - 10 = 20$
    $5(x - 2) = 20$

13. *Answer: (c)*
    If X only contains negative integers, then there are no positive integers in set X.

14. *Answer: (a)*
$x^2 - y^2 = (x - y)(x + y)$
$24 = (x - y) \times 6$
$x - y = 4$
$x + y = 6$
$x = 5$ *and* $y = 1$

15. *Answer: (d)*
$(x^{\frac{1}{8}}y^{\frac{1}{8}})^2 = (xy)^{\frac{1}{4}} = 3$
$xy = 3^4 = 81$

16. *Answer: 20*
$x = \frac{20}{5} = 4$; $y^2 = \frac{20}{4} = 5$
$xy^2 = 4 \times 5 = 20$

17. *Answer:* $\frac{3}{5}$ *or* .6
$\frac{Part}{Whole} = \frac{45}{45+22+8} = \frac{45}{75} = \frac{3}{5}$

18. *Answer: 7200*
Distance = Time × Speed
One Hour = 60 × 60 Seconds
Total Feet = 2 × 60 × 60 = 7,200 ft.

19. *Answer: 25*
Use the exterior angle theorem.
$a + a + 10 = 2a + a - 15 \quad \rightarrow \quad a = 25$

20. *Answer: 4*
Let x be the number of \$20 bills and y be the number of \$10 bills.
$x + y = 12, \ y = 12 - x$
$20x + 10y = 160$
$20x + 10(12 - x) = 160$
$120 + 10x = 160$
$10x = 40 \quad \rightarrow \quad x = 4$

SECTION 4

1. *Answer: (b)*
Let x be the number of students taking 5 APs and y be the number of students taking 4 APs.
$x + y = 20 \quad \rightarrow \quad y = 20 - x$
$5x + 4y = 85$ *(substitution rule)*
$5x + 4(20 - x) = 85$
$x + 80 = 85 \quad \rightarrow \quad x = 5$

2. *Answer: (b)*
The Perimeter of ΔXYZ: $\sqrt{9} \times 6 = 18$
Side Length of ΔXYZ: $\frac{18}{3} = 6$

3. *Answer: (d)*
$\frac{65}{4} < Average < \frac{67}{4}$
$16.25 < Average < 16.75$

4. *Answer: (d)*
$\text{Percent Increase} = \frac{\text{2013 Population} - \text{2012 Population}}{\text{2012 Population}} \times 100\%$
Total Population in 2012 = 25 + 35 + 20 + 15 + 40 = 135 thousand.
Total Population in 2013 = 15 + 30 + 25 + 15 + 35 = 120 thousand.
$\frac{120-135}{135} \times 100\% = -11.1\% \sim -11\%$

5. *Answer: (a)*
The LCM of 8 and 5 is 40.
Every 40 days, A and B will be on sale on the same day.
$\frac{365}{40} = 9.125$

6. *Answer: (d)*
$Slope = \frac{Rise}{Run} = \frac{0-2}{3-0} = -\frac{2}{3}$
y-intercept = 2
$y = -\frac{2}{3}x + 2$

7. *Answer: (A)*
When g(x) is equal to 0, the graph of the function intersects the x-axis.
The value of x is 1 when the graph intercepts x-axis.

8. *Answer: (b)*
Every 8 liters, (4+3+1), of drink, 3 liters of orange juice will be needed. So 4 liters of this drink, we need $\frac{3}{8} \times 4$ *of orange juice.*
Orange Juice = 1.5 liters

9. *Answer: (a)*
The hundreds has 3 choices (3, 6, 9) and the units digit has 5 choices (2, 4, 6, 8, 0). There are 10 possible values of tens digit (0 – 9).
Total = 3 × 5 × 10 = 150

10. *Answer: (a)*
Use the Pythagorean theorem.
$(x + 3)^2 + (x - 4)^2 = 13^2$
$x^2 + 6x + 9 + x^2 - 8x + 16 = 169$
$2x^2 - 2x = 144$
$x^2 - x - 72 = 0$
$(x + 8)(x - 9) = 0$
$x = 9$ *or* -8 *(not applicable)*

11. *Answer: (c)*
$\frac{8\ People}{1.2\ Pounds} = \frac{200\ People}{x\ Pounds}$
$8x = 1.2 \times 200$
$x = 30$ *pounds of flour*

12. *Answer: (d)*
30% + 40% = 70% of the total number of graduates go to 2 or 4 years of college.
$0.7 \times 400 = 280$ *students*

13. *Answer: (d)*
2013^1 *has units digit of 3*
2013^2 *has units digit of 9* $(3 \times 3 = 9)$
2013^3 *has units digit of 7* $(3 \times 9 = 27)$
2013^4 *has units digit of 1* $(3 \times 7 = 21)$
2013^5 *has units digit of 3* $(3 \times 1 = 3)$
Only the units digit needs to be concerned.
So every fourth power of 2013 repeats its units digit.
$2014 \div 4$ *has remainder of 2*
2013^{2014} *has the same units digit as* 2013^2*, which is 9.*

14. *Answer: (c)*
$a^x \cdot a^4 = a^{(x+4)} = a^{10}$
$(a^4)^y = a^{4y} = a^{12}$
$x = 6$ *and* $y = 3$*, therefore* $x + y = 9$

15. *Answer: (b)*
AC = AB
The coordinates of B: (0, 3)
The coordinates of C: (–3, 0)

16. *Answer: (c)*
The relationship of the pressure and the volume of a gas is inversely proportional.
Graph c) represents the inversely proportional relationship: $PV = k$.

17. *Answer: (d)*
As the pressure increases, the volume of the gas decreases proportionately.
$P_1V_1 = P_2V_2$
$2 \times 10 = 5 \times V_2 \quad \rightarrow V_2 = 4\ liters$

18. *Answer: (b)*
$1 + (t - 3) \times 0.1 = 0.15t \quad \rightarrow t = 14$

19. *Answer: (c)*
Find the distance of $\overline{AB}$ *then divide it by 4.*
$\frac{AB}{4} = \frac{6-(-2)}{4} = 2$
The coordinate of point C could be (6 – 2) =4 or (–2 + 2) =0 or (4 – 2) =2.

20. *Answer: (a)*
As an exterior angle, x is equal to (180 – 70) plus a small interior angle. Therefore, $x > 110$.
x cannot be 105.

21. *Answer: (b)*
C is located in the quadrant IV which has positive x and negative y coordinates. (a, –b)

22. *Answer: (a)*
Use the same ratio number to compare
Pear : Apple = 3 : 4 = 15 : 20
Pear: Orange = 5 : 7 = 15 : 21
Apple : Orange = 20 : 21

23. *Answer: (a)*
$v = \sqrt{\frac{2K_e}{m}}$
Since K_e *is a constant, v is inversely proportional to the square root of m.*
Only a) presents the inversely proportional relationship.

24. *Answer: (c)*
$(\frac{1}{2} - \frac{1}{3}) \times 360^o = 60^o$

25. *Answer: (b)*
$2^{2x} + 2^{(2x+2)} = 5 \times 2^{2x}$
$5 \times 2^{2x} = y \quad \rightarrow \quad 2^{2x} = \frac{y}{5}$
$(2^x)^2 = \frac{y}{5} \quad \rightarrow \quad 2^x = \frac{\sqrt{y}}{\sqrt{5}}$

26. *Answer: (d)*
The four terms can be rewritten as w, w+d, w+2d, and w+3d
The Sum of the Sequence = w + w + d + w + 2d + w + 3d = 4w + 6d = 2(2w +3d)

27. *Answer: (c)*
Increasing every year by 4% is to multiply $(1 + \frac{4}{100})$ *for each additional year.*
$C(n) = (1.04)^n \times 2500 = 2500(1.04)^n$

28. *Answer: (b)*
There are 20 years between 2014 and 2034 and 5 leap years in between.
Therefore, the total number of days between Feb. 28, 2014 and Feb. 28, 2034 is 365 × 20 + 5 = 7305 days.
The remainder of 7305 divided by 7 is 4.
So 4 days after Friday is Tuesday.

29. *Answer: (d)*

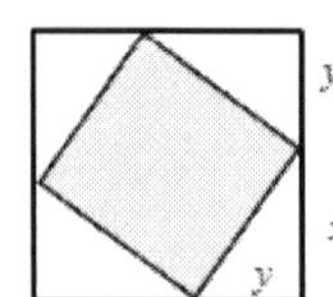

Four similar triangles.
Area of Big Square = $(x+y)^2$
Area of Gray Square = $(\sqrt{x^2+y^2})^2$
$x^2+y^2 = \frac{13}{25}(x+y)^2$
$x^2+y^2 = \frac{13}{25}(x^2+y^2+2xy)$
Divide by y^2 on both sides.
$(\frac{x}{y})^2 + 1 = \frac{13}{25}(\frac{x}{y})^2 + \frac{13}{25} + \frac{26x}{25y}$
$\frac{12}{25}(\frac{x}{y})^2 - \frac{26x}{25y} + \frac{12}{25} = 0$ *(multiply each term by 25)*
$12(\frac{x}{y})^2 - 26(\frac{x}{y}) + 12 = 0$
To simplify the calculation, set $(\frac{x}{y}) = z$
$12(\frac{x}{y})^2 - 26(\frac{x}{y}) + 12 = 12z^2 - 26z + 12$
$6z^2 - 13z + 6 = (2z-3)(3z-2) = 0$
$z = \frac{x}{y} = \frac{3}{2}$ *or* $\frac{2}{3}$
Or apply quadratic formula to solve for z:
$z = \frac{-b \pm \sqrt{b^2-4ac}}{2a} = \frac{-(-13) \pm \sqrt{(-13)^2-4\times6\times6}}{2\times6} = \frac{13\pm5}{12} = \frac{3}{2}$ *or* $\frac{2}{3}$
Since $x > y$ *so* $\frac{x}{y} = \frac{3}{2}$

30. *Answer: (a)*
For every half-life of two days, the radioactive material will be halved.

Day	Mass (grams)
0	100
2	50
4	25
6	12.5
8	6.25

Only graph a) fits the data above.

31. *Answer: 12*
b is the y-coordinate which, since $\overline{AC} = 2\overline{AB}$, *is double the x-coordinate in length and extends in the positive direction.*
$2 \times |-6| = 12$

32. *Answer:* $\frac{5}{6}$ *or .833*
Total Area – White Area = Shaded Area
$\pi(6)^2 - \pi(3)^2 + \pi(2)^2 - \pi(1)^2 = 30\pi$
Probability = $\frac{Shaded\ Area}{Total\ Area} = \frac{30\pi}{36\pi} = \frac{30}{36} = \frac{5}{6}$

33. *Answer: 68*
$a + b = 180^o$
$4a - 160 + a = 180^o \rightarrow 5a = 340 \rightarrow a = 68^o$

34. *Answer: 6.75*
There are 3 similar triangles between l_1 *and the first 3 squares.*
Their heights of those triangles have the same ratio as the ratio of the lengths of sides of the squares.
The first triangle has height of $3 - 2 = 1$.
So the height of triangle is half of the length of the square.
The second triangle has height of ½ (3) = 1.5
The third triangle has height of ½ (3 + 1.5) = 2.25
The length of 3rd square = 3 + 1.5 = 4.5
y = Length of 3rd Square + the height of 3rd triangle = 4.5 + 2.25 = 6.75

35. *Answer: 5*
ΔOAB is a right triangle with hypotenuse $\overline{OA}$, *so use the Pythagorean theorem.*
$OB = OC = 3$
$AC = x \quad AB = 2x \quad AO = 3 + x$
$(2x)^2 + 3^2 = (3+x)^2$
$4x^2 + 9 = x^2 + 6x + 9 \quad 3x^2 = 6x \rightarrow x = 2$ *so* $AO = 5$

36. *Answer: 27*
Use the Pythagorean theorem to find the lengths of sides of the right triangle.
$cos(b^o) = \sqrt{1-0.6^2} = 0.8$
$cos(b^o) = 0.8 = \frac{9}{AB} \rightarrow AB = 11.25$
$AC = AB \times sin(b^o) = 11.25 \times 0.6 = 6.75$
$11.25 + 6.75 + 9 = 27$

37. *Answer: 3*
There are three intersections between $y = x$ *and* $y = x^3 + 2x^2 - 3x - 4$

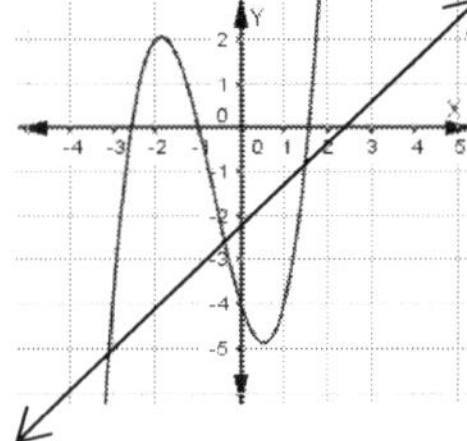

38. *Answer: 78.5*
Rewrite to the equation in standard form.
$x^2 - 4x + 4 + y^2 + 2y + 1 = 20 + 5$
$(x-2)^2 + (y+1)^2 = 5^2$
The center of the circle is (2, −1) *and the radius is 5.*
The area of the circle is $\pi r^2 = 25\pi = 78.5$.

SAT Math Mock Test No. 7

SECTION 3 

Math Test – NO Calculator 25 MINUTES, 20 QUESTIONS

Directions:
For questions 1-15, solve each problem, choose the best answer from the choices provided, and fill in the corresponding circle on your answer sheet. **For questions 16-20**, solve the problem and enter your answer in the grid on the answer sheet. Please refer to the directions before question 16 on how to enter your answers in the grid. You may use any available space in your test booklet for scratch work.

Notes:

1. **No calculator** is allowed for this section. All numbers used are real numbers.
2. Figures that accompany problems in this test are intended to provide information useful in solving the problems. They are drawn as accurately as possible EXCEPT when it is stated in a specific problem that the figure is not drawn to scale. All figures lie in a plane unless otherwise indicated.
3. Unless otherwise specified, the domain of any function *f(x)* assumed to be the set of all real numbers *x* for which *f(x)* is a real number.

References:

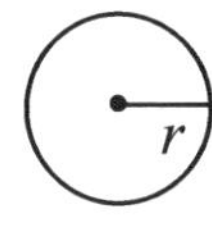

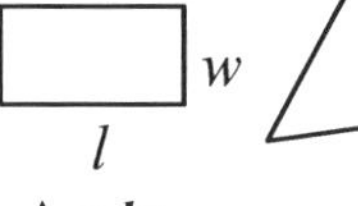
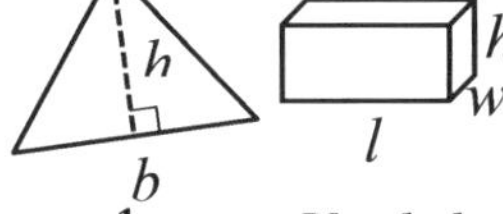
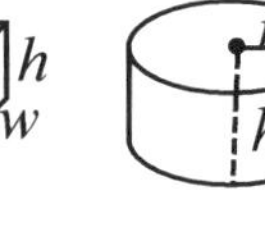
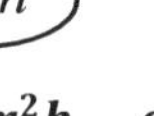
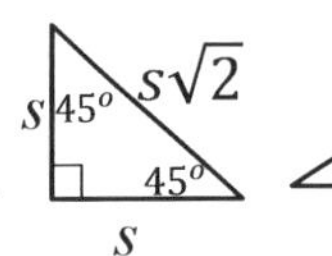
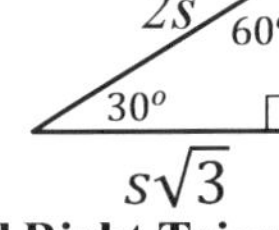

$A = \pi r^2$
$C = 2\pi r$
$A = lw$
$A = \frac{1}{2}bh$
$V = lwh$
$V = \pi r^2 h$
$c^2 = a^2 + b^2$
Special Right Triangles

The number of degrees of arc in a circle is 360; the number of radians of arc in a circle is 2π.
The sum of the degree measures of the angles in a triangle is 180.

1. If $x^{\frac{1}{4}} = \sqrt{3}$, then what is the value of x?
   a) 1
   b) 3
   c) 9
   d) 27

2. If $3(x^2 - 2) = 21$, which of the following is the value of x?
   a) –2
   b) –1
   c) 2
   d) 3

3. What is the least value of integer x such that the value of $2x - 5$ is greater than 7?
   a) 7
   b) 6
   c) 5
   d) 4

4. If x and y are positive integers and $8(2^x) = 4^y$, what is x in terms of y?
   a) y
   b) y^2
   c) $2y$
   d) $2y - 3$

5. If $\frac{8}{\sqrt{x+4}} = 2$, what is the value of x?
   a) 12
   b) – 3
   c) 0
   d) 3

6. If $x = 1$, what is $2y(6 - 5x)$ in terms of y?
   a) $2y - 10$
   b) $2y$
   c) $12y - 10$
   d) $12y$

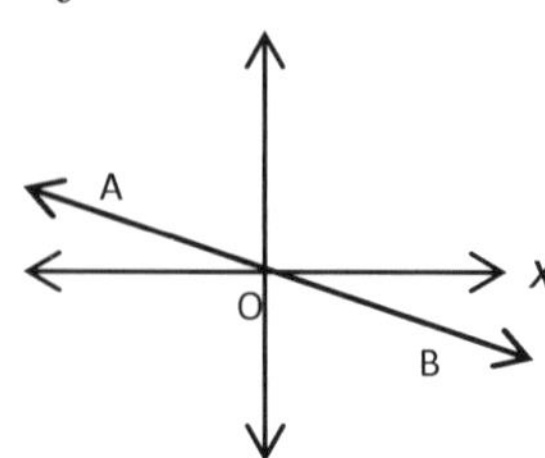

7. The coordinates of point A in the figure above are (a, b), where $|a| > |3b|$. Which of the following could be the slope of AB?
   a) -1
   b) $-\frac{1}{2}$
   c) $-\frac{1}{3}$
   d) $\frac{-1}{4}$

8. Which of the following could be the sum of 9 numbers if the average of these 9 numbers is greater than 9 and less than 10?
   a) 91
   b) 90
   c) 85
   d) 81

9. What is the product of the slopes of all four sides of a rectangle if all four sides' slopes are not equal to zero?
   a) -2
   b) -1
   c) 0
   d) 1

10. If the average (arithmetic mean) of a and b is m, which of the following is the average of a, b, and $4m$?
    a) $2m$
    b) $\frac{5m}{2}$
    c) $3m$
    d) $\frac{7m}{3}$

11. If $0 > xy$ and $y > 0$, which of the following statements must be true?
    $x < 0$
    $x < y$
    $x > 0$
    a) I only
    b) III only
    c) I and II
    d) II and III

12. If x, y, and z are all integers greater than 1 and $xy = 15$ and $yz = 21$, which of the following must be true?
    a) $z > x > y$
    b) $y > z > x$
    c) $y > x > z$
    d) $x > z > y$

13. Which of the following must be a factor of x if x is a multiple of both 12 and 8?
    a) 10
    b) 24
    c) 27
    d) 30

14. If $x = 2y^2 + 3y + 4$ and $z = -y - 1$, what is x in terms of z?
    a) $2z^2 - 7z - 9$
    b) $2z^2 - 7z + 9$
    c) $2z^2 + z + 3$
    d) $2z^2 - z + 3$

15. The price of green tea leaves is D dollars for y ounces and each ounce makes x bottles of green tea drink. In terms of D, x, and y, which of the following expressions shows the cost of making 1 bottle of green tea drink?
    a) Dxy
    b) $\frac{yD}{x}$
    c) $\frac{xy}{D}$
    d) $\frac{D}{xy}$

Directions:

For questions 16-20, solve the problem and enter your answer in the grid, as described below, on the answer sheet.

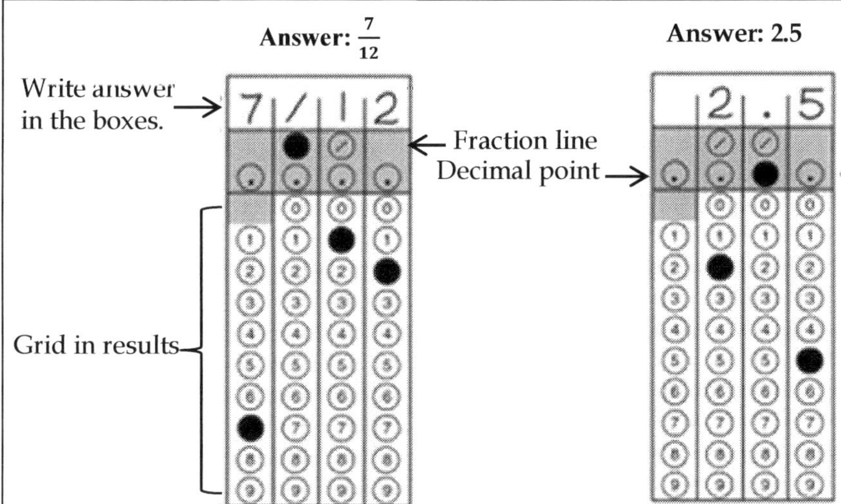

Answer: 201
Either position is correct.

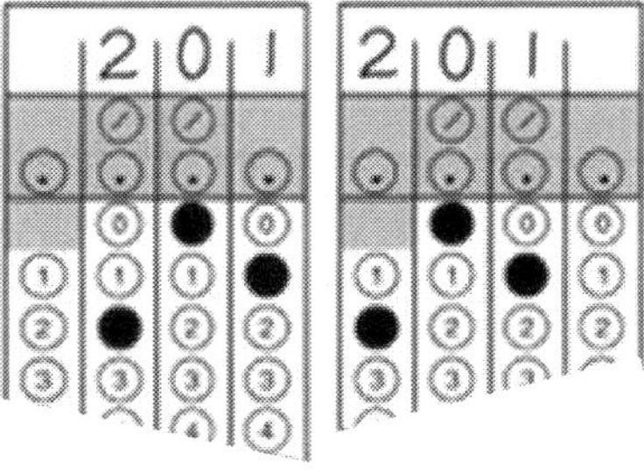

Note: You may start your answers in any column, space permitting. Columns not needed should be left blank.

- Mark no more than one circle in any column.
- Because the answer sheet will be machine-scored. **You will receive credit only if the circles are filled in correctly.**
- Although not required, it is suggested that you write your answer in the boxes at the top of the columns to help you fill in the circles accurately.
- Some problems may have more than one correct answer. In such case, grid only one answer.
- No question has a negative answer.
- **Mixed numbers** such as $3\frac{1}{2}$ must be gridded as 3.5 or $\frac{7}{2}$. (If 31/2 is gridded, it will be interpreted as $\frac{31}{2}$, not $3\frac{1}{2}$.)
- **Decimal Answer**: If you obtain a decimal answer with more digits than the grid can accommodate, it may be either rounded or truncated, but it must fill the entire grid. The acceptable ways to grid $\frac{2}{3}$ are:

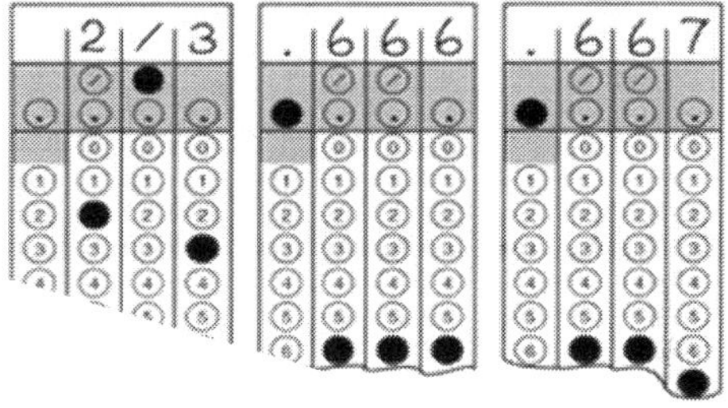

16. In a certain game, points are assigned to every word. Each "m", "a", and "t" in the word is worth 3 points, and all other letters are worth 2 point each. What is the sum of the points assigned to the word "mathematics"?

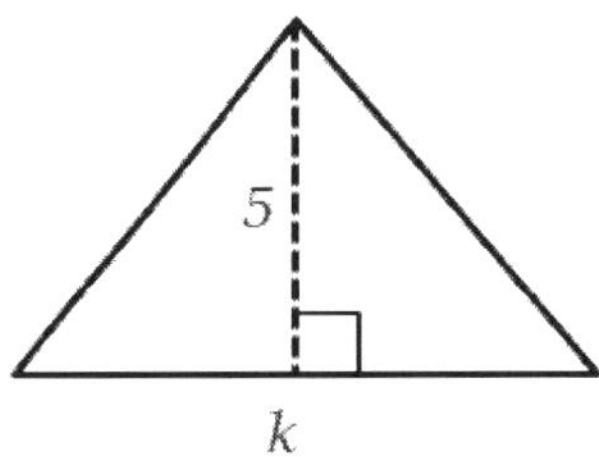

17. In the figure above, if the area of the triangle is 15, what is the value of k?

18. The function $g(x) = (x - 3)(x - 1)$. If $g(a + 1) = 0$ and $a > 0$, what is the value of a?

19. Megan has 7 blue cards, 3 black cards, and 5 red cards in her pocket. She takes out a card at random and puts it aside because the card is not blue. She then takes out a second card randomly from her pocket. What is the probability that the second card will be a blue card?

20. If 3 less than the product of 6 and a number is equal to the product of 3 and the square of the number, what is the number?

SECTION 4 

Math Test – Calculator **55 MINUTES, 38 QUESTIONS**

Directions:

For questions 1-30, solve each problem, choose the best answer from the choices provided, and fill in the corresponding circle on your answer sheet. **For questions 31-38**, solve the problem and enter your answer in the grid on the answer sheet. Please refer to the directions before question 31 on how to enter your answers in the grid. You may use any available space in your test booklet for scratch work.

Notes:

1. Acceptable calculators are allowed for this section. All numbers used are real numbers.
2. Figures that accompany problems in this test are intended to provide information useful in solving the problems. They are drawn as accurately as possible EXCEPT when it is stated in a specific problem that the figure is not drawn to scale. All figures lie in a plane unless otherwise indicated.
3. Unless otherwise specified, the domain of any function $f(x)$ assumed to be the set of all real numbers x for which $f(x)$ is a real number.

References:

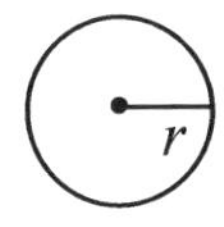

$A = \pi r^2$
$C = 2\pi r$

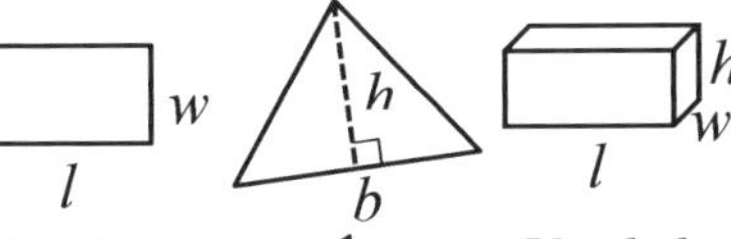

$A = lw$ $A = \frac{1}{2}bh$ $V = lwh$

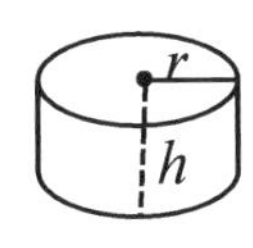

$V = \pi r^2 h$

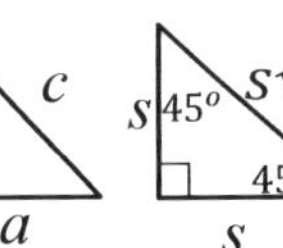

$c^2 = a^2 + b^2$

s, 45°, $s\sqrt{2}$, 45°, s; $2s$, 60°, s, 30°, $s\sqrt{3}$

Special Right Triangles

The number of degrees of arc in a circle is 360; the number of radians of arc in a circle is 2π.
The sum of the degree measures of the angles in a triangle is 180.

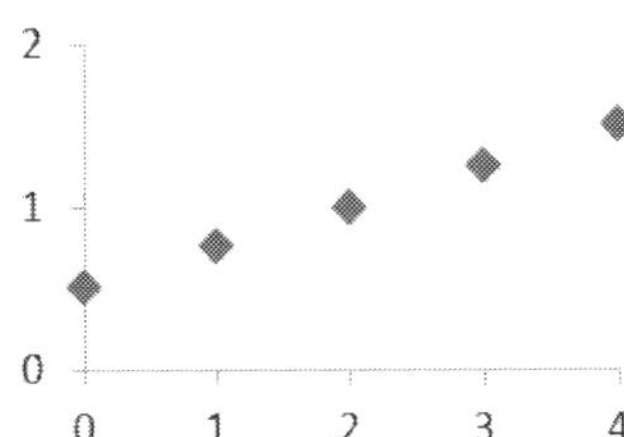

1. Which of the lines described by the following equations best fits those points above?
   a) $y = \frac{1}{4}x + \frac{1}{2}$
   b) $y = \frac{1}{4}x + 1$
   c) $y = -\frac{1}{4}x - \frac{1}{2}$
   d) $y = -\frac{1}{2}x + \frac{1}{2}$

2. Equation $(x + 3)(x + a) = x^2 + 4x + b$ where a and b are constants. If the equation is true for all values of x, what is the value of b?
   a) 8
   b) 6
   c) 4
   d) 3

3. If $(0.10) \times y = 10^2$, then y =?
   a) 0.01
   b) 0.001
   c) 100
   d) 1000

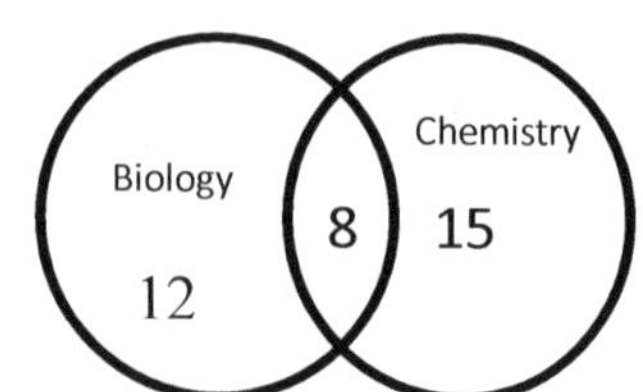

4. The Venn diagram above shows the distribution of 35 students at a school who took biology, chemistry, or both. What percent of the students who take both chemistry and biology?
   a) 15%
   b) 20%
   c) 23%
   d) 25%

5. Which of the following could be the coordinates of point R in a coordinate plane, if points P(2, 1), Q(-1, 4), and R(x, y) lie on the same line?
   a) (0, 2)
   b) (3, 2)
   c) (0, −2)
   d) (1, 2)

6. The following are coordinates of points on the xy-plane. Which of these points is nearest to the origin?
   a) (0, −1)
   b) $(-\frac{1}{2}, 0)$
   c) $(-\frac{1}{2}, -\frac{1}{2})$
   d) $(\frac{1}{2}, \frac{1}{2})$

7. In the figure below, the vertices of an isosceles right triangle, an equilateral triangle, and a regular pentagon intersect at one point. What is the value of a + b + c?

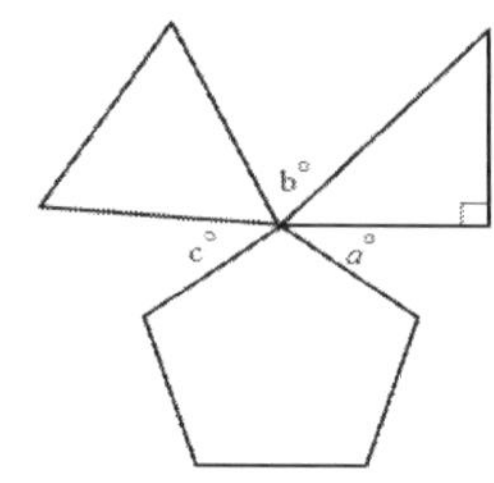

   a) 90
   b) 100
   c) 135
   d) 147

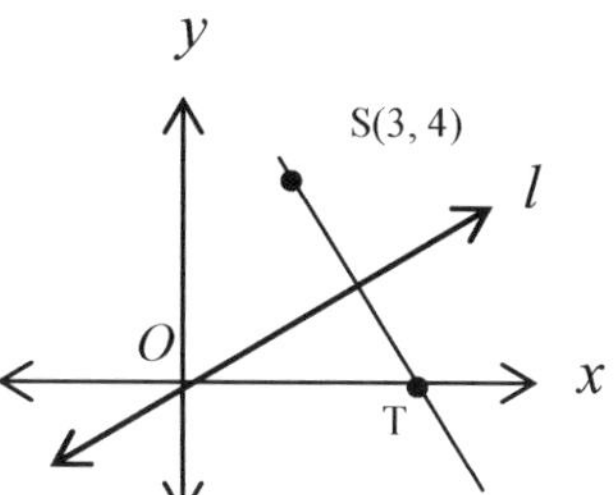

8. Line l intersects ST between S and T and also passes through the origin. Which of the following could be line l's slope?
   a) −2
   b) −1
   c) $\frac{1}{2}$
   d) $\frac{3}{2}$

9. If $\frac{a^3}{b^2}$ is an integer, but $\frac{2a+9}{b}$ is not an integer, which of the following could be the values of a and b?
   a) a = 5, b =5
   b) a = 3, b = 2
   c) a = 6, b = 3
   d) a = 6, b = 4

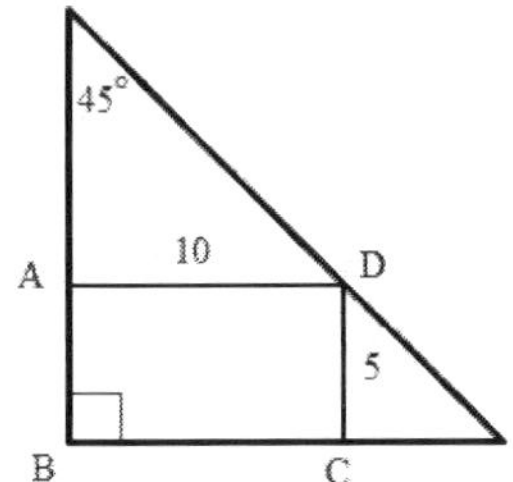

10. In the figure above, if ABCD is a rectangle, what is the area of the triangle?
    a) 150
    b) 122.5
    c) 112.5
    d) 100

11. Segment $\overline{AB}$ is the diameter of a circle with center O. Another point C lies on circle O. If AC = 5 and BC = 12, what is the area of circle O?
    a) $\frac{169}{2}\pi$
    b) $\frac{169}{4}\pi$
    c) 100π
    d) 50π

12. If a movie is 100 minutes long, what fraction of the movie has been completed 25 minutes after it begins?
    a) $\frac{1}{5}$
    b) $\frac{1}{6}$
    c) $\frac{1}{4}$
    d) $\frac{1}{3}$

Questions 13 – 14 refer to the following information:

The unemployment rate is officially defined as the percentage of unemployed individuals divided by all individuals currently willing to work. To count as unemployed, a person must be 16 or older and have not held a job during the week of the survey.

According to the Bureau of Labor Statistics, below is a comparison of the seasonally adjusted unemployment rates for certain states and the percent change from August 2015 to September 2015.

State	Rate (August 2015)	Monthly Percent Change from August 2015 to September 2015
New York	5.2	↓ 2%
Pennsylvania	5.4	↓2%
South Carolina	6.0	↓ 5%
California	6.1	↓ 3%
Arizona	6.3	– 0%
New Mexico	6.7	↑ 1%

13. The unemployment rate in South Carolina has dropped from August to September. According to the data shown in the table, what was the unemployment rate in September 2015 for the state of South Carolina?
    a) 5.9
    b) 5.8
    c) 5.7
    d) 5.6

14. If about 530,000 residents of New York were unemployed in August 2015, approximately how many New York residents were willing to work in August 2015?
    a) 9,900,000
    b) 10,200,000
    c) 99,000
    d) 102,000

15. Positive integers x, y, and z satisfy the equations $x^{-1/2} = \frac{1}{3}$ and $y^z = 8$, $z > y$, what is the value of $x + y + z$?
    a) 5
    b) 7
    c) 14
    d) 15

16. For all numbers p and q, let $p@q$ be defined by $p@q = (p + 1)^2 \times (q - 2)^2$, what is the value of 7@5?
    a) 24
    b) 576
    c) 729
    d) 884

5, 13, 29, 61, ...

17. The leading term in the sequence above is 5, and each successive term is formed by multiplying the preceding term by x and then adding y. What is the value of y?
    a) 1
    b) 2
    c) 3
    d) 4

18. The width of Mitchell's room is 3 feet less than its length. If the area of his room is 180 square feet, what is the width of his room in feet?
    a) 9
    b) 12
    c) 14
    d) 15

Questions 19 – 20 refer to the following information:

The kinetic energy of an object is the energy that the object possesses due to its motion. Kinetic energy is equal to half of the product of the mass and the square of its velocity.

The momentum is the quantity of the motion of a moving body, measured as a product of its mass and velocity.

19. If two bodies, A and B, have equal kinetic energies and the mass of A is four times as much as the mass of B, what is the ratio of the momentum of A to that of B?
    a) $\frac{1}{2}$
    b) $\frac{1}{4}$
    c) 2
    d) 4

20. If two bodies A and B as described above have equal momentum, what is the ratio of the kinetic energy of A to that of B?
    a) $\frac{1}{2}$
    b) $\frac{1}{4}$
    c) 2
    d) 4

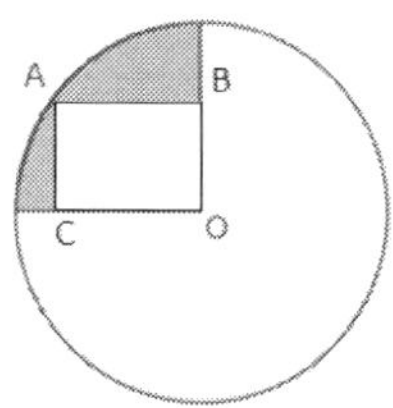

21. In the figure above, rectangle ABOC is drawn in circle O. If OB = 6 and OC = 8, what is the area of the shaded region?
    a) $24\pi - 24$
    b) $25\pi - 24$
    c) $25\pi - 48$
    d) $\frac{25\pi}{2} - 48$

22. A rectangular box is 25 inches long, 30 inches wide and 10 inches high. What is the least number of cubic boxes that can be stored perfectly in this box?
    a) 30
    b) 36
    c) 60
    d) 65

23. The ratio of 1.25 to 1 is equal to which of the following ratios?
    a) 2 to 1.5
    b) 3 to 2
    c) 4 to 3
    d) 5 to 4

24. Let <I, J> be defined as any integer greater than I but less than J, such as <–2, 4> = { –1, 0, 1, 2, 3}. Which of the following has the same elements as the intersection of <2, 6> and <3, 9>?
    a) <–2, 2>
    b) <–1, 3>
    c) <–3, 2>
    d) <3, 6>

25. Find the product of 5 and the sum of m and 5. Then, find one-fifth of the difference between that product and 5. In terms of m, what is the final result?
    a) $m - 5$
    b) $m - 4$
    c) $m + 4$
    d) $m + 5$

26. The quadratic function f is given by $f(x) = ax^2 + bx + c$, where a is a negative real number and c is a positive real number. Which of the following is the possible graph of $f(x)$?
    a)

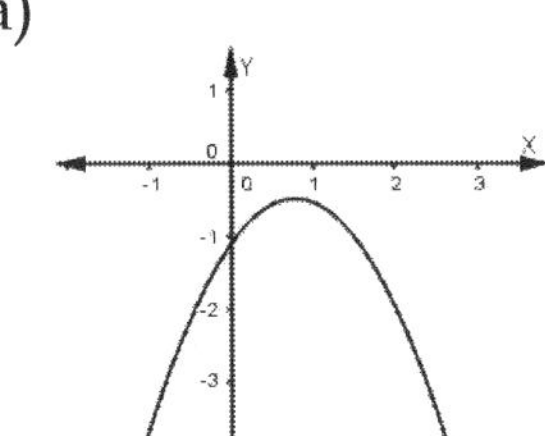

    b)

    c)

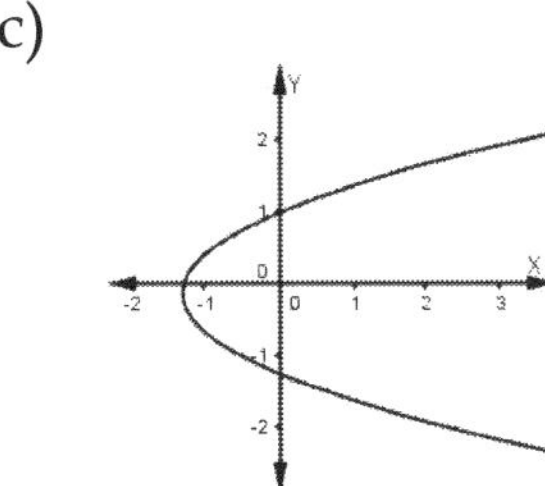

    d)

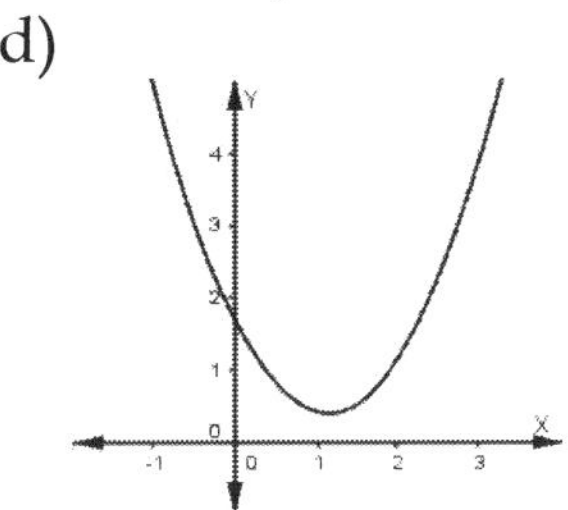

27. In the figure below, what is the value of $a + b + 2c + 2d$?

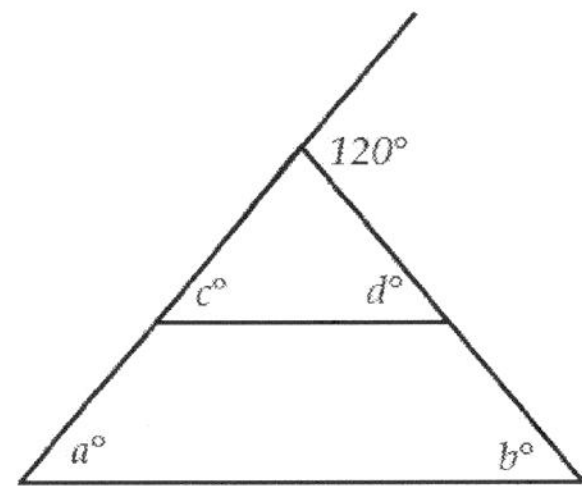

Note: Figure not drawn to scale.
    a) 240
    b) 300
    c) 360
    d) 380

28. When the number 99 is divided by the positive integer N, the remainder is 4. For how many different values of N is this true?
    a) One
    b) Two
    c) Three
    d) Four

29. The term *half-life* is defined as the time it takes for half of a sample of radioactive material to decay. It is constant for any amount of the radioactive material. Initially, there are 100 grams of a radioactive material which has a half-life of one day. Which of the following graphs could model the mass of the radioactive material left as a function of time?

a)

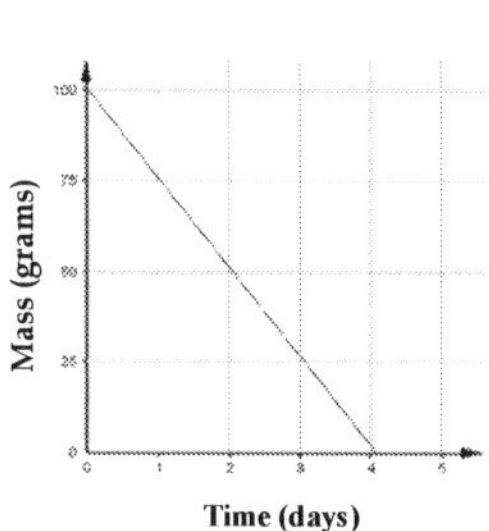

b)

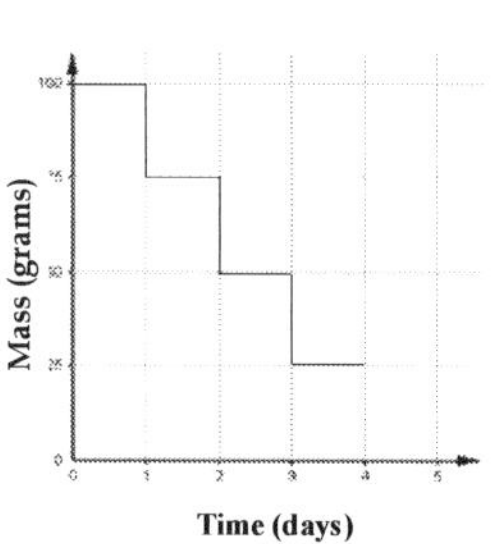

c)

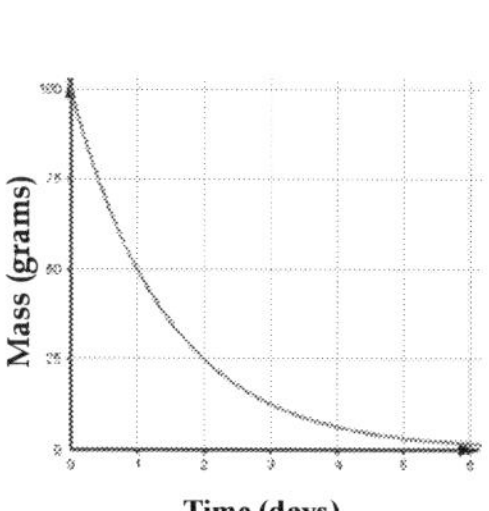

d)

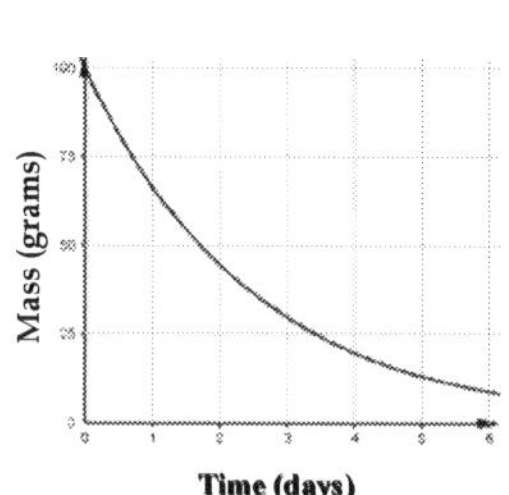

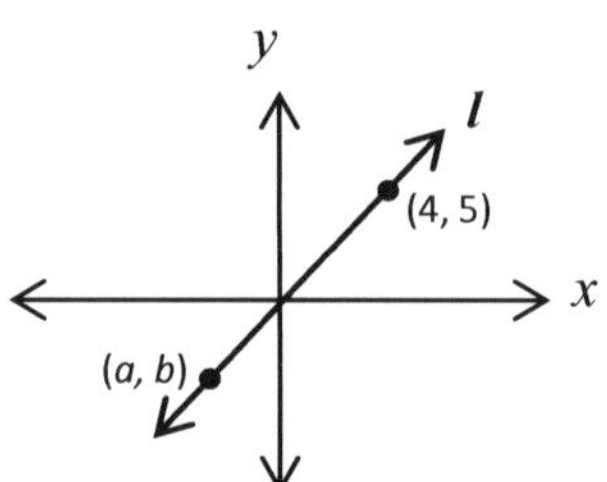

30. In the figure above, line l passes through the origin. What is the value of $\frac{b}{a}$?

a) 1
b) 1.25
c) 1.33
d) 1.5

Directions:

For questions 31-38, solve the problem and enter your answer in the grid, as described below, on the answer sheet.

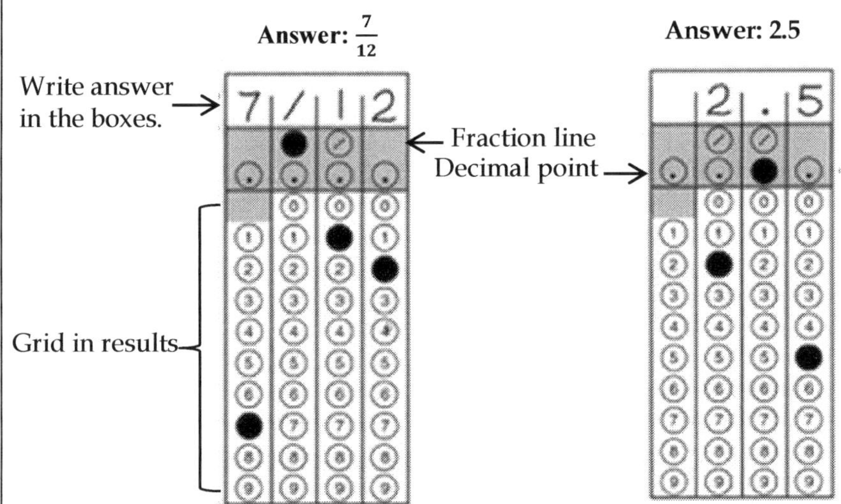

Answer: 201
Either position is correct.

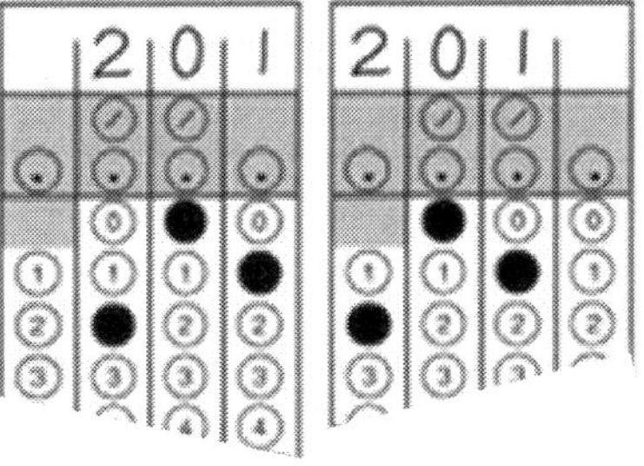

<u>**Note:**</u> You may start your answers in any column, space permitting. Columns not needed should be left blank.

- Mark no more than one circle in any column.
- Because the answer sheet will be machine-scored. **You will receive credit only if the circles are filled in correctly.**
- Although not required, it is suggested that you write your answer in the boxes at the top of the columns to help you fill in the circles accurately.
- Some problems may have more than one correct answer. In such case, grid only one answer.
- No question has a negative answer.
- **Mixed numbers** such as $3\frac{1}{2}$ must be gridded as 3.5 or $\frac{7}{2}$. (If 3 1 / 2 is gridded, it will be interpreted as $\frac{31}{2}$, not $3\frac{1}{2}$.)
- **Decimal Answer**: If you obtain a decimal answer with more digits than the grid can accommodate, it may be either rounded or truncated, but it must fill the entire grid. The acceptable ways to grid $\frac{2}{3}$ are:

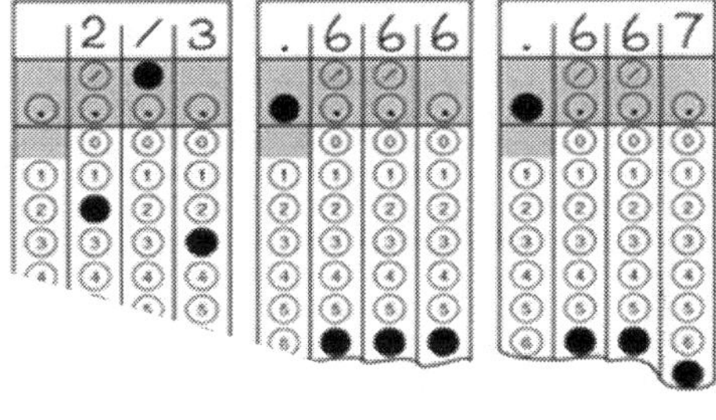

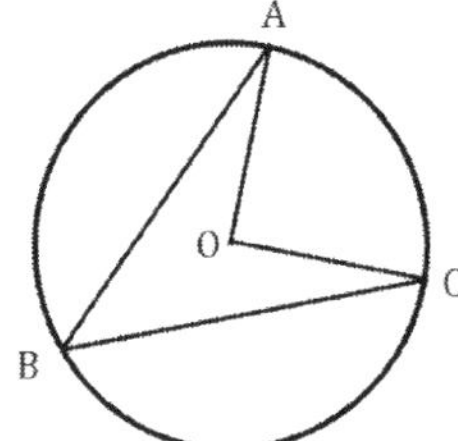

31. In the figure above, if $\widehat{AC}$ has arc length equal to $\frac{1}{4}$ of the circumference of the circle, what is the value of $m\angle ABC$ in degrees?

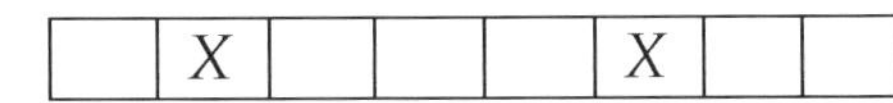

32. The figure above represents eight chairs that will be assigned randomly to eight students, one student per chair. If Sam and Chris are two of the eight students, what is the probability, in fraction, that each will be assigned a chair indicated by an X?

33. In a recent town election, 80 percent of the 16,000 people voted. Of the voting people, 55 percent voted for current mayor and 150 votes were invalid. How many people voted for other candidates?

34. A movie company invited a total of 600 people to complete their review survey after watching a new release movie. Of the 420 people who finished that survey so far, 55 percent are male and 45 percent are female. Assuming all 600 people will eventually complete the survey, how many of the rest of the respondents must be female in order for half of the total respondents to be female?

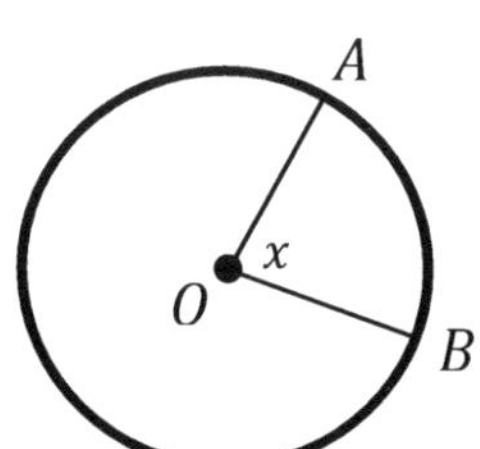

35. In the figure above, the circle has center O and radius 5. If the area of the minor sector $\widehat{AB}$ is between 9 and 14, what is one possible integer value of arc length s?

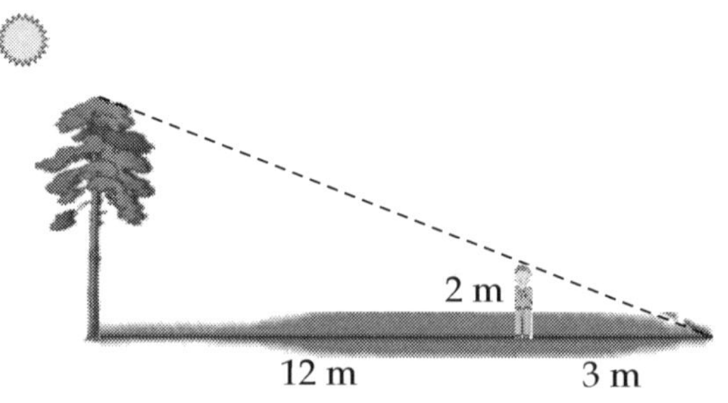

36. Sam walked 12 meters away from the base of a tree as shown in the figure above. At the point he was standing, he noticed that his shadow reached the same spot on the ground as the shadow of the tree. If Sam is 2 meters tall and his shadow is 3 meters long, how high is the tree, in meters?

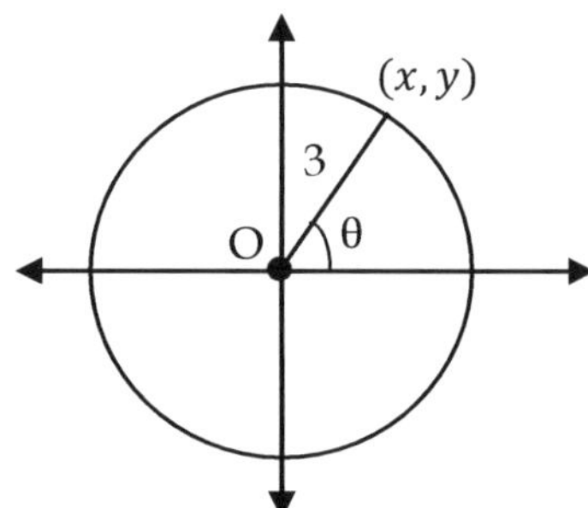

37. In the xy-plane above, O is the center of the circle with a radius of 3, and the measure of $\angle\theta$ is $\frac{\pi}{3}$ radians. What is the value of $x + y$? (Round your answer to the nearest tenth.)

38. If the center of the circle defined by $x^2 + y^2 - 4x + 2y = 20$ is (a, b), then $a + b = ?$

SAT MATH MOCK TEST No. 7 ANSWER KEYS

Section 3									
1. C	2. D	3. A	4. D	5. A	6. B	7. D	8. C	9. D	10. A
11. C	12. A	13. B	14. C	15. D	16. 28	17. 6	18. 2	19. 0.5	20. 1

Section 4									
1. A	2. D	3. C	4. D	5. C	6. B	7. D	8. C	9. A	10. C
11. B	12. C	13. C	14. B	15. C	16. B	17. C	18. B	19. C	20. B
21. C	22. C	23. D	24. D	25. C	26. B	27. C	28. C	29. C	30. B
31. 45	32. $\frac{1}{28}$	33. 5610	34. 111	35. 4or5	36. 10	37. 4.1	38. 1		

SECTION 3

1. *Answer: (c)*
$(x^{\frac{1}{4}})^4 = x$
$(\sqrt{3})^4 = 9$

2. *Answer: (d)*
Divide both sides by 3.
$3(x^2 - 2) = 21$
$x^2 - 2 = 7$
$x^2 = 9$
$x = \pm 3$

3. *Answer: (a)*
$2x - 5 > 7$
$2x > 12$
$x > 6$
The least value of integer is 7.

4. *Answer: (d)*
Given that $8(2^x) = 4^y$*, then*
$2^3 \times 2^x = 2^{2y}$.
$2^{3+x} = 2^{2y}$
$3 + x = 2y$
$x = 2y - 3$

5. *Answer: (a)*
$\frac{8}{\sqrt{x+4}} = 2, \quad \sqrt{x+4} = \frac{8}{2}$
$\sqrt{x+4} = 4$
$x + 4 = 16$
$x = 12$

6. *Answer: (b)*
Replace x with 3 in the equation.
$x = 1, \quad 2y(6 - 5\times 1) = 2y$

7. *Answer: (d)*
A line with a negative slope descends from left to right; therefore, the slope of the line in the graph is negative.
$|a| > |3b| \rightarrow \frac{1}{3} > |\frac{b}{a}|$

8. *Answer: (c)*
Sum = Number of Elements × Average
$9 \times 9 < Sum < 10 \times 9$
$81 < Sum < 90$

9. *Answer: (d)*
The product of the slopes of two perpendicular lines is −1.
The product of the slopes of all four sides of rectangle is $-1 \times -1 = 1$.

10. *Answer: (a)*
The average of a, b, and 4m is equal to the sum of a, b, and 4m divided by 3.
$a + b = 2m$
$a + b + 4m = 2m + 4m = 6m$
Average: $\frac{6m}{3} = 2m$

11. *Answer: (c)*
If $xy < 0$ *and* $y > 0$ *then* $x < 0$
A positive number is always greater than a negative number.
$y > x$

12. *Answer: (a)*
The only common factor of 15 and 21 other than 1 is 3, so $y = 3$.
$x = \frac{15}{3} = 5$
$z = \frac{21}{3} = 7$

13. *Answer: (b)*
The LCM of 12 and 8 is 24.

14. *Answer: (c)*
Plug in $y = -1 - z$ to the first equation and then apply FOIL method and the distributive law.
$x = 2(-1-z)^2 + 3(-1-z) + 4$
$= 2(1 + 2z + z^2) - 3 - 3z + 4$
$= 2z^2 + z + 3$

15. *Answer: (d)*
$D = y \text{ Ounces} \times \frac{x \text{ Bottles}}{1 \text{ Ounce}} \times \text{Price of One Bottle}$
$\text{Price of One Bottle} = \frac{D}{xy}$

16. *Answer: 28*
$3(m) + 3(a) + 3(t) + 2(h) + 2(e) + 3(m) + 3(a) + 3(t) + 2(i) + 2(c) + 2(s) = 28$

17. *Answer: 6*
$15 = \frac{1}{2} \times 5 \times k$
$k = 6$

18. *Answer: 2*
Substitute x with (a +1).
$g(a+1) = (a + 1 - 3)(a + 1 - 1) = 0$
$a(a - 2) = 0$
$a = 2$ *(Given that $a > 0$)*

19. *Answer:* $\frac{1}{2}$ *or .5*
After first taking, there are 7 blue cards and a total of 14 cards left in her pocket.
Probability to get a blue card : $\frac{7}{14} = \frac{1}{2}$

20. *Answer: 1*
Let x be the number.
$6x - 3 = 3x^2$
$x^2 - 2x + 1 = 0$
$(x - 1)^2 = 0$
$x = 1$

SECTION 4

1. *Answer: (a)*
$\text{Slope} = \frac{\text{Rise}}{\text{Run}} = \frac{1-\frac{1}{2}}{2-0} = \frac{1}{4}$
$y\text{-intercept} = \frac{1}{2}$
$y = \frac{1}{4}x + \frac{1}{2}$

2. *Answer: (d)*
This is an identity equation question. The two expressions have the same coefficients for corresponding terms.
$(x + 3)(x + a) = x^2 + (3+a)x + 3a$
By comparison, $3 + a = 4$ *and* $3a = b$
$a = 1$ *and* $b = 3$

3. *Answer: (d)*
Divide both sides by 0.1.
$(0.10) \times y = 100$
$y = \frac{100}{0.1} = 1000$

4. *Answer: (c)*
$\frac{8}{35} = 0.23 = 23\%$

5. *Answer: (d)*
$\text{Slope} = \frac{\text{Rise}}{\text{Run}} = \frac{4-1}{-1-2} = -1$
Point-slope-form: $y - 1 = -(x - 2)$
The point (1, 2) satisfies the above equation.

6. *Answer: (b)*
Distance to the Origin $= \sqrt{(x-0)^2 + (y-0)^2} = \sqrt{x^2 + y^2}$
(b) Has the shortest distance of $\frac{1}{2}$ *from the origin.*

7. *Answer: (d)*
The base angle of an isosceles right triangle is 45°, each interior angle of an equilateral triangle is 60°, and each interior angle of a regular pentagon is 108°.
$a + b + c + 45° + 60° + 108° = 360°$
$a + b + c = 147°$

8. *Answer: (c)*
OT has a slope of 0 and OS has a slope of $\frac{4}{3}$*, so the slope of line l should be between 0 and* $\frac{4}{3}$.

9. *Answer: (a)*
Try out the values of a and b from answer choices.
a). $\frac{5^3}{5^2}, \frac{19}{5}$
b). $\frac{3^3}{2^2}, \frac{15}{2}$
c). $\frac{6^3}{3^2}, \frac{21}{3}$
d). $\frac{6^3}{4^2}, \frac{21}{4}$

10. *Answer: (c)*
Both legs of the triangle have length of 10 + 5 = 15.
So the area of the triangle: $\frac{1}{2} \times 15 \times 15 = 112.5$

11. *Answer: (b)*
ΔABC is a right triangle.
$AB^2 = AC^2 + BC^2$
$AB = \sqrt{5^2 + 12^2} = 13$
Radius $= \frac{1}{2}(13) = 6.5$
Area $= \pi \times 6.5^2 = 42.25\pi = \frac{169}{4}\pi$

12. *Answer: (c)*
$\frac{25}{100} = \frac{1}{4}$

13. *Answer: (c)*
Let the unemployment rate in September be x.
$\frac{x - 6.0}{6.0} = -0.05$
$x = 5.7$

14. *Answer: (b)*
Let the number of residents who were willing to work be x.
$\frac{530{,}000}{x} = 5.2\%$
$5.2x = 53{,}000{,}000$
$x = 10{,}192{,}308 \approx 10{,}200{,}000$

15. *Answer: (c)*
$x^{-½} = \frac{1}{3}$, $x = (\frac{1}{3})^{-2} = 3^2 = 9$
$8 = 2^3 = y^z$
$y = 2$ and $z = 3$
$x + y + z = 2 + 3 + 9 = 14$

16. *Answer: (b)*
Replace p with 7 and q with 5.
$7@5 = (7 + 1)^2(5 - 2)^2 = 576$

17. *Answer: (c)*
$13 - 5 = 8$
$29 - 13 = 16$
$61 - 29 = 32$
So each successive term is multiplying the proceeding term by 2 and adding 3.
$13 = 2 \times 5 + 3$, so $y = 3$
$61 = 29 \times 2 + 3$ (double check the answer)

18. *Answer: (b)*
Let the length be x, then the width is $x - 3$.
$x(x - 3) = 180$
$x^2 - 3x = 180 \rightarrow x = 15$
$15 - 3 = 12$
The width of the room is 12 and the length is 15.

19. *Answer: (c)*
Let the mass of A be $4k$ and the mass of B be k.
$\frac{1}{2}(4k) \times (v_A)^2 = \frac{1}{2}(k) \times (v_B)^2$
$\frac{v_A}{v_B} = \frac{1}{2}$
$\frac{Momentum\ of\ A}{Momentum\ of\ B} = \frac{4k \times v_A}{k \times v_B}$
$= 4 \times \frac{1}{2} = 2$

20. *Answer: (b)*
Momentum is measured as a product of mass and velocity.
$4k \times v_A = k \times v_B$
$\frac{v_A}{v_B} = \frac{1}{4}$
$\frac{K_e of\ A}{K_e of\ B} = \frac{\frac{1}{2} \times 4k \times v_A^2}{\frac{1}{2} \times k \times v_B^2} = \frac{4}{16} = \frac{1}{4}$

21. *Answer: (c)*
OA is the radius of the circle and the shaded area is the area of the quarter circle minus the area of the rectangle.
Radius $= \sqrt{OB^2 + OC^2} = \sqrt{6 + 8} = 10$
Shaded Area = Area of $\frac{1}{4}$ Circle – Area of Rectangle =
$\frac{1}{4}(\pi \times 10^2) - 6 \times 8 = \frac{1}{4} \times 100\pi - 48 = 25\pi - 48$

22. *Answer: (c)*
Cubic boxes' length, width, and height have the same length, so the number of cubic boxes must be a common factor of 25, 30, and 10. To find the minimum number of boxes, we need to find the GCF (greatest common factor) of these three numbers.
The GCF of 25, 30 and 10 is 5, so there are $\frac{25}{5} \times \frac{30}{5} \times \frac{10}{5}$ cubic boxes.
$\frac{25}{5} \times \frac{30}{5} \times \frac{10}{5} = 60$

23. *Answer: (d)*
You can multiply the numerator and denominator by the same factor to get an equivalent ratio.
$1.25 \times 4 : 1 \times 4 = 5 : 4$
Or just simply convert the ratios to decimals and compare, such as $5 \div 4 = 1.25$.

24. *Answer: (d)*
Intersection of <2, 6> and <3, 9> = {3, 4, 5} ∩ {4, 5, 6, 7, 8} = {4, 5}
(d) <3, 6> has the same elements of {4, 5}.

25. *Answer: (c)*
$\frac{5(m+5)-5}{5} = \frac{5(m+5-1)}{5} = m+4$

26. *Answer: (b)*
A negative value of a will make the quadratic function's graph open downward and a positive value of c will show that the function has a positive y-intercept.

27. *Answer: (c)*
$120 = c + d = a + b$
$a + b + 2(c + d) = 120 + 2 \times 120 = 360$

28. *Answer: (c)*
Find all the factors of (99 − 4) that are greater than 4.
$95 = 5 \times 19$
The total number of factors of 95: (1+1)(1+1) =4
N must be greater than 4, so we need to deduct factors that are smaller than or equal to 4 which are 1.
The total number of different values of N: 4 − 1 = 3

29. *Answer: (c)*
For every half-life of one day, the radioactive material will be halved.

Day	Mass (grams)
0	100
1	50
2	25
3	12.5
4	6.25

Only graph c) fits the data above.

30. *Answer: (b)*
$\frac{b-0}{a-0} = \frac{5-0}{4-0}$
$\frac{b}{a} = \frac{5}{4} = 1.25$

31. *Answer: 45*
$m\angle ABC = \frac{1}{2} m\angle AOC = \frac{1}{2} \times \frac{1}{4} \times 360^o = 45^o$

32. *Answer:* $\frac{1}{28}$
The arrangement that we want is an arrangement where six students choose from 6 chairs and two students (Sam and Chris) choose from the 2 chairs marked with an X. Then we will divide the number of special arrangements by the number of possible arrangements, where Sam and Chris are not constrained to the two chairs with Xs.
$Probability = \frac{Special\ Arrangements}{Total\ Arrangements}$
Total Arrangements = 8!
Special Arrangements = 6! × 2!
$P = \frac{6! \times 2!}{8!} = \frac{2}{8 \times 7} = \frac{1}{28}$

33. *Answer: 5610*
Total Votes – Votes for Current Mayor – Invalid Votes = Votes for Other Candidates
Total Votes = 16000 × 0.8 = 12800
Votes for Current Mayor: 12800 × 0.55 = 7040
Votes for Others = 12800 – 7040 – 150 = 5610

34. *Answer: 111*
We need 300 females but only 189 (420 × 0.45) females who complete the survey so far.
300 – 189 = 111

35. *Answer: 4 or 5*
Area of the Sector $= \frac{1}{2} r^2 \theta$
$9 < \frac{1}{2} 5^2 \theta < 14$
$\frac{18}{25} < \theta < \frac{28}{25}$
$s = r\theta$
$3.6 < s < 5.6$
$s = 4\ or\ 5$

36. *Answer: 10*
Let the height of the tree be x.
The two triangles are similar, therefore their corresponding sides are proportional.
$\frac{3}{12+3} = \frac{2}{x}$
$x = 10\ m$

37. *Answer: 4.1*
$x = r\cos(\theta) = 3 \times \cos\left(\frac{\pi}{3}\right) = 1.5$
$y = r\sin(\theta) = 3 \times \sin\left(\frac{\pi}{3}\right) = 2.6$
$x + y = 4.1$

38. *Answer: 1*
Rewrite to the equation in standard form.
$x^2 - 4x + 4 + y^2 + 2y + 1 = 20 + 5$
$(x-2)^2 + (y+1)^2 = 5^2$
The center of the circle is (2, −1) and the radius is 5.
$a = 2, b = -1$
$a + b = 1$

SAT Math Mock Test No. 8

SECTION 3 

Math Test – NO Calculator **25 MINUTES, 20 QUESTIONS**

Directions:

For questions 1-15, solve each problem, choose the best answer from the choices provided, and fill in the corresponding circle on your answer sheet. **For questions 16-20**, solve the problem and enter your answer in the grid on the answer sheet. Please refer to the directions before question 16 on how to enter your answers in the grid. You may use any available space in your test booklet for scratch work.

Notes:

1. **No calculator** is allowed for this section. All numbers used are real numbers.
2. Figures that accompany problems in this test are intended to provide information useful in solving the problems. They are drawn as accurately as possible EXCEPT when it is stated in a specific problem that the figure is not drawn to scale. All figures lie in a plane unless otherwise indicated.
3. Unless otherwise specified, the domain of any function *f(x)* assumed to be the set of all real numbers *x* for which *f(x)* is a real number.

References:

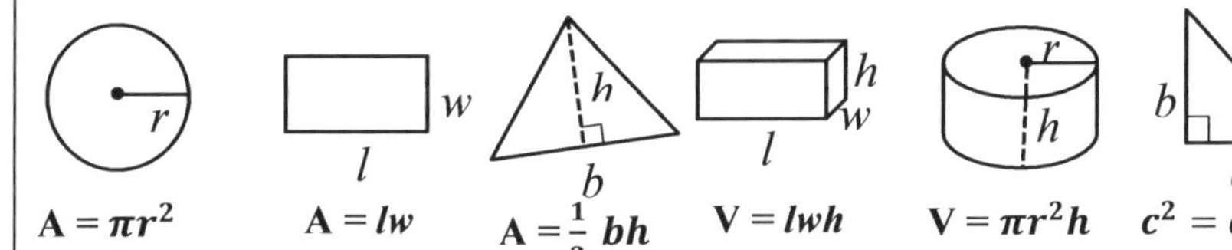

$A = \pi r^2$ $C = 2\pi r$ $A = lw$ $A = \frac{1}{2}bh$ $V = lwh$ $V = \pi r^2 h$ $c^2 = a^2 + b^2$ **Special Right Triangles**

The number of degrees of arc in a circle is 360; the number of radians of arc in a circle is 2π.
The sum of the degree measures of the angles in a triangle is 180.

1. A, B, and C are three points on a line in that order. If $\overline{AB} = 20$ and $\overline{BC}$ is 10 less than $\overline{AB}$, what is the length of $\overline{AC}$?
   a) 30
   b) 38
   c) 35
   d) 32

2. If $y > 0$, what is 20 percent of $50y$?
   a) $10y$
   b) $12y$
   c) $14y$
   d) $20y$

3. In the figure below, if $a = 2c$, and $b = 3a$, what is the value of c?

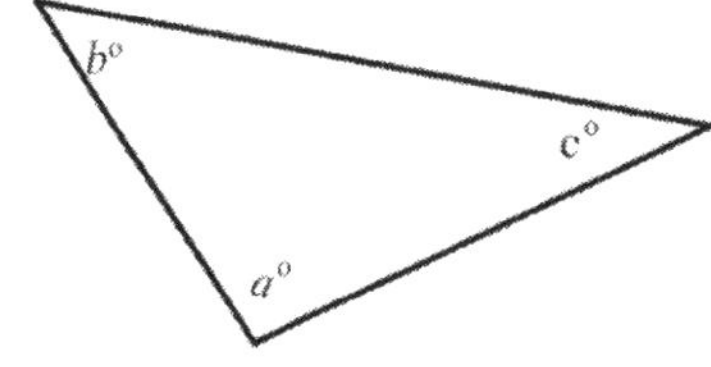

Note: Figure not drawn to scale.

   a) 18
   b) 20
   c) 28
   d) 34

4. If $x > x^2$, which of the following must be true?

   I. $x < 1$
   II. $x > 0$
   III. $x^2 > 1$

   a) I only
   b) II only
   c) I and II only
   d) I and III only

5. A rectangular solid has dimensions of $a \times b \times c$ where a, b and c are positive integers. Its volume is v and its surface area is s. If v is odd, which of the following must be true?

   I. a is odd.
   II. Both b and c are odds
   III. s is even.

   a) I only
   b) I and II only
   c) I and III only
   d) I, II, and III

6. If $x > 0$ and $x^y x^{\frac{1}{2}} = x^{\frac{1}{4}}$, what is the value of y?
   a) $\frac{1}{2}$
   b) $\frac{1}{4}$
   c) $-\frac{1}{4}$
   d) $-\frac{1}{2}$

7. Which of the following expressions must be negative if $x < 0$?
   a) $x^2 - 2$
   b) $x^5 - 1$
   c) $x^4 - 3x^2 - 1$
   d) $x^6 + 3x^2 + 1$

8. Point Q lies on the line with equation $y - 3 = 2(x - 3)$. If the x-coordinate of Q is 2, what is the y-coordinate of Q?
   a) 2
   b) 1
   c) 0
   d) −1

9. On a certain farm, every sixth tomato picked is rotten, and every fifth tomato picked is green. If a famer randomly picks a tomato from the farm, what is the probability that the tomato will be both green and rotten?
   a) $\frac{1}{5}$
   b) $\frac{1}{6}$
   c) $\frac{1}{30}$
   d) $\frac{1}{20}$

10. Which of the following is an equation of the line that is perpendicular to the y-axis and passes through the point (2, 1)?
    a) $y = 1$
    b) $y = -1$
    c) $y = x$
    d) $y = -x$

11. At West Hill High School, some members of the Key Club are on the math team and no members of the math team are freshmen. Which of the following must also be true?
    a) No members of the Key Club are freshmen.
    b) Some members of the Key Club are freshmen.
    c) Some members of the Key Club are not freshmen.
    d) More tenth graders are on the math team than are on the Key Club.

12. If $\frac{x}{y} = 4$, $x = 4z$, and $z = 6$, what is the value of y?
    a) 6
    b) 7
    c) 8
    d) 10

13. If the sum of three numbers is 54, what is the average (arithmetic mean) of the three numbers?
    a) 9
    b) 12
    c) 15
    d) 18

14. In the xy-plane, line l passes through the origin and is perpendicular to the line $2x + y = b$, where b is a constant. If the two lines intersect at the point $(3a, a+1)$, what is the value of b?
    a) 3
    b) 15
    c) 9
    d) 12

15. When the number 13 is divided by the positive integer p, the remainder is 1. For how many different values of p is this true?
    a) Six
    b) Five
    c) Four
    d) Three

Directions:

For questions 16-20, solve the problem and enter your answer in the grid, as described below, on the answer sheet.

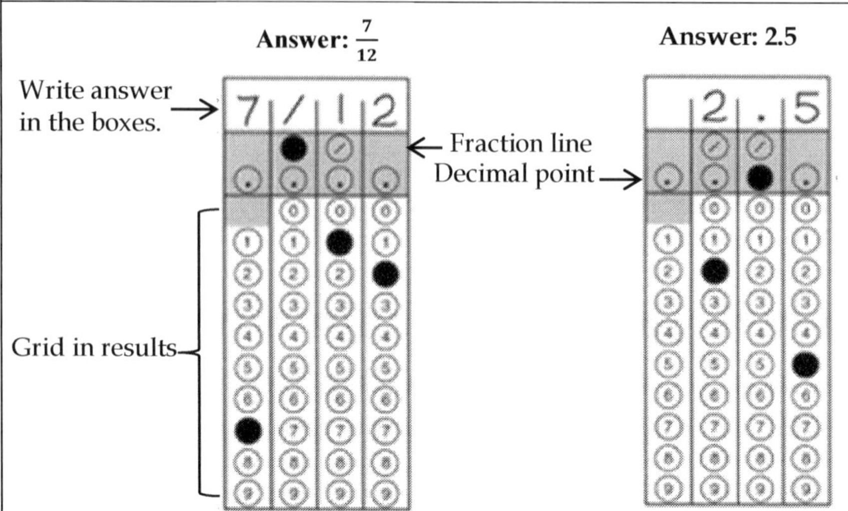

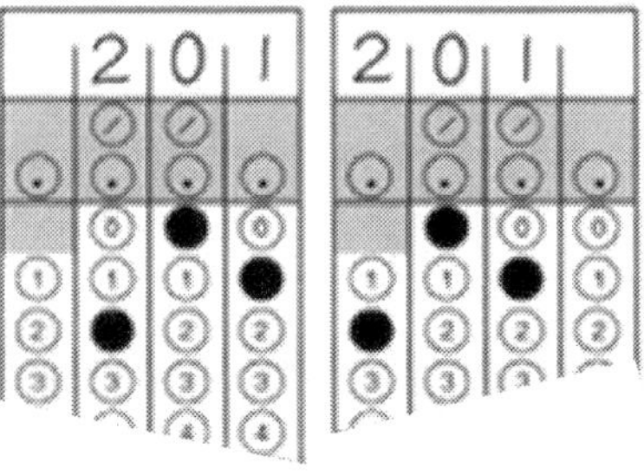

Note: You may start your answers in any column, space permitting. Columns not needed should be left blank.

- Mark no more than one circle in any column.
- Because the answer sheet will be machine-scored. **You will receive credit only if the circles are filled in correctly.**
- Although not required, it is suggested that you write your answer in the boxes at the top of the columns to help you fill in the circles accurately.
- Some problems may have more than one correct answer. In such case, grid only one answer.
- No question has a negative answer.
- **Mixed numbers** such as $3\frac{1}{2}$ must be gridded as 3.5 or $\frac{7}{2}$. (If 3 1 / 2 is gridded, it will be interpreted as $\frac{31}{2}$, not $3\frac{1}{2}$.)
- **Decimal Answer**: If you obtain a decimal answer with more digits than the grid can accommodate, it may be either rounded or truncated, but it must fill the entire grid. The acceptable ways to grid $\frac{2}{3}$ are:

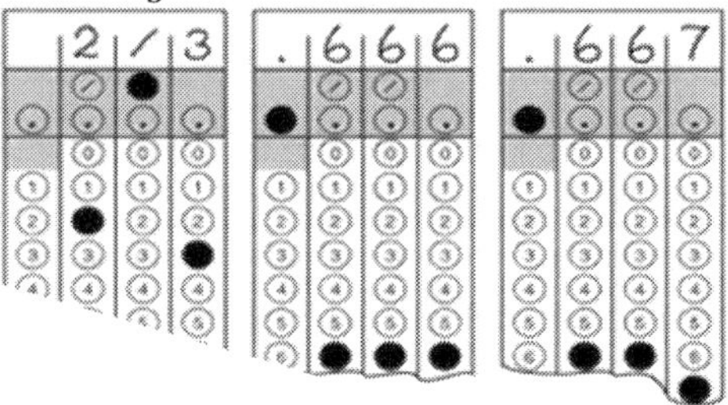

16. A bag contains only red, white, and blue marbles. If randomly choosing a blue marble is three times as likely as randomly choosing a white marble, and randomly choosing a red marble is twice as likely as randomly choosing a blue marble, then what is the smallest possible number of marbles in the bag?

17. If $3x^2 = 5y = 15$, what is the value of x^2y?

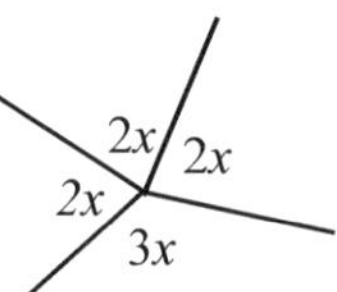

18. In the figure above, four line segments intercept at a point. How many degrees is x?

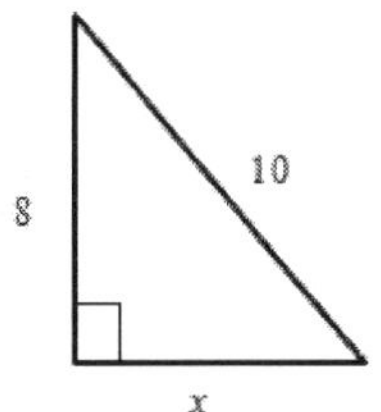

19. In the right triangle above, what is the value of x?

20. If $x + 2y = 5$, what is the value of $x + 2y - 1$?

SECTION 4 

Math Test — Calculator **55 MINUTES, 38 QUESTIONS**

Directions:

For questions 1-30, solve each problem, choose the best answer from the choices provided, and fill in the corresponding circle on your answer sheet. **For questions 31-38**, solve the problem and enter your answer in the grid on the answer sheet. Please refer to the directions before question 31 on how to enter your answers in the grid. You may use any available space in your test booklet for scratch work.

Notes:

1. Acceptable calculators are allowed for this section. All numbers used are real numbers.
2. Figures that accompany problems in this test are intended to provide information useful in solving the problems. They are drawn as accurately as possible EXCEPT when it is stated in a specific problem that the figure is not drawn to scale. All figures lie in a plane unless otherwise indicated.
3. Unless otherwise specified, the domain of any function *f(x)* assumed to be the set of all real numbers *x* for which *f(x)* is a real number.

References:

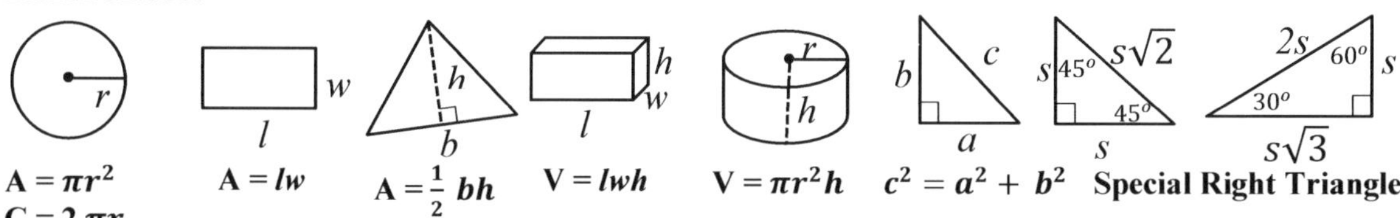

The number of degrees of arc in a circle is 360; the number of radians of arc in a circle is 2π.
The sum of the degree measures of the angles in a triangle is 180.

1. The median of a set of 15 consecutive integers is 35. What is the greatest of these 15 integers?
   a) 42
   b) 41
   c) 40
   d) 38

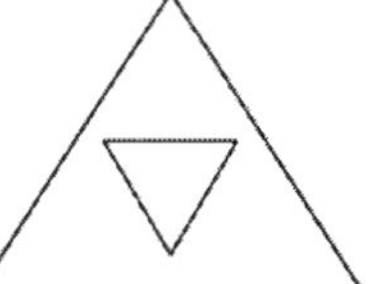

Note: Figure not drawn to scale.

2. Two equilateral triangles are shown above with the ratio of their side lengths equal to $\frac{1}{2}$. What is the ratio of their areas?
   a) $\frac{1}{3}$
   b) $\frac{1}{\sqrt{3}}$
   c) $\frac{1}{6}$
   d) $\frac{1}{4}$

3. A car rental company charges \$50 per day for the first 5 days, and \$45 a day for each day after that. How much will Tom be charged if he rents a car for two weeks?
   a) \$455
   b) \$525
   c) \$555
   d) \$655

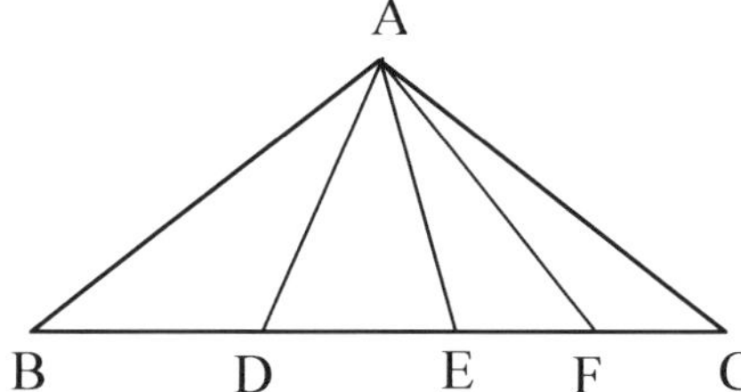

4. In the figure above, if segment AD bisects ∠BAE, segment AF bisects ∠EAC, and $m\angle BAC = 110^\circ$, what is the value of $m\angle DAF$ in degrees (Figure not drawn to scale.)?
   a) 60°
   b) 55°
   c) 45°
   d) 40°

5. Five erasers cost as much as 3 pencils. If Matt bought one eraser and one pencil for \$1.60, how much does one pencil cost in dollars?
   a) 0.50
   b) 0.60
   c) 1.00
   d) 1.10

6. 36 marbles, all of which are red, blue, or green, are placed in a bag. If a marble is picked from the bag at random, the probability of getting a red marble is $\frac{1}{4}$ and the probability of getting a blue marble is $\frac{1}{2}$. How many green marbles are in the bag?
   a) 9
   b) 10
   c) 12
   d) 15

7. A cube has 2 faces painted green and the remaining faces painted red. The total area of the green faces is 32 square inches. What is the volume of this cube, in cubic inches?
   a) 9
   b) 27
   c) 36
   d) 64

8. In the xy-plane, line l passes through the origin and is perpendicular to the line $3x + 2y = 2b$, where b is a constant. If the two lines intersect at the point $(2a, a - 1)$, what is the value of b?
   a) – 13
   b) – 12
   c) −6
   d) 12

9. Megan began a one-way 10-mile bicycle trip by riding very slowly for 5 miles. She rested for 30 minutes and then rode quickly for the rest of the trip. Which of the following graphs could correctly represents the trip?
   a)

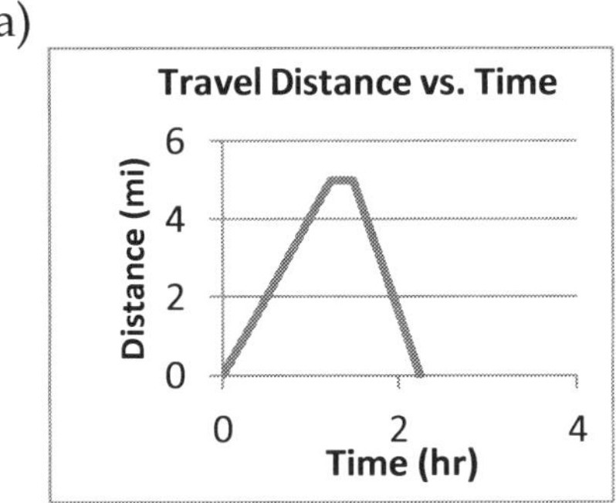

b)

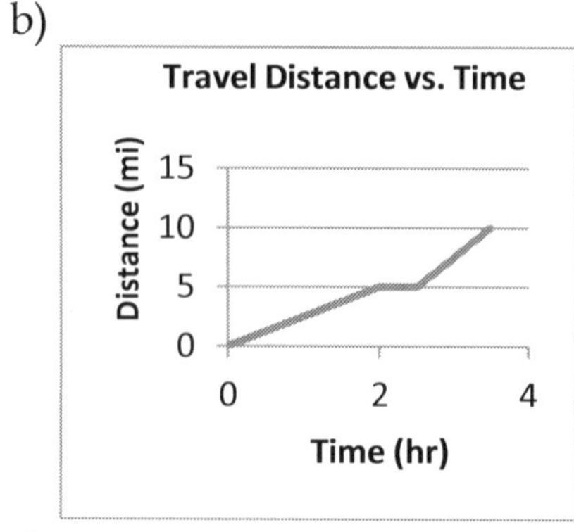

c)

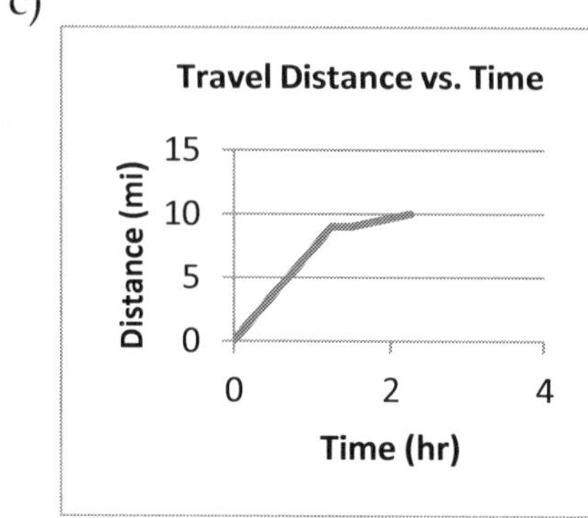

d)

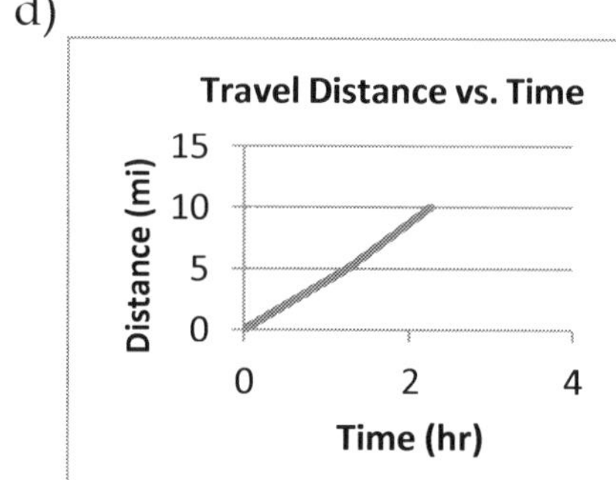

10. The table below shows the number of students in Mr. Jang's class that are taking 1, 2, 3, or 4 AP classes. After a new student joined the class (not shown in the table), the average (arithmetic mean) number of AP classes per student became equal to the median. How many AP classes is the new student taking?

Students Taking AP Classes	
Number of APs	*Number of Students*
1	6
2	4
3	5
4	4

a) 5
b) 4
c) 3
d) 2

11. From the graphs below, how many more graduates went on to a four-year college in 2013 than in 2012?

2012 Graduates Plans
total number of graduates: 400

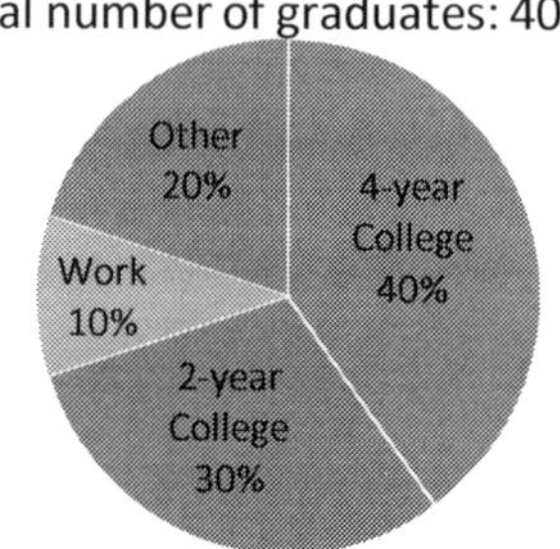

2013 Graduates Plans:
Total Number of Graduates: 420

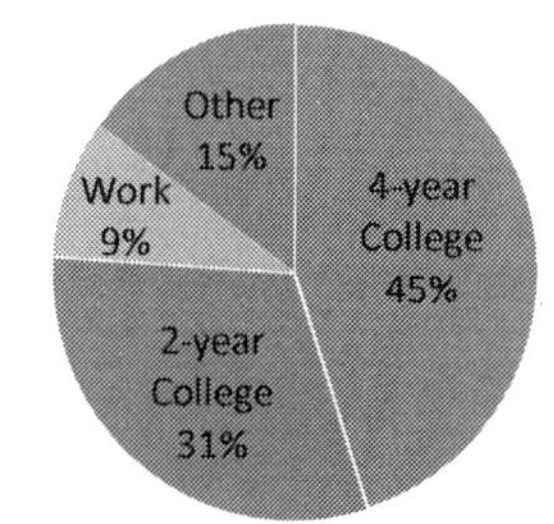

a) 29
b) 32
c) 33
d) 35

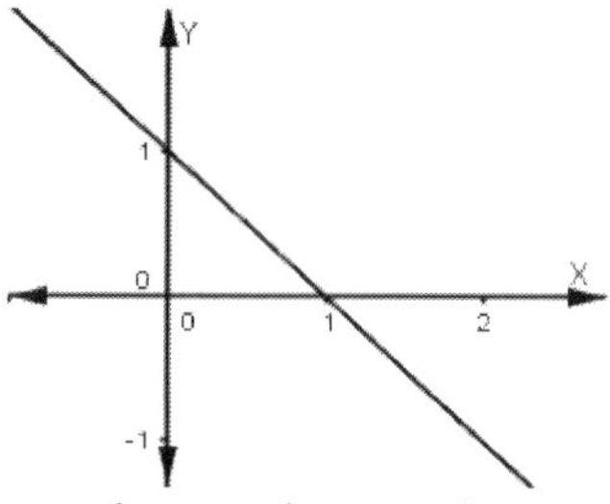

12. The figure above shows the graph of the line $y = mx + b$, where m and b are constants. Which of the following best represents the graph of the line $y= -2mx + b$?

a)

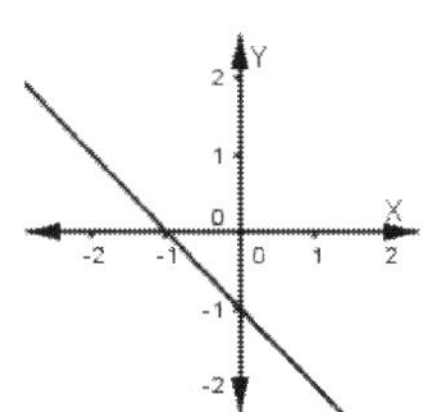

b)

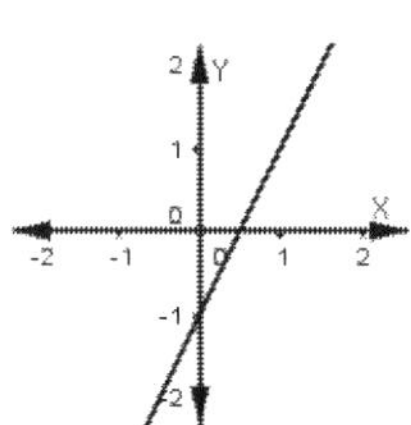

c)

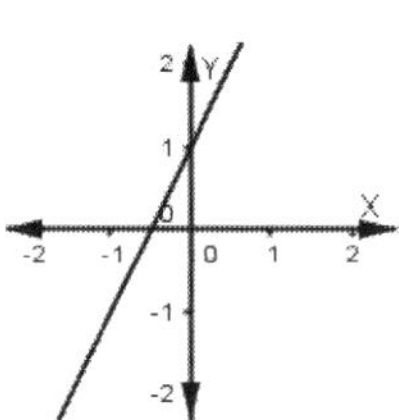

d)

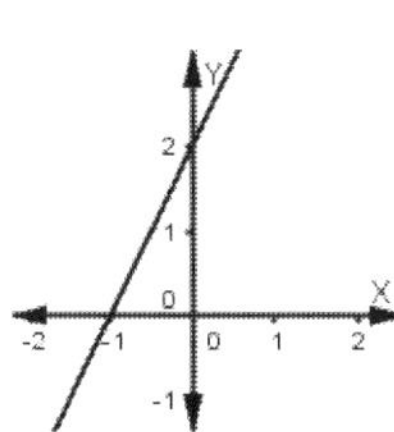

13. If $f(x) = x^2 + x^{3/2}$, what is the value of $f(3)$ =?
    a) $3 \times (1 + 3\sqrt{3})$
    b) $(1 + 3\sqrt{3})$
    c) $3 \times (1 + 3\sqrt{3})$
    d) $3 \times (3 + \sqrt{3})$

14. In ΔABC below, ∠ACB is 90°. Which of the following segments has the longest length?

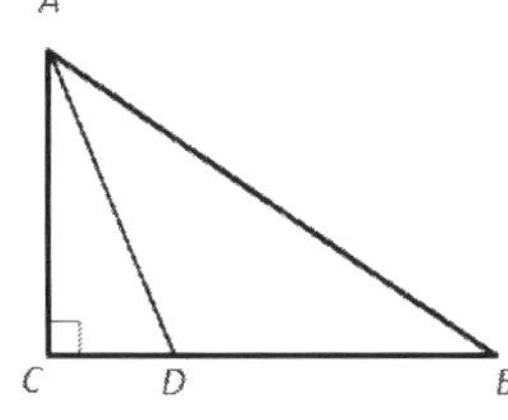

    a) Segment AD
    b) Segment AC
    c) Segment CB
    d) Segment AB

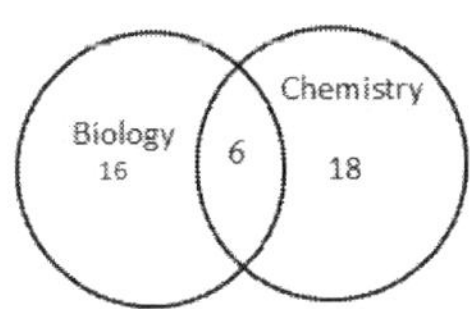

15. The Venn diagram above shows the distribution of 40 students at a school who took biology, chemistry, or both. What percent of the students studied chemistry?
    a) 30%
    b) 45%
    c) 50%
    d) 60%

16. On an Algebra final exam, class A has an average score of 90 with 15 students. Class B has an average score of 86.5 with 20 students. When the scores of class A and B are combined, what is the average score of class A and B?
    a) 86
    b) 86.5
    c) 88
    d) 88.5

17. 104 students are in the freshman class. If the ratio of male students to female students is 6 : 7, how many more female students than male students in the class?
    a) 8
    b) 10
    c) 14
    d) 15

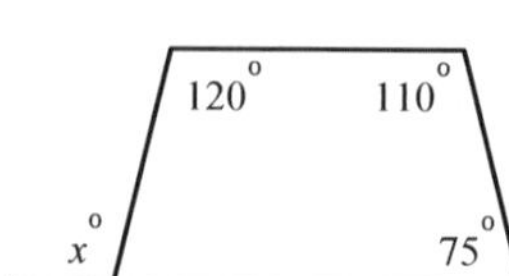

Note: Figure not drawn to scale.

18. What is the value of x in the figure above?
    a) 90
    b) 100
    c) 125
    d) 120

19. How many points do the graph of function, $f(x) = (x - 1)^2$, cross the x-axis?
    a) 0
    b) 1
    c) 2
    d) 3

20. In the xy-coordinate system, $(k, 9)$ is one of the points of intersection of the graphs $y = 2x^2 + 1$ and $y = -x^2 + m$, where m and k are constants. What is the value of m?
    a) 13
    b) 12
    c) 10
    d) 8

Questions 21 – 22 refer to the following information:

The kinetic energy of an object is the energy that the object possesses due to its motion. Kinetic energy is equal to half of the product of the mass and the square of its velocity.

The momentum is the quantity of the motion of a moving body, measured as a product of its mass and velocity.

21. If two bodies, A and B, have equal kinetic energies and the mass of A is nine times as much as the mass of B, what is the ratio of the momentum of A to that of B?
    a) $\frac{1}{3}$
    b) $\frac{3}{4}$
    c) 3
    d) 5

22. If two bodies A and B as described above have equal momentum, what is the ratio of the kinetic energy of A to that of B?
    a) $\frac{1}{9}$
    b) $\frac{1}{3}$
    c) 3
    d) 9

23. Joan has $25 and wants to buy a dozen of red pens at $0.60 each and two dozens of blue pens at $0.8 each. Without counting sales tax, how much more money does she need?
    a) $1.00
    b) $1.40
    c) $1.50
    d) $2.00

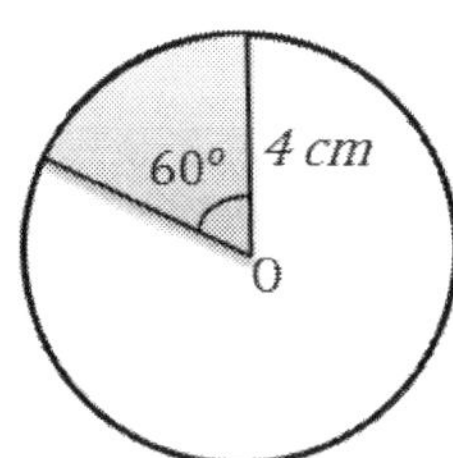

24. In the figure above, the circle has a center O and radius of 4 cm. What is the area of the shaded portion, in square centimeters?
    a) $\frac{1}{2}\pi$
    b) $2\frac{2}{3}\pi$
    c) $2\frac{3}{4}\pi$
    d) 3π

25. If x and y are non-zero integers, what is x percent of y percent of 2000?
    a) xy
    b) $5xy$
    c) $10xy$
    d) $\frac{1}{5}xy$

26. A ramp is 30 meters long and set at a 30° angle of inclination. If you walk up to the top of the ramp, how high off the ground (in meters) will you be?
    a) 15
    b) $15\sqrt{2}$
    c) $15\sqrt{3}$
    d) 18

27. One of the angles of a rhombus is 120°. If one side has length of 3, what is the area of the rhombus?
    a) 3
    b) $3\sqrt{3}$
    c) $4.5\sqrt{3}$
    d) $6\sqrt{3}$

28. To get a job done, a machine needs to produce x boxes of toys, in which each box contains y toys. If this machine runs 10 hours per day and produces an average of z toys per minute, how many days will it take to finish the job?
    a) $\frac{xy}{z}$
    b) $\frac{xy}{60 \times 10 \times z}$
    c) $\frac{xy}{60 \times 60 \times 10 \times z}$
    d) $\frac{60 \times 10 \times xy}{z}$

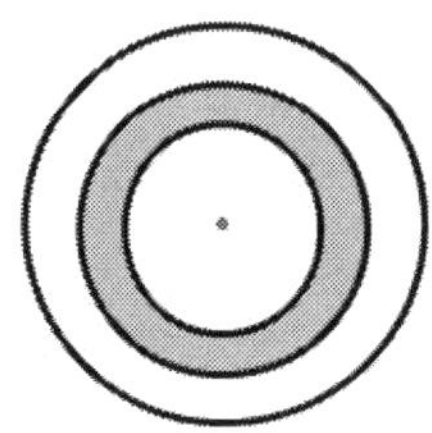

29. The figure above consists of three circles that share the same center. The circles have radii of 2, 3, and 5 respectively. What is the probability that a randomly chosen point will be in the shaded region?
    a) $\frac{1}{5}$
    b) $\frac{1}{4}$
    c) $\frac{5}{16}$
    d) $\frac{7}{16}$

30. Machine A makes 250 toys per hour. Machine B makes 350 toys per hour. If both machines begin running at the same time, how many minutes will it take the two machines to make a total of 1800 toys?
    a) 180
    b) 150
    c) 130
    d) 120

Directions:

For questions 31-38, solve the problem and enter your answer in the grid, as described below, on the answer sheet.

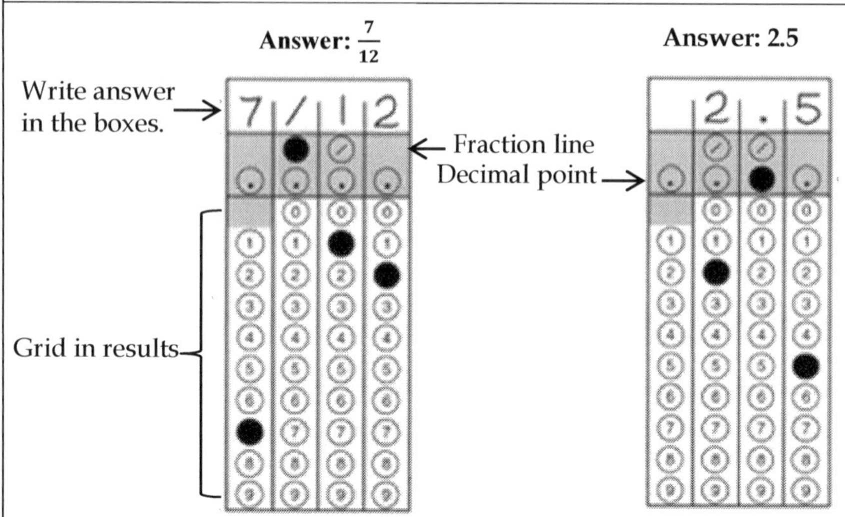

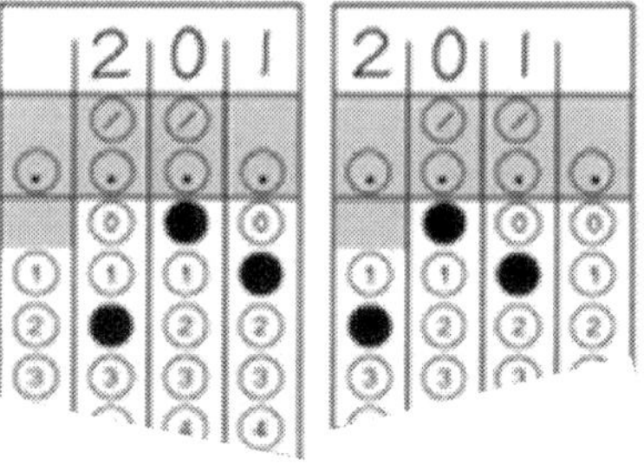

Note: You may start your answers in any column, space permitting. Columns not needed should be left blank.

- Mark no more than one circle in any column.
- Because the answer sheet will be machine-scored. **You will receive credit only if the circles are filled in correctly.**
- Although not required, it is suggested that you write your answer in the boxes at the top of the columns to help you fill in the circles accurately.
- Some problems may have more than one correct answer. In such case, grid only one answer.
- No question has a negative answer.
- **Mixed numbers** such as $3\frac{1}{2}$ must be gridded as 3.5 or $\frac{7}{2}$. (If 3 1 / 2 is gridded, it will be interpreted as $\frac{31}{2}$, not $3\frac{1}{2}$.)

- **Decimal Answer**: If you obtain a decimal answer with more digits than the grid can accommodate, it may be either rounded or truncated, but it must fill the entire grid. The acceptable ways to grid $\frac{2}{3}$ are:

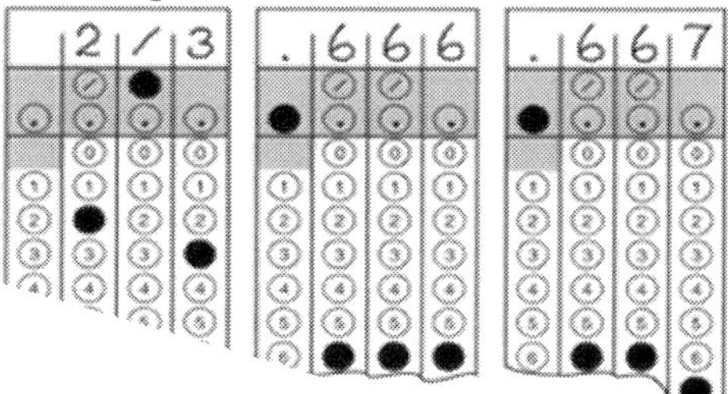

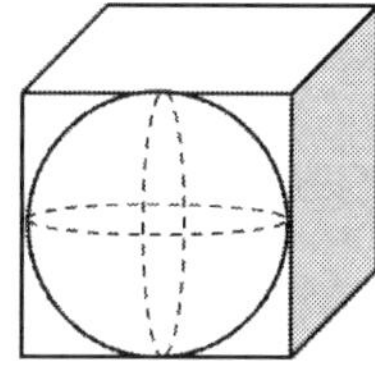

31. In the figure above, a cube has a volume of 64 cubic units. What is the length of the diameter of a sphere that is inscribed in the cube?

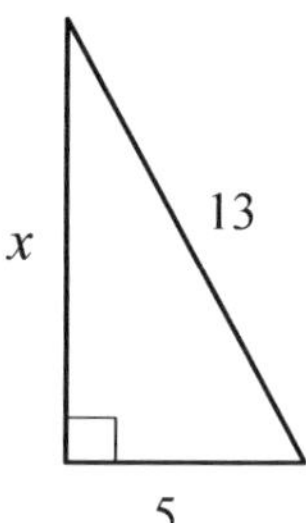

32. In the right triangle above, what is the value of x?

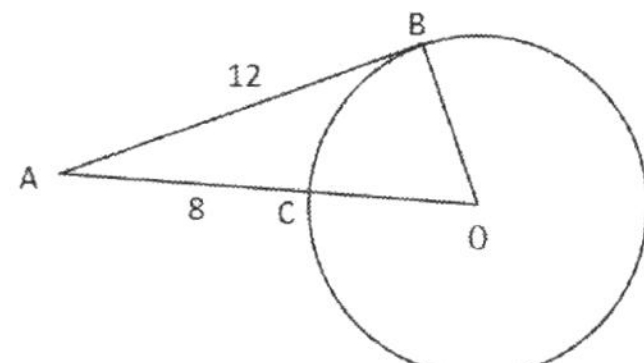

33. In the figure above, AB is tangent to circle O, $\overline{AB} = 12$, and $\overline{AC} = 8$. What is the area of ΔOAB?

34. Monday morning, Jason starts out with a certain amount of money that he plans to spend throughout the week. Every morning after that, he spends exactly $\frac{1}{3}$ the amount he has left. 6 days later, on Sunday morning, he finds that he has \$64 left. How many dollars did Jason originally have on Monday morning?

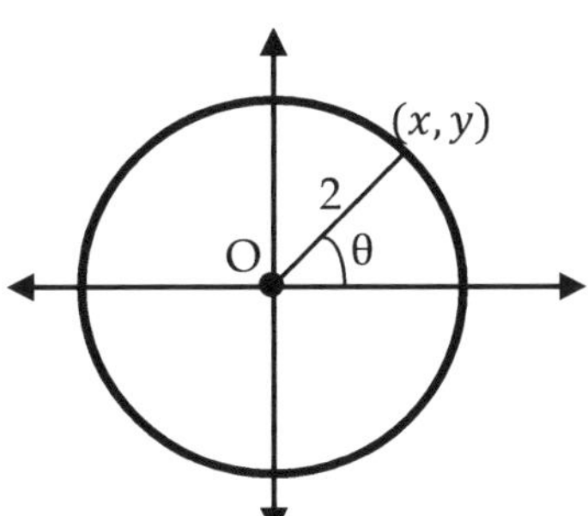

35. In the xy-plane above, O is the center of the circle with a radius of 2, and the measure of $\angle\theta$ is $\frac{\pi}{4}$ radians. What is the value of $x + y$? (Round your answer to the nearest tenth.)

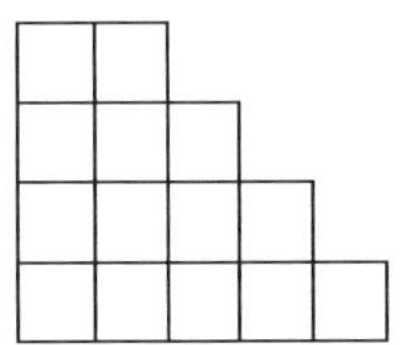

36. The figure above shows an arrangement of 14 squares, each with side length of x inches. The perimeter of the figure is P inches and the area of the figure is A square inches. If $21P = A$, what is the value of x?

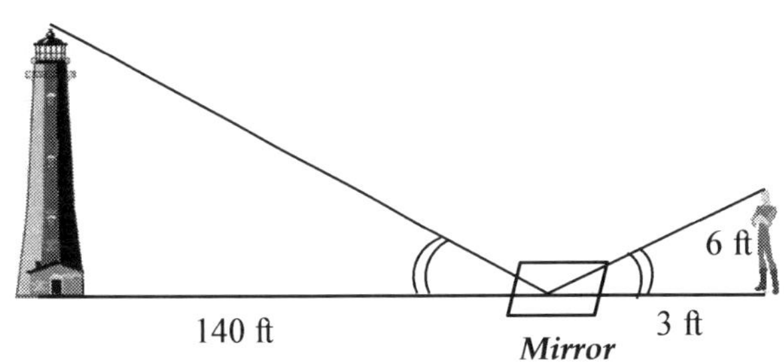

37. John places a mirror on the ground 140 feet from the base of a lighthouse. He walks backward until he can see the top of the lighthouse in the middle of the mirror. At that point, John's eyes are 6 feet above the ground and he is 3 feet from the mirror. Find the height, in feet, of the lighthouse.

38. In the xy-plane, the point (1, 2) is the minimum of the quadratic function $f(x) = x^2 + ax + b$. What is the value of $|a-b|$?

SAT MATH MOCK TEST No. 8 ANSWER KEYS

Section 3									
1. A	2. A	3. B	4. C	5. D	6. C	7. B	8. B	9. C	10. A
11. C	12. A	13. D	14. B	15. B	16. 10	17. 15	18. 40	19. 6	20. 4

Section 4									
1. A	2. D	3. D	4. B	5. C	6. A	7. D	8. A	9. B	10. A
11. A	12. C	13. D	14. D	15. D	16. C	17. A	18. C	19. B	20. A
21. C	22. A	23. B	24. B	25. D	26. A	27. C	28. B	29. A	30. A
31. 4	32. 12	33. 30	34. 729	35. 2.8	36. 27	37. 280	38. 5		

SECTION 3

1. *Answer: (a)*
   Given that the points A, B, C are in order.
   $BC = 20 - 10 = 10$
   $AC = AB + BC = 20 + 10 = 30$

2. *Answer: (a)*
   20 percent of $50y \rightarrow 20\% \times 50y = 10y$

3. *Answer: (b)*
   $a + b + c = 180$
   $2c + 6c + c = 180 \quad \rightarrow \quad c = 20$

4. *Answer: (c)*
   $x > x^2 > 0$
   $x - x^2 > 0$
   $x(1 - x) > 0$
   Since $x > 0$
   x must be smaller than 1.

5. *Answer: (d)*
   $v = abc$
   If v is odd, then a, b, and c must be all odd numbers.
   $s = 2(ab + bc + ca)$
   s is always an even number if a, b, and c are positive integers.

6. *Answer: (c)*
   $x^y x^{\frac{1}{2}} = x^{(y+\frac{1}{2})} = x^{\frac{1}{4}}$
   $y + \frac{1}{2} = \frac{1}{4} \quad \rightarrow \quad y = -\frac{1}{4}$

7. *Answer: (b)*
   If $x < 0$*, then the result of an odd power of x is negative and the result of an even power of x is positive.*

8. *Answer: (b)*
   $y - 3 = 2(2 - 3) \quad \rightarrow \quad y = 1$

9. *Answer: (c)*
   For every multiple of the LCM of 5 and 6, there will be a tomato that is both green and rotten.
   LCM of 5 and 6 is 30.
   Probability $= \frac{1}{30}$

10. *Answer: (a)*
    The line perpendicular to the y-axis is a horizontal line. The value of the y coordinate is constant for a horizontal line.
    $y = 1$

11. *Answer: (c)*
    Some students on Key Club also on math team in which there are no freshmen.

12. *Answer: (a)*
    Plug the value of z into $x = 4z$.
    $x = 4 \times 6 = 24$
    $\frac{x}{y} = 4, \ \frac{24}{y} = 4, \ 4y = 24, \ y = 6$

13. *Answer: (d)*
    Average $= \frac{Sum}{3}$
    $\frac{54}{3} = 18$

14. *Answer: (b)*
    The line of $2x + y = b$ *has a slope of* -2.
    Line l is perpendicular, so it should have a slope of $\frac{1}{2}$.
    We also know that it passes through the origin.
    $y = \frac{1}{2}x$

$a + 1 = \frac{1}{2}(3a)$
$2a + 2 = 3a \rightarrow a = 2$
point (6 , 3) passing through $2x + y = b \rightarrow$
$12 + 3 = b \rightarrow b = 15$

15. *Answer: (b)*
Find all the factors of (13 − 1) that are greater than 1. The factors of 12 that are greater than 1 are 2, 3, 4, 6 and 12.
4 different values of p.

16. *Answer: 10*
Blue: White = 3: 1
Red : Blue = 2 : 1
Red : Blue : White = 6 : 3 : 1
The smallest possible number of marbles in the bag is 10.

17. *Answer: 15*
$x^2 = \frac{15}{3} = 5$
$y = \frac{15}{5} = 3$
$x^2 y = 5 \times 3 = 15$

18. *Answer: 40*
$360^o = 2x + 3x + 2x + 2x$
$360^o = 9x \rightarrow x = 40^o$

19. *Answer: 6*
Use the Pythagorean theorem.
$x^2 + 8^2 = 10^2$
$x = 6$

20. *Answer: 4*
$(x + 2y) = 5, \ 5 - 1 = 4$

SECTION 4

1. *Answer: (a)*
The median is the 8th number of 15 consecutive integers. That means there are 7 integers less than the median and 7 integers greater than the median. The greatest integer is the 7th consecutive integer after 35.
$35 + 7 = 42$

2. *Answer: (d)*
The ratio of two triangles' areas is equal to the square of the ratio of their sides.
$(\frac{1}{2})^2 = \frac{1}{4}$

3. *Answer: (d)*
Two weeks have 14 days.
$50 \times 5 + 45 \times 9 = 655$

4. *Answer: (b)*
Since segment AD and segment AF bisects ∠BAE and ∠EAC respectively, ∠DAF will be half of ∠BAC
$\angle DAF = \frac{110°}{2} = 55°$

5. *Answer: (c)*
Let the price of one eraser be x and the price of one pencil be y. The price of 6 erasers = The price of 3 pencils.
$5x = 3y, \ x = \frac{3}{5}y$
$x + y = 1.60$
$\frac{3}{5}y + y = 1.60$
Solve for y to get the price of one pencil $1.00.

6. *Answer: (a)*
The probability of getting green marbles: $1 - \frac{1}{4} - \frac{1}{2} = \frac{1}{4}$
$\frac{1}{4} = \frac{x}{36}, \ x = 9$

7. *Answer: (d)*
Let x be the length of the side. The area of one face is x^2. The total area of the two green faces is then $2x^2$, which is equal to 32.
$2x^2 = 32 \rightarrow x^2 = 16 \rightarrow x = 4 \ (x > 0)$
The volume of cube:
$x \times x \times x = 4 \times 4 \times 4 = 64$ *cubic inches*

8. *Answer: (a)*
The line of 3x +2y = 2b has a slope of $\frac{-3}{2}$.
Line l is perpendicular, so it should have a slope of $\frac{2}{3}$.
We also know that it passes through the origin.
$y = \frac{2}{3}x$
$a - 1 = \frac{2}{3}(2a)$
$3a - 3 = 4a \rightarrow a = -3$
point (−6 , −4) passing through $3x + 2y = 2b \rightarrow$
$-6 \times 3 - 4 \times 2 = -26 = 2b$
$b = -13$

9. *Answer: (b)*
Slower speeds have smaller (flatter) slopes. Resting speeds have horizontal slope. Higher speeds have bigger (steeper) slopes.

10. *Answer: (a)*
There are 20 students after a new student joined the class. If the student is taking 2 or less APs, the median is 2. If the student is taking more than 2 APs, the

median is 2.5.
If median is 2 and the new average is 2, then the new student needs to take $20 \times 2 - (6 \times 1 + 4 \times 2 + 5 \times 3 + 4 \times 4) = -5$ *AP classes (which is not possible).*
If the median is 2.5 and the new average is 2.5, then the new student needs to take $20 \times 2.5 - (6 \times 1 + 4 \times 2 + 5 \times 3 + 4 \times 4) = 5$ *AP classes.*

11. *Answer: (a)*
In 2013, the total number of graduates going to 4-year college is $420 \times 0.45 = 189$.
In 2012, the total number of students heading to 4-year college is $400 \times 0.4 = 160$.
$189 - 160 = 29$

12. *Answer: (c)*
The graph of $y = mx + b$ *shows the slope equals* -1 *and y-intercept is 1.*
$m = -1,\ b = 1$
$y = -2mx + b = 2x + 1$ *with a positive slope and positive y-intercept.*

13. *Answer: (d)*
The value of f(3) is calculated by replacing x with 3 in the function.
$3^2 + 3^{3/2} = 9 + 3\sqrt{3} = 3(3 + \sqrt{3})$

14. *Answer: (d)*
In a triangle, bigger angles will always face longer sides. No angle in ΔABC will have degree greater than 90, so the side facing ∠ACB will be longest.
AB > AD > AC and CD.

15. *Answer: (d)*
Among the total 40 students, there were (18 + 6) students studied chemistry.
$\frac{24}{40} = 0.6 = 60\%$

16. *Answer: (c)*
This is ***not*** *the average of the averages since the classes have different number of students! The final average is the sum of all students' scores divided by the total number of students.*
We know that the sum of all the students' scores in one class is just the average multiplied by the number of students.
$Average = \frac{15 \times 90 + 20 \times 86.5}{15 + 20} = 88$

17. *Answer: (a)*
Female students : $104 \times \frac{7}{13} = 56$
Male students : $104 \times \frac{6}{13} = 48$
$56 - 48 = 8$

18. *Answer: (c)*
The sum of a quadrilateral's interior angles is equal to 360°.
$120 + 110 + 75 + (180 - x) = 360$
$x = 125$

19. *Answer: (b)*
The graph of f(x) intersects the x-axis when f(x) = 0.
$0 = (x - 1)^2 \rightarrow x = 1$

20. *Answer: (a)*
Plug in the values for x and y into both equations.
$2(k)^2 + 1 = 9 \rightarrow k^2 = 4$
$9 = -k^2 + m$
$9 = -4 + m \rightarrow m = 13$

21. *Answer: (c)*
Let the mass of A be 9k and the mass of B be k.
$\frac{1}{2}(9k) \times (v_A)^2 = \frac{1}{2}(k) \times (v_B)^2$
$\frac{v_A}{v_B} = \frac{1}{3}$
$\frac{Momentum\ of\ A}{Momentum\ of\ B} = \frac{9k \times v_A}{k \times v_B} = 9 \times \frac{1}{3} = 3$

22. *Answer: (a)*
Momentum is measured as a product of mass and velocity.
$9k \times v_A = k \times v_B$
$\frac{v_A}{v_B} = \frac{1}{9}$
$\frac{K_e of\ A}{K_e of\ B} = \frac{\frac{1}{2} \times 9k \times v_A^2}{\frac{1}{2} \times k \times v_B^2} = \frac{1}{9}$

23. *Answer: (b)*
The cost of buying 12 red pens: $12 \times 0.6 = 7.2$
The cost of buying 24 blue pens: $24 \times 0.8 = 19.2$
Joan would need 7.2 + 19.2 = \$26.4, so she has \$1.40 short.

24. *Answer: (b)*
The area of the shaded portion is $\frac{60}{360}$ *of the area of the whole circle.*
Shaded Area $= \frac{60}{360} \times \pi \times 4^2 = \frac{8}{3}\pi = 2\frac{2}{3}\pi$

25. *Answer: (d)*
x percent of y percent of 2000 →
$\frac{x}{100} \times \frac{y}{100} \times 2000 = \frac{xy}{5}$

26. *Answer: (a)*

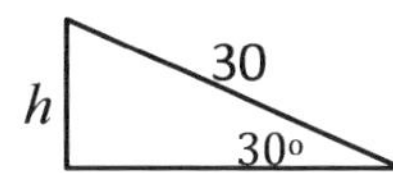

$h = 30 \times sin(30^o) = 30 \times 0.5 = 15$

27. *Answer: (c)*

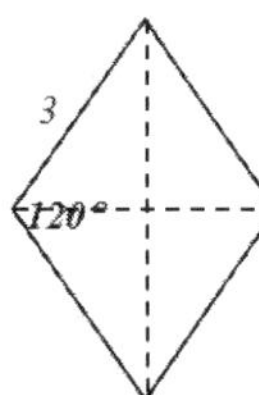

30−60−90 triangles are formed by the diagonals of the rhombus. The length of longer diagonal is $\frac{3}{2}\sqrt{3} \times 2 = 3\sqrt{3}$ *and the length of shorter diagonal is 3.*

Area of Rhombus $= \frac{1}{2} \times 3 \times 3\sqrt{3} = 4.5\sqrt{3}$

28. *Answer: (b)*

Number of Days $= \frac{Total\ Work}{Work\ per\ Hour}$

Total Number of Toys to Make= xy

Machine runs 10 hours (10 × 60 minutes) per day.

Number of Toys Made per Day $= z \times 60 \times 10$

Number of Days $= \frac{xy}{60 \times 10 \times z}$

29. *Answer: (a)*

The probability that a randomly chosen point will be in the shaded area is equal to $\frac{Area\ of\ Shaded\ Region}{Total\ Area}$

Area of Shaded Region = Area of Medium Circle – Area of Small Circle

$\pi \times 3^2 - \pi \times 2^2 = 5\pi$

Total Area $= \pi \times 5^2 = 25\pi$

Probability $= \frac{5\pi}{25\pi} = \frac{1}{5}$

30. *Answer: (a)*

Total Time $= \frac{Total\ Toys}{Total\ Rate}$

Total Rate = 250 toys/hour + 350 toys/hour = 600 toys/hour

Total Time $= \frac{1800\ toys}{600\ toys/hour}$ *= 3 hours = 180 minutes*

31. *Answer: 4*

Diameter of Sphere = Length of Side of Cube

Length of Side of Cube $= \sqrt[3]{64} = 4$

32. *Answer: 12*

Use the Pythagorean theorem.

$x^2 + 5^2 = 13^2$

$x = 12$

33. *Answer: 30*

ΔABO *is a right triangle with hypotenuse* $\overline{AO}$*, so use the Pythagorean theorem to find OB.*

OB and OC are radii and let their length be r.

$12^2 + r^2 = (8 + r)^2$

$144 + r^2 = 64 + 16r + r^2$

$80 = 16r \rightarrow r = 5$

Area of $\Delta OAB = \frac{1}{2} \times 5 \times 12 = 30$

34. *Answer: 729*

Jason spends $\frac{1}{3}$ *of his money each day, so he has* $\frac{2}{3}$ *of his money left next morning.*

Let Jason have \$x on Monday. On Sunday, he will have:$(\frac{2}{3} \times \frac{2}{3} \times \frac{2}{3} \times \frac{2}{3} \times \frac{2}{3} \times \frac{2}{3})x$ *dollars left.*

$\frac{2^6 x}{3^6} = 64$

$x = 3^6 = 729$ *dollars*

35. *Answer: 2.8*

$x = rcos(\theta) = 2 \times \cos\left(\frac{\pi}{4}\right) = 1.414$

$y = rsin(\theta) = 2 \times \sin\left(\frac{\pi}{4}\right) = 1.414$

$x + y = 2.8$

36. *Answer: 27*

The perimeter P is equal to 18x and its area is equal to $14 \times x^2$.

$21P = A$

$21 \times 18x = 14x^2$

$14x^2 - 378x = 0$

$x^2 - 27x = 0$

$x(x - 27) = 0 \rightarrow x = 27\ (x > 0)$

37. *Answer: 280*

The two triangles are similar, therefore their corresponding sides are proportional.

$\frac{x}{140} = \frac{6}{3} \rightarrow x = 280\ feet$

38. *Answer: 5*

The vextex of the quadratic function $f(x) = x^2 + ax + b$ *is* $(-\frac{a}{2}, f\left(-\frac{a}{2}\right))$

$-\frac{a}{2} = 1$

$a = -2$

$2 = (1)^2 - 2(1) + b$

$b = 3$

$|a - b| = |-2 - 3| = 5$

SAT Math Mock Test No. 9

SECTION 3 

Math Test – NO Calculator **25 MINUTES, 20 QUESTIONS**

Directions:

For questions 1-15, solve each problem, choose the best answer from the choices provided, and fill in the corresponding circle on your answer sheet. **For questions 16-20**, solve the problem and enter your answer in the grid on the answer sheet. Please refer to the directions before question 16 on how to enter your answers in the grid. You may use any available space in your test booklet for scratch work.

Notes:

1. **No calculator** is allowed for this section. All numbers used are real numbers.
2. Figures that accompany problems in this test are intended to provide information useful in solving the problems. They are drawn as accurately as possible EXCEPT when it is stated in a specific problem that the figure is not drawn to scale. All figures lie in a plane unless otherwise indicated.
3. Unless otherwise specified, the domain of any function *f(x)* assumed to be the set of all real numbers *x* for which *f(x)* is a real number.

References:

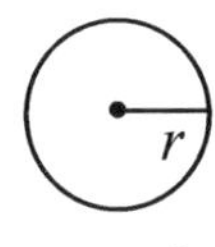

$A = \pi r^2$ $C = 2\pi r$ $A = lw$ $A = \frac{1}{2}bh$ $V = lwh$ $V = \pi r^2 h$ $c^2 = a^2 + b^2$ **Special Right Triangles**

The number of degrees of arc in a circle is 360; the number of radians of arc in a circle is 2π.
The sum of the degree measures of the angles in a triangle is 180.

1. What is the least value of integer x such that the value of $2x + 1$ is greater than 13?
   a) 7
   b) 6
   c) 5
   d) 4

2. If $3x + 5 = 4x + 2$, what is the value of x?
   a) 1
   b) 2
   c) 3
   d) 4

3. If $2x + 3 = 11$, then $6x - 2$?
   a) 20
   b) 22
   c) 24
   d) 26

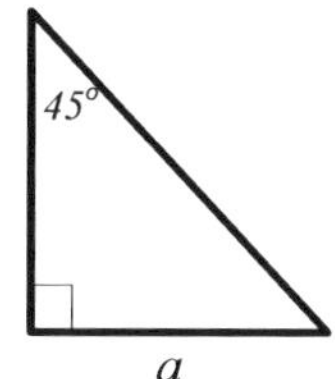

4. In the figure above, the perimeter of the triangle is $8 + 4\sqrt{2}$. What is the value of a?
   a) 3
   b) 4
   c) $2\sqrt{2}$
   d) $4\sqrt{2}$

5. How many different positive four-digit integers can be formed if the digits 0, 1, 2, and 3 are each used exactly once?
   a) 10
   b) 12
   c) 15
   d) 18

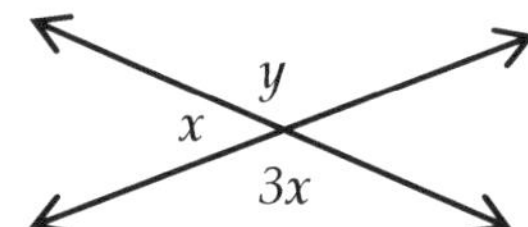

6. In the figure above, what is the value of $3x + 2y$?
   a) 405
   b) 135
   c) 270
   d) 360

7. In the xy-coordinate plane, lines m and n are perpendicular. If line m contains the points (0, 0) and (2, 1), and line n contains the points (2, 3) and (−1, a), what is the value of a?
   a) 6
   b) 9
   c) 0
   d) −9

8. If the average (arithmetic mean) of a, b and c is m, which of the following is the average of a, b, c and d?
   a) $\frac{2m+d}{3}$
   b) $\frac{m+d}{2}$
   c) $\frac{3m+d}{4}$
   d) $\frac{m+2d}{2}$

All numbers that are divisible by both 5 and 10 are also divisible by 15

9. Which of the following numbers shows that the above statement is FALSE?
   a) 45
   b) 30
   c) 25
   d) 20

10. If $3x < 2y$ and $4y < 9z$, which of the following is true?
   a) $3x < 9z$
   b) $3x > 9z$
   c) $6x < 9z$
   d) $6x = 9z$

11. If $x + y = 9$, $y = z - 3$, and $z = 2$, then what is the value of x?
   a) −8
   b) −6
   c) 10
   d) 3

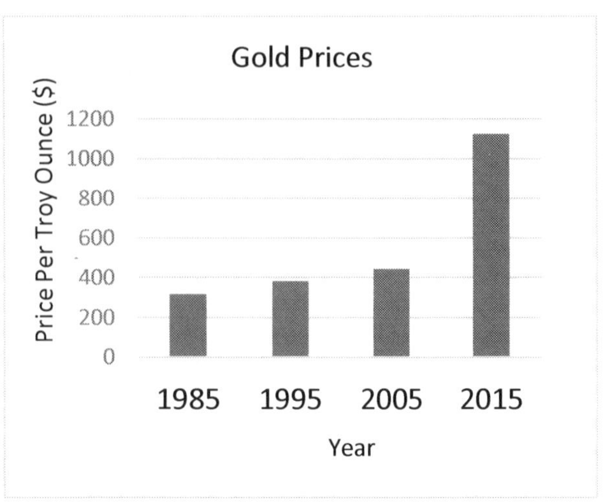

Annual Average Gold Price from 1985 to 2015 (U.S. dollars per troy ounce)

12. The figure above shows the change of the annual average gold price between 1985 and 2015, in U.S. dollars per troy ounce. A troy ounce is a traditional unit of gold weight. In 1985, a troy ounce of gold had an annual average price of around $317. Based on the information shown, which of the following conclusions is valid?
    a) A troy ounce of gold cost more in 1995 than in 2005.
    b) The price more than doubled between 2005 and 2015.
    c) The percent increase from 1985 to 2015 is more than 300%.
    d) The overall average gold price between 1985 and 2015 is around US $550.

13. If $\frac{x+3}{2}$ is an integer, then x must be?
    a) a prime number
    b) a positive integer
    c) an odd number
    d) a multiple of 2

14. If $x = 2(3z^2 + z + 4)$ and $y = -z + 3$, what is x in terms of y?
    a) $6y^2 - 38y - 68$
    b) $6y^2 + 38y - 132$
    c) $6y^2 - 38y + 68$
    d) $6y^2 + 38y + 68$

15. If $|x - 2| = p$, where $x < 2$, then $x - p =$
    a) 2
    b) 2−2p
    c) $2p-2$
    d) $2p + 2$

Directions:

For questions 16-20, solve the problem and enter your answer in the grid, as described below, on the answer sheet.

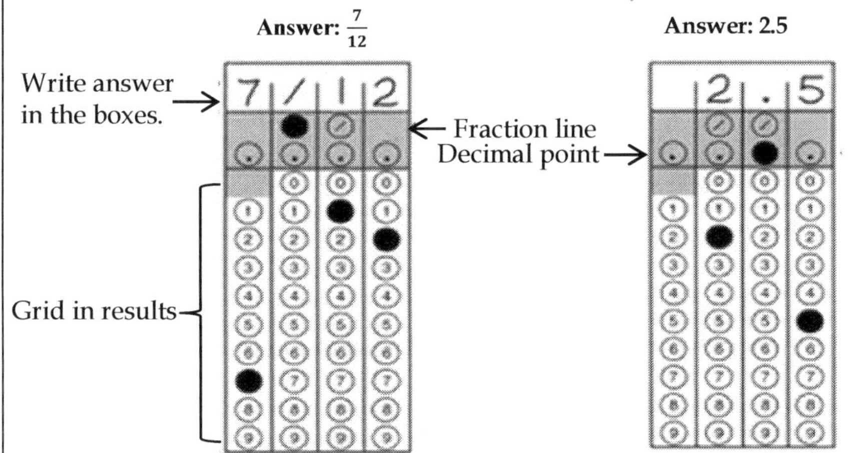

Answer: 201
Either position is correct.

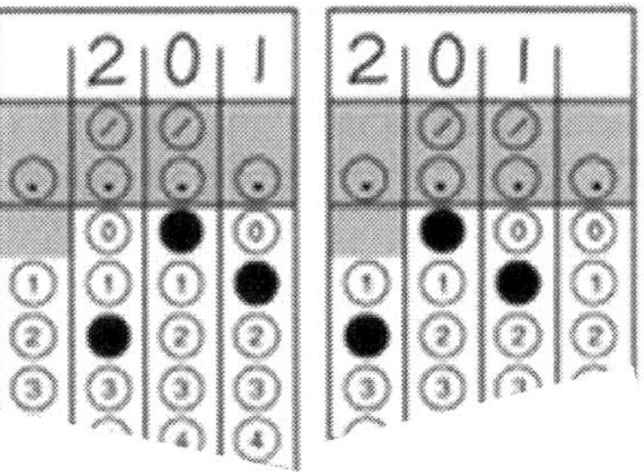

Note: You may start your answers in any column, space permitting. Columns not needed should be left blank.

- Mark no more than one circle in any column.
- Because the answer sheet will be machine-scored. **You will receive credit only if the circles are filled in correctly.**
- Although not required, it is suggested that you write your answer in the boxes at the top of the columns to help you fill in the circles accurately.
- Some problems may have more than one correct answer. In such case, grid only one answer.
- No question has a negative answer.
- **Mixed numbers** such as $3\frac{1}{2}$ must be gridded as 3.5 or $\frac{7}{2}$. (If 3|1|/|2 is gridded, it will be interpreted as $\frac{31}{2}$, not $3\frac{1}{2}$.)
- **Decimal Answer**: If you obtain a decimal answer with more digits than the grid can accommodate, it may be either rounded or truncated, but it must fill the entire grid. The acceptable ways to grid $\frac{2}{3}$ are:

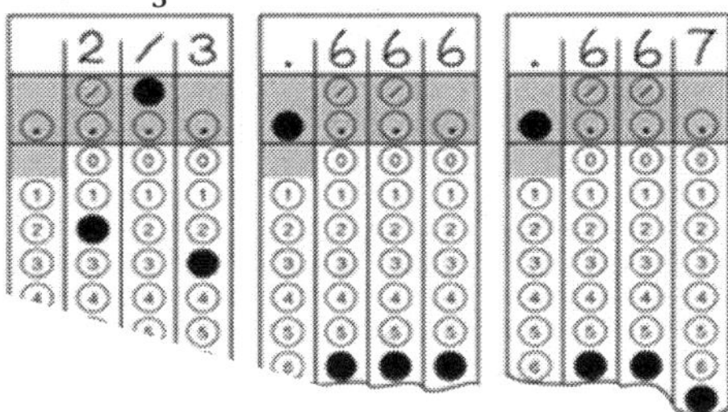

16. Let the function f be defined by $f(x) = 3x + 1$. If $f(a+3) = 25$, what is the value of $f(2a)$?

17. A bag contains 20 tennis balls, 7 of which are yellow, 5 pink, and the rest blue. If one ball is randomly chosen from the bag, what is the probability that the ball is blue?

18. If Mega has \$80.00 and she spends \$30 on clothes and \$20 on food, what fraction of the original \$80.00 does Mega have left?

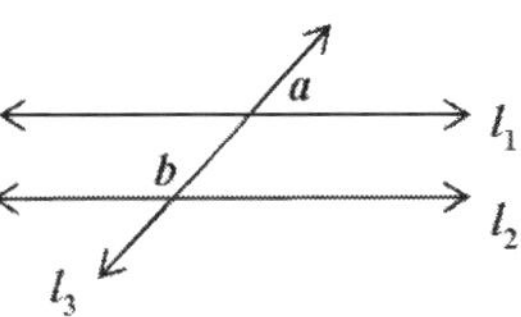

19. In the figure above, $l_1 \parallel l_2$ and $b = 3a - 20$. What is the value of a, in degrees?

20. In quadrilateral ABCD, $m\angle A = m\angle B = 120°$, and $m\angle D$ is $10°$ less than 4 times of $m\angle C$. Find $m\angle D$.

SECTION 4

Math Test — Calculator **55 MINUTES, 38 QUESTIONS**

Directions:

For questions 1-30, solve each problem, choose the best answer from the choices provided, and fill in the corresponding circle on your answer sheet. **For questions 31-38**, solve the problem and enter your answer in the grid on the answer sheet. Please refer to the directions before question 31 on how to enter your answers in the grid. You may use any available space in your test booklet for scratch work.

Notes:

1. Acceptable calculators are allowed for this section. All numbers used are real numbers.
2. Figures that accompany problems in this test are intended to provide information useful in solving the problems. They are drawn as accurately as possible EXCEPT when it is stated in a specific problem that the figure is not drawn to scale. All figures lie in a plane unless otherwise indicated.
3. Unless otherwise specified, the domain of any function *f(x)* assumed to be the set of all real numbers *x* for which *f(x)* is a real number.

References:

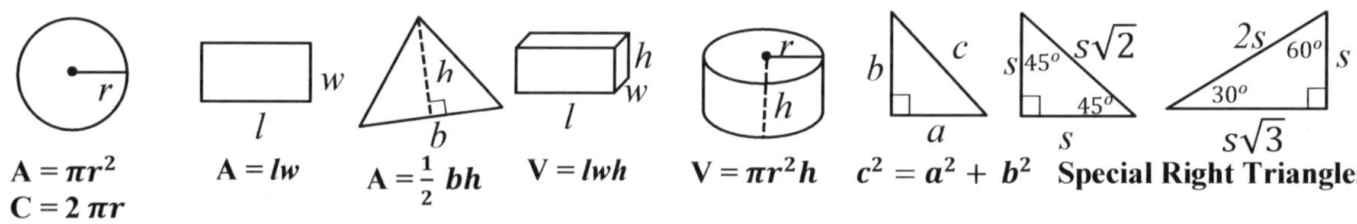

$A = \pi r^2$ $C = 2\pi r$ $A = lw$ $A = \frac{1}{2}bh$ $V = lwh$ $V = \pi r^2 h$ $c^2 = a^2 + b^2$ **Special Right Triangles**

The number of degrees of arc in a circle is 360; the number of radians of arc in a circle is 2π.
The sum of the degree measures of the angles in a triangle is 180.

1. Triangles A, B, and C are different in size. Triangle A's area is twice the area of triangle B, and triangle C's area is three times the area of triangle A. What is the area of triangle C, in square inches, if the area of triangle B is 10 square inches?
   a) 20
   b) 40
   c) 60
   d) 80

2. In the circle below, a regular hexagon ABCDEF is inscribed inside a circle. What is the ratio of the length of arc AFE to the length of arc ADE?

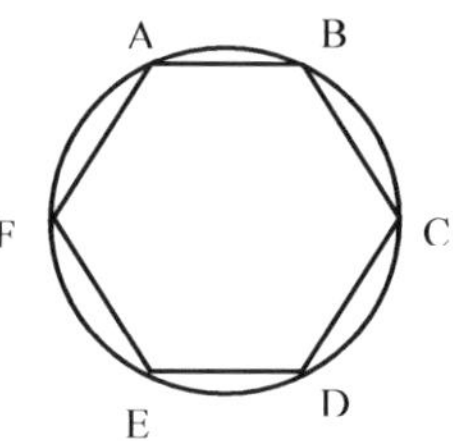

   a) 1 to 2
   b) 2 to 3
   c) 2 to 5
   d) 3 to 2

3. If a number was rounded to 20.3, which of the following could have been the original number?
   a) 20.24
   b) 20.249
   c) 20.35
   d) 20.25

1, 5, 21, 85, *t*, 1365, ...

4. In the sequence above, what is the value of *t*?
   a) 34
   b) 51
   c) 53
   d) 341

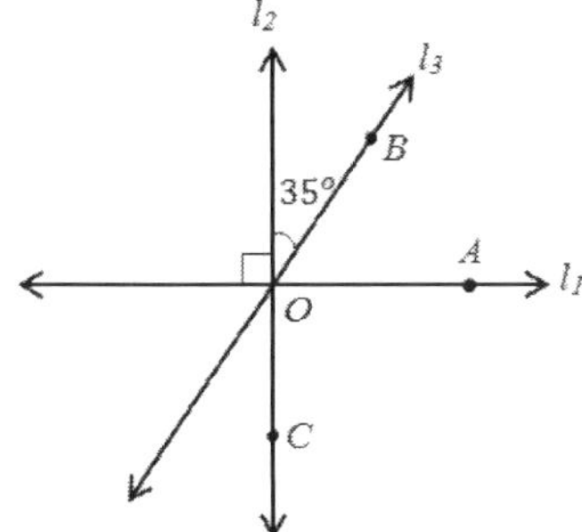

5. In the figure above, lines l_1, l_2 and l_3 intersect at point O and l_1 is perpendicular to l_2. What is the value of $m\angle BOC$, in degree?
   a) 145
   b) 130
   c) 100
   d) 95

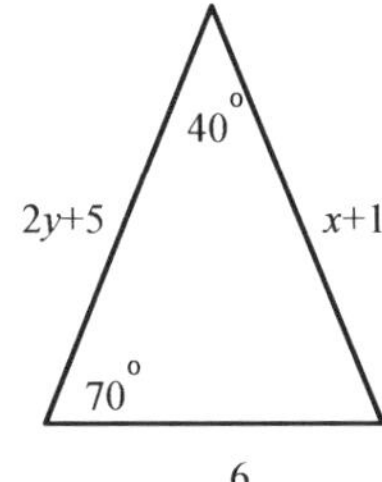

6. In the triangle above, which of the following must be true?
   a) $x = y$
   b) $x = 5$
   c) $x < y$
   d) $x = 2y + 4$

7. The three interior angle measures of a triangle have the ratio 3 : 4 : 5. What is the measure, in degrees, of the largest angles?
   a) 60°
   b) 70°
   c) 75°
   d) 85°

8. In a high school pep rally, a student is to be chosen at random. The probability of choosing a freshman is $\frac{1}{4}$ and the probability of choosing a sophomore is $\frac{1}{3}$. Which of the following cannot be the total number of students in the pep rally?
   a) 120
   b) 144
   c) 150
   d) 156

9. If y is directly proportional to x and y is equal to 30 when x is equal to 4, what is the value of y when $x = 8$?
   a) 15
   b) 45
   c) 60
   d) 70

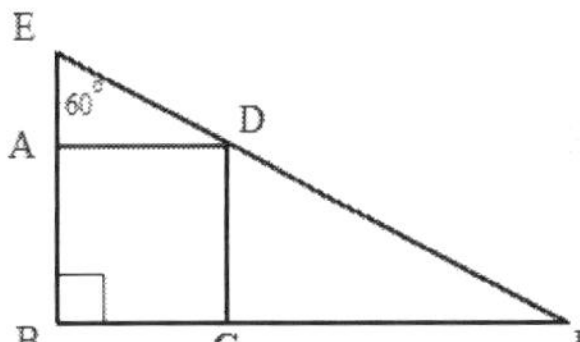

10. In the figure above, if ABCD is a square with area of 9, what is the area of triangle BEF?
   a) 9
   b) 12
   c) $9(1 + \frac{2\sqrt{3}}{3})$
   d) $9\sqrt{3}$

11. 8 players participate in a tennis tournament. A game involves two players and each player plays two games with each of the other seven players. How many games will be played in total at this tournament?
    a) 45
    b) 50
    c) 56
    d) 108

12. A car rental company calculates the price of renting a car by adding the fixed rental fee with an additional charge for every 10 miles traveled. If the charge to rent a car and drive 50 miles is $120 and the charge to rent a car and drive 200 miles is $165, what would be the price, in dollars, to rent a car and travel 300 miles?
    a) 178
    b) 186
    c) 195
    d) 225

13. Set S is a set of consecutive integers whose sum is a positive even integer. If the smallest integer in the set is −5, what is the least possible number of integers in the set?
    a) 8
    b) 12
    c) 10
    d) 11

14. A company sells boxes of marbles in red and green. Helen purchased a box of marbles in which there were half as many green marbles in the box as red ones and 15 marbles were green. How many marbles were in Helen's box?
    a) 30
    b) 40
    c) 45
    d) 50

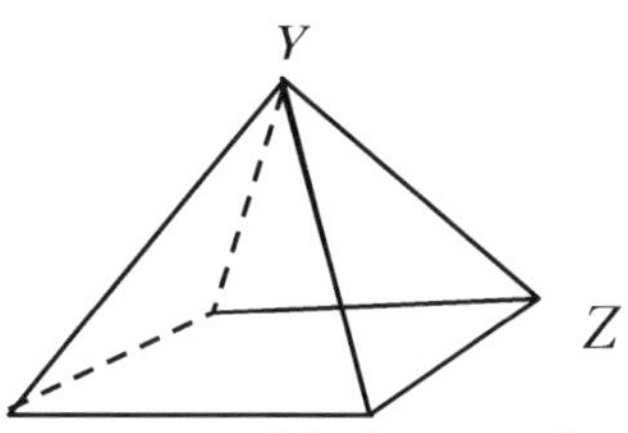

15. The square pyramid shown above has volume 72 and height 6. What is the length of YZ?
    a) $6\sqrt{3}$
    b) $3\sqrt{3}$
    c) $3\sqrt{6}$
    d) 6

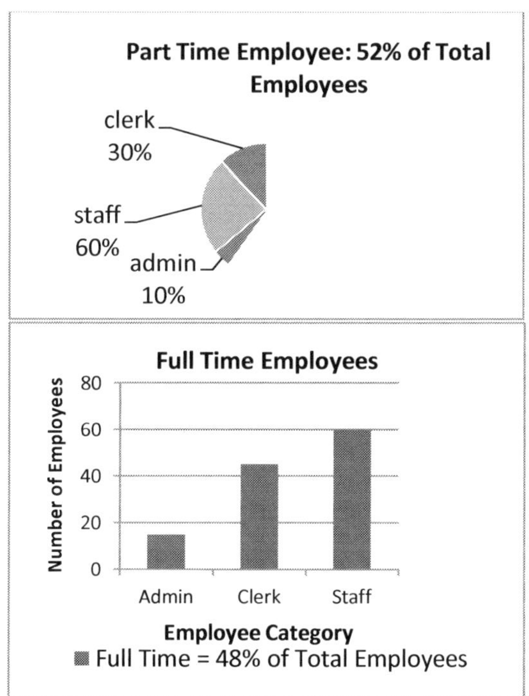

16. According to the graphs above, how many part time administrators at Oak Town High School?
    a) 10
    b) 12
    c) 13
    d) 20

17. For all numbers j and k, let $j@k$ be defined by $j@k = (j + 1)^2 \times (2k - 2)^2$, what is the value of 6@3?
    a) 228
    b) 338
    c) 544
    d) 784

18. The center of a circle is the origin of a rectangular coordinate plane. If (−5, 0), (0, 5), and (5, 0) are three points on the circumference of the circle, what is the probability that a randomly picked point inside the circle would fall inside the triangle formed by those three points?
    a) $\frac{1}{2}$
    b) $\frac{1}{3}$
    c) $\frac{1}{\pi}$
    d) $\frac{2}{\pi}$

19. If $x > y$, $w < z$, and $x < w$, which of the following must be true?
    $y < z$
    $w < y$
    $x < z$
    a) None
    b) II and III
    c) I and II
    d) I and III

20. The operation ♣ is defined for ordered pairs of numbers in the following way: (w, x) ♣ $(y, z) = (wy + xz, wz + xy)$. If (a, b) ♣ $(c, d) = (a + 2b, 2a + b)$, what is (c, d)?
    a) (1, 1)
    b) (2, 1)
    c) (1, 2)
    d) (2, −1)

21. A "square-root-factor" is an integer greater than 1 with exactly three positive integer factors: itself, its square root, and 1. Which of the following is a square-root-factor?
    a) 128
    b) 81
    c) 64
    d) 49

22. Sam drove from home at an average speed of 40 miles per hour to her working place and then returned along the same route at an average speed of 30 miles per hour. If the entire trip took her 2.1 hours, what is the entire distance, in miles, for the round trip?
    a) 36
    b) 72
    c) 84
    d) 90

23. If $f(x) = \frac{2-x^2}{x}$ for all nonzero x, then $f(2)$=?
    a) 1
    b) 2
    c) 3
    d) −1

24. If $z = \frac{3x^3}{y^2}$ what happens to the value of z when both x and y are doubled?
    a) z is divided by 2.
    b) z is divided by 4.
    c) z is not changed.
    d) z is doubled.

25. If each edge of a rectangular solid has a length that is an integer greater than one, which of the following could be the volume of the solid, in cubic units?
    a) 9
    b) 15
    c) 18
    d) 21

26. In the xy-plane, the point $(-1, 2)$ is the minimum of the quadratic function $f(x) = x^2 + ax + b$. What is the value of $|a - b|$?
    a) 0
    b) 1
    c) 2
    d) 5

27. If 15% of x is equal to 10% of y, which of the following is equivalent to y?
    a) 200% of x
    b) 150% of x
    c) 100% of x
    d) 75% of x

28. A parallel circuit has two or more paths for current to flow through and has more than one resistor as shown below. In a house, there are many electrical appliances that connect in parallel so they would not affect each other when their switches are turned on or off.

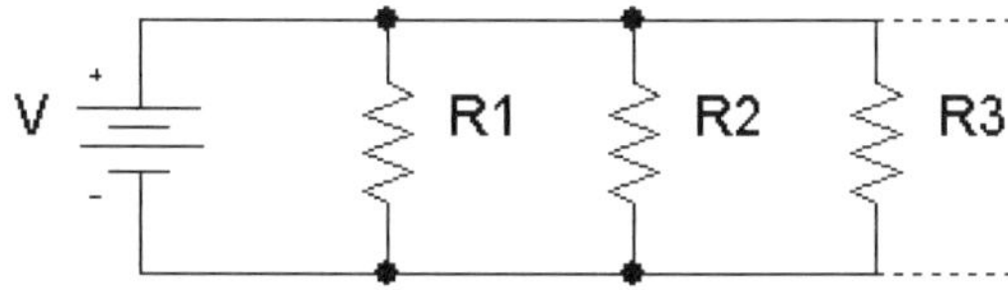

The total resistance, R_{Total}, in a parallel circuit can be calculated by the following formula:

$$\frac{1}{R_{Total}} = \frac{1}{R_1} + \frac{1}{R_2} + \frac{1}{R_3}$$

If three resistors are connected together in parallel and the resistors have values of 10 ohm, 15 ohm, and 30 ohm respectively, what is the total resistance of the circuit?
    a) 55 ohm
    b) 12 ohm
    c) 6 ohm
    d) 5 ohm

29. The cost of a long-distance call using phone company A is $1.00 for the first three minutes and $.20 for each additional minute. The same call using the phone company B is charged flat rate at $0.22 per minute for any amount of time. For a call that lasts t minutes, the cost using company A is the same as the cost using the company B, what is the value of t?
    a) 5
    b) 10
    c) 15
    d) 20

30. There are 100 students in the school pep rally. What is the largest number of n students such that the statement "At least n student birthdays in this pep rally falling in the same month" is always true?
    a) 8
    b) 9
    c) 10
    d) 12

Directions:

For questions 31-38, solve the problem and enter your answer in the grid, as described below, on the answer sheet.

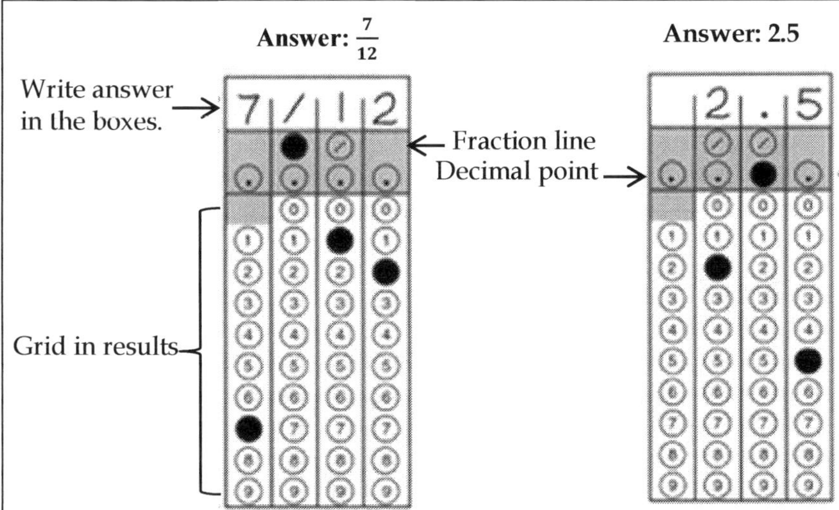

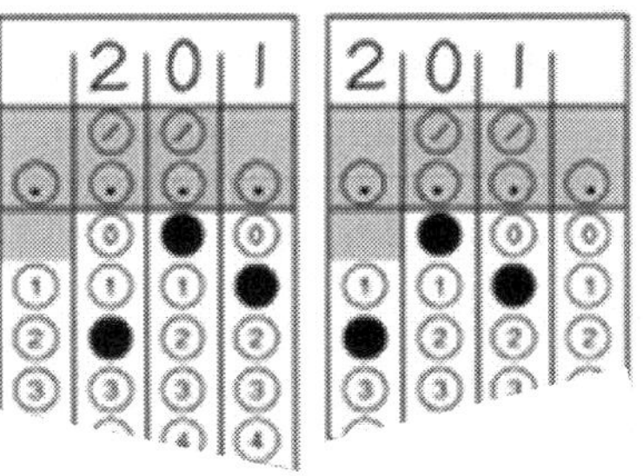

Note: You may start your answers in any column, space permitting. Columns not needed should be left blank.

- Mark no more than one circle in any column.
- Because the answer sheet will be machine-scored. **You will receive credit only if the circles are filled in correctly.**
- Although not required, it is suggested that you write your answer in the boxes at the top of the columns to help you fill in the circles accurately.
- Some problems may have more than one correct answer. In such case, grid only one answer.
- No question has a negative answer.
- **Mixed numbers** such as $3\frac{1}{2}$ must be gridded as 3.5 or $\frac{7}{2}$. (If 3 1 / 2 is gridded, it will be interpreted as $\frac{31}{2}$, not $3\frac{1}{2}$.)

- **Decimal Answer**: If you obtain a decimal answer with more digits than the grid can accommodate, it may be either rounded or truncated, but it must fill the entire grid. The acceptable ways to grid $\frac{2}{3}$ are:

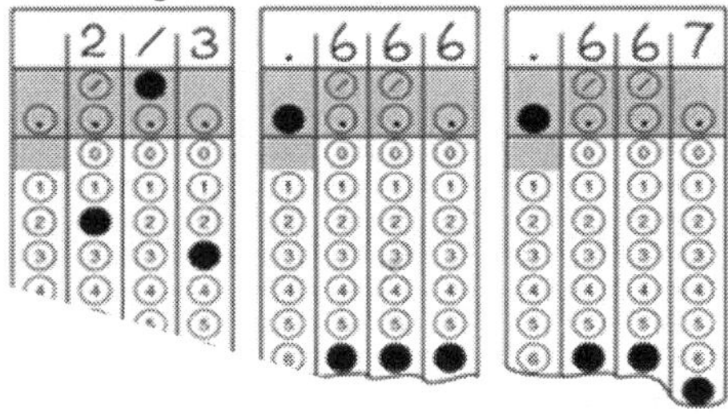

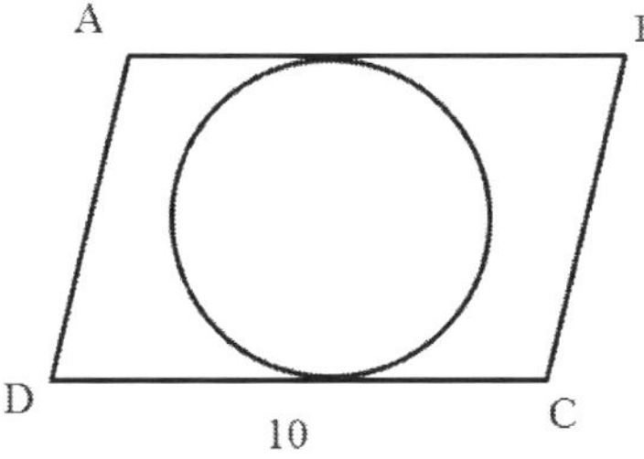

31. A circle is tangent to two sides of a parallelogram ABCD as shown in the figure above. If the circle has an area of 9π, what is the area of the parallelogram ABCD?

32. At an intersection, a complete cycle of the traffic light takes 70 seconds. Within each cycle, the red light lasts for 30 seconds and the yellow light 10 seconds. If a driver arrives at the intersection at a random time, what is the probability that the light is green?

33. There are 12 red boxes, 18 blue boxes, and 20 white boxes. If a blue marble is randomly placed into one of these boxes, what is the probability that it will be placed in a box that is the same color as it?

1.313113111311113. . .

34. The decimal number above consists of only 1s and 3s. The first 3 is followed by one 1, the second 3 is followed by two 1s, and the third 3 is followed by three 1s. If such a pattern goes on, how many 1s are between the 94th 3 and the 98th 3?

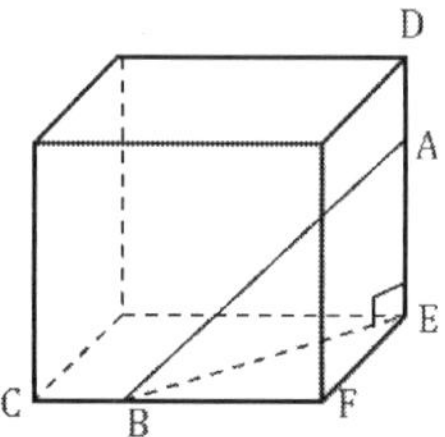

35. The cube shown above has edges of length 5. If $\overline{CB} = \overline{AD} = 2$, what is the length of $\overline{AB}$? (Round your answer to the nearest hundredth)

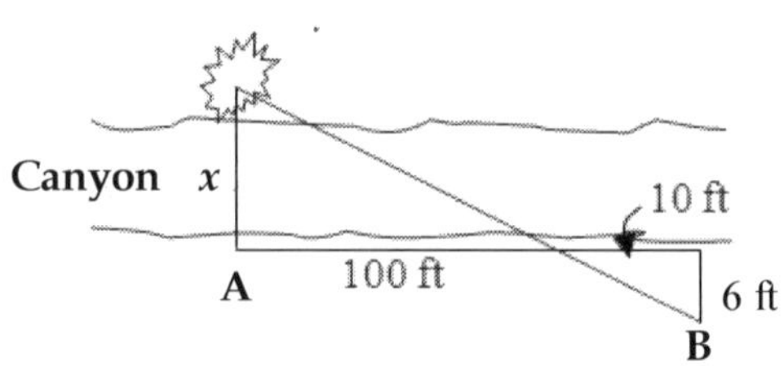

36. A bush fire is sighted on the other side of a canyon at points *A* and *B* as shown in the figure above. Find the width, in feet, of the canyon.

37. In a triangle, one angle measures $x°$, where $\sin x° = \frac{4}{5}$. What is $\cos(90° - x°)$?

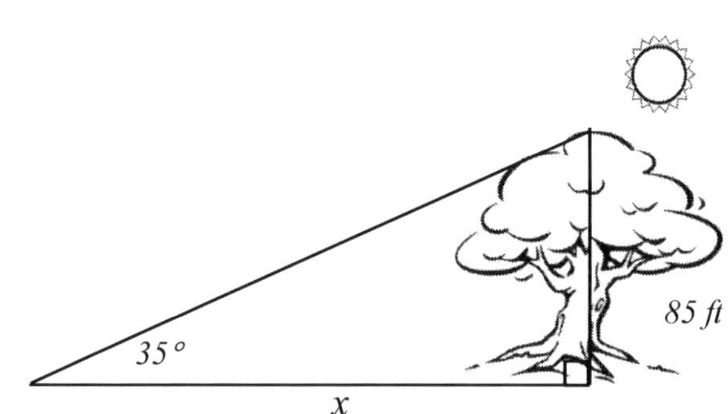

38. When the Sun is 35° above the horizon, how long is the shadow cast by a tree 85 feet tall? (Round your answer to the nearest whole number.)

SAT MATH MOCK TEST No. 9 ANSWER KEYS

Section 3									
1. A	2. C	3. B	4. B	5. D	6. A	7. B	8. C	9. D	10. C
11. C	12. D	13. C	14. C	15. B	16. 31	17. $\frac{2}{5}$	18. $\frac{3}{8}$	19. 50	20. 94

Section 4									
1. C	2. A	3. D	4. D	5. A	6. D	7. C	8. C	9. C	10. C
11. C	12. C	13. B	14. C	15. C	16. C	17. D	18. C	19. D	20. C
21. D	22. B	23. D	24. D	25. C	26. B	27. B	28. D	29. B	30. C
31. 60	32. $\frac{3}{7}$	33. $\frac{9}{25}$	34. 382	35. 6.56	36. 60	37. $\frac{4}{5}$	38. 121		

SECTION 3

1. *Answer: (a)*
   $2x + 1 > 13$
   $2x > 12$
   $x > 6$
   The least value of integer is 7.

2. *Answer: (c)*
   $5 - 2 = 4x - 3x$
   $3 = x$

3. *Answer: (b)*
   $2x = 8,\ 6x = 24$
   $6x - 2 = 24 - 2 = 22$

4. *Answer: (b)*
   The length of the hypotenuse is $\sqrt{a^2 + a^2} = a\sqrt{2}$.
   Perimeter of triangle: $a + a + a\sqrt{2} = 8 + 4\sqrt{2}$
   $a = 4$

5. *Answer: (d)*
   Thousands digit can only have 3 choices(1, 2 or 3)
   Hundreds digit: 3 choices
   Tens digit: 2 choices
   Units digit: 1 choice
   $3 \times 3 \times 2 \times 1 = 18$

6. *Answer: (a)*
   $3x + x = 180°$ *and* $y = 3x$
   $4x = 180°$
   $x = 45°$
   $3x = 135° = y$
   $2y = 135 \times 2 = 270°$
   $3x + 2y = 135 + 270 = 405°$

7. *Answer: (b)*
   If two lines are perpendicular, then the product of their slopes is −1.
   $\frac{1-0}{2-0} \times \frac{3-a}{2-(-1)} = -1$
   $3 - a = -6$
   $a = 9$

8. *Answer: (c)*
   The Average of a, b, and c is equal to the sum of a, b, and c divided by 3.
   $a + b + c = 3m$
   $a + b + c + d = 3m + d$
   Average: $\frac{3m+d}{4}$

9. *Answer: (d)*
   Find the number that is divisible by 5 and 10 but not divisible by 15.

10. *Answer: (c)*
    Multiply both sides of the first equation by 2.
    $(3x < 2y) \times 2 \rightarrow 6x < 4y$ (1)
    $4y < 9z$ (2)
    Combine both inequalities (1) + (2):
    $6x < 4y < 9z$

11. *Answer: (c)*
    If $z = 2$, *then* $y = 2 - 3 = -1$.
    $x + (-1) = 9$
    $x = 10$

12. *Answer: (d)*
    Percent Change: $\frac{1100-310}{310} \times 100\% \approx 255\%$
    Overall Average: $\frac{310+390+420+1100}{4} = \$550$

13. *Answer: (c)*
$\frac{x+3}{2} = n$
$x + 3 = 2n$
$x = 2n + 3$
$2n + 3$ *is odd if* n *is an integer.*

14. *Answer: (c)*
Write z in terms of y.
$z = 3 - y$
$x = 2[3(3-y)^2 + (3 - y) + 4)]$
$= 2[\ 3(y^2 - 6y + 9) + 7 - y]$
$= 2(3y^2 - 18y + 27 + 7 - y\ )$
$= 2(3y^2 - 19y + 34)$
$= 6y^2 - 38y + 68$

15. *Answer: (b)*
$|x - 2| = p$
If $x < 2$, *then* $|x - 2| = -(x - 2) = 2 - x$
$2 - x = p$
$x = 2 - p$
$x - p = 2 - p - p = 2 - 2p$

16. *Answer: 31*
Substitute x with (a + 3).
$25 = 3 \times (a + 3) + 1$
$25 = 3a + 10$
$a = 5$
$f(2a) = f(10) = 3 \times 10 + 1 = 31$

17. *Answer:* $\frac{2}{5}$ *or .4*
The number of blue balls : $20 - 7 - 5 = 8$
Probability $= \frac{8}{20} = \frac{2}{5}$

18. *Answer:* $\frac{3}{8}$
$\frac{80-30-20\ dollars}{80\ dollars} = \frac{30}{80} = \frac{3}{8}$

19. *Answer: 50*
$a + b = 180^o$
$3a - 20 + a = 180^o$
$a = 50^o$

20. *Answer: 94*
$A + B + C + D = 360°$
$120° + 120° + 4x - 10° + x = 360°$
$x = 26°$
$4x - 10° = 94°$

SECTION 4

1. *Answer: (c)*
$A = 2B,$
$C = 3A$
If $B = 10$, *then*
$A = 20, C = 3 \times 20 = 60.$

2. *Answer: (a)*
The arc ADE is 4 times the arc AB and arc AFE is 2 times the arc AB (since the polygon is regular).
AFE : ADE = 2 : 4 = 1 : 2

3. *Answer: (d)*
According to the rounding rules, the original number can be in the range:
$25.25 \le x \le 25.34$

4. *Answer: (d)*
Examine the first few terms to figure out the pattern.
$1 + 4^1 = 5$
$5 + 4^2 = 21$
$21 + 4^3 = 85$
$85 + 4^4 = 341 = t$
$341 + 4^5 = 1365$ *(Doing this is to verify that the answer is correct.)*
This is also a sequence constructed by multiplying the previous term by 4 and then adding 1 to the product each time to get the next term.
$1 \times 4 + 1 = 5$
$5 \times 4 + 1 = 21$
$21 \times 4 + 1 = 85$
$85 \times 4 + 1 = 341$
$t = 341$
$341 \times 4 + 1 = 1365$ *(Doing this is to verify that the answer is correct.)*

5. *Answer: (a)*
$m\angle BOC = 180 - 35 = 145\,°$

6. *Answer: (d)*
The degree of the 3rd interior angle is $180^o - 40^o - 70^o = 70^o$.
Since this triangle has two angles that are 70°, it is an isosceles triangle.
$2y + 5 = x + 1$
$x = 2y + 4$

7. *Answer: (c)*
We can define the measures of the three angles to be 3x, 4x, and 5x.
$3x + 4x + 5x = 180^o$
$x = 15^o$
$5 \times 15 = 75^o$

8. *Answer: (c)*
The total number of students must be a multiple of 3 and 4 which is 12. Note that the number of students must be a whole number.
Only (c) is not a multiple of 12.

9. *Answer: (c)*
$\frac{30}{4} = \frac{y}{8}$
$y = 60$

10. *Answer: (c)*
Each of these triangles is a 30–60–90 triangle.
The Area of Large Triangle $= \frac{1}{2} \times \overline{BE} \times \overline{BF}$
Side of Square $= \sqrt{9} = 3$
$\overline{BE}$ *(faces 30°angle)* $= 3 + \frac{3}{\sqrt{3}} = 3 + \sqrt{3}$
$\overline{BF}$ *(faces 60°angle)* $= 3 + 3\sqrt{3}$
Area $= \frac{1}{2} \times (3 + 3\sqrt{3})(3 + \sqrt{3}) = 9 + 6\sqrt{3}$
$= 9(1 + \frac{2\sqrt{3}}{3})$

11. *Answer: (c)*
This is combination. The number of ways to select m objects from n objects (n ≥ m), where order does not matter:
$$C_m^n = \frac{n!}{m!\,(n - m)!}$$
Choose any 2 players from 8 players to play a match.
$C_2^8 = 28$
Each match has 2 games.
$28 \times 2 = 56$ *games*

12. *Answer: (c)*
Let initial charge be \$x, and the fee for every 10 miles be \$y.
$x + 5y = 120$
$x + 20y = 165$
$15y = 45, \quad y = 3, \quad x = 105$
For traveling 300 miles, the total charge is
$105 + 30 \times 3 = 195.$

13. *Answer: (b)*
The last integer must be more than 5 and must be an even positive number. Because the integers in the set have to be consecutive, all positive integers less than or equal to 5 will cancel out their negative counterparts.
The integer 6 is the first integer greater than 5. So we include the next integer, 6, to the set, which gives us a sum of 6, an even sum.
Therefore the integers in the set:
$\{-5, -4, -3, -2, -1, 0, 1, 2, 3, 4, 5, 6\}$

14. *Answer: (c)*
Let g be the number of green marbles and r be the number of red marbles.
Translate "half as many green marbles as red ones" into an algebraic statement: $g = \frac{1}{2}r$
Plug $g = 15$ *into the equation to get* $r = 30$
Therefore, $15 + 30 = 45$.

15. *Answer: (c)*
If center of the square base is O, then ΔYOZ is a right triangle.
Volume $= \frac{1}{3} \times$ *Area of Base × Height = 72*
Let x be the length one side of the square.
$\frac{1}{3}x^2 \times 6 = 72$
$x^2 = 36$
$x = 6$
Length of Diagonal of Square $= 6\sqrt{2}$
$YZ = \sqrt{\left(\frac{Diagonal}{2}\right)^2 + Height}$
$YZ = \sqrt{(3\sqrt{2})^2 + 6^2} = \sqrt{54} = 3\sqrt{6}$

16. *Answer: (c)*
Number of Full Time Employees = 15 + 45 + 60 = 120 employees.
Full time employees comprise of 48% of the total.
0.48 × Total Employees = 120 employees
Total Employees = 250 employees
Part Time Employees = 250 × 0.52 = 130 employees
130 × 0.1 = 13 part time administrators

17. *Answer: (d)*
Replace j with 6 and k with 3.
$6@3 = (6 + 1)^2 (2 \times 3 - 2)^2 = 49 \times 16 = 784$

18. *Answer: (c)*
Radius of the Circle = 5
Area of the Circle $= \pi (5)^2 = 25\pi$
Area of the Triangle $= \frac{1}{2} \times 5 \times 10 = 25$
Probability $= \frac{25}{25\pi} = \frac{1}{\pi}$

19. *Answer: (d)*
Draw a number line and locate w, x, y and z on the line.

smaller ← y • x • w • z • → larger

Only (I) and (III) are correct.

20. *Answer: (c)*
(w, x) ♣ (y, z) = (wy + xz, wz + xy)
(a, b) ♣ (c, d) = (ac + bd, ad + bc) = (a + 2b , 2a + b)
By comparison between (ac + bd, ad + bc) and (a + 2b, 2a + b), d is equal to 2 and c is equal to 1.
(c, d) = (1, 2)

21. *Answer: (d)*
The square root of the number must be a prime number.
Only $\sqrt{49}$ *is a prime number.*

22. *Answer: (b)*
Let one trip have x miles.
Time $= 2.1 = t_1 + t_2 = \frac{x}{30} + \frac{x}{40}$
$2.1 = x(\frac{1}{30} + \frac{1}{40})$
$x = 36$
Entire Distance $= 2 \times 36 = 72$

23. *Answer: (d)*
Plug x = 2 into the function.
$f(2) = \frac{2-(2)^2}{2} = \frac{-2}{2} = -1$

24. *Answer: (d)*
If x is doubled, then x^3 *will be 8 times as the original x and* y^2 *will be 4 times as original y.*
$\frac{8}{4} = 2$, so $\frac{x^3}{y^2}$ *will be doubled.*

25. *Answer: (c)*
The volume should be the product of at least 3 integers greater than one.
Among the answer choices only 18 can be the product of 3 integers greater than 1.
$18 = 2 \times 3 \times 3$

26. *Answer: (b)*
The vextex of the quadratic function $f(x) = x^2 + ax + b$ *is* $(-\frac{a}{2}, f\left(-\frac{a}{2}\right))$.
$-\frac{a}{2} = -1$
$a = 2$
$2 = (-1)^2 + 2(-1) + b$
$b = 3$
$|a - b| = |2 - 3| = 1$

27. *Answer: (b)*
$\frac{15}{100}x = \frac{10}{100}y$
$y = \frac{15}{10}x = \frac{3}{2}x = 1.5\,x = 150\%\,x$

28. *Answer: (d)*
$\frac{1}{R_{total}} = \frac{1}{10} + \frac{1}{15} + \frac{1}{30} = \frac{1}{5}$
$R_{total} = 5\ ohm$

29. *Answer: (d)*
$1 + (t - 3) \times 0.2 = 0.22t$
$1 + 0.2t - 0.6 = 0.22t$
$0.4 = 0.02t$
$t = 20$

30. *Answer: (b)*
It is a probability question.
The least students can have birthdays in the same month is when every month has the same number of students' birthdays for the first 96 students.
$96 \div 12 = 8$.
The rest of four students' birthdays spread into 4 different months.
So at least 8 + 1 = 9 students' birthdays will be in the same month.

31. *Answer: 60*
The area of the parallelogram ABCD is equal to its base multiplied by its height.
Base × Height = 10 × Diameter of Circle
$\pi r^2 = 9\pi$
$r = 3$
$d = 2r = 6$
Area of Parallelogram = 10 × 6 = 60

32. *Answer:* $\frac{3}{7}$ *or .428 or .429*
The green light takes 30 seconds.
$70 - 30 - 10 = 30$
Probability of Green Light $= \frac{30}{70} = \frac{3}{7}$

33. *Answer: 0.36 or* $\frac{9}{25}$

$Probability = \frac{Number\ of\ Successful\ Events}{Total\ Number\ of\ Possible\ Events}$

$\frac{18}{12+18+20} = 0.36$

34. *Answer: 382*

Following the pattern, find the number of 1s between the 94th 3 and the 98th 3.

94 + 95 + 96 + 97 = 382 ones

35. *Answer: 6.56*

$BF = 5 - 2 = 3$

$EF = 5$

$EA = 5 - 2 = 3$

$AB = \sqrt{EA^2 + EB^2} = \sqrt{BF^2 + EF^2 + EA^2}$

$AB = \sqrt{3^2 + 5^2 + 3^2} = \sqrt{43} = 6.56$

36. *Answer: 60*

The two triangles are similar, therefore their corresponding sides are proportional.

$\frac{x}{100} = \frac{6}{10}$

$x = 60\ feet$

37. *Answer:* $\frac{4}{5}$ *or* 0.8

$\cos(90^o - x^o) = \sin(x^o) = \frac{4}{5}$

38. *Answer: 121*

$tan(35°) = \frac{85}{x}$

$x = \frac{85}{tan35°} = \frac{85}{0.7002} = 121$

SAT Math Mock Test No. 10

SECTION 3 

Math Test – NO Calculator **25 MINUTES, 20 QUESTIONS**

Directions:

For questions 1-15, solve each problem, choose the best answer from the choices provided, and fill in the corresponding circle on your answer sheet. **For questions 16-20,** solve the problem and enter your answer in the grid on the answer sheet. Please refer to the directions before question 16 on how to enter your answers in the grid. You may use any available space in your test booklet for scratch work.

Notes:

1. **No calculator** is allowed for this section. All numbers used are real numbers.
2. Figures that accompany problems in this test are intended to provide information useful in solving the problems. They are drawn as accurately as possible EXCEPT when it is stated in a specific problem that the figure is not drawn to scale. All figures lie in a plane unless otherwise indicated.
3. Unless otherwise specified, the domain of any function *f(x)* assumed to be the set of all real numbers *x* for which *f(x)* is a real number.

References:

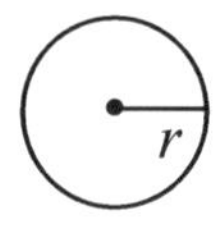

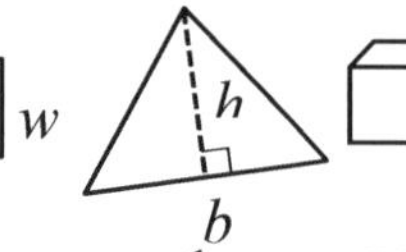

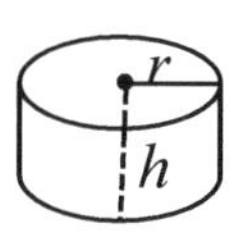

$A = \pi r^2$
$C = 2\pi r$

$A = lw$

$A = \frac{1}{2}bh$

$V = lwh$

$V = \pi r^2 h$

$c^2 = a^2 + b^2$

Special Right Triangles

The number of degrees of arc in a circle is 360; the number of radians of arc in a circle is 2π.
The sum of the degree measures of the angles in a triangle is 180.

1. The average (arithmetic mean) of 7, 14, and x is 16. What is the value of x?
   a) 25
   b) 26
   c) 27
   d) 28

2. If $2x + 1 = 9$, what is the value of $\sqrt{5x - 4}$?
   a) 4
   b) −4
   c) 3
   d) −3

3. In the figure below, what is the value of $a - b$?

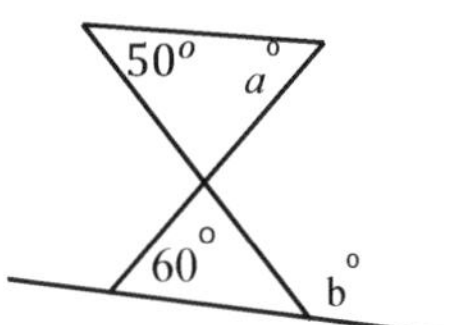

   a) 10
   b) 15
   c) 20
   d) 25

4. Let $wx^2 = y$, where $wxy \neq 0$.If both x and y are multiplied by 3, then w is
   a) multiplied by $\frac{1}{3}$
   b) multiplied by $\frac{1}{9}$
   c) multiplied by $\frac{1}{18}$
   d) multiplied by $\frac{1}{27}$

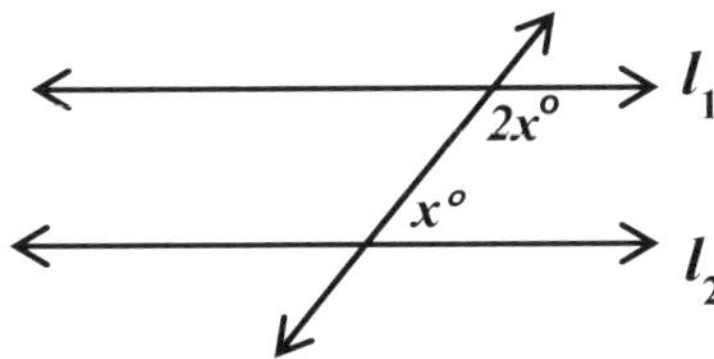

Note: Figure not drawn to scale.

5. In the figure above, $l_1 \parallel l_2$, what is the value of x?
   a) 45
   b) 50
   c) 60
   d) 70

6. If $y = x\sqrt{3}$ and $x \neq 0$, what does x^2 equal in terms of y?
   a) $\frac{y^2}{3}$
   b) $3y^2$
   c) $\frac{9}{y^2}$
   d) $\frac{y^2}{9}$

2, 4, 6, 8

7. In the list above, if we add a positive integer P to the list, which of the following could be the median of the new list of five numbers?
   I. 4
   II. 5
   III. 6
   a) I only
   b) I, II only
   c) I, III only
   d) I, II, III

8. Let $*m$ be defined as $*m = m^2 + 4$ for all values of m. If $*x = 3x^2$, which of the following could be the value of x?
   a) −2
   b) 1
   c) 2
   d) $-\sqrt{2}$

9. If $3x - 2 = 4$, then $3x + 4 =$?
   a) 10
   b) 11
   c) 12
   d) 14

10. If $x^2 - 16 = 0$, which of the following could be a value of x?
    a) −4
    b) −8
    c) 2
    d) 8

11. If $3x + 1 = a$, then $6x + 1$?
    a) $a + 3$
    b) $a - 3$
    c) $2a - 1$
    d) $2a + 1$

12. When $3x$ is added to 13 and the sum is divided by 5 subtracted from x, the result equals 4. What is the value of x?
    a) 33
    b) 29
    c) 24
    d) 18

13. X is a set of numbers whose average (arithmetic mean) is 6. Y is a set that is created by tripling and subtracting 3 to each number in X. What is the average of the numbers in the set Y?
    a) 10
    b) 15
    c) 16
    d) 18

Questions 14 – 15 refer to the following information:

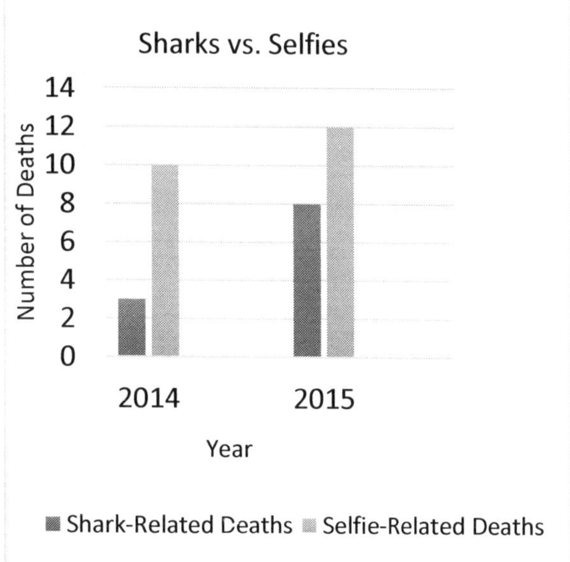

News outlet *Reuters* reports that taking a selfie is actually a dangerous endeavor, and that many people have been injured or died while taking a selfie. The figure above shows that more people around the world have died by taking selfies than by shark attacks in the years of 2014 and 2015. There have been twelve recorded selfie deaths in 2015 compared to eight people dying from shark attacks. The most common selfie-related deaths have been due to falling or being hit by a moving vehicle.

14. What is the percent change of total deaths from 2014 to 2015?
    a) 50%
    b) 70%
    c) 100%
    d) 233%

15. What is the difference between the percent changes of shark-related deaths and selfie-related deaths from 2014 to 2015?
    a) 20%
    b) 147%
    c) 167%
    d) 187%

Directions:

For questions 16-20, solve the problem and enter your answer in the grid, as described below, on the answer sheet.

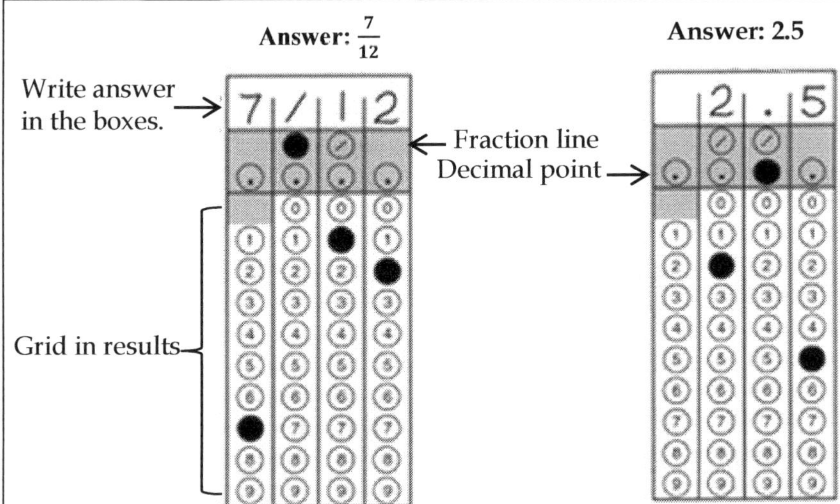

Answer: 201
Either position is correct.

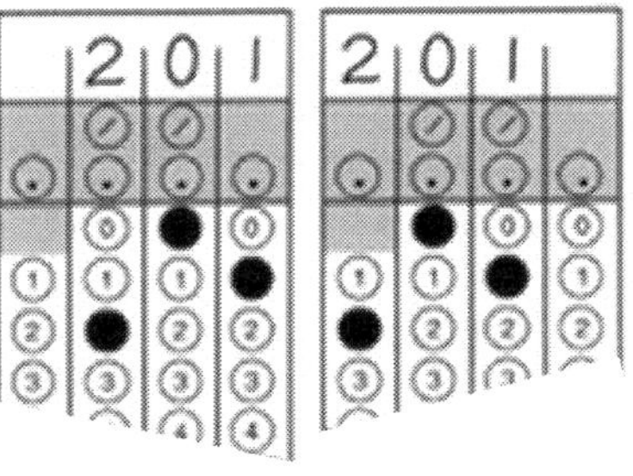

Note: You may start your answers in any column, space permitting. Columns not needed should be left blank.

- Mark no more than one circle in any column.
- Because the answer sheet will be machine-scored. **You will receive credit only if the circles are filled in correctly.**
- Although not required, it is suggested that you write your answer in the boxes at the top of the columns to help you fill in the circles accurately.
- Some problems may have more than one correct answer. In such case, grid only one answer.
- No question has a negative answer.
- **Mixed numbers** such as $3\frac{1}{2}$ must be gridded as 3.5 or $\frac{7}{2}$. (If 3 1/2 is gridded, it will be interpreted as $\frac{31}{2}$, not $3\frac{1}{2}$.)
- **Decimal Answer**: If you obtain a decimal answer with more digits than the grid can accommodate, it may be either rounded or truncated, but it must fill the entire grid. The acceptable ways to grid $\frac{2}{3}$ are:

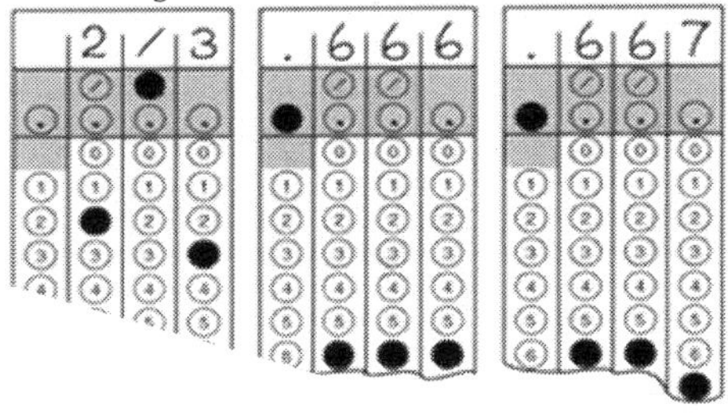

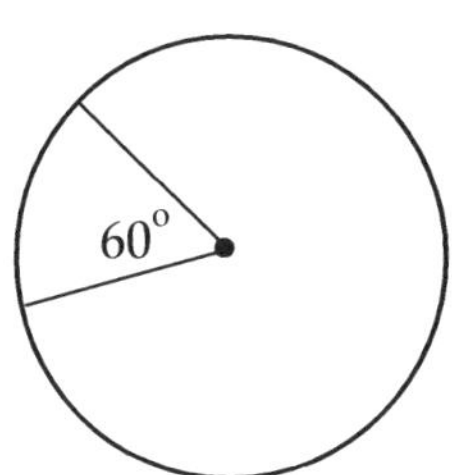

16. In the figure above, a piece with a 60° center angle has been cut out of an 18-ounce pie. How many ounces was the piece of pie that was cut out?

17. A circle with center at coordinates (4, 3) touches the x-axis at only one point. What is the radius of the circle?

18. The function $j@k = (\frac{j}{k})^j$. If $j@k = -8$ when $j = -3$, what is the value of k?

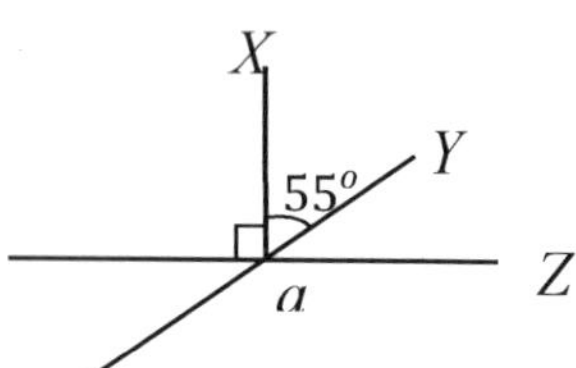

19. What is the value of a in the figure above?

20. Ms. DePietro provides some markers to her Arts class. If each student takes 3 markers, there will be 1 marker left. If 5 students take 4 markers each and the rest of students take 2 marker each, there will be no markers left. How many students are in Ms. DePietro's Arts class?

SECTION 4 

Math Test – Calculator 55 MINUTES, 38 QUESTIONS

Directions:

For questions 1-30, solve each problem, choose the best answer from the choices provided, and fill in the corresponding circle on your answer sheet. **For questions 31-38**, solve the problem and enter your answer in the grid on the answer sheet. Please refer to the directions before question 31 on how to enter your answers in the grid. You may use any available space in your test booklet for scratch work.

Notes:

1. Acceptable calculators are allowed for this section. All numbers used are real numbers.
2. Figures that accompany problems in this test are intended to provide information useful in solving the problems. They are drawn as accurately as possible EXCEPT when it is stated in a specific problem that the figure is not drawn to scale. All figures lie in a plane unless otherwise indicated.
3. Unless otherwise specified, the domain of any function *f(x)* assumed to be the set of all real numbers *x* for which *f(x)* is a real number.

References:

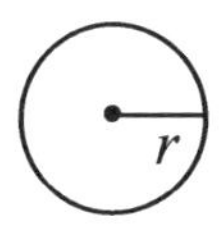

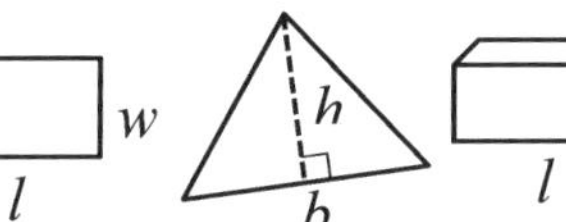

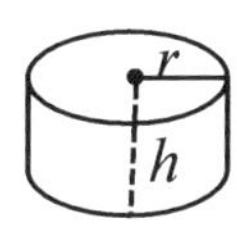

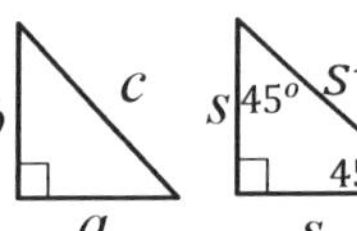

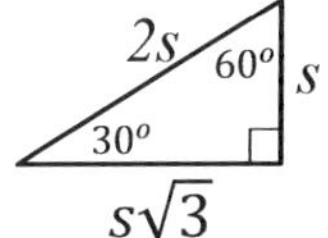

$2s$ 60° s 30° $s\sqrt{3}$

$A = \pi r^2$, $C = 2\pi r$ $A = lw$ $A = \frac{1}{2}bh$ $V = lwh$ $V = \pi r^2 h$ $c^2 = a^2 + b^2$ **Special Right Triangles**

The number of degrees of arc in a circle is 360; the number of radians of arc in a circle is 2π.
The sum of the degree measures of the angles in a triangle is 180.

1. The number of water lilies in a pond has doubled every five years since $t = 0$. This relation is given by $y = (x)2^{t/5}$, where t is in number of years, y is the number of water lilies in the pond at time t, and x is the original number of water lilies. If there were 800 water lilies in this pond 10 years after $t = 0$, then what was the original number of water lilies?
   a) 100
   b) 150
   c) 180
   d) 200

2. In the figure below, points A and B lie on circle O. If $\angle AOB = 2y^o$, what is the value of x in term of y?

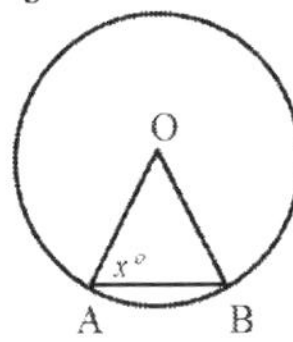

   a) y
   b) $90 - y$
   c) $180 - y$
   d) $90 - \frac{1}{2}y$

3. How many pounds of flour are needed to make 18 rolls of bread if 20 pounds of flour are needed to make 120 rolls of bread?
   a) 3
   b) 4
   c) 5
   d) 3.5

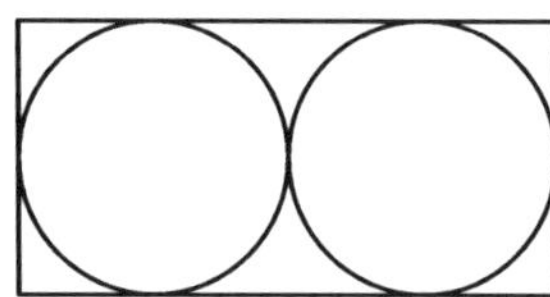

4. In the figure above, two congruent circles are inscribed in a rectangle. If the area of one circle is 4π, what is the area of the rectangle?
   a) 24
   b) 27
   c) 32
   d) 36

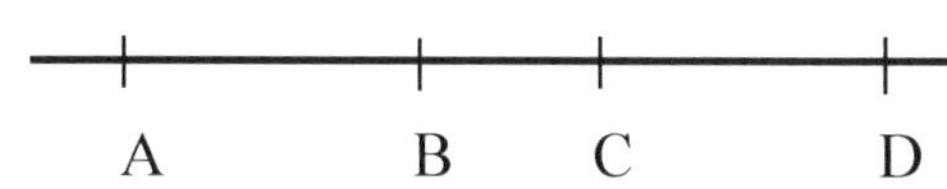

5. In the figure above, AC = 12, AB = 2BC, and AB = CD. What does AD equal?
   a) 16
   b) 18
   c) 20
   d) 21

6. If John gives Sally \$5, Sally will have twice the amount of money that John will have. Originally, there was a total of \$45 between the two of them. How much money did John initially have?
   a) 25
   b) 20
   c) 18
   d) 15

7. If $\frac{2}{5}$ of a number is 30, what is $\frac{1}{15}$ of that number?
   a) 3
   b) 4
   c) 5
   d) 6

8. The total population in all five cities increased by approximately what percent from 2012 to 2013?

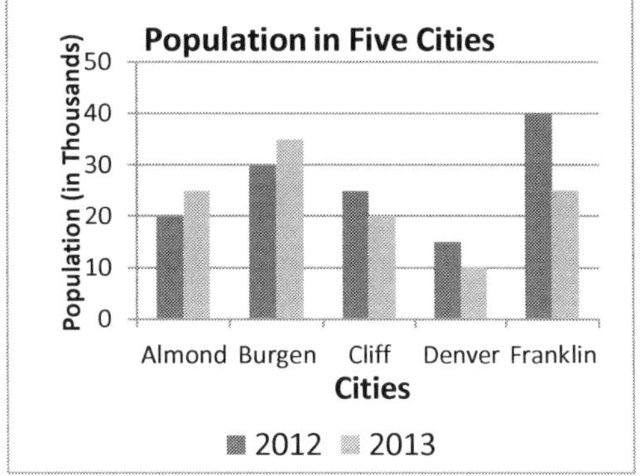

   a) 13.5%
   b) 11.5%
   c) −11.5%
   d) −13.5%

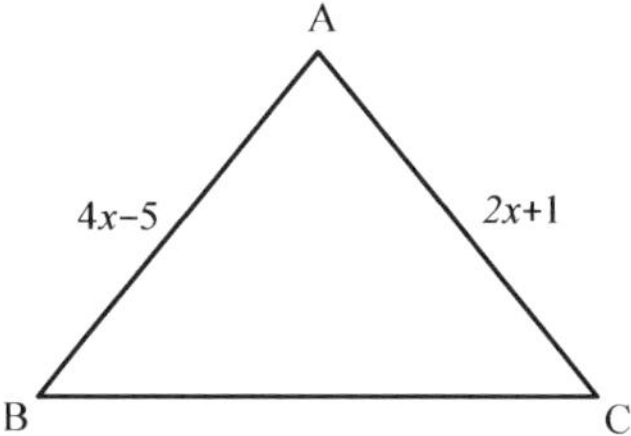

9. In the figure above, if ΔABC is an equilateral triangle, what is the perimeter of ΔABC?
   a) 12
   b) 15
   c) 18
   d) 21

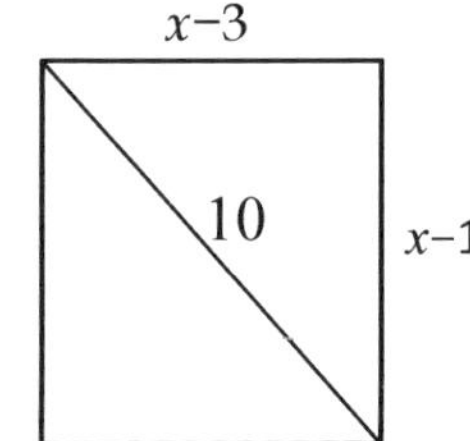

10. The figure above is a rectangle. What is the value of x?
    a) 5
    b) 6
    c) 9
    d) 10

11. he number of DVDs that have been checked out of the local public library in a particular week was recorded in the table below. If the median number of DVDs checked out for the whole week was 83, which of the following could have been the number of DVDs checked out on Saturday and Sunday, respectively, of the same week?

Local Library Checkout Records	
Day of the Week	*Number of DVDs Checked Out*
Monday	*77*
Tuesday	*81*
Wednesday	*82*
Thursday	*83*
Friday	*86*

    a) 78 and 82
    b) 79 and81
    c) 80 and 87
    d) 84 and 87

12. If the fraction $\frac{1}{7}$ equals the repeating decimal 0.1428571428571.., what is the 303rd digit after the decimal point of the repeating decimal?
    a) 1
    b) 4
    c) 2
    d) 8

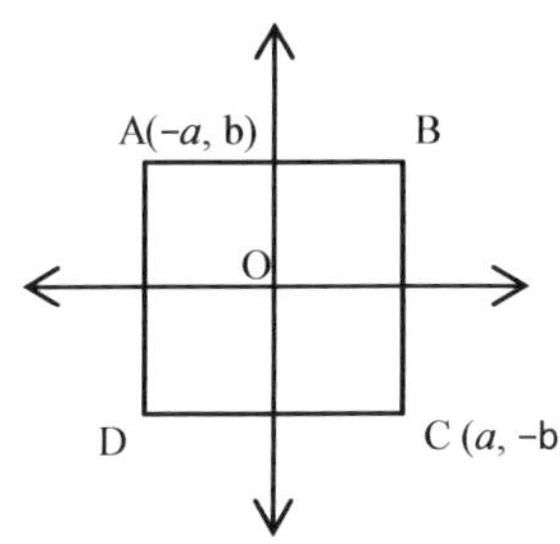

13. In the figure above, rectangle ABCD lies on the xy-coordinate plane. If the origin is located at the center of rectangle, which of the following could be the coordinates of point B?
    a) (a, b)
    b) $(a, -b)$
    c) $(-a, -b)$
    d) $(-b, -a)$

14. If set A = {1, 3, 8, 10, 15} and set B consists of all the even positive integers less than or equal to 10, how many elements are in the union of the two sets?
    a) 0
    b) 3
    c) 8
    d) 9

15. What would be the least amount of money needed to purchase exactly 31 tickets according the table below?

Bus Ticket Price	
Number of Bus Tickets	*Price*
1	*7.5*
Book of 6	*40*
Book of 12	*75*

    a) $207.5
    b) $202.5
    c) $200
    d) $197.5

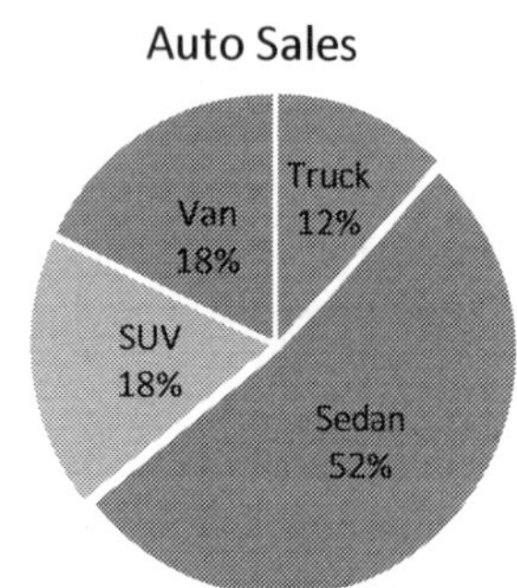

16. The pie graph above represents the automobiles that were sold by a dealer in 2010, according to their records. If the dealer sold 50 more Sedans than all others combined, how many automobiles did it sell altogether?
    a) 1,000
    b) 1,150
    c) 1,250
    d) 1,500

17. If no wallpaper is wasted, how many square feet of wall paper is needed to cover a rectangular wall that is 6 yards by 8 yards (1 yard = 3 feet)?
    a) 432 square feet
    b) 384 square feet
    b) 378 square feet
    d) 324 square feet

18. Ken, Justin, and Tiff have read a total of 90 books from the library. Justin read 3 times as many books as Ken and Tiff read 2 times as many as Justin. How many books did Justin read?
    a) 9
    b) 18
    c) 27
    d) 36

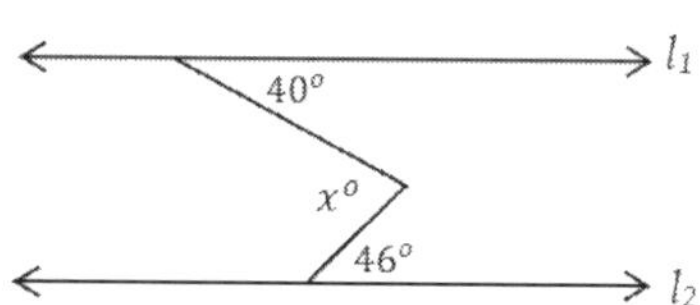

19. In the figure above, lines l_1 and l_2 are parallel. What is the value of x?
    a) 90
    b) 86
    c) 80
    d) 76

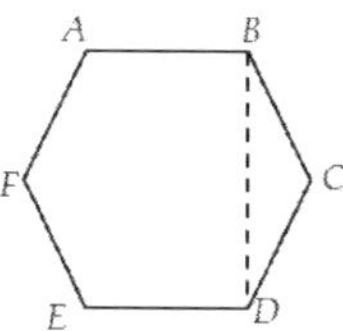

20. In the regular hexagon as shown above, if length of $\overline{AB}$ is 6, what is the length of $\overline{BD}$?
    a) 12
    b) 9
    c) $6\sqrt{3}$
    d) $6\sqrt{2}$

21. In the figure below, $c = 130$. What is the value of $a + b$?

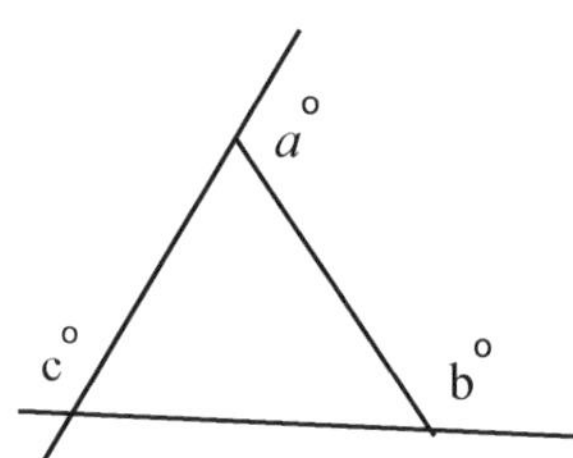

    a) 140
    b) 180
    c) 210
    d) 230

22. In a sequence of numbers, the leading term is 2. Each successive term is formed by adding 1 to its preceding term and then multiplying the result by 2. What is the fourth term in the sequence?
    a) 30
    b) 32
    c) 42
    d) 46

23. If $x > y > 0.1$, which of the following is less than $\frac{x}{y}$?
   a) $\frac{x+0.1}{y+0.1}$
   b) $\frac{2x}{2y}$
   c) $\frac{x-0.1}{y-0.1}$
   d) $(\frac{x}{y})^2$

24. When r is divided by 12, the remainder is 9. What is the remainder when $r + 1$ is divided by 4?
   a) 0
   b) 1
   c) 2
   d) 3

25. The monthly cost of renting an apartment increases every year by 3%. John paid $500 per month this year on his rental. What is the monthly cost for John's rental n years from now?
   a) 500×0.03^n
   b) $500 \times 1.03 \times n$
   c) 500×1.03^n
   d) $500 \times 1.03^{n-1}$

Questions 26 – 27 refer to the following information:

Density describes how compact or concentrated a material is. It is defined as the ratio between mass and volume, or mass per unit volume. The formula to calculate the density is:

$$Density = \frac{Mass}{Volume}$$

26. The standard gold bar held in gold reserves by central banks and traded among bullion dealers is the 400-troy-ounce (12,441.4-gram) Good Delivery gold bar. If the density of the gold bar is 19.3 grams per cm^3, what would be the volume of the Good Delivery gold bar, in cm^3?
   a) 592.8
   b) 644.6
   c) 696.4
   d) 748.2

27. If a cylinder gold block has a diameter of 4 centimeters and height of 15 centimeters, what would be its mass, in grams? (Gold has a density of 19.3 grams per cm^3.)
   a) 3,638
   b) 3,949
   c) 9,100
   d) 14,552

1, 2, 3, 4 , 5, 6

28. A three-digit integer is to be formed from the digits listed above. If the first digit must be even, either the second or the third digit must be 5, and no digit may be repeated, how many such integers are possible?
   a) 12
   b) 15
   c) 18
   d) 24

29. If the sum of all consecutive integers from –41 to x, inclusive, is 42, what is the value of x?
   a) 49
   b) 45
   c) 43
   d) 42

30. July 4th, 2014 is a Friday. What day of the week is July 4th, 2050?
   a) Sunday
   b) Monday
   c) Thursday
   d) Friday

Directions:

For questions 31-38, solve the problem and enter your answer in the grid, as described below, on the answer sheet.

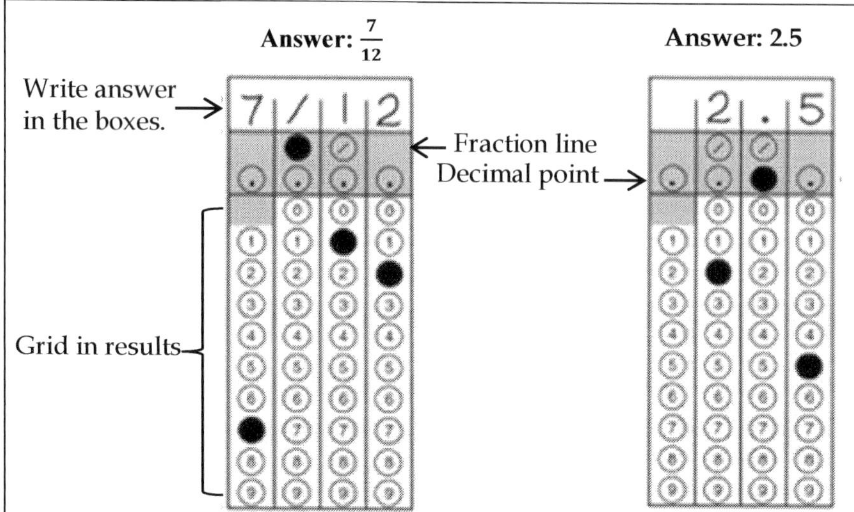

Answer: 201
Either position is correct.

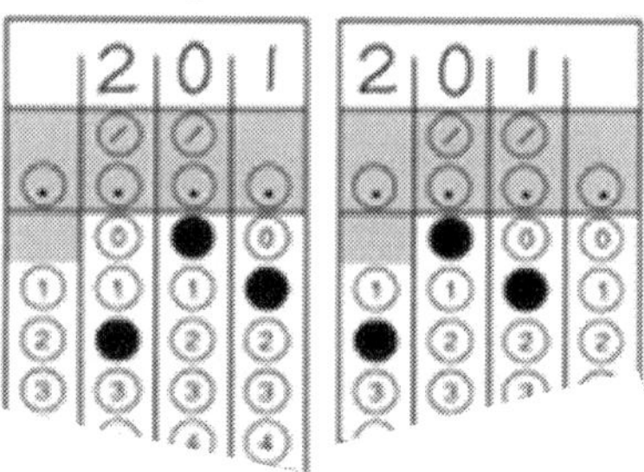

Note: You may start your answers in any column, space permitting. Columns not needed should be left blank.

- Mark no more than one circle in any column.
- Because the answer sheet will be machine-scored. **You will receive credit only if the circles are filled in correctly.**
- Although not required, it is suggested that you write your answer in the boxes at the top of the columns to help you fill in the circles accurately.
- Some problems may have more than one correct answer. In such case, grid only one answer.
- No question has a negative answer.
- **Mixed numbers** such as $3\frac{1}{2}$ must be gridded as 3.5 or $\frac{7}{2}$. (If 31/2 is gridded, it will be interpreted as $\frac{31}{2}$, not $3\frac{1}{2}$.)
- **Decimal Answer**: If you obtain a decimal answer with more digits than the grid can accommodate, it may be either rounded or truncated, but it must fill the entire grid. The acceptable ways to grid $\frac{2}{3}$ are:

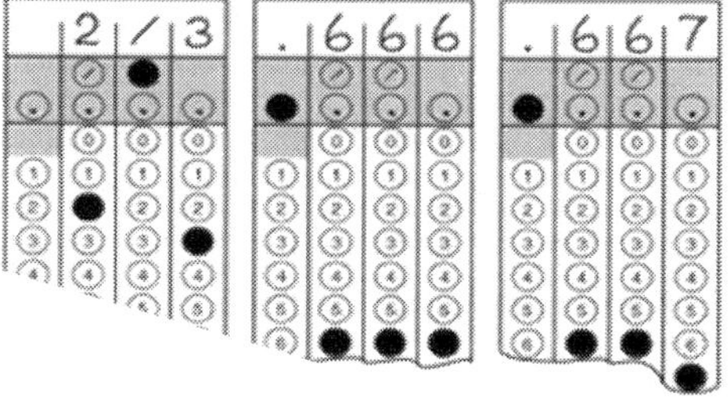

31. In the figure above, if the area of parallelogram OABC is 16, what is the value of x?

32. If the average (arithmetic mean) of 35, 50, 20, and x is 40, then find the value of x.

33. Gina drove at an average of 40 miles per hour from her house to a bookstore. Along the same route, she returned at an average of 60 miles per hour. If the entire trip took her 1 hour, how many miles did Gina drive in total?

34. In a poll, 20 people supported the current city mayor, 20 people were against him, and 10 people had no opinion. What fraction of those polled supported the city mayor?

35. In a junior high school with seventh and eighth graders, there is the same number of girls as boys. The eighth grade has 220 students, and there are 5 boys for every 6 girls. In the seventh grade there are 5 boys for every 4 girls. How many girls are in the seventh grade?

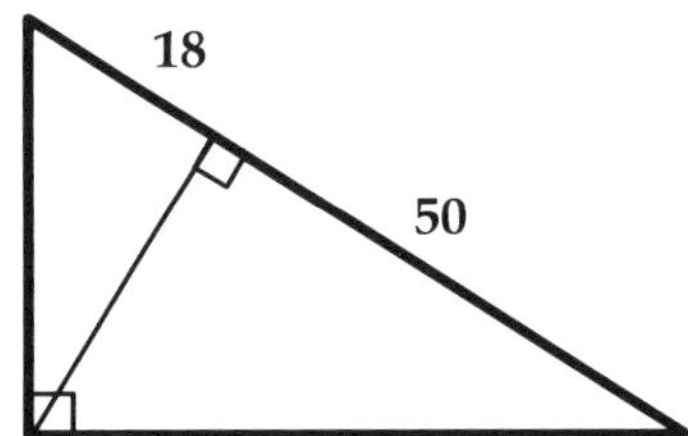

36. The graph above is a right triangle. Find the area of this right triangle?

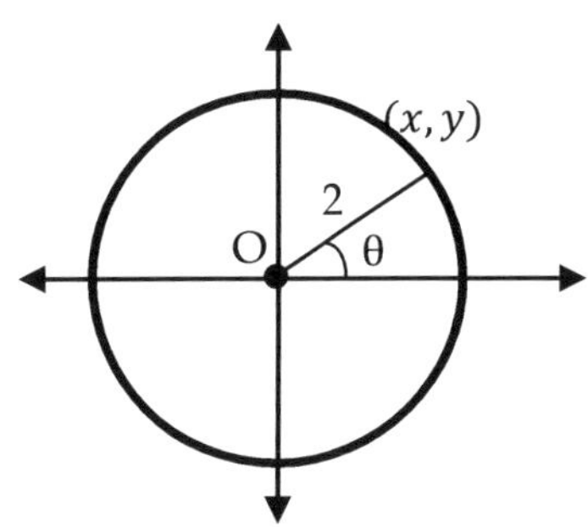

37. In the xy-plane aboye, O is the center of the circle with a radius of 2, and the measure of $\angle\theta$ is $\frac{\pi}{5}$ radians. What is a the value of $x + y$? (Round your answer to the nearest tenth.)

38. The length of a rectangular piece of cardboard is 15 inches longer than its width. If a 5-inch square is cut from each corner of the cardboard, and the remaining piece is folded up to form a box, the volume of the box is 1,250 cubic inches. Find the sum of the length and the width, in inches, of the original cardboard.

SAT MATH MOCK TEST No. 10 ANSWER KEYS

Section 3									
1. C	2. A	3. A	4. A	5. C	6. A	7. D	8. D	9. A	10. A
11. C	12. A	13. B	14. C	15. B	16. 3	17. 3	18. 6	19. 145	20. 9

Section 4									
1. D	2. B	3. A	4. C	5. C	6. B	7. C	8. C	9. D	10. C
11. D	12. C	13. A	14. C	15. D	16. C	17. A	18. C	19. B	20. C
21. D	22. A	23. A	24. C	25. C	26. B	27. A	28. D	29. D	30. B
31. 2	32. 55	33. 48	34. $\frac{2}{5}$	35. 80	36. 1020	37. 2.8	38. 55		

SECTION 3

1. *Answer: (c)*
   The average of these three numbers is 16, so the sum will be 3 × 16 =48.
   $7 + 14 + x = 48$
   $x = 48 - 21 = 27$

2. *Answer: (a)*
   $2x + 1 = 9$
   $x = 4$
   $5(4) - 4 = 16$
   $\sqrt{16} = 4$

3. *Answer: (a)*
   Since the two triangles share an angle with the same measure, the sum of their other two angles must be equal.
   $a + 50 = b + 60$
   $a - b = 10$

4. *Answer: (a)*
   $w\,(3x)^2 = 3y$
   $w = \frac{3y}{9x^2} = \frac{1y}{3x^2}$

5. *Answer: (c)*
   Consecutive interior angles are supplementary.
   $2x + x = 180$
   $x = 60$

6. *Answer: (a)*
   Divide by $\sqrt{3}$ on both sides of the equation $y = x\sqrt{3}$.
   $x = \frac{y}{\sqrt{3}}$ *(Then square both sides.)*
   $x^2 = \frac{y^2}{3}$

7. *Answer: (d)*
   P can be any positive integer, so there are a few cases.
   $P < 4$: The median would be 4.
   $P = 5$: The median would be P.
   $P > 6$: The median would be 6.

8. *Answer: (d)*
   $^*x = x^2 + 4,\ x^2 + 4 = 3x^2$
   $x^2 = 2,\ \ x = \pm\sqrt{2}$

9. *Answer: (a)*
   Use opposite operations.
   $3x - 2 = 4$
   $3x - 2 + 2 = 4 + 2$
   $3x = 6$
   $x = 2$
   $3(2) + 4 = 10$

10. *Answer: (a)*
    $x^2 - 16 = 0$
    $x^2 = 16$
    $x = \pm 4$

11. *Answer: (c)*
    $3x = a - 1$
    $6x = 2 \times (3x) = 2 \times (a - 1) = 2a - 2$
    $6x + 1 = 2a - 2 + 1 = 2a - 1$

12. *Answer: (a)*
    $\frac{3x+13}{x-5} = 4$
    $3x + 13 = 4(x - 5)$
    $3x + 13 = 4x - 20$
    $33 = x$

13. *Answer: (b)*
If we triple and subtract 3 from each element in X, we will triple and subtract 3 from the mean of X as well.
$6 \times 3 - 3 = 15$

14. *Answer: (c)*
Total selfie-related deaths: $10 + 12 = 22$
Total shark-related deaths: $3 + 8 = 11$
Percent Increase $= \frac{22-11}{11} \times 100\% = 100\%$

15. *Answer: (b)*
Percent change of selfie-related deaths: $\frac{12-10}{10} \times 100\% = 20\%$
Percent change of shark-related deaths: $\frac{8-3}{3} \times 100\% = 167\%$
Difference: $167\% - 20\% = 147\%$

16. *Answer: 3*
Weight of Whole Pie : 360º = Weight of Piece : 60º
$18 : 360^o = x : 60^o$
$\frac{18}{360} = \frac{x}{60}$
$x = 3$ *ounces*

17. *Answer: 3*
The circle is tangent to the x-axis, since otherwise it would touch the axis at zero or two points (try drawing it out to see). Its radius is the distance from the center to the x-axis which is 3.

18. *Answer: 6*
$J = -3$
$(\frac{-3}{k})^{-3} = -8$
$(\frac{-3}{k})^{3} = \frac{1}{-8}$
$\frac{-3}{k} = \sqrt[3]{\frac{1}{-8}} = \frac{-1}{2}$
$k = 6$

19. *Answer: 145*
$a + (90 - 55)° = 180°$
$a = 145°$

20. *Answer: 9*
Let x be the number of students in Ms. DePietro's Arts class.
$3x + 1 = 5 \times 4 + (x - 5) \times 2$
$x = 9$

SECTION 4

1. *Answer: (d)*
Plug in t = 10 and y = 800 in the function.
$800 = (x) \times 2^{(10/5)} = x \times 2^2 = 4x$
$x = 200$

2. *Answer: (b)*
ΔOAB is an isosceles Δ.
$2x + 2y = 180$
$x + y = 90$
$x = 90 - y$

3. *Answer: (a)*
20 pounds : 120 rolls = x : 18 rolls
$\frac{20\ pounds}{120\ rolls} = \frac{x\ pounds}{18\ rolls}$
$120x = 20 \times 18$ *(Cross multiply)*
$x = 3$ *pounds*

4. *Answer: (c)*
The length of the rectangle is 4r and its width is 2r.
$\pi r^2 = 4\pi$
$r = 2$
Area of Rectangle $= 4r \times 2r = 8 \times 4 = 32$

5. *Answer: (c)*
The length of $\overline{AC}$ *plus* $\overline{CD}$ *is equal to the length of* $\overline{AD}$.
$\overline{AB} = \frac{2}{3} \times 12 = 8$
$\overline{CD} = 8$
$AD = AC + CD = 12 + 8 = 20$

6. *Answer: (b)*
Let J be the amount of money John initially had and S be the amount of money Sally initially had. Together, they originally had $45.
$J + S = 45$
$J = 45 - S$
After John gives Sally $5, John will have J – 5 dollars and Sally will have S + 5 dollars. Therefore: $S + 5 = 2(J - 5)$.
$S + 5 = 2(45 - S - 5) = 80 - 2S$
$S = 25$
Plug J = 45 – S into the equation above to get J = $20.

7. *Answer: (c)*
Let the number be x.
$\frac{2}{5}x = 30$
$x = 75$
$\frac{1}{15} \times 75 = 5$

8. *Answer: (c)*
Percent Increase = $\frac{\text{2013 Population} - \text{2012 Population}}{\text{2012 Population}} \times 100\%$
Total Population in 2012 = 20 + 30 + 25 + 15 + 40 = 130 thousand.
Total Population in 2013= 25 + 35 + 20 + 10 + 25 = 115 thousand.
$\frac{115-130}{130} \times 100\% = -11.5\%$

9. *Answer: (d)*
All sides are equal in length.
$4x - 5 = 2x + 1$
$x = 3$
Perimeter = $3 \times (2 \times 3 + 1) = 21$

10. *Answer: (c)*
Use the Pythagorean theorem.
$(x - 1)^2 + (x - 3)^2 = 10^2$
$x^2 - 2x + 1 + x^2 - 6x + 9 = 100$
$2x^2 - 8x + 10 = 100$
$x^2 - 4x - 45 = 0$
$(x - 9)(x + 5) = 0$
$x = 9$

11. *Answer: (d)*
If the median number of DVDs checked out for the whole week was 83, the number of DVDs checked out on either Saturday or Sunday should be more than 83.

12. *Answer: (c)*
Every 6 digits are repeated.
The remainder of 303 divided by 6 is 3 so the 303rd digit is same as the 3rd digit after the decimal point, both of which are 2.

13. *Answer: (a)*
B is located in the quadrant I which has positive x and y coordinates.
(a, b)

14. *Answer: (c)*
$A \cup B = A + B - (A \cap B)$
$A = \{1, 3, 8, 10, 15\}$
$B = \{2, 4, 6, 8, 10\}$
$A \cap B = \{8, 10\}$
Number of Elements in $(A \cup B) = 5 + 5 - 2 = 8$

15. *Answer: (d)*
The lowest price for 31 tickets is to purchase 2 books of 12, 1 book of 6 and 1 single tickets.
$75 × 2 + $40 + $7.5 = $197.5

16. *Answer: (c)*
Solve this problem using proportions.
There were 4% (52% − 48%) more Sedans sold than all other cars combined.
4% : 50 = 100% : x
x = 1,250 cars

17. *Answer: (a)*
$(3 \times 6) \times (3 \times 8) = 432$ square feet

18. *Answer: (c)*
Let k be the number of books Ken read, j be the number of books Justin read, and t be the number of books Tiff read.
$j = 3k$
$t = 2j = 2(3k) = 6k$
Given that $k + j + t = 90$
Substitute for j and t:
$k + 3k + 6k = 90$
$k = 9$
$j = 3k = 27$

19. *Answer: (b)*

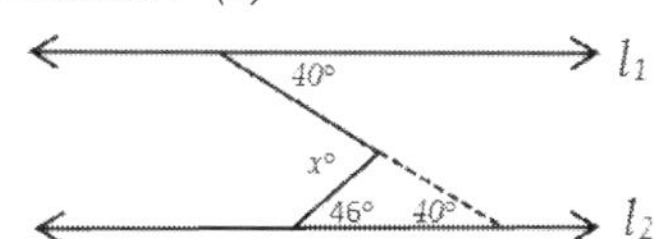

Use the exterior angle theorem.
$x = 46 + 40 = 86$

20. *Answer: (c)*

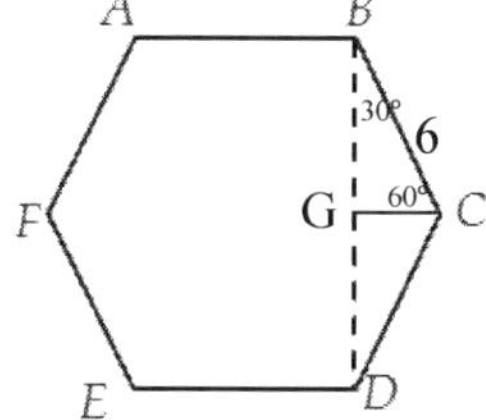

$\frac{(6-2)\times 180}{6} = 120$ (each interior angle)
ΔBGC is a 30–60–90 special right triangle.
$BG = BC \times \frac{\sqrt{3}}{2} = 6 \times \frac{\sqrt{3}}{2} = 3\sqrt{3}$
$BD = 2BG = 6\sqrt{3}$

21. *Answer: (d)*
The sum of any polygon's exterior angles is 360°.
$a + b + c = 360$
$a + b = 360 - c = 360 - 130 = 230$

22. *Answer: (a)*
$((((((2+1)\times 2)+1)\times 2)+1)\times 2) = 30$

23. *Answer: (a)*
$x > y > 0.1$
Plug in $x = 2$, *and* $y = 1$
Only answer (a), $\frac{2.1}{1.1}$, *less than 2.*

24. *Answer: (c)*
$r = 12 \times q + 9$ *(Remainder Theorem)*
$r + 1 = 12 \times q + 10$
Since $12 \times q$ *is divisible by 4, the remainder of* $r + 1$ *divided by 4 is equal to the remainder of 10 divided by 4, which is 2.*
Or just simply pick an easy number to try out this question, such as 21 (12 + 9) in this case.

25. *Answer: (c)*
Increasing every year by 3% is to multiply $(1 + \frac{3}{100})$ *for each additional year.*
$C(n) = (1.03)^n \times 500 = 500(1.03)^n$

26. *Answer: (b)*
$Density = \frac{Mass}{Volume}$
$19.3 = \frac{12441.4}{Volume}$
$Volume = \frac{12441.4}{19.3} = 644.6$

27. *Answer: (a)*
$Volume = \pi r^2 h = \pi \times 2^2 \times 15$
$Mass = 19.3 \times 60\pi = 3{,}638$

28. *Answer: (d)*
1st digit must be even: 3 choices
If 2nd digit is 5, then 2nd digit has 1 choice, and 3rd digit has 4 choices.
If 2nd digit is not 5, then 3rd digit is 5: 2nd digit has 4 choices and 3rd digit has 1 choice.
$3 \times 1 \times 4 + 3 \times 4 \times 1 = 24$

29. *Answer: (d)*
The sum of all integers from –41 to +41 is 0. The next term is 42.
Therefore $x = 42$

30. *Answer: (b)*
Count the number of days between July 4th, 2014 and July 4th, 2050.
There are 2050 –2014 = 36 years.
There are $\frac{2048-2016}{4} + 1 = 9$ *leap years in between.*
So the total number of days:
$36 \times 365 + 9 = 13{,}149$ *days*
The remainder of $13149 \div 7$ *is 3.*
Three days after Friday is Monday.

31. *Answer: 2*
Area of OABC = Base × Height =
$(x+2) \times (2x) = 16$
$2x^2 + 4x - 16 = 0$
$x^2 + 2x - 8 = 0$
$(x + 4)(x - 2) = 0$
$x = -4$ *(not applicable, x must be positive) or* $x = 2$

32. *Answer: 55*
$\frac{35+50+20+x}{4} = 40$
$x = 160 - 50 - 35 - 20 = 55$

33. *Answer: 48*
Let one trip have x miles
Total Time = $t_{go} + t_{back}$
$1 = \frac{x}{40} + \frac{x}{60} = x(\frac{1}{40} + \frac{1}{60}) \rightarrow x = 24$
Total miles: $2 \times 24 = 48$ *miles*

34. *Answer:* $\frac{2}{5}$
$\frac{Part}{Whole} = \frac{20}{20+20+10} = \frac{20}{50} = \frac{2}{5}$

35. *Answer: 80*
In the eighth grade, there are $220 \times \frac{5}{6+5} = 100$ *boys and 220 −100 = 120 girls.*
Let x be the number of girls in seventh grade.
Boys of 7th Grade : Girls of 7th Grade = 5 : 4
So the number of boys in 7th grade is $\frac{5}{4}x$.
The total number of boys in two grades is the same as girls:
$100 + \frac{5}{4}x = 120 + x$
$\frac{1}{4}x = 20 \rightarrow x = 80$

36. *Answer: 1020*

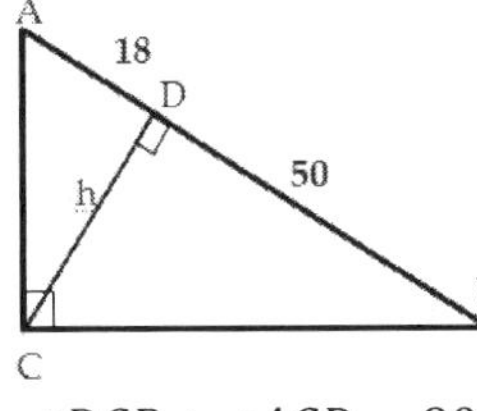

$\angle A + \angle ACD = \angle DCB + \angle ACD = 90°$
$\angle A = \angle DCB$
$\angle ADC = \angle CDB = 90°$
$\Delta ADC \sim \Delta CDB$
$\frac{CD}{AD} = \frac{BD}{CD} = \frac{h}{18} = \frac{50}{h}$
$h^2 = 18 \times 50 = 900$
$h = 30$
$Area = \frac{1}{2}(50 + 18)(30) = 1020$

37. *Answer: 2.8*

$x = rcos(\theta) = 2 \times \cos\left(\frac{\pi}{5}\right) = 1.618$

$y = rsin(\theta) = 2 \times \sin\left(\frac{\pi}{5}\right) = 1.176$

$x + y = 2.8$

38. *Answer: 55*

If the width of the cardboard is x inches, the length of the carboard is $15 + x$ *inches.*

After 5-inch square is cut from each corner and the cardboard is folded to form a box, the width will be $x - 10$, *the length will be* $x + 5$, *and the height will be 5 inches.*

The volume of the box is given, so $(x - 10)(x + 5)(5) = 1250.$

$x^2 - 5x - 50 = 250$

$x^2 - 5x - 300 = 0$

$(x + 15)(x - 20) = 0$

$x = 20\ inches$

20 + (20 + 15) = 55

Index

STAY TUNED FOR MORE BOOKS BY DR. JANG!

Dr. Jang's SAT 800 Series:

Dr. Jang's SAT 800 Math Workbook (2014, co-authored with Tiffany Jang)
Dr. Jang's SAT 800 Math Subject Test Level 2 (co-authored with Tiffany Jang)
Dr. Jang's SAT 800 Chemistry Subject Test (2015)
Dr. Jang's SAT 800 Physics Subject Test (2016)

Dr. Jang's AP 5 Series:

Dr. Jang's AP 5 Calculus AB/BC Workbook
Dr. Jang's AP 5 Physics 1 & 2 Workbook
Dr. Jang's AP 5 Physics C: Mechanics Workbook
Dr. Jang's AP 5 Physics C: Electricity and Magnetism Workbook
Dr. Jang's AP 5 Chemistry Workbook

Check Out More Services on Our Website:

www.DrJang800.com

The Goals of Dr. Jang's Books:

~For students:
To help you study based on your skill level.

~For teachers:
To help you plan lessons based on students' needs.

"Giving instruction based on each student's characteristics and ability will achieve the best educational results." ~ *Confucius*

Made in the USA
Lexington, KY
15 July 2016